Peterson Reference Guide to

Behavior

of North American

Mammals

THE PETERSON REFERENCE GUIDE SERIES

BEHAVIOR

OF NORTH AMERICAN

MAMMALS

MARK ELBROCH

AND

KURT RINEHART

HOUGHTON MIFFLIN HARCOURT
BOSTON   NEW YORK
2011

Sponsored by
the Roger Tory Peterson Institute
and the National Wildlife Federation

Copyright © 2011 by Mark Elbroch and Kurt Rinehart

For information about permission to reproduce selections from this book, write to
Permissions, Houghton Mifflin Harcourt Publishing Company,
215 Park Avenue South, New York, New York 10003.

www.hmhbooks.com

Library of Congress Cataloging-in-Publication Data

Elbroch, Mark.
Peterson reference guide to behavior of North American mammals / Mark Elbroch and Kurt Rinehart.
p. cm.
Includes bibliographical references and index.
ISBN 978-0-618-88345-5
1. Mammals—Behavior—North America. I. Rinehart, Kurt. II. Title.
QL739.3.E43 2011
599.15097—dc232
2011016052

Book design by Anne Chalmers and George Restrepo
Illustrations by Mark Elbroch and Kurt Rinehart

Printed in China
SCP 10 9 8 7 6 5 4 3 2 1

The legacy of America's greatest naturalist and creator of the field guide series, Roger Tory Peterson, is kept alive through the dedicated work of the Roger Tory Peterson Institute of Natural History (RTPI). Established in 1985, RTPI is located in Peterson's hometown of Jamestown, New York, near Chautauqua Institution in the southwestern part of the state.

Today RTPI is a national center for nature education that maintains, shares, and interprets Peterson's extraordinary archive of writings, art, and photography. The Institute, housed in a landmark building by world-class architect Robert A. M. Stern, continues to transmit Peterson's zest for teaching about the natural world through leadership programs in teacher development as well as outstanding exhibits of contemporary nature art, natural history, and the Peterson Collection.

Your participation as a steward of the Peterson Collection and supporter of the Peterson legacy is needed. Please consider joining RTPI at an introductory rate of 50 percent of the regular membership fee for the first year. Simply call RTPI's membership department at (800) 758-6841 ext. 226, or e-mail member ship@rtpi.org to take advantage of this special membership offered to purchasers of this book. For more information, please visit the Peterson Institute in person or virtually at www.rtpi.org.

Peterson Reference Guide to

Behavior

of North American

Mammals

CONTENTS

INTRODUCTION

This book attempts to capture and share portions of the rich, dynamic lives of many North American mammals. This is not a replacement for your *Peterson Field Guide to Mammals*, but a book to complement it. Think of the subtitle for this guide as "The Secret Lives of Mammals." Our emphasis is on behavior and how mammals survive, reproduce, and interact with other animals and the environment in which they live. This information will not only fascinate and inform, but also leverage your time in the field and allow you to see and know more of what is happening when you watch wild mammals.

WHAT IS A MAMMAL?

Mammals are warm-blooded animals with hair that feed their young with milk produced by the mother. Mammalian bodies regulate their own temperatures, and hair functions in many mammals as insulation and protection against temperature and weather. Lactation—the production of milk in mammary glands—allows mothers to provide sustenance to offspring as they develop outside the womb. These traits have allowed mammals to extend their collective range from pole to pole, to inhabit nearly every aquatic and terrestrial ecological community on earth, and to build incredibly complex societies.

LEARNING ABOUT MAMMAL BEHAVIOR AND NATURAL HISTORY

There are three easy ways to increase your knowledge of mammal natural history and behaviors: viewing wildlife, interpreting mammal tracks and signs, and delving into the literature—the books, articles, and other media that record and convey our collective knowledge of mammal life and behavior. Watching animals in the wild requires patience, stealth, and knowledge of where and how to find them. Of course, some species are more easily seen than others, and some places can make wildlife watching seem easy.

In the Lamar Valley in northern Yellowstone National Park, with some patience and a spotting scope, you can watch wild wolves, coyotes, bison, elk, Brown Bears, Black Bears, ground squirrels, Red Foxes, and others. Atop Mount Evans in central Colorado you can easily observe Yellow-bellied Marmots, American Pikas, Bighorn Sheep, and Mountain Goats. There are plenty of books, websites, and employees of parks and refuges out there expressly to help you find these places. Any opportunity to watch animals move and interact with each other is valuable, and you shouldn't wait until your next vacation to do so. Animals in zoos and wildlife parks are tremendously educational, and you can learn a lot from watching videos. Opportunities to watch urban and suburban wildlife abound, and even domestic animals provide us some insights into wild animals. Watching domestic cats hunt in the garden teaches us much about their wild counterparts. There is also new technology to help you watch wildlife at night, whether you are awake or not. New night-vision goggles expose nocturnal animals, and inexpensive remote cameras unobtrusively record mammal behaviors throughout the day and night while we are away.

Learning to interpret wildlife tracks and signs will open a window to the hidden behavior of wild animals. Scratches on the trail are territorial scrapes of coyotes; girdled saplings are sites of feeding Snowshoe Hares. This book doesn't teach you how to identify tracks and signs, but it supplies the critical knowledge necessary for finding and interpreting them. It will provide the "why" that is so important to understanding the bits and pieces you observe directly and indirectly through tracks and signs in the field. Some excellent field guides to wildlife signs are *Mammal Tracks and Sign: A Guide to North American Species* (Stackpole Books) and the *Peter-*

A fisher pauses to assess the photographer before retreating to a treetop to escape danger. © *Mark Elbroch*

A nursing gray fox caught with a digital remote trail camera. © *Mark Elbroch*

son Field Guide to Animal Tracks, 3rd ed. (Houghton Mifflin Harcourt).

There are literally tons of printed material written about mammal behavior and natural history. Information can be found in literary accounts of naturalists; in field guides to mammals, forests, and regions of North America; in magazine articles; and in scientific journals. Every resource has something to offer. At one extreme, scientific publications are frustratingly opaque to most people, but they are the foundation of our knowledge of wildlife behavior. At the other extreme, various Internet sites deliver easily accessible information, but often of unknown accuracy. The species accounts provided by museum and university websites are often quite informative, and Wikipedia, too, provides wonderful accounts for many species. For many mammals, there is also a host of printed books for readers of all backgrounds and interests.

Your local libraries and universities should have excellent books and journals, as well as special web-based search tools to help you find what you are after. Universities also maintain a staggering number of online subscriptions to the scientific journals that publish the latest research. The help of a librarian will be invaluable in learning to navigate the various different sources of information.

GETTING STARTED

Two handy concepts to help understand mammal behavior are *niche* and *fitness.* An animal's niche describes how an animal makes its living, including what it does and where it does it. Wolves are social predators of large ungulates, which they hunt by coursing, or running, in packs. Chipmunks are solitary, seed-hoarding, burrowing rodents. There are more technical definitions of *niche,* but for now consider it as a snapshot of what a particular animal "is."

Fitness, on the other hand, helps us imagine the "why." Fitness is the quality of success experienced by an animal. In ecology, it is measured by how well one reproduces—the continuation and proliferation of an individual's genes into the future. Evolution selects for behavior that improves fitness, and keeping this in mind allows us to better interpret behavior. An animal has high fitness when it produces numerous offspring that themselves produce many offspring. Having offspring is not enough to ensure the continuation of one's genetic heritage. An animal's offspring need to survive long enough to

A log ripped open by an American Black Bear searching for ant and other insect nests and pupae. © *Mark Elbroch*

The large feet of the Canada Lynx enable it to run in the deepest snow. © *Mark Elbroch*

breed, and their offspring too need to survive. Think of the measure of success as the number of grandchildren an animal has, since having grandchildren indicates successful production of offspring that were, in turn, able to survive and reproduce.

A species' niche is strongly influenced by its evolutionary heritage. Scientists use an evolutionary family tree to classify all living things based on how recently they shared a common ancestor. This book is organized phylogenetically, meaning "according to the evolutionary tree." What this does in a practical sense is group species together in families—the "branches of the tree" that contain closely related, and therefore similar, species.

You can improve your ability to understand any one species if you know something about the other members of the family. Many behaviors are common to entire families, and since space is limited, you might find an illustration for a behavior in another account in the same family as the one you are reading. That said, we wrote each species account to stand alone. If you are interested only in muskrats, walrus, or moles, you can find the relevant account and read the most economical, readable portrait we have been able to distill.

HOW TO USE THIS BOOK

Each species account follows the same organization, with information broken down into eight topical sections: Activity and Movement, Food and For-

aging, Habitat and Home Range, Communication, Courtship and Mating, Development and Dispersal of Young, Interactions among the Species (for example, Interactions among Armadillos), and Interactions with Other Species. We begin with a series of brief snapshots of the eight sections, which provide background terminology and useful concepts to interpret and understand the information in the book. Enjoy.

ACTIVITY AND MOVEMENT

Activity studies in the field usually rely on animals with telemetry collars (radio and GPS collars) that relay to researchers when an animal is active and how far they travel in a period of time. Daily movement is related to food or reproduction and habits of rest, grooming, and maintenance. If an animal is most active at night, it is called *nocturnal*, and if active during the day, *diurnal*. Many animals are *crepuscular*, which means most active in the twilight hours around dawn and dusk.

In North America, seasonal changes cause shifts in temperature, precipitation, and food availability and are a major factor in shaping mammalian ecology and behavior. Many behaviors are synchronized with the seasons, and often the length of daylight per day is the trigger. Breeding, migration, and hibernation all depend on changes in photoperiod (the amount of light per day) that trigger hormonal changes. External events also influence behaviors. When winter approaches and days grow shorter, a storm may cause a species migration, while at other times of year a storm will only cause animals to seek cover. With a redundant system, animals are less likely to migrate at the wrong time because of a freak snowstorm in July.

FOOD AND FORAGING

Most of a wild animal's life is dominated by its search for food. Food determines where animals are found, and over time, food selection significantly influences the shape of a mammal's jaws, teeth, tongue, and digestive system, as well as the manner in which it secures its food.

FORAGING

In the interest of survival, animals balance the benefits of a meal with the costs of foraging for it. Most animals maintain stable home ranges, allowing their experience to inform and refine their foraging. Foraging becomes more efficient when future searches are in areas that paid off in the past.

The theory of *optimal foraging* predicts that animals make choices that optimize their gain, compared with the costs that they incur while collecting it. Generally speaking, if two types of food are available, a mammal (whether carnivore or herbivore) should always choose the one with the greatest net benefit in terms of energy, or calories. The cost of foraging includes the energy invested in finding and "handling" the food. Handling includes attacking and subduing a source of food, accessing the food (for example, cracking a clamshell), biting, chewing, and digesting. When the calories spent foraging are deducted from the calories gained from the meal, the result is the *net energetic value* of the food. Of course foraging is more than just counting calories. The dangers posed by competitors and predators; the risks of starvation, illness, and injury; and changing environmental conditions all influence how and where a species forages.

TYPES OF EATERS

Different foods require different tools and foraging techniques. *Herbivores* specialize in eating plant tissues, *carnivores* eat other animals, and *omnivores* often eat everything. More specific terms also exist: *insectivores* eat insects and other invertebrates, *piscivores* eat fish, *granivores* eat seeds, and *frugivores* eat fruits.

HERBIVORES. For herbivores, catching and "subduing" their food is not much of a challenge. The biggest energetic cost is from digestion, which is impeded by cellulose (fiber), the structural support in plant tissues. Different portions and stages of a plant differ in their fiber content, and most herbivores show some selectivity for foods that are high

A moist bobcat sits perched on a rock after a frolic through morning dew. © *Mark Elbroch*

A group of dolphins cooperatively corral fish and trap the school against the surface of the water. Then they take turns swimming through the fish to forage. © Doug Perrine/SeaPics.com

in essential nutrients and low in fiber. Plant fiber can be broken down, but that requires the right tools and considerable time.

Many plant tissues are also toxic. Plants have a host of defenses, including thorns and spines, but chemical toxins are the most pernicious. Compounds such as tannins inhibit mammalian digestion by binding to enzymes in the mouth and stomach. They also bind to the proteins in the food itself, preventing their absorption. Mammals compensate by either avoiding or overcoming the effects of these compounds.

CARNIVORES. The term *carnivore* can be confusing. First, a carnivore is any member of the mammal families grouped together in the order Carnivora. In looser terms, a carnivore is a mammal that eats meat. All members of the order Carnivora eat other animals, but to very different degrees and under different circumstances. They range from the almost strictly meat-eating cats to the largely insectivorous skunks to the omnivorous dogs and raccoons to the largely herbivorous bears.

Meat is nontoxic, comes in nutritionally complete packages, and is comparatively easy to digest. But finding, pursuing, and subduing prey requires a lot of energy and drives numerous morphological and behavioral adaptations. Mammalian carnivores have teeth to hold and kill animals, shear meat, or crack hard-shelled invertebrates. Meat-eaters depend on sometimes taxing and dangerous capture and handling of prey, so they tend to specialize in certain types or sizes of prey to maximize their advantages and avoid competition with each other.

OMNIVORES. Omnivores can eat almost any type of food, but many of our omnivores in North America are primarily carnivorous or insectivorous. Omni-

vores take advantage of easily digested plant foods as well as readily available animal foods, but they lack special adaptations for catching, handling, or digesting any one specific kind of food efficiently. Bears and raccoons eat a variety of plant and animal foods, but sleep through the winter when the foods they can catch and digest are in short supply.

HABITAT AND HOME RANGE

HABITAT

Habitat is an animal's natural home, including the plants and animals and the climatic and physical conditions in which they exist. A species' *range* is the sum of all the habitats that it occupies. Many animals show some innate preference for different habitats and actively select them. Certain subspecies of deermice have an inherent preference for prairie or woodland habitats depending on their ancestry. This selectivity is both genetic and environmental. Deermice raised in a lab prefer their ancestral habitat (genetic inclination), but without

An American Mink with a trout pulled from a stocked pond. Carnivores that specialize on fish diets are also called piscivores. © Mark Elbroch

exposure to that environment to reinforce their preference, it will disappear after about 15 generations. To occupy a particular habitat, a species must be able to tolerate its local environmental stresses: heat, cold, aridity, snow, rain, and so forth. Animals are habitat specialists or generalists, depending on what resources they need and what obstacles they face. Mexican Long-tongued Bats are specialists that restrict their range to where saguaros and agaves grow, whose blossoms they feed on. Coyotes are a classic generalist species. They have wide environmental tolerances and find suitable food almost anywhere. Coyotes and other generalists are better able to pioneer new habitats and expand their ranges, whereas specialists are very limited in their ability to make these kinds of changes. However, specialization is a successful strategy to exploit particular niches and habitats, and a certain degree of specialization is often necessary to avoid competition with similar species.

HOME RANGE

A *home range* is the area in which an animal roams to find sufficient food and mates; it's where the animal lives and where you are likely to find it. A *territory* is an area within the home range that a mammal actively defends against others of the same species. Almost all animals have home ranges, but not all of them have territories. Within a home range there is often a smaller area that is used much more frequently, and we call this a *core area*. Home range size differs between species, regions, and individuals, and it can vary from season to season as well.

Larger animals, which need more food, usually use a larger area. When food is scarce or widely dispersed, home ranges are large, and when it is abundant or dense, they are small. Carnivores tend to have larger home ranges than similar-sized herbivores because animals are in general less abundant than plants. Access to mates is also an important factor in home range size. In most of our mammal species, female home ranges are determined by the availability of food and shelter necessary for rearing young, and the larger male home ranges are determined by access to multiple females. In addition to food and mates, scarce resting and denning sites, water, and protective cover from predators and harsh weather can all influence home range size and shape.

COMMUNICATION

Communication occurs when one animal's intentional behavior alters the behavior of another through some sensory message, or *signal*. Words are signals that signify concepts, and when we exchange them with someone else, we are communicating. Rather than words, wild mammals use pungent odors, grunts, growls, bared teeth, gentle

A Mexican Long-tongued Bat feeding on and pollinating the flowers of an agave. © *Merlin D. Tuttle/Bat Conservation International*

An American Pika amidst the rock jumble it calls home. © *Mark Elbroch*

An agitated female cougar communicates her displeasure with ears laid back and flat and a snarl to reveal her intimidating teeth. © *Mark Elbroch*

nudges, and a myriad of other nonverbal signs to communicate. Communication saves energy and can mitigate risks when conflicts can be resolved through signals rather than combat.

MODES OF COMMUNICATION

CHEMICAL (SCENT AND SMELLING). Chemical communication is particularly well developed in mammals. Communication by scent is essentially continuous: mammals' bodies constantly release a dynamic suite of scents, and their sensitive noses take in new information with every breath. The elimination of urine and feces is often under voluntary control, and their placement intentional. Mammals have many scent glands—regions of skin tissue that produce and secrete various chemical substances that convey a broad range of information. Some common scent glands are the interdigital (between the toes), suborbital (corner of the eye), tarsal (lower hind leg), oral, chin, and anal glands. These glands manufacture and release scents that reflect the internal chemistry of the individual, and they include a particularly powerful group of chemicals called pheromones.

Pheromones are a diverse group of organic molecules that elicit a behavioral response in the receiver. These compounds are present in all scents and are specific to the individual. Scent secretions reflect the animal's current state, and glands produce different secretions depending upon an animal's chemical condition. The result is an extremely varied and sophisticated system of signals that can communicate species and individual identity, sex, age, social status, health, reproductive condition, and much more that we have yet to discover.

To analyze these complex signals, mammalian noses include intricate, convoluted walls of bone inside the nostrils (called turbinate bones) to dramatically increase the surface area within the nose and the number of scent receptors that can be housed in the skin lining it. Many also have a vomeronasal, or Jacobson's organ that analyzes sexual pheromones produced and secreted during breeding. *Flehmen*, which looks like a grimacing facial expression, opens the pits to the Jacobson's organ in the roof of the mouth. This highly sensitive organ provides a detailed assessment of the breeding condition of a potential mate.

Aerial scents are fragile, and a gust of wind or a rain shower can erase them completely. Thus they are best suited for short-term, close-range communication, as with alarm scents. Most scent communication involves applying scents to static objects, to the animal itself, or to others of its kind. Applying scent to objects in the environment allows mammals to localize a scent and increase its effective duration. Scents persist longest in moderate environments, and too much rain or too much dry heat degrades them quickly.

AUDITORY (SOUNDS AND HEARING). Auditory communication is essentially instantaneous and can be projected over vast distances but is of short duration. These sounds are perfect for intense, short-range interactions such as alarms, greetings, fights, and parental care. Some sounds, like a wolf's howl, are adapted by some species for immediate, long-range contact.

Auditory communication includes both vocalizations and nonvocal sounds like foot-drumming, tail-slapping, and tooth-clicking. Social animals are often very vocal. The sounds of solitary mammals are usually limited to comfort sounds, like coos and squeaks, and harsh, aggressive sounds used to avoid conflict through intimidation. Sounds that have more complex social functions are innate but are modified by learning; over time, different groups can develop unique "dialects" of social sounds.

VISUAL. Visual communication is short-range, immediate, and can be very specific. It includes physical postures, movements, facial expressions, and even marks on static objects in the environment. Many threat displays clearly feature weapons such as teeth, flailing hooves, and horns and antlers and are accompanied by fluffed-up hair, vocal sounds, scent discharges, and other intimidation tactics. *Piloerection*—the raising of the hair—accentuates the animal's apparent size, and some species also have fur specially adapted for displaying, such as manes and longer hairs on the back, shoulders, and tails.

TACTILE (TOUCH AND FEELING). Direct physical communication through touching begins between a mother and her young. Adult tactile communication is usually exhibited by more social species in which mother-child behaviors are carried over to later life. Contact between social mammals also serves to build a common scent for group identity as well as to convey an animal's status within the group. In more solitary species, adult tactile communication is usually limited to courtship and mating.

COURTSHIP AND MATING

Unlike humans, most wild mammals in North America are only periodically capable of reproducing. Usually the trigger is lengthening daylight, and as winter wanes, hormonal activity increases and initiates sperm production in males and the estrous cycle in females. *Estrus* in animals is the cycle analogous to but different from the human menstrual cycle. (The term *estrous* is an adjective based on the noun *estrus*, the period of sexual receptivity immediately preceding ovulation.)

COURTSHIP

Courtship is the pattern of behavior that coordinates the reproduction of two individuals. Courtship ensures that copulation occurs with the highest potential for success, generally during ovulation, when an egg is released from the ovary and travels to the uterus. Various modes of communication serve to bring potential mates together, overcome aggressive and defensive impulses that might interfere with mating, and coordinate their biological readiness to mate and conceive.

MATING SYSTEMS

Mating systems exist on a spectrum ranging from perennial *monogamy*, in which a pair mates together for many years or until one of the partners dies, to *promiscuity*, in which both sexes mate with many members of the opposite sex each breeding season.

Monogamous mating, which is rare among mammals, tends to occur in species with low reproductive potential and long maturation times for the young. The most common mating system among mammals is polygamy, and more specifically, *polygyny* (from *poly-*, "many," and *-gyny*, "number of female partners"), in which males mate with multiple females and females tend to mate with only one male. Rather than enhance their chances of successful grandchildren by investing in the rearing of a single litter, males of most species compete to spread their genes to as many females as possible.

Wolves use howling to communicate with other pack members and advertise occupancy and territoriality to neighboring packs. © *istockphoto. com/Jim Kruger*

Pronghorn mating on the open range. © istockphoto.com/Cynthia Baldauf

Competition for mates leads to *sexual dimorphism*—differences in body size, shape, and appearance between males and females. The tendency of male mammals to be larger (and often more aggressive) than females and to carry horns, antlers, manes, and other weapons or badges of rank is directly related to sexual competition. For polygynous males, the obstacle to increased reproductive success is the presence of other males. Their ability to fight and intimidate their rivals is critical to their fitness.

DEVELOPMENT AND DISPERSAL OF YOUNG

When any egg is fertilized, it begins to develop immediately, and then it floats in the uterus until it implants in the uterine wall, where it develops until birth. The length of time between mating and parturition (birth) is the *gestation*. But when the gap between the ideal time to give birth and the ideal time to mate is different from the length of gestation, species exhibit *delayed implantation*. In delayed implantation, the embryo remains free-floating and enters suspended animation, allowing the pregnancy to go on "hold" for a few months.

Once mating has occurred and a female's eggs are actively developing, she enters the most demanding period of the year. She has to eat enough to nourish her growing embryos, and if her health or nutrition falters, she may spontaneously abort some or all of the embryos inside her. After successful gestation and birth, she must produce milk and protect her young from danger. If the young of the litter are killed by a predator or bad weather, the mother's energetic investments have been wasted. On the other hand, if she runs herself ragged, severely compromising her health to ensure the survival of this litter, she may endanger her own fitness and survival.

An American Mink family, with the adult female in the lead and three large juveniles looking on. © Mark Elbroch

One way to reduce the costs of carrying young is to give birth to them when they are relatively undeveloped. Newborns (neonates) that are underdeveloped and helpless at birth are called *altricial*. Extremely altricial young have no insulating fur, no ability to move themselves around, and no functional vision, hearing, or teeth. Essentially all they can do is nurse, and they must be kept warm, fed often, and protected from predators. The mother reduces the cost of carrying the litter, but incurs a cost of caring for them after they are born.

Precocial young are relatively well developed at birth. They have fur and open eyes and are generally able to move about quickly, sometimes within hours of their birth. Litters of precocial young tend to be smaller than those of altricial young.

As newborns mature, they become *juveniles*. Juveniles look like small adults, but they are not capable of sexual reproduction. Some mammals remain with their mothers even when they are sexually mature. These *subadults* are fully developed, but they need more time simply to grow or learn enough to make it on their own. The early family experience shapes later social behavior, allows for development of critical skills, and provides a period of protection and support for the young so that they have a good shot at surviving on their own when they disperse.

DISPERSAL

Dispersal is the one-way movement of young animals away from the area of their birth. There are risks associated with this, but it may be necessary in order for this young animal to gain access to food and mates, and possibly to avoid inbreeding. Populations of territorial species include residents and transients. *Residents* are usually mature adults with their own home ranges. *Transients* are the dispersed or dispersing juveniles that have not yet established their own home ranges. In populations that inhabit places where life expectancy is short, juveniles can disperse relatively easily, because territories regularly become vacant as individuals die. In dense, growing populations, those in which more animals are growing up and maturing than are dying, dispersers may have difficulty finding a vacant spot to call home and can spend long periods as transients.

INTERACTIONS AMONG THE SPECIES

Animal species are generally referred to as being *solitary* or *social*. These two conditions exist on a spectrum, rather than as two distinct alternatives. Some species are strongly solitary, while others form groups numbering in the thousands. In between are numerous species that form small groups or group together at certain times of year or under specific conditions.

Members of the same species, by definition, need

In this series of Red Fox pictures, two territorial animals first circle each other, then stand with front paws on each other's shoulders to gape and posture, and when this fails to resolve the dispute, fall into an all-out fight. © *Mark Elbroch*

Badgers and coyotes sometimes forage in each other's company. While the badger hunts below, the coyote remains above and is quick to snatch up any ground squirrel or prairie dog that pops up to escape the predator below. *TOP: © istockphoto.com/John Pitcher BOTTOM: © Outdoorsman/Fotolia.com*

the same things and compete with one another for food, habitat, mates, and other resources. In order to ensure an adequate supply of each, many species maintain territories from which others of their kind are excluded. Under certain conditions, the benefits of grouping can outweigh these costs. When food is hyperabundant, territoriality often relaxes and even among otherwise solitary species, ephemeral aggregations can occur. In other cases, grouping up may make for better foraging, while in still other cases groups may be better at finding and exploiting certain foods. Even if grouping does not improve feeding, teaming up to raise offspring may outweigh any negative costs associated with foraging.

Groups are more conspicuous to predators than individuals, but with the "many eyes" in the herd, each individual watches less (and eats more), and there are always some eyes on the lookout. In the event of an attack, the risk to each individual is reduced, since there is more prey available. Groups can further reduce the risk of predation by other means, including mounting a collective defense.

The most social animals have evolved the most complex systems of communication, since a particular sound or gesture is less costly than actually having to fight to assert dominance (or defend yourself) time and again. Solitary animals interact less and so can rely on more rudimentary signals.

INTERACTIONS WITH OTHER SPECIES

There are a host of different kinds of interactions between individuals of one species and individuals of another. Ecologists characterize these interactions based on whether the outcome is positive, negative, or neutral for either party. These interactions provide the impetus for many of the evolved traits we see in animals today.

Predation, the killing and eating of one organism by another, is beneficial to one organism and profoundly negative to the other. For many species, predation has been one of the most potent forces shaping their evolution. The defensive behaviors, the speed, agility, and wariness we see in many wild animals are rooted in predator avoidance. Social grouping is a behavioral way to reduce predation risk, as is risk-sensitive habitat use. The threat of being killed by a predator is more important than the killing in shaping prey behavior.

Parasitism is like predation, but rather than killing and eating it up, one organism lives off of the life or labor of another. The relationship is positive for the parasite, but bad for the host. Parasites are usually much smaller than their hosts and feed on them in some fashion. Ticks are parasites, but so are skunks stealing bits of meat from a cougar's kill or dolphins following crab fishermen and raiding their traps. The ticks feed on blood, and the others feed on the energy of cougars and humans. For clarity, a distinction is often made between parasites such as ticks and *social parasites* such as skunks and dolphins.

Competition is a constant between and within species, and the more ecologically similar two species are, the more likely they are to compete. Competition is a relationship in which the actions of one species reduce the fitness of another. Even the superior competitor "wastes" some energy in the process, so competition is a negative interaction for both individuals. *Exploitation competition* occurs when one species uses more of a critical common resource (such as acorns) than its competitor. *Interference competition* is a direct agonistic interaction between two individuals. *Apparent competition* exists when two species are both prey of the same predator. For instance, a large, growing moose population may support increasing wolf numbers, which in turn kill larger numbers of caribou in addition to the moose. The immediate cause of death to the caribou is predation, but within a system of apparent competition with moose.

Commensalism is a relationship in which one animal benefits, but the other animal neither benefits nor suffers. Two examples are a chipmunk responding to the alarm calls of a woodpecker, or when Arctic Foxes clean up the scraps at a Polar Bear kill.

The relationships above are not limited just to animals, and are evident in the profound impact mammals can have on their habitats. Mammal-plant interactions may entail predation and parasitism, but the important thing to note is the shaping influence mammal populations have on entire ecological communities. A *keystone species* is one whose presence increases biological diversity, and can shape entire ecosystems. Sea Otters enable the presence of kelp forests through their predation of kelp-eating sea urchins, and beavers create entire wetland ecosystems.

SPECIES
ACCOUNTS

OTHER NAMES: opossum, possum, grinner, bush rat (Dutch New Guinea), white-face (Algonquian), zorro pelón ("bald fox" in Spanish), tlacuache (Nahuatl). In Argentina they use a slang term meaning "stinker."

The Algonquian name for this animal—the word that Captain John Smith heard Pocahontas's people use when he arrived in the Americas—was *pasum* or *possum*. It was also preceded by a gruntlike sound, which contributed to our name "opossum." Captain Cook carried the name opossum to Australia and applied it to the arboreal, prehensile-tailed marsupials he encountered there. Today, "possum" is used generally for about 17 genera and over 40 species of animals known specifically as phalangers (referring to their opposable thumbs), possums, and cuscuses, while "opossum" is now used solely for our distinctive and not too closely related species.

The Virginia Opossum is the most-northerly ranging of 6 *Didelphis* opossums in North and South America. The Common, or Mexican, Opossum (*D. marsupialis*), which ranges from Mexico to Bolivia, is occasionally found just north of the US border with Mexico. The generic name *Didelphis* refers to the female opossum's two-branched uterus, for which the male has a matching forked penis. The specific name refers to the state of Virginia.

ACTIVITY AND MOVEMENT

DAILY

The opossum doesn't choose to hang by its tail, and pictures of adult opossums hanging upside down are surely posed by photographers. Though they can; small, young opossums can wrap their tails and hang, but they must be made to do so. Their tails aren't strong enough to be used as a "fifth hand" in swinging as monkeys do. Tails are used for steadying, stabilizing, and loosely grasping branches while climbing.

On the ground, they forage and travel in a slow, deliberate walk with each foot moving and being placed separately on the ground. They transition smoothly into an efficient trot when nervous or crossing exposed areas. As they trot, they hold their tails completely straight and sticking out behind them. They also gallop surprisingly quickly when pressed.

Opossums are capable, if not exactly agile, climbers. Their opposable thumbs, grasping tail, and ridged foot surfaces all contribute traction and stability. As swimmers, they are slow and strong, able to cross 100 meters of water with little apparent difficulty. They swim either by moving the limbs as when walking or by swinging the limbs on one side of the body in unison followed by the same for the other side; in either method, the tail gently sculls. An opossum was even observed once swimming underwater as a means of escape.

For all their reputation as being repulsive and unclean, opossums invest quite a bit of time in grooming. Their hind feet comb through the fur of the back of the head, sides, and upper body, and across the surfaces of the ears. Their feet remove parasites and debris from the fur, and periodic licking cleans the feet. Opossums use their forefeet and mouth to wash the face, in similar fashion to cats. Females concentrate some licking and cleaning on their pouches, especially if young are in it.

Opossums are highly nomadic—even mothers with young show little fidelity to their nests. They usually only spend two nights in any given place, never staying long enough to make runs or trails. Nests and rest sites, which they need to keep themselves warm when temperatures dip, may be old crow or squirrel nests, hollow trees or logs, brush piles, vine tangles, rock outcrops, culverts, attics, skunk or woodchuck dens—pretty much

A wonderful look at an adult female opossum and several of her young sticking out of her pouch between her hind legs. © *Mark Elbroch*

anything under cover offering the look and feel of a hole, crack, or crevice to which they can add debris for comfort and insulation. Opossums do not dig their own burrows, and so rely upon those dug by others, usually skunks and woodchucks. They may even share dens with other species, including skunks, tortoises, armadillos, raccoons, small mammals, rabbits, and other opossums. For example, in a study in New York, dens of a mother weaning her young consisted of woodchuck burrows near stone walls.

Opossums collect dried leaves, grasses, corn husks, and similar things in the mouth and then pass them under their body with their fore- and hind feet. Behind them, they curl the tail over the top of the bundle of debris and then lift it off the ground. Using their tail like this allows materials gathered on the ground to be effectively carried up into trees.

SEASONAL

Opossums are nocturnal, with activity peaks in the middle of the night during the warmest months of the year. In winter they are more active by day. They wander about most in the summer, perhaps because of dispersed food resources. Nightly rest sites are located near temporarily available food resources, like ripened fruit or nuts. An individual may travel up to 2.2 miles (3.5 km) in a night, but usually less than 0.3 miles (0.5 km) from the previous night's den.

Their general level of activity declines markedly as more time is spent both nest-building and feeding in response to cold temperatures. Despite lessened activity in winter, they do not hibernate. Cold winters kill and damage many opossums; signs of frostbite, which are often seen on the ears and tails of adults, can lead to gangrene and death. Winter weather is probably the biggest limiting factor for opossum populations, keeping their range at or south of the northern tier of US states.

FOOD AND FORAGING

Opossums are omnivorous, cannibalistic scavengers that eat just about anything. Many animals have been known to eat their own kind, but opossums do so even when other foods are available. One night during a cold, snowy winter, an opossum researcher watched three opossums feeding under a birdfeeder: two were eating seed near each other, while the third was busy eating the tail of one of its companions. The opossum having its tail eaten paid no attention; presumably because its tail was numb with cold. The naked tails (and ears) of opossums often suffer injury from freezing at the tips during cold winters. In this case, one unlucky individual seems to have had a freezing injury exacerbated by an opportunistic comrade. If the gnawing reached a more sensitive area farther up the tail, the victim would surely fight back. As it was, they all seemed quite happy.

Their number one food preference is insects, mostly beetles. They also eat mammals, reptiles (including poisonous snakes), amphibians, and songbirds, including the eggs of reptiles and songbirds. On beaches where sea turtles nest, they dig up and pilfer the nests. They will also eat any bird eggs they encounter, on the ground or up in trees. Much of the animal flesh they eat is probably carrion, and they also consume fruits, nuts, grass, and green vegetation. Opossums relish scavenging large carcasses and will linger in areas around road-killed deer or where farmers dump dead animals, feeding on sequential nights. Opossums don't present a threat to poultry.

HABITAT AND HOME RANGE

Opossums range across the eastern United States and up the Pacific Coast, reaching the southern edges of Ontario and British Columbia. They are largely absent from the Plains States and the arid Southwest.

Preferred wild habitat includes deciduous hardwood stands associated with streams. Areas with little cover (e.g., agricultural, grassland, residential) have the lowest densities. Population densities can vary from 1 animal per 50 acres (20 ha) to 1 per 4 acres (1.6 ha). Research in the southeastern United States shows that they prefer sapling-sized and older forests and avoid open fields and pole-sized pine stands. In the north of their range they are limited by climate and availability of food and den sites. Since European settlement, changes in land use have indirectly benefited opossums in many areas. A study of small nature preserves in San Diego County detected opossums more often as the surrounding areas were more urbanized. Mapping of roadkills in Massachusetts suggested opossums actually prefer urbanized areas to woodlands.

Different researchers have found widely disparate results for opossum home ranges. Their nomadic ramblings challenge the typical notion of a home range. Most estimates are based on tracking individuals for a single season or only a few months (because they usually don't live longer than that), further muddying the results. At the very least, their home ranges appear to be an aggregate of smaller areas surrounding different den sites. The dens, which they switch frequently, are usually about 975 feet (300 m) apart.

COMMUNICATION

Scent marks are made by males, which lick and rub their heads against objects. This behavior peaks around breeding time and can be elicited by exposure to the scent of other males or estrous females.

A male encountering the scent mark of another male might immediately mark over it or engage in his "fighting dance" described below. Females will also lick and rub, but not as vigorously as males.

Opossums are generally very quiet, but they do make a few standard sounds. During agonistic encounters they utter, in order of escalating intensity, hisses, growls, and screeches. Youngsters and adults also make a "metallic" clicking sound. The specific function of the sound is unknown, as is the manner by which it is made. It could be made by clicking the canine teeth together or by some action of the lips. Clicking is made by males in mating, adults in agonistic encounters, and females in the presence of young.

Encounters between opossums or with other species elicit open-mouth threats, called gaping or grinning. The moderate gape with which you might be greeted when coming upon an opossum can look every bit like a smile; a wide gape exposes the startling canines. When making threats, they will also hiss, growl, or screech. Fighting males "dance" at one another by lowering their hips, extending their forelegs, and waving their tails back and forth. They may click before and after, but otherwise the display is silent. Very intense interactions can also cause excretion of a smelly, greenish fluid from anal glands. Wild opossums caught by hand will growl, defecate, and excrete this foul-smelling fluid.

COURTSHIP AND MATING

The breeding season is long, running from January to July in the United States. Reproductive activity has two peaks. The first, from February to March, is the most intense and is followed by a second, less-intense pulse of breeding activity from May to July. Tropical opossums might be able to conceive and deliver three litters per year, but two is likely the maximum in North America. Males and estrous females most likely find one another by following scent marks until they locate the animal that made them. The female is receptive for about 36 hours every 3 to 5 days until she conceives. The female will spontaneously ovulate during this time, during which she will also briefly tolerate the approach of a male. The male mounts the female from behind, and together they fall over onto their right sides. Falling over seems to be a critical component to breeding. In observed cases in which they did not fall, or fell to the left, no sperm was found in the female's genital tract after mating.

DEVELOPMENT AND DISPERSAL OF YOUNG

For birth, the female retreats to a prepared den. The gestation period is only about 2 weeks. As a result, the young are hardly formed at birth. As birth approaches, the female appears restless, lays back her ears, and draws her tail up between her legs. When ready to deliver, she sits in a humped, semi-recumbent position and begins licking her genitalia as the young emerge, each so small that 20 could fit in a teaspoon. Each one of the young must crawl about 3 inches (7.5 cm) to the pouch. The babies have relatively well developed front legs and claws but only rudimentary hindquarters, so gravity provides direction and instinct provides the drive to reach a teat. The average litter is 8 or 9 young. Each female has an average of 22 ova, but there are only 13 teats and often only 7 to 10 of them can actually provide milk. If all or most of the ova are fertilized, surplus young die for lack of a teat on which to suckle.

Young opossums have a special structure in their throats allowing them to drink and breathe simultaneously. When they "attach" to the nipple, the tip swells in their mouth, helping to hold them on. This tight bond is unique among North American mammals. Over time the nipple elongates, allowing them greater freedom of movement inside and outside the pouch.

At 40 days, if the young are removed from the pouch by their mother, they can stand upright, walk a bit, and cry when disturbed. They are about

This opossum is gaping to expose her 50 teeth and communicate a threat. She may also hiss and snap. © *Mark Elbroch*

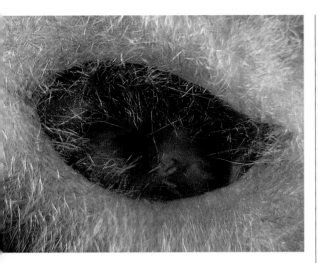

Tiny undeveloped neonates in the pouch. © *Mark Elbroch*

2 months old before their eyes open and they are able to detach themselves from the nipples, leave the pouch on their own, and crawl around. At this point, the nipples are elongated such that the young can suckle them from outside the pouch. In the third month they show excited interest in solid food and are weaned soon after.

Mothers offer little in the way of maternal care. Once juveniles detach from the teat, she no longer grooms or cleans them, and they must do this for themselves. The only tending she offers is to clean the pouch and the young that happen to be in it. As they detach from the nipples and emerge from the pouch, the mother will click to them, orienting them toward her. After 3 months, they passively wean themselves and begin to roam away from her.

INTERACTIONS AMONG OPOSSUMS

Agonistic encounters between opossums are usually avoided as much as possible. Females appear to be mutually tolerant except when one is in estrus, and then she is attacked by other females. One hypothesis for why females would attack a female in estrus is that she attracts the more dangerous males. Males attack one another more often than not, and these attacks can be fierce. Two males penned together in captivity will fight constantly until one is killed. Females also attack males when they are not sexually receptive.

Littermates may den together for days or weeks after weaning. Adult animals will also occasionally den together, usually females, but, rarely, a male and a female.

INTERACTIONS WITH OTHER SPECIES

When subject to extreme anxiety, some opossums feign death as an anti-predator defense, and this behavior has come to be known as "playing 'possum." They are not feigning death in the sense of just pretending—they actually faint in fear and enter a deathlike, catatonic state. An opossum in this state will curl up and its mouth will sag open. The animal will drool and excrete the green anal gland fluid. At this point, the opossum cannot simply get up and run if the opportunity presents itself. It is in a coma-like state in which its respirations and pulse are much reduced. It has completely "checked out" of the situation in hopes that whatever threat

Once young opossums have outgrown their mother's pouch, they travel about perched atop her back.

A frightened opossum feigning death in hopes that it will be left alone.

it faced will have lost interest and moved on by the time the opossum rouses. Arousal may be minutes later, or it may take hours.

Curiously, opossums don't seem to fall into this state that readily. They are much more likely to gape and snap, growl and hiss, and look for an opportunity to run away. Some authors mention how experience plays a factor, and that more experienced animals are less inclined to play dead. One author who tried to provoke the response in a number of animals found only 1 in 10 actually did it.

The chief foe of the opossum (other than winter weather) is the automobile, followed by dogs and owls, humans, and other predators, but not snakes. Opossums are uniquely resistant to the venom of crotalid snakes (rattlesnakes, copperheads, and water moccasins). If bitten, the opossum may display some of the symptoms of mild distress, but they abate quickly and the animal continues on its business. Young opossums may be preyed on by adults, but nonhuman predation has little effect on populations.

Opossums are carriers of a protozoan that can cause equine protozoal myeloencephalitis in horses. It is rare, but quite dangerous to horses. Opossums become infected by eating the remains of infected birds, and then they transmit it to horses by leaving their feces in stables and pastures.

West Indian Manatee
Trichechus manatus

OTHER NAMES: sea cow, sirenian, Florida manatee, mermaid (by the earliest European explorers).

Like cetaceans, manatees are entirely aquatic mammals that never leave the water. With dugongs, they comprise the order Sirenia, a group of mammals named after the mermaids in Greek mythology called Sirens. Sirens were beautiful monsters that lured sailors into shipwrecks with their enchanted, irresistible singing. Ironically, manatees have a small vocabulary of relatively brief, simple sounds. They are more likely named for their part-mammal, part-"fish" form. However, manatee vocalizations are proving more richly harmonic than we once thought and may convey detailed information. They also have fatty deposits in their skulls and jawbones similar to those known to enhance the hearing of such complex "speakers" as dolphins and porpoises.

ACTIVITY AND MOVEMENT

DAILY

A manatee's life appears very serene. They move slowly about in tepid tropical water, grazing languorously and resting frequently. The buoyancy of the water and their slow movements and frequent rests are all advantages for such large animals, and ones dependent on less than hardy seagrasses to sustain themselves. Manatees expend about one-third as much energy in a given day as terrestrial mammals of similar proportions do.

They are active at any and all times of day and night, showing no preference for either. Their activities can broadly be split into traveling, foraging, resting, and socializing, yet most of every day is spent alternating between periods of foraging and rest. Manatees may forage continuously for as long as 4 hours, with alternate intervals of rest for similar duration. They average 6 to 10 hours of respite per day, but as temperatures cool, resting periods become longer and may occupy most of a 24-hour period.

Manatees typically linger between 3 and 10 feet (1–3 m) below the surface of the water, which is, unfortunately, the depth of many boat propellers. When alarmed, they may dive to depths of 33 feet (10 m). Manatees dive for 2 to 5 minutes at a time, occasionally remaining submerged for up to 20 minutes. When they surface, they breathe through their noses, nostrils flaring widely, and sometimes spray forth water like a fountain.

Manatees often rest on the ocean floor, snoozing

in a hunched position during which their noses and flippers leave impressions in the soft sand. At approximately 4-minute intervals (occasionally much longer) they redistribute the air in their lungs to alter their buoyancy, causing them to float up toward the surface. They rise in the same hunched position in which they rest, but just below the surface, they arch their backs to break the surface and breathe, and then drift back down to hunch again at the bottom in the very spot from which they started. They may also rest near the surface, hanging limp, suspended in the water with their eyes closed as if they are in a trance. Naps near the surface are usually transitory and are quickly followed by longer rests on the sea floor.

Manatees also roll onto their backs or sides as they rest. At regular intervals they tuck their flippers in against their chests and stretch slowly forward and then backward, and then stretch again

Snorkeling tourists are a current conservation issue for the West Indian Manatee. While some animals approach and interact with swimmers, others retreat and are displaced from productive foraging areas. Long-term harassment could displace manatees permanently from a given area. © Collection Butorétoilé/Fotolia.com

at the end of their nap. If you are near enough you may hear them groan when they stretch forward.

Manatees swim in an undulating fashion at 2.5 to 6 miles (4–10 km) per hour, and their large flattened tails provide the thrust and propulsion. They can also sprint for short stretches at an impressive 15.5 miles (25 km) per hour. Manatees turn, bank, and roll by using the tail as both propulsion and rudder, and using their flippers as we would oars in a boat. To facilitate a sharp turn to the left they backstroke with their left flipper, while the right flipper strokes normally. Sometimes they propel themselves along the ocean floor by "walking" on their flippers.

Manatees explore their environments through touch, mouthing objects, tasting them, and using the stiff whiskers on their upper lips to feel out objects and potential food sources. Manatees are curious about new objects, such as anchor lines or crab traps in the water—often taking smaller objects into their mouths and rubbing and nibbling on larger ones. Their eyesight is poor and they bump into objects in murky waters. There is evidence, however, that the sparse hairs along their entire body may serve as tactile receptors. Thus the subtle movements of these hairs may communicate much about currents, stationary objects, and approaching animals.

Manatees invest great lengths of time in rubbing just about every part of their bodies on any suitable object or surface, whether it be natural or foreign. Rubbing is a means of communication by scent-marking, but manatees also seem to rub for the enjoyment of it, and they place themselves in very odd positions to be able to rub objects on a particular section of their body.

SEASONAL

Manatees avoid water temperatures below 68°F (20°C), and during cold spells they may fall prey to pneumonia. As the temperatures of ocean waters vary through the seasons and from year to year, manatees adjust their range and movements accordingly. During the summer a few manatees wander north, with occasional sightings as far north as Virginia and even Rhode Island. Then during the winter months they swim south to warmer waters. Yet even in Florida periodic cold swells create waters too cold for manatees to survive, and they seek refuge in natural and anthropogenic reservoirs of warmer waters. When temperatures dip below 50°F (10°C), manatees congregate en masse in warm bays.

Historically, manatees were likely more numerous in northern Florida, where large thermal hot springs helped congregating manatees stay warm and forage during the winter months, than they were in the south. But hunting pressure from Europeans drove the manatees farther south, and today up to 60 percent of southern Florida's manatees winter in and around Crystal River, where warm waters are expelled by 10 active power plants. Manatees exhibit site fidelity and return to the same winter refuges year after year, and they have become dependent upon these human-made warm-water refuges. Ironically, the proposed decommissioning of power plants could further threaten this endangered species.

FOOD AND FORAGING

Manatees are almost completely herbivorous and spend their time grazing the varied grasses and greenery that grow in shallow waters up to 10 feet (3 m) deep, where ample sunlight penetrates water to support photosynthesis. Manatees are known to eat at least 60 varieties of plants. In salt water they eat turtlegrass (*Thalassia*) and seagrass (*Syringodium*), and in fresh water they favor water hyacinths (*Eichhornia*) and pondweed (*Potamogeton*). Manatees also eat tiny mollusks and shellfish clinging to the vegetation, and they may even eat the occasional fish.

Manatees consume 66 to 110 pounds (30–50 kg) of vegetation per day, which is 8 to 15 percent of their body weight. They use their whiskers to locate and maneuver vegetation into their mouths. Unlike seals and other pinnipeds, manatees also have a greater range of motion in their forelimbs and can be seen handling and moving plants to their mouths with their flippers. Their incessant chewing can be

A manatee foraging on vegetation in the shallows of Florida's ocean waters. © Agostino (marco) Celentano/Dreamstime.com

heard beneath the surface of the water if you are near enough, and it is very hard on their teeth. As in elephants, when a manatee's teeth become useless they drop out, and replacements emerge from the back of the jaw, sliding upward and forward as if on an escalator.

Feeding so often on stringy plants means that bits and pieces sometimes become stuck in their mouth. Manatees try to rid themselves of these irritants. They invert their lips, open their mouths as wide as possible, and extend their jaws in a way that might dislodge the plant material. They also use their flippers to rub their gums and teeth in hopes of freeing particularly stubborn strands.

Since they spend so much time eating, they continuously excrete waste behind them as they go. Their scats are cylindrical and pass slowly from the body. It is often the case that partial scats are left hanging from a manatee as it continues to travel or forage, and only when pushed out by further excrement do they float away, degrading over the next several days.

HABITAT AND HOME RANGE

West Indian Manatees live in rivers, estuaries, and coastal waters in the Atlantic tropics, including southern Georgia, western and eastern Florida, the east coast of Mexico, and continuing south along the north coast of South America. Manatees often inhabit sluggish, brackish river mouths and saltwater bays. They have been found as far as 497 miles (800 km) inland in freshwater river systems. Small remnant populations of manatees also inhabit the Caribbean islands, including the Dominican Republic, Jamaica, Cuba, Haiti, and Puerto Rico.

COMMUNICATION

Mouthing, nudging, embracing, and nuzzling are common physical forms of communication and are often initiated by mature bulls. Manatees frequently mouth each other on various parts of the body, including the genitalia and anus, and it is suspected that they are interpreting chemical cues as a form of communication. At the surface manatees may be seen muzzle to muzzle in what is commonly called "kissing." Within winter congregations, physical play involving much contact, mouthing, nibbling, embracing, rolling, and chasing is common and shared among adults and calves.

Manatees rub to leave scent marks on prominent objects sticking up from the ocean floor—limestone ridges, crab traps, old metal debris, and protruding rocks. The manatees that follow use their mouths to "taste" the scent marks and are thought to be able to recognize individuals that rubbed earlier. At regular scent posts numerous manatees visit to add their own scents and check in on the scents of others.

Vocal communication in manatees is purely social and is not used for navigational purposes. Without the aid of vocal cords they somehow mysteriously produce high-pitched chirps. Chirps are distinctive to individuals and rich in harmonics. The intricacies of manatee calls may allow for a range of communication we have yet to understand. Calls are most frequent between cows and calves, which use them to keep tabs on one another. A cow may call to her calf up to 22 times per minute while traveling and 2 to 3 times per minute when feeding. Calves have also been seen immediately responding to their mother's calls from distances of 130 feet (40 m). Adult manatees in social exchanges call on average 6 times per minute. Manatees also vocalize in fear or surprise, and these calls are slightly longer than those used to communicate in other circumstances.

COURTSHIP AND MATING

Manatees breed throughout the year, though most calves are born in spring and summer. Manatees form short-term estrus herds composed of a single female and her suitors, several of which may end up mating with her. Over a period of 1 to 3 weeks while they are in estrus, females are often followed by up to a half dozen suitors (there is one record of pursuit by 17 males). Mature bulls form the heart of the estrus herd, while subadult males join and depart the fray over the duration of the female's estrus period.

Males relentlessly chase the female, mouthing her all over her body and embracing her, and since she flees their advances, the herd is in near constant motion. Males jockey for the position closest to the female, and when they bump each other, they may embrace and thrash their bodies in what might be one of the few moments of manatee aggression you are ever going to witness. When the cow finally allows a male to mate, usually in shallow water, the bull flips on his back and swims beneath her, mouthing her genitalia as he goes. When he is in position, he embraces her and copulation occurs, stomach to stomach. While in the embrace, which lasts perhaps 30 seconds, the pair often sink to the ocean floor, and other courting males mouth the female's back from above. After less than a minute's respite, she then may mate with a second male. When the female has had enough, she again attempts to evade her pursuers, which continue to chase and harass her. Eventually, as her estrus wanes, males lose interest in her and seek another estrous female to chase.

While males work themselves into a frenzy around an estrous female, they may engage in homosexual coupling. Male-male pairing can be seen throughout the year and is reported to be fairly common. Two to four males may begin by bumping into each other while chasing a female, or start by "kissing" at the water surface, before coming together into a mutual embrace during which they stimulate each other's genitalia. Male manatees may become sexually aroused even in the absence of an estrous female, and they may be seen chasing and harassing females not in heat. All their advances are

In this mating group, a male and female mate at the bottom of the pile, and other males mouth and touch the pair while they copulate.

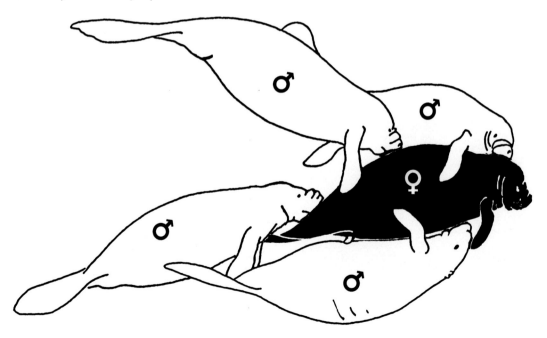

spurned by the females, which present the males with their backs. Yet a persistent male may pursue a female for several hours.

DEVELOPMENT AND DISPERSAL OF YOUNG

The exact gestation of the manatee is unknown but thought to be somewhere near a year. As a female approaches birth, she travels to a secluded backwater area to give birth to one calf (occasionally two) of over 3 feet (1 m) in length and weighing roughly 66 pounds (30 kg). The dark black calves can swim immediately, flapping their flippers as if trying to fly through the water. Within several days they learn to depend more upon their tails for propulsion. The cow and calf remain in the relative safety of the backwater area for several weeks, developing an intimate bond.

Calves that appear to be sucking on the posterior edge of one of their mother's flippers are nursing. The mammary glands are not located beneath the female on the belly, as with so many other mammals, but instead in their "armpits," tight against their bodies at the back edges of their flippers. Calves may nurse for 1 to 2 years, and researchers believe that such a long duration aids in teaching the calves seasonal migration routes, winter refuges, and where foods are most abundant. The cow-calf bond is so strong that they synchronously surface to breathe and remain in direct physical contact for much of the time.

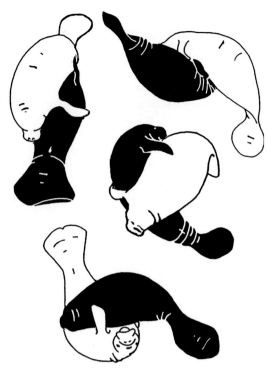

Various homosexual couplings in adult male manatees. Drawn after Hartman, 1971, "Behavior and Ecology of the Florida Manatee at Crystal River, Citrus County." Cornell University. Used with permission.

This calf is nursing. The mother's nipples are located just behind her flippers, in her "armpits."
© Steven David Miller/Animals Animals

Calves leave their mothers sometime after 2 years of age, but they do not become sexually mature until 4 to 8 years of age, when they would be considered full adults. It is not uncommon to find groups of three manatees of different sizes: the large mother, a small nursing calf, and an intermediate-sized, older calf now weaned but sharing the company of its mother for an additional year. Manatees have a very low reproduction rate, giving birth to a single calf every 2.5 to 4 years. Unlike many mammals, orphaned calves are sometimes adopted and cared for by other adults.

INTERACTIONS AMONG MANATEES

Manatees are sometimes social, forming small groups of 6 to 8 animals, though their relationships are usually short-lived. The only long-term bond is between a mother and her calf. During the summer months manatees are more isolated from one another and may encounter another of their kind only every few days. During winter, groups may be larger and have a more stable membership, and social interactions and play may consume many hours each day. In captivity, manatees socialize only with a subset of the animals present and exhibit clear preferences in their companions.

INTERACTIONS WITH OTHER SPECIES

These slow-moving water mammals are exposed to ample sunlight and are subsequently hosts to entire ecological communities. In fresh water, numerous green and red algae thrive on their backs and harbor a variety of invertebrate animals, including arthropods, copepods, and nematodes. In salt water, marine diatoms and barnacles encrust manatees. Fish peck at their backs to harvest microorganisms and sometimes irritate manatees enough that they attempt to swim away.

The manatee has few, if any, real predators other than humans. Sharks, crocodiles, alligators, and piranhas may kill a few, but this is only speculation. Poaching still occurs at varying levels throughout their range, and it is thought to be one of the leading causes of mortality for manatees living outside the coastal waters of the United States. In the United States, recreational boats, not hunters, kill and maim a huge proportion of the small number of remaining manatees. Manatees are well suited to hearing high-pitched sounds, but they appear to have difficulty interpreting low-frequency sounds, such as those made by boat motors.

Otters and dolphins have been seen cruising through groups of manatees, yet neither party responds to or interacts with the other. When startled by diving pelicans or other surprises, manatees dive to escape and then often return to investigate the disturbance.

Nine-banded Armadillo
Dasypus novemcinctus

OTHER NAMES: long-nosed armadillo, azototchli ("tortoise-rabbit" in Nahuatl), cachicamo (Spanish), tatu-hu (Guaraní).

Nine-banded Armadillos do not roll into a ball to avoid danger. The Three-banded Armadillo (*Tolypeutes matacus*) of South America can roll into a perfect ball, but the Nine-banded Armadillo can at best curl up and tuck its head and legs against its vulnerable belly. In South and Central America, a variety of armadillo species as small as rats and as large as medium-sized dogs not only roam natural environments but are also hunted for people's dinner tables. Nine-banded Armadillos are the only armadillos north of Mexico.

The generic name *Dasypus* is derived from the Greek term for "rabbit" or "hare," *dasypodis*. This was applied as a substitute for the Nahuatl (Aztec) name *azototchli*, meaning "tortoise-hare," as reported by the conquistador Hernández. The specific name *novemcinctus* is Latin for "nine-banded" and refers to the armored bands covering the torso.

ACTIVITY AND MOVEMENT

DAILY

Armadillos may be seen at any time of day, but are most often active during the evening hours between 6 and 11 p.m. and when temperatures are between 68° and 77°F (20°–25°C). Adults primarily restrict their movements to evenings and early night, but juveniles are much more active during daylight hours than are adults, and they start their evening foraging trips several hours earlier each night. Travel patterns are generally erratic and appear random, but some researchers report that armadillos follow their own trails when traveling. Juveniles are often seen foraging without their parents, and people mistakenly assume juveniles, which are smaller than adults, are orphans that need rescuing. On the contrary, they are just fine and should be left alone. When not active, armadillos are resting or sleeping in nests inside their burrows.

As they wander, they appear to always know exactly where they are and if disturbed, run immediately and directly to one of their burrows. In an interesting experiment, an armadillo was captured and removed from the site for 24 hours before being released in the vicinity of its capture. Once free, the animal ran a short distance and then began a slow circle, carefully sniffing the ground. At one point it paused as if having found something it recognized, looked around, and then turned and ran directly to and escaped through the only hole in the fence enclosing the site.

Smell is an important sense for armadillos and appears to function in orientation. In contrast, their eyesight is poor at moderate to long distances. Their hearing is decent but most sensitive to higher frequencies. They are more responsive to the noise of crunching leaves than to a human voice. Even while out in the open, armadillos can easily be approached if you are careful to keep quiet.

Armadillos move in a shuffling walk, a loping jog, and a fast trot. When not fleeing from danger they travel steadily, sniffing the ground, stopping to dig when they find something of interest. At the end of stout legs they have 4 toes on the forefeet and 5 on the hind. The central toes on each foot tend to be longest and sport large, robust claws for digging in hard, dry earth. They hold their nose close to the ground when digging and emphasize each tug at the earth with a low grunting sound. They often use their tail as a counterweight to brace themselves when digging and manipulating objects. While active, they will occasionally pause to assess their surroundings. Some pauses are simple stops. Others involve raising the nose up and sniffing the air or even rearing up on their hind legs and tail and sniffing the air, nodding their head up and down. Vigilance is important, both to check for predators and also to check for other potentially aggressive armadillos. Rearing up to sniff and listen now and again also helps a group of animals (e.g., mother and young) stay together.

Armadillos have been observed climbing up wire cages in captivity and up stock fences in the wild. They also swim, and like no other mammal. They can withstand a severe oxygen debt, and if the distance across the water is short, they simply walk across the bottom of the pool. If they must go farther, they walk into the water until they are submerged and then paddle like a dog. Lifting their nose above the surface, they gulp air and swallow it to fill their stomach. By sequestering air in their guts, which can be blown up to twice their usual volume, they increase their buoyancy and are able to paddle themselves across the surface of the water. Armadillos continue to gulp air as they swim and the longer the crossing, the higher an animal floats in the water.

Their tolerance for limited oxygen allows armadillos to be extremely active without oxygen for up to 4 minutes. Exercising with minimal oxygen is costly though, and they may need 4 hours to recover after such an episode. This is probably an adaptation to the high levels of exertion needed in tight, enclosed spaces when they dig their tunnels.

If there are armadillos around, you are bound to see their burrows. They dig their burrows using their noses and forefeet to loosen the earth and pass it into a pile under their bellies. Balancing on the forefeet and tail, they bring their hind feet forward of the pile and kick backward vigorously. The dirt shoots out from under them in a dusty plume extending several feet. Armadillos rely on burrows for safety and protection from both predators and temperature extremes. In central Texas each armadillo maintains 4 or 5 burrows. In the coastal plains, each animal uses 8 or 9 burrows, and in other locations armadillos might use up to 32 burrows over the course of a year. A single armadillo may actively use several burrows at any time.

They dig simple resting or escape burrows as well as burrows with nests for raising young. Simple burrows, those without branches or nesting chambers, may be for escape and not for sleeping. Nesting burrows tend to be longer and more complex than non-nesting ones, with averages around 6 feet (1.9 m) and 3 feet (0.9 m) respectively. Overall, burrows range from 1 to 22 feet (0.3–7 m) long, averaging 4.5 feet (1.4 m), and they may run 4 feet (1.2 m) or more below the surface.

Burrow entrances are about 8 to 9 inches (20–22 cm) wide, although this varies depending on soil, topography, and the age of the burrow. Tunnels narrow to about 7 inches (18 cm) inside and may terminate in an enlarged 13-inch-diameter (34 cm) nest chamber lined with vegetation. The vegetation shows no obvious structure and looks like it was simply crammed down the burrow to the nest chamber. Sometimes decomposing material is found outside of a burrow entrance, suggesting periodic replacement by the resident armadillo.

When gathering nest material, an armadillo scrapes a pile together under its belly and atop its hind feet. It uses its forefeet to hold the pile against its belly and hind feet and then shuffles and hops backward toward the den. It brings the material

An armadillo sits up to check for danger.

An underwater armadillo navigating its way across a pond. © *Bianca Lavies/National Geographic Image Collection*

into the burrow by backing in and raking the debris with its nose and forefeet. Armadillos are also reported to carry nesting debris back to the burrow in backward, bipedal hops, clasping the material to their bellies with their forefeet. Entrances show no particular orientation, but are usually tucked under shrubbery, roots, porches, or other overhead cover.

Some armadillos build surface nests. These consist of a depression the size of the animal's body roofed over with dry vegetation. Some can be approximately 2.5 feet (0.77 m) in diameter and 1.5 feet (0.46 m) tall. Where soils are saturated or likely to flood, as in Florida, they are often located atop tussocks of vegetation.

SEASONAL

As a primarily tropical animal, armadillos lack strong seasonal cycles in their behavior. Throughout most of their range they need alter their activity little from month to month. In North America, southern winters often mean increased rains, which can flood their burrows and foraging areas. In the rainy season they move to higher ground and will remain there until it passes. When things dry out they return to their original location. When conditions are severely dry they move toward moister areas, such as streams and creeks, where digging and foraging is easier.

FOOD AND FORAGING

Armadillos, with a narrow, elongated head and primitive, peglike teeth, resemble other mammals around the world that specialize in eating ants and termites. They do eat ants and termites, but they also eat many other things, including eggs, birds, reptiles, amphibians, and seasonal fruits. Overall, invertebrates (mostly insects) make up 90 percent of the items they are known to eat. In winter they eat mostly reptiles and amphibians, when they are slower and more easily captured. Recent research in Florida reveals that they are major predators of northern bobwhite quail nests. Occasionally armadillos eat baby rats, mice, and rabbits, but mammalian prey is rare overall. During the peak of their season in Texas, persimmon fruits and seeds make up 80 percent of the local armadillo diet. Their teeth are ill-suited to grinding green vegetation, but the soft, ripe flesh of fruits and berries is easily handled. They also seem to need fresh water to drink, which may encourage their inhabitation of wet habitats such as wetlands and ditches.

Emerging from burrows in the evening, they immediately begin to forage. They start by searching areas in brush and cover near their dens, and as night falls they move into more open areas. Armadillos forage as they travel, their nose to the ground in search of scents that betray any available meal. They dig shallow pits to feed on many insects and shuffle through any debris to forage on either invertebrates or fallen fruits. In the southern tip of Texas they dig deep among the roots of endangered sabal palms, and their excavations are sometimes so great they cause palm trees to tip over. In general, though, the armadillos are beneficial, as they eat parasitic beetle larvae along the roots that would have led to the quick demise of the tree. Camel crickets are superabundant in some Texas burrows. Their great numbers, as well as observations of an armadillo entering such a tunnel and feeding on the crickets, have led to some speculation that certain simple burrows may serve as prey traps.

HABITAT AND HOME RANGE

Mostly distributed in Mexico and Central and South America, the Nine-banded Armadillo was first recorded in the United States in south-central Texas in 1854. Since then, populations have established themselves in most of Texas north through Oklahoma and Nebraska and eastward through Missouri and Arkansas and into Tennessee. They live in all of the Gulf States as well as Florida, Georgia, and South Carolina. Their range expansion was boosted when armadillos were introduced to central Florida. Based on habitat preference and tolerance, they could continue to expand throughout all of the Southeast and up the Eastern Seaboard as far as Massachusetts.

Armadillos are limited by cold temperatures and lack of precipitation, which keeps them out of more-northerly states and the arid southwestern United States. Changes humans make on the land, such as large-scale irrigation systems, may have facilitated inhabitation of otherwise dry, open agricultural lands in Nebraska, and expansion of brushy habitats and built-up levees, roads, and ditches have helped armadillos expand into prairie and wetland habitats.

Armadillo home ranges are relatively small. Home ranges from 11 comparable studies throughout the species' range varied from 1.5 to 22 acres (0.6 to 9 ha) and averaged about 10 acres (4 ha). Home ranges tend to be smaller in moister areas where food may be more concentrated. Armadillos like forested areas for protective cover, but open grasslands and developed areas are their preferred foraging sites. Male home ranges are larger than those of females, and juveniles (1- to 2-year-olds) have the smallest home ranges. Female armadillo home ranges overlap broadly with those of other females. Males maintain home ranges exclusive of other mature males, but overlapping with females and nonbreeding males.

COMMUNICATION

Armadillos are mostly individualistic and communicate little with one another. Males and females communicate with a quiet *chuck* sound. These chucks are most often heard when males and females forage close to one another during the summer and are thought to be contact calls between mating pairs. They also grunt while digging and are said to utter a "buzzing" sound when running hard. A young armadillo was heard making a faint "purring" sound—it may have been vocal or mechanical—when trying to solicit nursing from an adult female.

Unwanted approaches by other armadillos are sometimes met with chasing, kicking with the back legs, and leaping attacks. They also have anal glands that exude a strong odor when the animal is scared or excited. Armadillos will drag their hind ends along the ground to mark during courtship and just after agonistic interactions with other armadillos. The anal glands of a female may become everted (turned inside out) during mating, serving a social or sexual function.

Their scats look like large marbles of dirt and insect remains, which they typically bury and/or urinate atop. Often an armadillo digs a shallow pit, defecates within it, and then buries it. Individuals observed in captivity tend to bury scats far from where they sleep. In the drier habitats of Texas, where scats hold their shape much longer, armadillo latrines holding numerous scats of various ages can also be found in shallow scrapes under cover.

COURTSHIP AND MATING

Mating occurs from June to November and peaks in July and August. Armadillos in some populations appear to be polygynous: most males mate with more than one female, most females have only one mate, and a few males monopolize most of the females. However, genetic tests in Florida did not indicate polygynous mating, so their actual mating system is not definitively known.

Excellent fieldwork has been done on pairing behavior, but little has been seen of actual mating. When a male approaches a female, he must establish a bond with her that will carry them through to the final act. A male must persistently follow a female. She will move and forage, and if he does not keep up, she will leave him behind. An unreceptive female might give an approaching suitor a sharp kick with her hind legs and walk off. Persistent males pursue, and long chases are possible before he is successful. Between mounting attempts, armadillos may also feed peacefully, side by side. Generally a male makes initial contact with a female only after she wags her tail, a visual signal that may also aid in spreading the scents being created by her anal glands. After she wags, the male quickly approaches and touches her on her back. Then he sniffs and nuzzles her hindquarters. Tail wagging is induced by male contact and increases as his attention increases. Little is known of the actual copulation, and some of the reports that exist are likely misinterpretations of aggressive encounters. One such report suggests that they must copulate belly to belly because of the limitations imposed by their carapaces. In truth, the male's penis is adapted to extend beyond the female's carapace to reach her genitals when he mounts from behind.

DEVELOPMENT AND DISPERSAL OF YOUNG

Typically armadillo gestation lasts 8 to 9 months, including a 3- to 4-month delay of implantation. Armadillos also exhibit super-delayed implantation, which is unknown in any other mammal. Females isolated from males in captivity give birth 1 to 2 years after their capture. Somehow these females store eggs fertilized during a previous mating and activate them when new mating opportunities are absent.

Young are born most often in March or April. Armadillos are most unusual in that they always give birth to 4 genetically identical clones (monozygotic quadruplets). The litter of 4 is precocial, and within a few hours of birth they are walking. The armor with which they are born is initially very pliable and gets progressively harder until adulthood. Aggression between young armadillos is very rare, and interactions are generally amicable. After the first few weeks they begin following their mother on foraging trips.

Young may remain with their mother for several months, even after they have stopped nursing. Juveniles often feed together early in the summer with or without their mother, and they sometimes form feeding coalitions with littermates that last into fall. By 9 months of age they are independent and solitary. They are sexually mature at 2 years and fully grown at 4 years of age.

Little is known of dispersal, but some observations suggest that dispersal occurs in the late summer and fall and covers distances of 0.75 miles (1.2 km). Sometimes juveniles disperse only short distances, and their home ranges overlap with those of their parents. Other times young armadillos travel far away and then return to their natal areas. One individual was recorded traveling 23 miles (37 km) before looping back to establish a territory where it was born.

INTERACTIONS AMONG ARMADILLOS

Other than breeding and rearing young, armadillos are generally individualistic, with differing tendencies toward territoriality. Armadillo populations are made up of adult males and females and juveniles 1 to 2 years old living on their own, but not yet breeding. Males aggressively exclude other adult males from their territory, but not juveniles and females. Adult females and juveniles have smaller home ranges than males with no territoriality.

Aggressive exchanges involve one armadillo chasing another or actual fights, sometimes leaving blood flecks on the carapaces of the fighters. Fighting includes scratching and often two animals rearing up and "boxing" at one another with their forefeet. Sometimes the animals roll and flip over while clasping onto one another, belly to belly. Males and

Four genetically identical offspring line up to nurse from their mother. © *Bianca Lavies/National Geographic Image Collection*

females can be equally aggressive, entering into the same number of aggressive interactions, but they do so under different circumstances. Females tend to be most aggressive toward juveniles and other females, and females with young can be extremely aggressive to any mammalian intruder. Males are most aggressive during the breeding season, and breeding males direct most of their aggression toward younger adults. Aggression in females serves to protect current litters and to encourage dispersal of juveniles. Male aggression likely results in greater access to mates.

Occasional observations report on amicable relationships of varying duration, including multiple adults sharing burrows and even multiple litters having been raised by different mothers in the same burrow. Sometimes, when a pair are feeding in the same field together but not moving as a pair, they maintain a constant spacing between them. These "neighbor" associations are most common in late spring (May–June) but can continue through October. Female-female associations are less common than male-female and male-male associations. Although they manage to coexist peacefully, sometimes aggressive interactions arise. Males and females have been seen in chases in which the male chases the female and, if he catches her, scrambles up on her back. Sometimes females and males jump into the air and claw at each other while airborne. Females may also claw at one another's bellies before launching into a chase. Chases range from 130 to 230 feet (40–70 m) and usually terminate when the aggressor delivers several double-hind-leg kicks to the other's carapace. Such is the strength of their legs that a well-placed kick can move the recipient nearly 6 feet (1.8 m).

INTERACTIONS WITH OTHER SPECIES

Predation on adults is not a significant factor in armadillo populations, but it can be a significant cause of mortality for juveniles during their first summer. Known predators of armadillos include most medium to large predators in their range, including alligators and domestic dogs. Two large studies of coyote diets in armadillo range turned up 1 percent and 0 percent of armadillo in the coyote stomachs. Similarly, a bobcat study in south-central Florida, where armadillos are abundant, did not indicate any armadillo predation. A bobcat there was seen stalking an armadillo by the sounds of its foraging and then, upon seeing the source of the sounds, the bobcat abandoned the stalk and walked off. Of all predators in the United States, Florida Black Bears are most likely to have armadillo remains in their stomachs and scats. In the tropics, predators include jaguars and cougars, which have the teeth and jaw muscles to puncture their protection.

When startled, armadillos sometimes "buck," leaping straight up into the air. © *Bianca Lavies/ National Geographic Image Collection*

The armadillo survival strategy is simply to flee and hide within their burrows. Under certain conditions they may freeze in response to an unknown threat. When pursued into a burrow they arch their back, bracing themselves solidly between the floor and roof of their burrows. When so braced, it is nearly impossible to extricate them. They do not roll into a ball for protection. In thickets and brambles, the armadillo may have some advantages when running away from danger, but it is no match for an able person over open ground. When alarmed, an armadillo might jump upward with an arched back, a behavior called a "buck," and then hit the ground running.

Armadillos interact commensally with a variety of species. Birds like fan-tailed warblers (*Euthlypis lachrymosa*) and ovenbirds (*Seiurus aurocapillus*) take advantage of foraging armadillos. They follow shuffling armadillos and quickly snatch up small invertebrates disturbed and uncovered by the larger animals. Armadillos also share burrows with cottontail rabbits, cotton rats, opossums, and skunks.

Armadillos are known to be carriers of Chagas' disease, which they probably get from eating infected insects or their feces. Many people know that armadillos can contract leprosy, possibly from bacteria in the soil. Fewer people know that there is no definitive evidence that they can transmit it to humans. Contact with armadillos is common, but leprosy in humans is very rare. Nevertheless, there is a low rate of infection among wild populations in the southeastern United States.

American Pika
Ochotona princeps

OTHER NAMES: cony, rock rabbit, whistling or piping hare.

Watching pika behavior requires patience, as they are small creatures the same color as the boulder piles they inhabit. You are far more likely to hear them than see them, since they emit sharp, loud calls that echo across expanses and down mountain slopes whenever they see an intruder in their realm. Should they spot you coming and call an alarm, they typically disappear into cracks and crevices. But if you wait patiently, they reappear. The species name *princeps* is from the Chipewyan name for the pika, which they call "little chief hare."

ACTIVITY AND MOVEMENT

DAILY

While the snowdrifts are small or absent, pikas can be seen aboveground for approximately one-third of the day. They are most active at dawn and dusk and on still, clear days. They spend up to half of this

A pika carries freshly harvested vegetation back to its cache. Note the shape of the hind foot, which is often hard to see in the wild.
© istockphoto.com/Frank Leung

time perched on a small rock under a protective overhang with a view, or on occasional forays onto high boulders to better survey their territories for intruders and potential predators. Pikas invest the remainder of their activity in foraging, in haying for the winter season, and in maintaining their territories, which they do either aggressively with other pikas or through scent-marking and vocalizations. In late summer pikas may make more than 100 trips into nearby meadows to forage and procure winter provisions every day.

Pikas operate in two speeds during the short alpine summer: *full stop*, when they forage, sunbathe, look for trespassers and predators, and vocalize; and *rapid motion*, bounding in and out of boulders and talus, where you might glimpse gray-brown blurs cruising across vegetation patches. Typically pikas use well-established trails, and animals that move into new areas invest time in creating a network of pathways to facilitate energy-efficient and fluid movement around their territories.

During inclement weather or high winds, pikas disappear into sheltered retreats. When out of sight they rest in a cupped nest of soft materials that they build deep within the crevices and safety of boulder-strewn slopes. In select habitats pikas may also dig a burrow underground in which to build their nest, but this is rare in North America.

SEASONAL

Warm temperatures can be fatal to pikas and hence influence their daily activity patterns. At high elevations where temperatures are cool, pikas may remain active throughout the day. At lower elevations they shift their activity to dawn and dusk to avoid being out during the hottest parts of the day. American Pikas die when exposed to temperatures of 77°F (25°C) or greater for just 30 minutes.

The winter activities of pikas still remain a mystery, given the inhospitable conditions of winter at high elevations and the deep snowpack that completely entombs the world of pikas until spring thaws. Pikas create networks of tunnels beneath the snowpack, in and around the talus slope. These tunnels connect their nests with food caches and latrine sites, as well as lead into nearby meadows where they still forage on cushion plants and other greenery.

FOOD AND FORAGING

American Pikas are herbivorous and eat a great diversity of green plants and woody vegetation over their range. Pika foraging behaviors can be split into two broad categories: *feeding* includes any foraging when a pika immediately eats what it collects, while *haying* entails the gathering of plants to store for winter consumption. In comparison with haying, feeding pikas tend to stay very near or within the protection of the talus and harvest a greater diversity of plant species. Feeding pikas first sit to look for danger, then quickly clip vegetation near the base, and then again briskly check for danger before eating on the spot or retiring to greater security to ensure that their meal isn't interrupted by an untimely death.

Pikas create one or several "haystacks" or "haypiles" of summer vegetation to sustain them through the winter. Haystacks are simple affairs that appear as if someone had either dumped several large buckets of greenery in a big pile in the open, or else stuffed them under a boulder. Most often they are tucked under a rock or log, where they are protected from the elements. For years it was thought that pikas first dried their harvest in the sun before amassing it in hidden caches. But this is not true. Pikas uproot, rather than clip, their harvest and then transport it directly to their haypiles for the coming winter.

Biologists still debate the primary function of haystacks. Some researchers believe they are the major source of sustenance for pikas during the winter. Many haystacks are large enough to keep a pika alive

A haystack of green vegetation created by an American Pika. © Mark Elbroch

for nearly a year, but others are so small they might not last through a winter season. Some researchers believe winter survivorship is more dependent upon continued foraging beneath the snow and that haypiles serve as reserves during particularly harsh winters. Pikas do continue to forage throughout the winter near their dens on cushion plants and lichens, and at lower elevations they may also debark the lowest limbs or trunks of shrubs to feed upon the cambium layer. Pikas also use accumulated snows to clip and eat overhanging whitebark pine branchlets at heights of 6 to 10 feet (2–3 m).

Haying pikas forage farther from the protection of rocks and for longer durations than feeding pikas. Haying farther from the talus leaves greater forage close to home, where it will be easier to access beneath the snowpack during the winter. Pikas harvest different plants at different times during the season, revealing some inherent understanding of when plants provide peak nutritional benefits, and/or an ability to differentiate between plants with different nutritional values.

Haying is a very complex behavior. Pikas select and harvest plants high in chemicals that would be poisonous if immediately ingested—such as those found in Alpine avens (*Geum rossii*)—but which become safe to eat if stored over time. The toxins in these plants break down and degrade as they dry and age. The toxic secondary compounds preserve the plants themselves and may even help preserve the haystacks within which they are stored. It's clear that pikas are strategically harvesting plants during the summer months that maintain their nutritional value longer than other species and become food when toxins degrade months down the line.

Like the rabbits, pikas exhibit coprophagy, which means that they reingest their own feces to better absorb nutrients locked in tough vegetation. Unlike rabbits, however, pikas sometimes store these soft cecal droppings for winter use. The first time through, the scats look like dark toothpaste squirted from a tube. Research has shown that there is higher energy value stored in soft cecal pellets than in stored vegetation in the haypile. After coprophagy, second-round defecations are small spherical pellets, resembling rabbit scats, except in miniature. Pikas create large latrine sites, where hundreds of these spherical scats accumulate, as well as defecate in smaller amounts in other areas throughout their range.

HABITAT AND HOME RANGE

The American Pika ranges throughout the mountains in the western half of the United States and then north into the mountains of southwestern Canada. The similar collared pika ranges throughout the northwest and into Alaska, north of the

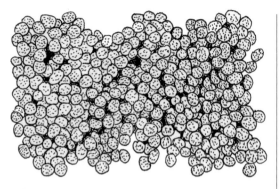

Life-sized scats in a small portion of a large American Pika latrine that stretched 2 feet long and was several inches thick.

range of the American Pika. In the southern Sierras and northern New Mexico, the southern limit of pika populations, they are only found above 8,000 feet (2,500 m), though they may be found at lower elevations in more-northern, cooler environments. In the far north they may be found at sea level.

The classic pika habitat consists of mountain talus slopes and rocky scree, intermingled with high meadows of lush vegetation that flowers, seeds, and wilts within the short, several-month alpine summers. Pikas inhabit the crevices created among boulder jumbles, where the rocks are at minimum 8 inches (20 cm) in diameter, though typically much larger. The boulders can't be more than 3 feet (1 m) in diameter, however, otherwise the spaces between them are large enough to allow predators entry. Occasionally pikas inhabit man-made habitats, such as the discarded tailing at the entrance of mines, rock walls along hiking trails, or lumber piles, which offer the same crevices and protection as boulder jumbles. High-altitude rocky talus is not contiguous across their geographic range, and thus local pika populations are relatively isolated from each other, their mountaintop homes like islands in an ocean of unsuitable habitat.

Pika home ranges vary from 957 to 2,630 square yards (800–2,200 m²), and the smaller core territories that they defend average about 55 percent of their home range, varying from 478 to 850 square yards (400–710 m²). Burrows of neighboring pikas may be as close as 82 feet (25 m) apart.

COMMUNICATION

The two common calls of the pika are both whistle-like sounds. The first is the "short call," which varies between geographic populations, and the second is the "long call," which is most often exhibited by males during the breeding season and is similar across their full range. The short call is produced with subtle variations in pitch and length and may be repeated and produced as a short series. It is

fundamental both to the maintenance of territory boundaries, when they are used to sound warnings to trespassing conspecifics, and to the safety and vigilance of the larger community, when short calls relay warnings about predators that have been spotted in the vicinity. Mating pairs or potential mating pairs also engage in short-call duets, alternately calling back and forth, which may serve to reinforce pair bonds between animals that are ferociously territorial for the majority of every year.

Pikas customize their short calls and the duration of the series of calls to match the potential threats in or near their territories. Deer and ground squirrels, which are not predators of pika, elicit much shorter series of calls from adult pikas than eagles, coyotes, and Canada Lynx. Juveniles seem not to distinguish intruders from potential predators and may call with the same length and intensity for a trespassing deer and a stalking coyote. Pikas sometimes delay in initiating a short-call series after spotting an American marten or weasel, and this is thought to aid them in avoiding unnecessary attention from their most dangerous predators. Pikas may be completely silent when they watch a weasel enter the talus slope they inhabit, since weasels can track and follow them into the narrowest passages beneath the rocks, where they would be safe from every other potential predator. Pikas are less active during high winds that reduce the effectiveness of alarm calls and make them more vulnerable to predation.

Both male and female pikas scent-mark with glands found on their cheeks, which they rub on rocks and other projecting surfaces throughout their home range. Scent-marking increases in areas where home ranges of males and females overlap, which suggests that scent-marking may play a dual role. Scents no doubt aid in the maintenance of territorial boundaries, but likely also advertise the sexual status and health of an individual to prospective mates. Pikas also urinate regularly at the entrance to regular trails within rock talus and near burrows.

COURTSHIP AND MATING

Female American Pikas may breed twice each year, but more often they raise a single litter. Their first breeding needs to be well timed to maximize the probability that their young succeed in finding their own territory. The first mating season occurs a month before the snows melt in spring, which may be as early as March in the southern portions of their range, but is more typically late May or June. If timed well, warm spring weather brings about a profusion of green growth and wildflowers just in time to support and sustain lactating females. And if a female times her mating perfectly, her litter disperses before others within the talus community

A pika sounds the alarm from an elevated perch. © *Kevin D. Mack*

and claims the limited number of vacant territories created by winter mortalities.

Females breed a second time if they fail to raise their first litter, but they have very poor success in raising a second litter if their first was successful. During times of environmental hardship or physical stress, females reabsorb fertilized eggs in the early stage of their development in order to limit their litter size, or they may stop their pregnancy completely if their health is poor.

Given the dispersal patterns of pikas, they often find themselves living adjacent to animals of immediate genetic relatedness, such as a parent or sibling, and thus they choose to mate farther away—as far as four territories away—with animals that are likely to be more distantly related. Aggression and territoriality between pikas suddenly recedes with the start of the breeding season, and so pikas are able to navigate farther away from their homes among the talus in search of potential mates. The breeding season is the only time during which pikas allow other pikas to trespass within their territories or to approach them without physical punishment.

Males seek out females in estrus and then chase them through the boulders. As he approaches her more closely he emits a long trill-like call. Unreceptive females give a loud, prolonged wail and sometimes turn on their suitor and become aggressive.

DEVELOPMENT AND DISPERSAL OF YOUNG

After a gestation of 30 days, pikas give birth to a litter of 2 to 4 altricial young, born with minimal hair and their eyes tightly closed. Young pikas are born with their incisors fully erupted and are more developed at birth than many other mammals. Females do not remain with the young, but return to the nest at 2-hour intervals to nurse them for approximately 10 minutes. During nursing young pikas emit soft chirps, which become more rapid and pronounced should they be disturbed or if the time interval between feedings is too long. They open their eyes at 9 days of age.

Juveniles rapidly develop aggressive territorial behaviors, and within a month of birth they no longer tolerate their siblings in close proximity. Juvenile pikas wean as quickly as 3 weeks of age, as they make their initial debut outside the nest, but more often wean closer to 6 weeks. Their mother instigates weaning by becoming increasingly aggressive toward youngsters attempting to nurse.

Pikas grow more quickly than rabbits and attain their adult size in as little as 3 months. By this age juveniles have become fiercely territorial and outwardly aggressive toward all conspecifics, including their mother and siblings, and disperse to establish their own territories.

INTERACTIONS AMONG PIKAS

Pika populations exist in isolated clumps within suitable talus slopes. Biologists have measured the distance between one pika's winter haypile and the haypile of its nearest neighbor and found the distance varies from 46 to 115 feet (14–35 m). The densely packed matrix of pika territories within a community typically alternate between male and female, so that the territory of one gender most often borders territories of the opposite gender. Territories are maintained with outward aggression, chasing, and physical fighting. Resident pikas chase intruders and attempt to bite their tails and rumps while still in pursuit. Physical battles sometimes involve standing "boxing matches," as in rabbits, and/ or tumbling wrestling matches persisting several minutes and punctuated with fierce and rapid biting to the opponent's head and neck. They may fight for up to 15 minutes and sometimes kill each other.

They are least territorial during the breeding season in late spring and June, when they wander farthest and have yet to begin constructing winter caches. In July and August pikas become viciously territorial and begin to create winter stores to sustain them through the long alpine winters.

As pika populations often exist on mountaintops cut off from other nearby pika populations, they are predisposed to genetic inbreeding. The success of dispersing young pikas establishing their own territories is often dependent on chance. Juveniles must discover vacancies in the talus slope where the previous occupant was the same gender. Should there be a lack of vacancies, juveniles are forced to set out in search of suitable habitat and are at great risk of predation or starvation. One research project removed resident pikas and found that their vacant territories were filled within a single night. Further, when the resident was reinstated by the researcher the next day, it had to fight the usurper to regain its territory.

Often juvenile pikas remain either in or adjacent to their natal ranges, and thus very close to their parents. Yet research has revealed that pikas avoid mating with animals of closely matching genetic stock, such as siblings and parents, and more often mate with more distantly related members of the community. Grandparent-grandchild and half-sibling unions are common. There is also speculation that pikas may disperse farther afield during the winter when snows provide them cover from predators.

INTERACTIONS WITH OTHER SPECIES

Pikas influence and shape their alpine environments through heavy foraging as well as moving and piling vegetation in specific places throughout the talus slopes. Pikas graze plants among and near the talus in predictable and heavy fashion on an annual basis, with the bulk of their harvesting occurring toward the end of summer when they begin to build their winter haypiles. Yet the plants that share habitat with and sustain pikas have adapted in ways that allow them to survive 60 percent annual leaf loss to grazing. Research on a Bellardi bog sedge (*Kobresia myosuroides*), an aster (*Erigeron* sp.), and an oxytrope (*Oxytropis* sp.) revealed that plants growing closest to pikas and suffering heavy annual grazing patterns regrow grazed leaves only at the start of summer, rather than late in the summer when they will inevitably be harvested again by the same pika.

Decomposing haystacks create patches of earth rich in nitrogen and carbon in an environment where plants are nitrogen-limited. Thus plants grow larger in areas atop or adjacent to old haystacks than anywhere else on the same slopes. Pika haystacks influence the vegetative structure, and then indirectly the insect pollinators and other grazers, in the alpine zones.

Pikas also share their alpine haunts with marmots, ground squirrels, chipmunks, and occasionally Bushy-tailed Woodrats. These community members work together to avoid their shared predators. Marmots, chipmunks, and ground squirrels have all been observed reacting to the alarm calls of pikas, and pikas in turn have sent up alarms in response to those made by other species. In California, woodrats may actually be competitors with pikas. In the eastern Sierras, pikas are absent in talus slopes occupied by woodrats, which would otherwise seem well suited to them.

The most significant predators of American Pikas are the long-bodied, short-legged American Marten, Long-tailed Weasel, and ermine, all of which are able to follow pikas into the crevices beneath the talus. Bobcats, Canada Lynx, Red Foxes, and coyotes also hunt pikas when they find them away from the protection of their boulders. Hawks and eagles are also quick to snatch a perched pika oblivious to their presence. Pikas are at the greatest risk of predation and other causes of mortality before they are 1 year of age and then again from the ages of 5 to 7. Wild pikas have been known to live up to 7 years.

Eastern Cottontail
Sylvilagus floridanus, and Allies

OTHER NAMES: cottontail, rabbit.

Rabbits are a most familiar animal. We grow up with caricatures of them in books, on television, and in theaters, and many people keep varieties of them as pets. Native rabbits inhabit nearly every corner of North America, and since we often see them up close, we have the opportunity to delve beyond the familiar hops and twitching noses into a fascinating world of behavior. Cottontail rabbits (genus *Sylvilagus*) are a highly successful group of mammals, and their success and wide distribution have established them as an integral part of many wildlife communities.

ACTIVITY AND MOVEMENT

DAILY

Eastern Cottontails are diurnal with two peaks of foraging activity each day. The first is 3 to 4 hours after sunrise, and the other is in the hour after sunset. During the day they tend to stick close to cover, resting and grooming. Grooming is the most frequent cottontail behavior after foraging. They groom their face by licking their paws and rubbing their muzzle, and they clean their ears by drawing them through their moistened front paws. They also scratch with their hind legs like a dog and twist about and directly lick the fur on their body and legs. They clean their feet with teeth and tongue, taking the time and attention to get down between the toes. Grooming often follows bouts of feeding or social interactions and is especially long for females that have just finished nursing.

Cottontails rest in beds called forms. These might be depressions scraped in the earth or mats of vegetation, such as grass, in the cover of herbaceous and shrubby vegetation. Screening vegetative cover is important for the cottontail's security, and forms are often surrounded on all sides by tall plants save for a beaten pathway in and out. Where possible, Eastern Cottontails take refuge in brush piles and protected spots such as hollow logs and the bases of large trees. Other cottontail species have been seen using the tops of stumps and holes and crotches in trees as resting sites. When at rest, Eastern Cottontails lie stretched out, with their bellies to the ground and legs extended to the front and rear. They also rest, lionlike, on their sides with hind legs casually extended and their heads up. Often they lie under cover, but sometimes they loaf in the open, exposed to the warming sun.

Before and after moving into the open, and peri-odically throughout their day, cottontails freeze, sitting rigid and still, watching and listening for danger. If all is clear, they continue about their business for a few moments before checking again. An alert cottontail perks up its head and ears and might sit up on its haunches or even stand up on its hind legs. Cottontails can move quickly and with great agility, bounding at 18 miles (29 km) an hour and covering 10 feet (3 m) in a single bound. But most of the time they move slowly in a series of deliberate hops. In a slow hop, the front feet reach out and the body stretches forward before the hindquarters hop ahead. Cottontails rarely walk using their hind feet independently, except for the Marsh Rabbit (*S. palustris*). Marsh rabbits often move about on soft, slick mud, and their basic gait is a four-legged walk just like that of a dog or cat. Many species of cottontails are known to swim using a dog paddle, with alternating walking-style strokes of the limbs. Brush Rabbits (*S. bachmani*), Swamp Rabbits (*S. aquaticus*), and Desert Cottontails (*S. audubonii*) also climb trees. The Riparian Brush Rabbit (*S. bachmani riparius*) is the greatest climber of all and relies on trees to escape high water levels in the coastal bay forests it inhabits.

SEASONAL

Cottontails do not hibernate, but instead remain active throughout the year and forage on top of the snow. They seek shelter from winter weather under piles of brush, rocks, or wood, and in burrows of other animals. In the West cottontails also

A cottontail loafing on its side.

A Desert Cottontail grooming and washing its face. © *Gordon and Cathy Illg/Animals Animals*

seek shelter in other animal burrows to escape both winter cold and summer heat. It is very common to find Desert Cottontails or Brush Rabbits resting in abandoned badger holes or in occupied ground squirrel and prairie dog burrows.

FOOD AND FORAGING

Eastern Cottontails feed primarily on herbaceous plants during the growing season and woody species during the fall and winter. The preferred foods in most areas are various grasses and clovers. They also feed on herbs such as dandelion and prickly lettuce, ragweed, dock, and plantain. During the winter they eat a wide range of woody plants, with apple trees and raspberry canes being favored wherever they can be found. Cottontails eat the buds and smallest stems of woody plants and chew on larger stems and trunks of saplings to strip away just the inner bark to eat. Herbaceous species continue to make up much of the cottontail's diet during the winter as well, as long as they are not covered by snow.

Cottontails forage for the majority of their active hours, feeding warily in the open. A feeding cottontail takes a number of bites, one after the other, nipping off the soft tips of grass and leaves. Once it has a mouthful, it raises its head and scans for danger as it chews. Anything that piques its curiosity causes the rabbit to stop chewing to better watch and listen for danger. Cottontails stretch out as they feed, extending their necks and shuffling their forefeet to get their mouths on all the food they can reach from where they sit. When they have nipped everything of interest within reach, they brace their forefeet on the ground and hop their hindquarters forward. For taller plants, they rise up on hind legs to nip off a choice bit and sit back, drawing it into their mouth with tongue and teeth. When feeding on tall seedheads they clip the stem and then slide it along the ground until the seeds are in front of their mouth and can be eaten. They chew with sideways motions of their lower jaws, grinding the food between their upper and lower incisors. They rarely drink, getting the water they need from the green vegetation they eat.

Cottontails practice coprophagy, the eating of their own feces. The plants they eat have cellulose fiber that is difficult to digest, and the rabbit does not have the ruminant's multi-chambered, fermenting gut to break it down. Long guts are better at digesting tough fiber, but the length of a rabbit's gut is limited by the cottontail's small size. Rabbits compensate for this by ingesting food twice, which effectively doubles the length of their digestive systems. The first-stage pellets (feces from fresh vegetation) are green and soft and are eaten directly from the anus as they emerge. The food is chewed a second time and a fresh dose of digestive enzymes aid in releasing yet more of the plants' nutrients. The second-stage pellets are dry, hard, round, and brown and consist of little but sawdust-like roughage. Cottontails are usually coprophagic in the daytime, allowing them to process food and gain nutrients while hidden out of sight.

HABITAT AND HOME RANGE

The Eastern Cottontail is the most widely distributed rabbit in North America. It ranges from the Atlantic Coast across the United States to the Rocky Mountains and into Arizona. They are absent from northern New England but extend into southern Canada in some small portions of Quebec, Ontario, and Manitoba. Eastern Cottontails have also successfully been released in parts of the West and are quite common in portions of Washington.

Eastern Cottontails favor a mixture of open areas such as pastures and young, shrubby woods, which afford them ample food, cover, and denning sites. European settlers in North America cleared trees and made small farmsteads, creating a patchwork of openings and young woods where Eastern and other cottontail populations flourished. The current trends toward huge consolidated farms in the

Midwest and the regrowth of forests in the East have led to a reduction in prime cottontail habitat and cottontail abundance.

Home range estimates for Eastern Cottontails vary between 2.3 and 6.9 acres (0.95–2.8 ha) for males and 2.3 to 3 acres (0.95–1.2 ha) for females. Cottontails are not territorial, and among Eastern Cottontails, home ranges overlap broadly. A number of animals may congregate in areas with plenty of food and cover.

COMMUNICATION

Interactions among cottontails are common and they communicate with one another through scent, sound, and visual displays. Scent communication is not as developed among cottontails as it is among the colonial European Rabbit (*Oryctolagus cuniculus*). In North America, only the very social Swamp Rabbits share the European Rabbit's well-developed chin glands, which dominant males use to "chin," or mark, branches, logs, and other objects. In contrast, male Eastern Cottontails can often be seen rubbing vegetation on the corners of their eyes when interacting with other rabbits in what may be a scenting ritual. Male and female cottontails may also urinate frequently as the breeding season approaches and during some of their courtship rituals.

Cottontails expressing dominance stand on extended legs, raising themselves off the ground in what is called the "alert posture." The hindquarters are usually higher than their shoulders and they hold their ears and tails erect. The alert posture is most common when a male confronts females and subordinate males in the breeding season and when females search for nest sites. A cottontail indicates submission by lying down on the ground with feet gathered under the body, neck drawn in, and ears laid back. When a female is seen crouching in a similar posture, but with her chin up and her head extended forward, she is threatening any rabbit, usually an amorous male, approaching her.

Male cottontails "rake" the ground with their forepaws in a ritualistic dominance gesture. It is seen in males searching for and fighting over breeding females. Eastern Cottontails rake by vigorously scratching the ground with both paws, most commonly during male-male interactions in the breeding season.

The cottontail's tail is also a visual signal. When the rabbit is placid, the tail is held down and the white is obscured. When the rabbit is frightened, the tail is raised and the white underside is highly visible. This may serve as a general alarm among rabbits, but it could also be intended for pursuing predators. When a rabbit runs and the white of the tail is exposed, it draws the pursuer's eye and may distract its attention from the body of the rabbit enough to give the rabbit a better chance at escaping. When you watch a rabbit moving at twilight, it is easy to track it as it moves, but when it stops, the underside of the tail is suddenly hidden again, and the rabbit seems to vanish.

Eastern Cottontails make two vocalizations that are common to all cottontails—a squeal and a distress cry. The squeal is high and loud and indicates agitation. Females squeal as they repel aggressive males, and males may also squeal during altercations. Distress calls are loud, high screams that have been heard from males bitten by females, rabbits caught by predators and researchers, and from young rabbits flushed from their nests. The distress cry puts other rabbits on alert and is contagious

Alert (a), submission (b), and female threat (c) postures. Drawn after Marsden and Holler, 1964, "Social behavior in confined populations of the cottontail and the swamp rabbit." *Wildlife Monographs.* Used with permission.

A wonderful look at the jump sequence in early courtship, during which mating pairs take turns jumping over each other until the female becomes more receptive to the male's advances. © *Ivan Brady*

among young in a nest. If one nestling cries out, its siblings take up the cry. Eastern Cottontail females have also been heard making another vocalization, a low, quiet grunt when approached on their nests.

When frightened, some cottontails thump a hind foot down on the ground, making a sharp, dull sound. An initial fright sends a Brush Rabbit dashing for cover, and if casually approached after this, the rabbit thumps its foot on the ground. It often repeats the thump every few seconds and may do so for many minutes, interspersed with more short dashes. Desert Cottontails thump when feeding in the open at night. Their single hard thumps (sometimes two in rapid succession) can be heard about 100 feet (31 m) away.

COURTSHIP AND MATING

Eastern Cottontails breed early and often. Breeding starts in the spring, earlier among more-southerly populations and later in the North. In Alabama, the first estrus can begin in January, while in Wisconsin it might begin at the end of March. Breeding usually occurs through October in the South and late August or September in the North. A female can bear a new litter every month during that time, and a single female can produce 35 or more offspring per year. Females born in the spring may bear their own litters before the onset of winter.

Courting unfolds over a few days as the males compete for access to females entering estrus. Female cottontails undergo a 7-day estrous cycle that culminates in a single hour when they are in estrus and receptive to mating. A few days before estrus,

they become very attractive to males that begin chasing them. In general, females are aggressive toward courting males, but as their estrous cycles progress, they exhibit more submissive behaviors. Males are the opposite: they start out somewhat passive in their approach, but become more and more excited and aggressive, battling among themselves and doggedly chasing the females in order to mate.

Several days before the female is due to be in estrus, a dominant male establishes himself as a "consort," staying near to her and chasing other males away. At first he stays back, guarding her, and the female passively accepts his presence. Eventually they begin to interact directly. Initially the male approaches the female in the alert stance and once he is within 3 feet (1 m) or so, she crouches down in her threat posture. What follows is a prolonged stare-down, called a "face-off," during which Swamp Rabbits, but not cottontails, squeak. If the male continues to advance toward the female, she responds aggressively, charging or lunging and rising up on her hind feet to strike at him with her forepaws. Despite occasional accounts of females bowling males over, pinning them down, and biting them repeatedly, physical contact is rare. Males typically retreat quickly from a female's aggressive attack, and if one is too slow, he may find himself pinned under the female's hind foot being bitten repeatedly.

The quick rush of either rabbit after the initial face-off can cause the other to leap straight up in the air as the charging rabbit passes beneath. After a jump, the two face off again and follow up with more charges and jumps. Eastern Cottontails usually jump over each other only a few times, after which the male seems to lose interest and moves off or begins to passively follow the female around without approaching her too closely. Swamp Rabbits may repeat the jump sequence up to 30 times.

Another common male response to an aggressive female is to "dash" at her. After he has evaded her charge, for example, he whirls about and from the alert posture dashes past her, throwing his rump at her and unleashing a spray of urine. Unlike jumping, wherein either sex may do the leaping and they often alternate back and forth, only males dash. The female just shakes her head and grooms herself. The male may dash up to 20 times, sometimes while running in circles around her. The chemicals in his urine and other aspects of the display likely speed up or further her estrus.

As the female comes closer to estrus her aggression diminishes. She may move away after a face-off and then the male follows close behind, frequently approaching to smell her hindquarters and attempt to mate. Often more than one male is attracted to the female, resulting in the dominant male chasing off his rivals. Chases of females are usually short (15–20 ft.; 4–6 m), but male-male chases can go hundreds of feet or more, and continuously without preliminary display. The female tries to escape, and the males jockey to be right behind her. The length and speed of these chases vary, and as the males tussle, the female sometimes slips away and crouches down, hidden in cover. The males sniff along her trail, and when they find her a new chase begins.

As a female finally enters estrus, the males become wild in their competition with each other, and their hierarchy is most sorely tested. Physical contact between males occurs as they face off and rush at one another. Some even knock a mounted male off the back of a female. Their usually rigid, linear hierarchy may experience temporary changes and even a general breakdown as high-rank males become exhausted and subordinate males temporarily displace them. It is not unusual during the long period of chases to see top-ranking males feeding and grooming side by side as others chase and seek the female.

When one male succeeds in separating an estrous female from the other males, he mates with her. When she is ready, she becomes submissive and crouches down as the male approaches. She signals the onset of estrus by standing with swayed back, upraised hips, and tail held erect, exposing her genital area. The male mounts quickly, clasping her midsection with his forelegs. Still the female often breaks away and is pursued by the male, and another mount is attempted when he catches her. Successful copulation is accompanied by 1 to 4 pelvic thrusts by the male, and then he jumps backward to break their connection and the female runs off. After a successful mating, the female runs until she has escaped the males, and then she feeds and grooms. The males continue to act excited, challenging and chasing one another, but they no longer seem interested in pursuing the female.

Other than the first cycle of the year, estrus occurs immediately after birthing a new litter. The general pattern of behavior is the same except that the females may be simultaneously making and lin-

A male "dashing" past a threatening female. Drawn after Marsden and Holler, 1964, "Social behavior in confined populations of the cottontail and the swamp rabbit." *Wildlife Monographs*. Used with permission.

Young Eastern Cottontails safely tucked away in their nest. © *istockphoto.com/Midwest Wilderness*

ing nests during the last hour of chasing. The final chase, ending in copulation, often occurs when the female emerges from her nest within an hour of having given birth.

DEVELOPMENT AND DISPERSAL OF YOUNG

Gestation lasts just under a month (28 days), meaning a rabbit can produce a litter each month for the 4- to 9-month duration of breeding. Northern rabbits have shorter breeding seasons, but they have larger litters. Eastern Cottontail litters average 5 young in the North and only 3 in the South. Estrus is highly synchronized among local females, and so are the ensuing births. The effect of this is that each female's litter is one of many scattered about the landscape. Predators can find only so many litters, so each litter has a better chance of survival if there are lots of others to choose from.

As they get ready to bear their first litters of the year in the spring, female cottontails excavate small depressions or cavities in which they build their nests. Eastern Cottontail burrows are usually slanting holes that average 7 inches (18 cm) long, 5 inches (12.7 cm) wide, and just under 5 inches (12.7 cm) deep. Cottontails can dig well, but they often search out existing cavities in which to nest. They can be found using holes made by woodchucks, even those still housing the woodchucks. Some cottontails, like Swamp and Brush Rabbits, often build their nests on the surface of the ground rather than in cavities. Cottontails often build a number of

nests, several of which, though not all, are used for rearing their numerous litters.

The nests themselves are masses of gathered vegetation and fur. Nesting females can be seen carrying the material they gather in their mouths, sometimes with stems extending 5 inches (12.7 cm) to either side. Dead, dry leaves, grasses, and stems of various herbs form an outer layer surrounding a thick inner layer of fur the mother rabbit plucks from her own body. Building the first nest of the season coincides with the female's molt. Her hair is in the process of falling out and being replaced; she just takes an active role in removing it. This allows her to use her fur for the young at little cost to herself. Hair is pulled from anywhere on her body except the abdomen. When she pulls out a clump of hair, it stretches her skin so far that when she releases the hair, her elastic skin bounces back and can knock her over, especially in the latter stages of pregnancy when she is also experiencing uterine contractions. Hair is carried to the nest and then deposited right before she gives birth.

At birth, baby rabbits are covered with fine hair. Their eyes are closed, but their hind legs and coordination are developed enough to allow them to crawl about. The mother leaves them in the fur-lined nest when she goes out to feed, covering them completely. The young develop very quickly, opening their eyes within their first week and moving about outside the nest by 2 weeks. By their fourth week they are on their own, having left or been forced from their natal nest by their mother, which is preparing to bear a new litter.

Cottontails are playful up until the end of their second month. Sometimes young rabbits play at adult courting behaviors while their mother is in estrus. Running and chasing are the main play activities, and often several young ones dash past one another taking turns chasing and being chased. Jumping and twisting is also common. The most commonly observed play is a single young rabbit dashing back and forth, up and down a run.

INTERACTIONS AMONG COTTONTAILS

Cottontails are generally not territorial and live solitary lives in overlapping ranges. Where food and cover are plentiful, numerous rabbits can live in a small area, and sometimes these congregations are defended by a cohesive group of males during the breeding season. In these cases, certain males mate only with females in the group they defend and not others. More typically, males work independently and all females are fair game.

Male cottontails relate to one another through a rigid dominance hierarchy throughout the year. In one study, only 1 percent of male dominance interactions resulted in changes of rank. Higher-ranking rabbits are more aggressive than lower-ranking ones and spend the most time asserting themselves. Aggression is also most likely between rabbits of near-equal rank. Among a group of rabbits observed in a natural habitat enclosure, the top two males accounted for over 80 percent of the aggressive interactions. Lower-ranking rabbits in that same study were limited in the area they could roam, and they were mostly relegated to areas rarely visited by females.

Dominant rabbits display aggression through the long-legged alert posture, paw-raking, and charging at their rivals to displace them. If the subordinate runs off, the dominant animal occupies its former position, except during the breeding season when the dominant may chase after the subordinate. Subordinate animals simply move away or adopt a low, submissive crouch, with ears laid back. They also commonly engage in short bouts of face-grooming and feeding during an interaction with a dominant—activities that allow the animal to expend anxious energy in a "neutral" direction.

Fighting is rare, but it does occur. Occasionally two males fight by rapidly circling and trying to bite the other on his side. They also rear up and box with their forefeet. Boxing is preceded by paw-raking and the alert posture, and if one of them is knocked down, the other tries to bite him and kick and rake him with his hind feet. In most cases, one rabbit gives ground early in the confrontation and dangerous combat is avoided.

Cottontail females may have a hierarchy, but it is not as rigid or linear as among males. Females rarely interact with other females in general and have been seen to be aggressive with one another only when they inadvertently came head to head when foraging and exploring. They never seek out other females to dominate (as high-ranking males do to their close rivals) and are often seen feeding peaceably alongside one another.

INTERACTIONS WITH OTHER SPECIES

Cottontails are the meat upon which most North American mammalian carnivore populations are built. Humans, too, are a major predator of cottontails for sport, meat, and fur. Against this onslaught, they must pit their wariness, the first line of defense for rabbits. They spend much of their time looking around for danger as they go about their business, sometimes sitting on prominences or standing to get a better view. They will even heed the alarm calls of birds and other animals feeding nearby. The next line of defense is to avoid notice by hiding. On the nest, they let a person approach very closely before they expose themselves by flushing and running. If hidden when it detects danger, a cottontail crouches down, belly to the ground and ears laid back, and stealthily slinks away. Slinking is particularly common in windy and rainy weather when rabbits spend more of the day than usual hunched in forms under vegetative cover.

If danger appears while the rabbit is out and about, it has to rely on its quickness and agility. They bolt for cover, bounding away at high speed, but it is a barrier of vegetation that offers them their best hope of survival. Once in concealing cover, the rabbit may double back, cross water, and use other tactics to throw off pursuit. Swamp Rabbits double back by climbing onto logs and walking along them. Then they jump off and run away on a perpendicular course for a short distance before hiding in thick cover and watching for pursuit.

The Eastern Cottontail was once implicated as a competitor with the rare and declining New England Cottontail (*S. transitionalis*), but this is not the case. The Eastern Cottontails just happen to survive in some habitats better than the New England Cottontails because they are better at spotting danger and making a timely escape. Experiments show the Eastern Cottontail's eye is slightly larger and more sensitive than that of the New England Cottontail. When exposed to a model owl, an Eastern Cottontail could detect it at 68 feet (21 m), while a New England Cottontail detected it only at 29 feet (9 m). Both species prefer young woods with abundant saplings and brush, but Eastern Cottontails successfully establish themselves in these sites, while New England Cottontails that try suffer higher rates of predation.

Northern Short-tailed Shrew
Blarina brevicauda

WITH NOTES on Water Shrew (*Sorex palustris*) and Allies.

To consider the life of a shrew is to consider what it must be like to weigh as little as a cotton ball, to catch and subdue other animals for food, and to have a metabolism that runs so fast you are in constant danger of starvation. Such are some of the challenges facing the many shrews that live all about us, largely unseen and unknown. Despite their small sizes and secretive natures, if you want to see a shrew, the first thing you have to do is slow down. It is not difficult to hear shrews rustling around in the duff and debris of the forest floor, and even calling out in high squeaks as they forage, but you will need to be still to do so. If you are lucky, you may see one dart from under a folded leaf to a rotten log nearby, but be watchful—they scurry so quickly they are difficult for the eye to follow.

ACTIVITY AND MOVEMENT

DAILY

Most shrews are almost always twitchy and active. They tend to rest with their noses and forelegs tucked under their bellies, but they are still for only a few minutes at a time. They rouse often, yawn, and groom a bit before going back to sleep. Familiar individuals housed together in a cage will lie together, constantly squirming to access the warmth at the bottom of the pile.

Shrews are unable to store a lot of fat, so they are never far from starvation and must quickly forage and then rest for long periods in order to stay alive. They can survive only a few hours without eating by virtue of their extremely active metabolisms and their small stomachs. Both Cinereus and Northern Short-tailed Shrews are active for only about 16 percent of a day, just 4 hours out of 24. Cinereus Shrews exhibit about 19 bouts of activity in a 24-hour period, each averaging a brief 11 to 12 minutes. Although the average is small, bouts are unlikely to be all the same duration. Shrews tend to have longer foraging bouts at dawn and dusk than in the afternoon, on cloudy versus sunny days, at night versus during the day, and in summer versus in winter. Generally, their activity increases as ambient temperatures and moisture levels increase, and most researchers find they are most active on rainy nights. Northern Short-tailed Shrews are active more often than Cinereus Shrews each day, but each bout averages only 4.5 minutes, with a distinct tendency toward longer bouts in the morning. There

are also occasional reports of Northern Short-tailed and other shrews climbing into shrubs.

Shrews use underground tunnels extensively, and you can recognize shrew holes in the woods by their small size. They might be only 0.5 inch (1.3 cm) or less in diameter. Short-tailed shrews are found more often belowground than above it, especially in cool weather. They use vole and mole tunnels as well as dig their own extensive tunnel networks. Their tunnels are usually in the top 4 inches (10 cm) of the soil, but go as deep as 20 inches (50 cm). They also extend their networks up into rotten logs and other surface features. They dig with their front feet, kicking the accumulated dirt away behind them with the hind feet. If the distance to the tunnel mouth is long, they will turn a somersault and push the dirt out with their noses. A short-tailed shrew can dig about 1 inch (2.5 cm) a minute, including frequent rest and nap breaks.

Water Shrews, which rely on their fur to protect them when foraging in cold water, must groom it often. Oils and air trapped in the fur keep it warm and dry, but after prolonged diving it begins to become saturated. Wet fur is worked with the hind legs, using the stiff hairs on the sides of the feet like combs. The feet press the water out of the fur and throw off droplets. After just 30 seconds or so, the shrew is dry.

SEASONAL

Cold temperatures present severe challenges to small-bodied mammals. Small bodies lose heat faster than large ones, driving up the metabolic cost

A Water Shrew perched with its prey. © *Ken Catania*

of survival. Many strategies for escaping winter's rigors are unavailable to shrews: they can't amass copious body fat deposits to support hibernation and they're too small to migrate. They must remain active all winter, and they do this under the snow. As snow cover accumulates, it creates an insulating blanket that protects the ground from the cold temperatures above the snow. Latent heat from the ground melts an extensive "subnivean" (below the snow) space with a floor of earth and a roof of snow. Provided the snow is thick enough, temperatures at ground level remain above freezing all winter, allowing shrews and other small mammals to forage for vegetation, invertebrates, mast, roots, bark, and whatever else they need.

FOOD AND FORAGING

Shrews are opportunistic, search-and-pounce predators. Rather like a marten or fisher, they canvass their range, investigating any spot that might harbor prey. Wild shrews eat anywhere from 50 to 150 percent of their body weight in food each day. The larger species need a lower percentage of their weight but a greater mass.

The diet is a function of the shrew's size, where it forages, and what prey is most abundant there. Most shrew diets are made up largely of insects, insect larvae, and invertebrates such as earthworms. General foraging niches of shrews are described as *hypogeal* (subsurface), *epigeal* (surface), and *aquatic*. Short-tailed shrews are hypogeal foragers that use any tunnels they can access, and the aquatic shrews (*Sorex palustris, S. alaskanus, S. bendirii*) are the aquatic foraging specialists and are never found far from water.

Water Shrews have a fringe of stiff hairs on their hind feet to aid in swimming as they forage in water. They have relatively acute vision and hearing, and they rely heavily on their sensitive whiskers to feel out prey when foraging. They are flush-pursuit predators that patrol for food and attack any small sources of disturbance underwater, usually caused by prey trying to escape. When dropped into a fish tank in complete darkness a Water Shrew can locate and capture a minnow in less than a second, provided the minnow moves. If the fish remains motionless, the shrew has difficulty finding it. As they capture their prey, they assess and recognize it by touch. In experiments, they prefer model fish to cylinders and other shapes. Once they capture prey, they rapidly sniff it by exhaling a small bubble of air onto the submerged object and then re-inhaling it, smelling the odors that the air absorbed. When they confirm that it is something tasty, they retreat to a terrestrial perch to eat. Other laboratory tests show that they do not use echolocation or electrical sensitivity while foraging, as some have speculated.

Foraging shrews are so quick that it has only been through slow-motion, infrared video that we have been able to see them at all.

Short-tailed shrews, in addition to having a little more weight to throw around, have toxic saliva, enhancing their lethality. The toxin, which attacks the respiratory and nervous system of its prey, is secreted from a duct below the lower incisors. It flows passively into the bite wound along the grooves between the teeth. In addition to being toxic, it may also aid digestion by breaking down proteins. Short-tailed shrews prey primarily on earthworms and insects, but eat a wide variety of other prey. Northern Short-tailed Shrews have a reputation for preying on voles, but voles often make up only a small portion of their diet. In one study, only 3 percent of Northern Short-tailed Shrew stomachs had vole hair in them. It should be noted that these studies of diet based on stomach and scat contents tend to over-report the number of hard items (e.g., insect parts) and under-report the number of soft items (e.g., mammal flesh) in the diet. This is especially true with a predator like the short-tailed shrew, which avoids eating at least some of the hair and the bones of mammalian prey.

During periodic booms in vole populations, short-tailed shrews may eat them more frequently, with more than half of the scats containing vole

A Water Shrew submerges and attacks its prey.
© Ken Catania

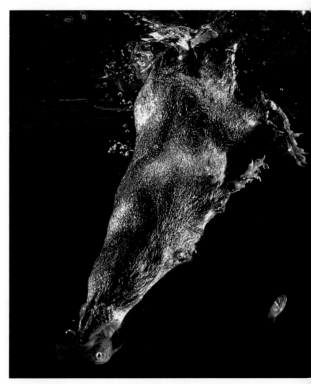

A Northern Short-tailed Shrew chewing on an insect. © *Andrew Jackson*

remains, although insects continue to be their primary food. It has been suggested that three short-tailed shrews could eat as many as 27 voles in a single winter season in a 1-acre (2.5-ha) area. Individuals seem to differ in their alacrity for attacking larger prey. In caged animals, some shrews appear fearful of voles, others attack "half-heartedly," and a few attack immediately and with vigor. Even so, an attack on a vole, initiated by a pounce and followed by gnawing bites to the head, may last a long time. One caged encounter unfolded over 11 minutes, as the vole dragged the shrew roughly about, attempting to dislodge its attacker, before finally succumbing to the wounds. Certainly, the reports of large prey taken by Northern Short-tailed Shrews are impressive. In addition to voles, they have been known to prey on other shrews, baby hares, salamanders, and various snakes, including a 24-inch (60-cm) water snake.

Short-tailed shrews store food for future consumption. Caching is most evident in autumn and winter or when prey is exceptionally abundant. A small item may be eaten immediately, but subsequent or larger captures are cached. Caches are revisited, sometimes by other short-tails, and the prey eaten. This behavior has been investigated among short-tailed shrews, but it may be more widespread. Food hoarding has also been observed in wild *Sorex* shrews in Europe.

HABITAT AND HOME RANGE

Shrews occupy every terrestrial habitat in North America from desert to tundra; Water Shrews even forage in streams, rivers, and standing water. Moist habitats generally support more shrews than very wet or dry ones, as the thick humus soil layer in moist habitats supports an abundance of invertebrate prey. Habitat use is also influenced by competitive pressures from other shrew species. Shrew species overlapping in range each focus on particular micro-niches, like rooting through mossy tussocks or scouring relatively open ground, thereby avoiding competition.

Shrews occupy small areas. For terrestrial shrews, a home range may be around 0.5 acres (0.2 ha) or less at any particular moment, depending on population density. Water Shrew home ranges, which include the terrestrial habitats immediately adjacent to their waterway, are less fixed, shifting along a watercourse as they follow shifting prey densities. Northern Short-tailed Shrew home ranges vary from 0.25 to 4.5 acres (0.1–1.8 ha). Their home ranges are thought to overlap and not be defended as a territory.

COMMUNICATION

Many shrews (especially those of the genus *Sorex*) are extremely vocal creatures, making a wide range of alarm, defensive/aggressive, courtship, and mother-young sounds. It is not uncommon when sitting quietly in the woods to hear shrews vocalize as they forage about the forest floor. Alarm calls have been described as short squeaks, chips, buzzes, and *chits*. An aggressive encounter entails staccato shrieks and rolling *churls*. Courtship chirp-twitters communicate receptivity. Mothers and young also communicate with twitters. Young squeak when cold or hungry and make clicks and barks to solicit

Agonistic postures of Northern Short-tailed Shrews. Drawn after Olsen, 1969, "Agonistic behavior of the short-tailed shrew." *Journal of Mammalogy.* Used with permission.

attention once they are moving and exploring beyond the maternal nest.

Northern Short-tailed Shrews use echolocation to navigate in complete darkness. They can tell if a tunnel is open or blocked out to a range of 24 inches (61 cm) by the echoes of their high-pitched squeaks. At ranges less than 12 inches (31 cm), they can perceive the tunnel around a 90° bend and discover openings as small as 0.25 inches (0.63 cm) in diameter. Most species of shrews have been heard making short squeaks and high-frequency pulses as they travel, which might serve for echolocation.

Short-tailed and other shrews have glands on their flanks behind the ribs, midway between shoulder and hip. These are most active in breeding males, and their secretions may darken the animals' fur on the flanks. Short-tailed shrews also have a scent gland on the belly that may be controlled by muscular contractions of the abdomen. Putting two shrews together in the same cage results in a release of odors easily detectable to humans. The scent may facilitate individual or species recognition and communicate reproductive condition during courtship. Other scent-related areas include the throat, ear, and the base of the tail. Feces may also be used in territorial marking as they are conspicuously deposited in latrines in tunnels and at burrow entrances. Water Shrews make latrines in hollows among rocks and debris along the shores of their home range.

Northern Short-tailed Shrews have an apparently unique and well-developed repertoire of aggressive display postures. Their display stances are all accompanied by a raised head, gaping mouth, and vocalizations. Commonly Northern Short-tails will stand on all four feet or rise up on their hind legs with the head toward their opponent. Other versions include leaning to one side with the forefoot nearest their opponent up in the air, and lying on their side with the belly toward their opponent, while waving the upraised fore and hind feet. Northern Short-tails even roll over onto their back, waving all four feet in the air while gaping and vocalizing.

Short-tailed shrews may need these elaborate displays to simply identify themselves as short-tailed shrews. Given their propensity for attacking voles, they may have evolved these displays to prevent accidental cannibalism. Despite having scent glands, their sense of smell is poorly developed and could require a more reliable system of recognition. They may still fight, but at least they won't attack out of hunger.

Aggressive combat begins when one short-tail directly approaches its opponent, with a raised head and a horizontal or down-pointed tail. Without any other preliminaries, it launches a lunging attack, aiming bites at the other. Many species of shrews also rear up and "box" with their forefeet. In the ensuing battle, the short-tails grasp one another and roll around on the ground. The combat is usually head to head, but sometimes they end up head to tail as they wrestle and struggle. After a few moments, the loser retreats, running or hopping away with its tail slightly raised. The victor rarely pursues.

COURTSHIP AND MATING

Breeding in shrews occurs in early spring through summer when food resources and warmer temperatures rebound after winter. Pregnant and lactating Cinereus Shrews have been trapped from April to August. The breeding season for the Northern Short-tailed Shrew extends from February to September. A Southern Short-tailed Shrew (*B. carolinensis*) was found lactating in December, suggesting broader mating seasons in more southerly latitudes. Most female shrews have a single litter of young in their first spring, although some breed multiple times. Females are sexually mature in their first autumn, but rarely breed that early except during a population irruption, fueled by some superabundant food.

As changes in daylight trigger hormone production in the spring, territories relax. Rather than defend their home ranges, males and females channel their energy into seeking out potential mates. Scent, auditory, and postural communication is likely critically important for species recognition during courtship as well as inhibiting their strong impulses to fight each other off.

In the Northern Short-tailed Shrew, for which we have observational data, at least 6 copulatory bouts per day are needed to ensure egg release, which occurs between 2 and 3 days after the first copulation. A pair may mate up to 20 times per day in bouts usually lasting 5, but sometimes as many as 25, minutes. The male and female sex organs are both shaped such that they become locked together, encouraging a connection adequate to induce ovulation.

DEVELOPMENT AND DISPERSAL OF YOUNG

Short-tailed and *Sorex* shrews gestate for about 3 to 4 weeks. Young Cinereus Shrews are rarely observed in field studies before June or after September. In the end, a litter of 5 to 7 young are born in a small insulated ball of woven, dried grasses. Short-tailed shrews make nests underground, in their tunnels. Their nests are balls of grass and vegetation and may be lined with the fur of dined-on voles. The entrances to the nest are constricted when the mother has young in the nest.

As always, existence is tenuous for shrews. A female that needs to eat 80 percent of her weight each day during the winter might need to eat 125 percent while pregnant and lactating. Only the mother cares for the youngsters, and her care is for the most part limited to grooming and nursing. A captive Northern Short-tailed Shrew was seen regurgitating

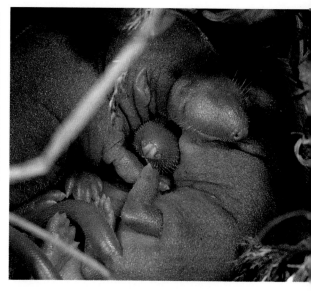

Newborn Water Shrews tucked up in a nest.
© *Ken Catania*

food for her offspring as early as 4 days after birth. No such behavior has been seen among Cinereus Shrews, but most of what happens in the nest is hidden from us.

Shrews are tiny and translucent at birth; their organs can be seen through the abdominal wall and the only hairs on their bodies are short whiskers. They develop rapidly, attaining adult appearance and 80 percent of adult weight in only 3 weeks. After the first week, guard hairs are growing in. At this stage baby Northern Short-tailed Shrews can make sucking sounds and baby Cinereus Shrews can chirp in response to disturbance. Young shrews are initially rather vocal, but this decreases as they age. Their eyes and ears open by their third week, and at around 25 days of age they are weaned.

When independent of their mother, young Cinereus Shrews remain together for a few days. When frightened, as by a passing shadow, they "caravan" and move as a train by pressing their snouts into the fur at the base of the tail of the sibling in front of them (in some species, they actually bite onto one another's rumps). They can move very quickly in this fashion, appearing like a furry snake slithering away in the debris.

Each summer sees 2 generations of shrews born,

A caravan of youngsters following an adult shrew. North American species usually maintain their contact by placing their snouts upon the back of the shrew in front of them, rather than by biting its rear end.

but most do not survive. Mortality is highest in the first 2 months of life. Only about 80 percent of shrews survive to sexual maturity, and fall litters have lower survival than spring litters. The 20 percent that do make it are further reduced by half in the following months. After parental and sibling bonds dissolve, young shrews disperse to find and create their own territories. Since mortality for adult shrews is high, most young are able to usurp adult territories, but when the population is growing, they may be forced to move into marginal and poor habitats. Most of the overwintering population each year is composed of juveniles that will be the breeding base of next summer's population. Ultimately few shrews live past 15 months.

INTERACTIONS AMONG SHREWS

Shrews are not especially sociable. Other than a mother with young or a male and female in courtship, Cinereus Shrews are generally fiercely territorial. Nevertheless, extremely high concentrations of shrews have been noted. In one case, many shrews, mostly Cinereus Shrews, ran about on the surface of the ground, rearing up and "boxing" other shrews as they encountered them. Several observers have reported these active concentrations, but no adequate explanations have been offered. In one account, an unusual concentration was observed during the day, but trapping the area at night resulted in no captures.

Multiple adult Northern Short-tailed Shrews have also been captured in close proximity to one another and in the same tunnels. Studies of their home ranges indicate that they overlap tremendously and that the short-tails are not territorial. These incidents, plus the continued association of Cinereus Shrew siblings after weaning, suggest that shrews may have some capacity for gregariousness, but the extent of their social behaviors is currently unknown.

Aside from seemingly aberrant aggregations, tremendous fluctuations in population density have also been recorded. In response to superabundant food (e.g., an insect outbreak), Northern Short-tailed Shrews have quadrupled their population size in less than a year. In cold winter temperatures, they may decline by 90 percent and recovery from such big crashes can take several years. Typically populations peak in late summer and then decline through the winter. They are lowest in the spring before the shrews begin breeding again. Much of the summer population rise could come not just from local breeding but from an influx of individuals immigrating into the area. One field study of Cinereus Shrews that occurred during a population irruption indicated a high rate of immigration in the summers.

The study also noted that the behavior, and apparently the biology, of the shrews changed markedly at the time. The shrews were much more irritable and excitable then they had been in earlier years of the study. As juveniles began mating early and the population began to rise, it became difficult to keep the shrews alive in the traps or in captivity. Shrews, with their high metabolisms, sometimes starve in a matter of hours when caught in a trap, but in most years of this study, they fared well; they could remain in the traps for 8 hours with fewer than 5 percent of the captured shrews dying. Suddenly, as the population irrupted, trap deaths shot to 25 percent even when traps were being checked every 2 hours.

INTERACTIONS WITH OTHER SPECIES

Some studies suggest that Northern Short-tailed Shrews and White-footed Deermice (*Peromyscus leucopus*) are competitors and that the presence of the mice aboveground limits the shrews in tunnels below. Others suggest that the mice extend their foraging aboveground into trees in order to avoid shrews. This raises the lingering question as to whether short-tailed shrews are significant predators of mice and voles. We do know the presence of short-tailed shrew scent acts as a repellent for North American Deermice (*Peromyscus maniculatus*), Meadow Voles (*Microtus pennsylvanicus*), and Red-backed Voles (*Myodes gapperi*), and that at times short-tailed shrews prey heavily on voles, especially their young. Otherwise their interactions remain largely unknown.

Shrews are a minor part of the diet of numerous mammalian, reptilian, and avian predators. Many cat owners find that their cats kill shrews but refuse to eat them. For their abundance within a habitat, they are underrepresented in most mammalian predators' diets. Some hypothesize that the distinctive odors of shrews function primarily as defense, making them distasteful. Birds don't seem to care, and hawks and owls take their fair share of shrews. Surely not common, but interesting, a Southern Short-tailed Shrew was once found in the stomach of a green sunfish (*Lepomis cyanellus*).

As predators of invertebrates, shrews are beneficial to most human interests, particularly when they prey on pest insects such as the larvae of sawflies which attack commercial timber. Intensive foraging by shrews does not control insect populations, but it can alter relative abundance or dominance among the species. If there is an outbreak of some insect, shrews may concentrate on them as a food, even migrating in from nearby to partake of the bounty. For these reasons, Cinereus Shrews were introduced to Newfoundland as biocontrollers of larch sawfly, a forestry pest.

Star-nosed Mole
Condylura cristata, and Allies

OTHER NAMES: taupe (French), topo (Spanish), alem8nska (Abenaki, in which "8" is a nasal sound).

Star-nosed Moles have 22 radiating, fleshy "tentacles" at the end of their snout. These tentacles are sensitive, tactile appendages covered with sensory receptors that respond to touch and, perhaps, seismic vibrations. The tentacles can move independently and flex 90 degrees forward and backward. Sometimes they are all pointed forward together, and at other times they are opened up like the petals of a flower.

All moles have several thousand sensitive tactile receptors called Eimer's organs on their snout, but Star-nosed Moles have 25,000 to 30,000 of them studding the entire surface of their nasal appendages. Though their tentacles are small, just 0.4 in. (1 cm) across, they contain more than 5 times the number of nerves of human hands. Their tentacles are not used to grasp or move anything; they are simply ultrasensitive "fingers" for seeing the world through touch. The Star-nosed Mole's nose is so sensitive and its brain is so highly attuned to that information that it has been referred to as the "nose that looks like a hand but acts like an eye."

ACTIVITY AND MOVEMENT

DAILY

Moles alternate periods of activity and rest, each of which may last 3 to 4 hours. The majority of the day is spent sleeping or resting: Star-nosed Moles likely spend over half of each day sleeping. When active, Star-nosed Moles take a little extra time to tend to their nose. They must take care of their sensitive

An excellent look at the fleshy appendages at the tip of the Star-nosed Mole's nose. © *Ken Catania*

When they are not sleeping, moles are found patrolling existing tunnels or excavating new ones. Most people believe moles are slow creatures, but this is not true. When aboveground, or traveling unobstructed tunnels, they move with surprising speed in a wriggling blur of gray. The sensory cortex of a mole's brain is devoted almost completely to the tactile capacity of the face and hands. Sensory vibrissae (whiskers) grow from the snout, head, shoulders, and possibly in the tails. When moving through their tunnels they hold their tail up, in contact with the roof, and may be using it as a tactile antenna.

Digging moles have unique arm and shoulder structures that allow them to generate the force needed to dig both extensively and efficiently. When digging, the upper arm is rotated with a motion similar to a human dribbling a ball or giving a high-five. The upper arm bones are short and broad and driven by strong muscles, allowing a twisting motion that scrapes away all but the hardest earth.

Moles do not "swim" through the dirt as many imagine. When digging, a mole twists its body to one side and reaches forward with one hand. That hand compresses or scoops earth while the other limbs brace against the tunnel walls. They make surface tunnels that result in long raised ridges of dirt by pushing the earth upward. These tunnels can be made quickly: the Eastern Mole (*Scalopus aquaticus*) can make surface tunnels at about 15 feet (4.6 m) per hour.

The mole digs deep tunnels where the earth is more compact by carving away the face of the tunnel and pushing the dirt over and behind its body. It digs first with one arm and then the other. Here, the dirt can't be merely pushed aside as in shallow tunnels and so must be removed completely from the tunnel. When dirt has built up behind the mole, it turns a sideways somersault and, holding one forefoot in front of its face as a "blade," bulldozes the waste back to a tunnel exit where it is ejected and deposited as a molehill. After ejecting these tailings, the mole plugs the hole, and it may backfill the whole exit tunnel as it shifts its activity farther along the new tunnel.

Molehills can be distinguished from gopher mounds by their uniform, volcano shape and often a lack of an obvious hole or hole plug. Only excavation of the mound will disclose the hole at its center. Gopher mounds have a hole with an obvious plug, and the dirt is mounded asymmetrically to one side of the hole in a fan or crescent.

Star-nosed Moles build few surface ridges and mounds. Their tunnel systems include shallow and deep tunnels, but with gradual transitions between

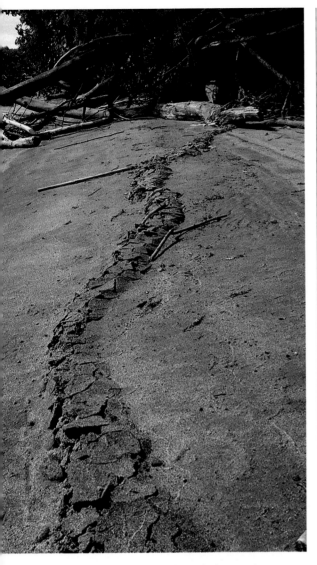

The raised ridge of earth made by a mole creating a shallow tunnel just beneath the surface of the earth. © *Mark Elbroch*

them, and no patterns to where shallow or deep tunnels are dug within their systems. They frequently have open tunnels exiting under the surface of water, and occasionally their tunnels open up and run across the surface as paths. The length of a Star-nosed Mole's burrow has only been recorded a few times. One burrow belonging to a male was 236 feet (72 m) long, of which 69 feet (21 m) was in boggy soils adjacent to water. A second male's burrow was 886 feet (270 m) long, of which only 66 feet (20 m) were in dry, upland soils covered in grass. The remainder was in the very wet soil adjacent to water.

Tunnel systems include rest and nest chambers, with the nest chambers being specifically for raising young. Nesting chambers are usually larger than simple resting chambers, although both have matted vegetation for insulation. The maternal nests of Star-nosed Moles are made of grasses, leaves, and straw. Unlike those of mice and voles, the vegetation is bundled together but not shredded. Resting chambers appear similar to maternal nest chambers, but smaller.

Most moles are good swimmers, but Star-nosed Moles have taken this to the extreme. They have nearly twice the lung capacity of other moles and are semiaquatic mammals that forage extensively in water. They hold their breath to dive beneath the surface of streams and ponds to snatch aquatic invertebrates. Their typical dives are about 10 seconds long, but they may remain submerged for up to 47 seconds. Their hind feet are proportionally larger than those of other moles, an aid in swimming. They often bend their nose upward in a "snorkeling" position when they swim. They are occasionally caught in muskrat and minnow traps and have been observed swimming under the ice during winter. They may swim more often in winter than in any other season because at that time aquatic prey are more readily available than terrestrial.

SEASONAL

Star-nosed Moles dig two types of tunnels, shallow and deep. Shallow tunnels occur in light, moist soils and are used mostly in summer. In drier soils and cold weather, moles use deeper tunnels for travel routes to other, moist foraging areas and as refuges from the cold. Shallow tunnels have the conspicuous ridge of raised soil where the mole plowed through just below the surface, compressing and pushing the dirt up out of the way. Deep tunnels can be dug more than 3 feet (1 m) below the surface where the earth never freezes. Northern moles remain active in deep tunnels throughout the winter.

FOOD AND FORAGING

Moles are opportunistic and eat animals, mostly invertebrates, in proportion to their availability in their immediate habitat. They prey most heavily on earthworms, but in hot summer weather, when the ground may get hard, moles can be quite active foraging on the surface.

Earthworms are a significant portion, if not the primary component, of the diets of all members of the mole family. The European Mole (*Talpa europaea*) hoards worms by biting their heads off and storing them in the walls of their tunnels and burrows. They augment their diet of worms and other invertebrates with some peculiar exceptions. Most species eat some vegetation, including truffles, but a few species consume a significant amount of it. Sometimes moles damage plant roots and bulbs in the course of their tunneling. This damage includes biting, but usually does not appear to be from eating.

The diets of Star-nosed Moles, like other species, are a function of habitat. They appear to be generalist, opportunistic predators of terrestrial and aquatic invertebrates. They also eat small vertebrate prey. Moles studied in habitats near large water bodies eat mostly aquatic worms and other water-dwelling invertebrates. Moles in habitats with only small ponds in the vicinity eat mostly earthworms and beetle larvae.

Moles have well-developed tactile senses and perhaps some ability to detect magnetic or seismic stimuli. They don't seem to use their sense of smell much in locating prey, and they don't attack prey until they touch it with their snouts. Their primary foraging tactic is likely blundering into tasty bits while plying their tunnels. Once a tunnel is made, the soil forming the walls dries out, and prey density drops compared to undisturbed, moister soils. Nevertheless, given the amount of energy it takes to dig tunnels rather than simply travel through them, foraging in existing tunnels is generally advantageous. Few tunnels, once made, go unused by one individual or another.

Star-nosed Moles move quickly along their tunnels, their nose swinging from side to side, tentacles waving, touching all over the tunnel as it passes. Should an insect go untouched, it is often not detected. If the nose does find something, the mole moves like lightning to grab and dispatch it and then tears it into pieces and quickly gulps it down. Although scent doesn't appear to be used for prey location, it could be used for prey recognition. The smelling ability of Star-nosed Moles may be used to track prey, even underwater. On land, moles test scents by puffing air onto an object and then rapidly inhaling the air again, along with molecules of whatever they smell. Star-nosed Moles use this same technique underwater. Scent molecules diffuse into the bubbles and are smelled when the mole re-inhales the air; they can actually smell the surrounding water when sniffing in the bubbles. Laboratory tests show that Star-nosed Moles (and Water Shrews, *Sorex palustris*) can use this technique to follow scent trails on the bottom of a holding tank. They might also use this ability to detect hiding prey.

HABITAT AND HOME RANGE

Moles inhabit all but the most arid and rocky habitats, where the earth is too compacted for efficient digging. Various mole species inhabit the eastern half of the United States and the West Coast. They are absent from the Southwest, Rocky Mountain, and Northern Great Plains states. The Star-nosed Mole has the most-northerly distribution, extending well up into Manitoba, Ontario, Quebec, and Newfoundland. Perhaps its ability to exploit aquatic environments in the winter allows it to thrive where no other moles do. Its range also includes the Great Lakes states and New England and extends southward along the Atlantic Coast to southern Georgia.

Moles require moist soils and overhead cover, which helps guard against solar drying. Not surprising for the most aquatic of the North American moles, Star-nosed Mole burrows and tunnels are constructed in or near wet, marshy areas, lakes, and streams. Some tunnels open underwater, allowing safe access to water, even under winter ice. Tunneling is most extensive around buried rocks, fallen logs, and roots, which provide structural support.

Home ranges vary by quality of habitat. The only thorough investigation of mole home ranges in North America was done on Eastern Moles, and it sampled only 12 individuals. In that study, males' home ranges averaged 2.7 acres (1.1 ha) and females' averaged 0.67 acres (0.27 ha). Home ranges in poor habitat might be 10 times the size of those in good habitat.

Tunnel systems of two Star-nosed Moles and a nest (the star symbol). Drawn after Hickman, 1983, "Influence of semiaquatic habit in determining burrow structure of the star-nosed mole." *Canadian Journal of Zoology.* Used with permission.

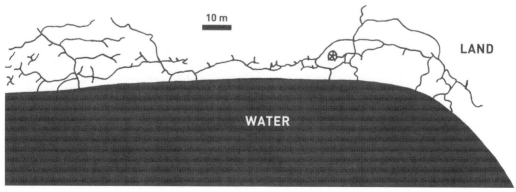

A Star-nosed Mole blowing bubbles while swimming, which captures scents of potential food items underwater. © *Ken Catania*

Mole densities are usually much smaller than those of small rodents because of their carnivorous habits and relatively large home ranges. Estimated densities of moles in various habitats range from 0.25 to 1.2 moles per acre (0.59 to 3 moles per ha) but might be as high as 12 per acre (30 per ha).

COMMUNICATION

All moles have a variety of scent glands on their belly, head, chin, throat, wrist, and near the anus. The most developed of the glands in the Star-nosed and other moles are the flank glands, located on the sides of the body between the last ribs and the hind legs. All Star-nosed Moles have these glands, but they are functional only in males and then only during the breeding season. When active, the glands secrete a golden waxy substance like ear wax, which builds up on the sides of the animal, discoloring its fur.

European Moles (*Talpa europaea*) use anal gland secretions as spatial markings at the intersections of

tunnels, defining territories and regulating the use of shared areas. This could be true for North American moles, as well. Urine also likely functions in scent-marking, and the high water content of earthworms can support copious urine production.

Moles also form substantial latrines, but it's unknown whether they serve any communicative function. Many can be found aboveground, at an open burrow entrance below a log or other such cover. Large latrines may hold up to 50 scats. Their 1-inch (2.5-cm) droppings are decidedly large for such tiny creatures. When a mole is eating earthworms, the droppings look like curved tubes of moist mud; otherwise they are composed of the shiny parts of insects.

COURTSHIP AND MATING

Little is known of the breeding behavior of moles. Most of what is known is simply the timing of when reproductive males and females are caught by researchers. Moles appear to breed in early spring and summer. Most of the male Star-nosed Moles studied around Ithaca, New York, appeared to be in peak reproductive condition from late February until late May. Females enter estrus repeatedly if they have not bred. Females typically appear to be able to breed after their first year, and bear only 1 litter per year. Male and female Star-nosed Moles, however, may breed during their first year, when they are only a few months old.

Female Star-nosed and other moles that have mated exhibit a copulatory plug. This is a blockage of the vagina created by secretions from glands in the male. It prohibits other males from mating with that female and possibly displacing his semen. Breeding is a costly endeavor for males and females. Males often forgo foraging in order to travel and seek out mates. Females have the burden of fueling developing young and suckling them after they are born. Throughout the winter and spring, Star-nosed Moles store excess calories as fat in their tails. This fat may then serve as an energy reservoir during breeding. Animals caught before or during the breeding season usually have fat tails, while those caught later in the summer have thin ones.

DEVELOPMENT AND DISPERSAL OF YOUNG

Gestation lasts 4 to 6 weeks, and litters averaging 5 young are born from late March to early August, with the majority of them in April or May. Star-nosed Moles give birth in maternal nests, built underground but high enough to avoid typical flooding danger. Young Star-nosed Moles are altricial, naked but for tiny vibrissae on the snout. The eyes are visible through the skin and the hands are relatively well developed. They have tiny claws at the ends of the fingers. In about 10 days they begin to develop fine hair. Their nasal appendages are noticeable early on, having begun to form *in utero*. In newborns, they are pressed back along the snout and covered by a thin membrane. It is only later that they separate and flex forward into their normal arrangement.

Young moles appear to remain dependent on their mother for about 4 weeks. After 4 weeks of nursing, they are ready to be weaned and disperse, mostly within their mother's territory. Dispersal can include movements above ground and through water, contributing to its danger and uncertainties. Given their swimming abilities, water is not likely to be a hindrance to dispersal, but the dense clayey soils associated with wet areas could be.

INTERACTIONS AMONG MOLES

Some researchers report that Star-nosed Moles are gregarious, but data are sparse and conclusions difficult to make. Most studies of this species are based on examination of captured individuals, and it is not uncommon for multiple individuals to be captured in a single location. Of course, reproductive males and females can be found together during breeding season, but they have also been found in the same tunnels at other times of year and may even overwinter in pairs or small groups.

The North American moles may be similar to the European Mole, in which home ranges are largely exclusive. Males do not overlap with other males, but do overlap with multiple females. Females may or may not overlap with one another. Some areas are shared and used at different times by the neighboring moles. Anal gland secretions are important territorial markers, and when a mole is removed, its territory is quickly invaded by other moles.

INTERACTIONS WITH OTHER SPECIES

Moles are a minor prey item in many predators' diets. Hawks and owls are a mole's most likely predators, although they are eaten by a host of other carnivores from weasels to foxes. Predation by large fish cannot be discounted for Star-nosed Moles, but gulping a live mole can be troublesome. In one account, a dead gull was found on a beach with a dead mole half-emerged from a ragged hole in the gull's throat. Apparently the gull gobbled a live mole, tail-first, and as it tried to swallow it, the mole clawed and dug its way out of its captor. The gull must have been flying at the time and crashed to earth, killing the mole on impact.

Mole tunnels, especially those near the surface, are used by other animals for refuge and travel, including toads, shrews, mice, and voles. Southern Short-tailed Shrews (*Blarina carolinensis*) use deep mole tunnels as refuges from cold winter temperatures, much as moles do themselves.

Mexican Free-tailed Bat
Tadarida brasiliensis, and Allies

OTHER NAMES: Brazilian free-tailed bat, guano bat.

Many bats, and Mexican Free-tailed Bats in particular, benefit our lives through the control of insect pests. Mexican Free-tailed Bats target several key agricultural pests, including fall armyworm, cabbage looper, and the corn earworm (also called cotton bollworm). One thousand Mexican Free-tailed Bats eat an estimated 25 pounds (11.25 kg) of insects per night, and given that some colonies number in the millions, they remove millions of pounds of agricultural pests and other insects every night across the southern portion of the United States and northern Mexico. In just eight counties of southern Texas it is estimated that Mexican Free-tailed Bats save the cotton industry between $122,000 and $1,725,000 every year. Bats consume moths early in the growing season (before they lay their eggs) and likely prevent the need for one or two additional pesticide applications. Reducing pesticides on crops provides not only an economic benefit but also a health benefit for people and the environment.

ACTIVITY AND MOVEMENT

DAILY

Flight is surely the most conspicuous behavior of bats. Flight characteristics are variable across species and intrinsically linked to wing shape and foraging strategies. The general performance of a wing is predicted by its aspect ratio—the ratio of a wing's length to width. A high-aspect wing is long and thin, and a low-aspect wing is short and broad. Long, thin wings are more aerodynamic and allow for faster flight. They are ideal for bats that forage in open country or commute long distances to foraging areas or during migrations. Short, broad wings are slower, but allow for greater maneuverability and hovering, which is ideal for bats that forage in forests or other arenas with numerous obstacles. Mexican Free-tailed Bats have long, thin wings and are fast fliers that forage in open areas. They fly at a minimum of 11.5 miles (18.5 km) per hour just to remain in the air and can attain speeds up to 25 miles (40 km) per hour. They fly in excess of 31 miles (50 km) to foraging areas and may forage over 154 square miles (400 km²) in an evening.

Echolocation allows bats to navigate night skies at high speed and in low light when eyes are handicapped. Numerous animals use echolocation, but it is arguably most highly developed in bats, which use it to both navigate and hunt. During echolocation, bats emit sounds that bounce off objects and

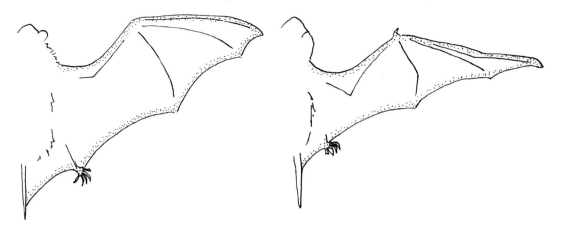

Wings of a Little Brown Myotis, left, and a Mexican Free-tailed Bat, right. The narrower, proportionately longer wing of the free-tailed bat has a higher aspect ratio. Also note the "free" tail in comparison to the tail of the Little Brown Myotis.

return to them. Based on the timing and quality of the returning echoes, bats are able to construct a three-dimensional image of their environment. Bats echolocate extensively to navigate until they learn the terrain. Then they rely so strongly on their memories that they "avoid" objects that have been removed from their environment and bump into others that are added.

When bats aren't flying they are roosting. The many diverse species of bats in North America have each adapted to take advantage of an equally diverse availability of day roosts: rock crevices (Pallid Bat, *Antrozous pallidus*), tree cavities (Silver-haired Bat, *Lasionycteris noctivagans*), under loose bark (Long-legged and California Myotis, *Myotis* spp.), in shrub and tree foliage (red bats, *Lasiurus* spp.), or in attics (Little Brown Myotis, *Myotis lucifugus*). Several *Myotis* species cling to walls behind framed pictures or shutters. Bridges where cracks allow for seasonal expansion of concrete are ideal roosts. People also increasingly construct wooden bat boxes, attaching chicken wire so that bats may better grip one side, or overlap burlap sacks where bats burrow between the layers.

Mexican Free-tailed Bats roost in caves and under highway bridges in colonies of up to 2 million animals. So many bats in one place creates complications, but the Mexican Free-tailed Bat is physiologically and behaviorally adapted to withstand them. Their bodies are adapted to the high levels of ammonia given off by decomposing feces, or guano, a compound that can be deadly to other animals in such high concentration. They also swarm in circles below their roosts to move air in and out of caves. Mexican Free-tailed Bats also roost in smaller groups in attics and old buildings with domed ceilings.

In smaller aggregations, Mexican Free-tailed Bats tend to exit their roosts in the evening to forage in diffuse patterns, beginning within 16 minutes of sunset. Larger colonies more typically exit en masse just prior to sunset, and immense, undulating, serpentine columns of ascending bats may stretch several miles long and be visible from many miles away. They may exit in one great effort or in several groups, the first including the largest number of bats. During each mass exit bats flow forth for 15 to 20 minutes at a time, broken by gaps of several minutes when no bats emerge. Mexican Free-tailed Bats typically remain aloft and forage for 4 hours before returning to their roosts for a break. They leave their roosts for a second time after midnight and return just prior to dawn.

SEASONAL

Bats are widespread in North America because they can enter torpor to save energy when insects are less abundant. Bats are tiny and thus subject to much more rapid heat loss than larger mammals. The energetic costs of flight are also far greater than those of walking or even running. In order to meet their high energy demands, bats need to eat far more than most mammals in proportion to their body size. Yet food availability varies through the year, and bad weather may make foraging flights difficult, if not impossible. Torpor allows them to conserve energy and to survive periods of fasting.

During torpor, a bat reduces its body temperature to within several degrees of the ambient temperature and slows its breathing and heart rate. They can wake themselves at any time, but while torpid their bodies consume one-fifth, and in rare cases only one-ninth, as much energy as they would in their normal state. Torpor is short-term; when it continues for long periods it becomes hibernation. Some bats in northern climates use torpor every day in their day roosts to minimize energy expenditure and then fully arouse each evening to feed.

Hibernation is triggered by ambient temperatures. Bats lose body heat so quickly that in cold northern winters they would quickly freeze regardless of how many insects they could eat. Hibernation is not free, however. The body still requires fuel and is possible only in bats that have sufficient fat reserves to nourish them while they are inactive. Bats preparing for hibernation frequently forage closer to their roosts in order to save energy and eat enough to gain weight every day. Bats require 20 to 30 percent of their body weight in fat deposits to successfully enter and emerge from hibernation. Heart rates of actively flying bats may be as high as 800 beats per minute, and in roosting animals it might be 250 to 450. Eastern Red Bats drop their heart rates to 10 to 16 beats per minute during hibernation, and Big Brown Bats (*Eptesicus*) to 40 to 60. Captive Little Brown Myotis have remained in hibernation for up to 140 days (wild bats hibernate for shorter periods) and taken single breaths at intervals of 60 to 90 minutes. Because Little Brown Myotis hibernate, they use only one-eighth the energy that Mexican Free-tailed Bats use in a given year. In the wild, hibernation periods are more frequently interspersed with arousals, during which animals warm themselves by shivering and increasing blood flow.

Bats are quite selective about where they hibernate. Many species hibernate deep in specific caves where ambient temperatures along the ceiling remain stable between 36° to 50°F (2°–10°C). Bats also often prefer moist caves, which reduces the water they lose while in hibernation and the frequency with which they would need to wake to drink.

An alternative to hibernating to withstand the rigors of winter is to simply avoid them and migrate to warmer climates for part of each year. Some populations of Mexican Free-tailed Bats are migratory, moving south for the winter and returning in the spring. Populations of Mexican Free-tailed Bats inhabiting warmer climates east of Texas do not migrate and remain active throughout the year, and several isolated populations in California and Oregon where climates are moderate are also year-round residents. Mexican Free-tailed Bats in southeast California, Nevada, southwest Utah, and western Arizona migrate south to southern California and the northern portions of the Baja California peninsula. Those inhabiting eastern Arizona, southwest Colorado, and western New Mexico migrate to the western coast of central mainland Mexico. Those remaining in eastern Colorado, Oklahoma, and Kansas move south into southern Texas and northern and eastern Mexico. Migrating Mexican Free-tailed Bats move up to 20 miles (32 km) per day and travel for distances up to 1,143 miles (1,840 km). One bat flew the 795 miles (1,280 km) from Carlsbad Caverns, New Mexico, to Jalisco, Mexico,

Mexican Free-tailed Bats emerging in the evening from under Highway 80 west of Sacramento, CA.
© Mark Elbroch

in 69 days. They typically return to the same summer grounds each year, though a small percentage relocate to other colonies.

Depending upon their migration routes, some Mexican Free-tailed Bats make efforts to gain additional weight in fat reserves for their flight south, while others do not. Fat reserves reflect the certainty and abundance of food reserves en route. All populations gain weight prior to their northerly migrations, when spring foods and weather are more variable.

Mexican Free-tailed Bats cluster in large colonies but vary their spacing depending upon the temperature. In warm temperatures, they maintain loose colonies, but when temperatures drop below 75°F (25°C), they begin to roost more closely together. Tight clustering helps prevent hypothermia and death. When temperatures are very hot, blood vessels in their ears and wings dilate to aid in heat dissipation. They also salivate on their wings to lower their body temperature through evaporative cooling.

FOOD AND FORAGING

Bats are aerial, nocturnal foragers of diverse foods, including numerous insects, pollen, fruit, nectar, fish, and the blood of living animals. In North America, insectivorous bats are by far the most common, though the preferred foraging style of each bat varies widely. Some species "hawk" insects, meaning they catch them in flight. Hawking bats sometimes catch insects in their mouth, especially the larger ones, but smaller insects are often caught in a pocket created in the stretched skin surrounding the bat's tail, or a wing, and then quickly moved to the mouth while in mid-flight. Others "glean" insects from leaves, bark, or other surfaces, or "trawl" across water surfaces for insects or even small fish. Still others "fly catch," making short flying strikes to catch insects they spy from a perch. Insect prey varies from tiny midges (Little Brown Myotis) to flying beetles (Big Brown Bat) to moths (Mexican Free-tailed Bat).

A select few species of moths account for 90 percent of the diet of Mexican Free-tailed Bats. Until quite recently it was assumed that Mexican Free-tailed Bats foraged 20 to 49 feet (6–15 m) above the ground. Innovative thinking and new technology have revealed that most of their feeding occurs between 600 and 3,200 feet (200 to 1,000 m) above the ground, and some hunt higher than 1.9 miles (3,000 m). There are an estimated 100 million Mexican Free-tailed Bats inhabiting the roosts of central Texas, and they eat 2 million pounds of insects every night. And in particular they target the number one insect enemy of agricultural America.

Billions of corn earworm moths emerge just af-

Two Little Brown Myotis hibernating. Note the condensation building up in their fur, which aids them in water retention and allows them to remain in torpor for longer periods. © *McDonald Wildlife Photog./Animals Animals*

ter dusk in the agricultural areas of the Lower Rio Grande Valley of Mexico and ascend on high to surf prevailing winds to the north, arriving in central Texas just before dawn. Mexican Free-tailed Bats in Texas forage twice each night—at sunset and in the hours before dawn. Corn earworms are up to 39 percent of their meals in their first foraging trip, and then comprise as much as 96 percent of their diets during their second foraging bout in the predawn. Bats ascend to great heights to feast upon clouds of migrating moths.

Not all bats in the world use echolocation in foraging and navigation, but all bats in North America do to varying degrees. Echolocation begins as a series of sonic pulses produced in the larynx during the upstroke of flight, when the movement of the wings naturally compresses the chest. Sounds created in the larynx exit through the mouth or nostrils. Leaf-nosed bats (family Phyllostomidae) have complex nose shapes that focus sounds into beams that they can aim. Large and sensitive ears are the receivers for the returning echoes. Many species also have a tragus—a large projection of skin that sticks up in the middle of the ear and partially blocks incoming sounds. The tragus splits the returning echo, allowing it to pass to either side of the ear, thus improving the bats' ability to determine the direction from which the sounds are coming. High-frequency sounds must be loud and intense in order for them to travel any distance and then rebound with enough power for bats to hear them. The combination of supersensitive hearing and the generation of such high-intensity sounds could lead to hearing damage. When bats produce sounds the muscles in their ears contract, separating the bones of the middle ear and rendering them deaf for a fraction of a second. As soon as the sound is emitted, their ears "open" and they are able to receive the near-instantaneous rebound.

Echolocation frequencies range from 20 to 200 kHz and are beyond the hearing of humans. Lower-frequency sounds travel farther than high-frequency sounds. High-frequency echolocation is effective only within a range of about 16 feet (5 m). However, high-frequency sounds are less likely to be detected by insect prey and allow bats to detect smaller objects. In a typical foraging scenario, bats begin with low-frequency sweeps to locate targets and then in-

crease the frequency and rate of their chirps to refine their image of the target, its range, and movement as they close in. Along the way, bats change the rate of their pulses and their frequencies to allow them to determine the relative shape and even texture of the prey species. When in close pursuit of prey, bats twist and turn in the night sky, demonstrating the maneuverability that is critical to many species' success. Bats are often echolocating in dense swarms, especially when entering and exiting roosts. Researchers are still attempting to decipher how the calls of one bat do not interfere with those of another. Evidence suggests that bats may recognize their own calls and that each may be distinctive. While in flight Mexican Free-tailed Bats also home in on the feeding buzzes of their fellows in order to locate patches of insects in which to forage.

Not all bats rely on echolocation when foraging. Big Brown and Pallid Bats use echolocation much less than other native bats and augment their hunting by listening for rustling and incidental sounds made by the wings or legs of moving insects. They also use vision to spot and attack prey. On moonlit nights, California Leaf-nosed Bats (*Macrotus californicus*) use echolocation only one-third of the time, relying primarily on sight to catch prey. Pallid Bats

A Pallid Bat flying off with a large centipede it just captured on the desert floor. © *Merlin D. Tuttle/Bat Conservation International*

capture large insects and arthropods, such as cockroaches and scorpions, by landing on the ground and chasing them down. The bats "run" on all fours, using both their hind feet and the knuckles on the leading edge of their folded wings.

Other North American bats feed on nectars, fruits, and blood. Mexican Long-nosed (*Leptonycteris nivalis*) and Mexican Long-tongued (*Choeronycteris mexicana*) bats feed on the nectar of the saguaro cactus and various agaves in the deserts of Arizona and south into Mexico. They also feed on the ripe cactus fruits. There are 3 species of vampire bats in North America, and 1 is found in southern Texas. Common Vampire Bats (*Desmodus rotundus*) have become more abundant in Central America in recent years because of human disturbance. We replace native forests with cattle ranches to feed our insatiable appetite for beef, and cattle provide easy meals for vampire bats. Cattle and horses in that part of the world commonly show the signs of vampire bat feeding—bloody lower legs or blood dripping from the neck.

Vampire bats have modified canines for fur or feather clipping, large, razor-sharp incisors for slicing skin, anticoagulants in their saliva to prevent the blood from clotting, and a grooved tongue to guide the blood flow into their throat. They typically land on the ground to approach their slumbering victims in a shuffling gait, and with people they most often attack the feet.

HABITAT AND HOME RANGE

Bats inhabit nearly every habitat in North America, excepting the coldest tundra in the far north. The only terrestrial mammal native to the Hawaiian Islands is the Hoary Bat (*Lasiurus cinereus*). The Mexican Free-tailed Bat is one of the most widely distributed mammals in North and South America. They inhabit the southern half of the lower 48 states from coast to coast, as well as all of Mexico and Central America and portions of South America stretching south into Chile and Argentina. Home ranges are often not quantified for the extremely wide-ranging and migratory free-tailed bats.

COMMUNICATION

Bat calls are a hot topic in current bat research, since they can be recorded and analyzed to identify species sharing a large roost or hawking insects together in the air. The chips, churrs, and squeaks of bats can be identified to species using computer software, and there is evidence that individuals might produce distinctive calls as well. When you stand below a large colony of Mexican Free-tailed Bats, the chorus of buzzes, chirps, and squeaks is near deafening. Their vocalizations build to a crescendo as they prepare to exit their roosts to for-

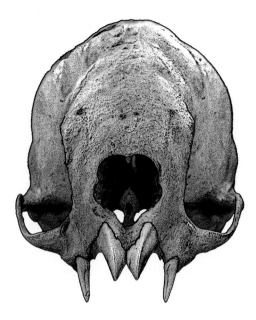

Anterior view of a vampire bat skull. The two large central teeth are the modified incisors with which they slice their prey to start the flow of blood.

age for the first time during the evening. What they are communicating to each other as they remain packed like sardines in their roosts remains one of the many mysteries of bat behavior.

The gular (throat), or hedonic, glands in male Mexican Free-tailed Bats are well developed and likely play a role in territoriality and breeding. Males are said to smell sweeter than the musty females because of secretions from this gland. The glands of males become larger and more active in the breeding season, when they rub secretions on roost ceilings and walls. They also rub their penis on the same surfaces during the breeding season, and it is assumed that these secretions convey sexual status, readiness, and perhaps territoriality. Male-male fighting is occasionally observed in the breeding season. Crawling around their roosts, they may confront each other and gape in aggression, opening their mouths wide to show their teeth. They may also grapple and bite, attempting to dislodge and drop each other into space.

Bat colonies have a very characteristic odor easily identifiable by humans. Odors may also play a role in how bats locate or use roosts. Experiments with new nest boxes have revealed they are more likely to attract new residents if they include odors from previously occupied structures.

COURTSHIP AND MATING

Monestry (one annual estrus) is the rule in temperate bats. Mexican Free-tailed Bats are promiscuous—both males and females mate with several partners. In Florida, female Mexican Free-tailed Bats ovulate for 3 weeks in March, and the breeding season lasts approximately 5 weeks. In Texas mating occurs from mid-March to mid-April.

The polygynous males exhibit two distinctive approaches to mating. Some males prefer one over the other, while others employ both depending on the situation. The first method is to be aggressive: a male locates a female in the colony, uses his teeth to seize her by an ear, head, or neck, and drags her to the side where he holds her temporarily captive. The female fights and resists, but the male overpowers her. The male then mounts the female from behind, biting the back of her neck to maintain his hold, and emits mating chirps while they mate. When the pair disengage it's not uncommon for the female or both partners to be bleeding from wounds on the head.

The second strategy is all about stealth. A male sneaks in quietly among a cluster of females, keeping his ears back and eyes closed. He mounts a fe-

male in estrus and begins to surreptitiously mate with her. In these cases females may groom, or even appear to be resting, as if completely undisturbed by the male. After mating, a copulatory plug appears in the female, but it is easily removed; several males may mate with a female, giving her little rest in between. During the breeding season, the floors below roosts are covered with expelled copulatory plugs, which look like translucent grains of rice.

DEVELOPMENT AND DISPERSAL OF YOUNG

Gestation in Mexican Free-tailed Bats lasts 11 weeks. In Florida, females give birth to one young, twins, or even triplets during a 2-week interval in June. Females remain in a head-down position, and birth occurs in about 90 seconds. Mothers use their claws to strip away the thin membrane surrounding the newborns as they emerge. Unaided by their mother, newborns take about 15 minutes to locate a nipple. They are nearly naked and their skin is smooth and slightly pigmented. Their skin darkens quickly and they soon appear a dark purple by flashlight.

Mexican Free-tailed Bats place their young in collective nurseries, called crèches, and adult females take turns watching over the youngsters while the others fly off to forage. Females carry their young in flight only if a roost is disturbed. Somehow they correctly identify and nurse their young among all the others in about 8 out of 10 tries, and pups do successfully nurse from other females from time to time. The females appear to use olfactory and vocal cues to identify and locate their pups, and pups themselves recognize their mothers and move toward them.

Youngsters shed their baby teeth by 2 weeks and their adult dentition has fully erupted by 6 weeks. By 5 to 6 weeks they are covered in thick, black fur. Juveniles gain weight quickly and some attain adult weights in just 3 weeks, though most require longer, attaining their full size by 2 months. Young females become sexually mature at 9 months, but males do not breed until their second year.

INTERACTIONS AMONG MEXICAN FREE-TAILED BATS

Mexican Free-tailed Bats often segregate their roosts by sex. Some of the largest and most renowned roosts in the United States, including Eagle Creek Cave in Arizona and Carlsbad Caverns in New Mexico, are strictly maternal roosts of pregnant females. Most males in migratory free-tailed populations do not migrate but stay to the south in their winter ranges. Mating occurs before migration, and females arrive to their summer ranges already pregnant. Those small numbers of males that do journey north typically roost on their own in bachelor roosts of up to several hundred animals.

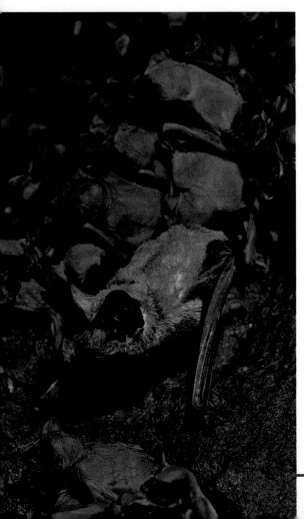

Look closely to differentiate the adult Mexican Free-tailed Bat that remained behind to defend and care for the numerous young in this communal nursery. © Merlin D. Tuttle/Bat Conservation International

Why bats roost in such large aggregations is a question we may never fully answer. In maternity roosts, females take turns watching the juveniles and are afforded more time to forage. There may also be an information exchange between roost members about particularly productive areas for foraging. Another possibility is that group hunting for specific prey is more efficient than hunting alone. Groups also provide greater safety. Should predators be lurking near roost exits, an individual is less likely to be eaten with greater numbers of companions at their side. Bats also use each other to conserve and share heat through huddling, and in this way save energy.

INTERACTIONS WITH OTHER SPECIES

Many bat species roost together. Mexican Free-tailed Bats roost with Big Brown Bats, numerous *Myotis* species, Pallid Bats, and Peters's Ghost-faced Bats (*Mormoops*). Rock wrens, phoebes, and cliff swallows also build their nests in caves and under bridges used by bats. Watch for swallows swarming and diminishing as they disappear into their nests for the night just as the bats emerge and leave for their evening foraging. Mexican Free-tailed Bats may even huddle in cliff swallow nests during cold snaps.

Wherever so many small mammals gather, predators are certain to be present. Mexican Free-tailed Bats have numerous avian and terrestrial enemies. Kestrels, red-tailed hawks, peregrine falcons, kites, barn owls, and great horned owls are among those that pluck them from the sky when they emerge each evening and return in the predawn. Rat snakes, coachwhips, and copperheads attack them while they roost. Raccoons climb cave walls to pluck them from the ceilings, and they join striped and hog-nosed skunks, roadrunners, and opossums below to catch and eat bats that fall from the roost, including numerous young. Young bats fall from roosts at a rate of 5 to 20 animals per hour, providing a feast for scavengers waiting below. Numerous beetles, including flesh-eating dermestids, and other invertebrates swarm over the guano and remains beneath large bat roosts, and they too prey on juveniles that fall and land below. Dermestid beetles are a substantial cause of mortality for juveniles, which fall and are not yet old enough to fly.

Insects that are prey to bats have also evolved defenses against them. Numerous moths and beetles are able to hear ultrasonic sounds and can alter their flight patterns or even drop to the ground in an attempt to evade capture. A few moths even create ultrasonic clicks of their own, which may startle and divert an incoming bat at the last moment or jam the echolocation in some way that provides acoustic camouflage.

Bobcat
Lynx rufus

OTHER NAMES: wildcat, red lynx, bay lynx, barred bobcat, bob-tailed cat, cat lynx, gato montés (Mexican Spanish).

Canada Lynx
Lynx canadensis

OTHER NAMES: lynx, Canadian lynx, niutuuyiq or nuutuuyiq (Inupiaq Eskimo), loup-cervier (Canadian French), be-jew or pe-zu (Ojibwa).

The bobcat is a close relative of the Canada Lynx. Both fill a similar niche and, when living together, compete for food and space. Deep snow favors the lynx; otherwise aggressive bobcats usually displace them. Bobcats, by virtue of smaller feet relative to their size, have four times the foot load (body weight supported per square inch of foot surface) of lynx, and this disadvantage, when moving and hunting in deep snow, contributes to a near-perfect separation between bobcat and lynx ranges. Bobcats monopolize the southern portions of North America and lynx roam across the far north. Though elusive and well camouflaged, bobcats are the easiest of our wild cats to see, and for this very reason are perhaps the most exciting.

ACTIVITY AND MOVEMENT

DAILY

Bobcats and lynx tend to be crepuscular, but they may also be active throughout the night or day, especially in areas with minimal human presence. In general, daily activity and movement of both bobcat and lynx tend to peak around dawn and dusk, closely mirroring the activity patterns of rabbits and hares, their primary prey. Daily and weekly travel distances differ considerably by region, sex, age, weather, and even individual. In general, they travel 1 to 4 miles (1.6–6.4 km) in 24 hours. In Oregon and Montana, male bobcats traveled 3 times as far as females. In a South Carolina study, both sexes on average traveled 4.4 miles (7 km) in autumn, whereas in winter, males moved more (6.3 miles; 10 km) than females (3.8 miles; 6 km).

Bobcats and lynx generally move in a walk, leaving a neat zigzagging line of tracks behind them. They travel in straight lines between bedding and hunting areas and weave through thick vegetation when hunting. When they decide to move from one area to another, their trails switch from meandering patterns to straight lines. Similarly, they shift from slower to faster gaits. They usually forage and

A portrait of a Canada Lynx in a snowy northern forest. © *Mark Elbroch*

explore in a slow walk, but use either a fast walking gait, sometimes called an amble, or a trot to cover distance more quickly. When chasing prey or running from larger predators they lope and gallop, and at high speeds lynx make great rabbitlike bounds of 10 feet (3 m) or more.

Lynx and bobcats spend a lot of time resting. Lynx are more comfortable in the open than bobcats and sometimes lie in the snow near vegetation, rather than in it. An exposed ledge may allow a warm nap in the sun, but bobcats prefer to bed under some sort of cover and often upon a soft mattress of leaves or debris. Where available, beds are often in steep, cliffy areas with thick vertical cover and sparse ground vegetation. In flatter terrain and swamps they bed in rock crevices, hollow trees, logs, and brush piles, or beneath root wads, ledges, or blow-downs. Except when they are guarding a large cache, bobcats and lynx generally switch rest-

ing sites day to day. They will reuse well-protected sites time and again over their lives, and a well-used hillside can hold numerous kidney-shaped impressions of resting bodies, deepening with repeated use.

SEASONAL

Bobcats and lynx are active all winter. Lynx are well adapted to moving about in deep snow and usually hunt the same areas throughout the seasons. Where Snowshoe Hare populations cyclically increase and decline, lynx may disperse into new areas when hares are scarce. Dispersing adults typically depart their ranges in spring and early summer. One lynx traveled 684 miles (1,100 km), and cases of animals traveling 311 miles (500 km) are not uncommon.

The mobility of bobcats is hampered by 6 inches (15 cm) of snow, as is access to most of their prey. If the snow is even deeper, bobcats curtail their movements and shift their activity to less-snowy areas. They may seek out thick forest cover or cliffy areas where the steep terrain sheds snow. When they must move in soft snow, bobcats (and also lynx) often walk on logs, snowmobile trails, and packed animal trails.

FOOD AND FORAGING

Bobcats and lynx are almost exclusively carnivorous, and they exhibit none of the dental adaptations for grinding fibrous foods that are present in bears and dogs. Rabbits and hares are their primary prey. Snowshoe Hares can make up as much as 97 percent of lynx diet in many areas, although they eat other flesh, chiefly Red Squirrels and grouse. In addition to rabbits, bobcats eat a wide range of animals, and mice and voles are a bobcat staple. Among northern bobcats, especially larger-bodied males, White-tailed Deer are an important winter prey. Elsewhere they eat various small and medium-sized mammals, birds, and reptiles.

In the spring, bobcats kill deer fawns, and during a hare decline in Newfoundland, lynx were known to prey on caribou calves less than 2 weeks old. Lynx pounced on them from forest cover and suffocated them with a bite to the throat, dragging them into cover to feed. There are also records of lynx killing adult mule and White-tailed Deer and their fawns, and lynx scavenge any ungulate carcass they encounter. Bobcats sometimes kill livestock, mostly chickens, but very few overall. Grass occasionally shows up in their diets. They may ingest it accidentally in the course of regular feeding or eat it as a purgative as do domesticated cats. Bobcats occasionally consume other carnivores, including raccoons, skunks, and foxes.

Bobcats only rarely successfully hunt adult deer, and large male bobcats are the most successful. A bobcat may wait in a spot from which to leap onto the back of a passing deer or stalk in and attack them while they are bedded. In a White-tailed Deer (*Odocoileus virginianus*) study in the Florida Everglades, bobcats killed 33 tagged fawns and 6 radio-collared adults from 1989 to1992. Florida deer are small, increasing the chances of a successful hunt by a bobcat. One of the Florida deer killed was an adult male that weighed 106 pounds (48 kg), approximately four times the weight of a large male bobcat.

Bobcats kill deer with a powerful, suffocating bite to the throat, often delivered while clinging to the deer's back. They try to twist the deer's neck around to the back, forcing the deer onto its side to pin it down and finish it off. Those deer that are killed but not dragged away to cover show the characteristic death form: the head twisted backward and positioned diagonally under the shoulder, leaving the throat exposed. Bobcats partially or completely cover large carcasses with debris in the classic caching style of a cat.

Approximately half the time bobcats and lynx are expert stalkers and ambushers. In areas of high cottontail or hare density they follow well-worn runs and wait, sphinxlike, in "hunting beds" for rabbits to appear. In open woods and pastures, bobcats use "lookouts," where they sit and watch for prey from a distance. Bobcats and lynx also hunt by meandering through areas frequented by their prey, aiming to spot the prey before being detected. When a hare or squirrel is detected, the cat stalks slowly closer. In exposed terrain, cats crouch low and slink across the ground with painstaking patience. It could take nearly 15 minutes to cover 3 feet (1 m) of ground. For minutes on end, they can remain frozen but for nervous, or excited, flicks of their short tail. Once a cat has maneuvered to within striking distance, it finishes with a rush and a pounce. With its sharp, curved claws extended forward, it grasps and subdues its prey. Bites to the head or the base of the skull (nape of the neck in larger prey) finish the successful hunt.

Bobcats sometimes eat their prey immediately, but more often they carry it off to some concealing cover. They eat small mammals and birds whole. They pluck large birds before eating them. Bobcats sometimes pluck or shear the hair of large mammals prior to feeding by nipping off mouthfuls with their incisors. When eating large prey, they start at the hindquarters, the meatiest portion of the carcass. They consume meat and organs, cutting away the ribs to expose the internal organs. Cats in general are unable to synthesize fat-soluble vitamin A from beta-carotene, so their only source of vitamin A is the liver, lungs, adrenal glands, and kidneys of their prey. They usually avoid eating the bones of large prey and the intestines of rabbit-sized and larger prey. Instead, they discard the bones after

A juvenile lynx chasing a Snowshoe Hare, the lynx's primary prey. © FotoliaII – Fotolia.com

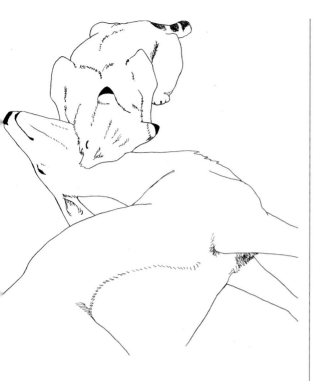

A bobcat with a secure grip on the throat of a White-tailed Deer.

using their rasplike tongue to remove the most stubborn, clinging meat.

After a bobcat has made a kill, there is a brief period, perhaps 10 to 20 minutes, during which it seems oblivious to the presence of observers. Perhaps it is adrenaline, but bobcats can be approached just after a kill and tend not to respond to an observer at all. Bobcats have been seen bumping into human observers or walking right past them while dragging their prey to cover. But be warned, after those few minutes, they come back to their senses and crouch, hiss, and threaten anyone too close.

Bobcats and lynx cache prey by covering it with earth and debris, usually, but not always, returning later to finish the meal. When feeding on Snowshoe Hares, lynx may make the effort to cache a hind leg and attached scraps, but only in times of real scarcity would they return for such a meager meal. When lynx do return to a food cache, they typically do so within 48 hours of making it. Bobcats are most likely to cache larger prey. In one instance, a bobcat killed a large raccoon, pulling it, torpid, from where it slept in a jumble of boulders and dragged it 650 feet (200 m) over and around logs, to a cache under a massive downed log. After a hefty meal of nearly half of the raccoon, the bobcat covered the remains with leaves in a pile with a mink's tail and an entire gray squirrel.

Adult bobcats consume more medium to large prey (hares and deer) than juveniles, and in some studies, females kill more small mammals than males. One hypothesis for why male and female bobcats are of different sizes is so that they can exploit different foods and avoid competing with one another. It is certainly true that smaller bobcats are less able to kill deer or defend their meals against others. On the other hand, females may simply eat more small mammals because they hunt more intensively within smaller home ranges. This might minimize the vulnerability of the kits left behind in the den. Males, being larger, may also be able to consume larger quantities of food at one time, making large prey particularly rewarding.

HABITAT AND HOME RANGE

Lynx typically inhabit coniferous forests or mixed woods, where hardwood patches are intermingled with conifers. In northern Maine, lynx are particularly associated with large, 11- to 26-year-old fir-hardwood forest disturbances created by spruce budworm outbreaks or by clear-cut logging. Lynx may benefit from herbicide treatments of clear-cuts that inhibit hardwood growth and allow conifers to get a head start. Lynx hunt extensively in these areas, where hares are provided good cover among

A bobcat straddles a goose and attempts to retire to cover to feed in peace. Rather than drag large prey items backward, it is more characteristic of bobcats and other felids to straddle their prey and move forward.

After feeding for an hour, a bobcat caches a deer carcass in a dry riverbed. (Remote camera)
© *Mark Elbroch*

the conifers and good forage among the younger hardwoods.

Home ranges for Canada Lynx vary with geographic location, season, and prey availability. When hare density in the far north is high, home ranges are typically 5 to 7 square miles (13–18 km²) for females, and 5 to 15 square miles (4–40 km²) for males. When hares are scarce, males and females may forage over 194 square miles (500 km²) or more. In southern populations, home ranges vary from 15 to 97 square miles (40 to 250 km²). In Maine, while snow is on the ground, females use areas nearly 3 times those they use in summer. Conversely, males occupy slightly smaller areas during winter than summer. At low hare densities, lynx densities average 3 animals per 39 square miles (100 km²), but at high hare densities, up to 45 lynx can share that same amount of land.

Bobcats live in an incredible variety of habitats across North America, gravitating to uneven terrain and rough, rocky features interspersed with dense cover. The amount of area that a bobcat uses is strongly tied to habitat quality: cover for stalking prey, denning sites, availability of mates, protection from competitors, and high prey availability. In the North, where prey is less dense and bobcats are larger than in the South, home ranges are larger and bobcat populations less dense. The highest densities of 1 bobcat per 0.3 to 1.6 square miles (0.8–4 km²) are in California chaparral, Arizona scrub grasslands, and in Alabama bottomland hardwood forest openings. The lowest densities, 1 bobcat per 9 to 11 square miles (23–27 km²), are reported from coniferous forests, sagebrush grasslands, and desert canyon country.

Male home ranges average 127 square miles (325 km²) in upstate New York, 44 square miles (112 km²) in Maine, and 1 square mile (2.6 km²) in Alabama. Males need home ranges that overlap the ranges of several females. Female bobcats need home ranges that supply adequate food for them and their offspring, and that are close enough to their dens that they may be on hand to defend their young if need be. Accordingly, female home ranges are smallest when they are breeding and rearing their young.

COMMUNICATION

White marks on the back of the ears are common among wild felines and are present in both bobcats and lynx. These marks highlight movements of the ear that communicate the cat's disposition, just as white marks around the eyes and mouth accentuate facial expressions.

Bobcats and lynx use urine and feces as well as body scents to communicate with one another. Scent marks are made by rubbing the cheeks and neck on various objects. These are the same behaviors you see in housecats: their solicitous gestures of rubbing on people's legs and hands serve to mingle scents and reinforce social relationships. Housecats can also be seen rubbing their cheeks on couches and the like just as their wild cousins do on similar objects in their home ranges. Well-marked rocky outcrops can show discoloration and clinging hairs shed during cheek-rubbing. Just as housecats scratch up the arms of couches, bobcats and lynx occasionally scratch up the bark of trees. This "claw sharpening" may be primarily a means of depositing scent.

Bobcats and lynx mark with urine by lifting their tails and spraying it backward with amazing accuracy. As the cat passes a tree, rock, rotting stump, or sprig of vegetation, it steps sideways with one hind leg to position its rear end directly in front of the object, sprays a bit of urine, and then walks on. Lynx might spray up to 20 times in a mile (1.6 km) of travel. Scent posts are often reused time and again, and in dry climates bobcat urine accumulates and stains tree trunks and rock surfaces. In winter you can also find urine frozen in place beneath cliff ledges where it was deposited on a protected wall.

Bobcats also make "scrapes" in dirt and debris, and they may or may not spray urine or defecate in them. Whereas bobcats, lynx, and housecats may gather up a pile of debris with their front paws to cover a recent defecation, only the bobcat makes scrapes with its hind feet, first one and then the other. This is the manner of marking in cougars and jaguars as well, and it results in a swath of bare ground backed up by a neat pile of debris. Bobcat scrapes are commonplace where their numbers are high and less so in the Northeast where they are less abundant. Lynx are not known to make scrapes.

Bobcat vocalizations include caterwauling—a shrill, discordant screeching common during breeding—and hisses, puffs, spits, and growls when threatened. Lynx, too, spit when threatened. The classic open-mouthed hiss of a cornered cat clearly displays its sharp teeth. This is the primary weapon threat of these cats and is meant to warn off an intruder before the cat must attack to defend itself.

COURTSHIP AND MATING

Bobcats and lynx are polygynous: males seek to mate with as many females as possible. Lynx breeding peaks in March and continues through May. Bobcat breeding peaks in February and March. In the southern portion of its range, breeding starts sooner and continues longer. Less bounded by limits of harsh winters, breeding in the extreme south can happen at any time of year; litters have been reported in every month. Successful breeding in lynx, and likely bobcats as well, is linked to prey availability. When hares are plentiful, up to 92 percent of adult female lynx and as many as 79 percent of yearlings breed, but when hares are scarce, pregnancy rates drop to 30 to 64 percent in adults and approximately 10 percent in yearlings. When hares are abundant, lynx may raise kittens every year, but during years of scarcity lynx may breed only every other year.

A bobcat scratches with its claws, which helps shed outer layers of keratin to sharpen its claws and also deposits scent from glands on its feet.

The ice-blue eyes of a lynx kitten. Their dens are made in crevices, under fallen logs, and in thick protective vegetation. © *Mark Elbroch*

Actual mating has been observed more often in captive bobcats than in lynx. As estrus approaches, females frequently cheek-rub, body-rub, and urine-mark their territory, no doubt relaying information about their sexual status. Females make loud and frequent vocalizations. A female flicks her tail and holds it upright, visual signals that also help disperse her scent. Male testosterone levels rise during breeding, driving them to seek out females. A female won't have to wait long before a suitor approaches and begins courting her. She shows interest in males she encounters, arching her back, vocalizing, and circling him should he linger. If a male approaches a female that is not in estrus, she'll attack and repel his advances with teeth and claws.

When she is nearing estrus, the two court, engaging in playlike behavior. They run together, often bumping into, chasing, and leaping at each other in mock ambushes. This courtship serves to synchronize the two, behaviorally and hormonally, for mating. When she is receptive, the female arches her back and moves her tail to one side to invite mating. The male mounts from behind and bites her neck during intercourse. Mating is short, perhaps 5 minutes, but repeated up to 16 times daily for several days. When the male separates from the female, he contributes nothing further to the rearing of the kittens.

Bobcat dens are located in secure areas, such as rock crevices, hollow logs, upturned root wads, and thick brush. Here a young kitten explores the end of its hollow log. © *Mark Elbroch*

DEVELOPMENT AND DISPERSAL OF YOUNG

There is usually only 1 litter per year unless the first is lost. Gestation lasts 2 months or a little more. Usually 2 to 4 kittens are born between April and June. The mother must come and go as she hunts for the food she needs to keep herself vigorous enough to make milk for her young ones. When hares are scarce, only 1 or 2 lynx kittens are born per litter, and in Alberta during a Snowshoe Hare decline, 95 percent of kittens died before their first birthday.

Birth takes place in dry, well-hidden, relatively inaccessible dens. Female bobcats move their litters from the natal den to up to 5 maternal dens over the course of their kittens' development, either to avoid predators that may find the den or because of a build-up of parasites within it. These dens are cov-

ered, protected sites that might be in caves, brush piles, or even abandoned beaver lodges. Lynx dens are typically found within tangles of wind-blown trees, young evergreens, intertwined stands of young willows, or under fallen logs or rock overhangs. They only rarely reuse a den site unless there are no other options. Den and resting sites are important features of a female's home range, influencing the range's size and configuration.

The newborn kittens are blind and helpless. Bobcats remain exclusively in the den for their first 4 to 6 weeks, while lynx kittens begin to walk around during their fourth week and follow their mother on explorations at 5 weeks. At 6 months, bobcat kittens may travel alone close to the den. Juvenile lynx are actively hunting by 7 months but do not reach their full adult size until they are between 1 and 2 years old.

Juvenile bobcats typically disperse in fall, whereas juvenile lynx wait until spring, just before their mother has a new litter. Bobcats, for which dispersal is better known, may hang about in their natal territory for several months prior to dispersing or settling nearby. Males usually disperse earlier and farther than females, who may take over part of their mother's home range. Dispersal distances noted for bobcats vary from straight-line movements of 4 to 23 miles (6 to 37 km) followed by quick establishment in a vacant home range, to long periods of transience, lasting 4 months to 4 years. Transients wander between centers of activity, usually relocating every 30 to 60 days. Widespread dispersal in heavily hunted populations is probably uncommon because of high turnover of potential home ranges.

INTERACTIONS AMONG BOBCATS AND AMONG LYNX

Bobcats and lynx are individualistic, and adults rarely associate with one another except when courting and mating. A female with young is the basic social unit. Even where two adult cats' ranges might overlap, they avoid one another through scent-marking behaviors.

INTERACTIONS WITH OTHER SPECIES

The lives of Canada Lynx and Snowshoe Hares are inextricably intertwined. Snowshoe Hares follow an 8- to 11-year boom-bust cycle, with their numbers 10 to 25 times more abundant during peak years than during lows. The lynx follow suit, with their numbers increasing 10 to 17 times in size as hare populations grow, and subsequently crashing when hare numbers plummet. When Snowshoe Hare populations are high, lynx breed more often, produce larger litters, and more successfully raise kittens to dispersal age. When hares are abundant, lynx focus their hunting strategies upon hares and

A bobcat crouches low, ready to pounce or flee. © *Mark Elbroch*

increase the percentage of them in their diet, sometimes to the exclusion of all other potential prey species.

Snowshoe Hare cycles across North America do not occur simultaneously, but seem to begin in central Canada and radiate outward. Peak hare populations in central Canada are followed 2 to 4 years later by booms in the western and eastern portions of North America. Some hare populations in the southern parts of their range (i.e., the US border with Canada and the lower 48 states) do not experience these boom-bust cycles at all, but persist at stable, low densities. Southern lynx populations are similar to the population densities and dynamics of northern populations during low Snowshoe Hare years.

Bobcats compete with other carnivores sharing their territory. A study of carnivore community interactions in the Santa Monica Mountains of southern California showed that coyotes occasionally kill bobcats. Coyotes could be a significant source of mortality for bobcats in other areas, too, but in that study there was no evidence that coyotes excluded bobcats from hunting in certain areas. The bobcats in the California study were also able to minimize contact with the nocturnal coyotes by being more active in the daytime. Bobcats in the Santa Monica Mountains occasionally killed gray foxes, and elsewhere they are the leading cause of death for endangered San Joaquin Kit Fox pups.

Cougars and farm dogs also kill bobcats, but humans are their greatest threat. Fishers are known to kill subadult lynx, and bobcats to kill fishers. Bobcats respond strongly to the presences of humans. Bobcats exhibit low and dramatically restricted range of activity where human activity is high. They avoid the times and sites of highest human activity. Where they appear active in residential areas is also where low-density housing development reaches into areas of high bobcat density (e.g., California and Arizona). Here, some cats are probably forced to accommodate human development in their home ranges in order to retain any territory at all.

Lynx and bobcats share very similar hunting strategies and prey preferences, thus making it difficult for the two species to share habitat. Where they share range, lynx typically stick to the higher elevations, where deeper snows give them the competitive advantage, and bobcats take control of the lowlands, where they assume the dominant role and exclude lynx through aggressive interactions. Where lynx are at low densities, they are known to occasionally hybridize with bobcats. Researchers are concerned that lynx-bobcat hybrids will dilute and threaten lynx populations in the southern portions of their range, where lynx are in the greatest need of protection.

OTHER NAMES: mountain lion, puma, catamount, Florida panther, lion, león (Spanish), leão (Portuguese).

One of the relics of folklore that still persists today is the presence of the black panther—an onyx, melanistic form of the mountain lion. In Florida nearly every cougar, locally called panthers, has been monitored since birth and none are black. Yet in Florida every year, "black" panther sightings far outnumber yellow. There are several old anecdotal records of black panthers having been shot in South America more than 100 years ago, but in the 100,000 shot or cataloged throughout the Americas since that time, not one cougar skin has been black.

The greater cat family is broadly divided into "large" and "small" cats. Even though cougars may reach considerable proportions, the shape of their eyes, nose, and feet are more akin to smaller cats. Cougars can also purr, a trait of small cats, but are unable to roar like true large cats. Thus cougars are considered "small cats," and their young are called kittens instead of cubs. The specific name *concolor* means "single color" and refers to their uniform pelage.

ACTIVITY AND MOVEMENT

DAILY

Cougars are most active during the twilight periods when day and night meld. They also move frequently during periods of darkness. When cougars inhabit areas where humans are present, be it suburban parks or remote logging operations, they become more nocturnal. But even then, they may move short distances at any time of day.

Cougars spend most of each 24-hour cycle resting in beds. Resting is critical for temperature regulation in both high heat and bitter cold. It also allows a cougar to conserve energy, in preparation for hunting prey larger than itself. During the heat of summer, cougars require shade to regulate their body temperature, and they rarely leave their beds. In the desert Southwest they lie in the deep shade of large boulders or in thick brush. In cooler temperatures, they select beds in which the sun will reach and warm them. Cougars sometimes bed very close to human activity. Research in southern California has documented them bedding only slightly more than 330 feet (100 m) from busy hiking and horseback-riding trails. When the foot traffic stops with nightfall, the cats emerge and use the very same trails to commute about their home ranges.

Cougars patrol their territories and hunt in a walking gait, giving them a stealthy and fluid grace. When traveling, cougars often use paths of least resistance, including trails, dirt roads, and sandy washes. Then when they hunt, cougars weave through cover and zigzag across the landscape, using both wind and terrain to their advantage. In steep country a cougar will hunt from the ridges, moving along them, but traveling just out of sight of the next drainage. Periodically it loops up to the crest to scent and listen for prey below. Then it loops down and around to move into the wind toward its quarry. Alternatively, cougars weave across the landscape, pausing every few hours in areas prey species frequent, waiting patiently for up to 2 hours for a target to appear.

Wandering is fundamental to cougar natural history. Even when cougars discover areas of high prey abundance, they leave the area to invest time in other parts of their range, and then wander back at some point in the future. Males wander farther and wider in a given night than females, though long-distance events have been recorded for both sexes.

A male cougar pauses to look up from his meal. He plucked and opened the deer carcass just behind the ribs. © *Mark Elbroch*

In southern California it is not unusual for cougars to hunt areas intensely from several weeks to a month and then disappear and not return to them for 2 to 3 months' time. Females with kittens may move only several miles per night (3–4 km), while a typical adult moves 4 to 5 miles (6–8 km). On occasion a traveling animal may cover up to 20 miles (32 km) and completely relocate to a new part of its range overnight.

Cougars trot when they wish to cover ground quickly, and bound and gallop when fleeing potential predators or chasing down prey. Vertically they can leap more than 10 feet (3 m), and horizontally, 20 to 25 feet (6–8 m). Cougars are competent tree climbers, and they sometimes swim. Florida panthers were documented swimming from the mainland to Sanibel Island, where they hunted the abundant raccoons. Cougars groom and maintain their coat in typical feline fashion: they lick their paws and use them to wipe their head and ears.

SEASONAL

Seasonal shifts in movement and behavior vary depending upon geography and other factors. Weather doesn't affect cougars directly so much as it affects the movements and locations of their prey. Where deep winter snows drive deer and elk to lower elevations or to the southern sides of mountains, the cougars follow. During warmer months, both ungulates and cougars seek out the cooler north slopes.

FOOD AND FORAGING

Cougars are highly efficient killers of live prey and specialist hunters of Mule and White-tailed Deer in North America. They lie in wait, or stalk, slinking low to the ground, with ears alert until their prey is within a striking range of approximately 50 feet (15 m). When they are able to get close enough to their quarry, their chances of catching it are great. In one study, cougars were successful in 37 of 45 attempted hunts. Cougars have small lungs and hearts, and if they are too far from their prey when they are detected, they are quick to give up pursuit.

Cougars explode into chase and pounce upon their prey. They grip their quarry rodeo-style, clinging tightly with sharp, retractable claws, including the enlarged claws of "toe 1" on the inside of their front feet. With their victims bucking and struggling beneath them, they deliver a killing bite to the back of the neck or skull. On larger prey and animals with head ornaments that protect the back of the head (such as the horns of Bighorn Sheep), they hook the head with a paw and yank backward to expose the neck, sometimes sliding down to one side for better access. Then the cougar bites and severs the windpipe, killing by suffocation. Unlike other

A cougar grips the throat of a bighorn ram, exhibiting the classic kill technique they use when their prey has large head ornaments (such as antlers or horns).

carnivores, the nerves in a cat's daggerlike canines run to the tips, providing them a reflexive means of directing their teeth between vertebrae and other bones. In older cougars the teeth are always worn enough to expose the nerve endings.

Throughout North America their predominant prey is deer. Cougars are hypercarnivores and eat little vegetation at all, though they will consume grasses to aid in the cleaning of parasites and hair from their gut. In addition to deer, they hunt elk, Bighorn Sheep, moose, and feral hogs when available, as well as a great diversity of smaller prey, including coyotes, foxes, raccoons, rabbits, ground squirrels, beavers, opossums, skunks, and peccaries. Cougars seem to seek porcupines when they are available, and where the two species overlap the front limbs of mountain lions often carry embedded porcupine quills too numerous to count. Cougars also eat domestic sheep, goats, cattle, dogs, cats, and occasionally horses, as well as scavenge carrion. Research with captive-raised kittens suggests that cougars recognize an animal as potential prey only once they have eaten it. One captive kitten didn't kill opossums encountered on walks until it had been fed road-killed opossum, after which it killed the very next opossum it found.

The age-old question as to how many animals a cougar kills per year is only now being properly documented with the advent of GPS technology, which allows researchers to track cougars more efficiently. Energetic models predicted that adult female cougars would require a deer every 16 days if they had no kittens, a deer every 9 days if they had

three 3-month-old kittens, and a deer every 3 days if they had three 15-month-old kittens. Recent field efforts, however, have documented kill rates 2 to 3 times as high. Part of this disparity is due to the fact that cougars do not always finish their meal, or may have it stolen by Black Bears or other scavengers.

Cougars kill disproportionately more older males and young deer. Male deer tend to be solitary, providing better opportunities for stalking them undetected. During and after the rut, males may also be less aware of their surroundings or in a weakened condition. Young deer are also desirable because their smaller size makes them less dangerous and easier to manage. Where cougars eat Bighorn Sheep, they eat more males because their massive horns obstruct their vision and thus they are more easily stalked from behind. Hunting large ungulates is risky. In one study 27 percent of cougar mortalities were the result of injuries or deaths incurred from hunting larger game. Unlike wolves and bears, cougars kill very quickly to minimize their chance of injury.

Once an animal has been killed, a cougar drags it to a secluded spot, leaving a beautiful dragline on the landscape. That is, unless its prey is too large to move. Adult females inhabiting the southern rim of the Grand Canyon are relatively small, yet they feed nearly exclusively on elk. When they drop an elk, they feed where it lands.

When under cover, cougars pluck their prey, pulling great tufts of fur from one side behind the rib cage. Then they open the carcass and remove the rumen (stomach) like a surgeon, to be discarded before any serious eating. Sometimes a cougar will start with the meat from the inside of the hind leg adjacent to the hole in the abdomen. More often, it will first shear the ribs close to the spinal column, moving up toward the head. Once the ribs are consumed and out of the way, the cougar gorges on the protein- and blood-rich internal organs, including the liver, lungs, and heart. Cats are unable to synthesize vitamin A, thought to be essential in reproductive processes in pregnant females, so they must get it directly from the internal organs of their prey. The cougar also makes a point of ingesting the most nutritious portions of the carcass first in case it is pushed off its kill before it is finished eating.

A typical meal for a wild cougar is between 6 and 10 pounds (2.7–4.5 kg) of meat per sitting, though captive cougars have eaten up to 22 pounds (10 kg) of meat in a 24-hour period. After the initial meal, cougars often cache their prey by covering it with debris, though they may also just leave it as it is. Caching behaviors vary from individual to individual and from season to season. Cougars are less likely to cache prey remains in cold weather. Covering a carcass reduces its scent, minimizing visits

A male cougar's cached Mule Deer. © *Mark Elbroch*

from scavengers and potential competitors. It also slows spoilage by insulating the meat and reducing insects' access to it.

Cougars defend their caches from other animals; occasionally a coyote or bobcat that attempts to steal from a cougar is killed and finds itself cached along with the remains of a deer. Wolves and Black and Brown Bears, however, can and do displace cougars and steal their food. Yet there is nothing but anecdotal evidence suggesting that cougars defend their caches from humans or that it is especially dangerous to investigate a cougar's kill. Cougars may bed immediately adjacent to their kills or up to 1.5 miles (2.4 km) away. Certainly the cat is nearby if the kill is fresh, but it is highly unlikely to confront you to protect it.

In very warm weather meat spoils before they have time to eat it, and they may abandon carcasses before finishing them. This may be one reason cougars hunt more small and medium game in the hot summer months than at any other time of year. Males are most likely to leave a kill with some parts uneaten, and females with kittens are most likely to remain until little is left.

HABITAT AND HOME RANGE

The cougar is the most widely distributed terrestrial carnivore in the Americas, ranging from central Canada south to the tip of South America. Once cougars ranged from coast to coast in North America, but they were successfully extirpated throughout much of the East, save a tiny, remnant population in Florida. Cougars can be seen in nearly every habitat across their range as long as it provides

them cover to hunt and remain undetected. They tend to avoid expansive open areas, such as large agricultural tracts and meadows. They are also absent in extreme open deserts and the grasslands of the Great Plains.

Population density and home range size of cougars seem to be strongly correlated with prey availability and prey vulnerability. Prey vulnerability is a function of suitable stalking terrain—varied topography or dense vegetation. In general, a typical cougar density in North America is 1 animal for every 39 square miles (100 km²). Home ranges are incredibly variable. Those of females have been recorded from as little as 21 to as many as 264 square miles (55–685 km²). Male home ranges are larger and overlap those of several females. They are typically 200 to 350 square miles (515–900 km²), but sometimes larger.

COMMUNICATION

Communication between cougars is primarily olfactory, so as to mitigate potential fighting, but includes visual and auditory components as well. Chemical communication through scrapes, scats, urine, scratching, and rubbing is essential in maintaining territories as well as for relaying information about sexual status and availability. A cougar scrapes with its hind feet only, first with one foot and then the other, repeating the process several times to create a neat pile of debris and/or soil at one end of parallel swaths of exposed earth. Both males and females create scrapes, though males do so far more often than females. All males use scrapes to delineate their territories, whereas it

An adult male scratches an old log to mark his territory. © Mark Elbroch

appears that some females never or only rarely make scrapes.

Scrapes are often made in softer substrates, such as pine or leaf litter, or where other debris has accumulated. Scrapes are found most often where topography funnels movement under ledges, along ridges, in dry drainages, and at forested mountain passes. They are also found around kill sites. In some areas, numerous scrapes accumulate over time. In Arizona under a large ponderosa pine, cougar scrapes completely covered an area at least 20 by 30 feet (6 x 9 m). Where adult male ranges overlap little, cougars leave scrapes along territorial boundaries. In areas where they overlap greatly, such as the Southwest, scrape sites are sprinkled more broadly across their ranges. They function like community bulletin boards, perhaps emphasizing dominance and advertising which male is presently using that area. Both males and females visit scrape sites, and investigating cougars exhibit a flehmen response to inhale the scents of other cougars as deeply as possible. In a California study, remote cameras recorded a male scraping, then a female investigating his scrape an hour later. Both cougars were tagged,

and their location data revealed that they spent the next three days together, during which time it is assumed they mated.

Cougars have four common vocalizations: the caterwaul, the growl, the hiss, and the chirp/whistle. Caterwauls are advertisements meant to attract mates. Females often begin caterwauling when they are investigating scrape sites where neighboring males post their scents. Caterwauls are repetitive vocalizations somewhat akin to those of mating housecats and a mix of yowls of high and low pitch. Cougars may produce caterwauls for long durations and at intervals over several hours.

Agitated cougars point their ears backward and flatten them against their skull. They also growl in a low rumble. If a cougar is unable to run from an aggressor or if the aggressor is foolish enough to continue its approach, a cougar will intersperse growls with long, high-pitched hisses. These are produced with the mouth wide open to reveal their intimidating canines. Aggressive lions may also stand stiff-legged with their head raised, hackles erect, and tail twitching. Agitated lions may also bluff-charge at approaching humans, though this is rare and most often exhibited by females with kittens.

The chirp or whistle call comes most often from cougar kittens separated from their mother. The call is birdlike in pitch and duration and carries a great distance through wooded terrain. Very young kittens use the chirp/whistle almost continuously to call their mother to let them nurse. Adults may also produce a similar call as a greeting or to keep tabs on one other. Wild adult females returning to their litters may greet them with purrs, chirps, and low whistles.

The infamous cougar scream, which has been horrifically described as sounding like a woman or child being tortured, is still debated to this day. Earlier researchers documented such a call and said it was very rare. Yet numerous cougar biologists, many of whom have studied cats for more than a decade, say they have yet to hear such a sound. When a scream is heard, it is more likely made by another animal, such as a fisher, raccoon, or large owl.

COURTSHIP AND MATING

Females may go into estrus at any time of year, and thus mate and have litters throughout the year as well. However, the majority of litters are born from late spring though the summer. A female's estrus period lasts 4 to 12 days, during which she is vociferous and receptive. If she does not mate then, it is believed that she will come into estrus again approximately 2 weeks later and continue to do so at regular intervals until she succeeds in breeding.

Male mountain lions roam across large areas and attempt to mate with all receptive females within their range. Females, because of the stability of their home ranges, often mate successively with the same male at approximately 2-year intervals. When a male discovers signs of a female in estrus or hears her caterwauling, which she does at regular intervals, he yowls in response and moves quickly to catch up with her. The female is the instigator and louder of the pair when caterwauling. One female in New Mexico was heard caterwauling 10 times in succession for a total of more than 500 vocalizations. Once a male appears, the pair will forage and travel together until her estrus is complete.

Females are especially playful just preceding and during estrus and may be seen batting shrubs, rolling, and soliciting attention from the male. Periodically he approaches her from behind to sniff her posterior and test whether she truly is in estrus. When he tests her scent, he exhibits a flehmen response, recognizable by his facial expression, which resembles an angry, growling lion, yet is completely silent. The female either allows him to mate or threatens him with snarling and hissing. When she is finally receptive, he mounts her from behind, and she arches her spine downward, elevating her rump. He may grasp the back of her neck in his mouth and wrap his front limbs around her torso for stability. Actual mating is brief, lasting a minute or less, but what males lack in individual mating performance, they make up in repetition, mating as many as 9 times in an hour and 70 times per day.

DEVELOPMENT AND DISPERSAL OF YOUNG

Pregnant females select a den in dense cover that provides security and temperature regulation. Dens are typically found in dense shrubby cover or in rocky terrain where boulders or fissures provide accessible cavities. After a gestation of 3 months, females give birth to 2 to 3 kittens, though on occasion they have 4.

The kittens are born with dense, bold, black spotting and with their eyes and ears tightly closed. They nurse 8 to 12 times per day for their first few days, when their mother is nearly always at their side. After this period the female begins to prolong her foraging forays and invest more time in hunting. Kittens gain weight rapidly and open their eyes for the first time between 7 and 15 days of age. After 4 weeks, they weigh as much as 10 pounds (4.5 kg) and are the size of housecats. Their first set of canines appears between 20 and 30 days, and by this point their mother may have moved them to a different den site. She may move them several times before they are old enough to accompany her as she travels about her territory.

By the time the kittens are 4 weeks old, the female may spend less than half of her time at the den site, and when they are several months old she may leave them for an entire day or even two, completely on their own. An observer who worked in a fire tower in California found himself next to a cougar's den for a short period and observed the female pouncing on grasshoppers until the youngsters started mimicking her and trying their own luck—thus the female may actively mentor her kittens in hunting behavior. Kittens walk in an unsteady manner when they are several weeks old but are agile on the ground and capable tree-climbers by 8 weeks.

Kittens begin to accompany their mother to her kills as early as 8 weeks of age but may continue to nurse for another month. Typically the female will make a new kill, return to her last kill where she'd left her kittens to finish the carcass, and escort them to the new one. After she has eaten her fill, rested, and left her kittens under cover with food, she moves on in search of the next meal. While she has few, small kittens, each meal earns her several days' respite, but when she has several large kittens, she may rest only the night before moving on to hunt again. Females with young tend to operate at 85 to 90 percent of their typical body weight, such are the demands of hunting for more than one.

The black spots begin to fade when the kittens are 4 months old, though remnant markings can sometimes be seen much longer. At about 6 months, just as their permanent teeth begin to appear, they begin accompanying their mother on select hunts, and by 8 months they begin to accompany her on every hunt. Their piercing blue eyes begin to fade at the same time and by 16 months they are the golden brown of an adult.

There are several records of orphaned kittens surviving on their own at 6 to 8 months old, but overall, orphaned kittens less than a year old have little chance of survival. A mother that has become separated form her kittens will search for them where she last saw them. Orphaned kittens linger where they last met up with their mother and return repeatedly to that site for many days.

Kittens disperse between 1.5 and 2 years of age, occasionally slightly younger, setting out on their own to establish territories. Females may reach sexual maturity between 1.5 and 3 years of age and mate in their first year on their own. In southern California, adult females sometimes escort their young far from their core home range and "drop them off." The mother may even abandon them in her territory and move away to establish a new home range of her own. Their mother may leave them at a kill site and never return or confront them aggressively if they try to follow her. Simultaneous with the breakup of the family, the female tends to enter estrus to begin the cycle all over again.

Dispersing cougars are called "transients," and they are usually hungry and inexperienced. Transients

A defensive adult female communicates her agitation by standing stiff-legged and putting her ears back. The kitten between her legs seems oblivious to the threat. © *Mark Elbroch*

are the most likely to be involved in human encounters and depredation on domestic animals, because they are seeking unoccupied habitats and run into human settlements in their search. Occasionally, dispersing kittens of the same litter will travel together for several months. Dispersers are often killed by resident adult male cougars as well, and this intraspecific killing is thought to be one of the major causes of mortalities for dispersing subadults. They also frequently fall victim to vehicles when attempting to cross highways. Males typically disperse farther than females and may range as far as 310 miles (500 km). The longest recorded dispersal is that of a female in the Rockies that traveled 830 miles (1,340 km).

INTERACTIONS AMONG COUGARS

Cougars are solitary animals, except for brief encounters for mating and the temporary familial units of a female and her kittens. New GPS tracking technology has shown that both males and females mingle peacefully with family groups (mothers and kittens) from time to time. Male cougars sometimes kill kittens and occasionally wipe out unattended litters. Researchers hypothesize that newly dominant males do this in order to kill their predecessor's offspring and cause the females to reenter estrus, enhancing their own reproductive success by increasing mating opportunities. In Florida populations, females go into heat almost immediately after losing their kittens. However, in cougar populations throughout the West, females enter estrus after several months' time, so the male would need to continue to check in on her to know when she next became receptive.

The amount of overlap in cougar home ranges varies across western North America. In studies in the Rockies, females overlapped with one another, but males rarely overlapped with other males. More recent research throughout the Southwest, including studies in southern California, show partial overlap among males and among females. Overlapping cougars employ a time-share system, meaning that when one cougar is present in a shared area, the neighboring cat is in a different part of its range.

INTERACTIONS WITH OTHER SPECIES

Long-term research in Idaho and elsewhere has revealed that cougars do little to impact healthy deer and elk herds they hunt, killing only 1 to 3 percent of those herds per year. Herds are more heavily influenced by winter severity and forage quality. But cougars do affect herd behavior, forcing elk and deer to be more evenly distributed on the landscape as opposed to reducing their numbers. However, when an ungulate herd is already in decline because of disease, severe winters, or reduced forage due to fire suppression, cougar impacts are more severe and can accelerate the herd's decline. In such instances cougars may be responsible for killing up to 20 percent of a deer population in a given year.

Cougars can also severely limit the recovery of newly introduced ungulate populations and small populations in general. Desert Bighorn Sheep are classified as endangered and persist in small populations. For these sheep, cougar predation is a significant barrier to their reproduction and proliferation. As a result, managers often remove cougars from the area around Bighorn Sheep to aid their recovery efforts. Yet removing all cougars creates a vacant area that draws in transient cougars, thus perpetuating cougar culling. Research in Canada and California has shown that certain cougars become Bighorn Sheep specialists, but most remain active deer hunters. Now in California managers remove only problem cougars, leaving those that are hunting deer to hold their territories on the landscape and keep out transients that may turn out to be Bighorn Sheep killers.

Cougars compete with other large and medium carnivores when they are present. Competition with jaguars in the tropics is little understood, yet where the two species overlap cougars tend to hunt smaller prey than do jaguars, or else, in areas of varied habitat, jaguars hunt in the moister wetlands while cougars hunt larger deer inhabiting the drier uplands. Black and Grizzly Bears both commandeer cougar kills, forcing cougars to hunt more often. Cougars in Montana and other bear-rich areas have been recorded hunting smaller prey and hauling carcasses into trees, as leopards do in Africa to avoid having meals stolen by hyenas and other predators.

In addition to having meals stolen, adult cougars are occasionally killed by Grizzly and Black Bears and by packs of wolves. In one instance, biologists in California were investigating a Bighorn Sheep mortality by helicopter. When they flew over the site, they were surprised to spot a Black Bear rather than a cougar. Upon further investigation, they discovered that the bear was eating the cougar that was assumed to be responsible for killing and caching the Bighorn Sheep.

Encounters with wild cougars are rare and attacks on humans even more so. However, they do occur. Should you encounter a curious or aggressive cougar in the wild, yell and make lots of noise, throw rocks or anything available, and make yourself appear as large and formidable as possible. Typically they flee when they realize you are human. Should the cougar attack, fight *hard*, since cougars abandon prey that does not easily succumb, and fight *long*, for cougars focus-lock on their prey, a lock that will persist for several minutes regardless of the abuse it is suffering.

OTHER NAMES: song-dog, brush wolf, prairie wolf, sunmanitu (Lakota), wa-ya (Cherokee), o'kome (Cheyenne).

The coyote plays varied roles in the folklore of indigenous cultures in North America: trickster, demigod, prophet, teacher. Native stories about Coyote center on his cunning, mischief, magic powers, and often his apparent lack of morals. He plays larger and more important roles in myths and legends than his larger and more formidable cousin, the wolf. Perhaps our continuous attempts at coyote control in North America have revealed why.

While we successfully culled or wiped out wolves, cougars, Grizzly Bears, and Black Bears over vast regions of the continent in our war against predators, the coyote is now more widespread than when Europeans arrived in North America. Coyotes have proliferated in the face of a century of intensive persecution and have again and again confirmed their intelligence and adaptability in the face of adversity; they have indeed proven worthy of rich folklore.

The English *coyote* is a borrowing of the Mexican Spanish word, which is a variation on the original Nahuatl (Aztec) word *coyotl*. The species name *Canis latrans* is Latin for "barking dog."

ACTIVITY AND MOVEMENT

DAILY

Coyotes may be active throughout the day but are most active during early morning and near sunset. In open terrain in the West, coyotes may be seen hunting or traveling in grasslands and meadows at any time, but in areas of high human activity or where they are heavily persecuted, coyotes typically become more nocturnal. They remain invisible by moving where terrain provides them cover and restricting their movements to times they are least likely to be spotted. They rest under cover and in areas where they can easily detect potential dangers approaching. They sometimes curl up on hummocks in thick, shrubby swamps, or sleep atop boulders on hillsides where sounds and smells are carried over large distances. Unlike felines, which prefer to sleep under cover, coyotes typically bed atop rocks or other structures.

Coyotes travel in a relentless ground-eating trot, slowing to walk only when something catches their interest and they pause to investigate. It is not unusual for them to travel several miles without ever breaking stride, pausing, or slowing. Coyotes can run up to 45 miles (72 km) per hour for short distances.

Coyote packs move in single file in open terrain and often step in each other's foot prints. When following tracks of coyotes, you might think you are following one animal, and then as they enter canopied forest and spread out so as better to detect prey, the tracks of one coyote may quickly become many. Residents prefer to remain within their territories, and even when pushed or pursued they generally circle back when they hit their borders.

SEASONAL

As the seasons change, so do the coyote's hunting strategies, particularly in boreal regions. In the North coyotes rest more in winter and hunt or scavenge the carcasses of ungulates, like deer and elk. In spring and summer they are more active and make regular hunting forays in search of smaller prey. In milder climates where seasonal changes are less dramatic, coyotes do not shift their foraging strategies so dramatically, but they certainly focus on specific foods at certain times of year.

Resident coyotes do not make seasonal migrations, but in the northern winter they often reduce their activity to smaller portions of their home range where deer are gathering under conifers in shallow snow. Deep snow is also a hindrance to coyote activity, and they must select areas on the landscape where wind, forest cover, or sun limits snow depths. Coyotes are quick to take advantage of "anthro-packed snow"—meaning snowshoe, cross-country ski, and snowmobile trails—to better access and travel in areas that would ordinarily be inaccessible to them.

FOOD AND FORAGING

Coyotes are amazing examples of ecological generalists. They are intelligent and inquisitive and quickly recognize and adapt to new habitats and opportunities. The coyote's teeth are ideal equipment for processing any and all sorts of foods. Their sharp, stout canines grip and kill prey of all sizes; their carnassials shear both fruits and meat; and their back molars are flattened to chew meat, nuts, fruit, or whatever else a coyote might try to eat. If it fits in a coyote's mouth, a coyote somewhere has tried to eat it. In Missouri, one study identified 47 animal and 28 plant foods eaten by local coyotes. They sneak onto porches to eat dog food from bowls, steal from trashcans in urban centers, and leap to pluck apples from trees in orchards, as well as hunt and scavenge animal prey.

Across their range, rabbits and small rodents are fundamental in coyote diets. Seasonal prey abundances and mast crops also influence what coyotes eat and when. In winter, coyotes rely more heavily upon ungulates, mostly scavenged as carrion. In spring they eat increasing proportions of rodents;

in summer they add large numbers of insects, including Jerusalem crickets and grasshoppers; and in autumn they feast on fruits and nut crops. In addition to seasonal changes, coyote diets also vary by region. In areas of Arkansas coyotes eat more stolen poultry, and in other areas they prey heavily on sheep. In Yosemite National Park in California coyotes primarily patrol the roadways during the winter in search of roadkill.

Like Red Foxes, solo coyotes "mouse" for voles and other small mammals. They listen through snow or thick vegetation for the sounds that betray the presence of an animal, and then, in a graceful arc, leap and descend upon their victim, pinning it to the ground with their forepaws. Playful coyotes may even fling their prey into the air several times before giving it a quick chew and swallowing it whole. In California the stomach of a road-killed coyote contained the remains of 17 undigested California Voles caught that morning: 3 babies, 3 juveniles, and 11 adults. After a quick stalk to close the gap, coyotes rush ground squirrels and rabbits and grab them in their teeth. They rely principally upon vision to hunt, and then audition and olfaction in decreasing importance, although this varies depending on conditions.

In contrast to scavenging, coyotes actively hunt ungulates at two times of year: the fawning season and winter. Coyotes can be a significant limiting factor for fawn and calf survival in Bighorn Sheep, pronghorn, elk, and deer. During the several weeks from their birth until fawns and calves are old enough to outrun and outmaneuver predators, coyotes sometimes hunt them exclusively. They attack their throats and heads, sometimes shredding their ears in the chase. Fawn hunting is often a coordinated effort between a pair of coyotes or a pack, so that while one coyote distracts the fawn's mother, the other sneaks in to make the kill. Sometimes the deer is able to fight off her attackers and protect her fawns, but sometimes not.

Winter, when snows are deep, is the time when coyotes most often *hunt* large ungulates. Ungulates suffer a slow starvation each winter and weaken as the season progresses, especially males that may have entered the winter exhausted and starving from the rut. Compounding their nutrient and energy deficiencies, they struggle to move in deep snow. During late winters, icy crusts form atop deep snow, and light coyotes can run aloft while deer, elk, and others break through, cutting themselves on sharp edges and exhausting themselves in the effort. In addition to snow conditions, the health and stamina of the prey and the presence of the alpha pair in pack hunting are critical to hunting success. The number of coyotes is not as important as which coyotes participate. In packs of 7 or more coyotes, only the alpha pair attack deer and elk; their larger

Here are the fresh remains of 17 voles found in the stomach of a coyote struck by a vehicle.

A coyote pounces and arcs to pin and capture a Meadow Vole in an open meadow.

A coyote attacks a battered-looking Mule Deer in winter, when deer are physically taxed and more vulnerable to predation. © *Art Wolfe/Photo Researchers*

sizes and more aggressive demeanors ensure the greatest chances of killing their prey.

Coyotes attack the rump and legs of large ungulates as they run, and when they stumble or slow, coyotes attack the throat to end the ordeal. Ungulates protect themselves by fighting or fleeing, often running into water. In one instance coyotes chased a female elk into a creek and then waited patiently on the shore for 7 days until she emerged, at which point she was too exhausted to fight back and quickly succumbed to their attack. When both Mule and White-tailed Deer are present, coyotes more often attack Mule Deer. White-tailed Deer almost always flee coyotes, whereas Mule Deer are much more likely to stand their ground and defend themselves and other deer in their group. This difference may make them more vulnerable to coordinated attacks.

The carrion of large ungulate carcasses is also vital to northern populations of coyotes. The boon of winter-scavenged or killed meat propels breeding females through their pregnancy and ensures healthy development of their young. In Wyoming coyotes triple their summer intake of carrion during winter, and since the reintroduction of wolves in Yellowstone National Park coyotes in the park have increased their scavenging of large carcasses throughout the year.

Deer and other ungulates killed by coyotes can be difficult to distinguish from carcasses they are scavenging, especially if the coyotes have been feeding on the kill or carcass for more than a day. In fresh kills, look for signs of the chase, and on the carcass itself look for signs of biting and tearing at the flanks and rump of the deer as it ran. Once the carcass is down, coyotes scavenge and open fresh carcasses in much the same way. They typically start at the rump of the animal, feed on the hind legs, then open the abdominal cavity, remove the rumen, and then chew through the ribs to access the internal organs. As coyotes continue to feed, the carcass is dragged about, dismantled, and spread across the area.

Coyotes also form hunting partnerships with golden eagles, ravens, and badgers. Eagles and ravens guide coyotes to potential prey, or in the case of ravens, to carcasses that they need opened so that they can scavenge more efficiently. Badgers and coyotes have been observed hunting both ground squirrels and prairie dogs in cooperative fashion. Coyotes may in fact be taking advantage of foraging badgers, capturing prey that flee their burrows to escape badgers, rather than contributing anything beneficial in return (see American Badger, p. 182).

HABITAT AND HOME RANGE

Coyotes are habitat generalists and are found throughout North America in woodlands, grasslands, deserts, mountains, and urban and agricultural areas. They are absent only from northeast and north-central Canada and the exposed coastal areas of northern Alaska.

Coyote territories vary with geographic population, season, and pack status. Transients roam over large areas while established packs use smaller, distinct territories. The size of home ranges for resident pairs and individuals ranges from 0.8 square miles (2 km²) in parts of Texas to extremes of 26 square miles (68 km²) in males studied in Minnesota. More typically, home ranges vary from 1.5 to 6 square miles (4 to 15 km²) and are smaller in the desert Southwest than in the North. Home ranges are also generally larger when including suburban or urban areas.

Statistical home ranges created from point locations often vary between the sexes and between seasons of the year. In truth, a resident pair share the same territory but use different proportions of it at different times of year. Male home ranges likely appear larger using point locations because they wander beyond their territory borders more often than females, and so published home ranges likely include their territories *plus* some adjacent habitat. In Vermont during the winter males use on average 7.3 square miles (18.8 km²), while in summer only 4 square miles (10.4 km²). Females in Vermont average 4.6 square miles (11.8 km²) in winter and 2.5 square miles (6.6 km²) in summer. In Colorado females use on average 2.9 to 3.5 square miles (7.5–9 km²), and males 3.3 to 4.6 square miles (8.5–12 km²) in a given year.

COMMUNICATION

Coyotes employ body postures, vocalizations, and chemical cues in an elaborate tapestry of meaningful exchange. They use rich visual displays, in which mood and intention are well conveyed through complex combinations of position of the head, mouth, ears, legs, ruff, and tail. Coyotes communicate in a continuum of subtle and graded variations of expression—consider the height of the head and the position of the ears, which are clear indicators of aggression, or dominance. At one end of the spectrum, highly aggressive coyotes hold their head high and their ears erect and forward, and at the other end highly submissive coyotes roll onto their side and place their ears back. Less submissive animals remain upright but lower their head nearly to the ground.

Aggressive animals pull back their black lips, which contrast with their white teeth, to reveal their

INCREASING AGGRESSION

INCREASING FEAR ———▷

The facial expressions of coyotes exhibiting various levels of fear and aggression. Drawing by F. Jacobs, from Lehner in Bekoff, 2001, *Coyotes: Biology, Behavior, and Management.* Used with permission of the Blackburn Press.

canines and incisors. The corners of their mouth are forward, making the mouth look smaller, and the eyes are narrowed. The eyes too are bordered in black and white lines to emphasize their position. When communicating a defensive threat, the head is often low, but the mouth is open to reveal the teeth, and the eyes are open or narrowed. In full submission, the mouth is closed or only partly open to reveal the tips of the canines. Submissive animals also pull back the corners of their mouth, which rise slightly to make them look like they are grinning, an expression known as the "submissive grin." Coyotes approaching other coyotes on a carcass often dip their head, lower their ears, and gape to reveal all their teeth with a submissive grin. They are communicating their intention to peaceably approach the carcass. If coyotes at the carcass have fed enough to temper their appetites, they often back away to let the newcomer feed.

Aggressive animals raise their hackles—the fur

Three coyote body postures exhibiting (a) moderate submission while approaching others feeding on a carcass; (b) dominance and aggression toward others, with the legs stiff and tail held more parallel to the ground; and (c) extreme submission, with the back curled and the tail held beneath itself.

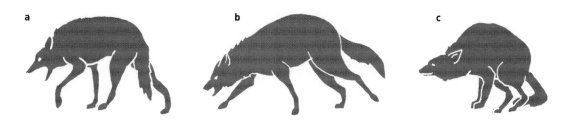

a   b   c

on their neck and shoulders—and hold their tail straight out behind them or even elevated to a 45° angle. Submissive animals either hold their tail low or, in extreme submission, tuck it completely between their legs. Sometimes they slowly wag their tail. Aggressive animals stand straight and may use a stiff-legged gait to convey their intentions. Submissive animals often curl their spine, lowering their hindquarters to further accentuate their submission, or even lower their entire bodies to the ground and grovel and crawl toward the dominant animal in an exchange.

Aggressive animals may also poke subordinates with their forelimbs, and subordinates sometimes raise one foreleg and leave it hovering and bent midair, like an ignored offer to shake hands, to signal their submission. Subordinates may also lick the chops of dominants like pups soliciting food, or whine and urinate during an exchange. Coyotes also display the "inguinal response": when one animal, usually the dominant, gently nudges the inguinal (groin) area of another, the latter reflexively lifts its leg to allow a closer inspection.

Coyotes often greet each other with characteristic displays of aggression and submission. The dominant animal stands tall and "ignores" the other coyote, and the subordinate lowers its head, licks at the dominant's chops, or briefly rolls over to display submission. Coyotes soliciting play from another often approach in a stiff, bouncing gait, with head up, eyes wide, and ears erect, and then they quickly retreat as if offering an invitation to start a chase. In a society built on dominance and submission, clear intentions are incredibly important. Playful coyotes wag their tail and may drop down into a play-bow, dipping their front legs, stretching out their forelimbs before them, holding their head erect, and keeping their hind end high with tail wagging. They may even bounce side to side, dropping into bows to encourage play in a potential partner.

Coyote vocabulary includes their emblematic howling and a host of barks, yips, snarls, and growls. Woofs or muffled barks are used in alarm when coyotes are surprised, as well as to call forth pups from the den. Coyotes growl in aggression and give huffs—rapid expulsions of air—in threat and aggression. They bark when alarmed as well as to communicate threat and challenge over longer distances. Coyotes may bark for up to 30 minutes should a threat persist. Barks may also turn into howls or yips to accentuate territoriality at a boundary after they chase out an intruder. Yelps and loud whines communicate submission to aggressors, and low whines and whimpers are used in greeting. Greeting coyotes may also produce a drawn-out bark, often described as "wow-wow."

Howling is territorial behavior that maintains spacing between packs through delineating boundaries and advertising the presence of alpha individuals that vigorously attack and repel invaders. Alpha animals howl both longer and more frequently than other members of the pack, and they howl more frequently along the periphery of their territories. Transients rarely if ever howl or respond

Coyotes exhibiting dominance and submission. The coyote on the left stands straight and holds its tail out straight to communicate its dominance. The coyote on the right curves its spine, lowers its head, and curves its tail beneath to communicate its submission. However, it gapes wide and "grins" to communicate that it isn't going to back off completely. In this way the coyote communicates that it intends no confrontation or threat, but still wants to approach. © *Dave Stiles*

A coyote throws its head back and howls.

serve as signals that an area has already been foraged and that it's not worth further investigation.

Scratching is the same behavior observed in domestic dogs, vigorously scraping backward with their hind and sometimes front feet after they defecate or urinate. Coyotes and dogs have scent glands between their toes, and they often scratch adjacent to scats or urine to deposit scent on the ground. Sometimes scratches are also made on their own.

The rate of scenting varies with the season, but it is not influenced by pack size. Scenting, like howling, peaks with the mating season in winter. In addition to showing ownership of territory to outsiders, scenting may also communicate sexual condition and facilitate sexual synchrony between the alpha pair during breeding. Transient coyotes scent-mark much less frequently than residents, and in one study were never observed to scratch the ground after defecations or urinations, a behavior frequently exhibited by coyotes holding a territory.

COURTSHIP AND MATING

Male-female pairs may mate together for up to 12 years, but not necessarily for life. Females have one "heat," or estrus, sometime between January and March, depending on geography and age of the female. Courtship begins as early as 2 to 3 months before breeding. There is a notable increase in scent-marking and howling at the beginning of the breeding season, and alpha males become increasingly attracted to the alpha female's urine and feces. The alpha pair also exhibit more aggression toward other members of the pack, as if to reinforce their hierarchy so as to dissuade others from intervening or participating in the mating season. This period, known as proestrus, is longer in the coyote than in other canids, suggesting the pair bond may be especially important in coyotes.

Mating pairs scent-mark in tandem as estrus approaches, which may help to synchronize their bodies to provide greater chance of reproductive success. As a female enters estrus, blood will be visible in her urine in snow. Before mating, females initiate nearly every paired scent-marking behavior. She squats and pees, and the male comes over to smell her urine and then lifts a leg to squirt urine adjacent to hers. After mating, the roles reverse, and males often pee first, with the female adding her scent afterward.

Female coyotes are in estrus for only 2 to 5 days each year. When she is ready for copulation, she will flag her tail to the side and tolerate mounting attempts. Coitus is brief, but the bulbous glandis at the base of the penis swells and becomes wedged in the vagina, resulting in a copulatory tie. The male usually steps over the female's rump and the two remain connected, rump to rump, for up to 25

to howling from resident animals. Howling peaks in winter with the breeding season, simultaneously with the peak in alpha pair tandem scent-marking, discussed below.

There are three classes of coyote howl: lone, group, and group-yip howling. Lone howls are given by lone coyotes. They are loud and long and are associated with long-distance communication. Lone howls may provide the location of individuals separated from the pack and thus facilitate reunions. Group howling is simultaneous howling by two or more individuals in the same location. Group-yip howling is a cacophony of multiple individuals creating distinct patterns of howls and yips. Group howling and group-yip howling advertise territoriality and coordinate group hunting. Group howling and yip-howls are most frequent near sunrise and sunset, though they may be heard sporadically through the night. They sometimes signal transitions in their activity, such as the start or end of hunting.

Coyotes leave the majority of their scent marks along the boundaries of their territories, and most scenting is done by the alpha male and female of the pack. They repeatedly scent particular areas prone to intrusion by neighboring coyotes. Most of this scenting consists of raised-leg and forward-lean urinations, stereotypically dominant postures associated with dominant animals. Scats are placed at trail junctions, where latrines may accumulate, or on elevated surfaces along travel routes. Scats are found equally throughout the range of a coyote, whereas urinations and scratches are made most often along the periphery of territories. Scats may also minutes. Food supply and related coyote densities are the primary factors governing the number of reproductive females in a population. When prey populations are high and food is abundant, 60 to 90 percent of adult females and up to 70 percent of yearling females in a population breed. In some packs, the alpha male will mate with 2 females, and numerous pairs without territories breed as well. When yearling females participate in the breeding season, they typically mate later in the breeding season than mature females.

DEVELOPMENT AND DISPERSAL OF YOUNG

The den is the focal point of coyote social life from the birth of the pups until they are large and mobile (several months). Coyotes appropriate the abandoned dens of badgers, woodchucks, wolves, armadillos, and others, which they then enlarge and remodel, or they dig their own. Dens are found in brushy thickets on slopes, on steep banks, and in rock ledges. Dens are often oriented in order to maximize solar exposure, and their entrances are typically 1 foot (0.3 m) in diameter and slightly taller than wide. They often have multiple entrances and many interconnecting tunnels that run up to 25 feet (7.5 m) long. Dens are reused year after year and in excellent habitat, generation after generation. Dens studied in Yellowstone have been used for greater than 50 years, and perhaps much more.

Older females give birth earlier in the spring than young females. Gestation averages 63 days (with a range of 58 to 65), after which 4 to 9 pups are born in the dark in the protection of the den. The average litter size is highly variable and is affected by population density and the food availability during the previous winter. Litter sizes average 4 when coyote densities are high or food is scarce and 7 when coyote densities are low or food is abundant. Occasionally coyotes produce exceptionally large litters, and several records exist of litters of 12 or more. When food is especially abundant, a second female in a pack may also breed. The two breeding females produce a double litter and cooperatively raise them in the same den.

Newborns are blind, helpless, and approximately 6 inches (16 cm) long. Their eyes and ears open by 2 weeks. Young pups lie quietly with as much bodily contact as possible with littermates, and they respond vigorously to tactile stimulation. Captive pups show avoidance reactions to being picked up, and touching the scruff of their neck causes them to shrink away and bare their teeth. For the first 2 to 3 weeks, pups urinate and defecate only when stimulated to do so by adults, which establishes behavioral patterns that shape later social interactions. Coyotes typically move their offspring to other dens 2 to 3 times within their first month, possibly

in response to flea infestations as well as to minimize predation risk. Den switching is typically over short distances, but 1.2 to 2.5 miles (2 to 4 km) is not uncommon.

Between 25 and 35 days of age, pups form dominance hierarchies among themselves through vicious fights. They grapple, box, and scratch with their forelimbs and bite at each other's faces and ruffs. Three days of intense fighting establishes the hierarchy, after which fighting rapidly decreases in frequency and transitions into the more ritualized displays of aggression and submission also used by adults to reinforce social ranks. No serious injuries occur during this period, and slight size differences and sex make no difference in the outcomes of fights. The dominant pups are also not necessarily the most aggressive, and they play with the lowest-ranking animals (omegas) more than any other pup. Both highest- and lowest-ranking pups distance themselves from their littermates and become out of synch with their activities. In some cases, alphas may appear to initiate a large number of fights with omegas (though omegas may misinterpret play solicitation and respond aggressively). True fights are most common between near-ranking individuals, especially when dominance is unclear. Pups seem unable to accurately judge whether they can beat an opponent (an important skill among adults) and may initiate fights just to see what happens.

Pups emerge from their den and start to eat solid food as early as 3 weeks of age. Initially food is regurgitated by beta and alpha pack members. Pups are cared for by their parents and their "helpers," which are usually young from the previous litter. Adults within the pack are extremely protective of the den and only rarely are young pups left without a guardian lingering around the den entrance.

As time passes, the female increasingly walks off or growls when juveniles attempt to suckle. The pups are weaned between 5 and 7 weeks, during which time they spend more time exploring and playing outside the den. During the summer pups are moved to and remain at "rendezvous sites," which function as aboveground dens and are where the pups await the return of parents with food. They attain adult proportions at 9 months.

Should pups disperse, they typically do so in autumn and early winter, as food becomes scarce. Pups may make several forays and explorations before they finally disperse to a vacant or occupied territory adjacent to their own or much farther away. Typical dispersals range from 30 to 99 miles (48 to 160 km) but have been recorded as long as 338 miles (544 km). Dispersing coyotes are at great risk of death as they cautiously travel through unfamiliar and potentially unfriendly terrain; they average just 7 miles (11 km) per week. On average, only 2

A nursing adult female with a litter of young coyotes. © *Tom & Pat Leeson/Photo Researchers*

pups in each litter survive until their first birthday.

Some pups choose to stay in their parents' home range and help raise the next litter. Philopatric coyotes—those that remain within their pack—tend to be alpha pups that may move into an alpha position when a parent dies. However, if they choose to stay, high-ranking pups sometimes become stuck in beta positions within their natal packs and may decide to disperse at a later point in order to lead a pack. Low-ranking coyotes more often attempt to establish themselves in either adjacent or distant territories. Dispersers in Yellowstone National Park were low-ranking pups or beta animals that spent little time with other pack members. They tended to suffer poor access to shared resources, especially ungulate carcasses during the winter. As the benefits of remaining in their natal pack dwindled, they set out in search of better circumstances.

INTERACTIONS AMONG COYOTES

Coyotes are less social than wolves and operate equally well as individuals, pairs, or packs. A typical coyote "pack" consists of a mated pair (alpha pair), their current offspring, and one or two young from the previous year that stay on as "helpers." In Yellowstone prior to the wolf reintroduction, packs were as large as 11 adults and, including yearlings and pups, reached 23 individuals. Elsewhere in the country, coyote packs remain much smaller. Territories of resident packs are stable and are clearly delineated on the landscape.

In every coyote population there are some number of transient or territorial pairs and lone ani-

mals. In some parts of the continent, especially in areas where they are heavily persecuted, adult pairs are the general rule rather than coyote packs. Unlike breeding foxes that share each other's company only during the mating and denning seasons, coyotes tend to spend the entire year in pairs or packs. Occasionally adult pack members other than the breeding pair hunt alone for periods of the year outside of the breeding season. Lone coyotes, also called transients, do not breed or maintain territories and may wander far and wide in order to eat and avoid severe harassment from other coyotes. Pairs without territories also often wander farther than packs and, along with lone coyotes, usually travel the peripheries of pack territories to avoid conflicts.

The alpha pair are the primary enforcers of territories and are involved in most confrontations with intruders. Unlike in wolves, territorial defense rarely results in mortalities or serious injuries. Coyotes more often chase and use ritualized displays to push intruders from their territories. Pursuit stops at the boundary of their territory, and the resident animals howl and scent-mark to enforce their border. If they were chasing animals from a neighboring pack, their neighbors in turn howl and scent-mark when they are back on their own ground. While under the guidance of the same alpha pair, pack territories rarely shift on the landscape. Most boundary shifts occur when one or both alpha animals are killed or die.

What exactly governs pack size in coyotes still remains a mystery. It was once believed that the size of localized prey governed pack size and that where prey are small, coyotes would remain in pairs or trios. Following this logic, larger packs would form where larger prey require additional claws and teeth for hunting, and this is not always the case. Current research suggests that perhaps pack size increases as coyote densities increase to improve group defense: larger groups can defend better territories with higher quality forage. A competing hypothesis is that pack size increases with density because juveniles have nowhere else to go, and so remain within their natal territories.

INTERACTIONS WITH OTHER SPECIES

Coyotes are subordinate to wolves, but dominant over foxes. In what has become a classic example of canine interactions, wolves completely wiped out the abundant coyote population on Isle Royale in Michigan within 5 or 6 years after they successfully crossed an ice bridge and populated the island in the 1950s. As a result, the tiny Red Fox population on the island blossomed under greater tolerance from wolves than from coyotes.

Coyotes compete with, displace, and kill Swift, Kit, gray, and Red foxes. Foxes avoid coyotes by using the periphery of coyote territories more than the interior, by moving into more protective habitat when they are present, and by denning in close proximity to humans, who are more tolerant of foxes but actively target coyotes. In Maine, Red Foxes made their own territories along the periphery of coyote territories and completely avoided riparian zones within coyote territories. Coyotes can also be tolerant of Red Foxes, most often when food is plentiful. During a study in Yellowstone National Park, coyotes were most aggressive to Red Foxes in the presence of a carcass, but otherwise they were not aggressive toward them in a little over half of their interactions.

Coyotes also sometimes compete with and kill bobcats and Canada Lynx. Where they overlap most in diet, these cats and coyotes employ slightly different habitats or hunting styles to minimize their negative interactions. Coyotes and bobcats more often coexist than interact. In areas where coyotes overlap with Canada Lynx, they both predominantly hunt Snowshoe Hares, yet they do so in different habitats. Coyotes are less able to hunt in deep snow than lynx and select habitats under dense forest canopies where the snow cover is less.

Thirty years ago in central New England, when coyotes were rare, bobcats primarily hunted White-tailed Deer during the winter. When coyotes returned and proliferated, they appropriated the deer-hunting niche, and bobcats have since shifted to primarily hunting Snowshoe Hares and smaller prey. In southern California, coyotes killed 2 bobcats and 7 of 24 collared gray foxes during a 2-year study. During the same time period at the same study site, coyotes also killed a badger, and the remains of other smaller carnivores were found in their scats. However, in a similar study in northern California, where prey were more abundant, coyotes, bobcats, and gray foxes coexisted at high density with no evidence of competition or interspecific killing.

Wolves and cougars are the greatest threats to coyotes, other than humans. Coyotes will sneak in to steal from carcasses killed by wolves and cougars, and where these larger predators are present coyotes feed on large ungulate carcasses throughout the year. Alpha coyotes take greater risks than subordinates and are most likely to sneak in to feed. Even with their increased vigilance while feeding at wolf and cougar kills, they are occasionally discovered and chased off. Should the wolves or cougars actually catch them, they are killed. Cougars also hunt coyotes opportunistically, but in general they coexist peacefully.

Wolves, on the other hand, can severely limit coyote populations and sometimes actively seek them out. In one case in Yellowstone National Park, shortly after the release of wolves in the park, a pair of wolves were seen digging out a coyote den. The entire pack of coyotes encircled the wolves, whining, but were unable to do anything to stop them. The wolves pulled the pups out one by one, shook them until they went limp, and then departed the area.

Coyotes can also be a serious threat to small isolated populations of wolves, not through aggression or violence, but through breeding. Female wolves unable to locate mates of their own species will mate with coyotes. Red Wolves persist at critically low numbers, and for this reason managers exclude coyotes from the area around Alligator National Wildlife Refuge in North Carolina to protect one of the last remaining Red Wolf populations. There is speculation that the smaller eastern timber wolf may have also crossbred with coyotes for similar reasons when their numbers were low, and this is why coyotes in the Northeast all carry wolf genes and are larger than in other parts of the country.

Coyotes are often blamed for killing housecats, but research has shown that cats are only a minuscule part of their diets. Certainly they kill the occasional housecat, but only rarely. The legend of coydogs, a hybrid coyote-dog offspring, is in fact based on truth. Coyote hybridization with dogs is thought to be very rare and is best documented in the Southeast, where 12 of 112 coyotes carried domestic dog genetics from a historic interbreeding. Elsewhere in the country, skull measurements have been used to identify potential hybrids, but other than in the Southeast little genetic evidence exists to support speculation.

Wolf
Canis lupus

OTHER NAMES: Gray Wolf, timber wolf, Arctic wolf, Mexican wolf, loup (French), lobo (Spanish), sungmanitu (Lakota).

Perhaps no other animal in North America so stirs the imagination and is so controversial. Indigenous North Americans both hunted and respected wolves, and few tribes, if any, ever attempted to exterminate them. Centuries ago, European settlers arrived with entrenched anti-wolf sentiments, and since then, we have waged war on wolves. Through guns, traps, and most effectively, poisons, we managed to completely extirpate breeding populations of Gray Wolves from the lower 48 states excepting only northern Minnesota. During that time we invented and perpetuated myths and legends about the ferocity of wolves, many of which survive to this day.

Wolf attacks on people in North America are exceedingly rare. Before 2005 there were only 16 records of wolves biting humans in North America, of which only 6 were severe and none were fatal. In 2005 wolves believed to be habituated to people killed a man jogging in the early hours in northern Canada; he is the first fatal attack recorded in North America.

ACTIVITY AND MOVEMENT

DAILY

Wolves are highly social and live in packs of 5 to 8 animals, sometimes more; packs of up to 36 wolves have been reported. The social cornerstone of wolf society is the mating pair, which in terms of pack dynamics is also the alpha pair. The alpha pair form the long-term foundation of any pack, which may include several other adults, yearlings from the previous year's litter, and pups from the newest litters. Wolves are also found in pairs and alone. Lone wolves form less than 15 percent of a wolf population in a given region.

Wolves are forever moving, covering vast distances in search of prey. They spend 28 to 50 percent of their lives traveling. Their stamina is legendary, and it led to Inuits and other northern peoples cross-breeding wolves with dogs to improve the endurance of their sled teams. Wolves trot at 5 to 6 miles (8–10 km) an hour and may cover up to 45 miles (72 km) in a single night. Wolves can run up to speeds of 38 miles (64 km) an hour and sustain a fast run for 20 minutes. They are also excellent swimmers and will cross rivers and lakes.

Wolves converge on an elk in Yellowstone. © *Douglas Smith, NPS/Yellowstone National Park*

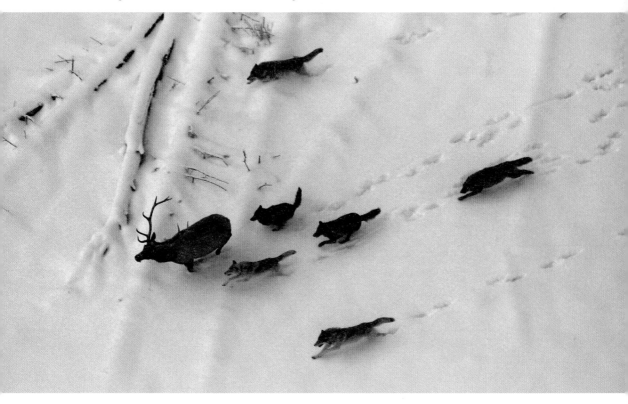

This wolf is exhibiting a play-bow, which is an invitation for a partner to play.

Wolves typically travel throughout the night, and peak activity periods occur at dawn and dusk. Wolves travel paths of least resistance to conserve energy, including trails, dirt roads, survey lines, lakeshores, and mountain passes. In winter they use ski and snowmobile trails, plowed and unplowed roads, and frozen lakes and rivers. Traveling wolves move in single file in open terrain and then fan out as they crest hills or enter forests, perhaps to better detect prey and be in position to chase and capture it. Most forays and travels are led by one of the alpha pair. In Yellowstone, pack leadership while traveling is shared equally between alpha males and females, although sometimes subordinate pack members are allowed to lead.

When wolves aren't hunting or traveling, they rest and, periodically, play, especially the younger animals. They sleep on their sides, or sometimes on their bellies. In cold weather they curl up with their nose under their tail. They bed at the edges of meadows, on rises in forested habitats, and on slopes where scents and sounds carry. When they play, they chase, ambush, and wrestle each other. Play brings the pack together, reinforcing bonds and the hierarchies that govern pack dynamics in a nonaggressive manner. Play is an opportunity to practice the physical skills of fighting without the inherent dangers of true combat.

SEASONAL

In tundra, wolves follow migrating caribou each spring and fall and annually commute more than 100 miles (160 km) from tundra to taiga (coniferous forest) and back again. In Nunavut, packs leave denning areas in autumn, follow caribou throughout the winter, and return to the tundra in spring to give birth. The longest migration of individual wolves, those following migratory woodland caribou, is 225 miles (360 km). If prey is sufficient on their range, wolves may not migrate with caribou and instead switch to hunting deer or moose.

Wolves may migrate one year when alternate prey is scarce and not the next if it is abundant.

FOOD AND FORAGING

Wolves are primarily hunters of large ungulates, but will hunt and eat prey of a great diversity of sizes, all the way down to Snowshoe Hares. Wolves hunt bison, deer, moose, elk, caribou, muskox, Bighorn Sheep, and Mountain Goats. They exhibit regional and local prey preferences, though generally they favor the most abundant local ungulate. In the Midwest their diet is dominated by White-tailed Deer and supplemented by moose, while in most of the West elk are their primary prey. In the North, moose is the dominant prey, and in the far north it's caribou, occasionally supplemented with muskox.

That wolves rarely eat anything smaller than a rabbit is a misconception purposefully and successfully perpetuated in Farley Mowat's book *Never Cry Wolf* in an attempt to improve public perceptions of wolves—and it worked. In many northern areas wolves prey heavily on beavers during the summer months, and along beaches of the Northwest they scavenge seal carcasses. They catch and eat salmon when rivers in Alaska are bulging with fish, and when they are well fed, they may strip only the brain and roe of the fish before discarding the rest to scavengers.

Pack size has often been attributed to local prey size, with larger packs forming to more efficiently handle larger prey. However, this is only a general pattern. Packs that hunt caribou and elk are larger than those hunting deer and moose. In Minnesota and Michigan, packs that hunt moose and deer are of similar size (7 to 8 animals), whereas in other parts of North America those that hunt moose are nearly twice as large as those hunting deer.

On Isle Royale in Michigan, where wolves hunt moose exclusively, individual wolves in smaller packs eat more of every kill. This suggests that the costs of sharing often outweigh the gains of increased muscle and teeth in larger packs. However, scavengers steal more meat from poorly defended kills made by lone wolves or smaller packs. In one study, ravens consumed up to 37 pounds (17 kg) of meat at a carcass per day. Since a single wolf consumes a kill more slowly than a pack, a lone wolf can lose 66 percent of its kill to ravens, but a pack of 10 on the same-sized carcass would only lose 10 percent. This may be part of the explanation of why packs that hunt larger prey are often larger than packs that hunt smaller game.

Wolves cover tremendous areas in search of suitable prey. The average distance between kills made by a single pack on Isle Royale is nearly 30 miles, which only hints at the twisting, circling, and chasing that were required to secure that meal. Wolves search for vulnerable animals, compromised in some way. They target the young, old, and inferior, but opportunistically kill healthy animals when deep snows hinder their defense or escape.

When wolves detect potential prey, they stalk in close, keeping themselves concealed until they are close enough to launch an attack. With smaller prey such as elk calves, beavers, and hares, they attempt to sneak in and catch them unawares with a quick dash or short chase. With large prey, wolves approach them and then reveal themselves; they prefer their prey to run. When large ungulates stand their ground, wolves usually halt, approach slowly, and attempt to scare their prey into running. Should they refuse to run, wolves may circle them and wait, periodically trying to force them to move.

Once a herd or animal is running, wolves only rarely rush right in and attempt a kill. Rather, they lope adjacent to or just behind the herd, conserving their energy while seeking an individual more vulnerable to attack than the others. In general, chases are 1 to 2 miles (2–3 km) long, after which the wolves either give up or select a target and move to separate it from the herd. When prey are healthy or do not display some vulnerability, wolves move on in search of easier prey. Most hunts are unsuccessful, and on Isle Royale, less than 8 percent of moose attacks end in meals.

One to three wolves from the pack carry out the attack while younger pack members hang back

---

A pack feeds on an elk that attempted to escape by taking to water. © *Douglas Smith, NPS/ Yellowstone National Park*

and watch. Alphas are most often involved in the attack, but other adult members of the pack may contribute as well. The degree to which wolves co-operatively hunt is still debated. Wolves have been observed splitting up, with one group driving prey toward the other, which then either cuts off the prey or waits in ambush. What may appear to be coordinated tactics or intent may be individual wolves simply cueing off their prey and packmates.

Unlike cougars, wolves do not kill their prey with a single, penetrating bite. Instead they slash and cut at their victim's hind legs and flanks. As the prey slows, the wolves bite and hold on. They often clamp down on the rump and nose. Just as a ring through the nose can pacify the largest barnyard bull, wolves with a strong nose-hold can sap the fight out of an elk in an instant. Whether on the run or held at a standstill, their wounded and exhausted prey succumbs and collapses. The teeth of wolves are stout and well rooted, so that they can grip their prey and be carried along for short rides. The canines suffer tremendous strain as a wolf holds fast to its prey. Hunting large game is not easy, and wolves that cling to the nose or legs of bison or moose are flung from side to side, slammed into trees, or dragged across the ground. Wolves can break ribs and be trampled or killed during hunts. When the wolves finally succeed in bringing down their prey, it is not unusual for them to begin to feed while their victim is still alive.

At large carcasses, the alpha pair typically feed first, although they may lie down and rest from the exertions of the hunt while the others open the carcass. Thereafter the order in which pack members feed clearly conveys their position in the hierarchy. Wolves feed for 14 to 30 minutes per bout, and sometimes longer. They eat the nutrient-rich organs first, and then the thick slabs of tender meat along the spine (tenderloin) and the large muscle masses of the legs. Everything is eaten and everything is essential to balance the diet of wolves. The hair provides some nutrients and helps pad large bone fragments as they pass through the digestive tract. Bones provide calcium and phosphorus, and the intestines of their prey include scarce B-complex vitamins and complex fatty acids. Wolves feed until their stomachs and sides are engorged. Wolves can hold up to 19 pounds (9 kg) of meat in their stomachs, and when they are sated, they sleep for as long as 5 hours. Should the carcass be large enough, they awake and feed again. In Alaska, eight wolves killed and completely consumed a yearling caribou in 3 hours. Small prey are consumed in their entirety, and nothing may remain except the matted vegetation or snow where the wolves lay, or a bit of hair or blood.

When wolves are full, they begin caching excess

meat as far away as 3 miles (5 km) from the kill site. Wolves may either gorge and carry meat in their stomachs, or pick up a convenient chunk, such as a leg, and carry it off. They dig holes to bury the meat and then cover them with a layer of soil and debris. They can control the amount of meat they regurgitate at any one time, and they may make several caches per trip. Wolves cache most often in summer. In winter caching is rare, and wolves almost always finish their kills. When prey is less abundant, wolves rely on old caches to sustain them or fast until the next opportunity. Wolves have been known to go several weeks without food.

In winter, when carcasses freeze solid, smaller animals cannot chew the meat and so the rate at which they steal meat slows or stops altogether. This aids healthy wolves, which are among the few mammalian predators with the teeth and musculature to reduce rocklike frozen meat into smaller chunks. However, the oldest wolves with worn teeth may struggle to feed and may starve.

In Yellowstone wolf packs kill on average 1 elk every 2 to 3 days, but they may go up to several weeks without making a fresh kill. Predation rates increase in late winter, a time of abundance for carnivores, when prey is more vulnerable. In late winter a pack of 10 wolves in Alberta killed a deer, moose, or elk every 2.7 days. In the latter half of winter in Wood Buffalo National Park, wolves killed 1 bison every 7.8 days. During the winter wolves consume water through their prey, but during summer they require open water from which to drink.

HABITAT AND HOME RANGE

Historically, Gray Wolves inhabited nearly every habitat in North America except those in the Southeast, which were the sole domain of the Red Wolf. Smaller subspecies of Gray Wolves inhabited the desert Southwest and eastern Canada, and larger Gray Wolves lived throughout the West and farther north throughout western Canada and Alaska. Today Gray Wolves are confined to the Rocky Mountains, the coastal ranges in the Pacific Northwest, and the Great Lakes states in the lower 48 states, but they still range over most of Canada and Alaska. Wolves are intelligent, flexible, and adaptable; they are found in mountain habitats, boreal forests, tundra, taiga, and coastal habitats wherever there is adequate prey. They are expanding rapidly in the lower 48 states. As of 2008 there are confirmed breeding pairs in Washington and Oregon, and dispersing animals from the Greater Yellowstone Ecosystem have crossed into Colorado.

In wolves, pack territories are synonymous with home range. The size of their territories is correlated with prey abundance and size, but it is also influenced by numerous other factors, including latitude. The farther north a pack is, the larger its territory. Where deer are numerous in northern Minnesota, territories average 30 to 60 square miles (78–153 km²) and are sometimes smaller. In Alaska, wolf territories are among the largest and may range up to 2,500 square miles (6,475 km²). Wolves that migrate with caribou herds travel even farther and may wander annual areas of 24,600 square miles (63,058 km²). They do not defend such vast areas, and they do not inhabit a territory or home range in the traditional sense.

Lone wolves (transients) cover larger areas, shifting about and being chased off by residents. Wolf densities are influenced by human hunting and trapping across their entire range. The highest recorded density of wolves is 1 wolf per 10 square miles (26 km²) in the Northwest Territories of Canada, where they are supported by high concentrations of migrating caribou. Similar densities were seen on Isle Royale when wolf densities peaked and on the west side of Glacier National Park when packs were largest.

COMMUNICATION

Wolves communicate much with their bodies, conveying complex messages with their eyes, mouth, ears, hackles, tail, and stance. To simplify the tremendously complex world of wolf communication, it serves to consider their various behaviors as a continuum from dominance to submission, or from aggression to fear. An aggressive, dominant

These illustrations show two extremes of submission behavior in wolves. In (a) the moderately submissive black wolf exhibits a defensive snap at the dominant wolf. In (b) the black wolf displays extreme submission.

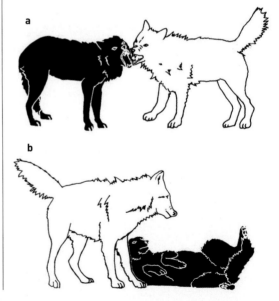

wolf stands erect with stiff, straight legs, head held high, ears forward and erect, teeth bared, mane bristling, and with its tail held vertical. Aggressive animals also sometimes wag their tail from side to side. Submissive or fearful animals cower low, bend their legs, draw their tails around or beneath themselves, draw their lips back into a "submissive grin," and lay their ears back flat. Submissive wolves may also repeatedly thrust out their tongue in nervous licking and wag their tail. Passive submission is the extreme form of submission and is exhibited when a wolf rolls onto its back and draws its paws up toward its body; it may simultaneously urinate.

Dominant animals often aim "fixed stares" at subordinates, which may in turn exhibit submissive behaviors, including tucking the tail, lowering the ears, and crouching. Subordinates may also grovel toward alphas and then reach up to lick their mouths, much like pups seeking food. A look from an alpha animal is enough to remind others of their place. When alphas are feeding, the approaching pack members that act most like pups will more quickly and successfully join in on the feast. Dominant males may mount subordinate animals and bite the back of their neck. In more intense interactions, dominants may even ambush and attack subordinates or crouch unseen within the pack and stalk toward them. Subordinates adopt a belly-up position, with their neck exposed, as the ultimate gesture of submission.

In addition to dominance interactions, wolves also exhibit numerous visual cues that promote pack well-being, cohesiveness, and amicability. Packs physically come together and rub each other with their muzzles and sides before a group howl or a hunt. Wolves also make "play-bows" like dogs and coyotes when inviting another member of the pack to play. While keeping their hindquarters standing, they drop their front ends and stretch out their front legs. They may also wag their tails.

Most auditory communication in wolves is made in close proximity. They whine, whimper, and yelp in amicable and submissive exchanges. They whine in both greeting and submission, though more often in submission. Yelps are also most often given in submissive contexts and are produced by a subordinate animal when a dominant wolf makes contact with it. Wolves growl and snarl in offensive and defensive encounters and when defending against other species. They make quiet woofs, like closed-mouth barks, when danger is looming or threatening. Woofs may call other nearby adults to aid in defense; they may also communicate to pups to lie quietly under cover or return to the den. Barks are often made under similar circumstances, but they are louder and draw attention to the animal making them. Barking near a den may both announce

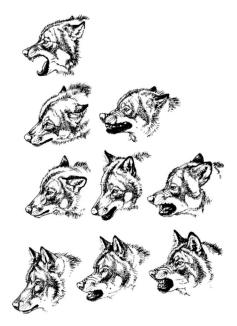

In this montage of expressions, a wolf's fear increases from top to bottom and its aggression (or likeliness to attack) from left to right. From Zimen (1981). Used with permission of Random House Publishing.

an intruder and reveal that the den is defended, or it may be an attempt to draw intruders away from the site. Wolves also make bark-howls under extreme stress, which is a combination of a deep bark and a shortened howl.

Howling is long-distance communication, and wolves react to howls from as far away as 6.6 miles (11 km) in forested habitats and up to 9.6 miles (16 km) in open tundra. Individual wolves have distinctive howls. Howling may be a call to assemble the pack or to aid separated wolves in coordinating hunting efforts. Howling also seems important in maintaining territories and avoiding other wolf packs. Howling advertises where packs are on the landscape and implies that they aim to hold that ground. Wolves are also more likely to howl in response to howls of other wolves, or of researchers, when they are at kills, and the more food that remains the more likely they are to reply. Wolf packs that reply to howls of neighbors or researchers stand firm, as if ready to fight. Those that don't respond tend to move away from the source of the howling. Howling rates are highest during the breeding season and while rearing pups.

Alpha wolves howl more often than subordinates, and the higher a wolf's status in the pack the more often it howls. For lone wolves, howling rates depend upon their prior pack status. Solo wolves howl in 2- to 14-second bouts for up to 9 minutes at a time. Solo animals howl most frequently just prior to and during the breeding season and are apparently seeking to contact potential mates. Agonistic howls are lower pitched than other types. Pups make higher-pitched howls that crack like a teenage boy entering manhood and intersperse their howls with lots of yapping.

A wolf's sense of smell is likely its strongest sense, and the one with which they most explore their world. Wolves use scent-marking to convey complex messages, and the tremendous advantage to olfactory messages is that they can be "received" long after the message is left. Wolves have various glands all over their bodies. Glands below the hackles are opened when hairs are erected and may play a contributing role to communication during aggressive and submissive encounters. Scent-marking includes urination, defecation, and scratching in conspicuous sites and on conspicuous objects along trails. Wolves frequently leave urine to mark their territories, most often along their boundaries. Alpha animals mark more often and in different positions than subordinates. Alpha males mark the most frequently, raising their hind legs high when urinating. The alpha female too will often raise a leg, though the stance is somewhat different. She pulls her leg up and forward rather than straight up, to precisely place her scent. Subordinate and juvenile females squat in typical canine fashion, and juvenile and subordinate males stretch forward, straightening both their hind legs in their version of a squat. The alpha pair scent-mark together, called double or tandem marking, more frequently prior to and during the breeding season. Newly formed pairs tandem-mark even more than pairs that have been together for several years.

Scent marks are placed approximately every 787 feet (240 m) throughout their range, though with twice the frequency along territory borders as within core areas. In addition to territorial functions, urine marking likely conveys information on reproductive and sexual status, as well as individual identity. Wolves also sometimes urinate on old caches after they have been emptied, in what may function to save them or other pack members from wasting time and rechecking them in the future.

Wolves place scats along travel routes and at trail junctions. Captive wolves often defecate most where their caretakers enter their enclosures, as if to create an olfactory fence to inhibit intrusion. Anal sac secretions may or may not be deposited on feces. Little is known about their function, yet alpha males deposit anal secretions more than other wolves and most often prior to and during the breeding season. Wolves sometimes stand stiff-legged and scratch and rake the earth and debris adjacent to urine or scat. This could leave additional scents from glands found between the toes, as well as smells from the fresh earth. Scratching creates a visual and olfactory marker that points to the scent mark.

Like dogs, wolves sometimes roll in foul-smelling substances, like decaying old carcasses, to pick up the scent for themselves; researchers are unsure exactly what the function of such a stench would be—is it like cologne and supposed to be attractive to mates? Captive wolves are more likely to do this than wild animals. Lone wolves scent-mark and howl in areas where wolf packs are not established, but do not where resident packs exist. Trespassing animals do not mark until they return to their own territory.

COURTSHIP AND MATING

Wolves mate from January to April depending on latitude, and northern wolves breed later than those in the south. A pack has 1 to 3 breeding-age females, but typically only the alpha pair mate and produce pups. Alpha animals usually maintain their tenure within a pack for 3 to 4 years, though 8 years has been documented. For the few months before estrus, the alpha pair sleep within 3 feet (1 m) of each other, which is closer than at any other time of year. They can also be seen nuzzling, interacting, and scent-marking in tandem more and more often.

Courtship may last days or months, during which a mating pair may copulate only once or up to 11 times. Courtship includes a great deal of sniffing, nipping, head rubbing, snout grabbing, tail wagging, and general play. Either the male or the female may place a paw over the neck of the other. A receptive female lifts her tail and moves it to one side and allows the male to mount her. Mounting may begin oriented sideways but is soon brought around to the rear. The male grasps the female around the shoulders and thrusts several times until the pair become locked in a copulatory tie. He steps over her hips and the two remain stuck, back to back, for up to 30 minutes, during which time several ejaculations occur. Pairs more often mate repeatedly to ensure that the female becomes pregnant.

Yearling females come into heat about 2 weeks later than experienced breeders, and should they become pregnant, they have smaller litters. In areas where wolves are only lightly hunted or trapped, approximately 60 percent of adult females breed. In areas where they are heavily exploited, up to 90 percent of females breed, allowing wolves to produce greater numbers of pups to counter their losses. The increased breeding is among second female breeders within packs and females in pairs without territories, neither of which ordinarily have the opportunity to breed.

DEVELOPMENT AND DISPERSAL OF YOUNG

Wolves often use the same dens year after year, and they are found close to the heart of a pack's territory to increase their protection. Dens are cleaned out, remodeled, and often expanded and prepared before the arrival of the pups. The locations of dens vary across habitats. In the frozen tundra of the far north, wolves use caves, rock crevices, and shallow pits. In other areas, they select well-drained, easy-to-dig soils, where structural support such as tree roots ensure that walls and ceiling of tunnels and whelping chambers won't collapse on them. Den burrows may be up to 30 feet (9 m) long and terminate in large whelping chambers up to 4 feet (1.2 m) in diameter. Some have multiple entrances and interconnecting tunnels.

After a gestation of 61 to 64 days, females typically give birth to as few as 1 or as many as 11 pups. The average litter is 6. Pups are typically born to coincide with the time when local ungulates give birth, to take advantage of easier prey. Pups are blind and helpless at birth but instinctively move toward their mother's belly and wave their head from side to side until they encounter a nipple upon which they clasp and suckle. Their mother and other adults lick them to stimulate urination and defecation until they are mature enough to walk outside to defecate on their own. The alpha female remains with the pups for at least 2 months, while the male and other pack members hunt and provision them. Should they be disturbed at a den site, wolves quickly move to a different den. Mortality of pups from disturbance has never been recorded, and abandonment of pups is exceedingly rare. Den sites within 0.6 miles (1 km) of human activity are usually abandoned permanently.

Their eyes and ears open between 11 to 15 days after birth. Pups make high-pitched squeals and screams as they wriggle to locate nipples in their first few weeks, after which time these vocalizations become increasingly rare. Pups also moan when suckling or resting in their first few weeks, and they continue to produce these vocalizations at lesser frequencies as they mature. Pups have most of their milk teeth by 3 weeks, by which point they are wriggling and crawling about to explore the den interior. After 3 to 4 weeks pups growl and squeak more often in interactions with littermates, and they also start to bark at sounds made outside the den. Pups are weaned slowly starting as early as 5 weeks, but some may continue to suckle until 10 weeks.

By 5 weeks they are spending much more time aboveground, playing, exploring, and napping at the mouth of the den entrance. When they wander too far from the den, an adult female picks them up in her mouth and carries them back to the den. Between 5 and 10 weeks pups grow rapidly, becoming more physically capable and socially interactive. They quickly develop adult vocalizations during this time. After 8 weeks, pups are moved to an aboveground nest, or "rendezvous site," where they play and roam over an area of up to an acre (0.4 ha). The pack may linger 3 weeks at a rendezvous site but then they shift to another as far as 5 miles (8 km) away. When adults return with food, pups rush to greet them. The first pup to greet the adult jabs the adult's mouth with its nose, and this often induces regurgitation of the food carried home in its stomach. On days when foods are plentiful, pups cache what they can't eat around the den entrance or rendezvous site.

Play in pups is critical to their social and physical development. They are less agonistic than coyote and fox pups and spend more time in amicable interactions and switching roles when wrestling. They exhibit numerous behaviors that aid them as adults, including stalking, pouncing, biting, chewing, running, and play mounting. Rendezvous sites also have numerous "chew toys" lying about, from old bones and antlers to sticks torn off local shrubs and trees. Pups also entertain themselves by trying to dig up any ground squirrels that might have burrows in the area. Adults don't waste their energy on such tiny meals.

Juveniles attain their adult teeth between 4 to 6 months. Pups in good condition join the adult members of the pack in October to complete their training in hunting and killing. Healthy pups are 60 pounds (27 kg) by October, but others require several more months of subsidies before they travel with the pack. Size correlates well with survival; smaller pups are more likely to die. Juveniles attain their adult proportions by 12 months but continue to gain weight and fill out for several more years.

Pups on occasion disperse as young as 9 months, but most wait until they are 1 to 2 years old. Some remain with their natal packs until they are 3 or 4 years old. Dispersing wolves travel huge straight-line distances: 129 miles (206 km) in 2 months and 416 miles (670 km) in 81 days. A yearling female traveled 522 miles (840 km) from Montana's Rocky Mountains into central British Columbia before settling down. Dispersal distance is highly variable, but correlates with age. Younger dispersers travel as far as 532 miles (886 km), whereas older animals are more likely to seize nearby openings in neighboring territories.

Dispersing wolves may spend a few months to several years without a pack. They try to form new packs with dispersers of the opposite sex or join another established pack. In Minnesota the majority of dispersers (15 of 16 individuals) formed new packs. In Alaska most of them joined established packs (22 of 27). Dispersers may return to their natal packs 1 to 6 times before finally dispersing for good, and some may split time between their natal pack and another before finally settling into their

A young wolf jabs the side of an adult's mouth with its nose to solicit regurgitation and a meal. © *Mark Elbroch*

males. On rare occasions all-male packs have maintained a territory for up to a year, though these situations are temporary.

The alpha is not the largest or most aggressive wolf, but rather the wisest animal best able to keep the pack alive by avoiding unnecessary conflict. A notoriously "bad" alpha was the old leader of the Druid pack in the Lamar Valley of Yellowstone National Park, which maintained continuous bloody feuds with neighboring packs until the leader of the Leopold pack killed him. The Leopold pack leader has proven a very strong, capable leader that has maintained peace among packs in the Lamar Valley.

Wolf packs are described most often as being governed by a linear dominance, with alphas on top, then betas, all the way down to omegas. In truth, family dynamics are more complex than this. At times one animal is clearly dominant while another is clearly submissive, but the time of year, the familial relationship, how much food they have, the age difference between the two wolves, and whether breeding is at stake, are all variables influencing pack member dynamics and skewing traditional dominance hierarchies.

Every wolf is a potential alpha animal and breeder, but in areas where wolf populations are high, the potential is never realized for most. Where packs and territories are dense, wolves must either wait patiently for an alpha position to become available within a resident pack, confront an alpha and usurp a breeding position, disperse and somehow carve out a new territory among local wolf territories, or, on rare occasions when food is plentiful, become an extra breeder.

Where wolves are less numerous, dispersers of the opposite sex may find each other and the suitable, unoccupied habitat needed to create a territory and pack of their own. Lone wolves may be chased off, killed, or adopted by existing packs. Those who are adopted are often younger, just 1 to 3 years old, whereas those that are older tend to be attacked aggressively. Adopted wolves also tend to be males, and speculation is that they are sometimes the extra breeders of nondominant females in packs during times of food abundance, avoiding inbreeding between alpha males and their daughters.

Neighboring packs often share kinship. Packs split and merge, and dispersers from one pack often take up residence in neighboring territories. Adjacent wolf packs often overlap slightly with each other, and both packs generally avoid this area of overlap. Borders are buffers to avoid confrontation. One of the most common causes of death for wild wolves is attack by other wolves, and most wolf-wolf killings are at or very near territory boundaries.

Trespassing animals are attacked and often killed.

new pack for good. Most disperse either in fall or early winter or when intra-pack aggression peaks in spring around breeding.

Females deliver pups for the first time between 2 and 5 years old, and sometimes slightly later where food is in short supply. Males are sexually mature in their second year but don't usually breed for another year or more. Wolves may live to be 16, but 10 is probably old in the wild.

INTERACTIONS AMONG WOLVES

Wolves form territorial, tightly bonded social packs with variable membership. Typically an alpha pair lives with a few other adults, yearlings, and pups of the year. Numerous other combinations occur as members die and packs merge, split, and disintegrate. An older male or female may mate with a yearling and an alpha male may mate with two fe-

Attacks on neighboring pack members are relatively common and reinforce territorial boundaries. Trespassing seems to occur more often when prey is less abundant and is likely driven by desperation. However, aggression toward trespassing wolves does not diminish during times of prey abundance. The intensity of aggression by wolves toward their neighbors remains somewhat of a mystery.

INTERACTIONS WITH OTHER SPECIES

Wolves harass and kill numerous other carnivores—their competitors—with which they share habitat. Few species compete successfully with wolves, though Brown Bears may be the exception. The two species interact around large carcasses frequently, but typically the chasing, growling, nipping, and charging result in few serious injuries. Wolves have been known to kill Brown Bears, most often near large carcasses the wolves are defending or attempting to appropriate from a sow with cubs. Wolves have also been known to attack and kill Brown and Polar Bear cubs as well. They harass the sows from either side, and as the sow lunges one way, a wolf slips in and attacks the vulnerable cub. Since they rarely eat bears or cubs, their attacks seem driven by competition. There are also documented cases of Brown Bears killing wolves near carcasses, and bears are more often successful at pushing wolves from their kills than vice versa. Wolves are most aggressive and persistent when bears wander too close to their dens.

Wolf interactions with Black Bears are a different story. Wolves are clearly dominant over Black Bears, killing 9 bears in 26 recorded encounters in Minnesota. Six of those were sought out or discovered and then purposefully killed in their winter dens. They ate the bears they killed in only a few instances.

Cougars and wolves rarely fight, though wolves will steal a cougar's kill should they discover its whereabouts. In Canada and Wyoming, as wolves have reestablished themselves in areas where they were extirpated, cougars have retreated into areas with less wolf activity. In the Tetons, researchers are right now watching areas where cougars were once common become wolf territories instead; the cougars appear to just pick up and leave.

Wolves also harass and sometimes kill wolverines. In 8 of 14 records wolf packs successfully caught wolverines away from the safety of trees or crevices and killed them. Typically the wolves kill subadults and kits they dig out of dens, but occasionally adult wolverines are killed as well. Wolves also dominate coyotes and Red and Arctic Foxes. Wolves often actively seek out and kill coyotes and may completely exclude them from core areas within their territories. There has never been

a record of coyotes killing a wolf, even when coyotes far outnumber wolves in an encounter. Unlike coyotes, Arctic and Red Foxes are thought to benefit more from the company of wolves than to suffer from them, since they frequently scavenge their carcasses. Wolves kill numerous smaller carnivores. They have been documented digging up and killing American Marten, as well as killing golden eagles and ravens that attempted to feed at their kills. They even kill Striped Skunks.

Most of all, wolves provide a vital service as keystone carcass-providers in much of their range. Wolf kills are a bonanza for diverse species, and prey remains are pilfered by all of the above-named species and numerous others; 400 species of beetles have been recorded on elk carcasses in Yellowstone alone. Wolves also "play" with ravens. The birds swoop low at traveling wolves, and the wolves jump to try to catch them. A raven will stalk up to a sleeping wolf and peck at its tail and backside, only to flit away as the wolf lunges in an attempt to catch it. The bird lands just out of reach, and the pair may chase each other for several minutes at a time.

Wolves can reduce and even threaten some populations of large ungulates; however, herds preyed upon by wolves tend to be composed of healthier, stronger individuals because wolves target the young, old, and unhealthy. In addition, the very presence of wolves on the landscape influences where prey populations congregate, which can have cascading effects through natural systems. Wolves affect elk herds by killing individual animals, but they also cause elk to alter their behaviors and habitat use. The "ecology of fear" is a new concept used to describe the indirect influence of wolves on elk in Yellowstone. Whereas elk used to linger in woodlands and riparian areas for much of the year before the wolf reintroduction, they have since moved into areas where they command more of a view to reduce their "predation risk." These movements, though subtle, have had a dramatic influence on the environment. With the migration of elk away from riparian systems in Yellowstone, riparian areas have begun to recover. For decades the browsing pressures of all the grazers and browsers along riparian corridors were so intense that they precluded any new growth at all. Since the return of the wolf, aspen, willow, and cottonwood trees have once again begun to grow in Yellowstone's riparian areas. With the return of the trees, there has been an increase in both beaver activity and riparian songbird diversity.

The influence of top predators on vegetation is visible elsewhere as well. In Quebec in areas where wolves are absent, moose live at densities 7 times higher than in areas where wolves roam, and their browsing has effectively stopped new tree growth.

Common Gray Fox
Urocyon cinereoargenteus

OTHER NAMES FOR GRAY FOX: tree fox, zorro gris (Mexican Spanish).

Kit Fox
Vulpes macrotis

Swift Fox
V. velox

An occasional flash of gray may be all that you will ever see of the diminutive, inconspicuous gray fox. Often unnoticed throughout most of its range, it lives like a shadow among and in between us. Its flecked coat and stealthy habits keep it hidden in the light-dappled forests and shrubby habitats it calls home. Ground-nesting sparrows and other passerines scold and mob hunting gray foxes, so keep your ears alert and you just might discover their whereabouts. Gray foxes are among the least studied and least known carnivores in North America.

In evolutionary terms the gray fox was the first canid to diverge from the rest of the canid family and for this reason may retain ancestral traits lost in other canids. Their early divergence may also explain why they share many characteristics and behaviors with the more distantly related cats. Their claws are highly recurved and semi-retractable, which keeps them sharp. Gray foxes can rotate their forearms, enabling them to climb trees by hugging the trunks with their forelimbs and pushing upward with the hind. The gray fox also has the shortest leg-to-body ratio of all wild canines, giving it a low center of gravity helpful in climbing. It can attain heights of up to 60 feet (18 m) and jump from branch to branch. It descends trees either headfirst at a run, or more slowly, tail leading. British settlers found the gray fox to be poor sport after their native Red Foxes. A gray fox takes to burrow or tree almost immediately when pursued, providing little to no "chase" at all.

ACTIVITY AND MOVEMENT

DAILY

Gray foxes are crepuscular and nocturnal. Captive gray foxes studied in Texas ate 5 times and drank 4 times between 6 a.m. and 6 p.m., but ate 104 times and drank 28 times during the night. At rest, gray foxes prefer cover and protection and will lie in cavities, burrows, or brush piles, or even in a crotch or the branches of a tree. In cold weather they curl up in a ball, with their great bushy tail covering their nose, and rarely bed in the open like Red Foxes.

Like all canids, gray foxes explore and move about their range in a trot. When they are foraging their nose guides them to new resources on the landscape, and they leave twisting, winding trails through dense cover where prey abounds. They pause frequently to listen for potential predators and prey or before crossing more exposed country. When traveling to or from a foraging location, trails are straighter and often on paths or in more open terrain.

Gray fox trails will lead you on a tour of fruits and mast in season, as well as the burrows and nests of diverse rodents. In the West you'll discover the bulky nests of woodrats and burrows of kangaroo rats when you follow gray foxes. In the East they often corner and excavate Red Squirrels living underground during winter months. Look for foxes to slow to a walk when they smell or hear something of interest and to bound and gallop when pursuing prey or being pursued by predators.

Kit and Swift Foxes, by comparison, are creatures of open country throughout the West. The Kit Fox inhabits extreme deserts and dry grasslands in the Southwest, and the Swift Fox is a denizen of expansive grasslands in central North America. Underground dens are central to the lives of Kit and Swift Foxes, and, unlike other North American canids, they use them continuously throughout

A gray fox clings to the side of a tree. The gray fox is the most arboreal of the North American canids.

the year. They use several dens within any given year, and ownership of a particular den may float from one family to another from year to year. Dens are clumped in ideal habitat rather than sprinkled evenly through a fox's range. Up to 8 to 10 dens may be located in a 5-acre (2-ha) area. Their dens provide critical protection from predators and also serve as refuges from extreme temperatures in both northern winters and desert summers. Foxes typically dig their dens on raised ground or slopes that provide good drainage, though many are dug in flat, open terrain, with barely a throw mound to betray their presence.

Kit and Swift Foxes are nocturnal creatures. During the day foxes nap and lie about in the safety of their dens, coming aboveground for brief bouts of sunbathing in cool weather. Foxes emerge from their dens after dark and forage widely from 4 to 9 miles (6–14 km) each night. Kit Foxes gallop in short bursts of speed up to 25 miles (40 km) an hour, but it is their agility and ability to dodge and weave at high speed that save them when pursued by predators.

SEASONAL

Gray foxes expand their home ranges in autumn, when they may wander as much as 5 miles (8 km) in search of food. Males also wander widely in spring, foraging in support of their mates and pups. In the northern parts of their range movements become localized in winter, especially when soft and deep snows greatly hinder their mobility. During the snow season gray foxes tend to stay close to human infrastructure, traveling the network of maintained roads and well-packed hiking and snowmobile trails. They may also hole up for many days during and after snowstorms, waiting for snows to firm up for easier walking.

FOOD AND FORAGING

Gray foxes are the most omnivorous of all the wild canines, eating a great variety of foods, including mammals, birds, fruits, nuts, grain crops, and invertebrates. In a comparison of the digestive efficiency of gray and Red foxes, both were of equal efficiency in digesting mice, yet the gray fox was more efficient at digesting fruit.

Gray fox diets differ through the seasons and across the species' range. Throughout the year gray foxes eat a great diversity of small mammals and birds, and this ability to switch to whatever prey are most accessible allows them to adapt and succeed in wide-ranging habitats. Their smaller dentition, musculature, and bone structure are unsuited for large-game hunts, though there is a single account of a gray fox strangling a deer fawn during their denning season. Foremost among their prey

A Kit Fox lounges at the entrance to its den.
© *Stephen J. Krasemann/Photo Researchers*

are cottontails, tree squirrels, voles, mice, woodrats, black rats, and wide-ranging passerines. Gray foxes have keen eyesight and noses, yet they most often hunt small mammals using their superb hearing. They stalk in close, pounce, and pin their prey with their front paws, or they listen closely to detect movement of animals within nests or underground, and then dig to reveal them. People who have cared for gray foxes as pets claim they were as efficient mousers as any housecat.

Autumn is the time of fruits and mast crops, and gray foxes will eat considerable amounts of corn, domestic and wild fruits, and nuts. In different regions they might consume persimmons, wild cherries, blueberries, or prickly pear fruit, juniper berries, and mesquite beans. Their subsequent scats spread seeds far and wide. Yet gray foxes consuming only fruits suffer protein deficiency, so even during the fall they continue to hunt small mammals.

During the winter, gray foxes forage wind-fallen fruits and mast as long as they last, and they hunt mammals and birds. With the arrival of spring and summer they also eat amphibians and reptiles. Insects then become a major source of food. Grasshoppers and crickets, including the massive Jerusalem crickets, constitute much of their warm-season diet.

A gray fox carries a cottontail rabbit after a successful hunt. © *Ivan Brady*

Both Swift and Kit Foxes are more carnivorous than gray and Red foxes, but the Kit Fox exhibits the most specialized diet. Over much of their range, Kit Foxes situate their dens in the midst of the largest patches of kangaroo rats on the landscape and feed almost exclusively upon them. Unlike the specialist Kit Fox, Swift Foxes hunt a wide variety of prey. At the top of their menu is the Black-tailed Jackrabbit and Black-tailed Prairie Dog.

HABITAT AND HOME RANGE

Where gray foxes are present, they are usually relatively common. They are widespread in forests, woodlands, brushlands, and canyonlands across temperate and tropical North America. Their short legs exclude them from regions where deep snows accumulate, and they have not succeeded in colonizing areas without trees or shrubs, which conceal and protect them. They range only as far north as southernmost Canada and are absent from the northern Rockies and Great Plains in the United States. In the far north they utilize coniferous forests during winter, perhaps because the dense foliage mitigates snowfalls. Densities range from 1 gray fox per 0.4 square miles to 1 per 0.8 square miles (1–1.5 km²).

The home range of the gray fox varies by season and food availability. On average, home ranges are small, from 0.3 to 1.5 square miles (0.8–3.9 km²), and the distance traveled by gray foxes in a given night averages from 2.2 to 3.1 miles (3.5–5 km). Ranges generally expand in the fall and contract in the spring. They are smallest for denning females.

COMMUNICATION

Gray foxes may be solitary, but they are often found in pairs throughout the year or in small family groups before the pups disperse. More than any other fox, gray foxes exhibit extensive allogrooming, in which pairs groom each other and their pups to remove ticks and other pests. No doubt this strengthens familial bonds and is some form of communication. Gray foxes have the largest tail gland of any North American canid—extending half the length of the tail on the upper side. This gland, which is absent in most domestic dogs, is thought to be used in individual recognition.

Gray foxes make scent posts along travel routes, which likely serve to communicate territory, individuality, and sexual status. Scats and urine are often placed on elevated perches such as rocks, stone walls, and tree stumps, and groups of scats can accumulate with time. Gray foxes will also counter-scent other species: they roll, urinate, and defecate on the trails and scats of other mammals, most notably Black Bears, Red Foxes, fishers, and humans. They also roll to pick up the smell of something on the ground, such as the stench of some decaying carcass. Scents from scats, urine, and rolling are posted throughout their range.

The top fox is exhibiting an offensive threat, with arched back and raised head and tail. It may also bark. The fox below is exhibiting a defensive threat, with arched back and lowered head and tail. It may also growl.

The gray fox is often silent, but not always. Its bark is guttural and hoarse and is often repeated for long periods. Barks can rarely be detected beyond 985 feet (300 m) but are often heard when dens are approached at night or in disputes over territory. Foxes will also bark at humans when they encounter them unexpectedly. In antagonistic encounters and in distress, they may use growls and screams. They make whimpers and other doglike sounds when trapped or injured. They use coos and low whines in greetings and when adults are calling to their pups.

Gray foxes assume a threat posture if provoked and cornered, and, much like a cat, arch their back and extend their guard hairs. An offensive threat posture is one in which the fox holds up its head, and the tail might be held slightly higher as well. When on the offense they may bark. A fox in a defensive threat posture holds its head down and often curls its tail in between its hind legs. In a defensive posture they often growl and sometimes whimper. Another physical communication, leg-lifting, is discussed below (see Development and Dispersal of Young).

Rapid sequential barking (2 to 15 barks) is a common signal in both Swift and Kit Foxes, though ongoing research suggests that the frequency and patterns of barking are different in each species. Swift Foxes have been observed barking throughout the year, but the frequency with which they bark increases during the mating season and appears to serve a territorial function. In wild populations male Swift Foxes bark far more than females, and they bark most often from within their core territory, that small portion of their home range that does not overlap with other Swift Foxes. They also quickly respond with barks of their own to any barks made by an unknown fox within their core territories.

In contrast, Kit Foxes are silent through much of the year and have been observed barking only either immediately preceding or during the winter mating season. Barking in Kit Foxes serves to call an existing or potential mate. Barking wild Kit Foxes in California were often approached by their mate or a potential partner within minutes of barking, after which the pair would exhibit classic pair-bonding behaviors, including close contact and mutual grooming. Females were observed barking less frequently than males, but one female let loose with 65 barking sequences in a single hour during the breeding season. Her mate had recently abandoned her, and such intensive barking may have played a role in her search for a new male.

Wild Kit Foxes make chittering calls in two different contexts. They produce soft chitters when communicating with pups, or their mates, and exhibit loud, sharp chitters in agonistic exchanges over territory or resources with other Kit Foxes. Aggression is rare in Kit Foxes but may include chasing trespassing foxes and sometimes physical fights and biting. Distressed Kit Foxes make a distinctive vocalization with their mouth closed, which sounds something like a muffled bark or croak.

Like other canids, Kit and Swift Foxes communicate indirectly through scats and urinations. They mark prominent objects throughout their range, including old tires, fenceposts, and cow skulls. Both

A juvenile Swift Fox races across the prairie carrying a kangaroo rat. © *Rob Palmer Photography*

The juvenile Kit Fox on the left communicates subordinate submissive behaviors to the adult on the right. These are collared urban Kit Foxes in Bakersfield, CA, that are being monitored for research purposes. © Christine Van Horn Job

species form latrines, where up to 30 scats may be found. In Swift Foxes latrines are located both within exclusive core areas as well as within areas where their home ranges overlap those of neighboring foxes. In areas of overlap, all resident foxes use the same latrines, where they most often urinate, but also defecate with regularity. In up to 25 percent of Swift Fox visits to latrines in areas where pairs overlap, the animal sniffs the area but does not mark in any way. Latrines may serve a territorial function as well as that of a community bulletin board, where information on sexual status, health, and other information is passed between neighboring animals in a nonconfrontational fashion.

COURTSHIP AND MATING

Mating has been little studied in gray foxes, but the predominant pattern appears to be monogamy. It is unknown whether pairs stay together for consecutive years.

In areas where Red Foxes are sympatric, mating is thought to occur just after the Red Fox's season. It may occur from January to April, depending on geographic location (earlier in the South). The mating season can be inferred from playful paired trails of courting animals and looping chases through woodland and brush. You will also find blood in the female's urine when she is in estrus. Exact gestation in gray foxes is unknown but is estimated to be 60 days.

DEVELOPMENT AND DISPERSAL OF YOUNG

Gray foxes, like Red Foxes, sometimes den near humans to raise young within the umbrella of protection afforded by people against coyotes and bobcats. Their dens are typically earthen holes dug with southern or eastern exposure. They dig the dens themselves or modify another animal's burrow. Woodchuck burrows are often appropriated, and gray foxes have been recorded sharing burrow systems with resident woodchucks. They also den

in brush piles, rock crevices, hollow logs, dry drainage pipes, and beneath abandoned buildings. Dens disturbed by humans or other predators are often abandoned and the pups moved to a new location, so be very cautious about approaching them. One female gray fox was reported to feign an injured leg to draw a human intruder away from her den.

The average litter size is 4 but may be up to 7. Both parents contribute to raising the litter. In Red Foxes, females contribute more than males, but the relative contribution of male and female gray fox parents is unknown. Pups (or kits) open their eyes between 10 and 12 days and emerge aboveground by 4 weeks. When they first appear aboveground, play is innocent with frisky attacks on their siblings often directed at their white cheek patches. When napping in furry heaps, they chew on each other's ears, noses, paws, and tails.

The female nurses several times at night and

An adult female gray fox stands, with eyes tightly shut, as her pups jostle and nurse below. Another pup noses her mouth in hopes she might regurgitate some food.

during the day. By the fourth week, she stands in a straddle position to nurse, often closing her eyes for the duration. The parents carry food to the den several times a day, frequently at dawn and dusk, and often carry multiple prey items at one time. Occasionally they call the pups out to greet them with a low and long whine. Pups lick and nose the sides of an adult's mouth to solicit food by regurgitation, or to be given what solid foods are being carried. By 5 to 8 weeks of age, fighting among the pups over food becomes common.

By the fifth or sixth week play has become more aggressive, and a hierarchy is clearly established within the litter. This ensures the survival of the strongest and most dominant should food shortages occur. Submissive animals lift a hind leg and present their genitalia or are forced to sniff the genitalia of dominant siblings. In wolves, coyotes, and domestic dogs, leg-lifting is often accompanied by urinating, but not in foxes. Nor do North American foxes roll onto their sides in submission, like the larger canines. Even in captive adult animals which are submissive to people, leg-lifting can be solicited by approaching and touching the flank.

As the weeks progress, the pups explore farther afield and spend more time aboveground than below. By 6 weeks they spend much of every night exploring and playing aboveground. At 3 months of age they begin to accompany their parents on foraging trips. The pups attain their adult size and weight at approximately 7 months and disperse as independent subadult animals between 9 and 10 months. Pups may settle very close to their natal dens or wander as far as 54 miles (84 km). Females

Gray fox pups wrestle in play at the entrance to their den site. © *Mark Elbroch*

become sexually mature at 10 months but may not breed until the following season.

INTERACTIONS AMONG FOXES

Neither Kit nor Swift Foxes are territorial at any time of year, and home range overlap between neighboring animals can be large. The amount of home range overlap between foxes is directly related to kinship. In animals that share close relation (parent-offspring, siblings) home range overlap is often extensive, but in unrelated foxes, overlap is minimal.

Each pair, however, also maintains a core area within their territory that does not overlap with neighboring foxes, in which they raise their litters. Familial relation also governs the sort of interaction two overlapping foxes that encounter each other are likely to have. Related foxes are more likely to exhibit amicable exchanges, including nuzzling, allogrooming, and resting in close proximity to each other, while unrelated foxes are more likely to be aggressive toward each other and display threats and/or chase each other.

INTERACTIONS WITH OTHER SPECIES

Gray foxes are both hunter and hunted. They are known to limit and displace Long-tailed Weasels, but in turn are limited and displaced by coyotes. Bobcats may also be displacing gray foxes to a lesser degree. In a study in southern California, 12 of 24 radio-collared foxes died during the study period. Eleven of the 12 were killed by other animals: 8 by coyotes, 2 by bobcats, and 1 by an undetermined predator, possibly a bobcat or coyote. Gray, Kit, and Swift Foxes retreat from areas in which coyotes are present and return when coyotes have moved on. Through this dance of avoidance and exploiting different prey, foxes can occupy the same area as their competitors but minimize conflict. When pressed, they try to escape by running, hiding, or climbing trees. Gray foxes are also killed by great horned owls, golden eagles, and cougars.

Little is known about the competitive effects of Red Foxes and fishers on gray foxes. In the Northeast, where all 3 species coexist, they follow and mark each other's trails and steal each other's caches. Where Red and gray foxes overlap, it is also unknown how they divide habitat. In general, Red Foxes utilize more open terrain, though Red Foxes also use diverse forested habitats. When forests and woodlands are shared, Red and gray foxes rarely overlap in space *and* time; they appear to use time-share strategies to avoid interactions we have yet to understand.

Gray foxes rarely live longer than 4 to 5 years in the wild; 80 percent of the animals caught in one population were less than 1 year old. The vast majority of gray foxes do not live beyond 2, and yet there are old records of foxes living 14 to 15 years in captivity.

Arctic Fox
Vulpes lagopus

OTHER NAMES: white fox, polar fox, blue fox.

Arctic Foxes are circumpolar creatures of the far north and have numerous adaptations to help them survive the long, dark, frigid Arctic winters. Their shorter-than-average canid snouts, limbs, and ears all reduce heat loss and minimize the possibility of frostbite on the extremities. Their winter fur, 70 percent of which is thick underfur that functions like down on a bird, is twice as long as their summer coats. They keep their feet warm by increasing blood flow to their limbs and shielding their foot pads from the ice with a layer of fur. During fierce, windy storms, foxes hole up within snow shelters or in other cavities, such as rock crevices. They also conserve energy during winter months by resting more often and for longer periods than in the summer.

Vulpes is Latin for "fox," and *lagopus* is the combination of two Greek forms *lago* ("hare") and *pus* ("foot"); it is said to refer to the fur-covered pads on the Arctic Fox's feet, which is also characteristic of rabbits and hares.

ACTIVITY AND MOVEMENT

DAILY

Arctic Foxes are typically nocturnal and crepuscular, but they remain flexible and are active at any time of day that presents opportunities for foraging. Foraging foxes cruise their open landscapes in a rocking-horse lope, slowing to trots and walks when a scent or sight catches their attention. Most of their activity is devoted to foraging, for fuel is tremendously important in the far north where cold temperatures demand high metabolisms. When they are not foraging, they invest in territorial maintenance through scenting and barking, and when neither foraging nor maintaining their territories, they rest to retain their energetic reserves.

On occasion, Arctic Foxes take long trips and relocate to a completely different area. They have been recorded moving up to 15 miles (24 km) per day and over 621 miles (1,000 km) with time. One fox was documented traveling 696 miles (1,120 km) over 2 years, and a male in Canada moved 1,429 miles (2,300 km) in 3 years. Arctic Foxes are excellent swimmers, crossing rivers and streams with relative ease.

SEASONAL

Arctic Foxes are solitary for approximately half the year, from late summer until mid- to late winter. Then they rejoin their mates to breed and rear young in their summer-range den. Den sites are valuable assets in a landscape where much earth remains frozen in early spring and summer, and therefore several dens may be clumped where suitable habitat exists. Dens are also often used in successive years and even by successive generations. Researchers believe that some historic den sites may have now been in use for more than 100 years.

Den sites are often in sandy soils on hillcrests or more subtle mounds. They are also found along banks near streams where soils are softer, thawed or thawing. Whatever the local topography, the dens tend to be where sunshine is ample and less winter snow remains. Arctic Fox dens are found in open tundra, sand dunes, talus slopes, under boulders, in culverts, and within other human-made shelters. Dens may begin as a single-entrance affair, but over time they are typically enlarged and may eventually encompass an area over 60 square yards (50 m²) and include more than 100 entrances.

Coastal populations of Arctic Foxes often forage in distinctively separate summer and winter ranges. During the summer they forage and den in open tundra, but as the pack ice forms in the fall, they move over both land and ice to follow Polar Bears and scavenge at their kills. Arctic Foxes may wander the pack ice widely during the winter season and have been observed on ice 497 miles (800 km) from the nearest landmass and within 93 miles (150 km) of the North Pole.

FOOD AND FORAGING

Arctic Foxes are adaptable hunters of small mammals, birds, and even marine invertebrates, switching prey when necessary depending on local availability. They hunt by stalking and pouncing, and when voles and lemmings are at peak populations and especially abundant, Arctic Foxes eat little else. However, vole and lemming populations cycle every 3 to 4 years, peaking and crashing through the years, and when they are at low densities Arctic Foxes become particularly creative in supplementing their diets. Coastal Arctic Foxes are particularly dependent upon seabird and goose colonies, where they hunt both birds and eggs. They also hunt Arctic Hares and use their acute noses to locate small mammal and Arctic Ground Squirrel nests beneath the ground or snow, liberating them with rapid and efficient digs with their front paws.

Foxes also occasionally kill larger prey. They hunt newborn Ringed Seal pups when they are still in their birthing lairs, and there are also records of Arctic Foxes killing caribou calves. Arctic Foxes also scavenge dead animals, ranging from fish along the coast and riparian areas to remains of ungulates that died of starvation or were abandoned by wolves. Arctic Foxes shadow larger predators

Arctic Foxes follow Polar Bears closely throughout the winter, feeding on the remains of their seal kills. © istockphoto.com/John Pitcher

through winter months and live almost entirely as scavengers on their kills. They follow wolves in inland areas and Polar Bears along the coast. Where foxes are abundant, nearly every Polar Bear may have one or several foxes following behind it, all surviving off the scraps of seals it kills. Polar Bears often feed only upon the fat layer of seals, and leave much of the meat and most of the carcass behind.

Foxes also eat insects, snails, and any available berries, even when they're frozen and found under a layer of snow. Arctic Foxes will also readily habituate to human settlements and eat handouts or from garbage dumps. Starvation is not uncommon for Arctic Foxes, especially during winter months or during dispersal.

Arctic Foxes cache food during times of abundance. This behavior has been studied most in coastal habitats where seasonal seabird nesting provides a bountiful smorgasbord in the form of the birds themselves and their eggs. Two separate caches in Alaska contained the following: the first, 103 petrels, 6 tufted puffins, 4 auklets, and a guillemot; and the second held 125 auklets, 7 petrels, 4 puffins, and a common murre.

Foxes are more successful at catching eggs than actual birds. Foxes flush smaller birds off their nests to steal eggs or sneak in to steal eggs from larger birds while they are away. Foxes take advantage of any large animal moving in nesting colonies and displacing birds as they go, including biologists. As researchers push birds off their nests, foxes slip in to steal the unguarded eggs. Foxes near nesting goose colonies have been reported caching more than 1,000 eggs each per nesting season.

The cool permafrost provides ideal refrigeration for food items cached within it. Eggs themselves contain antimicrobial agents which protect against spoilage and make them an ideal food source for long-term storage. Some egg caches are retrieved and eaten nearly a year after they were buried by an Arctic Fox. When the geese have flown south, cached eggs still contribute 30 to 40 percent of the foxes' sustenance during the fall months and up to 30 percent of their sustenance the following spring. Spring use of cached eggs is dependent upon the availability of other fresher food sources such as lemmings and voles.

HABITAT AND HOME RANGE

Arctic Foxes use diverse habitats surrounding the North Pole. They range across pack ice and marine environments as well as northern forests and tundra from sea level to the alpine zone, wherever prey is abundant. In North America, Arctic Foxes can be seen from the southern tip of Hudson Bay in Canada, north to the Arctic Ocean and west across Canada and much of Alaska, including several of the Aleutian Islands, where they were introduced for fur farming and have since naturalized.

Summer home ranges for Arctic Foxes vary from 1.5 to 23.2 square miles (4–60 km²) depending upon geographic population and prey predictability and availability. Nonbreeding animals roam much far-ther during winter months, as do animals that have distinctive summer and winter ranges, such as those who roam the pack ice following Polar Bears. In one study, both summer home range size and the degree to which individual home ranges overlapped with other foxes were correlated with prey availability. In coastal environments where prey were both concentrated in small areas as well as predictable and dependable over time (e.g., a nesting goose colony), home ranges averaged a small 3.9 square miles (10 km²) and fox territories overlapped 76 percent with one another. Among inland populations where prey remained clumped in large patches, but was less consistent over time, home ranges averaged 8.9 square miles (23 km²) and their territories overlapped on average 50 percent with other foxes. Arctic Foxes with the largest home ranges of 20.1 square miles (52 km²) and the least overlap (17 percent) inhabited inland environments where prey were widely dispersed and unpredictable.

COMMUNICATION

Arctic Foxes are territorial from April to August, during the rearing of the young. They mark their territories with urine and conspicuously placed scats atop elevated surfaces, such as boulders, hummocks, and piles of bear droppings. Some scent posts, including porches of rural cabins and other human structures, are used again and again and accumulate many scats over time.

Arctic Foxes are able to discriminate between the barks of related family members and unknown animals; barks vary in length and tone, creating distinctive signatures. Barks may elicit flight from

An Arctic Fox in summer coat escapes a goose colony with an egg, and with a goose in close pursuit.
© Nicolas Lecomte

A dominant pup aggressively holds down another to assert its higher rank. © *Mark Elbroch*

trespassing foxes and whimpers and greetings from family members. Family members often change their course to intercept foxes that bark, while unknown animals move to avoid intercepting the calling fox, sometimes fleeing in the exact opposite direction. An Arctic Fox will chase an intruder from its territory and fight with the intruder if necessary. Arctic Foxes growl and bark in threat and alarm. When greeting known conspecifics or family members they coo and whimper.

COURTSHIP AND MATING

The breeding season for Arctic Foxes, which occurs during March and April, is late when compared with southern canids. Males and females rejoin each other after months apart and foraging on their own. Mating is very similar to that of other canids, with the pair playing with and chasing each other upon reunion and into the breeding season. Female Arctic Foxes have but a single estrus per year, with a breeding window usually lasting only 3 to 5 days. The male mounts from behind during the act of mating, and when completed, the pair remain in a copulatory tie for several minutes to increase the chances that mating will result in pregnancy.

Males and females are often monogamous and are thought to mate for life. After their annual separation, they rejoin, quickly establish and defend a breeding territory, and remain together through the whelping of the pups. However, there is flexibility in the monogamous model. Single males have been observed breeding with two adult females, with the threesome raising two litters together in the same den; the pups nursed from both females. Two mating pairs have also been observed peacefully raising their separate litters in the same den. It is also not uncommon for a mating pair to tolerate one or more additional females, which may be one of last year's pups, taking up residence within the den and contributing to the raising of the pups. Though in truth, these additional "helpers" rarely contribute much to the sustenance of the pups. They may contribute more in terms of den protection, just by being present while both parents are foraging afield.

DEVELOPMENT AND DISPERSAL OF YOUNG

After a gestation of 52 days, dark soot-gray pups, or kits, are born between April and July within the protection of the den. Each weighs less than 2 pounds and is altricial, with eyes and ears closed. Litters can be massive, with extreme records of up to 25 pups. Their potential fecundity reveals the high resource variability in the Arctic from year to year. Each female has from 12 to 14 teats, which is much higher than any other canid in North America, and they may all be put to use should a boon of resources lead to higher birth rates. On average, though, Arctic Fox litters are smaller. Inland Arctic Foxes average 6 to 9 pups per litter, while coastal populations average just 3 to 6. Litter sizes correlate closely with prey abundance, such as the cyclic lemming and vole populations found in some areas.

en their eyes for the first time when they [be]tween 14 and 16 days old, and their first set [of te]eth appears between 3 and 4 weeks of age. By [3] to 4 weeks they are beginning to emerge aboveground and play about the den entrance. Dominance hierarchies will already be obvious, as Arctic Fox pups are particularly competitive with each other. The female may initiate nursing, usually calling the pups forth from the den to nurse, or the pups themselves may initiate it, nuzzling her sides when they are hungry.

Pups are weaned at 6 to 7 weeks, by which time they have been transitioning to prey items brought to the den by their parents. As parents approach the den they emit a low chittering, which results in a bursting of pups from the entrance. A parent does not cut the food into pieces and evenly distribute it, but drops it before the first pup to arrive, and the pups are left to fight it out among themselves.

When the pups are younger the parents also regurgitate food. Females bring more food into the den than males, and they also regurgitate when solicited more than males. When prey is very low, both parents may abandon their den altogether and allow their pups to die. Competition among siblings may be so severe as to cause subordinate animals to die from starvation, especially in years when prey is less abundant. Pups have also been recorded eating each other.

While the parents are off hunting and resting, pups rest for more than 50 percent of the time. They spend about a third of their time playing, which often turns into hierarchical dominance displays. Parents begin to bring food to the den less often as the summer progresses, forcing the young to begin to hunt on their own. In their eighth week the pups shed their initial gray coats and slowly replace them with adult pelage. The adult male abandons his family in July, and the female abandons them within a month of the male's departure. The juveniles become independent between 12 and 14 weeks of age, and they quickly attain adult proportions.

Juveniles disperse during autumn, but often remain in their parents' range if adequate prey exists there through the first winter. They attain sexual maturity at 9 to 10 months, although females may not breed during their first year. Females born in a large cohort tend to breed as yearlings since cohort size is often reflective of food availability, whereas females from small cohorts more often wait until their second year.

INTERACTIONS AMONG ARCTIC FOXES

Arctic Foxes are territorial for approximately 6 months per year, while food resources are critical in successfully producing and raising pups. Arctic Foxes follow strong dominance hierarchies based on an individual's level of aggressiveness. However, foxes with familial ties are much more tolerant of each other, and their summer ranges may overlap tremendously. Unrelated foxes rarely overlap except under conditions of ample food availability. Even then, they overlap to a lesser degree than related animals.

INTERACTIONS WITH OTHER SPECIES

In dry tundra communities the enrichment of soils from fox scats around den sites is so dramatic that

An adult drops off a goose to its pups at the den.

it causes distinctive plants to grow. Young dens exhibit no changes in vegetation and look similar to the surrounding environment. Older dens exhibit greener growth and greater plant diversity fueled by accumulations of scats and prey remains. The oldest dens exhibit the most significant changes in surrounding vegetation, as well as countless decomposing den entrances and collapsed tunnels. These small oases can be counted from the air as a means of population estimates. In moister environments, dens are less conspicuous.

Arctic Foxes compete for prey with other small and medium carnivores, including weasels, wolverines, and numerous birds, such as jaegers and snowy owls. Yet where they coincide, their principal competitor is the Red Fox, with which they overlap greatly in hunting style and prey selection. Red Foxes are dominant over the smaller Arctic Foxes in almost every encounter, and from time to time they kill and eat adults and raid dens and kill their pups. In the coldest tundra in the North, the Arctic Foxes inhabit the wilderness areas and the Red Foxes tend to congregate around human habitations, where there is additional cover, a greater diversity of foods, and maintained roads and trails that make it easier to move about. Red Foxes also compete with Arctic Foxes for den sites and may exclude them from their historic dens. Evidence suggests Red Foxes limit the edge of the southern distribution of Arctic Foxes, and there is concern that Arctic Foxes are being pushed farther north as Red Foxes expand their northern range into areas that previously were the sole dominion of the Arctic Fox.

The effect of Arctic Foxes on nesting seabirds has been well studied and at times can be dramatic. Ducks, murres, and puffins all nest on the ground and are particularly susceptible to predation. In one study in northern Canada, biologists recorded that each Arctic Fox they monitored around a single goose colony was responsible for between 900 and 1,570 stolen eggs in a single nesting season. While these numbers are remarkably high, they accounted for only 4 to 8 percent of the total eggs produced by the geese, and thus were a relatively low threat to the goose population as a whole.

Arctic Foxes are small predators, but they are prey for numerous other animals. Eagles, snowy owls, jaegers, Polar Bears, Brown Bears, wolverines, wolves, and Red Foxes all kill Arctic Foxes. Numerous avian predators are known to kill the vulnerable pups, and they are also killed by dogs near human settlements, as well as trapped and shot for furs and as pests. However, they also experience occasional tolerance from larger predators. In one instance Arctic Foxes and Gray Wolves each raised litters within the same burrow system; they used separate entrances and in general avoided each other.

Red Fox
Vulpes vulpes

OTHER NAMES: cross fox, silver fox, renard (French).

European Red Foxes were introduced along the East Coast for sport hunting during the 1700s. Then in the early 1900s, Red Foxes with bright, healthy coats were moved all over North America to stock the burgeoning fur farms industry. However, Red Foxes are also native to northern North America, including New England, most of Canada, and the high-elevation forests of the western United States.

Coat color was long used to argue that Red Foxes were native to North America. The Red Fox is typically an orange-red animal, but "silver foxes"—Red Foxes whose fur is black with gray patches and silvery, frosted highlights—are more common in Alaska and western North America, and "cross foxes"—which have a black-brown cross on their back and shoulders, and whose fur shows a mix of the red and black color phases—occur at low prevalence throughout Alaska, Canada, and the western mountain ranges. Since the evolution of color variation within a species requires many generations and isolated geographic populations, researchers argued that the 500 years since Columbus arrived in North America was inadequate to justify the diversity of colors of North American Red Foxes.

Newer genetic techniques have revealed that coat color is not a useful indicator of whether an animal is native or not. The East Coast Red Foxes, which are all red, are all native, and those introduced to the area from Europe centuries ago for hunting have vanished without a trace. Red Foxes in the Midwest and low elevation areas in California, Washington, and Utah exhibit mixed genetic lineages because of translocations from other North American populations.

ACTIVITY AND MOVEMENT

DAILY

Red Foxes are mostly nocturnal and are particularly active during dawn and dusk. However, they can be active at any time of day, especially in the far north and during the denning season throughout their range, when the insatiable appetites of pups drive parents to hunt nearly continuously. Foxes spend 35 percent of each day foraging for food. They patrol their territories in an efficient and fluid trot at 4 to 8 miles (6–13 km) an hour and cover up to 6 miles (10 km) in their rounds. They slow to a walk when exploring and scavenging, following up scents and sights in an endless search for food. They actively hunt and forage even if they are full, caching the surplus in shallow holes throughout their range.

Foxes typically rest during the day in beds they create and often reuse. They'll bed completely out in the open when resting at night, but during the day they prefer vegetative cover, perhaps even inside an abandoned burrow or under a porch. Look for beds along woodland edges with an excellent view of open terrain. When they wake they stretch their limbs and then stand and drop their shoulders into an arch and bow, yawning to shake off their sleep.

During bad weather foxes retreat under cover, nestling up against an upturned root wad or the thick trunk of an evergreen tree, where they remain protected by the low-hanging branches, which form nearly waterproof tents and shed water. They also use simple, shallow dens that are sprinkled throughout their range, so one is always close by when needed.

In an instant a fox can switch from a standstill to a quick gallop to pursue fleet prey such as cottontail rabbits or to escape danger. They are among the fastest mammals on earth, able to run at 45 miles (72 km) an hour for short distances. Red Foxes are faster runners than domestic dogs, wolves, and coyotes. They are also nimble and able to dodge and weave erratically to baffle a pursuing coyote. Red Foxes are excellent swimmers, and light and agile enough to tight-rope leaning saplings and traverse the tops of stone walls and ledges with confidence.

SEASONAL

In the spring Red Foxes dig one or more dens in sandy soils or soft loams, or they may expand those dug by woodchucks or badgers to accommodate a fox family. Old dens may be reused and expanded each year. Prolonged use contributes to accumulations of sign such as bones and scats and can lead to enriched soils supporting more luxurious vegetative growth. Dens typically have several entrances, with at least one inconspicuous hole acting as an emergency evacuation route in the case of a predator coming to the front door. Tunnels may be up to 72 feet (22 m) long with a central whelping chamber in which the family sleeps and nurses.

Red Foxes are winter-active and nonmigratory. Their winter coat is longest, thickest, and richest in color in December. In winter foxes curl up and lay their long brush over their face to minimize heat loss. Deep snows hinder their movements, but not to the extent of gray foxes or coyotes. Foxes may retreat under cover for one or two days when fresh, soft snows accumulate more than 8 inches (20 cm). After they emerge they primarily travel upon the trails of other animals, where snows have been packed down. Northern Red Foxes are larger and heavier than southern populations, and they have a 12 percent larger foot-area-to-weight ratio, which provides them slightly better "snowshoes" for navigating northern landscapes in the many months of snow cover.

FOOD AND FORAGING

Red Foxes are omnivorous, yet they are principally hunters of small mammals. Their primary prey include rabbits, squirrels, pocket gophers, mice, and voles, though they will hunt a great diversity of small and medium mammals when the opportunities present themselves: muskrats, woodchucks, opossums, weasels, raccoons, and deer fawns, as well as the carrion of nearly any species. Red Foxes can eat as much as 1.5 pounds in a sitting, and consume 5 to 8 pounds of food per week.

The Red Fox employs one of several hunting strategies when attempting to catch live prey. When "mousing," its head is high and its ears are erect and tipped slightly forward. It pauses often, moving silently along paths or walking slowly through fields, listening for the rustling of foraging rodents in tall grass or moving beneath the snow. Once it has located a potential target, it listens carefully to pinpoint the location of the prey, crouches, and

A Red Fox stretches after an afternoon nap, in preparation to forage for the evening.

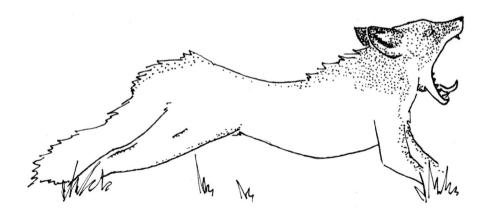

A Red Fox with a freshly caught deermouse sticking out of its mouth. © *Mark Elbroch*

then pounces in a graceful arc up to 16 feet (5 m) in length. It leads with its forepaws, pinning its intended prey to the ground where the fox can quickly dispatch it with a bite and a chew. It may pick up and fling voles and mice in the air, like a cat playing with its food. Then it slides the prey to the back of the mouth, chews several times, and swallows it whole.

Catching other prey requires stalking to close the distance before the fox can dash in or pounce on it. Stalking Red Foxes crouch low to the ground and slink forward like a hunting cat, pausing where cover offers protection or when the prey animal is looking up. Foxes attempt to close the gap sufficiently to pounce on birds of every kind, including pheasants, grouse, woodcocks, jays, and smaller songbirds. Often they pounce as the bird lifts off and pluck it from the air. Rabbits are more often caught with the teeth, after being flushed and then run down. Sometimes, when a tasty morsel escapes down a burrow, the Red Fox curls up and grabs a nap on its front doorstep. When the prey reemerges, the fox grabs it.

Of 434 hunts observed in the Canadian Rockies, Red Foxes successfully caught their prey in 32 percent. They were successful in only 2 percent of their attempts on birds and 23 percent of their small mammal hunts. Their rate of capture was exceedingly high for insects. Red Foxes rarely search for insects but instead snack on them as they move. They eat grasshoppers, beetles, earthworms, and numerous other invertebrates. They employ the same strategy with reptiles and amphibians, pouncing upon them when opportunities present themselves. In coastal areas foxes are notoriously dedicated and efficient hunters of nesting seabirds and waterfowl, and they eat their eggs, too. In North Dakota, as well, one study revealed that Red Foxes were the principal cause of mortality for nesting ducks.

On occasion Red Foxes exhibit "killing frenzies" in seabird colonies and chicken coops. Foxes have killed more than 200 gulls in a nesting colony in a single night, when fog and darkness provided confusion and cover. They carry away and cache as many carcasses as they can but inevitably waste much when they kill so many.

When a fox's appetite is sated, it continues to hunt and forage. Should it be successful, it caches its surplus in small holes dug throughout its range. Foxes dig shallow excavations, gather the dirt in a neat pile next to the hole with their front paws, and then make their deposit before carefully covering the cache with their nose. Red Fox caches are all but invisible and very difficult to detect. They cache eggs, small mammals, and birds, and fox biologists have even discovered ducks buried alive! Foxes return to their caches within several hours to several days, relying primarily on memory to locate and recover up to 96 percent of them. Memory provides the map to the cache, and it's likely that smell pinpoints the exact spot where they buried food.

Red Foxes invest time in hunting, and they also spend time "scavenging," which is the thorough investigation of areas for any available meal, including caches made by other foxes, insects, berries, and foods discarded by hikers and campers. Scavenging foxes systematically explore with their sensitive nose held low to the ground, following any and all scents that betray a meal. Their urine marks help them keep track of which areas they have already investigated, economizing their effort. While they scavenge, they dribble urine, averaging more than one urination per minute, to delineate the areas they have finished checking. In much of their range, Red Foxes forage along roads, where they quickly collect and consume any roadkills they encounter.

Red Foxes also eat fruits and nut masts in season. When fruits are ripe, the scats will be completely composed of blueberries, huckleberries, or apple skins. They occasionally eat grasses, sedges, and tubers.

HABITAT AND HOME RANGE

Red Foxes are the most widely distributed terrestrial carnivore in the world, inhabiting nearly every continent in a remarkable display of ecological plasticity. In North America, they can be found across Canada and in every US state except Hawaii. Red Foxes are common in eastern woodlands, especially where habitats mix and create "edges" along the borders of open habitats, including meadows, yards, and agricultural lands. Long-legged Red Foxes do well in deep snow, and their dense coats keep them warm, even in the far north where their range overlaps that of the Arctic Fox in tundra environments. Red Foxes also inhabit coastal dune ecosystems as well as alpine forests in the eastern Appalachians and the much higher western Sierras.

Red Foxes are absent throughout much of the desert Southwest, where surface water is unavailable. They persist in reduced numbers in the canyonlands and red-rock country. Increased irrigation near human settlements in dry parts of the country is allowing them to invade habitats previously uninhabitable to them. Red Foxes thrive in suburban and urban environments, where they are quick to take advantage of food scraps and man-made cavities where they can sleep and raise pups.

Red Fox densities are highly variable and correlate with food availability. Home ranges defended by mating pairs range from 0.6 square miles (1.5 km²) in urban environments, or where food is abundant, to 6.2 square miles (16 km²) in areas where food is scant, such as the northern tundra. Typical home ranges throughout their range are 1.9 to 2.3 square miles (5–6 km²).

COMMUNICATION

Red Foxes communicate vocally, with visual displays, and through scent. The most easily recognized vocalization of the Red Fox is their monosyllabic alarm bark, which is relatively high pitched and sometimes sounds similar to the caw of a crow. Barks are often given once or twice per minute and repeated from 5 to 15 times in a series. They serve primarily as alarms, and they may be given as a fox retreats. Barks are most common during the spring, when adults bark to alert pups back at the den that dangers are lurking nearby. Red Foxes also growl, whimper, and whine. When greeting conspecifics, they mew and coo or emit short whimpers.

Neighboring foxes and those that share a familial bond use posturing and ritualized displays of aggression and dominance, while unfamiliar foxes tend to engage in more violent exchanges. Red Foxes have a broadside display in which they stand sideways to an opponent, arching their back like a cat and erecting the hair along their spine to look as large as possible. Dominant or aggressive animals sometimes run sideways toward an opponent to maintain the broadside display. Dominant animals approaching subordinates may use a stiff-legged walk and a direct stare. Subordinates signal submission by gazing at the ground or to either side.

A pair of displaying Red Foxes may rise up, placing their forepaws on each other's shoulders, while "gaping" or "jawing." They make raspy, throaty low growls while each shows the other its teeth. In slightly more aggressive encounters the pair may tip over, with the dominant assuming the top position, pinning the subordinate down. Such ritualized displays sometimes turn into real fighting or a chase during which the dominant animal pursues the subordinate to the edge of its territory.

The most common form of submissive behavior in adult foxes resembles the behaviors exhibited by pups soliciting food from their parents at the den. Subordinates grovel before the dominant animal, whipping their tail side to side in excitement. They crawl forward on their belly, and then reach up, licking the mouth of the dominant animal in appeasement.

The tail and ears also communicate clear signals of status and intent during an exchange. A dominant animal about to attack another fox will hold its tail straight out behind it or slightly elevated at an angle. A submissive animal will tuck its tail either along one side of its body or between its legs. A curved, arching tail, with tip pointing down, communicates an invitation to play. Offensive animals hold their ears up and forward, while defensive and

The Red Fox on the left exhibits clear submission and groveling to the dominant animal on the right.

Two male Red Foxes settle a territorial dispute with aggressive posturing and contact. Both foxes gape at each other and whine, but clearly the dominant animal in the exchange is the animal on top. © *Mark Elbroch*

subordinate animals lay them flat and back; like bears, playing animals stick their ears out to either side.

Urine scent marks and scats advertise presence, dominance, and sexual status. They also establish whether food caches or carcasses remain viable. Red Foxes employ any of 12 different positions to urinate upon precarious perches and signposts they choose along their travel routes. Look for urinations and scats on elevated objects, such as stumps, rock walls, low-hanging foliage, and on novel objects such as an old shoe or large bear scat. Both males and females squat and lift their legs depending upon the circumstance, and all foxes leave only tiny, token quantities of urine when they pee. Red Fox urine has a very distinctive odor, especially during the second half of winter, when the smell becomes increasingly strong and their scent posts can be smelled hundreds of yards away. It's often described as a "skunky" odor because it is reminiscent of the defensive compounds sprayed by Striped Skunks.

Foxes urinate up to 70 times per hour when they are scavenging. They also mark next to food remains to indicate that they have already harvested any potential meal. Traveling foxes, ones that may be moving between foraging areas or returning to their dens from a night out, mark their territories with less frequency, on average 1 scat and 13 urinations for every 1.9 miles (3 km) of trail. Red Foxes often urinate or defecate upon the signs of other carnivores, including bears, fishers, and gray foxes, and they sometimes roll on the tracks of other species.

Foxes have a large subcaudal gland on the upper end of their tail, which is thought to be used in recognition between individuals. Family members often smell each other's tails in greeting.

COURTSHIP AND MATING

Males join females in early winter, and they spend 2 weeks in courtship, hunting, playing, and chasing each other. Red Foxes typically mate in January or February, but in some regions they may couple as early as December. Each female is in estrus for only 1 to 6 days once each year. The average length of copulation is 26 minutes, but it may last as long as

67. After mating, the pair are stuck in a copulatory tie, unable to detach from one another for a short time. The bulbous glandis at the base of the penis enlarges and becomes wedged in the female to better ensure the successful infiltration of his sperm. Once breeding has occurred, the pair split up and hunt as individuals. They rejoin each other when the female takes to her natal den to give birth, and the pair work together to raise the litter.

Red Foxes remain together as a monogamous pair for an entire season, and they sometimes mate with the same partner in successive years. During times of abundance, males may breed with two females, which then den in close proximity to each other. He brings food to both to sustain them while the pups are very young and contributes to the raising of both litters. In these cases the vixens are extremely tolerant of each other, and they may share close kinship. On occasion two females mate with the same male and raise their young in a communal den. The pups of both females then nurse from either female.

DEVELOPMENT AND DISPERSAL OF YOUNG

After a gestation of 50 to 55 days, females give birth to an average of 3 to 6 pups, or kits (the range is from 1 to 12). Newborns are charcoal gray with whitish or light brown highlights. Their eyes are closed at birth and open for the first time when they are between 8 and 9 days old, and their coats pale or change to buff by 8 to 14 days. At 3 weeks pups begin to walk and gain coordination. The pups may be moved several times to other den sites, especially if disturbed, and on occasion litters are split for a duration and raised in two separate dens.

Between the ages of 25 and 35 days old, pups fight frequently and viciously for access to food and to establish a dominance hierarchy among themselves. The weakest, lowest-ranking pup will be the first to die of starvation in times of food shortage, and the most dominant the last. Intense fighting coincides with their emergence from the den, after which the den becomes more conspicuous. The pups spend more and more time exploring, wrestling, and eating on the surface, trampling vegetation and spreading prey remains and small twisted scats across the ground. Pups increasingly lose their gray pelage, which is replaced with fur the color of sandy soil and dry grass, ideal camouflage near the den site.

By 4 to 5 weeks aggression within the litter is almost entirely replaced with sibling play and mock fights. Mock fights and mock hunts, where they chase and pounce on flowers, bugs, or anything else that catches their attention, are ideal training for their adult lives to come. Weaning is gradual, but lactation subsides after about 5 weeks.

The male participates in feeding and rearing the kits, at least early in the season. Often males provide less and less as the kits mature, and then they disappear altogether. Parents appear to provide as diverse a diet as the landscape supports, teaching their offspring the great diversity of potential foods available. When a parent arrives at the den with food, it drops it to the ground and calls the pups forth with a low vocalization. The first kit to arrive grovels before its parent, wagging its tail back and forth as it crawls closer, and then it reaches up and licks and nibbles the corner of the adult's mouth. Then the kit grabs the food and runs off to hide from its littermates or to at least find a defensible position from which to protect its prize. Subordinate animals are often forced to relinquish all or part of their meals by dominants, but all pups growl and threaten any other pup that tries to steal from them.

At up to one-third of dens an adult fox other than a parent is present and contributes to the rearing and feeding of the pups. These are most typically female pups from the previous year that have not yet dispersed. When one or two helpers are present, all the females form a strict hierarchy, with the breeding female at the top.

During the summer months pups begin to accompany their parents on forays and then more and more often explore and forage on their own or with other siblings. Their coats change to their adult coloration when they are between 9 and 14 weeks of age, and they attain adult size at 6 months.

Dispersal begins in late August and peaks in the early fall, although some animals do not leave their parents until the start of winter. Males typically disperse earlier and farther than females, moving 5 to 31 miles (8–50 km) before establishing their own territory. Females typically move but 3 to 9 miles (5–15 km). In exceptional cases, foxes may disperse as far as 187 miles (300 km). Dispersing foxes are at great risk from resident animals they encounter. Fights over territory are vicious, and dispersing animals receive the brunt of the violence.

At low densities, female pups often mate and yield pups in their first year, but when densities are high, females generally fail to raise young until their second winter. Males are sexually mature by 10 months and may participate in their first winter's breeding season.

INTERACTIONS AMONG RED FOXES

Other than their mates and pups, Red Foxes do not tolerate each other. Encounters are always aggressive in nature, but vary to the degree of violence depending upon the familiarity between two animals. Interactions between neighboring animals or those related by blood are ritualized, depending more on display than combat. Ritualized fights include at-

An adult male bites down on the snout of a pesky pup that continued to solicit food from him after it had already been fed. © *Mark Elbroch*

tacks to the shoulders, which are morphologically adapted to absorb blows, whereas true fights are directed at the head and neck of their opponents. Males encountering each other during the mating season employ broadside displays and ritualized gaping to settle most dominance disputes. However, territorial challenges at every time of year are barroom brawls, with animals twisting, tumbling, growling, and biting. Red Foxes can be seen bombing out of nearby woods to attack and bloody trespassing foxes and defend their territories.

INTERACTIONS WITH OTHER SPECIES

Red Foxes have very different relations with coyotes and Gray Wolves, as was best illustrated on Isle Royale in Michigan when wolves migrated to the island across an ice bridge decades ago. At the time of their arrival the island was ruled by coyotes, which kept Red Fox numbers at a minimum. Within 5 to 6 years the wolves killed every coyote on the island, and as a result the Red Fox population increased substantially. In general, coyotes are significant competitors with and predators of Red Foxes, and Gray Wolves are more tolerant of them. In agricultural Canada and Vermont, Red Foxes tend to den near people, which provides them protection against coyotes. People shoot coyotes throughout the year, but killing Red Foxes is more tightly restricted, and many people also enjoy or tolerate Red Foxes more than coyotes.

However, relations with coyotes and wolves can be slightly more complicated. Studies in Yellowstone National Park show that coyotes often tolerate the presence of Red Foxes when food is not involved, but are most likely to attack them when defending or stealing a carcass from a scavenging fox. Wolves, too, are not always tolerant. On Isle Royale wolves sometimes kill Red Foxes. In one instance, wolves feeding on a moose they had killed chased down and caught an inquisitive fox, shaking it violently until it went limp. Then they tossed it aside and returned to their kill. Nearby researchers approached the fox to examine it, but after lying prone for a long duration, it stood up, its fur matted and askew, and then trotted off into the woods, away from the wolves and their kill.

Golden eagles, cougars, bobcats, lynx, and domestic dogs are also predators of Red Foxes. Humans are a principal predator as well. Foxes are shot or trapped for furs and sport and to defend domestic fowl and livestock. Red Fox populations are suppressed by controlled killing to protect nests of endangered birds, including least terns, snowy plovers, and clapper rails, and occasionally to control the spread of rabies.

Red Foxes also kill endangered Kit Foxes and compete with them for denning sites and food. In southern California the ever-expanding irrigation of lawns and agriculture in desert habitats is facilitating the invasion of Kit Fox habitat by Red Foxes. In the North, Red Foxes compete with and sometimes kill Arctic Foxes; some argue that Red Foxes limit the southern geographic distribution of Arctic Foxes.

Crows and ravens can be seen following foxes with food in their mouths. They are waiting for the fox to dig its cache so they can move in to steal it. Should the fox become aware of their shadows in the sky, they simply continue to travel with their food until the birds give up and move on.

OTHER NAMES: Black Bear, cinnamon bear, spirit bear, blue bear (Pacific Northwest), kaskitew mask-wa (Cree), asikkiááyu (Blackfoot), oso (Spanish).

One of greatest marvels of Black Bears is their ability to disappear into a den for the winter and emerge again, months later, and resume their normal lives. While in the den in hibernation, Black Bears do not eat, drink, or defecate. Not only do they retain their waste, they recycle it metabolically, as a source of water and protein. Osteoporosis, or reduction in bone mass, is common in humans who become inactive for any length of time, but not in bears. Over 90 days of inactivity, black bears lose 23 percent of their muscle mass, whereas humans lose 90 percent over the same time period. While they are in a den, bears lose about half a pound (0.23 kg) per day and up to a third of their overall weight by the time they emerge in the spring. Females nursing new cubs expend the most energy and lose the most weight.

Black Bears are too large to achieve the radical temperature changes of hibernating small mammals, yet they do decrease their body temperature by 7° to 8°F (4°C) and their metabolism by 50 to 60 percent. Their heart rate slows from 40 to 50 beats per minute to 8 to 19. Their higher body temperatures and greater metabolic processes allow them to become active relatively quickly should they be disturbed and need to defend themselves, as well as to nurse newborn cubs in the heart of winter. The key to successful hibernation is enough feeding in the fall to pack on layers of fat, and access to abundant spring foods to recover from their winter fast. Poor feeding conditions in spring and summer lead to additional weight loss and sometimes starvation.

ACTIVITY AND MOVEMENT

DAILY

Black Bears are solitary animals, except during the breeding season and when a female is caring for her cubs. Black Bears are shy and retiring creatures that run at the slightest provocation. Yet if they feel secure, they'll materialize from the forest shadows with which they so well blend to investigate what scared them. Bears have excellent senses of smell and hearing, which they use to detect other animals and food at great distances. They spend much time pausing to listen to sounds in the distance, to assess whether they might betray danger. If they are curious about something just out of view, they rear up on their hind legs to get a better look.

Black Bears walk at a faster rate than we do, meandering through forests, grazing as they move. Their waking hours are devoted to finding and eating food, but they rest frequently, including long pauses spent standing and longer bouts lying down. Resting accounts for about 50 percent of their time. In wild areas Black Bears are typically diurnal, feeding throughout the day and sleeping a large portion of the night. In areas where humans are present they shift and become more active at sunrise and sunset (crepuscular), and during the night.

Bears bed for short duration just about anywhere they feel secure. They'll curl up in the berry bushes in which they are feeding, or plop down at the base of a tree for a rest. Bears are more selective of places where they rest for longer periods of time, preferring the security of areas where they can either see, smell, or hear potential predators approaching. Bears often bed on hummocks in shrub wetlands, in thick brush, or in forests rarely visited by people. They often use the base of a large tree that they can climb in an emergency. Bears reuse regular bedding sites time and again, and some beds become deep with regular use. Occasionally bears also prepare a mattress upon which to sleep, using cut vegetation or low-hanging branches from nearby shrubs and trees. When temperatures dip below freezing, bears quite regularly build mattresses, which may be either a few hemlock branches or elaborate mats of laurel foliage 5 inches (12.7 cm) thick. One naturalist described a bear's winter bed as resembling an eagle's nest that had fallen out of a tree.

Bears in Idaho move about a mile (1.6 km) each day. On average males travel slightly longer distances than females, and both sexes tend to use well-established runs when they travel from one feeding area to another. At a glance, bears give the impression of shuffling, but a more careful study reveals a nearly silent, efficient, flowing gait. Their head swings low from side to side, and their feet roll forward, barely lifting off the ground. But don't be fooled. Black Bears move like lightning when they want to and can run up to 35 miles (56 km) an hour for short distances. It is a myth that bears cannot run downhill.

SEASONAL

Black Bears increase their daily activity through the spring and summer, peaking at the end of August or early October, when wild foods are most abundant. As fall begins, their metabolism changes and they become better at assimilating carbohydrates and turning them into the fat needed to survive the winter months. Thereafter their activity levels decline until they enter hibernation. It is during fall when bears wander farthest in search of high-quality foods. Territorial boundaries dissolve, and they

A first-year cub peers down at the photographer from high in an aspen tree. © *Mark Elbroch*

often congregate in food-rich woodlands and feed in close proximity to each other. Sows have been recorded traveling 125 miles (200 km) away from their territories to forage through the fall on localized nut crops, only to return to their territories in time to den.

Not all Black Bears become inactive during winter months. Southern bears may den up for only a month or two, and in the southernmost populations Black Bears may not den at all. In parts of Mexico and southern California, pregnant females enter dens to give birth, but males remain active throughout the year.

Several weeks before a bear enters its den, its body systems begin to slow down in preparation for hibernation. Its blood circulation slows and it eats less and begins to defecate and urinate less as well. During this time bears are essentially sleepwalking—sitting and lying more frequently and for longer durations. Females with cubs enter dens first, followed by sows without cubs, and last, mature males. Fat bears, those that fed well earlier in the season, enter their dens before thin bears, which remain active and continue to attempt to accrue the necessary reserves to survive the winter and early spring when good food is still scarce.

We are not exactly sure what complex biochemical and physical processes trigger a bear into hibernation. We believe food availability and weather play larger roles in sending bears scrambling for their dens than does temperature. Black Bears typically enter their dens sometime between September and December, depending on latitude and food availability. When nuts of trees are abundant, denning may be delayed, and from time to time bears in the North can still be seen wandering around in the snows after New Year's Eve. However, a severe snowstorm at any time during the fall can put an abrupt end to fall activities, and then bears seem to disappear overnight.

The den sites bears select are diverse, and individual bears may learn what makes a better den site as they age. Inexperienced bears might select sites that remain exposed to weather, while older bears increasingly select more secure areas. You may discover the exposed back of a bear amid accumulating snow where it just curled up atop the ground. Female bears generally select more secure sites than males. Dens can be found inside hollow trees of suitable girth, under root wads, in underground burrows the bears excavate or find, under porches, in brush piles, under boulders, in caves, or even in aboveground pits they dig. Black Bears often prepare their den sites by lining the chamber or bowl with branches of coniferous trees, grasses, and other vegetation. Once they are inside, they may partially or completely plug the entrance.

Look carefully on the left of this photo for the eye and nose of this Black Bear. The bear is within a den dug inside a hollow Douglas fir, with the soft, decomposing innermost wood forming the mattress beneath it. © *Jacob Katz and Mark Elbroch*

Bears may change dens up to 4 times in a given season, and a sudden midwinter warm spell may cause bears to go out for a stroll in the melting snow. If they are disturbed, they relocate to a new den. Although the same bear rarely uses the same den in consecutive years, an excellent den may be used by several different bears over a longer span of time.

Bears emerge from their long winter rest from March through May, depending upon latitude. Northernmost bears den longer than their southern counterparts to avoid the harsher and longer winters. Adult males are the first to emerge, and females with cubs are the last. Families also linger for several days at their dens, while single animals move into foraging areas almost immediately. Shortly after they begin to wander aboveground, they excrete a fecal plug that formed during the winter. It takes several weeks of activity for their appetites and blood circulation to increase to full operation. Should temperatures rise quickly, bears often overheat as they adjust from hibernation to normal blood circulation, and they seek to cool themselves in stream pools, ponds, and wallows.

Overheating is a serious issue for a dark, often black, animal in warm areas. During the summer, shade is critical to the life of bears, especially in the desert Southwest or the heat of summer at high altitudes in the West. Rarely will a Black Bear be out and about in full sun during the warmest months, when the tips of their fur reach well over 100°F (38°C); this could lead to life-threatening heat exposure. Black Bears maintain muddy wallows at natural springs in which to roll and bathe to cool down; they also seem to enjoy splashing and swimming in streams and ponds.

FOOD AND FORAGING

Black Bears seek foods that are abundant and easy to digest. They vary their diet with the seasons, switching to new resources as they become available. Black Bears would eat continuously, but they are limited both by the rate at which they can shovel food into their mouths and metabolize new foods, and by the size of their gastrointestinal tract. They are generalist omnivores that eat a great diversity of foods. Bears use sight, smell, and their excellent memory to locate and select the choicest items—those with the most protein and carbohydrate (sugar) and the least amount of fiber (cellulose). From past experience, bears know where and when to look for specific foods. Smell may lead them to a food source, such as a carcass, but it is believed that sight is their primary means of foraging at close range. Color vision helps them distinguish between ripe berries and leaves. They defecate on average every 4.5 hours, sowing seeds of grasses and fruits as they go.

During spring bears graze on the tender green shoots of new grasses and a wide range of herbaceous and woody vegetation. In wetlands they dig for cattail rhizomes and also eat their new growth. They ascend aspens to eat their newly emerging leaves. Over much of their range, spring bears also feed heavily upon carcasses of various ungulates killed by harsh winters. Carcasses that are putrid and decayed are still worth visiting to lap up the writhing maggots and other insects.

Spring is also the season during which bears strip the bark of trees to feed on the inner bark, or cambium. In northern Montana they commonly strip western larch, and in the Pacific Northwest they strip fir trees. Bears use their teeth to strip away the outer bark and then to scrape away the sugar-rich cambium layer. Bark-feeding is controversial in forest plantations, because bears often girdle and kill the tree in the process. Some bears feed extensively in this way, and they can easily be identified if you glimpse their teeth. The high-sugar diet rots their teeth quickly and turns them black as well, just as it would any person who ate so much sugar and disregarded oral hygiene.

The start of summer sees many bears at their most carnivorous, when for several weeks they prey upon deer fawns and the calves of elk and moose. One mature sow in Minnesota was exceptional at locating fawns and ate six in a single day. She plodded

A hot Black Bear takes a dip in a shallow pool in a California riparian area to cool off and refresh itself. © Mark Elbroch

along in her typical slow foraging gait and then caught the faintest whiff of a nearby fawn. In a flash she was transformed into a bloodhound, and nose to ground she rampaged, crisscrossing the area, scouring until she located the tiny deer, pouncing on it to subdue and kill it. Black Bears eat the youngest fawns in their entirety, and they suck down their tiny legs like we do spaghetti. In several studies in the West, Black Bears killed and ate significantly more elk calves than did coyotes, despite the latter's reputation. During the moose calving season in Alaska, mature male Black Bears congregate in areas where moose calves are most abundant, excluding 2-year-olds and female bears from the area.

Black Bears continue to graze through the summer, as well as dine on fruits as they ripen. Serviceberries are the first fruits to ripen in the Northeast, and they announce the start of the summer berry season for bears. Summer is also the season during which Black Bears eat the most insects. They dig up yellow jacket (ground hornet) nests, and in years when hornets are widespread you may find seven or more large excavations within several hundred yards of each other. Bears also rip open logs during the summer to feast on the pupae and larvae of ants and beetles.

Fall is when bears feast on the diverse berries, fruits, and nut crops that they depend on for their high levels of proteins and carbohydrates (sugars). Bears have a tremendous advantage over competing deer, coyotes, and foxes because rather than wait for fruits and nuts to drop to the ground, they can climb to harvest them. In New England they climb serviceberries in the summer and wild cherries, oaks, and American beeches in the fall. Once up in a tree, a bear finds a good spot to hold its weight and then bends and breaks limbs in toward itself, so that it can feed on nuts and fruits growing far from the trunk. It also breaks branches completely off, using both its teeth and the incredible strength in its arms. Once it has liberated the nuts on the branch, it pushes it down beneath it out of the way. As a bear continues to forage, it may stand on the growing accumulation of branches below it, packing it down. Biologists refer to these collections of branches by the slightly misleading term "bear nests." On rare occasions a bear might take a nap atop a pile, but bear nests in trees are signs of feeding, not resting.

Bears crack hard nuts more easily than deer or squirrels do, and they eat with a delicacy contradicting their size. They often take one nut into their mouth at a time, crack it open, separate the meat from the shell, and then dribble shell fragments out either side of their mouth. The trick to gaining enough nutrition is to eat continuously. In Minnesota a single bear was observed eating 2,605 hazelnuts in a single day, which is about 7 pounds of food.

Bears are intelligent and opportunistic and eat almost anything that can be ingested and provide some nutrition. They dig up vole nests to eat the young, stalk Yellow-bellied Marmots and woodcocks on the ground, and climb trees to pilfer eggs and fledglings of woodpeckers and raptors. They raid garbage cans, dumpsters, and backpacks, as well as gardens and orchards. They can clean out a melon patch in a single night, or strip a plum tree in a lazy afternoon. Black Bears also occasionally hunt and eat domestic calves and sheep.

HABITAT AND HOME RANGE

Black Bears are the most widely distributed of the 3 North American bears, with a historic distribution stretching from the East to West Coast and from northern Alaska to southern Mexico. Today they inhabit about 60 percent of their previous range, utilizing a great diversity of forested habitats in varied climates and at all elevations. They are absent in the driest and hottest deserts of the Southwest and Mexico, the harshest coastal regions of the far north where Polar Bears and Brown Bears dominate, on prairie grasslands, and wherever human populations and activities exclude them. Because of human persecution, Black Bears are absent from much of the Midwest and remain only in several threatened, remnant populations in the Southeast of the United States.

Black Bears inhabit forested habitats, whereas other bears favor open terrain. In the East and Northeast, Black Bears do well in nearly every forest type, whereas in the Southwest they inhabit higher elevations, especially where juniper berries, pine nuts, and manzanita fruits are plentiful. Typical home ranges for females are 4.6 to 19.3 square miles (12–50 km²), and for males, 45.2 to 77.2 square miles (110–200 km²). In rich areas where fruit and nut crops are plentiful, home ranges may be as small as 0.8 square miles (2 km²) for females and 1.9 square miles (5 km²) for males. Black Bear densities across their range vary from 1 bear for every 0.5 to every 5 square miles (every 1.3–13 km²).

COMMUNICATION

Scent-marking plays a large role in maintaining a comfortable distance between overlapping bears, as well as allowing males and females to communicate during the breeding season. Females dribble urine nearly constantly as they go, and these chemical cues are thought to strengthen their territorial boundaries and exclude other adult females. Bears also straddle and walk over saplings to deposit urine along travel routes; the females do this by first dribbling urine down the long hairs attached to their vulvas (which are often mistaken for penises) and then dragging them over vegetation.

Bears mark trees and shrubs visually and with scent. They decapitate evergreen saplings and other trees, sometimes climbing 40 feet (12 m) up to remove the top 3 feet (1 m) of a large tree. They bite through them with their teeth while pulling the top with their forelimbs. Most often such sign is associated with "gateways," or points of access to feeding areas such as nut crops or wetlands. On large trees they may rub the base with their flanks in passing, or pause long enough to bite the exposed roots as they rub. More often they stand to rub, claw, and bite the main trunk. Bears often rub the trunk with their backs, like they are relieving an itch, and then extend their head back over one shoulder to bite the trunk with their canines. They may also rake the bark over a shoulder with their claws, and they bite and claw the trunk while they face the tree as well. Rubbing is exhibited regardless of whether they claw or bite the tree, and you can find their hairs stuck in the bark, sap, or along the lowest branches of trees they mark if you look closely. Bears mark trees along their travel routes time and again, and over time sign accumulates and can be dramatic. Repeated biting may eat away at the tree trunk and eventually cause the tree to snap. Bears also love to mark telephone poles, signs, front porches, and other human objects in just the same way.

Some think the height of a bear's mark somehow reflects its status within the bear community and that new bears in an area seek the mark-trees of the resident animal to check their height against his. This conjecture smacks more of human interactions than those of bears, and there is no evidence to support it. Black Bears sometimes climb to mark higher on a tree, especially younger, smaller bears. Bears are also reluctant to give up an old rubbing post even when it falls over and will roll on and mark them where they lie in the dirt. Marks are visual, but they are also covered with scents that convey individual identity, sex, breeding condition, and possibly even social status. Bears do not need the height of a mark to determine something about a resident bear—they need only use their noses.

We think that bears mark areas most important to them in order to alert other bears to their presence. Sows mark trees most often during the fall, which may serve to create a territorial zone around critical fall foods. Males, on the other hand, mark most often during the spring, when defending mating opportunities becomes important. Bears that encounter a tree marked by another bear are most likely to over-mark if it was made by a bear of the same sex; males over-mark male scents and females over-mark female.

Bears also scent-mark with their feet. They travel the same routes repeatedly throughout their ranges, and multiple bears use well-established trails. Along certain sections of trails, bears step in exactly the same spots as their predecessors, and over time zigzags of deep, worn circles appear in the debris or ground. With stiff, straight front legs, they deliberately emphasize the normal twist of their front feet while they walk, as if rubbing scent into the earth. Some bears walk through such a section of trail and then loop back to do it again. Short sections of "bear trails" in which they follow in each other's footsteps are often found near mark-trees, wetlands, and dumps in the Northeast, and are associated with wallows, mark-trees, and abundant food in the West.

Black Bears make a great number of vocalizations, including huffs, moans, chomps, bawls, grunts, whines, clicks, and the occasional growl. Cubs whine and moan when distressed or separated from their mother. Distressed cubs and even scared adults in trees create long, low moans, sounds not unlike whale song. Cubs also produce a noisy smacking when nursing, which one naturalist described as a rapid, motorlike buzz. Adults sometimes make similar noises when they are content. Bears use explosive woofs and huffs to scare off potential competitors and when they are afraid. They may also rattle their teeth or "jaw-pop" in an intimidating manner, or utter a long huff as a challenge to another bear.

The position of the ears best betrays a bear's intention to play and not to fight. Curious or alert bears hold their ears erect and forward. Playful bears spread their ears so they stick out to either side, and aggressive bears, including those on the defensive, put their ears back and lay them flat against their skulls. Look for younger bears to stand on their hind legs, lower their heads, and stick their

A juvenile vocalizes during a playful exchange with a sibling.

This bear stands straight and tall, pushes out its elbows, dips its head, and spreads its ears in a classic invitation to wrestle.

ears out. They approach each other like sumo wrestlers with short steps and then swipe and grapple with their forepaws.

Threat displays are generally sequential and predictable. A bear will stop and stare at a competitor or potential predator with head held low and ears back. It may pant audibly or otherwise vocalize its discomfort. With ears flattened, upper lip curled, and snout narrowed, bears stick out their "elbows" to appear larger and then charge forward in a great explosion of air and blurry black speed. They either veer off into cover at the last moment or stop short of their target with a great slap of their forelimbs on the ground or nearby tree trunk along with an intimidating explosive exhalation of air. But such a display to a human is often the surest sign that they don't mean to attack. Bears also walk with stiff front legs in an exaggerated gait to exhibit discomfort and fear.

COURTSHIP AND MATING

The breeding season runs from June to September, though mating is most common in June and July. Cubs remain with their mothers for more than 1 year. Environmental factors such as food availability as well as the long period of parental care influence how often a female may breed. Females breed every 2 years in eastern populations, but in some western populations females typically breed every 3 years or more.

During the breeding season males wander widely in search of sows in estrus. Males repeatedly visit as many females as they can, stopping in for a few hours to check whether or not they have entered estrus and are receptive. During this time, males are intolerant of each other, and dominant males oust subordinate animals to secure their rights to a given mate. Battles between similarly matched males are violent and may result in serious injuries. Research in North Carolina showed that the three largest boars in a study of 23 males fathered 91 percent of the cubs monitored over 3 years.

Boars follow the scent marks of estrous females to locate them. A boar tracks an estrous female by her scent and lingers in her periphery until, by some subtle cue, she indicates she is ready to mate. Should he attempt to move in before she is ready, she will rebuff his advances with swatting blows and aggression, so he waits patiently until she is ready. When he finally comes in close, he smells her urine, licks her face and genitalia, and without much further ado, mounts her from behind and grasps her around the midsection with his powerful forelimbs. The female often responds little for the duration of copulation, and she may even shuffle a few steps and graze on grasses while the male continues. The male may bite at her neck, and the pair may begin to quiver as mating progresses. Copulation lasts as long as 30 minutes, after which they lie down, together or separately. They mate several times each day for up to 5 days and then go their separate ways.

Black Bears are promiscuous; both males and females mate with multiple individuals. Females can conceive multiple times with different mates, and perhaps a quarter of litters include multiple cubs with different fathers.

DEVELOPMENT AND DISPERSAL OF YOUNG

A female's fertilized eggs remain in suspended animation until mid-November or December, when the embryos implant in the wall of the uterus (called delayed implantation). The embryos then actively gestate for 60 to 70 more days, and the cubs are born in January or February in the darkness and security of their mother's winter den.

The number of cubs in a litter varies from 1 to 6 (average 2 to 3) and depends on the age of the mother and her nutritional status in early winter. Young bears and bears in poor health or with less fat have smaller litters. Thus the largest litters are born to older sows, in excellent health and with ample fat reserves gathered the previous summer and fall during a particularly bountiful year. Females breed for the first time between 2 and 8 years of age, though a typical age is 4 or 5. If in poor health or lacking the fat to sustain lactation, females may reabsorb fetuses before birth or abandon the cubs after they are born. On rare occasions a female mates while still rearing cubs, though typically estrus does not occur in lactating females.

Tiny newborn cubs are furred but blind, toothless, and helpless. They wriggle up their mother's mass with little help from her until they locate a nipple and begin to nurse. The female wakes enough to make sure they are well situated and to lick them clean, and remains conscious enough to respond to their cries if they need her. Lactating females lower their body temperatures by only a few degrees during their winter dormancy, compared to the 7° to 8°F (4°C) of females without new litters. Thus they provide new cubs all the warmth they require.

From the moment cubs exit their dens for the first time, they are filled with energy and mischief. They are continuously frolicking, wrestling, climbing, tumbling, biting, and playing while exploring their environment. Sows sit, stretch their legs out, and recline back to expose their nipples for the cubs to nurse. The cubs each climb her like a mountain, find a nipple, and coo and hum as they suckle. Nursing bouts typically last 4 to 5 minutes and end when the female either pushes the cubs away or rises up, sending them tumbling to the ground.

After they emerge from the den, Black Bears use trees to protect their youngsters from danger. Sows teach their cubs to climb trees at a moment's notice, which they communicate with a quick and forceful woof or two relaying potential danger. A female eventually leaves her cubs for short periods so that she may move more quickly and forage on her own or in areas where safety is a concern. She often leaves cubs at the base of or even up in a large tree with rough, easy-to-climb bark and ample limbs for additional purchase. Some naturalists fondly refer to these trees as "babysitter trees" since they provide the protection cubs need while their mothers are away.

An adult sow lounges back against a boulder to allow her cub to climb atop her and nurse.

Cubs are weaned during their first summer. While cubs are with their mother they are trained in where and when diverse foods are available, which is essential to their adult survival. They must eat well to gain enough weight to survive the coming winter, even though they will den with their mothers. During their second winter they will have their mother's warmth but not her milk to sustain them. First-year cubs generally enter their dens weighing between 40 and 70 pounds (18–32 kg), depending upon geographic range.

Yearlings disperse in June, at about 16 months of age, when their mother chases them off and focuses her attention on the new breeding season. Males typically disperse 8 to 136 miles (13–219 km) from their mother's range, and sometimes farther, and enter a very dangerous stage of their lives. Many yearlings die before they establish a territory of their own. Nearly all female cubs remain in a portion of their mother's home range. The sow gives up these areas and enlarges her range elsewhere to accommodate her daughters.

INTERACTIONS AMONG BLACK BEARS

Black Bear territoriality is somewhat flexible, and home ranges stretch, shrink, merge, and separate throughout the year. Females are more territorial over most of their range than males, and other than in the fall they generally maintain exclusive territories. Female-female fights over territory are fierce and result in deaths. In the Sierra Nevada Range, female Black Bears defend only portions of their territories and overlap more with each other than in other parts of the country. Fall is the time when territorial boundaries fade away and bears wander farthest in search of food. Males overlap with each other and wander much farther than females. In Minnesota male bears typically overlapped with 2 other adult males and between 7 and 15 adult females. In years of low food availability, bears wander farthest. In areas where food is particularly abundant, such as a big hazelnut crop or a salmon run, bears congregate in large numbers. In these cases, bears keep a respectful distance between themselves and in general ignore each other.

Adult males are intolerant of dispersing subadults and bears attempting to establish their own ranges. Residents chase them off and engage them in sometimes deadly physical contests. Subadults actively avoid encounters with large boars and nervously search for solace. Females too are intolerant of subadult trespassers. In one instance an adult female with cubs chased a young male up a tree, climbed up after him, bit him in the posterior several times, and then ripped him from the tree. When he hit the ground, he took off running.

Cannibalism in Black Bears is considered rare,

Two cubs stand and face each other, ears to either side to communicate their intention to play and not fight. © Mark Elbroch

but it does occur. Most instances are adult males killing cubs. This is assumed to occur when the cubs are not their own and may facilitate further breeding opportunities with the mothers. A female that loses her cubs enters estrus during the next breeding season, and if she lives within the range of the cannibalizing male he has a chance to father her next litter. However, adult males have also been documented killing subadult males and females, adult females with cubs, and even cubs that they sired. The basic hypothesis of increasing mating opportunities may be too simplistic to account for this mysterious behavior.

INTERACTIONS WITH OTHER SPECIES

Over much of their range adult Black Bears have few predators other than man. Brown Bears and wolves are likely the reason why Black Bears rarely leave forested habitats, where they climb trees to escape danger. Cubs are sometimes killed by Brown Bears, wolves, coyotes, bobcats, lynx, and cougars. Wolves harass and infrequently kill bears they catch out in the open. They also dig Black Bears out of their winter dens, kill them, and only sometimes eat them before they leave. Brown Bears also occasionally kill adult Black Bears and eat them. Where Black and Brown Bears overlap, competition is reduced through subtle differences in their foraging patterns and habitat use. In a study in western Montana, Black Bears ate more insects than Brown Bears, but fewer roots, pine nuts, and mammals. They also utilized more forested habitats than Brown Bears, and

they denned at lower elevations on gentler slopes.

American Black Bears are distinctive among North America's large carnivores because of the intensity with which they interact with humans. Given the millions of interactions between people and Black Bears in dumps, campgrounds, suburbs, and the backcountry across North America each year, the rarity of bear attacks only confirms how tolerant and restrained they are, even in the face of human intrusion. Most reported attacks occur when people are crowding and feeding bears and involve bluff charges and displays rather than physical contact. Bears are solitary creatures and not accustomed to touch. Do not give in to the temptation to touch a habituated bear, for it may swat you as it would any bear that violated etiquette.

From 1900 through 2000 there were 52 confirmed cases of humans killed by Black Bears in North America. The rare Black Bear hunts people as it would large game, and its hunting behaviors are markedly different from the visual and auditory cues preceding loud bluff charges. Hunting bears stalk their victims, often approaching from behind, attempting to sneak into striking distance without being detected. Should you feel threatened by a Black Bear, be loud and assertive. Yell, and throw things. Pick up something to use as a weapon, but *never* corner the animal. Give it a clear avenue of escape. Bear aggression is typically a display of fear, and it will escape if it has the chance. However, if a bear attacks with the intent to kill, do not "play dead." Fight for your life.

Brown Bear
Ursus arctos

OTHER NAMES: Grizzly Bear, Kodiak bear, silvertip.

The Lewis and Clark expeditions encountered and killed many Brown Bears, and they wrote about them with some trepidation. They sent their specimens to George Ord, who without having ever seen a living Brown Bear gave them the name *Ursus horribilis* to reflect their rumored savagery and brutal nature. Indigenous people throughout the West also respectfully feared the strength and power of Brown Bears. Foraging Tutchone women in the Yukon never called bears by their name so as not to draw their attention, and they respectfully walked around bear defecations so as not to insult them. Many tribes refused to hunt bears, or did so only under special circumstances. Athabaskan hunters quickly poked out the eyes of bears they killed so that the bear wouldn't know who'd committed the hunt and come back to exact revenge.

The bears encountered by Lewis and Clark were called "grizzly bears," and they were considered a species distinct from the Brown Bears of Europe and other parts of the world. Today all Brown Bears are classified as a single species, and certain regional populations as subspecies. The Grizzly Bear of the Rocky Mountains is now called Brown Bear, *Ursus arctos horribilis*.

ACTIVITY AND MOVEMENT

DAILY

The daily regimen of Brown Bears is governed by foraging, but varies with food availability and the presence of humans. When food is scarce—or in contrast, when seasonal foods are especially abundant—bears may be active at any time of day or night. Yet when foods are of average availability, or when people are common, bears more typically restrict their movements to crepuscular or nocturnal hours. Bears forage for long periods and intersperse these with breaks for rest and digestion. Beds are typically adjacent to foraging areas, sometimes in a sheltered, dry spot with a view, but often not. In alpine areas bears sometimes bed in tiny clumps of trees adjacent to meadows, and in riparian zones in tall grass and other thick vegetation near water.

When grazing, or when foraging on distributed food sources such as ground squirrels and nut caches, bears eat as they meander. They shuffle about in a deceptively slow pigeon-toed walk, with their head held low and swinging side to side. Despite the slow gentleness of this locomotion, they can transition into a full gallop at amazing speed

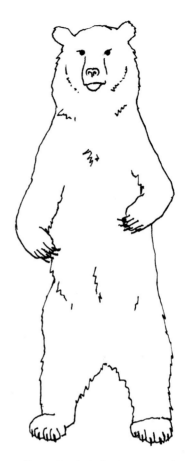

A Brown Bear stands to better assess its surroundings for danger.

when they need to bluff charge an opponent or escape potential danger. Bears may wander anywhere while they forage, but they often travel well-used bear trails when commuting through their range, especially in areas where bear densities are high or dependable foods appear in the same places year after year (e.g., garbage dumps, salmon runs). Depending upon substrate, moisture, and the density of bears in the area, these trails can take on a variety of forms. Bears also create worn trails as part of an elaborate form of scent-marking, and travel paths and scent trails are sometimes difficult to differentiate in the field. Subtle zigzagging compressions created by each passing bear carefully placing its feet in the tracks of a previous animal are signs of scent-marking. Paired ruts where the left feet and the right feet wear in separate paths, or wide, worn, or muddy paths that look like human-made trails, are more characteristic of commuting trails.

SEASONAL

Other than several weeks each year when bears are distracted by mating, Brown Bears focus their entire lives upon feeding and gaining sufficient weight to

A Grizzly Bear feasting on an elk carcass stolen from the wolves that had killed it near Glacier National Park, MT. © David Moskowitz/www.davidmoskowitz.net

survive the winter. Brown Bears become extremely obese year after year, without subsequent health risks. In bears, increased lipids and fats do not increase the risk of arteriosclerosis and heart attack. Quite the contrary, in fall a fat bear is a healthy bear with the highest chances of survival.

Like Black Bears, Brown Bears hibernate in dens for the cold months of the year. By some archaic definitions bears do not actually *hibernate*, but rather become dormant in a state called torpor. For 3 to 7 months of the year they do not eat, drink, urinate, or defecate, and their heart rate and body temperatures lower considerably. Their summer heart rates of 40 to 50 beats per minute dip to a mere 8 to 10 during dormancy. Their body temperature dips only by 10° to 12°F (4°–5°C), allowing them to wake more quickly than if they were in true hibernation, but still gradually. Weight loss in bears is achieved primarily through the loss of fat tissue, rather than of muscles, bones, or organs. Skinny bears that enter hibernation utilize muscle reserves to survive winter denning and may starve or exit their dens in spring too weak to regain their health.

Several weeks before entering their dens, bears begin to slow down, in what researchers call "pre-denning lethargy." Brown Bears typically take to their dens between late October and December and reappear as spring creeps into the mountains sometime between March and May. Bears with the highest fat reserves are often the first to den up, while those with low reserves may stay active until winter storms force them into dens. Bears may periodically rise in a warm spell during the winter to wander around in the snow until temperatures dip again, and they return to their dens to resume their rest.

Brown Bears den in various shelters, depending upon geographic range. In general they choose well-drained, safe locations. In the central Rockies, Brown Bears often wander into the highest elevations and dig their own dens near or above tree line, where protective layers of snow linger longest. Occasionally bears use the same den year after year. In the Brooks Range of Alaska, where melting is unlikely, most bear dens are at lower elevations and on southern slopes, to minimize the energy needed to dig out from their dens in the spring. Bears may den in rock crevices or caves or dig under the root systems of trees. Along the Pacific Coast and in flat terrain they may also den inside large-diameter trees with hollow trunks.

Adult males are the first to emerge from their dens in the spring, followed by subadults and females without cubs, and last by females with newborns. Most females lose more weight than males during hibernation because of the energy investment required to produce and sustain offspring. Lactating females lose 35 to 40 percent of their fall body weight, while males lose only 25 percent. Bears may remain in "walking hibernation" for 10 to 14 days after their emergence. During this time they may appear sleepy and rest frequently as their metabolism and appetite slowly return.

FOOD AND FORAGING

Brown Bears are adaptable omnivores and eat a great diversity of foods. Some Brown Bears survive primarily on plants and supplement their diets with meat only when the opportunities present themselves or during seasonal boons. Here we shall split Brown Bears in North America into two large categories—inland bears and coastal bears—and discuss their diets separately.

When inland bears emerge from their dens in early spring, they dig up the roots of various plants to sustain themselves. Should they find winter-killed ungulates, meat is a welcome boon of energy. In Yellowstone spring bears travel to elk and other ungulate wintering areas where they may also successfully hunt and kill those weakened by the winter or bogged down in deep, soft snows.

Warm spring temperatures bring forth new greenery, and Brown Bears graze on the succulent new grasses, sedges, and forbs. Brown Bears also seek tubers in spring. Bears dig up and eat the roots of pea vines as they wander old streambeds in central Alaska. Bears to the south dig young pocket gophers out of their nests, as well as gopher caches of bulbous oniongrass roots. Spring begins the calving season for the numerous ungulates that live within the Brown Bears' range. In the southern parts of their range, grizzlies hunt elk calves, deer fawns, and moose calves, and in the north, muskox, moose, and caribou calves. Bears may feed on little else for up to a month, or until young, ungainly ungulates are fast enough to outmaneuver them. Brown Bears use their sensitive noses to sniff out calves at rest in long grass or stalk and chase them until they are separated from their herds.

As summer wanes into fall, fruits of all sorts come into season, and Brown Bears eat them all. Huckleberries and blueberries are favored foods of Brown Bears, though they consume raspberries, elderberries, blackberries, and any domestic fruits they encounter with gusto. Then as fall begins in earnest, nut and seed crops become widely available. Whitebark pine seeds are a seasonal specialty of the Brown Bears in some areas in the Rocky Mountains. They sometimes gather the seeds themselves under prolifically abundant trees, or quite often they procure them by digging up and robbing caches of hundreds and hundreds of cones set aside by Red Squirrels.

Fall is also the time for hunting ground squirrels and marmots after they have retreated to their hibernacula for winter hibernation. The long claws and powerful arms of Brown Bears are premier digging tools, and ground squirrel "hunts" sometimes result in craters 6 feet deep with only some wisps of dry grasses to betray the nest that was destroyed to eat the animals within. Digging also provides access to roots that are swollen with calories stored for the following spring. Grizzly Bears in the northern Rockies climb into the higher elevations to rototill large expanses of alpine meadows to devour quantities of glacier lily bulbs.

Yellowstone grizzlies are an exception to the inland Brown Bear seasonal pattern. Up to 95 percent of their energy intake each year is from meat rather than vegetation, because of the rarity of fruit and the abundance and diversity of Yellowstone ungulates. Winter-killed bison, elk, and deer are a much-needed feast for "starving" bears emerging from their dens. As spring gives way to summer there are elk calves to hunt, and now, with resident wolves in the area, there are carcasses to be stolen throughout the remainder of the year.

Coastal Brown Bears have a simpler seasonal menu. The spring and early summer are a time of tubers and grazing on the succulent new growth of sedges. Great numbers of bears graze like cows in large open meadows, and medium to small bears also dig up Pacific razor (*Siliqua*) and soft-shelled (*Mya*) clams at low tide on exposed mudflats. Bears can harvest clams as quickly as one per minute, but given the clams' small size they are not profitable food for large bears.

The salmon run begins around early July, peaks in mid- to late July, and continues, depending on the area, until December. During this time bears glut upon fish, and as they gain weight they become more choosy. They often eat only the protein- and fat-rich brains and roe (eggs). Most bears stick to the shallows where fish are slowest and easiest to catch, but you'll also see others that have learned to catch fish in deeper waters, where they submerge and actually chase fish underwater. Still others joust for positions above waterfalls and catch salmon as they leap from the water in attempts to move farther upstream. Young bears watch older ones to learn fishing techniques and develop their own style. As the salmon run wanes, berry crops peak and sustain bears into early fall. In the fall they also consume abundant seeds, such as pine nuts, along with tubers and grasses.

Bears typically hunt only ungulate calves, but hungry bears also stalk and hunt adult ungulates and other animals, especially injured, sick, or old ones, if they think they can catch them. In these cases bears stalk and hunt much like a large cat, stealthily creeping forward and using any available cover to close the distance to their intended prey. Brown Bears have been known to lie in wait to ambush Mountain Goats in the south and, in the far north, muskox. When a Brown Bear has made a kill or otherwise come to claim a carcass, it typically

Small to medium coastal Brown Bears on mudflats excavating mussels and clams.

rakes in surrounding earth and vegetation to cover and cache it. Caching is thought to minimize odors that might attract other bears, and to slow spoilage. Day beds and scats litter areas surrounding large caches, and sometimes the bear naps directly atop its prize. In Montana a grizzly discovered a moose carcass, cached it, and then slept atop the mound for several days, resting its head on one protruding hoof for brief naps. This scene was a delight to accumulating photographers, but keep in mind that bears vigorously defend their caches, and it is unwise to linger near one.

Bears also eat insects where they mass or swarm thickly enough to make the effort worth their while. They dig up hornets' nests and rip open ant-infested logs to consume the larvae inside. In the Rockies they also move into the higher elevations to take advantage of swarming army cutworm moths in the height of summer.

Foods pass through Brown Bears very quickly, and they defecate 5 to 10 times each day. It takes 13 hours for meat to be digested and defecated, and 7 hours for clover. Fiber is poorly digested by Brown Bears and is why those on a vegetarian diet do not attain the same incredible mass as their more carnivorous counterparts.

HABITAT AND HOME RANGE

Brown Bears are distributed in circumpolar fashion throughout the Northern Hemisphere, and when the glaciers last receded, Brown Bears may have patrolled most of North America. By the time the European settlers arrived, their eastern limits had withdrawn to the eastern edge of the Great Plains, at the edge of what is now Oklahoma. Within 100 years Brown Bears were eliminated from 98 percent of their range in the lower 48 states. Today they are confined to several small managed populations in the Rocky Mountains and Washington and several expansive and healthy populations in western Canada and Alaska. There are about 1,300 Brown Bears remaining in the lower 48 states, between 35,000 and 45,000 Brown Bears in Alaska, and likely more than 25,000 in Canada.

In North America Brown Bears thrived in diverse forested habitats from sea level to the peaks of the coastal mountains, as well as on tundra and prairie. Where they persist today they continue to use diverse habitats. A Brown Bear's home range will overlap with the home ranges of other bears of both sexes. Home range size and bear densities correlate with food and resource availability. Abundant resources result in smaller home ranges and higher densities, whereas sparse resources result in wide-ranging bears. Females have smaller home ranges than males, since males are larger and need more food to sustain them. Males also roam widely each year to mate with as many females as possible. Kodiak Island and Yellowstone National Park demonstrate two extremes on the spectrum of bear home ranges and densities. On Kodiak, where a reliable, concentrated annual bounty of salmon sustains the bears, male home ranges average 9.2 square miles (24 km^2), and female ranges average 4.6 square miles (12 km^2). In Yellowstone home ranges of males average 320 square miles (828 km^2) and of females 148 square miles (384 km^2). Tundra grizzlies roam the largest home ranges, with males averaging 4,150 square miles (6,700 km^2) and females as much as 1,300 square miles (2,100 km^2). On Kodiak, the bear density (number of bears per square mile) is roughly 20 times greater than in the Yellowstone area, which averages a single bear for every 19.3 square miles (50 km^2).

COMMUNICATION

Vocalizations are uncommon in Brown Bears except during fights, threats, or the whines and moans they make when distressed or wounded. Cubs vocalize more than adults, and their sounds often communicate hunger or fear when separated from their mothers. When you are close enough to hear, bears greeting on friendly terms may "chuff" to one another (give a rapid inhale-exhale) or smack their lips. Chuffing is also used by subordinates attempting to appease a dominant, and also during mating between males and females.

Huffs, snorts, and jaw-popping are tactics used by nervous bears attempting to unnerve a non-bear opponent, such as a human (and it usually works!). They may also bluff charge in combination with these vocalizations, storming in and then drawing up short, to turn and walk away from their target. Bears may bluff charge an intruder repeatedly without making physical contact, and then retreat peaceably.

The height and orientation of the head and body, and the position of their ears, are important signals between bears. Bears raise their heads and use a stiff-legged walk in both submissive and aggressive exchanges. Dominant and aggressive bears maintain frontal orientation, outstretch and lower their head in the direction of their target, and flatten their ears backward. They also open their mouth to display their impressive canines as they approach their opponent, and when they can, assume the higher position in uneven terrain. Subordinate animals drop their gaze, assume a sideways orientation, or even turn completely around to face away from the dominant animal. They may also back up slowly to avoid any contact with the dominant animal, or sit down, a subordinate behavior also exhibited by canines and felines.

Threats follow three distinct stages: confrontation, charge, and fight. Only 4 percent or less of agonistic interactions between Brown Bears involve physical contact. The vast majority do not proceed beyond the confrontation stage, which comprises the displays described above. Should neither bear submit to the other, they may engage in "jawing," a low-level exhibition of aggression in which two bears face each other, ears back, mouths partly open, and growl at each other. After jawing, one bear bluff charges the other. If neither bear submits, they fight. Bears stand on their hind legs to box and grapple their opponents with their front paws. Fights are vicious and fast. They swipe with their claws at each other's head and shoulders, and aim bites at their head and neck. Chunks of fur are ripped from their opponents and fly through the air in a great blur of

A coastal Brown Bear fishing for migrating salmon. © *Photogaga/Dreamstime.com*

Two Brown Bears "jawing" at each other, which is a low-level form of aggression. © istockphoto.com/
Scott Leigh

brown motion and deafening roars. The roars of fighting Brown Bears can be heard more than a mile away.

Should an opponent run from a charging bear or from a confrontation instead of hold its ground, the aggressor almost always chases it down and engages it in a fight. The running bear is at a distinct disadvantage and is usually severely injured by the pursuer.

Chemical communication is central to the lives of Brown Bears. Trees, telephone poles, signs, cabins, and other human structures of all sizes are scratched with claws, bitten, and/or rubbed. Brown Bears select the largest-diameter trees along their travel routes upon which to rub. They stand with their back to the tree and rub their back, shoulders, and back of their head on the rough bark of the trunk. Brown Bears occasionally add bites and claw marks to rubbed trees, but not as often as Black Bears do. They are more likely to do so when marking a human sign or structure.

Males rub trees most often during the breeding season and females most often during the molt. Both are spring and early summer events, and then rubbing by both sexes declines through the remainder of the year. Like Black Bears, Brown Bears also straddle saplings and urinate on them along travel routes. Bears also roll to scent-mark, and they form worn-in trails where their feet are placed in the same footsteps again and again to form a zigzagging trail of cleared circles, which may be several inches below that of the surrounding debris.

COURTSHIP AND MATING

Females breed every 2 years at their highest productivity, and every 6 years at their lowest. The average for Brown Bears in North America is slightly more than 3 years. The breeding season extends from mid-May through early July, during which a female is in estrus from 10 to 30 days, a length that varies year to year within individuals. Should a female not become pregnant during her estrous cycle, she may come into estrus a second time beginning a few weeks after the end of the first.

Brown Bears are polygamous and promiscuous, and females in estrus may be followed by multiple males. Males become aggressive toward each other during the breeding season, and they engage in fights to earn the right to mate. A male may have to win numerous fights against multiple challengers to defend his access to an estrous female. Old males carry numerous wounds from battles during the breeding season. Should a younger, smaller male approach a larger male with a mate, he is chased off and sometimes injured or killed. Females appear to mate with multiple males when circumstances allow, and where Brown Bear densities are high, it is not uncommon for females to breed with many males during an estrous cycle. She may even sire a litter with cubs of different fathers.

Courtship behaviors are not well documented in Brown Bears. In the Canadian Rockies males have been seen herding females onto isolated peaks and exposed ridges, where the two bears interact over several days or even several weeks. Both animals eat very little while they engage in their exchange. Males repetitively herd females back into the area when they attempt to leave, but when females successfully "escape" their area of confinement, they turn around and enter it again of their own accord. When a female is finally receptive, the male rises up behind her and grasps her around the midsection. The duration of actual copulation varies from 10 minutes to an hour, depending on the receptiveness of the female, the excitement of the male, and their freedom from disturbance.

The development of the fertilized egg quickly stops, and it remains free-floating in the uterus for approximately 5 months (delayed implantation). It then implants in the wall of the uterus while the female is in winter hibernation and completes an active development of 6 to 8 weeks.

DEVELOPMENT AND DISPERSAL OF YOUNG

While the females are tucked away in winter dens, they give birth to 1 to 3, and sometimes 4, tiny, blind,

A Brown Bear scratching and marking a tree.

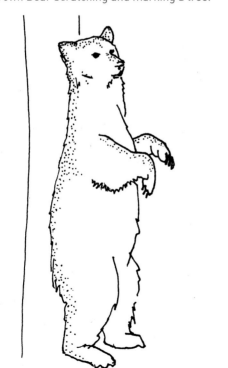

and helpless cubs between January and March. The fatter the mother, the earlier she gives birth, the richer her milk, and the greater chance her cubs have for survival. Cubs weigh approximately 1.1 pounds (500 g) and newborns crawl up their mothers to locate teats to which they attach.

By the time they emerge from the den 3 months later, cubs can each weigh 12 pounds (5.5 kg). They are round and furry, truly resembling teddy bears. Their rounded heads look too large for their bodies, and they tumble and play while they explore their world. Cubs of the year divide their time equally between playing and napping. They frolic beside their mother, wrestle, run about, and explore their new world with a curiosity characteristic of intelligent creatures. In their first summer they often have a necklace of white fur running across their back and chest that fades by their second year. Abandoned cubs are sometimes adopted by other bears, and a female may even adopt a cub while she has others of her own.

Cubs are generally weaned from milk before entering hibernation with their mother in the fall. Occasionally cubs are seen nursing in their second year. They den with their mother and share her body's heat. Cubs remain with their mother for 2 to 3 years, learning what to eat and where it can be found. Cubs often disperse with the arrival of adult males looking to mate with their mother. Females may also turn aggressive and chase their cubs away, after which time the cubs may tend to remain together for up to a month before they strike out on their own. Occasionally a cub stays with its mother into a fourth year, but this is rare. Siblings may also remain together for up to several years, or visit each other regularly as they establish their home ranges.

Females breed for the first time between 3 and 9 years of age, depending upon individual circumstances and geographic populations. On Kodiak Island, females breed for the first time between 3 and 6 years of age, while in the Yukon the average is 7. Males breed for the first time sometime after they are 4.5 years of age, but their opportunities may be limited by their ability to compete with older, larger bears. In a study in northern Canada, males required 14 years to reach 95 percent of their potential weight capacity, while females needed only 9. Females stop growing when they redirect their energy investments into reproduction, but males continue to grow since larger size makes them more competitive for breeding opportunities.

INTERACTIONS AMONG BROWN BEARS

Brown Bears do not defend their home ranges as a territory, but they do defend smaller zones around themselves, the size of which is determined largely by the availability of food. Bears may defend an

Wolves and a Brown Bear in a temporary truce dine together on a moose carcass killed by the wolves in Denali National Park, AK. © *John Eastcott and Yva Momatiuk/National Geographic Image Collection*

entire berry patch from others, but feed within a few yards of other bears at a salmon run.

Bears maintain peace with other bears through mutual avoidance and a rigid social hierarchy, with large males at the top, followed by adult females with cubs, followed by bears less than 3 years old of both sexes. Large bears dominate small ones, and when violence occurs, smaller animals can be injured or killed. Bear personalities are varied, however, and some bears engage in playful bouts with each other under crowded conditions, while others strictly ignore each other.

Salmon streams in Alaska highlight the differences in food consumption for high-, middle-, and low-ranked bears. Dominant bears consume twice as much fish as intermediate and subordinate bears, yet are no more competent fish catchers than bears in other social categories. Dominant bears eat twice the fish because they spend nearly twice as much time actually fishing as do the other social classes. Dominant animals can just fish, but subordinate animals need to split their time between foraging and watching out for other bears that may threaten them. Every 5 minutes they stand on their hind legs to search for dominant bears. In addition, dominant bears waste little time in traveling into cover to eat fish they catch. They are quite happy to eat their salmon in the open, where they run little risk of another bear trying to steal it. Lower social classes carry each catch as far as 650 feet (200 m) into deep cover to protect them, wasting precious foraging time in traveling back and forth from safe havens.

Just as during the breeding season, potentially deadly fights can occur on feeding grounds and elsewhere. Males not only kill subordinates, but they also eat them. Large males are also known to kill cubs and females, especially during the mating season when heightened testosterone levels contribute to heightened aggression. In Yellowstone, cubs are more often killed by other bears when their mothers join bear congregations to forage at trout streams than when they choose to forage in greater isolation in areas with less food. A female must weigh the potential benefits of food-rich habitats against the increased risks for her cubs and may avoid congested areas as well as the known haunts of large male bears. Of 57 cases in which bears killed bears, 25 of the victims were cubs of the year and 18 were females. Nearly all of the perpetrators were adult males.

INTERACTIONS WITH OTHER SPECIES

Brown Bear relations with Black Bears remain relatively unknown. Brown Bears do on occasion catch and kill Black Bears, but not often. Black Bears living among Brown Bears tend to remain within forested habitats and take to trees as a refuge if need be. There is evidence that in Alaska Brown Bears restrict Black Bear access to salmon resources, especially in low salmon years when Brown Bears completely exclude them from fishing.

Brown Bear interactions with wolves are varied, and they likely depend upon the particular circumstances, the mood and personalities of the animals involved, and their motivation (e.g., defending food, cubs, etc.). Large Brown Bears successfully steal carcasses from both wolves and cougars, and thus force them to hunt more frequently. Wolf packs successfully attack and kill grizzly cubs, yet females and their cubs also push wolf packs off carcasses. Cubs travel directly beneath their mother for protection as they approach wolves. When the wolves move to engage the bears the female lunges at them, and often the cubs do too, until they have slowly made their way to the carcass to feed.

Brown Bears can influence local ungulate herds through fawn and calf predation. During some years in Alaska Brown Bears kill 50 percent of moose calves in localized areas.

Brown Bears occasionally kill people, and their behavior can be unpredictable. Brown Bears are most passive where food is abundant and while they are in large congregations. Keep in mind that most Brown Bear interactions with people are territorial and not predatory. Here are some general rules: Do not interfere with a Brown Bear's cubs, or in some way separate them from their mother. Do not feed Brown Bears. Do not challenge a Brown Bear defending a food cache. Do not surprise a Brown Bear at close quarters—if you see one before it sees you, either retreat from the area quietly if you are at a safe distance, or make noise to let it know you are there. Never follow a Brown Bear closely or harass one—if you are charged, wait until the bear moves away and then retreat slowly from the area. Never run. Should the bear make contact, curl up into a fetal position and cover your neck with your hands. Others argue that you should attempt to intimidate the bear—be large and loud. This is not the recommended course of action, but it has proven effective in driving some bears away.

Polar Bear
Ursus maritimus

OTHER NAMES: ice bear, sea bear, white bear, nanuuq (Inuit), isbjørn (Danish).

The hairs of the Polar Bear are hollow. They lack pigment and can appear various colors that change with light conditions and season. In the 1970s it was discovered that Polar Bear fur absorbed ultraviolet light, and for years it was speculated that these creatures were somehow harnessing energy to keep warm while inhabiting a frigid environment. More recent research has revealed that the ultraviolet energy dissipates before it reaches the bears' skin, but perhaps it still warms trapped air in their coats and slows heat loss from their bodies.

ACTIVITY AND MOVEMENT

DAILY

Polar Bears are incessant wanderers, ambling along in a rolling gait as quickly as 3 miles (5 km) an hour. They may move as much as 31 miles (50 km) in 24 hours. Polar Bears are capable swimmers and can swim at 6 miles (10 km) an hour and for up to 40 miles (64 km) in a single go. They may also dive to depths of 10 to 15 feet (3–4.6 m), a tactic they often employ to escape human hunters in boats. Yet prolonged swimming can and does result in drowning, and it is hypothesized that later ice development and earlier ice breakups due to global warming may cause increased drowning in Polar Bears.

Polar Bears are most active for the first third of the day and least active for the last third. Overheating is a constant issue for Polar Bears, even when the temperatures dip to levels we might think impossibly cold (−40°F, −40°C). Normally heat dissipates through their foot pads and shoulders, but when they need to cool rapidly they pant and lie on the ice with their legs spread to expose the insides of their legs, where the fur is thinner and blood runs closer to the surface of the skin.

SEASONAL

In the far north ice forms a crust over the polar seas throughout the year. In summer this layer of ice shrinks around its edges, and then it grows again in winter. Most Polar Bears live nearly their entire lives on the ice, floating over sea, not land. In the warmest months they follow the receding ice northward and constrain their daily movements in order to remain on the ice. In the fall, as the extent of the ice increases again, the bears extend their ranges southward into shallower waters near shore where hunting is easier. Bears quickly disperse far and

The large paws of the Polar Bear are perfect paddles for swimming.

After a wrestling match with another male, an overheated Polar Bear lies flat out with its armpits and crotch on the ice to cool down.

wide as the ice sheets continue to solidify. If mid-winter hunting becomes sporadic and unsuccessful, bears spend more time sheltering and resting, awaiting changes in weather and ice that improve hunting opportunities.

In contrast, the Polar Bears of Hudson Bay do not follow the ice northward in summer. They are marooned along the bay's coastlines for the summer months. Food for bears is limited in the summer tundra, and these bears scavenge, forage, and hunt opportunistically, but eat very little overall.

Great congregations of bears gather near Churchill, Manitoba, on the western shore of Hudson Bay during October and early November. The bears await the winter freeze and the end of their season of privation at a spot where two rivers empty into the bay, lowering its salinity and allowing for the earliest freezing. Hundreds of bears pass their time around Churchill napping, wrestling, and walking about, waiting to set forth on the frozen bay. When the bay begins to freeze, the bears disperse overnight, as if by magic. When viewed from a helicopter, their dispersing trails weave intricate patterns, occasionally accented by spots of red where the new ice allows for successful seal hunts.

Unlike other North American bears, Polar Bears do not dig dens in which to hibernate during the winter months. But they do "shelter" throughout the year when weather is poor and hunting opportunities are limited. Bears dig into snowbanks and shelter for 25 to 150 days. In some areas, prolonged sheltering among males is rare, but everywhere in their range pregnant females dig dens in which to give birth and protect their cubs. In Hudson Bay this occurs just as the bay begins to freeze, and instead of returning to the ice to hunt and end their summer fasts, pregnant females move inland to dig their maternal dens and continue their fasts until the following spring.

FOOD AND FORAGING

Polar Bears are the most carnivorous of the bears, and most survive on little else but meat. Their principal prey is the Ringed Seal (*Phoca hispida*), but they also prey heavily on Bearded, Hooded, and Harp Seals. Polar Bears occasionally hunt walrus, though they are a difficult foe to overcome, and many bears that try are wounded and sometimes even killed. Polar Bears also scavenge the carcasses of seals, walrus, and whales they encounter.

In the southern parts of their range or when stranded on land during warmer months, Polar Bears eat anything that resembles food. They are curious and intelligent creatures, and their in-

A Polar Bear family atop a floating iceberg. As global warming reduces the ice pack, there is great concern about what will happen to Polar Bears. © istockphoto.com/Thomas Pickard

quisitive nature is an adaptive strength that allows them to explore and discover new sources of food. They scavenge in garbage bins near people and eat small mammals, bird eggs, and tundra fruits. Polar Bears have been documented stalking barnacle geese, glaucous gulls, and thick-billed murres, as well as successfully diving for and catching char and sculpin. They have also been observed hunting beluga whales, small white whales that congregate in Hudson Bay during the warmer months. On the Norwegian island of Svalbard Polar Bears are also known to hunt reindeer.

In the spring Polar Bears focus upon suckling Ringed Seal pups, and they may kill as many as 44 percent of seal pups born in a given area. Newborns are not a preferred food for Polar Bears, given that they offer a very small caloric reward for their efforts. In fact newborns killed at breathing holes by Polar Bears are often abandoned or only partially eaten. What Polar Bears really want is a pup that has had some time to nurse and grow.

Ringed Seal pups are essentially invisible on the landscape, hidden from view in snow caves excavated from beneath. The fact that Ringed Seals hide their young may be an anti-predator adaptation driven by ages of predation by bears. The mother seal maintains a hole in the ice between the sea and her snow cave, from which she can visit and nurse her pup. The hole also provides an escape hatch should a Polar Bear intrude from above. Typically, Polar Bears locate seal pups by scent, sniffing them out through up to a meter of snow and ice. Once a bear has targeted a pup it must move forward stealthily lest the tiny seal slide to safety through the ice hole. When the bear is close enough it rises up high on its hind legs and comes crashing down, driving its forelegs through the roof of the cave and, if all goes well, pinning its prey before it escapes.

Polar Bears are much more successful hunting subadult seals rather than older mature ones, and they hunt them in two principal ways. Primarily they hunt and ambush their prey by waiting still and alert over blowholes maintained by the seals. Alternatively they slowly stalk seals while they bask upon ice floes and shorelines. When a seal surfaces at a blowhole the bear lunges forward and pierces the head and neck of the animal with its long, tapering canines. The gap behind their massive canines is larger than in other bears and their cheek teeth smaller, allowing them to sink their canines into living prey more deeply than other bears, thus providing them greater purchase for the haul. Once a bear grasps a seal, it heaves the 200 pounds (90 kg) or more of seal out of the water—sometimes

A Polar Bear hunting Ringed Seal pups rises up on its hind feet to use its weight and strength to punch through the roof of the ice cave and catch its prey.

breaking a foot of ice in the process. The goliath strength of the Polar Bear is legendary, and the brunt that their teeth, jaws, and neck sustain in hauling seals from the polar seas is difficult to comprehend. Their sharp, recurved front claws grip their slippery prey and provide purchase on the slippery surfaces upon which they hunt.

When seals are hauled out on shore or on ice, Polar Bears stalk them using all available natural cover. They slowly creep, crawl, and slither forward until they are within striking distance, close enough to rush and grab the seal before it can dive to safety. Polar Bears also sneak up on hauled-out seals via water routes, thus cutting off their potential retreat right from the start. Numerous anecdotes describe bears covering their black noses with a white paw to improve their camouflage, but this may in fact be an Arctic legend.

Polar Bears feed most on the blubber of their prey, which they digest more easily than muscle and other tissue. Researchers estimate half the calories in a given seal are held in the fat layer, and thus a bear that quickly consumes the fat layer has most efficiently absorbed the most calories in the least amount of time. This might be particularly important where Polar Bear densities are higher and smaller bears are driven off carcasses by larger bears. Fat digestion also releases water, whereas protein digestion demands it. Thus a fat-rich diet might also aid the bear in an environment where fresh water, locked up in ice and snow, is limited.

When undisturbed, Polar Bears feed at a kill until they are sated and then often leave behind considerable waste. Mothers with cubs are more likely to finish a meal than adult males. Yet left-behind partial kills are not necessarily wasted, as Arctic Foxes depend upon Polar Bears to sustain them through the winter months, and hungry bears may also come along and find a meal abandoned by another bear.

The life of Polar Bears is a great swinging pendulum between feast and famine. Polar Bears accumulate a healthy layer of fat 2 to 4 inches (5–10 cm) thick to sustain them in cold temperatures, and to sustain females while they fast in their dens. Unlike other North American bear species, which enter a deep sleep only during the winter, Polar Bears can enter a hibernation-like state at any time of year in response to food shortages. These deep sleeps allow the body to conserve energy and avoid breaking down their own tissues for fuel when food is scarce. This allows the bears to await more favorable conditions when hunting is poor, or in the case of the Hudson Bay population, while they await the sea ice along the shores of the bay each summer.

HABITAT AND HOME RANGE

Polar Bears are distributed in circumpolar fashion around the North Pole, living on both northern landmasses and ice pack. North America includes their southernmost distribution, where the species' range dips south to include all of Hudson Bay in central Manitoba, Canada. Otherwise they are distributed only along northernmost Canada, including all the islands, and along the shorelines of northern Alaska. Only in North America do Brown Bear and Polar Bear ranges overlap, and then only in northern Alaska and the western Canadian Arctic.

Polar Bears inhabit the harshest and most inhospitable landscapes in North America, living upon sea ice or where ice and snow cover the land for most of every year, and vegetation is all but stunted growth. Polar Bears spend most if not all of their lives wandering the sea ice rather than patrolling nearby shores. Along the coast of northern Alaska and northwestern Canada, Polar Bears tracked for 16 years were located upon land only 7 percent of the time. The sea ice grows and recedes with the seasons each year, and now thanks to global warming has begun to shrink with each given year.

For years it was thought that Polar Bears wandered at random and that their movements were dictated by the presence and arrangement of the sea ice. In fact, Polar Bears select and reuse areas over many years and rarely venture beyond their bounds. Perhaps this is why they need to move so much, since the ice upon which they stand may be moving as fast as 10 miles (16 km) an hour in one direction. They must move constantly just to remain in place, and move even faster and farther if they actually wish to move opposite the flow of the ice.

Given the wandering nature of the beast, the area they use within a given year is vast, and the areas they use repeatedly over many years are truly difficult to comprehend. In the Beaufort Sea area, located just north of the Arctic National Wildlife Refuge, the average annual home range is nearly 58,000 square miles (150,000 km^2) and ranges from 5,000 to 230,000 square miles (13,000–600,000 km^2). Their multi-year ranges are even larger.

The world's population of Polar Bears is estimated to be between 22,000 and 25,000 bears, with 6,000 to 9,000 living along the coasts of Alaska, and 1,000 to 1,700 bears in Canada. North American bear densities are approximately 1 bear for every 15 to 54 square miles (38–140 km^2).

COMMUNICATION

Polar Bears exhibit a limited vocal repertoire. Perhaps the frigid, windy tundra and isolated nature of Polar Bears make vocalizations less important. Vocalizations are most often heard in aggressive encounters, as when males fight for the right to mate with females. Scent-marking among Polar Bears is also little documented, again perhaps because of the nature of life upon ice floes. Polar Bears wandering northern shores do occasionally straddle and urinate upon vegetation, just like other bear species.

Visual communication between Polar Bears is

A Polar Bear rips into a freshly caught seal, stripping away the more nutritious fat layer before it actually eats the meat. © Vladimir Seliverstov/Dreamstime.com

likely similar to visual communication in other bears. Ear placement and long stares are likely critical in communicating dominance and submission.

COURTSHIP AND MATING

In Alaska bears have been observed in pairs from mid-March through mid-May, while in other parts of the North they may start breeding slightly earlier or breed as late as mid-June. Males wander widely in search of females during the breeding season and aim to accompany them as they progress through estrus and become receptive to mating. Males engage in violent contests for dominance and access to mates. They face one another, rear up on their hind legs, and box and bite one another. Paired males quickly transition into a blur of blows with paws, claws, and teeth, all the while growling, snorting, and in every way giving voice to their ferocity. Regardless of season males who are of a breeding age and size can often be recognized by the scars they carry upon their nose, head, and neck, attained during the breeding season.

Males and females may spend several days together. The female is in estrus approximately 3 days, during which she may mate several times with whichever male or males accompany her at that time. After fertilization, the developing embryo becomes dormant before implanting in the wall of the uterus. This delayed implantation lasts until the egg begins to develop again in August or September, as the time approaches for the female to leave the ice to dig her maternal den.

Females are considered in prime reproductive health between the ages of 10 and 19, but females as old as 21 have been reported having successful litters. Females breed once every 3 or more years, and thus have a limited opportunity to produce young compared with other mammals. However, should cubs be lost in their first year, females immediately enter estrus, allowing them to improve their chances of replacing the lost litter. Females also seem to be able to reabsorb fetuses early in their development when they are not in the physical condition to successfully raise the litter. In these cases they abandon their den early to return to hunting and then breed again in the following spring.

Pregnant females in the North leave the ice pack in October or November to seek out an area in which to dig a den. In the Hudson Bay area these are the months when the ice reforms and all the bears should be ending their fasts. However, pregnant females continue to fast and dig into the snow and permafrost to create a den site. Polar Bear mothers may fast in their maternal dens, not eating, drinking, or urinating for 4 to 8 months. The vast majority of females dig their dens within 10 miles (16 km) of the coast, but some may go inland as far

as 73 miles (118 km). Dens are typically made on moderate to steep slopes with snow from 3 to 10 feet (1–3 m) deep, but may be dug on flat terrain as well. The most important feature of a denning site is its ability to catch and accumulate snow, which must cover the bear and her cubs to form a well-insulated and protective cave. Near Hudson Bay, dens are typically dug into a hill or hummock into the permafrost layer, forming a den as one might expect a Brown or Black Bear to dig. Sometimes only the bottom is dug into the permafrost while the roof is created by the snowpack. Permafrost dens are used time and again.

In areas where snow conditions are ideal, numerous Polar Bears congregate to dig their dens, yet each bear maintains a suitable distance from its neighbors and dens in isolation in its own protective cave. In contrast, some bears may den in snowbanks upon the sea ice. There are risks in such endeavors, and researchers have documented cubs lost to breaking ice, even after the mother desperately tries to carry the tiny bears to safety while holding them aloft in frigid waters. Those dens that survive through the winter may drift as much as 600 miles (1,000 km) and require a female to move significant distances to ensure she stays within or returns to her range.

DEVELOPMENT AND DISPERSAL OF YOUNG

Gestation is from 195 to 265 days. Typically 2 cubs, sometimes 1, are born in December or January in the blackness of their dens. Cubs are born weighing a mere 1.3 pounds (0.6 kg), blind, helpless, and with only a sparse fuzz of fur. In captive cubs monitored from birth, they do nothing but suckle their mothers for their first month of life and then begin to incorporate periods of rest. They gain weight quickly and are 22 to 33 pounds (10–15 kg) by the time they emerge from their den for the very first time 3 months later. Their emergence in late March or April coincides with the pupping season for Ringed Seals.

Upon emergence from maternal dens Polar Bear mothers typically linger at the den while they and their cubs acclimate to their new surroundings. They can be seen at the den entrance for up to 14 days, with the female spending much of each day lounging at the den entrance while the cubs explore and play in the nearby snow, resting little.

Females with cubs tend to avoid males, which on rare occasions kill and eat the cubs. When females with cubs intentionally intermingle with other bears, which is only in areas with abundant resources, they are particularly aggressive toward bears that approach their cubs, or to bears that their cubs approach. Where resources are scarce, females steer their families well clear of other bears.

Cubs may weigh as much as 220 pounds (100

As Hudson Bay Polar Bears await the formation of sea ice they congregate in large numbers, and males periodically stand and wrestle without any aggression. © *istockphoto.com/Dave Parsons*

kg) by 1 year of age and up to 308 pounds (140 kg) at age 2, although only 50 percent of cubs survive their first year. Cubs are weaned between 24 and 28 months of age, and sometimes as late as 36 months. Young females attain their adult weights by the age of 5, but may breed for the first time when they are 3.5 years old. More often females are 5 or 6 when they begin to breed, and their first litters are typically between the ages of 5 and 8. Males do not reach their full proportions until between 8 and 10 years of age, when they may begin to hold their own against other adult males and thus participate in breeding contests.

INTERACTIONS AMONG POLAR BEARS

Male-male contests are typical of the breeding season, yet subadult and adult males engage in play at other times of year. This behavior is most easily observed in Churchill, where great congregations of bears await the freezing of the bay each fall. Males of all sizes engage in play. A male will approach and engage a second, either through nosing the nose or face of the other bear or rearing up on its hind legs to entice a potential partner. More often than not a nose-to-nose communication is a more successful means of engaging a partner, and the pair then rise up and engage in silent wrestling for up to several minutes. Sometimes there is no clear winner, and in other instances one bear ends up on the bottom while the bear above pins it down with its mouth on the partner's neck or head. When the bears are clearly mismatched in size, it's the smaller bear that almost always ends up looking the winner, pinning the larger bear down with gaping maw. Some speculate that this encourages the smaller bears to be willing partners in the future, or that only partial effort on the part of the larger bear extends the encounter, which it is enjoying. When the wrestling stops, the bears often nuzzle, collapsing on the ice to cool off after the exertion. The exact function of male-male wrestling in the off season is unknown, but it may help bears become better judges of their own and others' strength. A bear that is an accurate judge of others will be more successful in knowing when to fight and when to retreat without risking injury during the breeding season.

INTERACTIONS WITH OTHER SPECIES

Arctic Foxes rely heavily upon Polar Bears to survive the winter out on the ice floes. Each bear may have several foxes that follow it and feed upon the remains of seals it has killed.

On occasion wolves successfully kill Polar Bear cubs. They surround and engage sows with cubs in open terrain. When the sow lunges at wolves to one side, she leaves her cubs vulnerable on the other, and a wolf sneaks in to grab them. Cubs successfully separated from their mothers are killed and often eaten by the wolves.

Little is known about how Brown Bears and Polar Bears interact in northern Alaska and Canada. In 2006 a hunter from the United States killed a Brown Bear–Polar Bear hybrid during a guided Polar Bear hunt on Banks Island, Northwest Territories. Genetic research confirmed that it was the first hybrid between the two species documented in the wild, and that the animal's parents had been a male Brown Bear and a female Polar Bear.

OTHER NAMES: aivuk or aivik (Inuit).

If you are ever fortunate enough to lift a walrus skull, you'll immediately be struck by its impressive weight. Their eyes are immediately atop the skull and surrounded by little bone. This allows them to see directly upward, which might be very useful when navigating fissures in the ice to air holes from below, as well as to keep a lookout for dangers while they forage with their muzzle buried in the sea floor trawling for bivalves.

A walrus skull is square, with a flattened facial profile. The space between their tusks and the rounded, heavy mandibles (jawbones) creates a perfect round opening when they open their mouth (see illustration). The opening is obstruction-free since walrus have few teeth in the front of their mouths, and its shape increases the pressure and power with which walrus can suck and squirt water while foraging.

Odobenus is derived from the Greek for "one who walks on or with its teeth," a name that comes from observations of walrus hauling themselves onto rocks and ice with their tusks. The tusks must be exceptionally strong to support such feats of strength, but so must other supporting structures in the body. There are two distinct populations of walrus in North America: those in the Northwest are called Pacific walrus and those in the Northeast, the Atlantic walrus.

ACTIVITY AND MOVEMENT

DAILY

The rotund, flabby bulk of the walrus is fluid and smooth beneath the water's surface, where they propel themselves forward with alternating kicks of their hind flippers. Walrus steer by twisting their bodies and with surreptitious flicks of their front flippers. In general, walrus are slow swimmers and average speeds of 4 to 5 miles (6.4–8 km) an hour. When alarmed they can swim at speeds up to 22 miles (35.5 km) an hour. Their nostrils and ears are valvular and shut tight while they are submerged. Walrus have numerous biological adaptations to aid them in deep-water dives and reduce the risks of pressure-related illnesses and tissue damage. For example, their large red blood cells contain enough hemoglobin to store five times the oxygen we can carry under similar conditions.

Daily routines follow one of two general patterns. Either walrus feed in the early mornings and then haul out for much of the remainder of the day, or they alternate between long periods of foraging and rest. Walrus may remain in the sea, switching between foraging and floating at the surface, for up to 56 hours before they return to land to haul out and spend approximately 20 hours sleeping and rejuvenating.

Like sea lions, walrus can hold up their upper torso while on land and propel themselves forward using their front and hind flippers. Yet the immense bulk of an adult walrus also requires that the chest support some of their weight while they move on land. Movement requires balancing the heavy body and head and thus appears more exaggerated and cumbersome than in seals and sea lions. Tusks may also be used when on slippery terrain or to help climb steep rocks or ice floes.

SEASONAL

Winter in the far north is a dark season of howling, frigid winds and storms that on occasion penetrate the thick blubber of walrus. When temperatures drop to their lowest and winds cut through the toughest skin like razors, walrus abandon their icy haulouts and take to the warmer Arctic waters to await the passing of the storm. Otherwise they huddle under the sunless skies of deep winter on

The anterior view of a walrus skull, with its jaws partially open to show the round opening of the mouth.

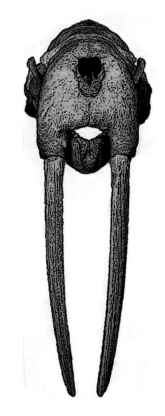

Loafing males turn red to release excess heat from their bodies while they lounge about at haulouts during the summer. © Matthis Breiter/Minden Pictures/National Geographic Image Collection

the great ice shelves and take intermittent trips down through the fissures in the ice to feed along the ocean floor. During the seeming inhospitableness of the dark, cold months, walrus also battle, display, and breed.

Winter is the only season during which all the adult males and females intermingle. Males in the Pacific population feed little during the winter season, providing greater resources for females and calves. The ever-changing and dangerous fissures in the ice sheets become the travel routes for walrus in search of food or when escaping predators or weather atop the ice. They can reopen frozen exits and entrances by battering the ice with their heavy heads, and they may also use their tusks to chip away at frozen entrances from above.

During the spring most adult males and females in the Pacific Ocean begin to separate, which allows for resource partitioning to better sustain the overall herd. Females migrate far to the north following the retreating pack ice, birthing calves en route and eventually arriving in the food-rich Chukchi Sea. Some males also make this trip and may intermingle with the females and calves or form all-male bands that forage on their own. The vast majority of males remain in the south and congregate in massive herds along rocky shores of remote islands in ice-free waters at the southern edge of their range. This separation of the sexes has not been well documented with the other races of walrus living around the Arctic, but they are assumed to exhibit similar movements.

The summer season is about feeding, molting, and sleeping in large social herds. Rookeries of females and calves congregate on ice floes in the north. The males congregate in impressive numbers on islands in the south and attract tourists from around the globe that brave sometimes rough seas to view them. When walrus are hauled out during the summer months they need to keep from overheating. They do this by diverting blood to their outermost layer of blubber, where capillaries along the surface of the skin dilate to release heat. Dilating capillaries also change the color of their skin, and sunbathing walrus turn red or deep pink. In contrast, cold walrus may appear grayish, with little blood being circulated through the outer skin.

In the fall females and calves begin their long trip back south, swimming ahead of the expanding ice sheets that form with the cooling temperatures.

A portrait of a Pacific walrus, with a close-up of the stiff whiskers it uses to aid in foraging along the murky sea bottom.

Eventually they rejoin the males in their winter breeding grounds and the cycle begins anew.

FOOD AND FORAGING

Walrus are specialist predators of benthic (sea floor) bivalves, including cockles, clams, whelks, and mollusks. In Atlantic walrus the most common prey species are bivalves of the genus *Mya*, which include the soft-shelled clams, steamers, and gapers. Walrus forage at depths up to 328 feet (100 m) deep and use their stiff mustache of whiskers to brush the ocean floor and sift out mollusks, echinoderms, and other benthic invertebrates. Walrus can manipulate their whiskers to grasp objects almost as well as we use our hands. Shellfish are positioned in the mouth and then their soft innards are sucked out (see start of account), swallowed in their entirety, and the hard shells discarded.

Typical foraging dives are between 5 and 10 minutes, but they may be as long as 25. Walrus descend quickly, averaging 2.5 feet (.76 m) per second, and spend approximately 80 percent of their time submerged moving along the ocean floor, before ascending at the rather rapid rate of 2.2 feet (.67 m)

per second to the surface for air. Walrus are living vacuum cleaners and eat up to 190 pounds (85.5 kg) of invertebrates each day. Walrus consume 6 clams per minute, 40 to 60 clams per dive, and they may eat up to 6,000 bivalves in a single feeding session consisting of numerous dives. As they plow along the ocean floor, hoovering up shellfish, they also eat snails, shrimp, crabs, and most any other small animal unlucky enough to be in their path.

Mollusks are unearthed in one of three manners. Walrus either plow furrows with their muzzles and forage as they go, or shoot powerful jet streams of water from their mouth to clear small areas, or use their forelimbs like brooms to brush sediments away. Feeding walrus are easy to detect when waters are clear enough, but difficult to see, since they are engulfed in great clouds of sediments that they create as they go. The signs of foraging walrus cover the sea floor. They leave furrows from 5.5 to 22 yards (5–20 m) long, as well as dig from 5 to 35 small, shallow pits per 2.5 acres (1 ha). In one of the few studies in which wild walrus were observed feeding, the animals predominantly used their right flippers to clear sediments. Researchers then followed up by measuring walrus skeletons and found that in 23 animals, their right forelimbs were significantly longer than their left.

Occasionally walrus eat slow fish. The odd rogue walrus may develop an unusual appetite for seal carcasses or actively hunt and consume young seals. Walrus have also been documented feeding on the skin and blubber of dead whales and raiding easily accessible seabird nesting colonies, where they hoover eggs and fledglings alike.

HABITAT AND HOME RANGE

The walrus is an Arctic-dwelling marine mammal with a circumpolar range. The population spanning Alaska and western Siberia, called the Pacific walrus, is considered separate and distinct from the Atlantic walrus population, which occupies the far northeast of Canada and Greenland. Walrus live on

A foraging walrus digs a trough along the sea floor, uncovering benthic bivalves upon which it feeds.

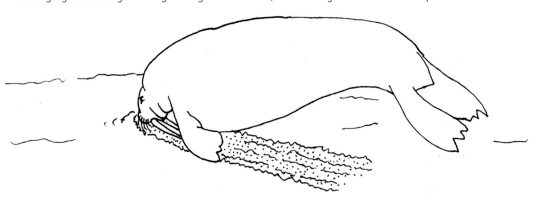

oceanic ice floes throughout the year, as well as haul out on rocks and sandy shores of small islands in the southern parts of their range.

COMMUNICATION

Walrus are social beasts, and in close proximity there are numerous squabbles occurring at all times within the herd. Dominance among walrus is based upon size and strength, but also upon the length and girth of an animal's tusks. They hold their tusks high and horizontal to the earth or water to communicate agitation and threat, and this behavior is often observed when males are clambering over and between each other in search of a resting spot at a rookery, or while males are maintaining their tiny breeding circles in frigid ocean waters. Walrus also cough, bark, and gnash their teeth to create a loud chattering sound intended to intimidate encroaching animals. Submissive walrus attempting to appease dominants erect their stiff mustache whiskers to communicate submission, and if this doesn't work they move away from the aggressor with speed.

When basking as a herd, walrus take turns acting as sentinels for the group. When an animal spots a potential predator, the sentinel utters a long, low whistle that sends the herd scrambling for the safety provided by ocean waters.

COURTSHIP AND MATING

Reproduction in walrus is a long-term investment. Females do not begin to ovulate until they are 6 or 7 years old; males are not sexually mature until they are 8 to 10 years old. Even then, younger males will not be able to compete with dominant bulls until they are about 15, and then, finally, they can begin to participate in mating. Walrus are polygynous, and sex ratios in a breeding colony may be as dramatic as 1 male for every 10 females. Males compete physically and through acoustic and visual displays for dominance in the herd and to attract females.

The breeding season runs from December into February during the dark Arctic winter. The males and females intermingle along the southern edges of the ice sheets that crept south during the autumn, and together they exhibit lekking behavior. Males competing for breeding opportunities set up small amorphous territories approximately 35 feet (11 m) apart in the ocean waters adjacent to ice floes where females haul out to rest. The boundaries of these territories shift and bend with pressures from other territorial males and the shifting ice itself.

Breeding males display both below and above the water, and their displays are likely both a challenge and deterrent to other males, as well as an attractant to females. Males submerge and "sing," emitting a series of metallic, bell-like sounds using unusual pouches in their throats. Next they produce a series of sounds similar to someone knocking on a door. Then the males surface and produce first a series of whistles and then a series of rattling sounds created by chattering their teeth. The riotous chorus of breeding males among the ice floes is said to be deafening, but with time, the females somehow differentiate among them and select a suitor. Having done so, an estrous female wiggles over to the edge of the ice floe, slips into the ocean to approach her chosen male, and then they mate. Occasionally males exit the water, chase females into the ocean, and then mate with them there, presumably by force.

During the breeding season males are less likely to respond submissively to the threat display of other males. When another walrus is not intimidated by displays, the threatening walrus immediately bluff charges its opponent. If this, too, fails to elicit submission, the pair battle with their swordlike tusks while roaring and growling with passion. The skin on the necks of breeding males is covered in ugly, wartlike tubercles that may be up to 2 inches (5 cm) thick. This armor serves as an outer layer of protection from a rival's stabbing tusks. Even so, males are sometimes killed by other males during courtship contests.

DEVELOPMENT AND DISPERSAL OF YOUNG

Walrus gestations are long, as is the time they invest in caring for and raising their calves. Eggs fertilized in the breeding season enter suspended animation (delayed implantation) until the summer months, before they resume their 10 to 11 months of development. In the following spring from April into June, which is a full 15 months after the breeding season, females give birth to a single calf or, on rare occasions, twins.

The walrus on the right exhibits dominance and a raised-tusk threat. The walrus on the left concedes its submission by turning laterally to the dominant animal.

An adult female reflexively clasps her calf close at the approach of a diver and potential danger. © *Paul Nicklen/National Geographic Image Collection*

Each calf is born at 120 to 140 pounds (60–65 kg) and approximately 4.5 feet (1.5 m) in length. Calves are born precocial and are completely dependent upon their mother for their first few weeks. During their first year of life walrus calves drink 7 percent of their body weight in milk every day (14 pounds of milk for a 200-pound walrus) and manage to triple their birth weight by their first birthday. They nurse less but continue to suckle for 2 to 3 years, gradually becoming more and more dependent on a diet of benthic bivalves. Calves disperse somewhere between 2 and 2.5 years of age, allowing females to breed and birth a single calf at roughly 3-year intervals, one of the lowest fecundity rates among mammals.

Be warned that females are said to defend their calves with dangerous attention. If threats are perceived, mothers typically clasp their calves to them, but if dangers persist, females may charge and attack. Walrus have also been documented going to great lengths to carry away their dead calves killed by hunters.

INTERACTIONS AMONG WALRUS

Walrus routinely lie in contact or even atop one another at haulouts, even when there is sufficient space to lie separately. A sleeping herd is a chorus of grunts, roars, groans, and rumbling vocalizations. Walrus joining the sleeping mass of bodies must negotiate a path to a free patch of ice and may need to threat display, bluff charge, or roar in order to gain passage beyond a series of challengers. On occasion calves are crushed and killed by adults moving about at haulouts.

INTERACTIONS WITH OTHER SPECIES

Like earthworms and pocket gophers on land, walrus are the bioturbators of northern sea floors. As walrus plow furrows in ocean sediments in search of bivalves, they stir up and release nutrients into the ocean, making them available to be used by diverse organisms. It's estimated that a quarter to half of the sea floor in the Chukchi Sea between northern Alaska and Russia is disturbed by walrus each year and that the entire Chukchi Sea floor is disturbed on a 3-year cycle. Such large-scale sedimentary movements are essential to the populations of zoo- and phytoplankton that form the foundation of Arctic food webs, but the larger effects of walrus bioturbation on Arctic oceans remain unknown, and are only now being researched and quantified.

Walrus appear to be feared by other smaller pinnipeds, and they routinely displace Ringed Seals and others at haulouts. Other than humans, adult walrus have little to fear from predators. Their thick skin and fierce tusks make them very difficult prey for Polar Bears and other top carnivores. Occasionally adult walrus and, more frequently, calves fall prey to orcas (killer whales) or large bears.

Two males exhibit their tusks to settle a dispute at a haulout area. © *istockphoto.com/Tersina Shieh*

Along the coast of California tens of thousands of Northern Elephant Seals haul out on the beaches to breed and molt each year. Elephant seals are the opposite of harbor seals in many ways. Bulls are huge, nearly 2.5 times the length of the average man and more than 25 times heavier. Such size makes their breeding battles extremely dramatic. They are without fear of humans or other land predators and provide stunning opportunities for observation in places such as San Simeon Beach and Año Nuevo State Natural Area in California, homes of some of the largest breeding colonies in the world. Their brief appearance onshore is accentuated by their lifestyle of huge migrations, during which they spend up to 10 months continually diving as much as a mile deep at sea.

Mirounga is derived from *miouroung*, a Native Australian term for the elephant seal. The species name means "narrow" (*angusti-*) "nose" (*rostris*), describing the bull Northern Elephant Seal's snout in comparison to the broader nose of the "lionlike" Southern Elephant Seal (*M. leonina*).

ACTIVITY AND MOVEMENT

DAILY

Seal movement on land is wormlike, with some assistance from the front flippers. Since they are unable to fully raise themselves up on their front flippers or walk on their hind flippers like sea lions and fur seals, seals simply lurch their bodies up off the ground, pull strongly with their front flippers, and scoot ahead bit by bit. Despite the awkward mechanics, their soft, blubbery flexibility and considerable strength contribute to a remarkable fluidity when moving across beaches and rocks.

Given their huge size and the warm temperatures at their rookeries, elephant seals are most active in morning and evening and least active at midday. When seals are hot they often flip sand onto their bodies with a sweeping motion of the fore flippers. Sand-flipping serves to protect the skin from the hot, burning sun, but it can also be a sign of arousal.

Seals swim by means of an alternate side-to-side waving of their hind flippers, with their neck retracted and their fore flippers usually held tight to the body. The hind flippers seem small compared to the seal's bulky torso, but they are flexible webs of flesh supported by long "toe" bones that splay, fanlike, when they "kick." The widespread flippers catch a large amount of water, providing a strong push, and then fold up compactly on the recovery stroke. Their front flippers, which are thicker and stouter, are used for maneuvering. Because of their blubber, they are neutrally buoyant—they neither sink nor float. Although water offers more resistance than air, elephant seals essentially swim the way astronauts float without gravity.

Male elephant seals spend 8 to 9 months and females up to 10 months a year at sea, often thousands of miles offshore, diving and breathing, diving and breathing, constantly. Adults do not haul out to rest, and they come ashore only twice a year to breed and molt. Diving down for about 23 minutes, they rarely pause for longer than 5 minutes on the surface before they dive again. During normal foraging they usually dive no deeper than 1,100 to 2,000 feet (350–600 m). However, the deepest dives recorded for both males and females are nearly a mile down (1,600m)! Among mammals, only sperm whales are known to dive deeper. The longest dive on record is nearly 2 hours long—think about holding your breath that long. At the bottom of deep dives, elephant seals slow their heart rate to 4 beats per minute to minimize oxygen use.

Seals exhibit a variety of different dive "shapes," depending on the sex and age of the animal and what it is doing. Most of their dives are foraging dives (see Food and Foraging), but even when migrating to and from foraging areas, elephant seals use a succession of dives rather than swim across the surface. Descending and ascending at angles, the seals can cover a large horizontal distance with each V-shaped "transit" dive. They are incredibly efficient underwater swimmers, and on the continental shelf, traveling by diving may help them avoid predators like sharks in the upper waters.

SEASONAL

Elephant seals migrate 11,000 to 13,000 miles (18,000–21,000 km) each year, making two separate round trips between their offshore feeding areas and traditional rookery beaches, first to breed and then to molt.

Bulls land at their rookeries in late November and December. Females arrive in mid-December and January and within a few days give birth to new pups. After caring for the new pups for a month, the females breed again, then wean their pups and depart for the open sea between late January and mid-March. They travel to their foraging areas and feed over a wide area spanning nearly 1,400 miles (2,240 km) north to south and 2,400 miles (3,840 km) from the coasts of Washington and Oregon out into the Pacific Ocean. Individual females wander within this area, following mobile, shifting concentrations of food. They spend 2 months feeding to restock their bodies after having fasted while on shore breeding. In April and May they return to

Male elephant seals resting against each other between episodes of startling violence. © *Tanguy de Tillesse*

the duration of their time on shore. Minimizing their energy expenditures, they spend much of their time sleeping. When sleeping, their heart rate and metabolism slow down, just as when they are diving. They sometimes even stop breathing for 5 to 20 minute intervals. The only thing that gets them moving is a fight or the opportunity to mate.

FOOD AND FORAGING

Elephant seal males and females forage quite differently. Male elephant seals mostly eat sluggish, benthic (bottom-dwelling) prey along the coastal shelf. This includes dogfish and other sharks, sculpins, ratfish, skates and stingrays, eels, hagfish, flatfish, and octopus. Females, juveniles, and to a lesser extent males, too, eat squid and fish at mid-depths between the surface and bottom.

Males generally forage using flat-bottomed dives and rapid ascents and descents. While at the bottom of the dive, they travel at a relatively constant speed, following the contours of the sea floor, picking off tasty tidbits. Females and juveniles mostly forage in the upper pelagic zone (below the surface, but well up from the sea floor) and chase their prey. They dive steeply down to the depth of their prey and zigzag up and down with extreme variations in speed as they pursue it. All elephant seals also use "drift dives" with long, shallow-angled descent and a shorter, steeper return. After catching something on a foraging dive, the elephant seal comes up for a breath and then glides slowly downward, processing, handling, and eating its food on the way. Rarely, male elephant seals make another kind of drifting dive, during which they travel all the way to the sea floor, but don't swim at all once they're there. What they are doing is a mystery.

Elephant seals are visual predators that forage in the twilight zone where sunlight barely reaches. Bioluminescent squid and fish—those that make their own light like fireflies—may be important prey items, but elephant seals may rely on their other senses more under these conditions. Many of the animals in the sea migrate up and down as light levels change, retreating lower during the day and then rising up at night. This lets them access the more abundant foods in the upper waters without leaving the relative protection of darkness. Elephant seals benefit from this, often meeting their prey closer to the surface on shorter foraging dives at night.

HABITAT AND HOME RANGE

Elephant seals breed on coastal and island beaches from Baja California north through California and into Oregon. Their populations have been growing over the past century, leading to an increase in the number and distribution of rookeries. They prefer beaches protected from waves and tide. They ap-

their southern rookeries to haul out and molt, going back to their foraging grounds in late May and June to spend the next 6 to 8 months feeding. They return to pup and breed in January.

Male elephant seals leave the rookeries once the females have all departed in February and March. Their foraging areas are north of the female foraging zone, in the Gulf of Alaska and along the Aleutian Islands. Males tend to use traditional migratory routes and foraging sites that they return to again and again. After 3 to 4 months of feeding there, they head back south to the rookeries to molt for 3 to 4 weeks in June and July. Once the molt is over they return to Alaskan waters to feed for another 5 months before heading to their rookeries to breed.

After pups are weaned they immediately molt and lose their black natal fur in favor of a silver coat that fades to light brown with wear. While molting they fast for 6 to 8 weeks before going to sea to forage. Juveniles seem to stay closer to shore; they are sighted foraging along the coast more frequently than adults. When they haul out they do so at times when the adults are at sea to minimize conflict. They haul out at the traditional rookeries in the fall, from September to November, for a month or so, but avoid them during the breeding season. They also haul out there to molt in April or May, depending on age and sex.

During the periods adult seals (and newborns) are on shore for breeding and molting, only the suckling pups eat. All other elephant seals fast for pear to have little concern for terrestrial predators, but juveniles are easily disturbed by humans, as are newly established colonies. Individual seals return to the same rookery beaches year after year.

At sea their foraging habitat is determined by availability of prey and avoidance of predators. Elephant seals are pelagic (off-shore, in upper waters) and benthic (at the sea floor) feeders. They are excellent divers, and by foraging in deep waters they can find food and avoid their only real threat: large sharks. Their foraging areas presumably support abundant prey, given that the seals can grow so tremendously large. They are hard-wired to visit these areas year after year, and doing so has allowed a rapid recovery of the species now that it is protected from hunting.

COMMUNICATION

Seals are limited in their social communication, especially on land, by virtue of their adaptations to life in the water. They cannot adopt many body postures and lack ears, tails, and erectile hair. Their aquatic lifestyle makes scenting ineffective and militates against showy adornments, like manes or horns, that other mammals use for signaling. The male elephant seal sports an elastic, tubular proboscis, or trunk, that is used in visual and vocal signaling, but interferes little with swimming and diving.

Elephant seals rely on visual and vocal threat rituals, and sometimes on combat, to establish dominance hierarchies. Vocal threats include snorts (expulsion of air through the proboscis) and growls, and might come from males or females. The primary vocal threat, the "clap threat," is made by the males when displaying for dominance. This strange and extremely loud sound is far from a roar, although it is often referred to as such. It is a resonant, metallic clapping sound that suggests the exhaust sound of a diesel engine. Clap threats are individually distinct and likely communicate identity, size, and status of the bull making them. The calls are learned, at least to some degree, and show dialectal variations between distant rookeries.

Males display visually by inflating and extending their proboscis. They turn their heads upward so that the end of their snout falls into their open mouth while they vocalize their clap threats. Vocalizations can be issued from the "low-rear" or the "high-rear" position, which refers to how high the head rears up, not how high the rear end is lifted. In the low-rear position, the body is mostly flat with just the head and upper chest lifted upward off the beach. In the high-rear position, half of the body is held erect and the fore flippers may even leave the ground. From this position bulls fight with wild lunging head swings, usually made with an open mouth, batting into the chest, head, and shoulders

of their rivals. They signal submission by backing away with the proboscis retracted. Females also use vocalizations, head thrusts, and biting, usually against other females on crowded beaches.

Elephant seal pups produce two calls that elicit their mothers' attention when in distress or wanting to suckle. Mothers are evidently able to discriminate between their own and others' young because they respond positively to their offspring but not to others. If the beach is very crowded, pups often get separated from their mothers, and the two call out to one another in an effort to reunite.

COURTSHIP AND MATING

Female elephant seals come ashore to give birth and, subsequently, to mate. Since they breed on land, a strong male can monopolize numerous females, using his size and aggression to limit access by other males.

In December and January bull elephant seals begin arriving and setting up small territories on breeding beaches. As females start arriving in January, they congregate thickly, and the bulls that hold the best beach spots have access to the most females for mating. The arriving females become the breeding harems of the "beachmaster" bulls. The females "join" a harem simply by grabbing a particular piece of beach. The older, stronger females grab the best beach sites, and these tend to be held by the strongest bulls. Actual harem membership fluctuates as beachmasters compete and boundaries shift. For the next 3 months these huge animals compete to control access to a harem of females that may number over 100.

Defending a harem means being always vigilant for trespassing males. Only large mature bulls, those 9 years old or more, mate, but younger and subordinate males try to sneak in and copulate with females if they think they can get away with it. Weaker males may hold territories in less attractive sections of the beach, and if another bull's harem is very large, an assistant beachmaster—a sort of institutionalized apprentice—can attach himself to the group. Other "satellite" males lurk along the edges.

If a "sneaker" is spotted, or a neighbor wanders too close, the beachmaster rushes to confront him, a boiling bag of blubber rippling with surprising speed across the beach. The beachmaster displays and threatens by raising his head with mouth open and inflated "trunk" hanging into his mouth. He utters his growling clap threat from a low-rear position. If submission is not immediate, or if the beachmaster is particularly full of steam, the two bulls face off, rearing up on their fore flippers until their heads are towering 8 feet (2.5 m) or more above the beach. At any point one can submit by retracting his proboscis and turning away. If the contest continues, they strike at one another's face, chest, and back with swinging strikes of the head. These are wild, forceful, open-mouthed swipes, and the canine teeth of bull elephant seals are larger than those of Grizzly Bears. Lots of superficial wounds to the head and neck are common; lips and eyes are ripped, teeth get broken, and in long battles the sand or frothing waves around the pair turns red with their blood. Fighting is exhausting, and should it continue for long, the bulls take breaks at intervals and lean against each other to remain upright. They may fight for 10 minutes, swapping powerful blows and savage bites, and then rest peaceably against each other for 20 minutes before they start in again.

The female's first priority is to give birth to the single pup she conceived the year before. A few days before the month of nursing nears its end, the female enters estrus again and mates, conceiving another pup to be born a year later on the very same beach. Once bred, she turns her full attention to resting and nursing her newborn, nearly weaned pup. Copulation occurs when a male crawls to, and partly on, an estrous female, pinning her head and neck to the sand with his mouth. He holds his near-side fore flipper over her back, immobilizing her, scoots his hips forward, and mates with her.

Once the female has bred and her pup is weaned, she soon takes to the sea. As she is heading back to sea she has to be careful to avoid male attention. Although she is no longer receptive, nearby males may attack departing females and force them to copulate. Very rarely, females may be injured or even killed in the process.

DEVELOPMENT AND DISPERSAL OF YOUNG

Gestation in elephant seals lasts about 11 months, including a 2- to 3-month implantation delay. Elephant seal pups are born in January within a few days of the female's arrival at the rookery. Male newborns, which are slightly larger than females, are nearly 5 feet (1.5 m) long and weigh 80 pounds (36 kg). The mother nurses her young for a month on milk that grows increasingly dense, with more fat and less water, as time passes. Fasting mothers lose nearly half of their mass to feed their pups. At weaning, pups weigh up to an astonishing 280 pounds (130 kg), a three-fold increase. Elephant seal pups molt immediately after weaning and fast on land for 6 to 8 weeks, during which time they lose about 20 percent of their overall mass.

Youngsters are inexperienced in how and where to get food, and they are physiologically limited in their ability to dive. Limited dive capacity may further limit their foraging and may expose young seals to predation by sharks and orcas (killer whales). Once an elephant seal pup enters the water for good and heads north, it has only a 50 percent chance of surviving its first 7 months until hauling out again in the fall. Up to 60 percent die before their first birthday.

Elephant seals are programmed to find their foraging areas and then return to the rookeries. In experiments, 8- to 10-month-old pups return to their

Male-male contests between elephant seals are bloody and ferocious, though the thick skin around their neck and head offers males some protection. © *Tanguy de Tillesse*

A mammoth male slides up behind the much smaller female to mate with her on the beach. © *Tanguy de Tillesse*

rookeries if captured and released up to 60 miles (100 km) away. Juveniles, those that have made the trip to their foraging grounds and back once already, are even better, traveling very direct routes and covering about 24 miles (39 km) per day.

Female elephant seals do not become successful breeders until they are 2 to 5 years old or older. Most males mate starting at around 8 years old, even though they are biologically mature years earlier. In order to compete socially for females, they need to be very big, and that takes time. Male elephant seals have a tremendous growth rate and an equally tremendous mortality rate. Only about 10 percent of bulls live to breed at 8 to 10 years of age. The highest male breeding success is among 12- to 13-year-old bulls, and only 1 percent of bulls survive to that age. That, plus intense competition for breeding territories, results in many fewer bulls than females at the rookeries. In one rookery there were 77 males to 306 females.

INTERACTIONS AMONG ELEPHANT SEALS

For all the drama and bluster of a fight between two 2.5-ton animals, elephant seals actually spend little time in aggressive conflict. Less than 1 percent of their interactions are agonistic, and most of those are visual and auditory displays. Almost all of the time the animals are on the beach is spent resting.

When necessary, females vocalize and fight with one another and attack others' pups. If a beach is crowded, adult females gape and growl, trying to maintain a bubble of safety around their own pups. Young nonbreeding males "wrestle" to practice dominance fighting.

One of the reasons larger and older females are more successful at rearing pups is that they are more socially dominant. Young female breeders are subject to the aggression of higher status females. This harassment leads to higher pup deaths among young females through being forced into poor sites on the rookeries, frequent and tiring interactions and displacements, direct injury to them and their pups, and separation from the pups. Separation is the leading cause of death among elephant seal pups; this and attacks by females on pups are more frequent when beaches are crowded. Some pups starve when they are unable to reunite with their mothers, some die from vicious bites from unrelated adult females, and others get trampled by displaying and clashing males.

On crowded beaches and in storms, elephant seal pups may be separated from their mothers. In this case a mother seal swims up and down the beach vocalizing and hauling out to sniff and inspect pups that she encounters. Pups, too, swim up and down the beach, searching for their mothers. In

A great white shark attacks a seal from below off the coast of the Farallon Islands near San Francisco, and launches out of the water gripping its prey.

some cases they never find one another, and if the pup is lucky it will be adopted by a foster mother. Elephant seal pups may be adopted by a female that has lost a pup, or they might be partially cared for by a number of females. However, an orphan trying to "steal" milk from a sleeping female will be attacked viciously if she arouses. Most orphans die of starvation or bite wounds.

INTERACTIONS WITH OTHER SPECIES

Elephant seals are preyed on by sharks, primarily great whites, especially when the seals pause, floating on the surface, to recover from the exertion of diving. Great white sharks along the central coast of California attack seals in the water surrounding their colonies. At Año Nuevo State Park, up to 13 white sharks have been spotted at one time from the peninsula near the seal rookery. Sharks sometimes attack seals as they are exiting or entering the water and nearly beach themselves in a spray of blood and water before disappearing back into the deeper, darker waters with their victim. White sharks near South Africa are famous for swimming up beneath a seal at such speed that they launch from the water and hang momentarily in the air, seal grasped in their jaws. These displays are less common along coastal North America, but are occasionally seen at the Farallon Islands near San Francisco, where sharks hunt harbor seals, sea lions, and elephant seals.

Elephant seals are also attacked and killed by orcas, though a large bull with his backside protected by a rock wall or shoreline can sometimes successfully fend off his attackers. Elephant seals, for all their size and ferocity, are amazingly docile toward humans. Their placidity onshore bespeaks thousands of years spent onshore with no fear of predation.

Sea Otter
Enhydra lutris

OTHER NAMES: chngatu (Atkan Aleut).

Sea Otters once ranged all along the northern Pacific Rim from Baja California north across the Aleutian Archipelago, north to the Pribilof Islands, and southwest to Japan. Their rich, dense fur is the key to their survival in cold waters, and it is highly desirable to humans. Sea Otters are also docile and easily approached, and human hunting nearly wiped them out by the late 1800s. Russian traders and adventurers had been traveling as far south as Baja California to hunt Sea Otters in specially designed kayaks, but they had managed to institute regulations to control their harvests. After the United States purchased Alaska from the Russians, unregulated harvests resumed, ushering in the species' near extinction within decades.

At the dawn of the 20th century over 800,000 Sea Otters had been killed for their fur, a prime pelt was going for $1,125 in London, and there were only approximately 1,000 to 2,000 Sea Otters remaining in the world. Yet under strict conservation protections, by the 1990s their numbers had increased to more than 150,000. Sea Otters still face a number of threats, although hunting for fur is no longer one of them. Today, changes in the oceanic food webs from over-fishing, changing ocean currents, and global warming are a much greater threat. Diminished populations of seals and sea lions could be causing orcas (killer whales) to switch to Sea Otters to sustain them off the coast of Alaska.

Enhydra derives from Greek and means "in water." *Lutris* is Latin for "otter."

ACTIVITY AND MOVEMENT

DAILY

Sea Otters are diurnal and even more aquatic than seals, very rarely coming ashore. They are equipped to live out their entire lives at sea; they mate and give birth while afloat and can drink seawater to quench their thirst. Where local population densities are high and shores are free of disturbance (e.g., humans) they may come ashore to rest.

In repose, Sea Otters float belly-up on the surface of the sea, sometimes anchoring themselves by wrapping up in floating kelp fronds. The amount of resting varies depending on availability of food, weather conditions, and sex and age. In newly occupied areas, where food supplies are plentiful, Sea Otters may spend less than 20 percent of their time feeding, more than half their time resting, and the remainder grooming, swimming, and interacting with other otters. In areas that Sea Otters have in-habited for a long time, reducing the amount of prey available, the average otter may spend nearly 50 percent of its time feeding. Females with pups may spend 13 or more hours a day feeding (and another 4 hours grooming their pup). In winter, when sea conditions are rougher and the water and air colder, Sea Otters expend more energy just lying on their back, so feeding time must be further increased.

In areas rich in food, Sea Otters may feed for short periods in early morning and evening. Else-where, feeding occurs throughout the day, with a shorter bout of resting. Where nocturnally active crabs are the chief food, Sea Otters feed mostly at night. However, in no areas are otters strictly diur-nal or nocturnal.

Grooming is critical to Sea Otter survival in the cold waters they call home. Sea Otters lack blub-ber, the thick layer of fat that insulates other marine mammals, so they rely on their fur to stay warm. Fortunately, Sea Otters possess the richest, thickest fur of any mammal. Humans have about 100,000 hairs on their entire heads, and dogs have about 56,000 hairs per square inch (9,000 per cm^2). River otters, which also spend much of their time swim-ming in cold waters, have an amazing 375,000 hairs per square inch (60,000 per cm^2). Sea Otters have an absolutely astounding 1,025,000 hairs per square inch (164,000 per cm^2). Of course, this luxuriant pelage also led to their decimation by fur hunters.

A Sea Otter's rich coat is only a good insulator if it is clean, waterproof, and filled with air. Ulti-mately it is the trapped air that buffers the loss of body heat to the surroundings. Grooming is so crit-ical to maintaining proper insulation that you can easily witness their stereotyped and often-repeated sequence of behaviors. After a bout of hunting or feeding, the animal engages in energetic somer-saulting and rolling followed by vigorous licking, rubbing with its forepaws, and blowing into the fur. The warm breath blown into the fur adds insulation and buoyancy. It floats on its back and rubs and blows its face, neck, paws, flippers, and tail.

Their broad, webbed hind feet are the site of the greatest heat exchange with their environment. Sea Otters are often seen holding them up in the air like solar panels to collect heat when floating on their backs on warm, sunny days. Despite this and their fur's insulation, keeping warm also demands a high level of metabolic activity. Sea Otters must produce 3 times as much heat as would a mammal of similar size living on land, and to do this they must eat 20 to 30 percent of their body mass in food every day.

SEASONAL

For much of the year large groups of mostly young males congregate in "male areas," sites near the frontiers of an expanding population or in patches of less-preferred habitats among well-established populations. Female areas occur in more estab-lished parts of the range, in areas suitable for pup-ping. They are often less discrete and less densely populated than the male areas. Mature males es-tablish and maintain breeding territories for at least part of the year in the female areas, often returning to male areas during nonbreeding seasons. In some populations these males may make seasonal trips of 60 to 90 miles (100–150 km) to and from male and female areas. Subadult males are rarely seen in the female areas. After young males leave their mother they disperse to a male area. How they find them for the first time is unknown.

After the breeding season males typically leave their territory and either move to a male area or re-main dispersed throughout the female areas, mill-ing about and using a more typical home range. Males may be prompted to travel to distant areas because frontier areas offer better food quality and availability. Pioneering of new areas as populations expand is led by males venturing from male areas into unexploited waters.

FOOD AND FORAGING

Sea Otters eat a variety of bottom-dwelling marine invertebrates and fish, but they consume all of their food at the surface. Their preferred foods are sea ur-chins, crabs, and clams. However, their diets vary tremendously by habitat and the length of time an area has been occupied. In the Aleutian Islands of western Alaska, where Sea Otter populations are well established, urchins and similar invertebrates are fewer and kelp beds are more developed, pro-viding protection and food to a greater abundance of fishes. Sea Otters there eat urchins and fish, but otters east of the Aleutians eat few fish. The fish they eat most are sculpins, greenlings, scorpionfish, and, best of all, lumpsuckers. These are all smallish fish that live in rocky nooks and crevices and feed on small invertebrates. Lumpsuckers are bulbous, chunky fish that swim weakly and spend their time clinging onto rocks with pectoral fins adapted into a suction disc. What's more, some lumpsucker spe-cies are superabundant, providing an occasional bumper crop of easily caught mouthfuls.

Behavioral studies show a wide range of feeding preferences within a population. One researcher re-marked on a "striking absence of generalists" among the female Sea Otters studied over many years, a fact which may minimize competition among otters in areas of high density. Coastal marine environments include a great diversity of potential foods, yet each requires relatively specialized skills for find-ing and securing them. One male otter discovered that octopuses often go into old cans, so he learned

A Sea Otter dismantling a large crab and using its stomach as a table. © *Kim Worrell/Dreamstime.com*

to search for and bite open discarded cans. Others learn to hunt seabirds. No single otter can master all the skills necessary for every available food, so they specialize and transmit these skills culturally from mother to young.

On a foraging dive, a Sea Otter investigates the nooks and crannies of the ocean bottom, peering into them and feeling for food with its long whiskers and sometimes its forepaws. Sea Otters are excellent at finding clams in muddy bottoms, much better than humans with diving masks, but how they find them is a mystery. Perhaps they detect the subtle movements of water from the clams' siphons or detect some electrical impulse.

If a Sea Otter collects a particularly large clam, something that can't be opened by prying or cracking with the teeth, it also needs to collect a rock from the bottom. After surfacing with the rock tucked under its armpit, the otter reclines and lays the rock on its belly as an anvil. Holding the clam in both forepaws, it lifts it overhead and repeatedly slams it down on the rock. It continues pounding until the shell loosens or cracks enough for the otter to pry it open with its teeth. Not all Sea Otters use anvils, but in the long term the rib cages of otters that do a lot of pounding get flattened from the banging.

HABITAT AND HOME RANGE

Typical Sea Otter habitat is kelp beds and rocky shores in cold marine environments. They usually live in water up to about 100 feet (30 m) deep, although they have been known to dive to depths of 325 feet (100 m). Whereas river otters are sometimes seen in the ocean, Sea Otters never forage in fresh water.

Territorial males defend small territories during the breeding season, where they exclude other males. These are a tenth or less the size of an actual home range, but are quite variable, measuring 10 to 550 acres (4–225 ha). Other males may occasionally pass through, but can't stop to forage or rest there. If they do, the territory holder vigorously chases them out, sometimes involving a brief fight. Females, in contrast, can enter male territories any time of year and are enticed to do so during the breeding season. Females are not territorial, and their home ranges average 7 to 10 square miles (18–25 km^2).

COMMUNICATION

Being so highly aquatic, Sea Otters lack much of the scent-marking behaviors of other otters. They do have well-developed olfaction, and they come ashore occasionally and defecate, but scent-marking is of little value to them. Most of their territorial interactions take place at sea, where olfaction is direct and short-range, rather than indirect through static marks. When joining a group of other resting otters, the newcomer approaches and sniffs many or all of the individuals.

Aural and visual communication includes splashing and vigorous kicking on the surface of the water as well as various vocalizations. Up to 10 distinct vocalizations have been identified, including screams, whistles, whines, hisses, snarls, growls, coos, and grunts. Most are rather soft and not heard by human observers. They are invariable for an individual, like the bark of your neighbor's dog. On the other hand, Sea Otter squeals, growls, and grunts are "graded" signals, ones that can vary along a continuum from mild to intense, like a human's smile. Graded signals are associated with animals that have complex social relationships.

Screams are loud, shrill, and individually distinct. They are made from an open mouth and can be heard for over 0.6 miles (1 km). Mothers and pups scream back and forth when separated or in distress, although the pups do most of the screaming. Whines are low-volume, low-frequency calls made with a closed mouth. Whines appear to be begging or solicitation calls and are uttered by young being groomed or attempting to suckle, or a male attempting to reach an estrous female for mating. Whines are interspersed with whimpers and squeals if associated with distress. Whines and squeals are used often during the mating season. Whistles are high-pitched, raspy, and tonal. These are uttered in stressful situations, as when an individual is captured by researchers. Squeals are rarely uttered on their own. Rather, they are used as squeal-whines or squeal-screams, graded calls indicative of elevating distress. Cooing is a close-contact call between mother and young or other closely bonded individuals. Grunts are used in stress-free situations and appear similar to cooing.

COURTSHIP AND MATING

Sea Otters are polygamous and can breed throughout the year. In Alaska most breeding occurs in the fall, September to November, with most births in May and June. In California breeding and birthing are much less synchronized, although a weak peak in pupping occurs from December to March, and mating 6 months before that. Females are not sexually mature until at least their third year. And

males are usually more than 5 years old before they are able to hold a territory and mate successfully. Females can breed every year, but may skip a year, especially in food-stressed populations.

The females control the mating process by choosing which males they visit. Some males try to sequester females within their territories by closely tending them, but ultimately males with "good" territories—meaning large, relatively protected by the coast, accessible to females, and with plenty of food—tend to mate more than males with poor territories.

Mature males establish their breeding territories in the vicinity of female areas. They defend them infrequently by fighting and mostly by splashing and kicking and by harassing intruders. They tolerate female "intruders" and also seek them out, swimming quickly to them on their belly, with their head above water. When a female is in the territory the male and female physically interact, sniffing, touching, nuzzling, and diving synchronously for food. This consortship may last several days, with mating occurring multiple times on one day. Coitus is aggressive. The female is belly-down in the water, and the male mounts her by climbing onto her back and biting her on the nose and face to secure himself as they mate and tumble about. Females have been known to drown while mating, and they can be injured by these bites to the face. The biting is so much a part of the process that nose-scars are used as field marks indicative of a female that has mated. Males often try to tend females for a few days after mating, to prevent them from mating with another male, although they are not always successful at doing so.

DEVELOPMENT AND DISPERSAL OF YOUNG

Gestation in Sea Otters typically lasts about 6 months but appears to vary among populations. The fertilized egg enters a state of suspended animation for about 2 months or more before implanting in the lining of the uterus to continue its development. Litter size is almost invariably one; in the rare case of twins, the mother must abandon one of them.

When born, a pup's fur is saturated and matted, which can be deadly. Pups need dry, air-filled fur for buoyancy and insulation. The first thing the mother does is pull the tiny pup, little bigger than her head, to her chest with her forelimbs and groom it thoroughly by licking and rubbing its fur. One mother groomed her newborn for 2.5 hours, took a short break, and then groomed the pup for another hour and 15 minutes. At that point the pup was dry and fluffy, so she repositioned it with her forepaws so it could have its first suckle. She laid the pup with its head down near her abdomen,

A Sea Otter pounds a clam on a stone anvil.

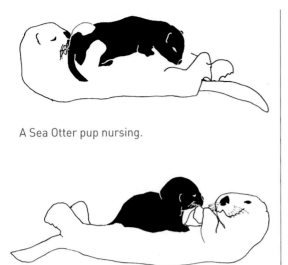

A Sea Otter pup nursing.

A Sea Otter pup begs for food on its mother's belly.

where her two nipples are located; she then continued to groom its back end and tail, which was near her face. Only after nearly 4 hours of constant grooming did she set it aside to float passively while she vigorously groomed herself for 10 minutes. Once done, she replaced the pup on her chest and had a well-earned rest.

The mother is in constant attendance of the pup, often clutching it in her forearms or carrying it on her belly. They are primate-like in their grasping of one another, hugging with their arms around each other's necks. At first, pups are suckled 6 times daily, and each bout averages just under 10 minutes. A small pup suckles while lying on its mother's chest with its head at her abdominal nipples. While the pup nurses, the mother grooms its tail and anogenital region. As pups get larger they lie crosswise, with their head and forepaws on their mother's abdomen and their body in the water. Mothers initiate suckling in small pups by putting them into position with their forepaws. As the pups grow, they begin to take the initiative.

When diving for food, the mother places a small pup aside to float and await her return. This is when the pups are most vulnerable and are sometimes taken by bald eagles and other predators. They are not only helpless (unable to swim or dive), but also readily draw attention to themselves. Often, when the mother dives, the pup begins calling for her and does so with increasing intensity until she returns. When mothers are present, pup vocalizing is followed by nursing and in some cases, lifting the pup to their face by "hugging" it around the neck, and then licking its face and head. This is unlike grooming and appears to be a specific comfort gesture.

When pups are about 2 months old they begin to dive. Their early fur is woolly and too buoyant for them to submerge, but as it gradually changes to its adult texture they can start learning to swim and forage for themselves. When they are very young their mothers give them castoff shells that they manipulate with paws and mouth. Some can be seen immediately attempting the stereotyped hammering motions they will later use to open tough shellfish. When its mother dives the pup remains on the surface, sometimes turning belly-down and putting its head underwater to watch its mother. As they begin to dive on their own, pups often obtain empty shells from the bottom. Upon realizing this at the surface, a pup scrambles onto its mother's chest and forces her to give up some food. With time, the duration of their dives and their proficiency at finding and processing food improves.

Mothers with pups can be seen feeding close to one another or resting together with their pups playing around them. In stormy seas a mother allows the pup to suckle while continually swimming back into the storm to regain her initial location. In prolonged rough conditions she seeks a sheltered cove or floats over a kelp bed where the water is calmer and she can anchor herself.

Mothers vigorously defend their pups. When threatened, the mother can clasp her pup to her chest and dive. Too much diving, as from a persistent, dangerous threat, can (rarely) result in a drowned pup. If a pup is captured (e.g., by researchers), the mother counterattacks, uttering human-

A young pup rides atop its mother in calm waters. © *istockphoto.com/Andrew Coleman*

A large raft of Sea Otters congregating in the relatively calm waters of a large California bay. © *Mark Elbroch*

like wailing screams. If a pup dies the mother might keep it with her for days, even after it begins to decompose.

Pups remain with and are dependent upon their mother for 5 to 6 months, longer in areas where food is less plentiful. The shortest dependencies are in areas where Sea Otters eat mostly clams; the longest are where they catch and eat more fish.

INTERACTIONS AMONG SEA OTTERS

Otters often rest together in floating congregations called "rafts." The higher the density, the larger the rafts; consequently, male rafts tend to be larger. Rafts of males in Prince William Sound, Alaska, average 70 to 100 animals but may include several hundred. The largest raft seen (western Alaska) comprised 2,000 animals. Occasionally, females with young form "nursery groups." These are simple aggregations in which each mother cares for only her own pup; there is no communal or cooperative parenting.

The underlying mechanism of their gregariousness is not clear. When feeding they spread out so as not to interfere or compete with each other. They do not seem to benefit from group foraging per se, but might glean information from others about where, when, and how to find good food. On the other hand, Sea Otters have been known to actively defend one another from predators, especially humans. They are relatively small mammals in dangerous waters, and they must split their time and attention between the surface and the depths, so they may derive some anti-predator benefits from sharing the lookout for predators.

INTERACTIONS WITH OTHER SPECIES

The effect that Sea Otters have had on rocky coastal marine communities has been very well studied and provides a strong example of the keystone species concept. A keystone species is one that has a disproportionate effect on an ecosystem relative to its abundance and increases local biodiversity. One consistent effect of Sea Otter habitation is that the average size and relative abundance of its primary prey decline measurably: relatively fewer and smaller sea urchins, abalone, crabs, and clams are around once the otters move in. This effect then changes the ecological relationships within the entire community, and striking changes can occur.

Several studies have shown that sea urchins, the primary prey of Sea Otters, increase dramatically in abundance when otters are largely absent from the coast. Sea urchins eat algae, including long "leafy" seaweeds such as kelp. As urchins flourish in the absence of otters, they turn forests of long, lush kelp into denuded underwater barrens. Where otters are found, they eat up most of the urchins and keep their numbers very low, and so the kelp beds thrive. With the growth of the kelp beds comes the return of a rich ecological community. Sea Otters have no significant direct interactions with kelp, but their suppression of urchin abundance allows the kelp to grow and flourish. This is known as a "trophic cascade," the effects of one organism's behavior cascade downward through a food web.

Sea Otters can be keystone species in other systems as well. Where bottoms are muddy there tend to be few urchins and also little kelp, which needs solid substrates to fasten itself to. In muddy substrate areas of the Kodiak Islands in Alaska, foraging Sea Otters churn the bottom, exposing old clamshells and depositing new ones. These exposed shells afford good traction for kelp, anemones, and others that without otters would lack footholds.

Along the Aleutian Islands and Alaskan peninsula, Sea Otter numbers have recently fallen as much as 90 percent. Although direct evidence is wanting, multiple lines of evidence suggest that predation by orcas is the primary cause. The northern Pacific is in the midst of a decline in fish populations and a resulting decline in harbor seal and Steller sea lions. These species are the common prey of certain orcas, which seem to have switched to taking Sea Otters instead. Sightings suggest a dramatic increase in the rate of orca attacks on otters, and throughout this period, no carcasses have washed up on shore, as they would if disease, pollution, or starvation were at work. Sharks are also a documented predator of otters, but are not implicated in the Alaskan decline. In the rocky shore communities where Sea Otters have declined, increasing urchin populations are once again deconstructing the resurgent kelp forests. At some sites, kelp density has dropped to less than one-twelfth what it was before 1990.

North American River Otter
Lontra canadensis

There are over 28 different common names for this species in North America, including: nearctic otter, loutre (French), fischotter (German), chah (Navajo), culinguq (Yupik), kolta (Klamath), neekeek (Ojibwa), saquenu'ckot (Algonquian), oshan (Choctaw), pat-cukee (Comanche), ptan (Lakota), nutria or perro de agua (Spanish).

River otters have a reputation for being playful, but this endearing quality may be exaggerated. Captive otters often wrestle, slide, retrieve objects from the water, and bat sticks and pebbles with their forepaws, but this is not necessarily indicative of wild behavior. Many of these behaviors may be displacement behaviors, a redirection of nervous impulses, caused by captivity. In the wild, juveniles do play, as do some adults, but play forms a much smaller proportion of daily activities than in the lives of captive animals or television programs would suggest.

ACTIVITY AND MOVEMENT

DAILY

River otters spend most of their time foraging, exploring, or moving about their home ranges, by day and night. Where otters live near people they are active from dusk until midmorning; where they are unlikely to be disturbed by humans they are more diurnal. Daily movements for family groups in Idaho were about 2.8 miles (4.5 km) in spring and summer and 1.7 miles (2.7 km) in winter.

In some areas otters make circuits along larger bodies of water, such as rivers and lakes, interspersed with periods of travel along smaller interconnecting streams. In this way they may travel a stream once every 7 to 10 days, depending upon the length of their circuit. In other areas they visit one body of water after another, following shorelines and minimizing overland travel. Sometimes they cross up and over low mountain passes to access watercourses on the other side. Their movements overland are typically direct and on their own well-worn paths. They use scats, scrapes, and rolls to mark these at the highest points of elevation and where they enter and exit the water.

Resting sites are an important feature of otter home ranges. They sleep either aboveground or in dens, which can be large complexes with many exits. These burrow-type resting sites are not dug by the otters, but are natural crevices and crannies. They might be under stumps and tree roots, amid jumbled boulders, or even in duck blinds and on boat docks. Beaver dams and bank lodges are ideal

An otter rises up out of the water to investigate farther ahead. © *Mark Elbroch*

and commonly used resting sites. Otters also lie in dense vegetation and sometimes scrape together a "nest" of vegetation as a bed.

When you depend on waterproof fur to keep you alive, you have to make sure you take care of your coat. Otters frequently groom themselves, most often by rubbing and rolling on the ground. They make "rolling sites" (also called haulouts, landings, and scrapes) where they roll and tumble on the ground in snow, vegetation, washed-up seaweed, sand, and grass. Rolling both cleans and dries the fur, fluffing it up and renewing its insulation. Any river otter that swims in the ocean also requires access to fresh water with which to rinse its fur in addition to regular grooming. Otters that are unable to roll and sufficiently dry their fur after swimming

A river otter rolls back and forth in the grass at a stream edge. Rolling distributes the oils that keep them waterproof and is also a means of scent-marking.

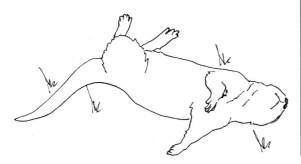

(e.g., captives with unsuitable ground for rolling) catch pneumonia and die. Some mutual grooming occurs between otters, more than would be strictly necessary for fur maintenance, suggesting a social function.

Otters move through the water by paddling with alternating kicks of the hind legs or vertical undulations of the body and tail. They twist and turn and undulate like they are made of rubber, their arms held to their sides when they are not using them to maneuver. Otters can swim up to 7.5 miles (12 km) per hour, dive to 65 feet (20 m), and spend up to 4 minutes underwater on a single breath. They are so proficient and casual-seeming it is hard not to imagine a look of bemusement on their faces as they slip in and out of the water.

The characteristics that make them so streamlined in the water make them more awkward on land. Nevertheless, they are able to walk and gallop well across the ground. Their most common traveling gait is a lope with head and tail outstretched and their back hunched high in the air. Where they can they slide on the ground—especially atop grass on steep slopes, and on flat ground and down hills in snow—sometimes over short distance and sometimes for hundreds of yards. Sliding is an efficient means of travel as well as, possibly, play.

SEASONAL

River otters are active year-round, often becoming more diurnal in the winter than at other times of year. Winter only really affects their basic activities when ice forms over water. As long as there is a hole somewhere nearby, they are perfectly capable of foraging under the ice. Where lowered water levels open air spaces under the ice, an otter may roam far and wide beneath the ice without needing to "surface" above it. Beavers maintain holes in the ice, which also benefit otters. Beaver lodges also provide den sites, and their impoundments contain otter food. Otters have been known to breach beaver dams beneath the ice, creating air spaces under the ice, and concentrating fish as the water flows out of the impoundment. They may emigrate to a new area if food is wanting, but they do not migrate. In mountainous areas heavy snows and deep freezing of waters can cause otters to abandon higher elevation sites for lower ones in winter. Otters are capable of moving long distances over land, including over high mountains, in order to access suitable habitat. Winter snow provides the opportunity to "toboggan," or slide. An otter slides in a manner similar to swimming—arms held in and sometimes pushing with the hind legs across snow. By combining running and sliding over favorable terrain, otters can reach land speeds of about 17 miles (27 km) per hour.

River otters often stand on shore when curious or checking for potential danger.

FOOD AND FORAGING

Fish is the staple of the otter diet, especially slower species. Bottom-dwelling fish are often eaten because they tend to freeze motionless on the bottom rather than scoot away to cover. By the time they realize the otter is on to them, it is too late. Otters catch more food by ambush than by prolonged chases. They have a notorious (and exaggerated) reputation as trout-killers, usually where they enter small stocked ponds and help themselves to the buffet. In natural systems otters rarely prey on fast species like trout. Various estimates of foraging success range from one-third to more than half of otter dives resulting in catches. During observations of a female European Otter (*Lutra lutra*) for 24 minutes, she caught 15 fish, each about the length of her head. The otter diet is almost entirely fish, but also includes frogs, crayfish, freshwater mussels, crabs, small mammals, birds, and reptiles. Otters typically go ashore to eat large catches. They lie on their belly and grasp fish with their forepaws. Then they chew them into smaller chunks using their cutting teeth located at the sides of their mouth. They may eat smaller items in the water, while they scull on their belly with their head up.

River otters forage along undercut banks and around docks, rocks, logjams, and clumps of vegetation, sometimes crawling up and over logs and other objects. Underwater, they roll rocks and push aside other objects to flush anything that may be hiding beneath. Otters initiate a dive by driving the head down and flipping the tail up. If the prey is clumped and relatively stationary, otters might use "patch-fishing," working one area intensively with repeated dives. For more mobile, dispersed prey they "swim-fish," patrolling and chasing underwater and resurfacing unexpectedly far from where they dove. Most fish associated with streams, rivers, and shoreline habitats retreat to cover when startled, which is where the otters catch them with a quick lunge or short chase. When they catch something, they grab it with their mouth and return to the surface to feed. They have also been known to swim up beneath swimming birds, grabbing them as they surface.

Cooperative fishing by river otters has been reported from a few locations. It most likely depends on prey abundance, among other factors. In coastal areas where it appears more common, schooling fish can dazzle and evade a single predator, but multiple attackers cause the cohesion of a school to break down. Multiple otters drive fish toward each other, or against rocks or shoreline, concentrating them and limiting their movements. As fish clump closer together, they become easier prey for the otters. Cooperative fishing allows coastal otters in Alaska to exploit higher quality prey than when fishing alone. Lone otters tend to eat intertidal fish and other nearshore fishes associated with the bottom. These species are less meaty and nutrient-

The trails of a pair of river otters traveling and sliding across a frozen lake in winter.

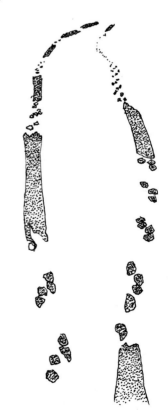

dense than the salmon and herring plying deeper waters in schools.

HABITAT AND HOME RANGE

North American River Otters live throughout most of North America, as far north as the tree line, and are absent only from the southwestern and Great Plains states. They are not exclusive to rivers; they also inhabit harbors, coastal bays, ponds, lakes, and swamps. They are most abundant in food-rich coastal areas such as estuaries and the lower reaches of streams and rivers, especially those with little or no human disturbance. Preferred inland habitats are lowland swamps and marshes connected to meandering streams and lakes. In addition to having food, it is important that the waters be clean. Otters are sensitive to pollution and avoid contaminated waters.

Within these habitats, river otters are drawn to areas with underwater "structure" like logs, roots, and rocks. These areas support more fish than gently sloping and sandy shores. Reservoirs may also be poor for fishing if water levels fluctuate greatly, but large reservoirs, such as the Quabbin Reservoir in western Massachusetts, can support an abundance of otters.

Home ranges are best expressed as linear distances of shoreline. In Idaho an otter might use 5 to 50 miles (8–80 km) of stream and lake shoreline. In areas without lakes, estimated home ranges might be twice that size. Along coastal Alaska there might be 20 to 80 otters along 63 miles (100 km) of shoreline. Individual males use about 22 miles (35 km), and females use about 9 miles (15 km). Most activity is concentrated in one or two high-prey-density areas within their home ranges. The most consistent quality of otter home ranges is that male home ranges tend to be larger than those of females. Those of lactating females tend to be the smallest, as their roaming is limited by caring for the pups. Home ranges tend to be largest in the North and where food is scarce.

COMMUNICATION

North American River Otters make shrill chirps, soft chuckles, and low purring grunts as contact calls. Soft grunts and chuckles are suitable for close-range communication, and chirps are used most when otters are farther apart. Taken by surprise or frightened, otters emit an explosive nasal snort as an alarm call. They snarl and hiss defensively when threatened and utter a scream when injured or under duress. Females caterwaul when copulating and chasing away unwelcome males. A caterwaul

A river otter emerges to stand on the thin layer of ice to eat the catfish it has just caught. © *Dan Kaiser*

is a shrill, discordant sound that is most commonly heard from domestic cats in heat.

River otters are active and frequent scent-markers. They have multiple scent glands on each hind foot that likely leave scents along their trails and at latrines. Like all of the other members of the weasel family, otters have highly developed anal scent glands. If the animal is afraid or enraged, it emits a strong, musky scent. Animals handled during field research discharge a whitish substance from their anal glands.

Just as we place billboards in areas with lots of traffic, otters mark sites of high "traffic," or use. This includes their rolling sites, but most of their scent-marking occurs in traditional latrines near foraging areas and dens. Otters leave scat in other conspicuous locations: atop prominent rocks on banks, under bridges, at tributary junctions. When they are scent-marking they arch their back and curl and undulate their tail. They paw, scratch, and tread on the spot, and then shoot a jet of feces or urine out onto the ground. Sometimes they create mounds of debris to serve as pedestals for their defecations, which can be several inches high and many inches across. Where otters are often active, entire forest floors may be swept into neat piles scattered at intervals near the shoreline. When an otter urinates, squirting forward if male or backward if female, nearby otters inspect this mark and are often induced to repeat the ritual themselves. The repeated and common use by a number of animals contributes to very large latrines.

Stinky latrines, which serve to fertilize the plant communities where they occur, are most obvious in coastal areas where otter densities are high. There you may find sites up to 65 feet (20 m) across and dotting the coast every 1,000 feet (300 m). More often, they are about 11 square feet (1 m²) and placed in prominent locations along an inhabited body of water. The scats, which in England are called spraints, are food remains: scales, bones, and bits of insect shells, and anal gland secretions. Sometimes there is also a yellow-greenish jelly that doesn't look like feces, but nevertheless comes from the intestines and not the anal glands. Traveling otters mark rolling sites and latrines as they are encountered. Two animals in Idaho marked 8 sites with scats along 1.5 miles (2.4 km) of stream bank. They also frequently defecate while swimming, so the absence of scat is not necessarily indicative of an absence of otters.

In Alaskan coastal populations, where there are both social and solitary otters, social otters communicate to others of their group through latrines: when they split up, information from the latrines helps them reunite. They use relatively few sites, but with great intensity, heaping them with their scat and scent. Nonsocial otters probably use scent marks to signal mutual avoidance, but breeding females also appear to use them in the defense of territories.

COURTSHIP AND MATING

The breeding season in otters lasts from about December to April. Active scent-marking likely ensures that estrous females will gain the attention of breeding males. Most males are not accomplished breeders until they are 5 to 7 years old, having not reached adult size until 3 or 4. Once a male and female locate one another, active courting ensues. This includes mutual chases in and out of water, wrestling, and mock fighting, including facing each other, lunging, and nipping at the other.

Copulation occurs in the water but can occur on land. The male grabs the female roughly, biting the back of her neck, often leaving a bleeding wound. Otters are induced ovulators: the act of copulation releases the female's egg from the ovary. Copulation may last from 15 to 75 minutes. It is vigorous, and the pair may take breaks to rest. Some females caterwaul during or after copulation.

DEVELOPMENT AND DISPERSAL OF YOUNG

Mothers raise their young in dens. These are similar to resting dens, although they are kept clear of scats and scent marks. They may be anywhere from immediately adjacent to the water to nearly half a mile away. Being out of flooding danger is critical, so they are often uphill from the water's edge. River otters often use burrows made by other animals for dens. They may use the abandoned burrows of woodchucks, foxes, and coyotes, as long as they are within reasonable proximity to water. As with resting areas, dens may also be in brush piles, downed logs, rotten stumps, and other natural shelters, depending on what is available.

Litters usually consist of 1 to 3 pups. Because of delayed implantation, total gestation is over 10 months, although active development of the embryo requires only 2 months. Because of their long delayed implantation, river otters sometimes give birth up to a year after mating, and just before their next breeding cycle. Pups are usually born between

Mating river otters.

Two otters at a roll site during winter. © *Jan Gottwald/Dreamstime.com*

February and March but can come as early as January and as late as May.

Birth can last 3 to 8 hours, during which the mother stands on all fours. Once the last newborn has emerged, the mother lies down, curling her body around them. The young, though altricial, are moderately well developed at birth. They are blind and toothless, but they are fully, if sparsely, haired and have claws, toe webbing, and whiskers.

The young are cared for by their mother and sometimes another adult helper, but not the father. Their eyes open after a month and they are able to move and play well after 5 or 6 weeks. In their third month the mother introduces them to solid food, and by their fourth month they are weaned. They could disperse after their fifth month, but they stay with their mother until they are 8 to 10 months old, during which time she helps provide them with food.

Otters are able to feed independently at 9 to 10 months and are abandoned by their mother shortly thereafter. Overall, the urge to disperse is variable: some animals of both sexes disperse long distances while others remain in their natal areas for years. Dispersal distances can be large, up to 125 miles (200 km). One individual dispersed so quickly as to cover 26 miles (42 km) per day, but typically they move about 2.5 miles (4 km) a day. In Alaskan coastal populations, males disperse more often than females, but for shorter distances, about 22 miles (35 km) on average, as opposed to nearly 38 miles (60 km) for females.

INTERACTIONS AMONG RIVER OTTERS

River otters are often seen alone or in small groups. Otters have been reported as solitary, possibly territorial, as well as highly social. In some studies they seem to establish home ranges that overlap one another, but then the otters mutually avoid one another and focus their activities within more-or-less exclusive core areas. Throughout their range the most persistent social unit is a mother and her young, although other social groups are possible.

Individual otters generally tolerate a high degree of overlap in their home ranges. Overlap is common between males and females, and sometimes there is overlap between animals of the same sex as well. Breeding females likely tolerate less overlap with other females because they need to avoid competition to maximize the food they get from a smaller home range.

In coastal Alaska male otters in particular are highly social, with most forming groups and only a few remaining solitary. Their groups can be quite large and last for multiple years, and they appear to improve otter feeding opportunities rather than provide protection from predators. In northern California male foraging groups along the coast consisted of 6 to 8 males that stayed together year-round. They hunted together, shared food and dens, and played with and groomed each other. When separated they chirp for one another and ignore males from other groups. During the breeding season in Alaska some male groups break up to find mates. Some individuals expand their home ranges and others move up to 16 miles (25 km) to completely different areas. When breeding ends they reunite in their shared range using latrines and scent stations to help find one another. Male groups have also been reported from several interior populations.

Females sometimes join these groups, but only when they are not actively raising a litter of pups. Females tend to maintain home ranges exclusive of other breeding females. Breeding females need a lot of food to carry them and their litter through until dispersal, and competition from other females can be deadly. In California the breeding female is the dominant animal, driving off any male that comes around. In Alaska adult females may still be the alpha animals, but males are often tolerated and their home ranges overlap those of several breeding females.

Female coastal otters may also be unusually tolerant of their weaned offspring (and possibly other nonbreeding females). In both Alaska and California females have raised litters with the help of another subadult or adult female, and it may happen elsewhere as well. These helpers tend to be females from an earlier litter that did not disperse and that remain to help provide food and protection for the young and play with them as they grow. Because breeding females tend to be territorial, young females may have trouble finding or making a breeding territory of their own and benefit from joining another family group for a while. In addition to easing the burden on the mother, helpers can gain experience in parenting and may eventually take over the parent otter's territory when she dies.

INTERACTIONS WITH OTHER SPECIES

River otters have a close relationship with beavers throughout North America. Otters do not generally prey on beavers, but they often use their constructions as resting sites. They have even been observed sharing lodges with resident beavers on at least three separate occasions. Beaver impoundments also create excellent foraging opportunities for otters.

Mink and otters, being semiaquatic predators, occupy similar niches and potentially compete. European Otters are known to hunt mink, but negative interactions between the North American animals have not been observed. The degree to which they compete probably depends on food availability. Otters are better divers and fish-catchers than mink, allowing them to exploit different foods and deeper waters. In coastal areas where food is abundant, they are unlikely to compete at all.

Humans are the primary predator of river otters, followed by wolves and to a lesser degree bobcats, coyotes, alligators, and orcas (killer whales). The sensitivity of otters to pollution makes them effective indicators of the health of aquatic ecosystems.

Wolverine
Gulo gulo

OTHER NAMES: glutton, skunk-bear, devil-bear, weasel-bear, Indian devil, carcajou (Canadian French).

Tales of the wolverine's ferocity may be exaggerated, but they are not completely fabricated. Wolverines' energy and attitude are disproportionate to their size. They are large enough to displace much larger carnivores from their meals and then carry their prize over vast tracts of land. Wolverines approach humans and other large carnivores in rapid charges, with back arched and fur erect. They snarl and growl, drooling continuously while they show their impressive teeth to their opponent. Many sensible creatures quickly withdraw from an advancing wolverine, but others are more reluctant to give up a large meal and stand their ground. Should the wolverine be forced to retreat, it returns in short order to attempt to intimidate its opponent again and again. Wolverines sometimes win a meal through sheer persistence when force and intimidation do not succeed.

Gulo is loosely translated from Latin to mean "glutton" (*gulosus* = "gluttonous"). Their rapid metabolism and long-range movements mean that they are always hungry and eat anything they can. Wolverines are notorious for stealing food, including animals caught in traps. They sometimes proceed down a trap line, consuming every animal caught and held. Early trappers in the far north despised them and actively hunted them down.

ACTIVITY AND MOVEMENT

DAILY

More than any other carnivore, wolverines cover ground. They patrol their territories in a relentless, shuffling lope, slowing to a walk only to investigate a potential meal or scent-mark, or as a break when soft snow tires them out. They pause at intervals and stand on their hind legs to test the air for scents, which betray potential food or threats. Wolverines are active throughout the day and night, alternating 3- to 4-hour periods of movement and activity with equivalent periods of rest. Clear nights, moonlight, bright auroras, and hunger may increase their nocturnal activity. Males tend to be more mobile than females, and their daily movements may exceed 19 miles (30 km). They travel much of their home range in 7- to 10-day blocks, looping continuously, marking their territory, and searching for food and potential mates. After 3 days, males in Montana are usually 40 miles (64 km) in a straight line from their

A wolverine slides down a snow-covered hillside on its back.

previous position. The actual distance the animals traveled, weaving and wandering as they hunted, is much longer. Females average 24 miles (38 km) of travel in the same amount of time. Wolverines loop their home range continuously, crisscrossing their own trails as they travel, and after 10 days they are often within 6 miles (10 km) of where they started.

Wolverines need to rest frequently, and when they do, they need a spot that is safe and secure from other predators. They often use cavities and other enclosed structures, and when none are available, they dig their own. They even dig and rest in holes immediately below large carcasses upon which they are feeding. On occasion they also rest atop the snow in oval depressions in areas of good visibility so that they are not surprised by a potential threat. In areas where wolves are common, wolverines also rest in trees to avoid harassment.

Wolverines are playful and are seen sliding on their backs in the snow, toying with objects, tumbling with their mates, and even playing with other individuals with which they may share a familial bond. They are capable swimmers and climbers and sometimes hunt from elevated perches.

SEASONAL

Wolverines have the lowest weight-to-foot-size ratio of any North American predator, meaning that their feet are exceptionally large for their size and well suited for travel in deep snow. But deep, soft snow can still hamper their ability to move around and causes them to shift their activities to areas under mature conifer cover, or where wind and sun compact or reduce snow cover. They are also quick to take advantage of compacted trails made by other animals, snowshoes, and snowmobiles. Both males and females move to higher elevations in summer and lower elevations in winter. In the far north wolverines spend less time in forests during the summer and less time on open tundra in winter.

Despite its limitations, if the snow conditions are suitable, winter may actually increase traveling opportunities for wolverines. Whereas they are unlikely to cross hot, dry plateaus between mountain ranges in summer, they might do so while snow and cold weather grip the land.

FOOD AND FORAGING

Wolverines fuel their insatiable appetites and rapid metabolisms primarily with the flesh of diverse ungulates, which they both scavenge and kill themselves. Wolverines are particularly well suited to scavenging, and cover vast distances in search of large carcasses. They are equipped with a heavy skull and jaws as well as the robust teeth and musculature needed to break large bones to feed on the marrow within. Wolverines cover their caches or carcasses with foul-smelling anal secretions that some believe deter other scavengers from feeding. They also follow the trails of lynx and foxes and steal any caches they may have left unattended.

Carrion is especially important to wolverines in winter. Along coastal Alaska wolverines gorge on whale and seal carcasses. Inland and elsewhere in North America they feast on any and every large carcass they encounter, whether it be moose, deer, caribou, or elk. Wolverines also kill large ungulates, including caribou and moose, most often when snows are deep enough to slow them down when they try to flee. In late winter, deep snow is sometimes covered by a hard crust, which provides wolverines ideal hunting conditions. Wolverines are light enough to remain aloft and run at full speed, while large ungulates break through, wallowing in the deep conditions and suffering the sharp, cutting edges of the ice.

Wolverines chase their prey, slashing at their

Wolverine sitting. © istockphoto.com/Anna Yu

exposed legs and leaving a bloody trail behind them. The chase persists until the ungulate succumbs to wounds and exhaustion and allows the wolverine to attack more vital areas. If the snows are deep enough and the crust strong, wolverines can attack the shoulders, neck, and head directly and end the chase much more quickly. In British Columbia they hunt caribou from trees, dropping down upon their back and chewing through their neck to sever the spinal cord or puncture the skull. Wolverine kills are bloody, messy affairs, and the thrashing, fighting caribou or moose leave a large area of red, packed snow and broken vegetation.

Wolverines also hunt smaller prey, including Snowshoe Hares, voles, lemmings, ground squirrels, marmots, porcupines, beavers, ptarmigan, geese, and other ground-nesting birds. They also eat fish and berries. Wolverines have stout arms used for digging, tearing, and turning rocks and carcasses. In Arctic Alaska, Arctic Ground Squirrels are an important summer food, and wolverines cache their carcasses to help sustain them into winter. They run down ground squirrels caught out foraging and dig them out from their burrows when they retreat underground. Wolverines also use a "mousing" posture and pounce technique typical of foxes and coyotes to catch voles and lemmings in tall grass or shallow snow. They kill Ross's and lesser snow geese in nesting colonies and sometimes steal their eggs. They also pilfer goose eggs and dead geese from Arctic Fox dens.

Excess food is cached in snow or under a few inches of soil. Wolverines make numerous caches during the summer and early fall, which they uncover to supplement their diet in winter when food is scarce. Caches are very important in the vicinity of maternal dens to sustain females while their kits are very young. They dig holes with their forefeet and cover their food with soil pushed by their feet and nose. Frequently used and large caches accumulate wolverine trail networks leading to them, like spokes of a wheel. Wolverines visit small caches only once.

HABITAT AND HOME RANGE

Wolverines are holarctic; they range across the boreal forests and tundra north of 37° latitude in North America and 50° in Eurasia. Historically they inhabited all of Alaska, most of Canada, and the northern tier of the lower 48 states. Their range extended down the Rocky Mountains all the way to Arizona and New Mexico. Large populations still occur over much of Canada and Alaska, and smaller populations persist in north-central Washington, central and northern Idaho, northwest Montana, and the Tetons in Wyoming.

Wolverines are never abundant, but are most common in remote northern wilderness. In Mon-

A wolverine at a caribou carcass. © *Peter Lilja/Animals Animals*

tana, wolverines use mature, montane forests, especially for winter and summer foraging. They avoid burned areas, wet meadows, and clear-cuts, yet gravitate toward open terrain at higher elevations. However, the lay of the land may be more important than the plant community covering it. Montane forests suitable for winter foraging and summer kit-rearing may be suitable if they are adjacent to subalpine cirques, which females rely on for safe denning in lingering snows. Wolverines require specific habitats at specific times. Development and recreation (skiing, snowmobiles, ORVs) may displace disturbance-sensitive wolverines just when those areas become most valuable to them.

In Alaska, average densities are 1 animal per 77 square miles (200 km^2), and in Montana densities are 1 wolverine per 25 square miles (65 km^2). Males maintain larger home ranges that overlap with those of several females. In Alaska, average annual home ranges vary from 207 to 257 square miles (535–666 km^2) for males and 41 to 50 square miles (105–130 km^2) for females. In Montana, male home ranges average 163 square miles (422 km^2) and those of females 150 square miles (388 km^2). However, given their propensity for long-distance travel, a wolverine on the move can cover 1,000 square miles (2,590 km^2).

COMMUNICATION

Given their low population densities and territoriality, wolverines rely on indirect communication with other wolverines. Urine, scats, and glandular secretions are spread liberally throughout a wolverine's home range and likely convey information on sexual status, territoriality, and even individual identity. Wolverines have scent glands on their face, abdomen, tail, and around their anal region. Their anal sac produces a very smelly, yellowish secretion that many find offensive. They also have plantar glands on the pads of their hind feet, which may allow for passive scenting of trails and other objects as they move.

Wolverines frequently deposit urine and scats on rocks, trees, logs, and other prominences, including the scats of other animals and steel traps set by people. Wolverines commonly mark saplings and larger trees isolated in meadows or prominently placed upon travel routes. They climb the tree trunks and rub their abdomen on them, while also depositing secretions from their anal sac. They scratch the bark with their claws and may even gnaw at branches, burls, or roots at the base of the tree. Sometimes they cling to the trunk upside down and scratch the ground or snow at its base. They will also scent and rub roots, and they may batter small saplings in the marking process, leaving broken limbs as evidence of their passing.

Wolverines rarely mark while they are hunting, digging for prey, or eating. Instead they travel purposefully to scent-marking sites to make a deposit or to check in and investigate. Marking sites are often well established and used over successive years. Claw marks may accumulate on bark and indicate previous visits. Wolverines typically mark 6 to 12 times per mile (1.6 km) of trail, and in one exceptional case an animal marked 20 times in 1.5 miles (2.5 km).

Little is known of the vocalizations of wolverines. They snarl and growl in a continuous undulating rumble when confronted by any other animal, and sometimes even in isolation when feeding or exploring. When trapped they growl, hiss, and snarl in intimidating fashion.

COURTSHIP AND MATING

Wolverines mate during the second half of summer, during which males wander and locate all the adult females within their range. Once a male finds a female he remains with her until they copulate. Females typically mate with the same male in successive years, as long as he remains the resident, dominant male that overlaps with them. In late winter and early spring, females give birth to the litters conceived the year before. When that litter is only a few months old the mothers enter estrus, usually in late July and early August. While receptive, the female initiates mating with the male that is

A wolverine hangs upside down on a tree trunk, scratching and marking both the ground and the trunk of the tree.

attending her by approaching him and presenting herself. He moves behind her and copulates while grasping her middle, and sometimes biting her nape should she start moving. After mating the pair roll in the debris and vegetation, take a brief siesta, and then begin the process all over again. Researchers observed a pair in Alaska copulating 4 times, each for 12 to 56 minutes. Repeated copulation may be necessary to induce ovulation or otherwise maximize the chances of fertilization. The pair bond dissolves after a few days, after which the male seeks another female in his range.

Once fertilized, eggs enter suspended animation and do not resume their development until winter. Delayed implantation, as this process is called, allows wolverines to both give birth and breed in the spring when movement is relatively easy and the young have the whole (albeit short) warm summer ahead to grow and develop before meeting their first winter.

DEVELOPMENT AND DISPERSAL OF YOUNG

Females give birth and rear their young in shallow earthen pits in dens they dig in snow at high elevations. Dens have 1 or more entrances, each 10 to 14 inches (25–35 cm) across. Their tunnels drop straight down or spiral toward the ground, where they follow the terrain for 3 to 177 feet (1–54 m) or more. Dens sometimes make use of natural cracks and spaces between rocks or roots. In Alaska, wolverine den sites are complex snow tunnels unassociated with trees or boulders. In Idaho, dens are associated with fallen logs or other structures in relatively open alpine terrain. Idaho dens access natural cavities under the logs and in talus, which they use as whelping chambers. Dens are rare in thick forests at low elevations.

Wolverines typically give birth to 2 kits between January and April. The kits are covered in fine, white fur, and their eyes and ears are tightly closed. They weigh 3 ounces (84 g) and are 5 inches (12.7 cm) long. A female rears her kits alone, carrying food to them in her stomach and regurgitating it for them. On occasion males approach dens, perhaps because of curiosity or because of the impending breeding season.

The family departs its den when temperatures rise above freezing for several consecutive days. Kits develop rapidly to match the short summer season in the far north and at higher altitudes. They are weaned after 7 to 8 weeks and begin to accompany their mother on forays in April or May. During their first 2.5 months, kit metabolism runs "hot" at 1.4 times the temperature of adult animals. This is perhaps due to their comparatively rapid development of high-energy tissues: the brain, heart, liver, and kidneys. After 2.5 months, at which time they

weigh 6.6 pounds (3 kg), they cool down. The cooling and slowing of their metabolism coincides with their weaning and may reflect changes in their diet.

Young wolverines attain adult size by winter, and some disperse as early as November. However, the average dispersal age is 13 months, and some linger in their natal range for up to 2 years. Some females reach sexual maturity at 15 months and produce their first litter at 2 years of age. Most males are sexually mature at 15 months but do not produce sperm until they are more than 2 years old. Wolverines may disperse as far as 235 miles (378 km).

INTERACTIONS AMONG WOLVERINES

Wolverines lead solitary lives in large home ranges, although there is some overlap between adjacent males and also between adjacent females. Females tend to exclude females other than their offspring from their home ranges, and males tend to exclude other males, but rarely through physical defense of their territories. Where foods are abundant, wolverines tolerate each other and may even feed in close proximity.

Wolverines do kill other wolverines. In one study 11 of 80 juvenile wolverines were killed by their own species. Adult females may commit infanticide and kill the kits of another female, and new males that supplant resident males may kill kits fathered by the previous male. Juveniles, too, are often killed by residents during their dispersal in search of their own territories.

INTERACTIONS WITH OTHER SPECIES

Wolverines are small and tenacious. They travel widely, climb trees, and hide in cavities and other shelters to protect themselves. They are the perfect top scavenger in the far north, which supports a diverse guild of large carnivores that hunt large ungulates, from cougars to wolves to Brown Bears. Wolverines confront and steal carcasses from bears and cougars, as well as meals from smaller carnivores, including lynx and Arctic Foxes. However convincing a wolverine may appear, though, some animals do stand their ground. In one case a very large male Black Bear fought with and killed a wolverine that attempted to steal a carcass the bear had claimed.

Other than man, the primary enemy of the wolverine is the wolf. Wolves dig out shallow dens and kill the kits, as well as chase down and kill juveniles, and in rare cases even adults. Females protect their kits by building dens under the cover of rocks or logs. Where they den in the snow, mothers dig long tunnels and tuck their bedding chambers down deep. Individual wolverines escape wolves by climbing trees. Wolverines—especially young, inexperienced individuals—are also occasionally killed by cougars, Black and Brown Bears, and golden eagles.

OTHER NAMES: fisher-cat, pekan (Canadian French).

American Marten
Martes americana

OTHER NAMES: pine marten, marten, wabachis (Cree).

Fishers and American Martens are bold, agile, arboreal hunters. Martens, because of their smaller size, are more inclined than fishers to climb trees. Fishers climb less than many suspect, and the heavier males climb very little. In Massachusetts, where gray squirrels are frequent in their diet, female fishers eat them far more than males. The squirrels' nests are also used as resting sites, which may be the primary reason for climbing. Fishers and martens have skeletal adaptations for climbing. Their ankles are adapted to allow the hind feet to rotate 180°, similar to how our hands rotate on our wrists. This lets them use the claws of their hind feet even when climbing down trees headfirst, like a squirrel. They sometimes climb snags, but usually just investigate them near the ground. Their tracks often ride up the side of a tree or boulder a few feet and then bounce off like a snowboarder riding up on a bank. Fishers have been known to jump 7 feet (2 m) between trees, as well as to leap to the ground when snows are deep and soft, leaving a print of their entire bodies behind. Martens will leap up to 18 feet (5.5 m) from a tree to land in deep snow, similarly leaving an impression of body, tail, and all four legs where they splash down.

ACTIVITY AND MOVEMENT

DAILY

Fishers and martens are neither strictly nocturnal nor diurnal; they are active at nearly any time of day or night. Their activity levels often peak around dawn and dusk, and they are least active around midday. Cycles of activity vary regionally, seasonally, and with prey availability and other factors. Martens studied in northern California are more nocturnal in winter and more diurnal in summer. In the summer they hunt diurnal ground squirrels. In winter these martens eat Snowshoe Hares, mice, and flying squirrels, all of which are active at night. Some fishers are more active in the daytime during the winter and least active in the middle of the night, when temperatures are coldest. Activity declines markedly during the midwinter period, when snow conditions make traveling and looking for food less efficient than lying up and waiting for better conditions. Late-winter sleet and warm days followed by cold nights result in icy crusts upon which fishers and martens can easily run and expand their movements.

Between periods of foraging and exploration, fishers and martens both carefully select places to rest, usually covered or enclosed sites: tree hollows, logs, stumps, squirrel and raptor nests, rock piles, brush piles, ground burrows, and even beaver lodges. The vast majority of their resting sites are in cavities or the canopies of trees, and they usually use these sites only once, but for varying durations. They can lie up for days after gorging or while feeding on a nearby cached kill or large carcass, and they will wait out winter snowstorms rather than waste energy struggling through deep, soft snow.

Fisher and marten trails wander widely but visit certain areas repeatedly, if not regularly. Points of interest shift throughout the seasons and include snags and trees used for denning by prey species, abandoned apple orchards, riparian corridors, and

A dark form of the American Marten climbs a tree in southern Alaska. © *Steven Kazlowski/ Getty Images*

An inquisitive American Marten in Montana. © *Mark Elbroch*

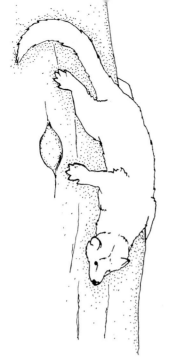

Fishers and martens can turn their hind feet 180 degrees to the rear and slither down trees headfirst.

dense conifer thickets. A trail sweeps through the forest, connecting old snags, nosing up to the bases of trees, brush piles, boulder jumbles, and other nooks and crannies potentially harboring prey. Periodically they may even stand on their hind feet to better assess their environment. You may see sharp turns where they have investigated spots just off their route of travel, where they smelled, heard, or even remembered something of interest. Some of these investigations will be accompanied by digging or scenting. Fishers can travel up to 18 miles (29 km) in 24 hours, but that distance is covered within a much smaller geographic range; fisher trails meander and loop in on themselves as they scour the landscape for food.

Fishers and martens use a variety of gaits while foraging and traveling. Gaits, like the gears of a car, exhibit grades of efficiency—some are good for high speeds and low power while others are for low speeds and more traction. When conditions for travel are good, fishers move in a long lope that leaves distinct track impressions either of all four feet or, when one of the hind feet lands atop the print of a forefoot, of what looks like only three feet. In more difficult conditions, such as deep, soft snow, they switch to a lope in which both hind feet fall into the prints left by the forefeet. It leaves a pattern of paired impressions repeated at intervals along the trail. If the snow is too deep or loose to allow this gait to be used efficiently, they may downgrade to a walk, the equivalent of creeping along in

first gear. Martens, being smaller and lighter than fishers, are better able to move in deep, soft snow. In the winter woods both species use the beaten runs of other animals and of their own to take advantage of firmer surfaces, improving the energy efficiency of movement. Sometimes they are able to discover and raid other predators' caches along these trails.

SEASONAL

In soft snow martens can plunge below the surface and tunnel down to find prey or shelter. They tend to do this around stumps and other ground debris that might harbor air spaces and mice or voles. Their small size not only allows this type of exploration, it may also demand it. The small, thin body of the marten holds heat poorly, and they must take shelter to conserve their energy in cold and inclement weather. Protected resting sites, including hollows in the snow, are critical to their survival. Martens caught out in the rain and unable to locate suitable cover can die from exposure. They also tend to be much less active in winter than they are in summer; they move an average of 16 percent of each day in winter, about a quarter as much as in summer (60 percent). Neither martens nor fishers hibernate, but martens may enter torpor, a hibernation-like deep

A fisher stands on its hind legs to investigate its surroundings. © Mark Elbroch

sleep that allows them to conserve the considerable amount of energy it takes to keep warm and well fed in winter.

FOOD AND FORAGING

The first thing most people think they know about fishers is that they eat porcupines, which is true. While trailing a fisher in the snow, you might be lucky enough to find a porcupine kill—a skin opened at the belly and turned inside out, as the fisher eats the carcass and avoids the quills. The skins are as clean as if removed by a trapper, and the carcass might be devoured down to the lower arms and legs—as far as the fisher's snout can poke into the skin of the limbs. Even so, the overall importance of porcupines to fishers is often exaggerated. The porcupine is just one member of the considerable list of animals eaten by fishers, which do perfectly well in habitats with few or no porcupines at all.

Fishers also have a reputation for eating housecats. Fishers are made the scapegoat for a long list of our complaints. Everyone in northern New England knows of a cat lost to a fisher—or so it seems. In fact, only 1 out of 1,000 fisher stomachs inspected in a New Hampshire study was found to contain the hairs of a housecat—and there's no way to know whether that fisher had killed it or been scavenging a cat killed by a car.

Food switching is the particular strength of generalist predators like martens and fishers: when one food becomes too rare to be worth pursuing, they switch to another. Fishers and martens both show tremendous flexibility in the prey they eat, but the bulk of their diets is small mammals. Snowshoe Hares are an important prey of fishers throughout their range. Porcupines may constitute as much as a third of the remains of fisher scats in some regions,

A fisher gripping a Snowshoe Hare in a fatal embrace. Drawn after illustration by C. Powell in R. A. Powell, 1993, *The Fisher: Life History, Ecology, and Behavior*. University of Minnesota Press. Used with permission of the artist.

but it is often absent or nearly so across much of their range. Squirrels are not represented as much as their abundance might suggest. Deer carcasses are an important food in the winter throughout the fisher's range, and there is even a report of a fisher killing a fawn in southern Vermont. In Massachusetts, New Hampshire, and Connecticut, raccoons are frequently preyed upon. Voles appear to be the most important prey of martens in the Northeast and parts of the West, and Red and Douglas's Squirrels in the remainder of the country. The largest regular prey of martens is the Snowshoe Hare, and they also eat reptiles, birds and their eggs, and even fish in some areas. One researcher checking on a radio-collared marten found it sleeping in a robin's nest, likely after eating the nestlings, while a pair of adult robins scolded overhead. Both species can kill animals larger than themselves and readily eat a wide range of animal flesh, carrion, and some fruit and nuts, although study of captive fishers suggests these latter foods may be taken only as a last resort.

Foraging fishers and martens use a variety of tactics. When searching an area they zigzag back and forth, sometimes crossing over their own trails investigating likely refuges of prey. As they move they investigate the trails of other animals they encounter, sniffing along them for a short distance. At other times they use a "directional search," and their trails move straight through the forest, apparently moving directly to an area of known or suspected prey concentration.

They are stalk-and-pounce predators that sneak in as close as possible and seize their prey in a quick rush. They dispatch prey with characteristic weasel attacks: a killing bite to the back of the neck or head while restraining their prey with a full-body embrace, or "bear hug." If they don't grab it right

A porcupine skillfully skinned by a large male fisher. © *Mark Elbroch*

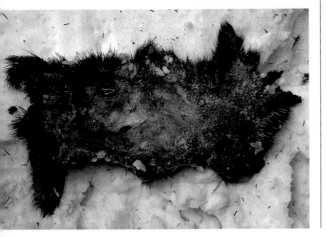

A fisher chews on a deer carcass in central Massachusetts. (Remote camera) © *Todd Weed*

away, they do not pursue their quarry a great distance. They have long, slender bodies and relatively short legs—better for probing in tight spaces than chasing things down. When attacking porcupines, fishers circle the animal and slash repeatedly at its face until it succumbs to the injuries. Evidence from snow tracking suggests that porcupines successfully defend themselves against fishers at least as often as not, even when caught in the open. The old tales of fishers attacking porcupines from the underside of tree branches or of flipping them over and attacking their bellies have never been corroborated. Their skill is in surprising their prey, not chasing it, and they can be very patient. In one case a female marten waited 30 minutes for a spooked ground squirrel to reemerge from its den, and when the ensuing attack failed, she waited over an hour longer before giving up as rain set in.

Martens often trap Red Squirrels in their underground cone caches and excavate to pull them out. Martens have also been seen using low branches of trees (4 ft.; 1.25 m, or lower) along the edges of sedge meadows to watch for Meadow Voles moving on the ground below. When a marten sees something of interest it pounces straight out of the tree onto its prey.

When fishers kill large prey or multiple animals in quick succession, they cache the remains for later consumption. Large prey items, such as raccoons or beavers, can require as many as 4 or more visits to fully consume. Caches are covered with snow, leaf litter, or other debris and are sometimes shoved under rock overhangs, boulders, or logs. Smaller prey items may never be reclaimed when newer hunting yields fresher meals, which might explain why Red and gray foxes invest so much time in following fisher trails.

HABITAT AND HOME RANGE

Fishers and American Martens both inhabit a wide range of forest types. Overall, they inhabit areas with a mixture of stands of different tree ages and types. On a finer scale, fishers like the tops of the trees or shrubs to make a roof over their head—across their range, they tend to avoid crossing large open expanses such as meadows and fields. They also prefer lots of low structure—branches, logs, downed wood, and debris. Their ideal forest habitats are dark and hard for humans to walk through. These areas also support high densities of small mammals. Both martens and fishers appear to have stronger preference for specific forest types in the West than the East. In the West, where younger and drier forests are more open, they prefer mature, old-growth and riparian forest types where there is lots of low structure and cover.

Martens appear to be more sensitive to habitat fragmentation and disturbance than fishers. Martens need a number of large, relatively undisturbed forest patches of at least 59 square miles (150 km²) connected by suitable corridors to allow travel between them. They tend to avoid potential home

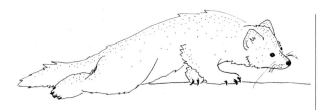

An American Marten splays its back legs and drags its hind end along the ground to deposit scents from its anal glands.

ranges where clear-cuts make up more than 20 percent of the area. They may also be limited to areas where deep, soft winter snows exclude fishers. Fishers do not move as easily in snow as martens, and they may avoid these areas. Because fishers are hypothesized to dominate martens and interfere with them, snowy areas may be the only refuges for martens from competition with fishers.

Home ranges of male fishers average 15 square miles (40 km²) with a range of 6 to 32 square miles (16 to 85 km²). Female home ranges average 5 square miles (15 km²) with a range of 1 to 12 square miles (4 to 32 km²). In addition to being smaller, female home ranges are more stable across seasons and from year to year—males redefine ranges frequently during ongoing competition with other males and when seeking females during the breeding season. Adult home ranges tend not to overlap with adult fishers of the same sex, except males in the spring when they wander widely to increase the number of reproductive females encountered.

Marten home ranges are about 8 to 12 square miles (20–30 km²) for males and 1 to 2.5 square miles (3–6 km²) for females. Male home ranges are 2 to 3 times larger than female home ranges, and 1 male may overlap 2 to 6 females, but not other males. When marten populations are at their peak densities in fall, when family groups disperse, there may be 3 to 5 martens per square mile (1.2–1.9 per km²).

COMMUNICATION

Fishers deposit scent as they travel, most frequently in the late winter and early spring. They have well-developed anal scent glands and glands or glandular tissue on the pads of the feet and on their bellies. Fishers are not known to spray from their anal glands like skunks, but they appear to leave secretions from these glands when scent-marking. They leave scat, urine, and scent secretions on small stumps and raised hummocks. Martens also splay their legs and drag their anal glands over the ground to deposit scent, and both species roll and drag their bellies to do the same. Fishers maul small saplings, biting them, and also roll on them or straddle them, urinating or leaving scat or glandular secretions. This is easily observed as winter turns to spring,

when male and female fishers rarely pass another fisher's scent without belly-dragging and urinating. Fishers frequently counter-scent, marking atop the tracks or scent marks of their prey species and other carnivores.

Because martens and fishers are so difficult to observe in the wild, descriptive records of their vocalizations mostly reflect defensive or agonistic circumstances during capture and handling for research. Calls that have been noted during capture and handling of martens include huffs, pants, chuckles, growls, screams, and whines. Martens huff in a rapid, accentuated exhalation, and "pant" in a series of less forceful huffs. The huff sounds somewhat similar to the hiss of a weasel and most likely expresses a low level of fear or unease. "Chuckles" are rapid bursts of sound that can be deep and throaty and interspersed with other rhythms and other sounds, including growls. Martens make a growl, and when in terror or pain they utter a high, prolonged scream. They whine in fear and discomfort.

Female martens make a clucking sound during courtship, and captive fishers make quiet cooing before mating and loud bawling during the act. People also claim to hear fishers scream in the wild, describing it as the scream of a terrified woman. Like disappearing housecats, wild screams are attributed to fishers more by virtue of their colorful reputation than by any clear evidence. One fisher was observed scolding a domestic dog with foot stamping and sounds not unlike a gray squirrel's. Though perhaps people are hearing male fishers fighting for breeding territory, for in these instances screeching and growling are common.

COURTSHIP AND MATING

Late-winter fisher trails are some of the most exciting tracks to follow. You will clearly see the size difference between male and female footprints as males run down the tracks of females and both are frantically scenting and marking their passage. When females of either species are reproductive (March–April for fishers and July–August for martens), males alter their behavior to increase their encounters with as many females as possible. Activity levels, scent-marking, and distances traveled increase dramatically. Along the way, males encounter one another and aggressively compete for access to females. Male fisher pelts often show signs of past fights, and one male fisher was captured with the broken canine of another fisher lodged in his back. Physical competition between males for access to breeding females is common among solitary carnivores and is one explanation for their pronounced sexual dimorphism; male fishers can be twice the size of females.

As estrus approaches, females squat and urinate

frequently and rub their belly on the ground and objects around them. This scenting probably helps males find them, and once they do, the two might court for 2 weeks, traveling together, playing and wrestling, and finally copulating. Should a female marten be ready to mate and the male not, she may go ahead and mount him to jump-start the process. In most cases this is not necessary. She signals her estrus by turning her hips up and exposing her genital area. The male mounts aggressively and pins her down by biting onto the back of her neck. Copulation lasts as long as 90 minutes and can happen 2 to 3 times in a day.

Male fishers and martens are polygynous and soon move on to find other females.

DEVELOPMENT AND DISPERSAL OF YOUNG

A female fisher gives birth to kits in late winter or early spring (February–March) and mates again within about 2 weeks. The developmental time for fertilized eggs is roughly a month, but the development is suspended through delayed implantation. Mating occurs in March and April, and shortly after the eggs have been fertilized their development is suspended. After 10 months active pregnancy resumes. Approximately 30 days later the young are born, followed by estrus and mating again for the following year's litter. Adult female fishers are pregnant for all but 2 weeks of every year.

Martens mate in July and August with a period of delayed implantation lasting 6 to 8 months. Fertilized embryos implant around February, and females give birth in late March and April after an active gestation of only 27 days. Litters of both species consist of 1 to 5 young and average 2 to 3.

The female bears the young in a natal den but quickly moves to a maternal den where they continue to grow. Fishers are more selective of natal (birthing) and maternal (kit-rearing) den sites than they are of foraging habitat, and the structure necessary for these sites is more prevalent in mature forest stands. A female fisher uses up to 5 dens per litter, so a significant number of sites must be available. Tree cavities are the most commonly used sites.

The kits are crawling around their unlined nests by 2 to 3 months of age. By the third month the young are weaned or weaning and eating solid food. By 4 months marten kits are full-sized and fisher kits, though still growing, are running and climbing well. Around this same time, aggressive behavior between mother and young and between littermates increases dramatically, typical of the social development of solitary carnivores. Aggression helps ensure that the strongest kits get the most food when there is a shortage, and increasing aggression and independence leads to dispersal.

The kits stay with their mother for the duration of the summer until they disperse in late summer or fall. Dispersing juveniles may wander and be attacked by resident adults as they search for a home range of their own. Often they must survive as nomadic "transients" in others' territories. Sometimes they eke out a living in only marginally suitable habitats, places without adequate cover or less prey. In most marten populations 50 percent of the animals have held their territories for more than 90 days, 10 to 20 percent have held a home range for only a short period, and nearly a third of the animals are transients without territories. There are more transients when the population is growing and fewer when the population is in decline. Juvenile mortality is high at this time, especially when the population is growing and there are few vacant territories for them to move into.

INTERACTIONS AMONG FISHERS AND AMONG MARTENS

Fishers and martens are aggressively territorial toward others of the same species, especially those of the same sex. For most of the year each species avoids others of a similar kind and they come together only to mate in the spring. In fur farms martens can live together amicably for most of the year, but must be separated around the breeding season and immediately after. Two of 35 radio-collared martens in a research study in Oregon were killed by their own kind.

INTERACTIONS WITH OTHER SPECIES

There is anecdotal evidence of fishers killing young lynx in Maine, and they could be doing the same to bobcats with which they share extensive range. Capable and aggressive predators, mature fishers have few real predators other than humans. Decades ago a trapper in California reported two fishers killed by a mountain lion. Other anecdotes tell of a fisher having killed a Red Fox, and another of a Red Fox that was seen successfully fighting off a fisher. Five coyotes were seen defending a deer carcass from a large male fisher that they escorted away from the carcass, but never engaged in direct fighting. In another account a female fisher was caught and killed on a frozen lake by a group of coyotes. In northern California the fisher's principal predator is the bobcat, which opportunistically pounces on them and kills them with bites to the head and neck.

Competition with fishers is considered a major factor in the local abundance of American Martens. There is little direct evidence to support this belief, but it is widely suspected that fishers readily kill martens they encounter and are the primary reason some marten reintroduction efforts have failed in the Northeast.

OTHER NAMES: weasel (United Kingdom), ermine (in winter).

OTHER NAMES: short-tailed weasel, stoat (United Kingdom).

OTHER NAMES: ermine (in winter), itunkasan (Lakota), bridled weasel (California).

OTHER NAMES: pispiza etopta sapa ("black-faced prairie dog" in Lakota), dlo ii liz-hinii (Navajo), namath (Hualapai).

Long held to be rapacious and bloodthirsty, the weasel simply does what it must to survive, and so is punished for its success. Like many predators, weasels have endured our negative misconceptions even as they exhibit an amazing natural history. Few other predators survive so exclusively on prey as large as or larger than they are, while simultaneously living under constant danger of becoming a meal themselves. Life expectancy for most weasels is less than a year after they become independent. A lucky weasel breeds for 2 years before dying, most likely because of predation or starvation.

Perhaps this contributes to their mythic ferocity and fearlessness. There are numerous reports of weasels attacking large animals, including people. In one popular story a dead eagle was found with a bleached weasel skull attached to its breast by clenched teeth. Apparently the eagle caught the weasel, but did not kill it immediately. The weasel fought back, mortally wounded the raptor, and then they both plummeted to their deaths.

Here we describe three species of weasels and the closely related Black-footed Ferret. Much of their behavior and natural history is applicable to all, but where it is specific to one species or another we have made note. The Black-footed Ferret is still so rare that little information is available on its wild behavior and ecology. Note, too, that "ferrets" that are bought and sold as pets in North America are the domesticated form of the European Polecat (*Mustela putoris*).

Mustela is Latin for weasel. *Frenata* means "bridled" and refers to the Long-tailed Weasel's varied facial markings. *Erminea* simply means "ermine," the term widely used for the white winter form of all weasels. *Nivalis* means "snowy," or "of the snow," and *nigripes* means "black feet."

ACTIVITY AND MOVEMENT

DAILY

Weasels are often on the move, seeking either food or mates, and they move in gaits peculiar to their long bodies and short legs. They walk at low speeds, but their bodies are ill-suited to faster walks or trotting. Speeding across open areas in anything but snow, they use bounding patterns similar to squirrels and rabbits. Especially in snow, they stretch out and touch down with their front feet, lifting them in time to have their hind feet land in the same area

A Long-tailed Weasel stands to investigate its surroundings. © *Thomas Woodruff/Dreamstime .com*

where the front feet were positioned just a fraction of a second before. Like this they bounce and careen with tails held high.

They also swim and climb, occasionally climbing high into trees to explore cavities and bird nests. Long-tailed Weasels usually initiate a tree-climb with a running leap, landing about 3 feet (1 m) up the trunk and scrambling farther up it in a spiral. Their hind feet can be reversed 180° so that they can climb down headfirst. Long-tailed Weasels are also the most aquatic of the small weasels, though not to the degree of the mink. Long-taileds frequently swim streams and the edges of ponds in their travels and will even take to water to hunt ducks and other animals.

Weasels may use a central den from which they make radiating forays to forage, or they may maintain a broader range, regularly marking and re-marking its boundaries. Home ranges of ermines often include several nests that they visit repeatedly. They use favored hunting territory near each base and move about along regular routes used by successive owners.

Ermines make circuits of their home range every 10 to 15 days, and Long-tailed Weasels make their rounds every 7 to 12 days. Weasels follow the same general "corridor" on each circuit, but vary their routes along it. They usually do not forage in the same area on two consecutive days, and their speed and the distance they travel decreases in areas of ample prey. Individuals may travel a circuitous route of up to 0.6 miles (1 km) during a foraging bout, but usually they travel much less.

The nests of most weasels are in the burrows of their prey and are used for resting and raising young. Among weasels, only the Black-footed Ferret digs, sometimes removing plugs from tunnels in order to reach prairie dogs inside. Nests are also made in hollow trees, rock piles, and other covered, protected cavities. The nest itself is in a depression or cavity lined with dry grass and leaves and, sometimes, the fur of previously eaten prey. Burrow nests of Long-tailed Weasels are in enlarged chambers about 2 inches (5 cm) wide. Radiating tunnels are used as latrines and food caches. The entrances to burrows of Long-tailed Weasels and ermines often have large latrines of scats to one side, along with the bones and hair of prey. Where nests are constructed in enclosed areas, caches are often nearby. In one instance, 17 mice were neatly piled in front of an ermine's nest.

Ferrets are nocturnal hunters rarely seen above the ground, preferring to spend most of their lives in the tunnels of their chief prey, the prairie dog. Weasels are active day and night, but at least the ermine is more diurnal in summer and more nocturnal in winter. They prefer conditions of dim light,

and their primary activity peak is around dusk. They are active only for about 10 to 45 minutes at a time, although sometimes for as long as 4 hours. Then they rest for 3 to 5 hours, alternating between bouts of activity and rest throughout a 24-hour day. Resting for the Long-tailed Weasel means sleeping, but it also means lolling around, wakeful and alert, but immobile. They might lie at the entrance to their burrow for half an hour or more with only their head showing. Long-tailed Weasels are less active in hot weather.

SEASONAL

Weasels are active year-round. The small, sinuous weasel body is perfectly designed for hunting small mammals in their burrows and under the snow. In severe winter climates, ermines, especially females, hunt mostly under the snow in subnivean space where mice, lemmings, and voles are active all winter. This melted-out gap between the snow and the earth provides free movement and insulation against the much colder air temperatures above. This insulation is critical to the survival of mice, and maybe for the weasels as well.

The downside of a long, thin, lightweight body is that it retains heat poorly. Because of the structure of their long back, weasels aren't even able to curl into a tight ball, as a dog does, to conserve heat. The best a weasel can manage is a loose curl, and they also have short fur that is a poor insulator. Some speculate that weasel fur turns white in winter, not as camouflage, but because white hairs, which are hollow, are better insulators than hairs filled with pigments. However, there is no evidence to support this notion. In any event, weasels must eat plenty and be judicious in the use of their surroundings to help retard heat loss. Home ranges typically contract in winter as they make frequent but short excursions from the warmth of the nest. Springtime sees longer movements as males search for mates. One male Long-tailed Weasel traveled a straight-line distance of 22 miles (35 km) in only 7 months.

FOOD AND FORAGING

The weasel body is designed to pursue and find prey in small, tight spaces. Their long body and short legs are not unlike those of dachshunds, tiny dogs bred by humans to chase badgers and rabbits from their burrows. Weasels hunt in tunnels and cavities and squeeze under logs, brush piles, and thick vegetation in search of prey. They also tunnel through snow and climb trees. Females, which are smaller than males, tend to hunt more often in tunnels, especially Least Weasels.

One of the limits imposed by hunting in tight spaces is on the size of the head and jaws. The weasel compensates with a combination of morphologi-

A Long-tailed Weasel grips its prey with all four limbs as it delivers a killing bite to the back of the head or neck.

cal characteristics and innate tactics: a long, skinny skull, a body-wrap, and a nape-bite. Their heads are short in height but long, providing ample anchorage for jaw muscles. The length of their skulls allows the jaw muscles to attach far behind the jaws, affording powerful bite strength in a compact package.

Weasels hunt by investigating the nooks and crannies where their prey is likely to hide. In the snow a foraging weasel often leaves a distinctive zigzagging trail, showing it has inspected every burrow and hole it encountered. They search on and under the ground and in trees and shrubs. They might hunt along Snowshoe Hare runs or in gopher burrows. Weasels cue strongly on movement and sound while searching, even tackling grasshoppers taking flight at their approach. If there is a mouse hiding under a log, its best strategy is to remain still, and then a hunting weasel might pass it by.

With smaller prey, weasels pursue in quick dashes ending in a pounce. After stalking or running down prey, weasels lunge and grasp their back or hindquarters and perhaps bite them to help hold on if the prey is large. In a scramble, the weasel swarms over its prey and wraps it up in a tackling, hobbling embrace with all four limbs. The entirety of the weasel's meager weight is used to subdue large prey and provide the leverage it needs to bite the neck or base of the skull, severing the spinal column or puncturing the braincase with its tiny, sharp canine teeth. When attacking prey in underground tunnels, with little room for maneuvering, weasels attack frontally in similar fashion, and if they can't reach the nape, they fasten their jaws on the throat to suffocate their prey.

When pursuing rabbits, which might outweigh a weasel 10 to 1, weasels make repeated leaps, bumping, grabbing, and biting the rabbit over and over again to wear it down. At the approach of a weasel, rabbits sometimes exhibit extreme panic, squealing in fear and even lying down, as if unable to flee. Some have suggested that rabbits simply die of "shock" rather than from wounds inflicted by the weasel, but in caged experiments, successful killing of rabbits is clearly due to physical injuries.

In captivity, Black-footed Ferrets use similar tactics to other weasels. In the wild, they seem reluctant to attack prairie dogs above ground and instead hunt mostly within the tunnels of prairie dogs at night. Prairie dogs are formidable opponents and kick sand and dirt at approaching ferrets to discourage them.

Once prey stops struggling, the weasel drops it. If there are other opportunities, as in a nest of voles, the weasel may attack again and again. When all the prey have been dispatched, a weasel begins feeding by licking the blood leaking from the wounds. This behavior has earned them the reputation of vampirism, but it is simply a means of getting all the sustenance they can from a kill. When the eating begins in earnest, weasels start with the head and brain, move on to the internal organs, and finally eat the muscular flesh.

The hunting preferences of the three weasel species vary by size. Least Weasels and ermines are small-mammal specialists, while Long-tailed Weasels are more general predators: their larger size allows them access to a wider range of prey. All species rely on voles and mice as their staple food; they account for 50 to 80 percent of their diets. Long-tailed Weasels commonly eat more rabbits than the other species, mostly young ones, and have been known to prey on muskrats, fox squirrels, and Snowshoe Hares as well. Weasels prey on most mammals rabbit-sized and smaller. They also eat birds and their eggs and nestlings, fish, snakes, lizards, frogs, beetles, grasshoppers, earthworms, and carrion. Long-tailed Weasels have been observed hunting ruffed grouse and ducks sitting on nests, and when they fail to catch the incubating bird, they break open and eat its eggs. Prairie dogs make up 80 to 90 percent of Black-footed Ferret diets, and a single ferret may eat 100 prairie dogs in a year. Ferrets also eat mice, ground squirrels, rats, rabbits, and other small mammals.

Diet varies by geography and season. Ermines sometimes live almost exclusively on hibernating jumping mice or, farther north, on lemmings, while spending a winter under a layer of snow. Late winter and early spring is when weasels most often prey on birds, nestlings, and eggs, which are readily available to an intrepid predator that can penetrate the densest shrub cover and travel into the treetops. It has long been noted that, like most predators, weasels seem to ignore the abundant shrews around them, though at certain times shrews form a significant portion of their diet. This may reflect the availability of other prey, or it could be a matter of taste. In one tantalizing case, a captive ermine showed a distinct preference for shrews over voles even when

A Least Weasel with its mouse prey. © *Eddie McDaid*

both were made available. Individual specialization can contribute to coexistence without competition.

The ability to switch among prey species is important during declines in populations of voles and other preferred prey. Weasels will kill poultry during periods when rodents are scarce; otherwise, they can live in a henhouse and do the birds and the farmer a great service by killing the mice and rats that plague them. Nevertheless, during one such rodent decline, a Long-tailed Weasel was observed killing a 3-day-old pig. In other, less spectacular cases, weasels turned to berries and juniper fruits when faced with a scarcity of voles. Males tend to be more flexible in prey choice than females by virtue of their larger size, just as the larger species are more flexible than smaller ones.

One way or another, weasels need to eat a lot to stay alive. For Long-tailed Weasels this might mean 1.5 voles per day. Captive adult Long-taileds maintain themselves on up to 30 percent of their body weight in food each day (2.6 oz.; 75 g). Ermines need a similar proportion, but the tiny Least Weasel might need to eat the equivalent of up to 60 percent of its mass (0.8 oz.; 24 g) each day. Least Weasels also need access to surface water; captives drink nearly an ounce (25 mL) each day, in numerous small doses.

Weasels cache excess food and may or may not visit their caches later on. They may defend caches from other weasels. Caches are a good way to take advantage of abundant prey. With a well-stocked cache, a weasel can hunt less and expose itself less to predators, allowing energy to be directed toward other tasks such as caring for young. Caches are made in passages of burrows used for shelter or other spots nearer a kill site. Long-tailed Weasels sometimes cache food in abandoned bird nests in trees. Caching and the surplus killing by weasels is the great fear of farmers with chickens. All those captive birds with no means of escape are ideal for weasels to kill and store for future use. But attacks on poultry are rare, and weasels do farmers more benefit than harm. In one case a weasel's cache of more than 100 rats was found, neatly collected in a tight heap, under the floorboards of a barn.

HABITAT AND HOME RANGE

Weasels inhabit all of the major biomes of North America, reaching from Mexico to northern Canada and Alaska. The Long-tailed Weasel ranges across all of the United States except the driest parts of the Southwest, and into the southern tier of Canada. The ermine is more northerly. It ranges across the northern tier of the United States, except the northern extension of the Great Plains, and throughout Canada and Alaska. The range of the Least Weasel includes Pennsylvania, Virginia, and West Virginia and covers a swath running northwestward through Quebec and the Upper Midwest to Alaska. Black-footed Ferrets formerly ranged over all of the Great Plains from Texas and Arizona to Alberta and Saskatchewan. Today they exist as scattered, small populations reintroduced to sites in Arizona, South Dakota, Wyoming, Montana, Utah, Colorado, and Chihuahua, Mexico.

Weasels select habitats, first and foremost, for availability of prey: large numbers of animals that are accessible through dens, burrows, and runways in and near overhead cover. Within any habitat, weasels must stick to cover for their own protection, but these are conveniently the same areas where they are likely to find their prey. In more open habitats, such as farmland and mature hardwoods, they stick to shrubby areas and hedgerows with abundant small mammals where they are also protected from raptors. Weasels are restricted to some degree to habitats containing fresh water for drinking and so are absent from true deserts. Other than that, they are present in all life zones from grassland to deciduous and coniferous woodland to tundra.

Among all weasels, males have larger home ranges than females. Males establish home ranges that overlap those of several females, but they are usually fiercely territorial toward other males. Similarly,

A Black-footed Ferret emerges from a prairie dog burrow. © *Joel Sartore/National Geographic Image Collection*

made by splaying their hind legs and dragging their anal glands on the ground after defecating. The anal glands can also be opened up to release a cloud of scent when the animal is very afraid, what researchers who frequently handle live weasels call a "stink bomb."

Weasels vocalize, although they are rarely heard by humans. Slight unease is signaled by a low hiss. If they feel defensive and pressed to stand their ground, they may emit a series of sharp, explosive barks and chirps. Extreme fear elicits a defensive screech, or squeal, along with a stink bomb. Screeches also accompany aggressive (nonpredatory) interactions. Screeches may be repeated up to 7 times and be accompanied by open-mouthed threats, sudden lunges, and hind-foot stamping. High anxiety or arousal is also signaled by a "bottlebrush" tail—raised hairs on the tail similar to the raised hackles of an aggressive dog. Under calmer conditions weasels make quiet, high-pitched trills. These sounds have been heard when animals are exploring, playing, or foraging as well as between mates and mothers and their young. In ermines a call described as a "zheep" signals interest between potential mates.

COURTSHIP AND MATING

Weasels appear to be polygynous, although ermines and others may be promiscuous. Mating is polygynous when a few males dominate breeding and mate with multiple females, while females typically mate with only one male. If the females mate with multiple males, undermining the breeding monopoly of local resident males, or if resident males are unable to exclude other males, then mating is said to be promiscuous.

Long-tailed Weasels and ermines most often breed between June and August, which is from 2 to 4 months after they've given birth to the litter conceived the previous summer. Adult females go into estrus after they finish nursing their litter, and young females born in the spring also participate in the summer breeding season, shortly after they are weaned. By the end of summer all females of all ages are fertilized. Black-footed Ferrets appear to follow a similar pattern, although few details are known. The peak of their breeding activity appears to be in March and April.

Long-tailed Weasels and ermines exhibit delayed implantation. After breeding in the summer, the fertilized eggs of females develop for 2 weeks (ermine) to 2 months (Long-tailed Weasel) and then go dormant. Instead of implanting in the uterine wall, they rest for 8 to 10 months. Then they implant in the uterus and continue developing for about 1 month, ending with the birth of the litter.

Least Weasels do not exhibit delayed implanta-

females aggressively exclude other females from their home ranges as well as actively avoid the resident male. Occasionally some overlap with members of the same sex is tolerated, usually when prey is scarce and the residents must roam farther to feed themselves.

Home ranges for Long-tailed Weasels average 30 to 35 acres (12–14 ha), but during prey declines may expand to 200 to 400 acres (80–160 ha). Male ermine home ranges average 37 acres (15 ha) and females average 10 to 25 acres (4–10 ha).

Population densities vary with prey availability, habitat, and season. Because weasels are so secretive, their densities are difficult to measure. In favorable conditions there can be 64 Least Weasels and 20 ermines per square mile (25 and 8 per km²). Long-tailed Weasel density, which is likely more stable and consistent than that of the others, is around 15 animals per square mile (6 per km²) when prey is plentiful.

COMMUNICATION

Weasels mark their territorial boundaries with urine, scat, and secretions from paired anal scent glands. Anal glands are highly developed and secrete individually distinct odors. Scent marks are tion, and their breeding system more closely resembles that of voles than it does other weasels. Least Weasels are opportunistic breeders that can repeatedly enter estrus and breed year-round. Males are sexually active throughout the year except December and January, when the stress of winter may force them to channel all of their energy into staying alive. Without delayed implantation, Least Weasels can respond directly to current prey conditions and breed rapidly when prey booms.

In Least Weasels, 2 annual litters are common, one in the spring (April–May) and one in the fall (August–September), although survival is lower for the young of the second litter. Females born in the earlier litter may breed in their first summer (at 3 months of age) at the same time their mother is breeding again. Fall babies are not sexually mature until the following spring.

In all weasels, males roam widely during the breeding season in order to find as many breeding females as possible. Long-tailed Weasels are in estrus for only about 3 to 4 days, and males locate them by scent. Smelling areas where she has urinated, he follows and finds her. When he catches up to her there is usually a scuffle as he tries to grasp her by the nape of the neck. A female might resist with anything from low chattering to a vigorous, prolonged physical resistance. She may be able to effectively resist a male for a while, until he gets her by the scruff. Females may even be dominant at this time. Male ermines are known to deliver food to estrous females as a courting or appeasement gesture.

Once the female is compliant, the male mounts her, clasping his forelimbs around her waist and curling his body to bring their hips together. Scruff-ing (grasping the skin at the back of the neck) pacifies most females, and a male ermine may drag a female around by her scruff while she hangs docilely like a youngster being carried by its mother. If the female continues to resist, the male pins her down until she relents. In Long-tailed and Least Weasels copulation may continue for 1 to 4 hours before the female breaks away, with periods of vigorous thrusting interspersed with rests. They may mate repeatedly over several days. In ermines each bout of copulation lasts only 2 to 20 minutes. Prolonged copulation may be necessary for proper sperm transport and fertilization. In other mustelids, short copulations have fewer successful fertilizations. Following copulation, the male may be tolerated and the two may even share a den. Or the female may violently drive him away.

DEVELOPMENT AND DISPERSAL OF YOUNG

The young are born in April or May. Long-tailed Weasels bear 4 to 5 young, and ermines usually 4 to 8. Birthing mothers alternate periods of rest with nervous movement about their nests, during which they experience violent labor contractions. The birth of each baby takes about 6 minutes, and once the young are born, the mother cares for them by wrapping around them and licking them as they lie in the curve of her belly.

Least Weasels bear litters averaging 5 to 6 young, about 5 weeks after mating. In Alaska, where Least Weasel populations are strongly affected by the abundance of prey, litters may include 13 young, enabling the Least Weasel to turn a bonanza of hyperabundant prey into numerous offspring.

Young weasels are born blind, helpless, and

A female ermine (short-tailed weasel) dashes across an opening carrying one of her youngsters to a new nest. © Roger Tidman/NHPA

mostly hairless, and they sleep together in a huddle. At 2 weeks of age they have fine, white fur, and young male Long-tailed Weasels are already larger than females. Their eyes don't open until after the first month, and shortly after that their first set of teeth is growing in and they can eat solid food. At and shortly after birth young Least Weasels make high squeaks, but by the time their eyes open squeaks are replaced by chirps. Weasels are weaned at 2 months of age, although in Long-taileds and ermines nursing might continue into the fourth month. By 2 to 3 months young weasels reach their adult proportions, but not weight, and are entirely self-sufficient. Least Weasels develop more quickly than the larger species. They begin weaning after only 1 month and may reach adult proportions by 2 months.

Young begin playing outside the nest during their second month. They are generally playful with their siblings, tackling and gnawing on one another, practicing the skills they need to survive. Around the third month they are fully grown and begin attempting to kill small rodents. The body-wrap and the killing nape-bite are innate, but their skills improve with experience. Black-footed Ferrets that watch their mothers kill prairie dogs are better hunters than those that do not. Practicing predatory motor skills in play with siblings or other objects also improves a youngster's killing efficiency. By the end of the third month typical predatory behavior is fully established.

Youngsters disperse 2 to 4 months after they are born. At this point they are likely to be aggressively repelled by their mothers and forced to wander to find a territory of their own. Life expectancy is short for weasels. Few see their second birthday, so there is a steady turnover of territories. Every population includes residents with territories that do most of the breeding and a few transients roaming in search of an opportunity. Young males are sexually mature at 1 year of age and may first breed in their second summer, when they are around 15 months of age. Without a territory of their own, they are unlikely to mate.

INTERACTIONS AMONG WEASELS OF THE SAME SPECIES

Weasels are solitary, polygynous (or sometimes promiscuous) carnivores. Home ranges are determined by access to critical resources: prey for females and breeding females for males. Even though males overlap with females, they usually avoid one another and establish contact only during mating season. Adult male weasels are usually dominant over all others, although breeding and pregnant females are more aggressive than other females and may be dominant over a male. Residents are also dominant over transients, and when territories are vacant nearby residents may take them over even if there are transients present.

Social relationships between weasels of a given species may change as prey and weasel densities change. When weasels are scarce they may not be territorial at all and may move from one area to another in a nomadic fashion. Sometimes they do this seasonally, being territorial in the summer and fall and then wandering more in the spring. When prey is scarce they may expand their territories and tolerate overlap with the same sex but maintain core areas for their exclusive use. Prey scarcity may also decrease tolerance, and resident males may start aggressively attacking the females that inhabit their territories as if they were trespassing males.

INTERACTIONS WITH OTHER SPECIES

Each of the weasels shares some of its range with at least one other weasel species. Ermines overlap in diet with both Least and Long-tailed Weasels, which can lead to competition. Where Long-taileds and ermines overlap, Long-taileds are usually less numerous and spend more time in forested habitats than ermines. The Least Weasel shares nearly all of its range with ermines. The two species likely coexist through a balance of competitive advantages. The larger ermine is better at taking larger prey, and Least Weasels are superior at catching small prey. When prey abundance declines only one weasel species persists, and the one that remains is determined by the size of the remaining prey.

Weasels are themselves prey for many species, including other weasels, coyotes, foxes, owls, hawks, eagles, snakes, domestic dogs and cats, and humans with traps, guns, poison, and cars. In some areas foxes and domestic cats limit weasel numbers, and their removal results in a rebounding weasel population. The white winter fur hides them in the snow, and black tail-tips distract raptors into attacking behind a fleeing weasel instead of right on it.

Least Weasel and ermine populations are particularly unstable, and their fortunes change along with those of their prey. Many vole and lemming populations experience periodic cycles of population booms and crashes, and populations of smaller weasels rise and fall with them, sometimes becoming locally extinct. Long-tailed Weasels are less susceptible to prey population crashes because of their larger size and their wider range of prey. In the Arctic, when lemming populations are in decline, Least Weasels continue to hunt them intensely, pursuing them into their last refuges, because they have few alternatives. The relentless pressure of their predation accentuates lemming population declines, which in turn leads to dramatic population declines in the weasels.

OTHER NAMES: mink, minx, water weasel, vison (French), ikusan (Lakota).

The mink coat is an icon of luxury, and it owes its rich look and feel to fur adapted to keeping mink warm and dry as they dive and swim, sometimes even under ice and snow. Although mink are still trapped in the wild, today most fur coats are made from the fur of mink raised in captivity on farms expressly for that purpose. The demand for mink fur led to the introduction of mink to the wilds of Russia and to the rise of mink farms around the world. Inevitably, animals escaped from these farms, and now feral populations of American Mink have established themselves across Europe and in South America. In Europe they have proven particularly troublesome, competing with European Otters (*Lutra lutra*) and European Mink (*Mustela lutreola*). Far more research has been done on mink as captives and introduced pests than as free-ranging native carnivores in North America. Here we use the word *mink* to denote the American Mink.

The scientific name of the American Mink probably originates from the Swedish word *vison*, which means "a type of weasel." The genus name *Neovison*, meaning "new mink," places the American Mink in a genus of its own, separate from that of the weasels (*Mustela*), with which it had been classified for many years.

ACTIVITY AND MOVEMENT

DAILY

Mink are mostly nocturnal, but it is not uncommon to see one out and about in the daytime, foraging or traveling about. They travel mostly on land, heading in and out of the water intermittently. They move in a walk with their back arched and their head down near the ground, or in a bounding lope with back arched, head up, and tail sticking out taut behind them. In the prairies, where they forage extensively in uplands (away from water), mink can cover up to 7.5 miles (12 km) in a single night. Elsewhere they travel much less. In a Tennessee study, for example, they moved less than 2 miles (5 km) per day.

Mink aren't particularly specialized to swimming; their bodies are essentially the same as those of fully terrestrial weasels. Nevertheless, they can dive nearly 20 feet (6 m) deep and can swim underwater for 114 feet (35 m). When they dive, they stroke either with left front and right rear together followed by right front and left rear, or they stroke with both front feet at the same time followed by both rear feet together. Surface swimming entails strokes of the forelimbs, with occasional strokes of the hind limbs to give a burst of power or to initiate a turn or dive. Mink are also skilled tree climbers. They can descend trees vertically and jump from tree to tree. Climbing may be primarily a defensive tactic, and they are known to rest in tree cavities up to 33 feet (10 m) off the ground.

Mink usually use underground burrows for resting and rearing young. They rarely dig these shelters themselves and instead take advantage of natural or preexisting shelters such as among the roots of bankside trees, rock and brush piles, culverts, and bridge foundations. They commonly rest in the abandoned burrows of muskrats, but they also appropriate the burrows of ground squirrels and beavers. Most dens have multiple entrances and are located within 6 feet (2 m) of water. They also rest in muskrat lodges and on the ground in clumps of emergent vegetation.

SEASONAL

Seasonal changes in water availability influence mink activity, and they retreat to permanent water sources when others dry up. Mink do not hibernate, but they are less active in winter than during the warmer months. Females are significantly less active while they are pregnant but are frequently on the move during the first 3 weeks after they give birth. They must roam to forage but return to the nest frequently to care for their young.

FOOD AND FORAGING

Mink are strictly carnivorous and eat a wide variety of mammals, fish, crayfish and crabs, amphibians, reptiles, birds, and even invertebrates. Small and medium mammals such as muskrats, rabbits, squirrels, voles, and mice are the most important prey in all seasons, making up 25 to 50 percent of a mink's diet. Some people maintain that muskrats are a primary prey of mink, but most mink prey only on juvenile muskrats they discover in burrows and

A mink foraging underwater.

lodges in the summertime. Prairie mink and those inhabiting the northwestern portion of the species' range are the largest mink, and they are the ones that prey on muskrats most frequently. At certain times of year waterfowl can be a significant portion of a mink's diet. They capture and kill adult ducks and take brooding hens right off the nest as well as eat eggs and nestlings. In Manitoba a male mink was estimated to have eaten 3 to 7 adult ducks, 15 to 25 nestlings, and 18 to 30 eggs in the course of a single nesting season.

Mink are weak swimmers compared to fish, so when fishing they focus their efforts on small and slow-moving fish, such as suckers (*Catostomus*), catfish, perch (*Perca*), dace (*Semotilus* and *Rhinichthys*), and shiners (*Notropis* and *Notemigonus*). Occasionally they prey on faster, larger fish like trout and salmon. These fish are most vulnerable in densely stocked ponds and in small spawning streams, especially naïve fish raised in hatcheries. Mink can quickly reduce the number of trout in a stretch of water, but their effect is limited to a small area, and the presence of other alternative prey may protect trout. In one study mink were shown to prefer to forage in portions of a stream that supported large numbers of trout, but the mink mostly fed on abundant crayfish that flourished there.

When foraging, mink move slowly along the edge of a waterway, searching visually for prey. Their eyesight is better in air than in water (unlike truly aquatic mammals), and they search by peering through the surface of the water, occasionally immersing their head to look below. They investigate any hiding place within 3 to 7 feet (1–2 m) of the water's edge—burrows, cavities in and under banks, or logs, stumps, and root wads—and at the ends of shallow riffles. They don't forage in expanses of deep water, but they do investigate small deep pools and places with submerged logs where their prey naturally congregate. Larger males hunting for rabbits and others in search of mice and voles hunt overland, and they may even find their way to neighboring farmsteads to seek out rodents among the grain bags and baled hay in barns. In prairie regions in particular they forage far into upland habitats. They also have excellent hearing and can hear the ultrasonic sounds made by rodents.

Mink take their quarry in a rush, grabbing it and delivering a killing bite to the back of the neck or skull. In times of excess they may cache what they

A mink carries a large trout away from a stocked pond toward the safety of the nearby river. © *Mark Elbroch*

Mink search for prey in the water by peering in from above.

kill and build up quite a stockpile. One account describes a mink cache in Illinois that contained 13 muskrats, 2 mallard ducks, and a coot.

HABITAT AND HOME RANGE

Mink inhabit temperate and boreal forests, prairie, tropical swamps, fresh- and saltwater coastal areas, and tundra. In general they are most numerous along waterways with lots of potential den sites and low, emergent vegetation. They are often associated with riparian habitat, which provides areas for home ranges as well as routes for long-distance dispersal. They are most abundant where the shore is lined with brushy vegetation, overhanging banks, and similar features, factors that contribute to increased terrestrial and aquatic prey abundance, as well as offering them cover and concealment. In coastal environments they prefer vegetated and tidal slopes that are protected from heavy waves. They avoid sand, pebble, and shingle beaches and prefer larger rocks and boulder fields where prey is more abundant.

Few radiotelemetry studies have been done on mink, so there are few data on their home ranges. In Tennessee 3 males occupied a nearly 5-mile (7.5-km) stretch of river. In Manitoba, where mink ranged across several small wetlands, average summer home ranges were 3 square miles (7.7 km²). In Europe it is evident that adult American Mink have larger home ranges than juveniles and that males have larger ones than females. Estimated home ranges for male American Mink in Europe are typically less than 3 miles (5 km) of shoreline and usually average around 1.3 miles (2 km). Shoreline home ranges are longest along rivers, intermediate along lakes, and shortest along the coast.

Densities of adults range from 0.25 to 1.8 mink per square mile (0.1–0.7 per km²), although they are limited by the availability of aquatic habitat. Densities tend to be lower along rivers and lakes and higher in coastal areas. Coastal mink home ranges tend to be smaller, and they are also more likely to overlap with other mink, even those of the same sex, than in other habitats.

COMMUNICATION

Mink, as largely solitary animals, interact infrequently. When they do they use vocalizations, postures and expressions, and potent scents. Mink have two anal scent glands, one on either side of the anus. These glands, also called anal pouches, are small pockets lined by glandular skin that secrete scent compounds. Anal pouches are used for marking and in defense, but they are closed off during defecation. Internal glands that empty directly into the rectum are responsible for scenting the feces (scat). Scats and urine are usually deposited in prominent locations and atop objects like logs, rocks, and clumps of vegetation, which may enhance the transmission of their scent. Mink also often defecate in muskrat latrines. Glandular scents are also applied directly by dragging the anal region along the ground. This anal dragging is assumed to deposit scent from the anal pouches, which can be squeezed by voluntary muscles to discharge their contents. Among captive mink, anal dragging is a common response to being moved to a new environment. The anal pouches can also be forcefully evacuated, and scent secretions can be shot up to 1 foot (30 cm) behind the animal. They don't squirt scent in the far-reaching, focused manner of skunks, but create a noxious cloud around themselves in times of stress.

A low-intensity response to danger is a hiss accompanied by aggressive (as opposed to defensive) posturing—an arched back, raised hair, and bared teeth. A mink holding off an aggressor often adopts this aggressive stance and hisses while swishing its tail back and forth and emptying its anal pouches, releasing a cloud of noxious odor. When cornered or severely frightened, mink scream as well as hiss. Screams are loud and last up to a full second. When a mink is in pain or extremely stressed, it squeaks. Squeaks are high-pitched and short: each lasts only a fraction of a second, but a series of them may be uttered in rapid succession. In contrast to these defensive and aggressive sounds, "chuckling" is a quiet, staccato sound that is common when mink are mating.

COURTSHIP AND MATING

The breeding season, which lasts 3 to 4 weeks, begins in February in the southern portions of the mink's range and April in the North. With the onset of breeding, males effectively abandon their home ranges and roam far and wide to locate estrous females, presumably through scent. Anal pouch secretions are individually distinct, and they or other scents deposited with scat and urine may communicate an individual's sex and reproductive condition as well. Once a male encounters a female he may stay with her for up to a few days. When she is in estrus they mate; copulation is vigorous and prolonged. The male usually clasps the female around the waist with his forelimbs and bites the nape of her neck, sometimes inflicting a bloody wound. Mating lasts an hour on average and has been observed (in captivity) lasting anywhere from 10 minutes to 4 hours, and the male may ejaculate multiple times.

Ovulation in mink is induced, either by the presence of the male or by the act of copulation. Once the egg is fertilized it goes into a sort of suspended animation before implanting in the uterus and actively gestating. In general we assume that mammals use delayed implantation to alter their "birth timing." The delay allows the timing of birth to be independent of the timing of mating, so these animals can mate and give birth at the best times of the year regardless of how long it takes for the fetus to develop. In mink the delay is very short, only 1 to 6 weeks, much less than the 3 to 11 months seen in other species (see accounts for fisher [p. 163], seals [p. 141], and Black Bear [p. 112]), and the delay hardly seems relevant to birth timing. Some have argued that delayed implantation in mink is just an inherited trait that mink do not need and, in evolutionary terms, are in the process of losing. Another hypothesis suggests that the delay is necessary for the peculiar way in which mink conceive their litters.

Female mink exhibit "superfetation," meaning they can ovulate and conceive even while already pregnant. Usually animals release multiple eggs simultaneously in order to conceive a litter. Mink can release eggs at different times, and they do so several times over the breeding season. One of the results of this is that females can bear litters in which the youngsters are sired by different fathers, which can be advantageous in reducing aggression from more males toward kits and broadening the gene pool of the litter. Captive females have been able to mate successfully multiple times over a period of up to 19 days. Hormonally, mink are only able to exhibit superfetation because of the implantation delay, and when mating is over, all the fertilized eggs implant and begin to gestate together. Some hypothesize that delayed implantation may have evolved as a means of superfetation and was only later adapted to the function of birth timing.

DEVELOPMENT AND DISPERSAL OF YOUNG

Young mink are born between April and June depending on geography, about 40 to 75 days after mating. Active gestation lasts about 30 days. Litter size averages 4 young but ranges from 2 to 8, and older females tend to have slightly larger litters than younger ones.

At birth the altricial young are tiny, blind, and helpless. They are pink and covered with silvery hairs, and they develop quickly. They open their eyes in their fourth week. A mink typically needs 150 calories or more each day, but nursing females need 3 times as much, and must forage frequently while also making frequent trips back to the den to look after their litter. Juveniles start eating some solid food brought to them by their mother after 2 weeks. They are fully weaned off of milk by 5 or 6 weeks, but are still dependent on their mother to bring them food. Any youngster that wanders too far from the nest is gruffly grabbed by the scruff by its mother and dragged back to rejoin the family.

When the young are 2 months old they begin hunting, practicing and honing their innate predatory skills. Although they are essentially independent at this time, they stay together with their mother until fall, when they disperse to find a place to spend the winter on their own. Dispersing juve-

An adult female mink drags a reluctant offspring who wandered too far from the protection of the nest.

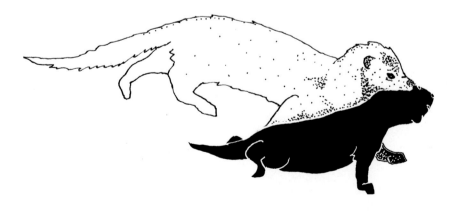

A family of mink peers out of a hollow log at a river's edge. The adult female is on the far left. Note her large front feet and webbed toes. © *Mark Elbroch*

niles travel to vacant (of mink) waters usually less than 28 miles (45 km) from where they were born. They mate for the first time in the following spring, when they are about 10 months old.

INTERACTIONS AMONG MINK

Mink are exceedingly solitary. Groups of mink that are sometimes seen are ephemeral: pairs traveling together during the mating season and groups of young with or temporarily without their mother. In addition to being solitary, they are also territorial toward mink of the same sex. Some overlap may occur between the sexes, but rarely within a sex. Among mink of the same sex, their home ranges have some areas that are exclusively their own and then there may be zones that are shared with neighbors. They maintain their territories by periodically traveling through them, checking on and refreshing their scent marks with scat, urine, and anal drags. Scats are more common in zones of overlap with other mink than in any other area in their home range, except in front of a den.

INTERACTIONS WITH OTHER SPECIES

Mink are preyed on by great horned owls, hawks, American Martens, fishers, coyotes, Red Foxes, bobcats, Canada Lynx, alligators, and North American River Otters. Their primary predator is man.

Although they overlap in range and habitat, river otters and mink do not usually compete, because they occupy slightly different niches. In most areas of overlap, their diets differ because otters are stronger swimmers and more aquatic than mink. They forage in deeper water than mink and consequently eat more fish. The smaller, more terrestrially adapted mink forages more along the edges of waterways and on dry land. In coastal areas where they overlap, their diets can be very similar, but mink prefer areas more protected from waves than those used by otters, so they are unlikely to encounter one another.

There is an anecdotal connection between populations of mink and those of muskrats. Early and current trappers maintain that mink cause declines in local muskrat populations. With the exception of northwestern mink, there is little evidence of mink killing and eating large numbers of muskrats. Recent analysis of decades of trapping shows that mink and muskrat populations cycle through regular periods of high and low abundance. As the muskrats rise and fall, so do the mink, peaking and declining a year or so after the muskrats. Although these cycles suggest a close predator-prey relationship between muskrats and mink, there is little direct evidence to support it. Further research is needed to determine their true relationship with one another.

OTHER NAMES: silver badger, New World badger, tejón (Spanish), hoka (Lakota).

The word *badger* is thought to have been derived from *bêcheur*, the French word for the European Badger (*Meles meles*). Early colonists recognized the bold black-and-white facial patterns of the American Badger as the New World counterpart to their European species and thus called it "badger." *Taxidea taxus* is Latin for "looks like a European badger." However, the two badger species are amazingly dissimilar. While European Badgers are social creatures living in family groups and inhabiting well-worn, complex burrow systems in woodland habitats, the American Badger is a solitary creature of open areas and prairies which constantly roams about its territory, digging new burrows in which to sleep.

ACTIVITY AND MOVEMENT

DAILY

Badgers are active both night and day over much of their range, except in coastal California, where they are strictly nocturnal. Badgers spend much of their time belowground, either napping or hunting. When badgers are foraging aboveground they meander in a walking gait with their nose held low to smell at the entrances of rodent burrows. They usually move only short distances, averaging 0.3 miles (0.5 km) per night. Yet badgers sometimes cover ground remarkably quickly and may move 8.7 miles (14 km) in just 4 hours. They utilize an efficient trot to cover long distances or to move between foraging patches. Badgers also lope and gallop when chased or for quick sprints to catch prey animals. The very features that make their bodies ill-suited to long sprints are what make them such unmatched diggers. Their preferred escape is down into the earth, either via an existing burrow or through one they make in a matter of seconds.

When badgers are in need of a long sleep or a break from hunting, they go underground. What may have started as a hunting excavation may be expanded into a sleeping refuge, or they may dig a burrow specifically for sleeping. Rest sites of California badgers can be differentiated from foraging digs by the volume of earth mounded at the burrow entrance. The mounds before dens in which a badger rested or spent the day cover an area of at least 1.1 square yards (1 m²), much larger than those created while hunting pocket gophers and voles.

Badgers may dig more than one den each night, or return to an old den near where they are foraging. Some badgers regularly operate out of a den site for several successive days before moving to a different part of their range, and then periodically return to the same den when foraging in the area. Others return to old den sites only on rare occasions.

Rested badgers typically exit dens in a ritualistic manner. Upon emerging they perch on the dirt mound out front to groom themselves, then sit peacefully to study their surroundings. They'll often loiter about the area for up to 15 minutes, exploring, scent-marking, and reentering the burrow from which they recently emerged, before finally setting forth to begin a foraging route.

SEASONAL

At higher elevations and in the northern portions of their range, badgers periodically reduce their heart rate by 50 percent in winter and become semi-torpid. Whether they go torpid or not, they tend to remain within the safety of their underground chambers, which mitigates temperatures, saving them a tremendous amount of energy. In studies of captive badgers, animals have remained belowground for up to 70 days during winter months.

Badgers also manage heat loss and retention through sleeping postures and plugging burrow entrances. They sleep curled in a ball during cold weather, but when it's warm they lie flat like a rug on either their stomach or back. During extreme weather badgers plug their burrow entrances. Plugging the entrance helps retain heat within the burrow during cold weather, and during hot weather, a plug serves to keep the outside heat at bay.

FOOD AND FORAGING

Badgers are specialist hunters of fossorial rodents and are well designed for subterranean excavation and hunting strategies. A badger's eyes have nic-

The spiraling burrow of a badger.

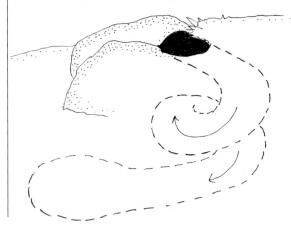

Badgers dig with their forepaws and then pass the dirt beneath them and to the sides. They expel it from their burrows with backward kicks of their hind feet as they back out of their holes. © *Mark Elbroch*

titating membranes to protect them from flying debris. Their ear canals are small, and their entire body is flattened, with a thick, muscular neck that enables the head to contribute to shoveling dirt. Their incredibly long, strong claws and partially webbed toes are also both adaptations that aid in digging, and their loose skin allows them to turn more easily in constricted tunnels.

Ground squirrels and prairie dogs are popular fare wherever they are available, and research on the energetic requirements of badgers suggests that an adult needs to eat 2.3 ground squirrels every day. During the nesting season badgers focus their efforts on locating young squirrels and prairie dogs that are still confined to the nest. With the start of summer, juveniles are more mobile and adults, too, and so may evade a badger digging within their tunnel systems. Before they break ground, many badgers plug extra entrances with soil, rocks, or even chunks of wood in order to limit the possible escape routes for squirrels within a tunnel system. Then they plunge in at an open burrow entrance and attempt to trap adults and juveniles in dead-end tunnels or within their sleeping chambers. Badgers also run down ground squirrels foraging aboveground, away from their burrows, and kill them with a swift bite across the chest, which crushes the vital organs and breaks ribs.

When ground squirrels enter their hibernacula in the fall to spend the winter months in deep sleep, badgers are still capable of finding and hunt-ing them, and take full advantage of their defense-less state. Such is their hunting success at this time that they often capture more than they can eat on the spot, and badgers cache more squirrels in the fall than at any other time of year. They have been observed carrying ground squirrels up to 145 yards (133 m) before caching them in either underground tunnels or buried within throw mounds of dirt at burrow entrances.

Badgers also eat numerous other rodents, including chipmunks, marmots, jumping mice, kangaroo rats, woodrats, voles, and pocket gophers. They also occasionally prey upon larger mammals when the opportunity presents itself, including cottontail rabbits, and, on rare occasions, Striped and spotted skunks.

In areas along the central coast of California, pocket gophers and voles form the mainstay of badger diets. They excavate the two species differently, although they tend to seek out nests of both, where helpless young are easy prey. When hunting voles, badgers make numerous shallow digs, so that the evidence left behind is a clump of 6 to 12 closely associated holes approximately 8 inches (20 cm) deep. When hunting pocket gophers they try to dig straight down into the nest chamber. Excavations are approximately 2 feet (60 cm) deep and appear singly or in pairs.

Badgers also revisit old excavation sites where secondary users, including ground squirrels, rabbits, reptiles, and invertebrates, may have since

An American Badger emerges from a California Ground Squirrel burrow where it had foraged and then rested through the day. (Remote camera) © Mark Elbroch

ing season to increase their opportunities for mating, and then shrink them again when the season has passed.

Badger home ranges do overlap, but female-female and male-male boundaries are more strictly delineated. Typically a male's home range overlaps with several females, and females within their range have slight overlap with each other. Evidence suggests that when females overlap greatly they are related, as with two siblings or a mother and her grown-up kit.

Badger densities vary tremendously depending upon prey densities. Where prey is scarce badgers persist at 1 animal per square mile (2.6 km²), yet in rich alfalfa fields where ground squirrels and voles are at amazing densities, badger densities may reach 5 or more animals per 0.4 square miles (1 km²).

COMMUNICATION

Badgers are notorious for their aggressive hissing and snarling when they are cornered, threatened, or disturbed—they quickly transform themselves into snarling dust mops with long claws and teeth. Often they make this racket while slowly backing up and swinging their head from side to side. They lower their head, raise their hackles, and roll back their

taken shelter and can be easily cornered. Along the coast of California, badgers regularly eat alligator lizards, king snakes, rattlesnakes, and large Jerusalem crickets, and they excavate and consume the larval catacombs of ground hornets. In portions of their range badgers may also prey upon the chicks and eggs of ground-nesting birds. Badgers also eat corn, fruits, mast crops, and honeybees along with their honey, as well as any carrion they discover.

HABITAT AND HOME RANGE

American Badgers are creatures of open plains and grasslands but are common in other dry habitats, ranging from high sagebrush to lowland cactus and ocotillo deserts. They also use dense shrub habitats, including mesquite thickets and chaparral. In California they are also associated with open oak woodlands. Movement studies have shown that badgers forage more often in open grasslands and desert, but where available they retreat into thicker cover to dig a sleeping chamber.

Home ranges for female badgers are about 1.9 square miles (5 km²) and up to 7.7 square miles (20 km²) for males in terrain where prey is readily found. Home ranges can be much larger in areas where prey is scarce. Male badgers in British Columbia use home ranges of up to 208.5 square miles (540 km²). In areas where the prey base is dense, home ranges for both males and females have been recorded at less than 1.2 square miles (3 km²). Males expand their home ranges during the breed-

The trail of a scent-marking badger, which dragged its hind end to deposit anal-sac secretions along a regular travel route.

lips to display impressive teeth. At their highest level of agitation they also elevate the soft tissues in the nose. Badgers can maintain a rolling growl for great lengths of time while digging or eating if they feel they are being watched, and they punctuate their growls with fierce snarls if further provoked.

Badgers also use chemical signals to communicate with one another and other species, though the importance of such signals is poorly understood. Like other mustelids, badgers release a pungent odor when disturbed. You can sometimes determine whether a badger den is occupied by making noise or digging at the entrance, and then sniffing deeply to determine whether scent has been discharged below.

Badgers sometimes drag their abdominal glands, and possibly their anal glands, on the mounds before their dens and in soft, sandy regions in their range. When they do this, they leave wide troughs as if they slid across the substrate. Such scent-marking may play an important role in maintaining territories and relay information about sexual status and dominance.

Compared to other carnivores, badgers appear to assign scat a lesser role in communication. Scats are often deposited belowground, or occasionally on their mounds before a burrow, where subsequent digging quickly buries them. You might find one or two by sifting through the soft dirt in front of den sites, but even then you'll be lucky if you find anything. Researchers in one study in California made hundreds of visits to dens known to have badgers inside, and only five scats were found on or near the mounds.

COURTSHIP AND MATING

Females enter estrus during the summer or early autumn, and mating occurs most often in July and August. Only about half of the females in a given population breed each year, and only about 25 percent raise young until an age when they will appear aboveground for the first time. Older females produce litters more often and are more successful in raising juveniles than younger ones. Male badgers are promiscuous and wander their territories, seeking to mate with any and all females within their range. Males expand their home ranges by two or three times during the breeding season and move at increased speeds in the hopes of locating a female on her single day of estrus. Males often monitor several females simultaneously and constantly move between them to check whether they are in estrus, and thus receptive to mating.

Copulations are prolonged, and one observation documented 21 minutes of activity. The male mounts from behind and grips the female's neck with his teeth. Once the egg is fertilized it enters a state of delayed implantation for up to 6 months in duration. Between December and February active gestation resumes, and the neonates are born approximately 6 weeks later.

DEVELOPMENT AND DISPERSAL OF YOUNG

Between March and early April, 1 to 5 young (typically 2 to 3) are born in a natal den, which differs from the typical badger burrow in being larger and having multiple entrances and chambers. Few badger dens have been excavated and investigated, but in those that have, some were bare and others lined with soft materials. Badgers may or may not use a dead-end tunnel or small chamber as a latrine site for themselves and the young.

Kits are born blind and scantly furred. They quickly grow into young badgers that by 4 to 5 weeks of age invest much of their time in wrestling and playing aboveground. Listen for their low grunts as they explore and play near their burrows. Even though they are mobile at this age, the mother will still carry them should she choose to relocate her den. Lactation continues for up to 8 weeks, though they'll begin to wean onto solid foods several weeks beforehand.

The youngsters disperse at varying times, generally between 10 and 12 weeks of age, when the female begins to leave them on their own for longer and longer. Males generally disperse farther than females, which sometimes set up territories adjacent to or overlapping with their mother. Dispersion may be far; one male badger was trapped 68.4 miles (110 km) away from his natal den only several months after he set out on his own. Dispersing females sometimes mate before their first birthday, but most do not. Males and most females are usually more than a year old before they begin to participate in the breeding season. Yearlings tend to maintain very small home ranges—typically less than 0.4 square miles (1 km^2) during their first year of independence. They will quickly expand it as they become full adults.

INTERACTIONS AMONG BADGERS

Much remains unknown about the social lives of American Badgers. They are solitary except during the mating season or when females are rearing young. Badger-to-badger in-fighting has been documented in field projects, yet the degree to which this influences populations remains a mystery. Occasionally larger, more dominant badgers kill young dispersers they discover trespassing in their home range.

INTERACTIONS WITH OTHER SPECIES

There is still some debate as to whether badgers truly cooperatively hunt with coyotes, their

A snarling badger lowers its head and lifts its nose to better expose its intimidating teeth. © *Mark Elbroch*

principal predator, or whether coyotes have learned to take advantage of hunting badgers. There is clear evidence in the National Elk Refuge in Wyoming that coyotes standing near ground squirrel burrows in which badgers are tunneling increase the efficiency with which they catch ground squirrels, which occasionally exit burrows in order to escape the badger beneath. However, it is difficult to know whether some squirrels might glimpse the coyote above and then retreat back into the burrow, thus increasing the hunting success of badgers as well. Badgers do remain submerged longer when accompanied by coyotes, and this may correlate with increased hunting success.

Coyotes, too, have been observed communicating the whereabouts of fresh ground squirrel sign to badgers. They do this either through vocalizations and signals while standing in the midst of new squirrel burrows or through corralling badgers toward fresh sign. Badgers and coyotes have been observed playing together for short stints and traveling together without antagonistic interactions for long periods. However, badgers that try to carry their prey aboveground stand to have it pilfered by the coyotes that accompany them.

Coyotes have killed tagged badgers in nearly every study to date in North America, and they seem to be badgers' principal mammalian preda-

tor after humans. Golden eagles also are known to kill youngsters, and bears, cougars, and wolves occasionally kill adults. However, badgers have often been observed successfully standing ground and even intimidating bears, cougars, and even motor vehicles. In fact the bold black-and-white facial markings of badgers may function much like the aposematic coloration in skunks and serve to warn potential predators of the inherent dangers in attacking a badger. If they choose to retreat, badgers can also burrow into tough ground and plug the hole behind them in less than 90 seconds.

Badgers have been conservatively estimated to dig between 1,100 and 1,700 burrows per year, resulting in 3 to 67 mounds per 2.5 acres (1 ha). At any given time only 7 percent of burrows are actively used by badgers, but burrows remain visible on the landscape for 7 to 10 years, depending upon local environmental conditions. Such large-scale tillage influences where nutrients gather on the landscape and where and what kinds of plants can seed and grow. Badgers increase the heterogeneity of soil types, nutrient pockets, and plant biomass so necessary for diverse and healthy ecosystems. Badger burrows are also used by numerous other species, ranging from black widows and tarantulas to lizards, snakes, burrowing owls, rabbits, rodents, and Striped Skunks.

WITH NOTES on Spotted Skunks (*Spilogale* spp.).

OTHER NAMES FOR SKUNKS: civet cat, polecat, maka (Lakota), xa′o (Cheyenne).

Most folks are familiar with the Striped Skunk's stench, a potent musk sprayed when the animal is disturbed or defending itself. *Mephitis* means "bad odor" in Latin, and it is the perfect description for both this family and genus. The English word *skunk*, borrowed from the Massachusett language, has survived history since the first European settlers arrived in North America.

Should you decide to try to remove a skunk from your house by yourself, be warned that the old adage that says skunks held aloft by their tail cannot spray is false. Certainly some skunks choose not to spray, but it is their choice, not yours. However, when a skunk's tail is held over its own anus or its anus is held to the ground, they *usually* refrain from spraying. It is best to approach skunks in live traps when they are curled up and asleep, and then cover them with a blanket. Should you approach them with a tarp or blanket while they are awake and agitated, they are almost certain to spray.

For those unlucky enough to be sprayed, or to have your pets sprayed, there are numerous folk remedies to aid in reducing and removing the smell from skin, clothes, and fur. Perhaps the most widespread folk remedy is a bath in tomato juice. If you ask skunk biologists, however, they are most likely to tell you, "Don't waste the tomato juice." As an alternative, many people swear by baths in citrus juice, such as lemon and lime, and still others insist that standing in wood smoke completely breaks down the chemical odors. The remedies considered most effective include hydrogen peroxide or white vinegar. Start with a quart of either liquid and add a third to a half cup of baking soda and a tablespoon of liquid dish soap. The mixture should be mixed, applied to affected areas, and allowed to soak in for up to 5 minutes. (Warning: hydrogen peroxide bleaches fur and human hair if allowed to soak too long.) Avoid the eyes! Rinse and repeat if necessary. Do not store any excess solution, because hydrogen peroxide and baking soda is an unstable mixture. Treat yourself to a fresh batch for each treatment.

ACTIVITY AND MOVEMENT

DAILY

Skunks emerge from day beds and burrows as the sun is setting and then forage for much of the night. They return to a covered retreat just before dawn, and only rarely are skunks abroad during the daylight hours. Occasionally they are still traveling in the early hours of the day, or they might forage on an overcast day. During the warmest months skunks tend to sleep aboveground within thick vegetation, which provides camouflage yet also allows heat to dissipate, or in shallow burrows. In cold weather, skunks rest in deeper cavities or burrows with greater insulation. Unlike Striped Skunks, spotted skunks are excellent climbers and also den and rest in tree cavities and rock crevices on cliffs.

Skunks typically meander in a walking gait as they forage, moving at speeds less than 1.2 miles (2 km) an hour. Skunks often forage along regular "routes." Such is the consistency of their patterns that skunks seen in an area during the evening can often be seen at the same time on successive evenings; they may forage in an area, making the same rounds for several days, and then move to forage in a different part of their range.

When traveling to foraging areas or crossing open areas in which they feel less safe, skunks move into a distinctive rocking-horse lope, in which they can travel for long distances. When they are fleeing for their lives or chasing off a potential threat, they move into a galloping gait and stretch out to their greatest potential. Galloping skunks may attain 10 miles (16 km) an hour, which is dangerously near the speed of a frightened person. Striped Skunks very rarely attempt climbing (except perhaps when an accessible garbage can is on the other side of a trellis) and do not take to water easily, though they can swim well when they must.

SEASONAL

From November to March in the northern part of their range, Striped Skunks hole up at various intervals, to escape from inclement weather and long cold spells. In the snowiest regions, they disappear for as many as 100 days each year, except for a brief period when males and females wander during the mating season in search of mates. The availability of sufficient dens and cavities is a limiting factor for Striped Skunks and is the reason they do so well near humans, where sewers, drains, porches, basements, and varied infrastructure create myriad holes and protected quarters. Skunks are also quick to procure the abandoned burrows of numerous other species, including muskrats, armadillos, badgers, and foxes. On occasion they are also found sharing quarters with another (perhaps reluctant) inhabitant, such as a gopher tortoise, or a willing inhabitant, such as a raccoon or opossum. Burrows they dig themselves tend to be 5 to 19.5 feet (1.7–6 m) long. Each one has one or more compartments lined in soft materials, such as grass, leaves, and other vegetation, that

A Striped Skunk lifts its tail, aims its hind end, and twists to keep an eye on the photographer, just in case it needs to defend itself and its litter. © *Mark Elbroch*

they use as a mattress and for insulation. Burrows often have more than one entrance as well, and a dead-end tunnel is used as a latrine.

While tucked away in dens during winter months they enter a profound sleep called torpor. This sleep is not technically hibernation, but serves the same function. In torpor Striped Skunks evade the rigors of winter and slow their metabolism in order to better live off of stored fat. During this time they may congregate in communal dens with related and unrelated individuals and survive months without foraging. A Minnesota study revealed that skunks lose up to 65 percent of their body weight over the winter and that some perish while underground because of insufficient reserves. After the winter the survivors are depleted of energy and must feed well to recover their health and vigor. Some skunks survive their winter dormancy yet emerge in spring in such a poor state that they are unable to rebound and perish before high summer. Parasites or dis-

temper further stress overwintering animals and can tip the scales of their survival. Particularly harsh winters may diminish skunk populations greatly in their northern range, but a succession of milder winters allows for an increase in their numbers.

FOOD AND FORAGING

Skunks forage in an exploratory walk with their nose leading them to potential prey or food sources. Striped Skunks are true omnivores and ingest a great diversity of foods through the course of the year. For much of the spring and summer they feast on insects, often the larger beetles and their grubs, but also grasshoppers, crickets, tent caterpillars, and carpenter ants. Striped Skunks employ their strong claws to dig for their prey, leaving behind a scattering of small conical craters across the landscape; unlike spotted skunks, the innermost three digits of their tiny front feet are completely fused together to better support rapid, focused digging. Ask any homeowner whose lawn has become infested with grubs, as no doubt their once manicured grass became pitted with tiny skunk digs that were at first more distressing than the true problem. Skunks also dig up yellow jacket or other ground hornet nests, as well as attack honeybee hives, eating the larvae, honey, and adults. Sometimes they scratch at hives to draw out the adults, which swarm the skunk. They beat them down with their forepaws and eat them. One skunk killed by bees had 65 bee stings inside its mouth and on its tongue, and a stomach full of bees.

Striped Skunks also eat worms, snails, crayfish, mole crabs, amphipods, and small reptiles and amphibians, and they pounce upon small mammals and birds, including White-footed Deermice, voles, moles, and sparrows. When they are hunting beetles, grasshoppers, or other smaller prey, they spot them from a relatively close distance and then make several swift and agile bounds before pinning their prey to the ground with their front feet. Then they dispatch them with a quick bite from their sharp teeth. When they catch spiny caterpillars and noxious toads, they roll them in dirt to remove the spines and noxious chemicals on their skin. Then they eat them. The smaller spotted skunks are even more carnivorous and hunt insects and small mammals more exclusively.

Skunks also feed heavily on ground-nesting bird eggs when nests are congregated in nesting colonies (as with gulls and terns) or in small patches of woods surrounded by agricultural matrix. When nests are spread through the landscape they eat only the eggs from the occasional nest they bumble into

in their wanderings. They are able to bite and crack the eggs of smaller species. For the eggs of larger species, such as grouse and turkeys, they resort to other methods. They are sometimes able to bite the pointed tip of the egg to crack the shell and gain entrance. Skunks also "hike" the eggs through their hind legs, hurling them against some hard backstop to break them open.

As late summer turns to fall, Striped Skunks ingest a variety of fruits, including blueberries, wild cherries, wild grapes, rosehips, and blackberries. Skunks also feed on planted crops, including corn, and they relish compost piles with kitchen scraps or accessible garbage. Striped Skunks also eat carrion and will actually crawl into the open cavities of large carcasses, such as deer, to feed on the meat from within.

HABITAT AND HOME RANGE

The Striped Skunk inhabits nearly every type of environment in the lower 48 states, as well as much of southern Canada and northernmost Mexico, excepting the hottest, driest deserts and the coldest, snowiest wilderness. Skunk populations are most dense in and around human habitations, as well as in mixed habitats where logging and agriculture have created mosaics of habitat type. Striped Skunks are least numerous in contiguous northern forests.

The home range and densities of Striped Skunks are highly correlated with the availability of both food and den sites. Skunks typically occupy home ranges of between 0.6 and 1.9 square miles (1.5–5 km²). In suburban areas, where food and

A Striped Skunk stumbles upon the nest of a wild turkey and is quick to harvest a meal. © *Steve Maslowski/Photo Researchers*

protection abound, skunks need only 0.2 square miles (0.5 km²). In contrast, on the Saskatchewan prairie Striped Skunks defend territories measuring 4.6 square miles (12 km²).

Striped Skunk densities correlate with home ranges and, including juveniles, have been recorded as high as 38 animals per 0.4 square miles (1 km²). Unlike raccoons, skunks are typically more abundant in suburban settings than urban ones.

COMMUNICATION

Skunks often seem either completely oblivious to or unmoved by another animal's approach, including humans. When they feel threatened, they most often run away to avoid an encounter. Females defending dens are most testy and least likely to retreat, but any animal that is cornered and feels threatened when approached too closely will exhibit characteristic behaviors. First, skunks exhibit displays to deter aggressors. They hiss, growl, and arch their back, and simultaneously lift their tail up and over their back, and erect the hairs along their spine and tail to make themselves appear much larger than they really are. Next, Striped Skunks foot-stamp to communicate their agitation and to solicit responses from potential predators. Foot stamps may be with one or both front feet, or with all four feet simultaneously, when they bounce like aggressive pogo sticks either side to side, in one place, or, on occasion, toward the source of disturbance. In these cases they often stomp-stomp-lunge, stomp-stomp-lunge toward the potential threat.

A Striped Skunk rises up to deliver a foot stomp, and convey threat and agitation.

Arched backs and bouncing agitation are characteristic of aggressive interactions between Striped Skunks. Pregnant females and youngsters foot-stamp at the slightest disturbance, while other adults require greater stimulus to elicit this response. Skunks often bluff-charge potential threats, sometimes repeatedly, and if an animal turns and runs from the skunk, the skunk pursues, chasing off the disturbance before returning to its foraging.

Spotted skunks are the only skunks that consistently use handstands to communicate a threat. They keep their head up to keep an eye on whatever they are threatening, and their hind legs fall to either side, so that they appear like a gymnast simultaneously doing a handstand and a split. They can squirt their noxious musk from this position, but typically drop onto four feet to spray.

Cornered skunks of all kinds, or those tired of running, turn their hindquarters in the aggressor's direction. They hold their tail erect and out of the way, and then curve their spine in a U-shape so that they can maintain eye contact and continue to hiss and growl at the looming threat. Should they continue to feel threatened, they spray, which is discussed further under Interactions with Other Species. On rare occasions trapped skunks spray without any warning.

The use of scents in the communication of Striped Skunks is poorly understood. Skunks form latrines at intervals along their foraging routes, where great numbers of scats will accumulate if the site is protected and undisturbed. Latrines also form at the entrance to their winter dens.

COURTSHIP AND MATING

The breeding season for Striped Skunks starts in mid-February in the South and may last until mid-April in the northern part of their range. Peak breeding occurs in March. Females generally breed once per year, and research has shown that up to 96 percent of females in a population become pregnant each breeding season, which is remarkably high compared with other mammals. If a pregnancy fails or a female fails to breed the first time, she enters a second estrus in May.

Males and females begin to search out potential mates in their winter den sites in January, and travel as much as 2.5 miles (4 km) per night. When a male discovers a female in estrus, he enters her den, approaches her from behind, and sniffs and licks her vulva. Then the male mounts the female from behind, grasps her neck in his jaws, and may also attempt to further stimulate her by stroking her genital area with his hind foot. Mating may occur repeatedly over the course of several days, with each instance lasting less than a minute—perhaps just several quick thrusts.

An agitated spotted skunk exhibits a handstand, which is a threat behavior. © *Jerry Dragoo*

A female's estrus lasts 9 to 10 days, and only after copulation with a male does ovulation occur, creating the opportunity for pregnancy. Once a female has successfully mated she will ferociously attack any subsequent suitors. The male, however, is polygamous, and after mating with one female will seek out a second, third, and so on, until he has mated with each of the females in his defended territory.

DEVELOPMENT AND DISPERSAL OF YOUNG

The female constructs a natal nest within retreats created by human structures, in excavated burrows they dig themselves, or in the adapted burrows of badgers, foxes, woodchucks, muskrats, or tortoises. One week prior to giving birth the female becomes especially aggressive, charging and foot-stamping at any nearby disturbance. Striped Skunks exhibit variable delayed implantation, and their gestation period ranges from 55 to 77 days. Females that breed earlier in the season exhibit the longest gestations, and those that breed latest, the shortest. The neonates are born from the middle of May to mid-June. Litters average 5 to 8 young, but may range from 2 to 10. There was even a report of 18 in a lit-

ter in Pennsylvania. Skunks are born with their eyes closed and almost completely without fur, but their skin pigmentation mimics the bold black and white pelage to come. When between 3 and 4 weeks old their eyes and ears open, and they become capable of squirting musk from their anal scent glands. Juveniles are weaned between 6 and 8 weeks, and disperse from July through September, when they are about 2 to 3 months of age. Juveniles weigh only 1 pound (0.4 kg) at 60 days, but after that they quickly gain weight. By 3 months of age they'll weigh as much as 4 pounds (1.7 kg). Rapid growth continues into November, when it suddenly slows to the typical growth rates of adult skunks. Juveniles then participate in the breeding season just before their first birthday.

From 50 to 70 percent of young skunks will not survive their first year. In captive populations many females kill their litters if disturbed shortly after birth. In fact in one study, female infanticide was the principal reason that only 192 of 321 young captive animals survived to weaning. In other studies captive females sometimes adopted young skunks from other litters and nursed them as their own. Male skunks in the wild also enter burrows and kill and eat young. Females are thus secretive about their whelping dens and defend them vigorously.

INTERACTIONS AMONG STRIPED SKUNKS

Striped Skunks are solitary for much of the year, and other than females with their juvenile offspring, they forage individually. Each chunk of habitat is typically dominated by a large male that overlaps the home ranges of several females. Juvenile males (up to a year old) are tolerated until they approach a size large enough to challenge the resident, when they are chased off to find a territory of their own. Striped Skunks may congregate at large food sources, like a trash heap, and feed amicably as long as each maintains a small bubble of personal space around itself.

In the North, Striped Skunks may or may not enter a communal den in which to spend the winter. Females most often den communally and have been found in groups up to 11 strong. Sometimes a single male joins a group of females, or they may den on their own. Older males are more likely to den with a harem while younger males are more likely to be found on their own. Group huddling provides a means of energy conservation unavailable to skunks denning in isolation. Single skunks rely more heavily upon torpor to survive long winters. In one study younger male skunks denning in isolation were torpid an average of 50 times during the winter season, with each period lasting 8 hours and their mean body temperature dropping to 81°F (27°C). In contrast, huddling skunks on average

A bobcat confronts a Striped Skunk scavenging at the carcass it had claimed and cached. The bobcat departed, returning only after the skunk had left of its own accord. (Remote camera) © *Mark Elbroch*

entered torpor only 6 times during the same winter season, and each bout lasted only 5.5 hours at a mean body temperature of 88°F (31°C).

Those differences have a large impact on their overall fitness. Skunks that huddled in a group den emerged in the spring with 25.5 percent body fat, while those skunks that denned alone emerged with only 9.3 percent body fat and were thus at a great disadvantage for spring survival. The fact that every female in the study used a communal den suggests it could be important to successfully producing and raising offspring, or that the demands of raising young left her insufficient time to gain the fat reserves to survive the winter on her own. On the other hand, diseases are transmitted more readily during communal denning, making this behavior detrimental in the long run. In that case, what seems a good survival strategy in the short term may in fact prove fatal in the long term.

INTERACTIONS WITH OTHER SPECIES

Striped Skunks have numerous natural predators and are occasionally killed by foxes, coyotes, bobcats, cougars, badgers, fishers, domestic dogs, golden eagles, and great horned owls, which are said to have little if any sense of smell. However, predation on adult skunks is rare, and in numerous studies of skunks, researchers have reported no predation at all. In one experiment coyote presence was simulated with tape recordings of howling and by spraying bottles of coyote urine about the area, and skunks did not alter their behavior in any way to avoid these simulated hotspots of coyote activity. Skunks are often observed feeding alongside other carnivores, including foxes, raccoons, and bobcats.

All skunks have conspicuous black and white markings on their coats, which are easy for predators to see and, if they have any sense, avoid. Such aposematic coloration is a warning for potential predators that an animal is dangerous, poisonous, or foul-tasting. Historically it's been assumed that predators innately recognize and avoid animals with aposematic coloration, but research with skunks has revealed that learning is also involved. Predators with skunk experience are more likely to avoid them in the future. The notoriously well-developed scent glands of the skunks lie just inside the anus. In defense, they protrude from both sides of the anus to shoot an oily, yellow substance up to 16.5 feet (5 m) with deadly accuracy. They may also spray a finer mist a shorter distance to encircle the threat. Skunks aim for a predator's eyes, and a direct shot causes burning and temporary blindness. The substance they spray is called butylmercaptan, and it contains sulfuric acid. Most people have some experience with the smell, as a disturbed animal underneath a porch or in the yard, or an animal struck by a vehicle, often exudes the odor. Adult males spray the most often and the most easily. Skunks are able to spray multiple times, likely up to 4 times in a row, as they do not discharge their entire supply in a single event.

Skunks are responsible for 20 percent of the annual rabies reports around the country and are a particularly common vector in the Midwest and prairie regions of southern Canada. Rapid declines in local skunk populations are often attributed to regional outbreaks of rabies or canine distemper. Most rabid skunks die underground, which is why some rabies outbreaks aren't even documented.

Raccoon
Procyon lotor

OTHER NAMES: ringtail (not to be confused with *Bassariscus astutus*, whose common name is Ring-tail), masked bandit, mapache (Spanish), azeban (Wabanaki).

Raccoon is a trickster and mischief-maker similar to Coyote in western Native tales. Raccoon frequently delighted in tricking others just to see them wonder or fight, but just as often suffered from his own machinations. Part of that mythology likely stems from raccoons' more humanlike qualities. The shape of their forepaws makes it difficult to call them anything but "hands." Their fingers are elongate and naked and tipped with sharp claws, or nails. When they forage with their hands, their head is usually turned up or away, watching elsewhere. There are four times as many touch receptors in their hands as in the feet, and a tremendous amount of the cerebral cortex of the raccoon is devoted to the hands, with which they "see" in the dark. In addition to sensory equipment, the hands are the focus and outlet of much of their nervous energy. They have limited grasp; usually they hold and roll

Racoons often stand to gain new perspective.

objects between both hands. Raccoons caught in box traps will often busy themselves making little balls of mud this way.

ACTIVITY AND MOVEMENT

DAILY

Raccoons are active from sunset to sunrise with a peak of feeding activity around midnight. Occasionally they are active into the morning daylight. Raccoons travel most frequently in a lateral-swinging walk. The result is a trail of tracks paired side-by-side, front tracks beside hind ones. At faster speeds they pace, swinging both limbs on one side of the body at the same time. Top speed is achieved in a gallop. They can swim well and are excellent climbers. The joints in their hind feet can rotate 180°, which allows them to descend trees headfirst. When investigating something, they may stand on only their hind legs.

Daytime resting sites are important to raccoons. These might be sites suitable for winter dens or just a spot in the cover of thick herbaceous vegetation. They don't make any kind of "nest" for these lays except in coastal marshes. There they build up platforms of vegetation so that they may lie above the high tide. High up in a tree, a raccoon might rest by simply flopping down on a bare branch, feet dangling. If seeking more comfort, an enterprising raccoon might appropriate a gray squirrel nest, squashing and packing it down into a comfortable platform. Rest sites can be located anywhere within the animal's range, but all are located within less than half a mile (800 m) of water. Most are much

A raccoon cleans its hands after a stint of foraging. © *Mark Elbroch*

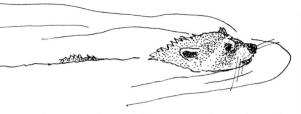

A raccoon dog-paddles across a river to forage in the city limits beyond.

closer: average distances from dens to water are between 220 and 340 feet (67–104 m).

Dens are important features of a home range. Some individuals reuse dens and resting sites on consecutive days and others don't. The differences are individualistic and could reflect different foraging conditions or strategies at night that put the animal close to or far from the previous day's rest site. Some dens also appear to be communal properties that might be used singly or in groups and be visited repeatedly by every raccoon in the area over the course of a year. Sometimes they are large with multiple chambers and entrances, such as a crevice network among boulders, and can be readily used by multiple individuals simultaneously.

SEASONAL

In the winter, cold temperatures and accumulating snow trigger a torpor that can last for months. Although not true hibernation, this winter sleep allows raccoons to avoid costly foraging in deep snow. They tend to den communally in winter in the northern extent of their range, but they disperse in the spring. It is often easy to find raccoon dens in late winter when males awake and emerge to seek out mates, leaving tracks to and from dens in the deep snow. In the warmer, less snowy parts of their range, they may sleep for a few days if the temperatures get unusually low, but they are generally active throughout the year.

Winter dens might be in trees or on the ground. Tree cavities used for dens are usually 10 to 39 feet (3–12 m) high. On the ground they may use old fox or woodchuck burrows, rock crevices, caves, brush piles, culverts, buildings, storm sewers, and nearly any natural or artificial structure affording some degree of cover and concealment. A raccoon was once found in a muskrat lodge, but with four frozen feet. They may switch to new sites after emerging in a warm spell in winter.

FOOD AND FORAGING

Raccoons are opportunistic omnivores that more often eat plant than animal matter. They forage by feeling about with their hands, searching under rocks, exploring every nook and cranny, even digging through mud. Given a relative abundance of food in streams and pond edges, they are predisposed to probe about in shallow water for food. They eat small items immediately and they may carry larger items to a boulder or bank to eat them.

Only captive raccoons engage in the iconic "washing" of food by dipping it repeatedly in water. An urban legend is that raccoons have weak throats and must soften foods before they eat them by dunking them in water. Searching for food in water, or "dabbling," is a fixed motor pattern that finds no expression in captivity, so washing becomes a substitute for the natural behavior. This animal lives by its hands and keeps them busy under all conditions. It is not unlike pet dogs chewing and shaking shoes and dolls—captive equivalents of evolved survival behaviors. Whether in water or on land, raccoons incessantly pat and probe with their hands, always searching, sensing, exploring.

The most important raccoon foods during fall and winter are fleshy fruits, nuts, and corn. Raccoons are most likely to feed heavily on animal matter in the spring before adequate plant foods are available. They rely heavily upon aquatic and other invertebrates: crayfish, grasshoppers, beetles, caterpillars, bees, ants, and wasps. Coastal raccoons eat crabs, oysters, mussels, some echinoderms (e.g., starfish, urchins), and some marine worms. Interior raccoons eat snails, slugs, and earthworms. They also eat rodents, young muskrats and rabbits, and even shrews and moles. They eat a variety of other, larger vertebrates, most often as carrion. They also eat human garbage, birds and turtles, and their eggs. They eat some frogs, but not many. Different areas support different food resources, so raccoon diets vary over the species' range, although what raccoons learn from their mothers likely accounts for efficient exploitation of different resources in different populations.

HABITAT AND HOME RANGE

Raccoons thrive in a variety of habitats, but those associated with water are the most important and productive. They inhabit woodlands, woodland-agricultural edges, fence-rows, shelterbelts, marshes, and swamps. Forested bottomlands have higher densities of raccoons, perhaps 50 animals per square mile (20 per km²), than other habitats that might support only perhaps 13 per square mile (5 per km²). They avoid open uplands (grassland and pasture) and bogs. Urban and suburban areas can have high raccoon densities, yet those neighborhoods close to woodland parks usually hold more raccoons than those dominated by open or industrial areas. Urban and suburban densities may reach 120 to 250 animals per square mile (50–100 per km²). Unlike Striped Skunks, raccoons increase from suburban to urban centers.

A foraging raccoon uses its hands to "see" beneath the surface of the water. This raccoon was pulling up underwater vegetation and then stripping it of freshwater snails. © *Mark Elbroch*

Home range sizes vary greatly by habitat and study, a testament to the general adaptability of raccoons. Males' home ranges tend to be larger than those of females. Raccoons in the northern Great Plains had home ranges approaching 7,413 acres (3,000 ha). In urban Cincinnati, males' home ranges averaged 40 acres (16 ha) and females' averaged 12 acres (5 ha). Most movements are localized around whatever food is available at the time, although the whole home range may be visited over a period of weeks. Raccoons also go on long excursions to temporary food bonanzas such as fruit or corn crops, where they may feed in large aggregations.

COMMUNICATION

Raccoons make a variety of vocalizations, including wild, bloodcurdling cries at night that are sometimes attributed to cougars and are the source of many folk legends. One researcher describes 13 unique calls, 7 or more of which are exchanged between mothers and young. Juveniles that are hungry or separated from their mother make a high-pitched "twitter" or squeal. Contented juveniles make a quiet, low purr and mothers purr while nursing. The common vocalization of the raccoon is the "chitter," which you may hear at any time while they forage and explore. Mothers also chitter and young whistle as contact calls. Chitters and whistles appear to be individually distinct. Individual recognition could be important in situations in which mothers raise young in close proximity to one an-

other. Multiple families forage together in urban areas and multiple litters have been raised simultaneously within a single brush pile.

A mother might warn a youngster with a short, explosive *MM!* A raccoon feeling threatened gives a sharp bark or screech accompanied by a head-down posture. Aggressive or fighting raccoons are scary and give fierce growls, snarls, and squeals. You may hear loud snarling and squeals coming from high in a good resting tree just before dawn, as a few raccoons sort out sleeping arrangements.

Visual dominance displays and threats include tail-lashing, teeth-baring, laying back the ears, raising the hackles, back-arching, and raising the tail. Threatened raccoons may make a series of sideways hops. Submissive gestures include head, body, and tail held down to the ground, and sometimes an actual retreat.

Scent-marking and neck- and anal-rubbing have been observed in captive raccoons. A juvenile raccoon was responsible for the neck-rubbing and the adult captives investigated these rubs, sniffing and urinating on them. Wild raccoons make latrines, mostly from summer through winter. Latrines are usually on the ground but have also been found on the limbs of trees as high as 39 feet (12 m). Latrines are also made under rock overhangs on slopes, in hollow logs, in attics, and atop logs and adjacent large conifers next to water sources. They might contain scats of one or more individuals; one observer recorded at least 3 raccoons using a single latrine. How latrines function in raccoon communities is unknown, but many species of animals and birds visit them and feed on undigested seeds. Raccoon latrines could serve as important information centers for a variety of species.

COURTSHIP AND MATING

Mating occurs in February and March throughout most of North America and a bit later in southern latitudes. Females that lose a litter or fail to breed may go through a second estrous cycle in May or June.

The only time males and females associate is during mating, when the males may seek out the females when they are still in their winter dens. Once a male finds a female, he establishes a 1- to 3-day "consortship," or tending bond, in which he may defend her from other males. Copulation lasts about an hour and varies in how aggressive it may appear. One female uttered shrill cries and occasionally attempted to bite the male.

Raccoon mating systems vary from polygyny to promiscuity. Typically, males maintain and conform to dominance hierarchies based upon size and weight, and dominant males control access to estrus females. Few males do most of the breeding, and many males show signs of injury from male-male confrontations. In one study, the most successful males consorted with up to 6 females in a breeding season, while others mated with few or none. Females often consort with only a single male, but females have been know to consort with up to 4. When estrus is highly synchronized, meaning local females come into estrus roughly simultaneously, dominant males cannot control access to all of them, and this allows more males an opportunity to mate.

DEVELOPMENT AND DISPERSAL OF YOUNG

Pregnant females reduce their activity and seek out suitable natal dens in the week before they give birth. Tree cavities offer ideal protection for newborns, but a variety of other den types have been used. Raccoons may give birth in rock crevices, caves, abandoned buildings, dry drainage pipes, and other cover. Their gestation lasts about 2 months, after which they give birth to a litter of 3 to 4 young in April in the North and later in the South.

Newborns are sparsely furred, and their eyes and ears are tightly closed. It takes a month in the nest before they are able to walk, and they begin moving about outside of their nests at 1.5 months. A few weeks later they begin eating solid food and begin to grow very rapidly. At this point they are roaming around as a group with their mother. Around late August and September the youngsters begin to roam independently. They will regroup with their

mother for winter denning if that is necessary, and finally disperse in the spring.

Young raccoons may not reach their adult size until their second spring or autumn, when they are also likely to disperse. In the North mothers reunite with their young of the year in late fall, and they den together through the winter. Then juveniles disperse in the spring. Sometimes pairs of yearlings will remain together through the spring, gradually separating as time passes. Females may remain nearby, and males move farther away. In southern regions like Texas, young raccoons never need to regroup with the family for winter denning, but familial bonds can still last up to and through their mother's next estrus and parturition. Males disperse more than females, and typical distances are between 6 and 19 miles (10–30 km), although on occasion a raccoon will travel up to 170 miles (275 km).

INTERACTIONS AMONG RACCOONS

Raccoons tend to be territorial in the North, and in other places where their home ranges overlap they avoid one another. Most reports indicate that amicable interactions between adult raccoons are rare, males especially. Even in feeding congregations, raccoons tend to avoid close proximity to one another. Yet, when raccoons are captured and kept together, animals drawn from the same general area assimilate to one another more readily than those drawn from disparate locations. Dominance hierarchies have been reported among wild raccoons visiting feeding stations, as well as raccoons traveling frequently in nonfamily groups, suggesting more complex relationships than simple avoidance.

In a study in Texas, males associated with one another in coalitions of 3 to 4 individuals throughout the year. They interacted frequently and positively. Their home ranges overlapped each other's strongly, but each coalition also excluded other male groups. Female home ranges in the same area were tightly clustered around limited aquatic habitats. Female clustering provided greater mating opportunities, and allowed successful coalitions to limit their male competitors to only those within their own groups.

Young males disperse, whereas females often move into portions of their mothers' home ranges. Mothers and daughters share available resources and may also engage in communal foraging and denning. One study found three generations of a matriline rearing pups in the same brush pile.

INTERACTIONS WITH OTHER SPECIES

Raccoon predators include coyotes, bobcats, Red Foxes, fishers, owls, and alligators. Fishers and bobcats attack and kill raccoons in their winter dens. In one case a fisher killed a raccoon slumbering in a

Curious young raccoons peek out from their tree den. © *Mark Elbroch*

tree cavity, but was unable to extract it. The fisher abandoned the wedged carcass, half sticking out of the tree, but stripped the exposed limbs to the bone before it departed. Overall, predation by other animals is probably not a significant factor in raccoon populations. Human harvests and disease (e.g., canine distemper, rabies) usually account for most adult mortality. Where there is no hunting pressure, vehicle collisions and attacks by domestic animals may be significant threats.

Raccoons are the primary terrestrial reservoir for the rabies virus. In the 1950s and 1960s, only the raccoons in Florida, Georgia, and South Carolina were known to have rabies. In the 1970s, rabies was found in West Virginia and Virginia, where several thousand animals from the South had been relocated by private hunting clubs. From there, rabies spread north and south along the Atlantic Coast. Now rabies can be found in raccoons from eastern Canada to Florida and from the Atlantic Coast to eastern Ohio and Tennessee. Raccoon rabies outbreaks also infect foxes, woodchucks, skunks, opos-

sums, rabbits, and domestic pets. Domestic cats are the most worrisome vector since they are often allowed to roam, have low vaccination rates, and can readily expose numerous humans and other animals. During an outbreak in Connecticut, domestic animals accounted for a minor portion of diseased animals, but they accounted for most of the human exposures.

Raccoons throughout their range are commonly infected with the raccoon roundworm (*Baylisacarus procyonis*), with infection rates higher in the North than the South. This worm lives in the gastrointestinal tract and does little damage to raccoons. The eggs of the worm are passed in raccoon scats, and then infect over 50 species of mammals and birds. Raccoon latrines provide a concentrated source of undigested seeds for rodents like White-footed Deermice, and raccoon roundworm can be a significant mortality factor for them in some areas. The disease can cause serious illness and even death in humans. The best means of protection is to avoid direct contact with raccoon scats and latrines.

Collared Peccary
Pecari tajacu

OTHER NAMES: javelina (Spanish), peccary, musk hog, chancho, pecarí, tajacu (South America).

Peccaries have a long history in North America: they may have evolved here 33 million years ago. Now, only the northernmost extent of the Collared Peccaries' range reaches the United States. Although they occupy the southwestern states, Collared Peccaries are not truly adapted to desert environments. Typical of tropical mammals, they have poorly insulated fur and little ability to conserve water. Although they need the warmth, it is energetically costly to stay cool in a hot, dry climate, for which they compensate behaviorally. In the summer they are crepuscular and nocturnal, while in winter they are active more during daylight hours. In the mountainous areas of Texas, New Mexico, and Arizona, local populations are extirpated by snow and severe cold.

The scientific names *Pecari* and *tajacu* come from native South American names for this animal. Some consider the Spanish term *pecarí* to have come from a word that originally meant "many paths through the woods."

ACTIVITY AND MOVEMENT

DAILY

Collared Peccaries time their activity to avoid extremes of heat and cold. Of their active hours, 75 percent or more are spent foraging or traveling to and from foraging areas. Peccaries travel in single-file lines and form well-worn runs between feeding, watering, and resting sites. Individuals compete for more forward positions when moving, and races sometimes occur in which two individuals trot and then run, each attempting to pass the other. When a group reaches a foraging site, individuals fan out and leave a slew of tracks, scats, and roughly chewed vegetation.

Peccaries have weak eyesight but sensitive noses and ears. They are not visually oriented and move about with their head down, sniffing the ground, occasionally lifting their nose skyward to sample the air. If you are downwind, and a bit stealthy, you may be able to approach to within 10 feet (3 m) of a peccary before it notices you. If it is alert to something close by, a peccary will try to get its scent by

Collared Peccaries make contact and rub each other's sides in greeting. © Mesquite53/Dreamstime.com

lifting its snout and moving downwind, but it may not appear to see the threat until it is almost on top of it. When they do detect a threat, however, they do not stick around long. Peccaries can run like lightning when pressed, streaking across the ground on their short legs, often disappearing into thick, spiny cover.

SEASONAL

Collared Peccaries move about less when the temperature is high, retreating to shade and water. Regular resting sites may be found under natural overhangs, in caves, in the shade of mesquite and palo verde trees, at the base of boulders, and under brushy, sloping banks. Bedding areas can be identified by their dished-out beds and tracked-up ground, accumulated scat, and radiating trails.

FOOD AND FORAGING

Collared Peccaries are generalist herbivores. Their digestive system is multi-chambered and allows digestion of fiber to a degree that rivals the ruminants. In their North American range they eat succulents (for example, agave, yucca, and cactus), mesquite and acacia beans, and some mix of browse, forbs, grasses, roots, tubers, and acorns depending on availability. They consume little, if any, animal matter. In the tropics javelinas eat many hard nuts, and some argue that their large interlocking canines provide support for the skull and limit lateral movements of the mandible, making their jaws more efficient nut crackers.

Collared Peccaries are notorious for eating the spiny pads of prickly pear and related cactus (*Opuntia* spp.), which they do without any visible ill effects. However, *Opuntia* is in fact very poor forage, lacking most important nutrients. Captive animals fed such fare *ad libitum* consumed up to one-third of their body weight in *Opuntia* each day, and then died in a matter of months from nutritional deficiencies. They most likely consume prickly pear cactus for its water content and depend upon other foods for nutrition.

HABITAT AND HOME RANGE

Collared Peccaries range from southern Argentina to the southwestern United States. In North America they inhabit two general areas: southeastern Arizona together with the adjacent corner of New Mexico, and an area extending from the southern tip of Texas northwesterly through western Texas to New Mexico. There are sporadic occurrences north of these areas.

North American peccaries inhabit dense thorn scrub, chaparral, oak woodlands, and desert scrub communities. They prefer areas with dense cover and abundant prickly pear cactus. In their tropical

A Collared Peccary rips into a prickly pear cactus pad. © *John Cancalosi/Ardea London*

ranges they inhabit all available wet and dry forest types. They are prevented from more northward expansion by winter cold.

A herd's territory occupies about 0.4 to 0.8 square miles (1–2 km²), and 0.4 square miles (1 km²) of occupied range could hold around 8 peccaries. The local population density varies by season and the resource availability. If resources are insufficient to support a resident herd, the territory may shift or expand, or the herd size shrinks.

COMMUNICATION

Collared Peccaries communicate with a great deal of physical touch, but each animal is protective of the space around it. Auditory and visual rituals and displays are used to prevent or allow close contact. Many of the displays peccaries make are graded. Graded signals change in quality to match the situation, as with feeding grunts. When feeding, a peccary makes low, repetitive grunts that indicate contentment, but if another peccary wanders too close, the grunt gets louder and the pitch begins rising and falling, warning the intruder to back off. If the intruder doesn't heed the message, the grunt gives way to a harsh growl that generally induces retreat.

In agonistic interactions, peccaries often growl at one another and clack their teeth together, making a distinctive sound. Teeth-clacking varies from light, rapid clicks (mild aggression) to harder clacks, to clacks accompanied by huffs and woofs (highly aggressive) of forcefully exhaled air. Aggressive stances and postures accompany the sounds. Visual displays of aggression, usually made by dominant animals toward subordinates, include direct, or "hard," stares with a tense body and wide-footed stance, and sometimes raised hackles. An open mouth is presented with head outstretched toward the opponent. The most intense visual threat is a lunge with an open mouth, and this usually occurs when a subordinate has blundered to within 3 feet (1 m) of a dominant animal.

Faced with aggressive displays, subordinate animals need to signal submission or suffer a beating. If the subordinate is more than 6 feet (2 m) away from the threatening dominant, it may just run off. If the aggressive display is of low intensity, a simple "head-away" gesture, made by lowering the nose nearly to the ground and turning the head away, could suffice. At close quarters, the subordinate first rocks back on its feet to show submission, and if this does not defuse the situation, it continues leaning back until it is crouching down on its rump and curls its forefeet under it. If that still is not enough, the subordinate lies flat on its belly, holding its chin to the ground, maybe even while pointing its head away. The lowered stance appeases dominant animals, and sometimes a subordinate "kneels" by lowering itself to its front "knees" when feeding alongside a more powerful animal. Submissive sounds that accompany these displays include whimpering "yips" and repetitive yelping. In some cases the target of the aggression doesn't submit and instead aims to defend itself. In these cases, the defending peccary will orient itself toward the aggressor, raise its hackles, and walk slowly backward.

When one animal is aggressive toward another and submission is not immediate, a "squabble" ensues. In a squabble, both individuals face one another, growling with open mouths, and simultaneously wag their snouts back and forth, often jostling and pushing one another with head and chest. Squabbles are relatively common, and on occasion a dominant animal simply presses its snout into another and the subordinate lies down. Squabbles can also escalate into real fights in which both animals lunge and attempt to bite one another in earnest. In a squabble, the winner is the one that makes the other lower its head first and stop squabbling. In a fight, the loser flees, often with at least minor injuries. These fights are rare and brief, but torn ears and noses bear witness to their occurrence.

Alarmed peccaries make an "uh" sound, lifting their nose to test for scent. When doing so they may have their hackles raised and hold one hoof off the ground, ready to flee as they wag their head back and forth and wriggle their nasal disc. If they cannot locate the threat, they may approach or try to circle downwind in a stiff-legged walk, with exaggerated foot-lifts and audible, stamping steps. If they flee, they huff as they do so. If highly alarmed (or aggressive) they make a resonant bark, often along with growling.

The vast majority of social interactions among peccaries are amicable. Amicable encounters begin with lifted snouts as they smell what is happening around them. One may walk slowly up to another as they sniff, closing the distance until their noses touch. Nuzzling and sniffing the nose leads to sniffing the body of the other animal and rubbing and nuzzling it with the snout. This rubbing often leads

A head-away appeasement gesture elicited by a hard stare (a). A subordinate peccary kneels when feeding next to a dominant individual (b). Peccaries in a squabble (c).

to the most important and common social behavior, the "mutual rub." In a mutual rub, two animals stand side by side, with their heads alongside the other's haunch. In this position, they rub heads on each other's hindquarters and back (where there is a large scent gland). They rub with sufficient force to jostle and move each other, and the pair often rub while walking in a small circle. Reciprocal grooming cements group identity and underscores dominance hierarchies. Social behaviors are seen most often when the herd is moving, playing, leaving a bedding site, or has been alarmed.

Marking and scenting behavior is crucial for group cohesion and territorial defense. Peccaries have large scent glands on their backs that can emit scent secretions up to nearly a foot (30 cm) as an alarm. Erecting the bristly guard hairs on their backs and rumps activates the dorsal gland and may be accompanied by a vigorous body shake. Peccaries often back up to objects and rub or squirt scent on them from their large dorsal scent glands, and they may also squat and rub directly on the ground. Defecation, urination, and pawing of the ground may be used in combination with glandular secretions to construct larger and more varied scent posts. Latrines of scats build up near bedding areas and along territorial boundaries. Those near bedding sites may be scent marks, or just incidental to the use of the sites.

When investigating scent marks, peccaries may rub their head on the scent-marked ground or even lie on their sides and "thrash" or roll, wiggling and squirming vigorously on the scent left by another peccary. Rubbing in scent marks and rubbing against other herd members spreads common scents across individuals of the group and may serve as marks of group membership.

COURTSHIP AND MATING

In their tropical range Collared Peccaries exhibit year-round reproduction, but in the hot southern areas where peccaries exist in North America, winter is the time for peccaries to breed. Peak breeding occurs in December and January, when increased precipitation and cooler temperatures produce more forage. The estrous cycle lasts 22 to 26 days, with a 2.5-day estrus when they are sexually receptive. Females in poor nutritional condition may not ovulate or participate in the current breeding season.

The dominant male in the herd attempts to mate with nearly all estrous females. As each comes into estrus, he forms a tending bond with her that lasts a few hours to a few days. A tending male rests his chin on the female's back or rump and engages her with many typical social gestures, like sniffing and nuzzling with the nose and mutual rubbing. To this repertoire he also adds successful and unsuccessful mounting attempts. Subordinate males are more likely to mate when several females are in estrus simultaneously and the dominant male is busy with one of the other females. The alpha male confronts or attacks subordinates attempting to breed. Even so, agonistic interactions between males are not more common during breeding than at other times of year, and subordinates that suffer attacks do not leave the group.

DEVELOPMENT AND DISPERSAL OF YOUNG

Mating occurs in late winter, and most females in a herd are pregnant in February, as days and nights are getting warmer. After a gestation of about 5 months females give birth in April or May. Females temporarily leave the herd and isolate themselves for the actual parturition. Litters are typically 2, but sometimes 3 or 4. Young peccaries are precocial and quickly stand to nurse for the first time after birth. After only a few days the mother and young rejoin the herd. The female and other females in the herd provide milk for up to 2 months, when juveniles are completely weaned.

Adults are highly tolerant of youngsters. Juveniles nurse from behind, and lactating females make no apparent effort to determine whether they are suckling their own young or another's. Little ones crawl atop adults while resting and feed mouth-to-mouth with them, snapping at them and even taking food from their mouths; they shoulder past adults when traveling in line and roam underfoot to the point of tripping them, all without eliciting hostility. When a herd is alarmed, the flight is orderly: the juveniles are kept together immediately behind the lead animal, which guides them to safety, and the rest of the adults follow behind, keeping themselves between the young and the threat. Youngsters are frequently seen playing. Play is a social bonding behavior and includes mock snaps, wrestling, chases, and quick dashes. It affords an opportunity to practice and learn the complementary agonistic displays and responses that will be necessary in adult life.

Natal dispersal, usually involving males, is very poorly understood in peccaries and may be uncommon. Peccaries have not been observed to show the behaviors common to deer and other families of chasing off subadult young in preparation for the next breeding. Adults have little success joining new herds, but some interchange does occur.

INTERACTIONS AMONG PECCARIES

Collared Peccaries are distinctive among North American ungulates in that they maintain mixed-sex herds throughout the year. Peccaries are intensely social animals, and these large stable groups keep in constant close contact with one another. Herds range from 9 to 13 animals on average. Social

Gaping peccaries communicate aggression, an uncommon agonistic display in their relatively peaceful societies. © Tom and Pat Leeson/Ardea London

relationships are based on physical contact, sounds, scent, and gestures at close quarters. The groups are structured according to a linear dominance hierarchy that includes both sexes but is headed by a dominant male. Herds are territorial, overlapping little or not at all with other herds.

Herds can and do temporarily fragment into smaller foraging groups. Such subgroups usually persist for only a day or less, but on occasion remain separated for several weeks. Subgroups form less often and tend to be smaller in the winter. When subgroups become increasingly isolated, a new herd may form. Fission is functionally complete when a splinter group remains isolated from its source group for an entire breeding season.

Agonistic interactions are relatively rare among Collared Peccaries, and violent fights are exceedingly infrequent, if they happen at all. When fights do occur, they may include biting, head-butting, or visual displays, such as mouth-gaping and head-lowering, which hint at physical fights. Attack displays are attenuated by well-developed submissive gestures, such as retreating, lying down, and rolling onto one's back.

Groups of peccaries defend their ground against other groups. Peccaries have been seen aggressively chasing one another across territory boundaries. In one case an intruding male was chased out of one territory, but as he was pursued about 330 feet (100 m) into his own territory, he turned and chased his former pursuer back across their mutual border. After subsequent, shorter chases the two stopped, staring at one another across the boundary, and then turned and walked away.

INTERACTIONS WITH OTHER SPECIES

Collared Peccaries suffer from habitat changes caused by cattle grazing and feral pigs. Research shows inverse relations between densities of peccaries and feral pigs, but specific effects have not been identified. Peccaries are pests to Texas landowners using feed for managing deer. Increasing urban populations, particularly in Tucson and Phoenix, have led to increased negative interactions with humans.

Adult Collared Peccaries are preyed on by jaguars, ocelots, cougars, and bobcats. Coyotes and raptors, particularly golden eagles, often prey on the young. When fleeing they run in single file, stopping occasionally and scenting and listening to assess their risk. If they are alarmed by a threat that they can't place, all the peccaries may flee in different directions for about 65 feet (20 m) before they stop and try again to place the threat. If they can place it, all the animals will flee directly away in the same direction and eventually regroup.

Cooperative defense by peccaries against coyotes and bobcats has been observed. In one case, adult peccaries moved forward and drove back an approaching coyote while the rest of the herd clustered around the juveniles and led them away. Against a bobcat, an entire herd bunched together and approached the predator as a group, causing the cat to flee. Peccaries are not entirely defenseless either. Peccary canines are dangerous weapons, and juveniles only a few weeks old will use them to slash intruders. White-lipped Peccaries (*Tayassu pecari*), which form large herds in the tropics, have been reported to kill ocelots and even jaguars in self-defense.

OTHER NAMES: elk (Europe), orignal (French), moos (Abenaki).

When hand-reared, moose can be trained to follow voice commands and can carry a 275-pound (125-kg) packload or pull a 600- to 800-pound (300–400-kg) sled at a walking speed of 3 miles (4 km) an hour. Moose can carry a load over steep ridges, through thickets and swamps, and across rivers without the slightest shifting of the contents. To discourage the effective resistance that moose-equipped guerillas could mount against his conquest of Siberia, the Russian general Jermak Timofeitsch outlawed moose husbandry, killed domesticated moose, and tortured moose-riders. What's more, horses panic at the sight of moose. The Estonian city of Tartu (Dorpat) once had to outlaw moose in the streets because of damage caused by crazed horses. In the late 1600s King Karl XI of Sweden tried to use moose as mounts for a special light cavalry unit that could swarm across inhospitable terrain and whose very appearance would cause disarray among the enemy. Ultimately this effort failed. Although individual moose are amenable in captivity, it is difficult to keep them long or in large numbers, because of the difficulty in supplying appropriate foods and their susceptibility to livestock diseases.

ACTIVITY AND MOVEMENT

DAILY

Moose alternate between perhaps 7 and 9 successive periods of foraging and rest throughout the day, spending up to 97 percent of each day eating and resting. During these cycles, they move from one feeding area to another, bedding in between to rest and chew their cud. They may use more than 5 different beds in a day. As we do when turning from work to lunch or back to work, moose stretch, yawn, shake, rub, and scratch themselves. Moose also play, most of which involves running and splashing around through water. They may also chase one another and play at fighting.

Moose, like other deer, travel in a walking gait. When pressed they speed up into a trot, often a straddle-trot in which the hind feet reach beyond the forefeet on the outside. Trotting moose exhibit the grace and mobility awarded by long, thin legs—they look like prancing stallions. The size and power of the moose allow it to move nimbly, gliding over obstacles, brush, and deep snow that forces other animals to leap, change course, or just plain stop.

Moose have been clocked running at 38 miles (60 km) an hour over *obstructed* ground.

Moose are adept swimmers, both above and below the surface. They will swim long distances, holding their head just above the surface of the water and paddling with their large hooves. While foraging in lakes or ponds, moose sometimes fully submerge in water up to 18 feet (5.5 m) deep. The longest dive recorded is 50 seconds. Moose can dive with so little disturbance to the water surface that all the ripples of their entrance fade before they resurface. They can also turn 180° while submerged and resurface at surprising distances from where they went under.

SEASONAL

Summers are short in the northern range of moose, and yet they must gain sufficient fat reserves in just 3 to 5 months to survive the upcoming winter. Breeding bulls lose 20 percent of their body weight from fall to winter, and so must regain hundreds of pounds each summer. Moose invest up to 12 hours a day in spring and early summer in foraging, and then less and less time as fall approaches.

Moose move locally within seasonal ranges, but the extent of movement varies greatly by locale and individual. Snow depth, despite moose adaptations, begins to hinder their movement at around 23 to 28 inches (60–70 cm) and is the primary factor for any seasonal migrations. Some moose travel 1 to 6 miles (2–10 km), sometimes much farther, on traditional migration routes to seek plant communities that offer them the resources they need in each season. Winter habitats include closed-canopy coniferous forest stands that offer protection from the wind

A moose dashes in front of a UPS truck in northern New Hampshire, where moose collisions are an increasing human safety concern. © *Mark Elbroch*

and accumulating snow. Often this means moving to higher or lower elevations to find the right cover. The importance of plant communities (apart from elevation) is underscored by the fact that migrations also occur in areas like Minnesota and the North Slope of Alaska, where the land is essentially flat.

Some moose remain on "summer ranges" all year, provided others migrate, reducing their density to a level that the area can support in winter. Diversity and flexibility of migratory patterns is the rule, not the exception, especially for moose in the West.

FOOD AND FORAGING

Moose are the largest members of the deer family and the largest of the "concentrate selectors"—ruminants that sample a wide array of plant material and concentrate their feeding on those of the greatest nutritional value at any given time. Moose can and do eat everything from moss to trees. Winter food is woody browse extending above the snowpack. Overall food intake is lower in the winter because this coarse food requires a 20 to 30 percent increase in retention time in the rumen. Availability of adequately nutritious winter browse is the principal ecological limitation on moose populations throughout North America. They reach out and grasp a tender twig between their lower incisors and their upper palate (all deer lack upper incisors) and jerk their head up and back to tear off the twig. They also straddle and bend small trees in order to reach the tender growth near the top, and they break large branches to get at new growth at their tips. Moose supplement twig browsing by feeding on bark, and heavily used wintering areas show substantial trunk-scarring of preferred species. Moose use their lower incisors to slice and cut strips of bark from young red and striped maples, balsam fir, aspen, and a select few other tree species.

Aspen, birch, alder, and willow are the predominant foods of moose throughout their range. In winter upwards of 75 percent of their diet may be conifers like balsam fir. Willows thrive in frequently disturbed, productive environments and have relatively weak chemical defenses against herbivores. Defensive compounds, such as tannins that are common in many species, not only taste bad but also disrupt absorption of essential nutrients like sodium.

Aquatic vegetation is richer in sodium and other essential minerals than woody browse and forms a major part of summer diets of moose in much of the species' range. Some consider the need for sodium to be the main impetus for aquatic foraging, but aquatics also are highly digestible and grow in great concentrations, making them economical to eat. Favored feeding areas might be bays in lakes and ponds with dense mats of potential food plants. Bur-reed, horsetails, and cattails are perhaps the most commonly reported aquatic food plants. Most of their feeding may be on smaller species that moose reach by dipping their head below the surface while wading, which is very difficult to document.

Aquatic foraging is not universal, however; some populations do little or none at all. This may be because they get sodium from other sources, including salt licks, which moose visit intensively wherever they are available. Where natural mineral deposits are rare, moose frequent roadsides and the areas they drain into to eat residual salt from winter road treatments. They may visit salt licks for up to an hour as many as 4 times a day, and as many as 6 moose may be seen congregating around salt in the spring and autumn.

HABITAT AND HOME RANGE

Moose, like other deer, thrive on upheaval. Forest disturbances, such as logging and fires, increase browsing opportunities for moose by encouraging new growth they can reach. Not all disturbances increase moose browse, though; the net effect depends on local soils and seeding conditions. The optimal moose habitat is that with climax plant communities interspersed with patches in various states of recovery and succession.

Moose habitat varies considerably across the species' range. Food and cover are the primary determiners of good habitat, and winter snow is one of the prime limiting factors. In the East, moose use wooded habitats in summer, preferably with stands of young aspen and birch. In the winter they move to thicker conifer cover like climax balsam fir communities. These stands block snow from reaching the ground, making travel easier under their canopies, and use of balsam fir stands increases when snow gets deeper than 30 inches (75 cm). Aquatic habitats are used often in early and mid-summer, but are not thought to be essential.

In the West, riparian willow stands are critical to survival. Moose like shrub communities: tracts of brushy, woody vegetation with lots of easily reached buds and young twigs. Most of these are ephemeral, springing up after storms, fire, and logging but eventually maturing into a forest. In contrast, riparian willow stands are permanent shrublands, kept ever-young and productive by frequent flooding and erosion. The effect is that of an orchard managed for moose forage. In some areas of the West, moose move to upland conifer stands in winter but in other areas, such as the Alaskan tundra, they remain in shrub communities year-round.

Moose home ranges average 2 to 4 square miles (5–10 km^2) but vary widely. Abundant snowfall will tend to reduce home ranges, temporarily or for the extent of the season, as the accumulating snow impedes movement. In interior Alaska, with its open habitats and low snowfall, moose home ranges may reach 117 square miles (300 km²). In a month-long period of high snowfall in Minnesota, moose confined their movements to stands of balsam fir 5 to 10 acres (2–4 ha) in size.

COMMUNICATION

As in other deer, the basic threat gesture among moose is a hard stare which is incorporated into head-high, head-low, and antler threats. Head-high threats are often accompanied by flailing attacks with the front legs. The head-low threat is associated with head-butting. Females use the head-high and head-low threats, and if their opponents do not back down they may rush in and strike with a stiff foreleg or rear up on their hind feet and flail with their forelegs. The head-low threat from cows or subordinate animals is considered by some as a high-intensity "scare threat," the last-ditch display of a cornered animal. Males also use kicking attacks, especially when their antlers are absent or still growing. Antler threats are specific to bulls after the velvet has been shed and is most often associated with rutting contests. Antlers may be held high or low, and the bulls tilt their head so that their nose points down, exposing the greatest surface area of their antlers to their opponent. In the low-antler threat, with ears laid back and hackles up, the bull's nose may nearly touch the ground.

The "challenger gait" is made when a bull seeks to intimidate a rival. The challenger walks around his rival with long, stiff-legged strides, presenting his bulky profile and swaying his antlers from side to side. This threat may emerge when two near-equal

ranking bulls encounter one another and neither one will back down. The two work up to low-antler threats before making physical contact. A bull shows submission and extricates himself before violence ensues by physically withdrawing.

During the rut, bulls thrash their antlers and wallow in rutting pits. Antler thrashing is an auditory display of the bull's vigor and strength. Bulls will swing and twist their antlers against shrubs or small trees, breaking twigs and limbs and making a noisy racket. A rutting pit (or wallow) is made by pawing a shallow depression with forefoot and squatting and urinating in it. They stomp their feet in the resulting muck as well as lie down and roll in it. Moose have excellent olfaction, and bull urine is strong enough that humans can smell it at great distances. Females rapidly approach these pits and get right into them to sniff and wallow. Females may even fight over access if they encounter each other there.

Both sexes of moose strip and rub trees as signposts. Females rub less often than males and usually in the middle of the rut, when most of them are in estrus. Female rubbing likely advertises their condition and location. Females will also defend their scent posts from other females, as well as aggressively displace rivals at rubbing posts and then over-mark them with their own scents. Males rub most toward the end of the rutting period. Their rubs may serve to attract females that did not breed earlier and may even stimulate or accelerate their estrous cycles. Before rubbing a pole-sized tree, a cow moose strips the bark with her incisors but does not eat it. Both sexes rub the tree with their foreheads, necks, and preorbital glands, located in

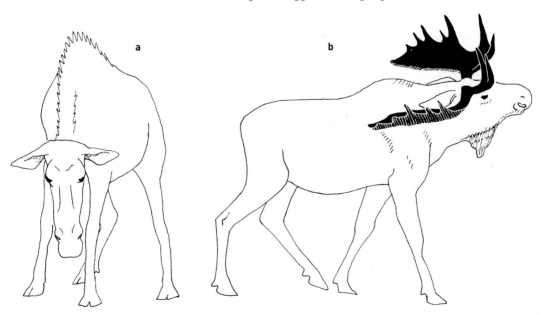

A cow moose's scare threat (a). The head-tilting, stiff-legged challenger gait (b).

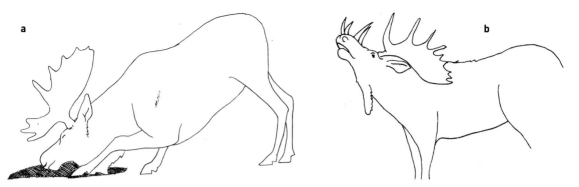

A bull in a wallow. Drawn after Geist, 1998, *Deer of the World*. Used with permission of Stackpole Books (a). A male calls as he trails a group of reluctant females during the rut (b).

front of their eyes. Males will also rub and scarify trees with their antlers.

Moose vocalizations are rudimentary and plain. Bulls make roaring bellows, grunts, and low-frequency "gulps" or croaks at regular intervals during the rut to advertise their presence to rivals and females alike. Cows grunt to their calves and moan to protest nursing by calves and in interactions with other females. They also use the call when being harassed by young bulls during the rut. The calves bawl and cry for attention and aid.

COURTSHIP AND MATING

Cows ovulate for the first time at 16 or 28 months. Earlier ovulation is more likely when food is abundant and rich. Poor range conditions may cause a delay in sexual maturity until as late as 40 months of age. A cow's most productive years are between the ages of 4 and 12, although they continue to bear young until nearly 20 years old. The annual estrus period lasts 7 to 12 days. Local females are synchronized, and the peak of the rut is sometime between late September and early October. Each cow is in estrus, receptive to mating, for only about 24 hours of her estrus period. If a cow fails to breed during her first cycle, she enters a second estrus about 3 weeks later. About 10 percent of females go into estrus a second time, causing a "second rut" in late October or early November.

During the rut, cows make a loud moan that can be heard up to 2 miles (3.2 km) away. Mature females are often pestered by persistent young bulls when they are not even in estrus, and the moan is made in protest. The moaning draws the attention of mature bulls, whose presence discourages the young bulls from harassing the cow. This interaction has led to the interpretation of the cow's moan as a mating call intended to draw in potential mates. In any event, it has been mimicked by generations of hunters using cones of birch bark to get the attention of rutting bulls.

Most North American populations are taiga, or woodland, moose, and they are mostly solitary and exhibit a tending-bond mating system similar to that of White-tailed Deer. As a female nears her short period of estrus, a rutting bull "tends" her, walking, feeding, and bedding with her until they are able to mate. Tundra moose in the open areas of interior Alaska and British Columbia are more sociable and are often found in groups. During the rut they form fluid groups of males and females in which the dominant male seeks to monopolize breeding with all the females he encounters. As the bulls compete for access to the females, the cows moan in annoyance at the harassment of amorous bulls, with whom they are not ready or willing to breed. During the second rut, when those few cows that haven't already bred come into heat again, tundra bulls form tending bonds instead of harems. Males focus on females during the rut and generally stop feeding. They dig 4 or 5 pits per day during the rut, in which they urinate and wallow, and thrash vegetation with their antlers. Moose dynamics around wallows are critical to the rut. Older males have more attractive urine, and when they create wallows in which to pee and roll, females may run from as far away as 100 yards (91 m) to soak in the smells and join the male in the wallow itself. They may even displace the bull before he is finished rolling himself. When more than one female appears at the edge of a freshly made wallow, they fight for access to it. Bulls, on the other hand, also try to keep the cows from rolling, though their attempts are in general unsuccessful. Biologists believe they do this to force females to rub the males themselves in order to gain access to the urine, which increases their mating opportunities. There is something in prime bull urine that is lacking in that of younger bulls, and so younger males sometimes try to sneak in and roll in large bull wallows to better attract a mate. When caught in the act, they are chased off.

Males also spar with one another. Sparring is ritualized antler fighting that usually occurs between young bulls or bulls of different status (size and age).

Large bulls do spar, but rarely and usually only in the period before the rut. Sparring is a ritual of controlled, low-level aggression, and sparring is often broken up by periods of other activities like feeding. The bulls approach each other in nonthreatening positions. Their heads are held down and out, but their ears are not back and their hackles are not up. Antlers are carefully positioned together and then the two push back and forth, grappling but not fighting all out. Among tundra moose, 2 to 3, usually young, subprime males might still get in a "scramble"—a grunting, running sparring match—in the period just after rutting ends. The noise attracts other bulls, and when a prime, mature bull shows up, the others scatter.

Sometimes when two large males of equal size meet, what begins as threats and pawing earth can quickly elevate to combat. Their antlers hook together with a loud, wooden crash, and the bulls begin pushing forcefully into one another. First one bull pushes harder and the other gives way for several steps. Then he digs in and begins driving his rival backward. They twist and turn their heads, trying to force the other to break contact. The speed and power exhibited in true fights is frightening. The sounds of exertion—the trampling of vegetation and the clamor of antlers clacking and sliding against one another—travel far and wide. Antler tines can break under the pressure. If one moose breaks away, the other will try to gore him in the side or rump. Usually the loser flees precipitously, but fights can go on for hours interspersed with displacement feeding and thrashing. Fights result in eye injuries, blindness, injured limbs, and injuries severe enough to lead to death.

Males approach a receptive female in a grunting, tongue-flicking, low-stretch posture. In the low-stretch, the head is held low with neck extended and the nose pointed upward. Often more than one male will approach a given female, prompting a contest if neither bull departs immediately. In tundra moose, males and females often congregate in arenas where males strut, fight, wallow, and mark. Antlers grow every year and therefore honestly reflect a bull's health and vigor. Bulls in their prime grow the largest and most symmetrical antlers, meaning their right and left antlers better match each other, and those still maturing or aging beyond their prime grow smaller, lopsided antlers. One researcher tested this hypothesis and constructed a moose suit for several fieldworkers, which he adorned with massive antlers. When the team entered the rut arena, all the large bulls melted into the surrounding brush, realizing they were outmatched.

If the female is nearing estrus she will allow the bull to tend her. They come together and touch noses. While tending her, he remains close, sniffing and nuzzling her and chasing off challengers. She tolerates his proximity and attention, but only to a degree. If he is too aggressive she will retreat. The male periodically tests whether she is in estrus by inhaling the scent of her urine, exhibiting the flehmen expression. When she is receptive, he follows her and attempts to lay his head across her rump. At this point the cow stops retreating and allows the bull to mount her, which he does repeatedly for a day or two.

DEVELOPMENT AND DISPERSAL OF YOUNG

Gestation is around 8 months long, and cows give birth to 1 to 2 calves in May and June. On rare occasions 3 are born, but more often families with 3 calves include an orphaned calf adopted by a mother with 2 calves of her own. Cows retreat to secluded, isolated areas to give birth. This birthing site is important in hiding the calves from predators. An expectant mother travels to her calving site by a circuitous, erratic route that is thought to thwart trailing predators. The mother also chases off other nearby moose shortly after she gives birth so that her calves imprint on her. Birthing territories tend to be at high elevations or in secluded islands of dense cover. They usually have good views of potential avenues of approach by predators and good forage like abundant willows nearby to nourish the mother during lactation. Mother and young remain in these areas for up to a month.

In the 2 or 3 days before birth cows may also do a lot more walking than usual, and when birth is imminent a mother's udders swell and she may secrete colostrum. Birth of a single calf takes 15 to 30 minutes on average and is done lying down. As soon as

Males crash together in fast and violent competitions to establish dominance and determine which animals gain access to females during the breeding season. © Michael S. Quinton/National Geographic Image Collection

the baby is born the mother begins licking it vigorously. This cleans and stimulates the calf and begins forging the bond between them. Within a few hours the calf is standing. The mother may lie down when nursing, a behavior unique to moose and caribou in the deer family.

The cow-calf bond is particularly strong among moose. Young moose are not "hiders" like deer fawns, they are "followers." A calf's defense is to stick close to its mother's heels and if threatened, hide behind her and her aggressive protection. Cows with calves sometimes defend rich summer food sources from other moose. They are not strictly territorial in terms of adhering to a certain area, but they maintain a "sliding territoriality" by protecting a space within which they wander from resource to resource. If the two should be separated for 10 days, the mother will no longer accept her own calf. If it is separated or in need of help or nursing, the calf uses a plaintive voice to call its mother and she comes running. The mother, in turn, often grunts to her calf.

Nursing continues for 5 months, and the diet of rich milk fuels rapid growth. Newborn calves weigh about 35 pounds (16 kg) on average, and while nursing they gain up to 2 to 4 pounds (1–2 kg) per day. By the time they are weaned in the fall they weigh 260 to 330 pounds (120–150 kg). Weaning in the fall allows females to be available for the rut. Even though juveniles remain with their mother, the biological demands of lactation are ended, and cows can devote their energies to new pregnancies through the long winter.

Biologists differentiate between two kinds of dispersal in moose: typical dispersal of juveniles from their mothers' ranges, and dispersal of adults and juveniles in response to poor food conditions, usually when populations are exceptionally dense. A certain level of male dispersal is always occurring, regardless of population density. These are mostly young, virile males that are driven off by their mothers and then aggressively dominated by the local bulls. They move and roam looking for a chance to work their way into a local breeding hierarchy. As long as forage is sufficient, females can be philopatric, establishing a home range that may overlap extensively with their mother.

The mother usually waits until the last moment to chase off her yearling, usually just a few days before giving birth to her next calf. One day the yearling awakes to find its mother aggressively rejecting its company. At first the youngster reacts as if mom is playing. When she rushes, the youngster bounces away and then comes skipping back for more fun, only to be met by flying hooves and more charges. When the rejection continues and the aggression is too obvious to ignore, the youngster starts hanging back farther and farther from its mother. Over a period of just a few days, the bonds of attachment are overcome by fear of the mother. The distance between them increases until the connection is broken and the juvenile begins its own wandering.

Newly independent juveniles often find comfort in one another, and small juvenile groups form up. They continue to try to follow other adult moose. Females are aggressively attending their new calves, but bulls may be tolerant of the company until the next rut. Most juveniles experience some weight loss as they adjust to fending for themselves. If they can't find food and gain weight, they are likely to be killed by predators. A minor difference in mass for a juvenile moose can make the difference between resisting an attack by wolves and succumbing to it.

When the population density nears or exceeds carrying capacity, dispersal increases. Under these conditions dispersing moose are not necessarily the strong young bulls out to make their own way; they are also any subordinate or weakened animals that are being excluded from patches of high-quality habitat by all the other moose. Where or when overall foraging is poor because of too many moose or moose having to survive in low-quality habitats, births are less frequent. When a female does not have a new calf, she allows her yearling to stay with her longer. Staying with its mother through spring and summer helps the yearling to better learn where and how to find food.

Much of what we know of moose calf behavior comes from domesticates or semi-domesticates. The strong innate attachment young form with their mothers can be transferred to human handlers. Hand-reared moose are very affectionate and are described as being more like 6-foot-tall dogs than livestock. They can learn to respond to voice commands, but they will follow only those of their individual trainers, not just any human. Young moose are programmed to learn and are very curious. One hand-reared suckling moose learned that it wasn't allowed in the house with muddy feet and started calling for a hoof-wiping before entering its keeper's house. When separated from its keeper, a young moose bawls and wails, its version of a dog's whine only much, much louder.

INTERACTIONS AMONG MOOSE

Moose are the most solitary of the North American deer. They need large ranges or ranges in dense habitats. The cow-calf bond is the only strong foundation of their social interactions. Much of the mother's behavior when the calf is young is to keep themselves separate from other moose. Most moose actively avoid one another as they roam about. In Alaska, however, moose are rather sociable and form groups, even outside of the rut. Their group sizes are larger in areas with less forest cover, suggesting that they group together as a defense against predators. In addition to predator defense, a common effect of grouping up is increased feeding efficiency because of shared vigilance among group members. Among Alaskan moose, however, feeding rates decline as group size increases because the moose are very aggressive and frequently disturb each other. The risk of predation appears to be encouraging the moose to be sociable, but they still carry the aggressive (toward each other) disposition of more solitary animals.

INTERACTIONS WITH OTHER SPECIES

Moose often appear placid and retiring when seen in the wild and have a reputation for dim-wittedness. In truth, they have little fear of most animals, including humans. When threatened they stand their ground longer and more often than other North American ungulates. Moose can run very fast through dense obstructions, but since they are large and have few predators, it is often economical to protect themselves through aggressive defense. They sometimes use a backward kick of the hind legs, like a horse, to defend themselves.

Still, moose are generally nonthreatening to humans and are likely to flee from cars and humans if they recognize them in time. Rutting bulls and cows with calves could be dangerous if pressed, and

moose-watchers would do well to be able to recognize threats and signs of anxiety. Moose at roadside licks in the northeastern United States are reasonably tolerant of humans watching them, and when spooked by loud people or large trucks they leave without conflict.

Although mature adult moose are capable of defending themselves against most predators, predation of calves and old animals is a significant cause of mortality in most moose populations. The moose-wolf system of Isle Royale, Michigan, shows that wolves are significant predators of calves and moose over 7 years old. The overall effect of wolves on moose depends on their relative abundances. At a wolf-to-moose ratio of 1:30 or less, wolf predation becomes the primary source of moose mortality, and moose numbers decline. Both Black and Brown Bears prey on moose calves as well. In Alaska some Brown Bears specialize on moose calves for 6 weeks each spring. One bear in Denali National Park was known to kill 8 moose calves in a single spring. Other common predators include cougars and dogs.

Humans are the major predators in many moose populations, even discounting vehicle collisions. Human hunting is skewed toward males since hunters value big antlers, but the most important element in determining which moose are taken by human hunters is access: moose populations in areas with ample roads and snow trails are subject to

Fighting females rise up to box with their fore hooves during the breeding season. © *Victor Van Ballenberghe*

more intense hunting pressure than remote populations. Roads and railroads are also significant direct sources of death from collisions, especially in areas of deep snow where the moose use them for easier travel.

We are currently witnessing a great resurgence in moose populations. Timber and forest regeneration and reduction of predators (including the regulation of human hunting) has allowed the steady southward march of moose into areas from which they were extirpated centuries ago. Just as moose are increasing, so are White-tailed Deer, which are extending their ranges northward, facilitating frequent contact between the two species. White-tailed Deer carry a meningeal worm, often called "brain worm," that can be deadly to moose (genus *Paraelaphostrongylus*).

Outbreaks of another small parasite, the winter tick (*Dermacentor albipictus*), have been linked to local moose population declines. Winter ticks are present in most of the moose's range (they are absent from Alaska), and sometimes moose can have huge numbers of them, up to 50,000 or more per animal. The ticks live on their hosts as larvae and nymphs in spring and summer, but do their blood-sucking in the winter and spring as adults. Some mammal species, like White-tailed Deer, are "programmed" groomers. They groom themselves automatically, removing tiny tick larvae whether they feel the little buggers or not. Moose are "stimulus" groomers, only actively trying to remove the ticks once they are an annoyance. When winter rolls around the White-tailed Deer may have only a few ticks to worry about, and they suffer little from them. By the time moose start grooming in earnest, the young ticks have grown into legions of adults that have attached and started feeding. At that point intense oral grooming, scratching, and rubbing only compounds the damage. The moose can become weakened from anemia and secondary infections, and extensive loss of fur can be fatal when combined with inclement weather and cold temperatures.

Moose browsing can stimulate greater nitrogen cycling as new shoots are turned into manure and spread about the forest. The benefits, though, are offset by severe browsing of overly abundant moose. In Newfoundland very high moose density significantly limits regeneration of balsam fir, white birch, and red maple. Local ecologists have added a category of "ungulate-induced" to their descriptors of plant communities in order to capture the forces at work. In other areas, too, moose browse damages young conifers and hardwoods, altering forest succession and composition, and excessively high populations of moose (or other herbivores like deer) increase the intensity of competition between them.

White-tailed Deer
Odocoileus virginianus

OTHER NAMES: whitetail, achtu (Lenape).

Mule Deer
Odocoileus hemionus

OTHER NAMES: muley, burro deer, black-tailed deer, black-tails.

The White-tailed Deer is the deer of the East, although its current range reaches far to the West as well. The Mule Deer is the common deer of arid, open western North America, and there are several subspecies of Mule Deer worth noting. The Rocky Mountain Mule Deer (*O. h. hemionus*) is the "textbook" form. Among the others are some called black-tailed deer or black-tails (Columbian Black-tail, *O. h. columbianus*; Sitka Black-tail, *O. h. sitkensis*), and they range along the Pacific Coast from northern California to Alaska.

Among these deer (and in the deer family generally) we see a spectrum of adaptation to open lands on the one hand and forests on the other. Most Mule Deer live in more open habitats than whitetails, and they are also more gregarious and less skittish than their cousins. Black-tails, which are Mule Deer but live in thick, wet forests, often fall somewhere in the middle.

Odocoileus means "hollow-toothed" and is formed from the Greek words for "tooth," *odous* or *odontis*, and "hollow," *koilos*. *Virginianus* means "of Virginia." *Hemionus* means "part-mule," in reference to their large ears.

ACTIVITY AND MOVEMENT

DAILY

Deer walk with delicate grace, moving and stopping to inspect vegetation as they forage. They can jump high, but usually duck and crawl under obstacles when possible. As they go, their head moves about on a long serpentine neck. They can turn their head and look directly behind them or nip a new shoot two feet off the trail without shifting their feet.

Deer do more eating than anything else, using different portions of their home ranges by day and night. The benefit of having a ruminating stomach, other than being able to digest coarse fiber, is the opportunity to fill it up and then retire to a safe location to process its contents. Deer prefer relatively succulent vegetation, which digests quickly and allows them to feed often, perhaps every few hours. They usually bed for a few hours or less at a time, resting, ruminating, and grooming.

Deer activity is highest at sunrise and sunset, and secondary peaks of activity occur at midnight and midday. During peaks of activity White-tailed Deer move perhaps half a mile over 2 hours as opposed to as little as a tenth of a mile during times of low activity. Yearlings move more and cover more ground than older deer or fawns. Males are typically on the move more often and travel farther than females. Overall, deer move between 1 and 4 miles (1.5–6 km) each day.

A whitetail spends most of its day in thick cover, alternating periods of bedding with short forays to grab choice bites of food. In the afternoon, with darkness approaching, longer movements into more open areas become safer, and deer travel from their bedding areas, in thick shrub and tree cover, to regenerating hardwoods, marsh, agricultural fields, or fruiting trees to do some heavy feeding with intermittent breaks to bed and ruminate. When morning comes, the deer feed heavily again and then return to thick cover in areas where they feel most safe to spend the daylight hours.

Bedding areas are often noteworthy for their thick, shady cover of trees and shrubs. Whereas the actual beds may not be reused, the general area is used repeatedly. Switching beds, even by only a short distance, can foil a stalking predator, as well as strand parasites like ticks that fell off in an earlier visit. Deer like to bed where they have a commanding view of the terrain, as on ridges, hummocks, and hill slopes. They sit, looking back over their trails, watching and listening for threats. Night beds are used opportunistically where they feed and can be found in open pastures and glades.

SEASONAL

Deer are flexible, adjusting their activity depending on environmental and other influences. Activity is inhibited by high summer temperatures, snow, heavy rain, gusty or strong winds, and intense cold. Seasonal peaks of activity occur in the spring, when the deer are readjusting their metabolism after the austerity of winter, and fall, when they are feeding heavily to lay on fat for the coming winter and breeding.

For all deer, traveling in deep snow can be exhausting, and cold winds rob their fur of its insulating warmth. In addition, winter forage is so nutrient-poor that deer have to minimize activity and heat loss and hope that they have enough fat from summer and fall foraging to see them through until spring. In the northern portion of their range, White-tailed Deer migrate to and congregate in winter "yards" in densely canopied conifer stands. The canopy of a deeryard reduces the snowpack by blocking up to 50 percent of the snowfall before it hits the ground. The trees also block wind and re-duce radiant and convective heat loss. Yarded deer wear in a network of runs, troughs followed by every deer, which ease movement and speed flight from predators. Most deeryards are traditional, as are summer home ranges, but the exact location and extent of the yard varies with snow, temperature, and wind conditions. Migration distances between summer home ranges and winter yards range vary from 3 to 15 miles (6–23 km).

Many, but not all, Mule Deer migrate between summer and winter ranges. Snow deeper than 1 foot (30 cm) makes movement difficult, and when deeper than 2 feet (60 cm), it forces them to evacuate an area. Migrants often have access to higher quality food, but they also suffer greater exposure to predation and other dangers along the way. Within a single population, some individuals stay in place year-round, while others migrate. Some shift between upper and lower slopes, and others make long migrations to distant ranges. Rocky Mountain Mule Deer usually travel around 9 to 19 miles (15–30 km) between seasonal ranges, but can go as far as 150 miles (241 km). Migrations can take up to a month or more, sometimes with long delays en route. Desert Mule Deer also need access to water and may migrate to permanent sources during the summer.

FOOD AND FORAGING

Deer are ruminants with multi-chambered, fermenting stomachs capable of digesting woody browse. Deer are often described as browsers of twigs and bark. In fact, they try to minimize woody fiber in the diet and maximize the protein and other nutrient content of their food through a strategy of opportunistically sampling a huge variety of plant foods. Among these, they focus most of their feeding on those species and parts of plants that are the most nutritious at any given time. Studies have shown White-tailed Deer feeding on up to 150 different species of plants, with 93 percent of their diet composed of only 47 species. Some Mule Deer can eat 788 different species of plants throughout the year: 202 shrubs, 484 herbs, and 84 species of grasses, sedges, and rushes. As with whitetails, only a small fraction of these species constitute the bulk of their diet at any given time.

HABITAT AND HOME RANGE

Deer occupy a variety of habitats, everything from farmland to cactus scrub to boreal forest to subtropical swamps. They favor younger, early successional habitats and a mixture of different habitat types. They thrive in agricultural and suburban areas where plants are highly nutritious and predators and human hunters are discouraged. Mule Deer range over most of western North America, from

Mexico to the southern Yukon and Alaska, favoring open forests and shrublands associated with steep, rough, and broken terrain. White-tailed Deer cover the eastern portion of the continent and extend as far west as Alberta, Oregon, and Arizona. Clearcutting in the North, irrigation in the Southwest, and agriculture across North America have allowed for range expansions by White-tailed Deer.

Food, which depends on rain, and suitable cover are the primary ecological needs driving home range size, shape, and location. Home range size for whitetails is often about 1 square mile (2.5 km²), although it differs greatly across the species' range. In sagebrush habitat, home ranges among nonmigratory Mule Deer average 18 square miles (45 km²) for males and 13 square miles (32 km²) for females. Annual home ranges for black-tailed deer, which live along the rainy Pacific Coast, average only 0.23 square miles (0.59 km²). Home ranges tend to be more linear than circular, allowing deer to sample a greater variety of habitats than if the home range were round. Male home ranges can be 50 percent larger than those of females, partly as a function of the fall rut, when males roam widely searching for breeding females.

In the Southwest and the mature forests of the Northeast, whitetail densities are rarely more than 10 deer per square mile (4 per km²). Hardwood bottomlands along the Atlantic coastal plain and a lot of Texas support 64 per square mile (25 per km²). Intensively managed small wildlife areas in oak-hickory forests can have over 200 per square mile (80 per km²). It's important to note that high densities are far from desirable, let alone sustainable. Like a horde of locusts, deer can decimate their habitats when they become overabundant.

COMMUNICATION

The eponymous white tail of White-tailed Deer is related in function to the light rump patches exhibited by open-country deer such as Mule Deer. The rump patch is a flight signal that warns other deer and helps keep a group together in flight. They also serve to notify the predator that it has been spotted and that the deer are on guard. Dense woodland ungulates, which also tend to be more solitary, rely on stealth for their escape and tend to exhibit cryptic rump coloration. White-tailed Deer use a mixed strategy with an "on-again, off-again" rump patch. When it serves them, they hold their tail low and sneak away undetected, but under other circumstances they raise their tail and wave a bright white flag as they flee. Muleys also hold their tail up as they flee.

Deer assume an alert posture when they encounter an unknown threat. They stand still with head held high and eyes and ears trained on the potential danger. A deer can stand motionless, seemingly, for hours. Eventually it moves, dropping its head as if to feed—but it's a ruse. More often than not, it picks its head up quickly again, as if to decoy some movement out of the unknown threat. Alert and agitated deer stamp their forefeet, sometimes once, sometimes more.

When feeling threatened, but unsure of the nature or position of the threat, Mule Deer adopt a stiff-legged, stilted walk. They hold their head low and move slowly and deliberately, almost menacingly. When the nature of a threat is clear (such as an obvious predator), Mule Deer may "alarm walk," which communicates alertness and agility rather then menace. The alarm walk looks a bit like a slow prance as the hooves are raised high off the ground with the head up and eyes and ears trained forward on the threat. It may communicate to the predator that it has been seen and that the deer is fit, healthy, and unlikely to be caught.

Deer aggressively enforce a "pecking order," and subordinates are always averting their eyes from dominant animals to appease them and avoid attacks. Mild aggression is shown through a direct, "hard" stare with dropped-back ears. It is a form of intimidation from a dominant animal and a challenge when coming from a subordinate. Females and males without antlers, or with antlers in velvet, use a head-high threat (head up, nose angled down, ears back) to signal readiness to "strike" with upward kicks of the forelegs. A head-high threat delivered while starting to rear up on the hind legs signals the intent to "flail" the opponent with down-

The upper position of the alarm walk. Drawn after Stankowich and Coss, 2008, "Alarm walking in Columbian black-tailed deer: Its characterization and possible antipredatory signaling functions." *Journal of Mammalogy*. Used with permission.

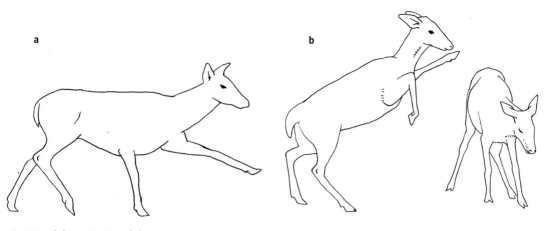

Striking (a) and flailing (b).

ward slaps of the forefeet if necessary. When antlers are mature and hard, annoyed bucks may snap into an antler threat: head held low and nose downward so that the antlers are pointed at their opponent. Aggressive bucks charge their rival with their head up and ears upright. They also use "head-tosses" (rapid lifting of the muzzle) to warn off subordinate competitors approaching a nearby female during the rut.

The intimidation display between rival whitetail bucks is the "sidle." Standing sideways, the buck looks directly at his opponent with his head in an antler-threat position. He moves toward his opponent in the sidling, or sideways ("sidelong"), gait. He approaches directly, not circling, but with a sideways presentation that displays his size, physique, and weapons. While sidling, bucks may "rub-urinate," a scenting behavior in which they rub the glands on their hocks together and dribble urine over them. The Mule Deer equivalent of the sidle is the "crouch." Crouching bucks hunch their backs, draw their legs under their bodies, and raise and quiver their tails. Rivals can size one another up because, although the stance is not sidelong, they circle one another as they close in, periodically emitting loud snorts.

Deer make a variety of vocalizations ranging from grunts and snorts to bleats. A single brief, low grunt is a moderate threat used by both sexes, often accompanying postural threats. In more tense situations, as between rutting bucks, grunts may be followed by a few snorts (grunt-snorts). Dominant bucks use a complex call known as the grunt-snort-wheeze during the rut. This sound of a combined grunt and snort is followed by a 3- to 10-second wheeze through clenched nostrils while the body is held rigid and tense. This is an intense threat, and any opponent that does not immediately retreat is in for a fight.

During the rut, a buck guarding, or "tending," an estrous doe makes a tending grunt. This is a low, prolonged croaking sound that, among whitetails, has been likened to the sound of an unoiled hinge. Bucks also moan and bellow while pursuing does.

Many people have heard deer snort as an alarm for other deer and perhaps also to elicit a response from a potential threat. Free-ranging, tame deer have been observed bleating to one another as a contact call while on the move. Generally, a mother calls to her fawn with a low grunt and the fawn's answer is a mew. A series of bleats is a care-solicitation call and might be uttered by a hungry or anxious fawn; a suckling fawn whines. The basic bleating sound of adults and fawns is drawn out into a loud bawl when an animal is traumatized or restrained.

Chemical cues from urine and scent secretions are a major part of deer communication. There are 4 major scent glands in deer, with those of Mule Deer being larger and more obvious. The metatarsal gland on the outside of the lower leg produces a scent used in alarm. The tarsal gland on the inside of the hock ("ankle") may serve for individual recognition, likely communicating age, rank, and breeding status, as well. Deer sniff them when meeting, and rutting bucks rub them together and urinate on them ("rub-urination"), often when threatening another buck. Preorbital glands located in dark pits at the inside corners of the eyes are obviously flared in Mule Deer during dominance displays and when females are nursing. Whitetails touch them to vegetation when scent-marking. Finally, there is the interdigital gland between the toes, which likely leaves a scent while the deer walks and in other situations as well. Bucks also have glandular tissue in their forehead. Whitetails frequently rub their foreheads when making antler rubs or scrapes. Muleys sometimes do the same after thrashing, but rarely.

Mule Deer bucks thrash vegetation with their antlers. Raking the antlers back and forth in shrubs and branches, they make a noisy racket that serves

A buck rub-urinates.

as an auditory dominance display. Thrashing is the most common male display during the rut, alone or in conjunction with aggressive interactions between bucks, and the sound of it makes younger bucks flee. All bucks thrash, but larger bucks thrash more than others. Mule Deer bucks also sometimes grind the base of their antlers and forehead on small trees to mark them with scent, but not nearly as much as whitetail bucks. Whitetail bucks frequently rub their antlers and forehead on the trunks of trees and saplings, rubbing bark off and leaving a rich deposit of scent. Rubbing is most intense during and shortly after the velvet sloughs, before the rut.

Whitetail bucks also make "scrapes" with their front hooves, which serve as small versions of elk and moose wallows. They paw and scratch up the ground, exposing moist soil into which the buck urinates. Usually the buck reaches up and "tastes" a small branch 1 to 2 yards (0.9 to 1.8 m) above the scrape. He pulls it down, often breaking it, and then rubs it with his forehead, face, and preorbital glands, depositing scent. During the rut, whitetail

A Mule Deer deposits scent onto a small tree and then transfers that scent onto its own antlers.
© Les Voorhis/Royal Tine Images

A whitetail buck inspects and scent-marks the branch hanging over its rut scrape.

does inspect these scrapes but do not appear to urinate in them. During the rest of the year the ground scrape goes dormant, but bucks and does sniff and rub the overhanging branch, though not with the vigor or thoroughness seen during the rut.

Just as Mule Deer bucks will thrash in one another's presence, whitetail bucks use scraping as a dominance display as well as a signpost. A buck may make a scrape in the presence of a rival in order to assert his status. The number of scrapes, as with antler rubs, varies depending on the local deer population. The density of sign increases with greater numbers of mature bucks sharing a given area.

COURTSHIP AND MATING

Reproduction occurs in the fall and winter, depending on location, during a period of synchronous mating known as the rut. Each doe is able to conceive for only 24 to 36 hours during her month-long estrous cycle, and most females in an area are receptive over the same 1 to 2 weeks that define the rut. In most of the country the rut is in October or November, but in places like southern Texas it may not occur until January. Any females not bred in the rut can try again after another estrous cycle.

The rut has several phases characterized by different behaviors: sparring, chasing, tending, and breeding. The sparring and chasing periods together are sometimes called the pre-rut, and the tending and breeding phases, the rut proper. Deer often spend the summer in groups of adult males or in groups of adult females and their offspring. As the rut approaches, the bachelor groups that have been together since they cast their antlers in the winter begin to break up. Their antlers have regrown and their hormone production is on the rise in preparation to breed. They become less and less tolerant of one another and increasingly seek out and consort with female-based family groups. While still in velvet, bucks establish a pecking order through aggressive displays and fighting with their hooves. As the velvet sloughs off during or near September, sparring begins in earnest.

Sparring is a ritualized, nonaggressive mock fight. Among Mule Deer it is common between smaller bucks but rarely seen between mature males. One buck assumes the dominant role and the other the subordinate. Sparring whitetail bucks are generally of obviously different status so that one is clearly subordinate. In either case, after sizing each other up, the dominant buck presents his antlers. Once the subordinate engages its antlers, the two twist and push each other, but in a controlled manner.

In the midst of sparring, Mule Deer occasionally disengage, lift their heads, and turn them sideways to one another, a curious display known as profiling. After a few seconds of this, the sparring match resumes. Usually sparring proceeds in rounds: up to a minute or two of sparring followed by a shorter interval of real or ritualized feeding or resting. Occasionally the subordinate turns and moves quickly away, but unlike in a true fight, the "victor" almost never chases. Generally there is no true winner or loser in a sparring match. For Mule Deer, sparring plays a role in establishing dominance hierarchies among young bucks. For White-tailed Deer, it may clarify the hierarchy and each buck's position within it.

Deer are polygynous, and a rutting buck roams about breeding with as many receptive females as he can. Dominant bucks are those in their prime, old enough to be full grown but young enough to be quick and strong. Among Mule Deer, dominants roam in the vicinity of female groups while other bucks, called floaters, wander unpredictably. The mature bucks don't gather and herd harems of females, but they position themselves near a female group and seek to breed with all of its females. Often females cluster around mature bucks, which provide them a bubble of protection against any younger bucks that would otherwise harass them unmercifully. Several males may attach themselves to a female group, but in the end, only one of them will mate.

Whitetail doe "groups" are usually just one breeding female and last year's fawn(s). In more open habitats (like those of most Mule Deer), whitetail bucks also may try to dominate 10 does simultaneously, but usually these bucks expand their home ranges and spend most of their time on the move to contact more females. With a swaggering gait to accommodate his wide chest, his tracks can often be recognized in the fall by their larger size and the forthright vigor in the trail as he plows across the landscape searching for does.

Male whitetails spar at the onset of the rut, or breeding season. © *istockphoto.com/Tony Campbell*

A buck on the trail of a doe trots with his nose down, following her scent. As he catches up to her, she moves off and he pursues her at a distance of about 160 feet (50 m). The chase may continue for over 500 yards (455 m) before the buck breaks off and goes elsewhere. More than one buck may join in on the chase, but the most dominant male remains closest to her, and the others lag far enough back that they don't elicit an attack. Fawns trot next to their mother until the serious chasing begins, and then they fall behind.

Ideally, a buck would wander around and encounter females during their window of receptivity, and they would immediately mate. That way he could split his time between finding does and mating with them. In reality, the situation is compli-

A male White-tailed Deer exhibits a flehmen response, inhaling and analyzing the scents of a female to determine whether she is ready to mate. © istockphoto.com/Paul Tessier

cated. When a buck finds a doe he must determine whether she is receptive or nearly so. If she's not yet ready, he must decide whether to stay with her until she is receptive, or go look for another doe and run the risk of missing the one at hand.

When a doe urinates, the buck stops to smell it, and he often makes the flehmen expression—a lip-curled, open-mouthed, and head-up gesture. This engages the vomeronasal organ in the roof of the mouth to analyze the female's scent. He analyzes the urine's chemical signals and determines how close she is to estrus. Her scent may also trigger hormonal responses in him that prepare or induce him to mate.

A mature, rutting buck is a sight to behold. His neck is swollen with thick muscle and his antlers shine from being polished on shrubs and tree trunks. His forehead and tarsal glands are darkened with secretions. Mule and White-tailed Deer bucks frequently rub-urinate, a behavior likened to wallowing in elk and moose that serves as a means of intensifying personal scents and applying them to their bodies. A buck is a mobile scent post—the center of his own sliding "territory" surrounded by a zone of intolerance for potential rivals. White-tails make rubs and scrapes, and muleys thrash to warn off and discover rivals. As the period of active breeding approaches, whitetail bucks rub their antlers less and make more scrapes. Sparring also becomes less common, and interactions between mature males become more common.

Each buck is a good judge of his own power and position. A mature buck will investigate the smell or sound of a rival, while younger bucks will flee. Human hunters that try to sucker in big bucks by mimicking buck grunts or antler rattles know that you're as likely to scare a buck off this way as draw one in. A dominant buck will repel other bucks that may approach him or a doe that he fancies. Should another mature buck appear they might end up in a fight.

Bucks go through a series of escalating threats, which "filter" out competitors. Only closely matched bucks stay with one another through the build-up that precedes an actual antler fight. Most challenges end at a hard stare from the bigger buck. If not, the bucks exchange antler threats and then sidle or crouch toward one another. If neither one flees, it is time to lock antlers. In sparring matches the deer only loosely engage their racks, rattling their antlers together as they push and twist. If sparring is like fencing, a fight is like sumo wrestling, an explosive back-and-forth pushing match. Good, big antlers provide traction and leverage, but it is the force of the body pushing and the neck twisting that determines the outcome. They wrench against one another, trying to steal the other's balance and gore the

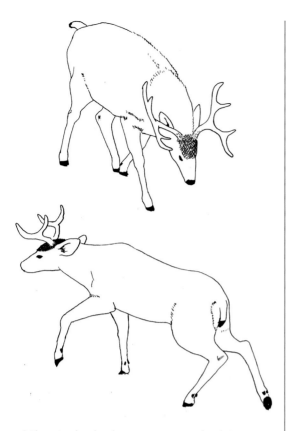

A threatening buck causes a young buck to move off submissively. Drawn after photo by V. Geist in Wallmo, 1981, *Mule and Black-tailed Deer of North America*. Used with permission.

opponent. The force they unleash can snap off antler tines. Mule Deer have a calmer demeanor, but once excited they are aggressive to the point of abandon. They fight until one suddenly breaks and makes a run for it, pursued by the victor, still intent on attacking. Typically fights between bucks last only 2 to 3 minutes, but afterward the pair are panting and exhausted from the intensity of the exertion.

When bucks first approach females early in the rut, the females aren't quite ready to mate, so they run and the bucks pursue. Whitetail bucks use "rush courtship"—they chase females relentlessly as they near their estrus. Bucks chasing does are notoriously single-minded, often to their detriment. They can end up struck by vehicles or picked off by predators, most definitely including humans, because they are distracted and easily stalked.

Mule Deer use "juvenile-mimicry" courtship. A courting buck approaches a doe from behind, holding his head shoulder level and extending his neck forward in a position called a head-low stretch. With his ears turned backward he extends his muzzle toward the doe's hindquarters. As he follows her he flicks his tongue, sniffs, and makes bleating

sounds, all signals suggestive of a young fawn seeking to nurse. He follows the doe closely, usually at less than 33 feet (10 m). She moves away from him, but within a small area, following an arc of maybe 16 to 65 feet (5–20 m). As she rambles the buck tries to head her off, blocking her travel, and when she stops and urinates, he nuzzles her backside and smells her urine.

Courtship is prolonged in Mule Deer. Their calm, unexcitable manner leads to long displays in order to release the next round of mating behavior. Overexcited bucks abandon juvenile-mimicry and resort to rush courtship similar to the courting of Whitetailed Deer, but even more energetic. A rushing muley buck bellows and moans menacingly as he aggressively charges a female and stamps his forefeet at her.

If the doe is close to estrus, the buck gives up looking for other females and stays close and "tends" her. As a doe enters estrus she is more interested in a buck's attention and flees less often, possibly even seeking the buck herself. By tending her, he can be present when she is most receptive and chase off any rivals that may come around. She continues to move about and the male follows, smelling and licking her urine and genital region. The doe keeps moving to stay ahead of the buck and may do so for up to a day. He follows her closely, sometimes laying his chin on her back as she walks and bedding near her. Sometimes the doe runs off at high speed for 325 feet (100 m) or so. The buck follows closely until he catches up to her and then continues to follow her every move. She has his undivided attention—he breaks away only for a few moments at a time to test her urine and chase off interlopers. Bucks mostly even forgo eating.

All along, the doe has been keeping her tail clamped down tight over her genitalia. When she is ready to mate, she pauses. The buck sniffs and licks her and slides his chin along her back and sides. If she is in estrus she may display the lordotic posture—a swayed back and upturned hips—and she moves her tail off to the side. Seeing his opening, the

The head-low stretch of a buck.

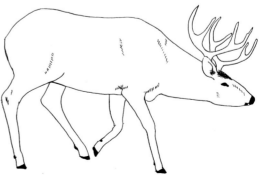

buck mounts her. At any time the doe can terminate the mount by walking forward, and there are commonly multiple mounting attempts before copulation finally succeeds. Copulation itself is brief and is accomplished in a single hard thrust that knocks the doe out from under him. The tending bond then dissolves, and a whitetail will head off in search of other receptive does. Muley bucks remain in the general area if they are keeping tabs on a group of females with more breeding does.

The rut is very hard on dominant bucks. Even if they escape injury by other males, they feed and rest little in their drive to mate. By the time the rut ends, their reserves are depleted and their aggression and energy is spent. Their ability to survive the winter depends on how well nourished they were going into the rut. Bucks contribute nothing to the rearing of fawns, instead concentrating on preparing for another round of mating in the next rut.

DEVELOPMENT AND DISPERSAL OF YOUNG

In early spring and summer, as the 6.5-month gestation nears its end, females prepare to give birth. The mating synchrony of the rut leads to birthing synchrony, when most fawns are born within a few days of one another. This provides some safety to the fawns from predators. If all the fawns are born at basically the same time in the spring, each individual has a reduced chance of being taken by a predator. If the births were spaced out over time, predators would have time to learn from experience and get better at finding and catching them.

When the does are ready to fawn they become restless. They chase off their yearlings and disperse to fawning territories—areas, usually within their home ranges, where does retreat for refuge from predators when they give birth. White-tailed (and black-tailed) Deer seek dense cover, and Mule Deer often seek high, rough, and steep ground. White-tailed does will defend these territories against other deer.

When giving birth, a doe lies on one side, neck outstretched and occasionally swinging back and forth with exertion. She licks the newborns and the birth area clean and eats the placenta, recapturing nutrients and hiding the evidence from predators. She delivers 1 or 2, and sometimes 3, fawns, depending on local population and forage conditions. Newborn fawns weigh about 4.5 pounds (2 kg) and they have a low life expectancy. Among Mule Deer, 30 percent of fawns may be dead by their first autumn, 50 percent by early winter, and 75 percent by spring. One hundred females might bear 160 fawns, but only 40 of them should be expected to survive through their first winter.

Young fawns rely on hiding rather than running for their safety for the first few weeks. They lie mo-

tionless in beds while their mother is off foraging and arouse to suckle when she returns. After nursing, a fawn wanders off about 30 feet (10 m) and freezes, lying down and remaining motionless until its mother returns. When an intruder is near, the fawn's heart rate and breathing slow down, enhancing its ability to hide, and twins hide separately, decreasing the chances that a single predator will get them both. Their coats, flecked with white spots, are easily lost in the dappled light of woodlands and thickets. Mothers don't travel far, usually bedding within about 80 feet (25 m) of their fawns, and when they return they approach with a stereotyped gesture of lowered head and outstretched neck. Wily researchers have been able to exploit this approach gesture by following new mothers using it. When they see it, they chase the mother off a short distance, and after a quick search of the immediate vicinity find the fawn and catch and tag it. A short while after the researchers leave, the mother returns and doe and fawn go about their business without the stress of long chases or tranquilizing drugs.

For the first few days of their lives the fawns are scentless, a distinct advantage when hiding from wolves, bears, and coyotes. Scentlessness is maintained by frequent grooming by the mother, including eating their feces and urine. The mother's licking is required to stimulate defecation and urination at first. Bottle-reared fawns need their backsides wiped by their human handlers with a sponge to mimic this; otherwise they develop fatal diarrhea.

At 3 to 4 weeks old the fawn is too active to sit still and hide while its mother forages. Around the same time, the mother's defense of the fawning territory relaxes. A more mobile fawn means that both can get on with the business of inhabiting her full home range. The doe begins to accept the presence of other does, and by 8 to 10 weeks the doe and her fawn are reintegrating with family groups.

Fawns outgrowing the hiding stage begin to run and buck and dodge and run back again. As fawns mature, the distance they venture from their mother increases, and they bleat to one another to keep in contact. The fawns are now following their mother around, jumping, playing, exploring, and learning how to take care of themselves. Play is common in summer but less so by fall when the young deer start to enter into adult relationships within the population. Fawns are weaned between 2 and 4 months of age, around which time they also molt, losing their spots.

After the fawns are born, yearling daughters may rejoin their mother once the new fawns are mobile, but males rarely do. Yearlings driven away from their mother are also rarely tolerated by other deer and often form exclusive yearling groups. Even when accepted by other deer, they stick to them-

A young whitetail fawn lies in the tall growth of an old field while its mother is away foraging. © *Mark Elbroch*

selves, forming a yearling subgroup. Since they are tolerated less, more males than females tend to disperse, going farther when they do so. Daughters often assume part or all of their mother's range as they mature. Eventually one of these yearlings may move to a new area. Most deer settle into a home range near their natal range, and few disperse long distances, as far as 100 miles (160 km).

INTERACTIONS AMONG DEER

Deer can be gregarious, but the degree to which they interact and operate as groups is attenuated by habitat. The more open the habitat, the larger the groups. Mule Deer live in more open habitats than whitetails and also form larger groups. Because of the many eyes sharing the lookout for danger, groups safely feed farther from cover than individuals and may do so in broad daylight. In a study in Alberta, Mule Deer in smaller groups were more

likely to be attacked and killed by coyotes than were deer in larger groups. In thick woods where one deer can hardly see another beyond a few yards, shared vigilance may not make anyone safer and might increase competition for choice foods.

Deer social groups exhibit gender-specific hierarchies in which dominance is driven by size and physical fitness in males, and by age in females. Both sexes use similar signals in the nonbreeding season: stares, laying back of the ears, head-high and head-low threats, rearing, and chases. Strikes and flails are meted out as necessary. Not all interactions are aggressive. Deer in groups also groom one another, usually around the head and neck.

The basic social unit is the milk group, a doe and her fawn(s). Family groups form with the addition of yearlings (last year's fawns), usually females, to the milk group. In more open habitats with high deer densities, deer often live in social groups of two or more generations of related females and their offspring. A mature, successfully reproductive female, called a matriarch, leads the group. The matriarch usually leads the movement of a group, followed by her fawns, with yearlings bringing up the rear. Yearlings are usually aggressive to fawns, but at times they also play with them. Yearlings are chased away by their mothers before fawning in the spring. Yearling bucks may be accepted back into their mother's group after the birth of the new fawns. Even so, they usually remain a bit removed from the group as a whole.

Outside of the rut, males live alone or in bachelor groups. These groups are small, usually 2 to 5 individuals, and their membership changes frequently. Bachelor groups break down in the fall as males become less tolerant of one another and begin competing for access to females. Sometimes males travel with female groups in the summer, and by the time the rut begins, nearly all doe groups have been joined by males.

Females are more likely than males to snort when they flee. Female deer in a local area tend to be related; each female shares and hands down her home range to her daughters, and evolution favors behavior that protects one's close relatives as well as oneself. Members of a buck group may not be related at all, and during the rut they are actually rivals. Close relatives share much of their genetic material, so when a doe sees a threat she snorts to alert her fawns and possibly other relatives nearby, perhaps enhancing their genes' survival. Bucks do snort, just not as reliably as does. If a buck sees a predator approaching, it may be in his best interest to quietly remove himself and leave his comrades to their own fates.

At times numerous family groups come together to form large aggregations. Groups of hundreds of Mule Deer occur, especially in very open terrain, snow-free pockets on winter range, and feeding areas with abundant spring growth. These are not true herds because each family group maintains its own independent organization and direction.

INTERACTIONS WITH OTHER SPECIES

Deer are keystone herbivores that can radically alter vegetation abundance and community structure, and they account for more agricultural damage claims than any other wildlife species. Moderate whitetail densities (20 per square mile; 8 per km²) alter plant communities enough to affect the local variety and abundance of songbirds. High densities hinder or completely suppress forest regeneration and could cause extensive reduction of eastern hemlock (*Tsuga canadensis*) in northeastern forests over the next 150 years. In openings in Pennsylvania forests, whitetail preference for Allegheny blackberry

(*Rubus allegheniensis*) shifted the ground cover toward hay-scented fern (*Dennstaedtia punctilobula*), which they do not eat. The ferns inhibit the establishment of tree seedlings and herbaceous ground cover, precluding the return of the original forest. In truth, many of the open, parklike forests of our national parks are the result of high densities of deer and other ungulates.

People, wolves, cougars, bears, coyotes, bobcats, and others prey upon deer. Dogs chase them but usually are bad at catching and killing adults unless the deer are hindered by snow, steep slopes, or similar conditions. Fawns are particularly vulnerable, especially as newborns, and many predators search for them where they hide.

When deer sense something dangerous they often stare, keeping the threat in sight, rather than fleeing out of hand. If the threat is far off, the deer may simply walk or sneak off in a safe direction. If the danger is more severe, full flight may be necessary. Whitetails gallop when in full flight. Their strategy is to move quickly along known trails through the woods. At high speed they thread their way through the forest, leaving as many obstacles as possible in the path of their pursuers. When they run they must pay attention to their flight, causing them to lose contact with the threat, so after an all-out sprint of a few hundred yards they slow to a trot, then a walk, and then stop to watch their back-trail. Although they may have to run again, they can keep tabs on the threat and avoid unnecessary exertion from rushing blindly on for a long distance if there is no pursuit. Black-tails, which often live in densely vegetated habitats with abundant obstacles and cover, are also apt to flee and hide quickly. They often have established hiding areas within their home ranges and head for these when spooked.

When open-country Mule Deer flee, they don't bolt like whitetails, rather they "stott." Stotting is a series of jumps made by pushing off with all four legs at once. The stott is not as fast as a gallop, with which they can reach 40 miles (64 km) an hour, but galloping is generally reserved for pursuing other deer in social chases. Stotting (up to 30 miles, or 50 km, an hour) is particularly effective for moving uphill and across broken, steep, and rocky ground that is difficult for predators to traverse. Mule Deer can bounce up steep mountains, sail over objects 4 feet (1.4 m) high, cross 26-foot (8-m) gaps, and change direction 180° in a single bound.

When Mule Deer suddenly become aware of a predator at close range, they often launch a vigorous attack, alone or as a group, wielding hooves and antlers as weapons. In one case a Mule Deer killed a cougar by puncturing its skull with a hoof. Deer in Alberta that defended themselves against coyotes by holding their ground were less likely to be killed

Stotting Mule Deer. Drawn after Geist, 1983, *Deer of the World.* Used with permission.

than if they ran. Aggressive defense is particularly important in protecting fawns. Responding to fawn distress cries, females may even attack predators to defend fawns other than their own.

White-tailed Deer are a vector for many parasites, including ticks, which cause diseases such as Lyme disease. White-tailed Deer carry a meningeal worm that doesn't adversely affect them at all but is deadly to moose. Moose catch the worm through contact with infected deer. As moose populations rebound and extend southward once again, and whitetail populations flourish and expand northward, they come into contact more and more often.

There is concern over competition between Mule Deer and cattle in the more arid portions of the West. In areas of intensive cattle grazing, deer home ranges increase to access sufficient forage to survive. When fawning, female movements are restricted, and intensive cattle grazing could threaten fawn survival. Mule Deer also seem to avoid elk, either by moving at different times or switching to different foods. Severe foraging by dense elk populations could have negative effects on local Mule Deer populations, and competition between elk and Mule Deer is exacerbated by the presence of cattle.

The eastern border of the Mule Deer's range overlaps that of the White-tailed Deer. Where they co-occur, the two species segregate themselves by habitat. Mule Deer prefer areas with less woody cover than whitetails. Grasslands and open woodlands depend on periodic low-intensity fires to encourage grasses and discourage the spread of trees and shrubs. Fire suppression and the presence of

livestock, which can overgraze grasses but ignore woody plants, have led to the transitioning of open habitats to more forestlike communities. These areas then become more suitable for whitetails than for Mule Deer. In their shared range, Mule Deer are usually found on relatively steep slopes with sparse or broken vegetative cover, and White-tailed Deer are found in lower, flatter areas with more cover. The exception to this general pattern is in the Southwest, the driest portion of their shared range, where Mule Deer inhabit the sparsely vegetated foothills and flats, and the whitetails live in the montane forests.

Competition with other large herbivores is not pronounced for White-tailed Deer, but when they feed heavily on acorns, small mammals such as mice become less abundant. A striking example of exploitation competition followed the introduction of whitetails to the small Anticosti Island in the Saint Lawrence River, Quebec, in 1896. Prior to the arrival of the deer, Black Bears and deermice were the only native mammals that fed on vegetation. Following the introduction, the deer population boomed, and by the 1950s the previously abundant bears were quite rare. Deer density since the 1960s reached a staggering 49 to 97 deer per square mile (7–15 per km^2). Although the population is now kept lower, the bears had already disappeared. The deer horde decimated the deciduous shrub species that produced berries critical to bear survival. Deer, gentle herbivores that they are, "killed off" the Anticosti population of one of the largest carnivores in North America.

OTHER NAMES: wapiti, red deer.

North American elk are now considered the same species as the European and Asian red deer. The most recent analysis lists 4 extant subspecies in North America: Rocky Mountain Elk (*C. e. nelsoni*); Roosevelt Elk (*C. e. roosevelti*) of California, Washington, and British Columbia; Manitoban Elk (*C. e. manitobensis*); and Tule Elk of central California (*C. e. nannodes*). Among European red deer, males are called stags and females are called hinds, whereas in North America we call them bulls and cows.

Elk once roamed widely across most of the United States and southern Canada. Tales from the original settling of the American Midwest include stories of settlers taming elk to pull the plow. They were reportedly sturdy and capable, but spent too much time standing and looking (for predators). Their behavior, particularly in the breeding season, is among the most intensively studied of all animals.

ACTIVITY AND MOVEMENT

DAILY

Cows and calves feed for up to 8 to 12 hours per day, mostly around dusk and dawn. Elk are susceptible to heat stress, so in spring and summer they forage in clear-cuts, pastures, and grassy openings but spend their days out of the direct sun. They retreat to shady areas with ample overhead cover, usually conifers, lingering banks of snow, and wet meadows. In some locations these areas provide seclusion from human disturbance as well as thermal protection. They also move to avoid insects in the summer, seeking higher, exposed, windy areas. On the other hand, they are well insulated against cold and may be seen feeding in the open during a storm. Rain and snow are little bother, but they avoid heavy winds, which chill them by stripping away the warm insulating air trapped within their coat.

A herd is noisy as it moves about. The cows and calves call to one another, and dominant animals enforce deference and submission from subordinates. They use various threats (see Communication), as well as kicking and biting. Other methods are more subtle. When feeding in a group, a dominant animal will commonly walk up and take over a nice patch of forage from a subordinate, forcing it to fend for itself elsewhere.

Elk appear to be curious and playful animals that do a lot of running and kicking up their heels. Cows, calves, and young bulls can be seen splashing and kicking in cool water; they paw at it with their front hooves and prance through the shallows. Sometimes groups of cows will engage in back-and-forth stampeding, individuals running with wild head-tossing and zigzagging routes. Occasionally two cows might leap around and chase each other in mock hostility. They have the peculiar tendency to try to outrace cars and trucks when on convergent courses. Instead of pausing to let the vehicle pass, they hurry to try to cross the road in front of them.

SEASONAL

The seasonal pattern of most elk populations is foraging in mountains in summer and retreating to lower elevations in winter, either to lower slopes or to valley bottoms. Not all animals go at the same time or to the same places. Where and when they go is largely learned through following their mothers. Calves born high in the Olympic Mountains that do not experience snow during their first winter do not learn to go down the mountains for summer foraging.

Throughout the winter mature bulls tend to roam independently, and younger males may be in small groups. Post-rut bulls are often weak, and their solitary existence removes them from the protection of the herd. Elk often winter up where deep snow and the cover of the trees help offset their risk of predation, seeking out windswept ridges and other small pockets of favorable foraging conditions. Overall, bulls travel much more widely than females.

One of the greatest migratory elk spectacles occurs each winter near Jackson Hole, Wyoming, where approximately 7,500 elk, half of one of the largest herds in the world, move from the surrounding mountains onto the valley floor and winter in the National Elk Refuge. The refuge, managed by the US Fish and Wildlife Service, was created to prevent large winter die-offs and to segregate elk from cattle ranches in order to protect ranchers' hay supplies. The refuge is managed to enhance elk winter habitat, and when deep or crusted snow prevents the elk from grazing or the natural forage is depleted, refuge personnel provide supplemental feed.

FOOD AND FORAGING

Grass, green or dry, is the staple food for elk throughout the year, but they include forbs and browse when possible or necessary. Grasses and sedges are extremely productive plants, but they are very high in fiber so they take longer to digest than do tender young herbs and leaves. Aspen and willows are the most heavily used species for browse. Aspen is highly palatable, and elk eat its leaves in spring and fall. In late fall elk will dig to reach leaves buried under snow. Elk also browse the twigs and bark of aspen, sometimes destroying young stands in the process. They eat willow leaves and shoots in spring and into the summer. They also browse willow heavily in winter, along with chokecherry. Elk are attracted to natural mineral licks wherever they are available. The Roosevelt Elk of the northwestern United States and neighboring Canada have been seen licking the rotten wood of western hemlock (*Tsuga heterophylla*), perhaps for its mineral content.

For Rocky Mountain Elk a typical seasonal round begins in the spring with dried grasses and browse while the animals are in low-elevation bottomlands. As new growth emerges they turn to eating leaves and shoots of aspen, chokecherry, and willow. As the green-up continues the animals follow reced-

Aspens freshly stripped by winter-feeding elk. Note the black scars where elk have stripped bark in years past. © *Mark Elbroch*

ing snow to high-elevation summer ranges where a wide variety of grasses, sedges, herbs, trees, and shrubs are available. With fall they eat a lot of drying grasses and sedges as they move down-slope for the winter. Over the winter, elk dig down through snow to gain access to dry grass, as well as browse woody plants. In the depth of winter most acceptable foods are running out and spring is still a month or two off. At this point they may eat cattails and other low-nutrient foods.

HABITAT AND HOME RANGE

Elk prefer open woodlands rather than continuous forest or continuous grasslands, and they inhabit a wide range of habitats, including shrub and sagebrush steppe, montane woodland, and deciduous forests. The best range consists of closed-canopy forests for cover interspersed with grassland, shrubs, and water. Clear-cuts and burned areas are important for their high-quality forage. Bulls, especially, depend on patchy sources of high-quality forage, and vegetation regenerating from small burns can be critical to their survival.

In some areas winter snow may force them onto south-facing slopes and into river bottoms at the lower elevations of their range. Deep snow makes woody browse one of the only foods available, so elk spend more time in woodlands than in the open. In spring and summer they follow the regenerating plant life into open, higher country.

The amount of area the animals need is great in areas of low average rainfall. In the dry sagebrush steppes of Idaho and Washington, reported summer home ranges are 45 and 95 square miles (115 and 250 km²), respectively. In the Black Hills of South Dakota, summer home ranges cover 40 to 60 square miles (100–160 km²); winter ranges are 40 to 140 square miles (100–350 km²). In Crater Lake National Park of Oregon, summer home ranges are roughly circular and cover 4 to 12 square miles (10–30 km²). Individuals range over 1 to 5 square miles in early summer in California coastal redwoods and Idaho cedar-hemlock forests.

COMMUNICATION

When elk are suspicious they adopt an alert posture. They stand with head held high and pointed upward, ears tilted backward, eyes and nostrils flared, and tail erect. They raise their body up a bit, and one hind leg might be cocked with the hoof held off the ground, ready to initiate flight. Their tension is obvious and it is difficult for them to stand still. They might ultimately ignore an insignificant threat; if the threat is severe they might flee, or one or more animals may charge it. They may also learn to avoid areas where they are repeatedly alarmed.

The halting, high-stepping "warning" gait and

Cows show (a) normal and (b) alert postures. Drawn after Geist, in Thomas and Toweill, 1982, *Elk of North America: Ecology and Management.* Used with permission.

the side-to-side head movements that they use to change their vantage points when on alert are easily observed and interpreted by other elk. Prolonged, high-pitched bleats called alarm "squeals" are associated with warning gaits. Mothers contact their young with barks, but when they flee, they become silent.

The light rump patches on elk serve as a flight signal, not to other elk so much as to predators. If wolves are approaching a herd of elk and the elk recognize the threat, the rump patches will make it obvious that they have started running away. The wolves must either abort their hunt or initiate their chase early, which increases the odds that the elk will outrun them.

Elk milling about in the open are notably noisy, constantly vocalizing to one another. Vocal cohesion helps elk locate one another when they are separated by short distances. They emit calls from the alert posture—head high and horizontal, ears up and forward, nostrils flared, and tail down. Their calls are short, high-pitched bleats that are usually repeated several times with short intervals between them. When cows utter calls, it elicits responding calls from the calf, and paired vocalizations precede nursing. Calls are also exchanged between adults.

Other calls include contact calls drawn out into squeals, which serve as alarm calls. These are most commonly heard from calves and yearlings. The alarm call for cows is a "bark." They also make a "clatter," a popping sound used as a warning or

when they are agitated. When sparring, bachelor bulls emit "sparring squeaks," a continuous string of quiet, high-pitched squeaks. The rapidity and volume of squeaks increase if the bachelor is sparring with a master bull, a mature male that is capable of maintaining a harem, especially as the master drives the younger bull backward.

The undulating bugles of bull elk during the rut carry considerable distances and are a sure sign of fall in the Rocky Mountains. Bugles are long, eerie, whining whistles used to communicate with both cows and other bulls. The bugling posture is similar to that of the broadside display, with low, outstretched neck and slightly upraised muzzle. Bugles are individually unique sounds that are used primarily for male-female interactions and incidentally for male-male contests. Bull elk also "yelp" during the rut. They yelp while in a low-stretch posture, often simultaneously moving in a stiff-legged gait and emitting small jets of urine.

A master bull bugles frequently when his harem is dispersed. He'll also bugle and yelp when interacting with one or more females, or while trying to herd or control his harem. Some bulls bugle when digging and wallowing. Bachelor bulls also bugle, but rarely. In a study of Roosevelt Elk in northern California, master bulls bugled an average of 1.8 times per hour while entire bachelor herds barely managed 1 bugle every 5 hours. A master bull will bugle in response to another male intruding on his harem, usually causing the interloper to flee, but both bugling and yelping are less frequent in male-male interactions than when herding cows.

Threat displays consist of head-high and head-low threats. The head-high threat presages dangerous, flailing kicks from the front legs. The bite threat is like a head-high threat with the nose raised up and lips pulled back to expose their small upper canines. Bite threats are accompanied by tooth-grinding and hissing. The grinding usually stops in a few moments if there is no overt movement by the intruder. Head-low threats are made with the head and neck held low and extended forward from the shoulder. The ears are laid back and the muzzle is tilted slightly upward so the antlers are tilted back. This posture, also called a low-stretch, is most commonly used by the male when herding his cows.

Antler threats are a variation of a head-low threat with the nose pointed to the ground so that the antler tines bristle forward. Bulls "snap" their antlers and quickly bring them to bear to threaten intruding and wandering cows. Bulls may also use charges that end with a slap of the forefoot on the ground and a series of sharp grunts. Cows may use the antler threat even though they have no antlers. They will present their head as if they did have antlers and may even butt an opponent, but they don't usually rush at one another.

Submission in response to a threat or display of

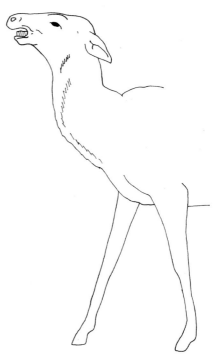

An elk displays the bite-threat. Drawn after Geist, in Thomas and Toweill, 1982, *Elk of North America: Ecology and Management*. Used with permission.

A male bugles to advertise his ownership of a harem. © *Lee Kirchhevel/Dreamstime.com*

dominance is signaled with a lowered neck and ears, extended muzzle, and chewing motions, called "jawing." The whole body may also be lowered slightly. Subordinate animals threatened as they are resting may crouch or lie flat—like an infant hiding. Grazing elk that are challenged by a dominant animal may simply turn away, averting their gaze, or trot off in a classic example of feeding displacement.

Scent posts are the elk version of a rub-tree such as deer and moose make. An elk begins making a scent post by sniffing a tree about 3.25 feet (1 m) off the ground. Then it uses its incisors or antler brow tines to peel or scrape off the bark. The animal alternates licking with peeling, but doesn't eat the bark. Once the bark has been removed from a section of a tree, elk rub their forehead, preorbital glands (located at corners of the eyes), neck, and shoulders on it. Both sexes and all ages of elk create scent posts, but master bulls do it most often and usually for longer. Unlike thrash-urination and wallowing, which only occur during the rut, scent posts are made year-round and are not re-marked.

COURTSHIP AND MATING

Antlers harden in August, and bulls start rubbing off the velvet and sparring in September. Sparring, quite distinct from fighting, is a ritualized interaction to test and reinforce dominance in the period leading up to the rut. Among White-tailed Deer, sparring is reserved for two bucks of obviously different status; a mature buck will offer a little resistance to a younger one. Among elk, sparring occurs between two equals. One bull will solicit an approach from another with a nod. They carefully approach one another with lowered heads swinging side to side. Antlers are engaged slowly with weaving motions of head. Once they are engaged, the bulls push against one another and twist their heads. The bout lasts a few moments and then they disengage. Peaceful disengagement is honored and eyes are averted to forestall overt aggression. Younger bulls emit a squealing sound to appease the aggressive impulses of their opponents.

The rut runs from September through October, and most breeding occurs early in October. The exception to this pattern is Tule Elk in central California, which begin rutting during the summer while the bulls are still in velvet, and their calves are born during the wet, mild winters. The rut through the remainder of North America occurs just before winter so that the calves will arrive in the spring, early enough to ensure that they experience a full growing season in which to fatten up before their first winter. In the southerly portions of their range, milder winters allow more liberal calving times so the rut may be spread over a longer season.

Rutting bulls engage in display and marking behaviors that create signs of their activity on the land. "Horning" and "thrashing" are terms that refer to vigorously raking the antlers through low vegetation and against small trees. The antlers break up branches, strip off bark, and tear up turf and vegetation. One of the most frequent behaviors of rutting bulls is the thrash-urination. They thrash their antlers side to side through low vegetation, dig into the ground, and throw bits of earth and plant material up into the air. All the while, the penis is unsheathed and swinging, soaking the belly and neck and surrounding ground with urine. The behavior is a signal of strength and vigor as well as a means of display that "enhances" the bull's odor during the rut.

Only bulls thrash-urinate, and dominant bulls do so more frequently than bachelors. This is the most frequent scenting display during the rut, and it is linked to direct aggression between bulls. Thrash-urination occasionally precedes sparring and real fights. Dominants do it when subordinates approach, causing the subordinates to flee. During the rut, master bulls do this every time they urinate. In one study, Roosevelt Elk master bulls thrash-urinated more than once every hour. Bachelor bulls averaged only once every 4 hours, and yearlings were not observed exhibiting this behavior at all.

Wallows are made by rutting bulls on damp, soft ground, in much the same way they thrash-urinate. A bare, churned-up patch of earth is exposed by thrashing and digging with the antlers and pawing up the ground with the front hooves, while interspersed with episodes of bugling. As the wallow is being dug, the bull urinates in the pit and onto his neck and mane. Once the pit is dug, the bull lowers himself and rolls and rubs his mane in it, caking himself in his odors. He may continue to urinate from an erect penis throughout. Bulls make several wallows and reuse them frequently. They can also be seen resting in them for long periods.

After wallowing, the bull may move off and rub his neck on a scent post tree. As with thrash-urination, wallowing is most frequent among the dominant master bulls, but other elk may investigate these sites. Calves and cows that visit wallows show signs of considerable excitation. Calves jump and bound; cows may paw and dig in the wallows with their heads, roll in them, jump about, and chase off other approaching cows. Wallowing is relatively rare among Tule Elk, presumably because of scarce appropriate ground.

Elk form harems because cows are already in herds, allowing relatively few mature bulls to control many females. The bulls gather harems by seeking out and attaching themselves to existing cow-calf groups. Young bachelor bulls are driven out of their herds by dominant master bulls as they form and tend their harems. Large groups of year-

Sparring males warm up for the true fights to come during the breeding season. © *Liquidphoto/ Dreamstime.com*

ling and bachelor bucks aggregate and try to steer clear of the harem masters. The yearling calves of harem cows take the brunt of the bull's displeasure. They are caught between their attachment to their mother and his aggressive intolerance of potential rivals. Their alarm calls are frequent during the rut as they go to their mother for comfort but are chased off when the master bull comes by. In particularly open habitats (where groups are largest) and where there is a high male-to-female ratio, several dominant bulls may preside over large mixed-sex, mixed-age groups. The master bull still performs the vast majority of the breeding, but in large groups the chances of "sneaky copulations" by younger bulls is higher.

If a cow wanders, the master bull herds her back to the group, bugling, threatening, tooth-grinding, hissing, and posturing. The herding posture of the master bull is a low-stretch with neck out, antlers and ears laid back, and nose upward. In this attitude he circles a cow, approaching her tangentially at a trot or rapid walk. He will avert his gaze from her and may grind his teeth, yelp, and flutter his abdomen. He displays his side to her, and for this reason this behavior is also called the broadside display. The shaggy, contrasting neck mane and massive antlers of a bull elk function here as visual signals. A variation of this herding behavior is for the bull to block the cow's route, first broadside in the herd-

ing posture, then by whirling and snapping his antlers at her. He may also charge her, pulling up short with a few sharp barks. Usually the cow quickly and submissively returns to the group. After herding his cows, the bull will turn away and bugle. When not actively herding, the master bulls are wallowing, thrashing, and bugling, sending the auditory, visual, and olfactory signals of their strength and vigor. Sometimes two bulls will challenge one another directly.

True fights are rare. Most interlopers are driven off by various displays and threats. The herding gestures that drive females before the bull are themselves modified threat displays. Fights between bulls are preceded by loud bugling until the opponents are in sight of one another. As they work to close the distance between them, they pause to thrash vegetation and flutter their abdomens as they do when thrash-urinating and wallowing. They approach one another frontally, but when they are about 20 paces apart, they turn sharply away. They may circle one another or walk parallel to each other separated by 6 paces or so, for approximately 500 feet (150 m). They avoid eye contact. Their body postures are normal, but with their antlers tilted forward and their heads slightly raised. The parallel march may develop into a trot and both bulls may bugle during the whole contest. At the end of a run, they suddenly reverse course and repeat the process in the opposite direction, thrashing with their antlers at the turn-around.

The bulls seem to behave as if the other isn't there, but these are all displays for the benefit of the opponent. Sometimes one bull will incline his antlers toward the other, and at this challenge, they close the distance and engage. With antlers enmeshed they push forcefully against one another and twist their heads. Fighting bulls are soon breathing heavily—their bodies crouched close to the ground with legs spread wide. At any moment they may break and one may flee. When this happens, the victor leaps after him with horns down, uttering short, sharp barks. The loser may be gored before he can escape, but there is not a lengthy pursuit.

Throughout the rut, bulls often forgo feeding as they divert their attention and energy toward maintaining their status and harems. As the breeding season wears on, the original dominants tire and weaken and are sometimes unseated by younger bulls. These younger bulls didn't have the strength to control a harem early in the season, but now they do. On rare occasions, even yearling spike-bulls form coalitions that, together, can unseat a harem master.

Mating presents a serious dilemma for females. They are compelled to mate and desire the bull's approach, but out of self-protection they wish to flee as he nears. He has, after all, been chasing and frightening them and others full-time since the rut began. To pacify the cow so she will allow his approach, he must clearly communicate his nonaggressive intent. Males court estrous females with head high, chin down, and tongue out. The bull may even accentuate this stance by dropping his hips. In this attitude the bull makes a frontal approach toward the cow, "plopping" softly with his tongue while flicking it out. If she tolerates his approach, he precedes to lick her entire body. She may turn and lick him in return or touch her muzzle to his. Usually she retires submissively, inducing a bugle. If she starts jawing, making accentuated chewing motions with her jaws, it's a signal of impending flight. The submission display is exaggerated in courtship by snakelike motions of the cow's head.

Occasionally a female will actively court an old bull. She will approach and rub her neck and head on him. Once she has his attention, she makes a series of coquettish jumps and runs, eliciting a following response that may lead to mating.

As the female enters estrus, the short period of receptivity during her estrous cycle, she licks dominant males more and also allows herself to be licked more. The bull appeases her jawing with jawing of his own. When she is ready to mate and the bull courts, she stands with a slightly spread-legged stance and lifted tail. He hangs his head and chin on

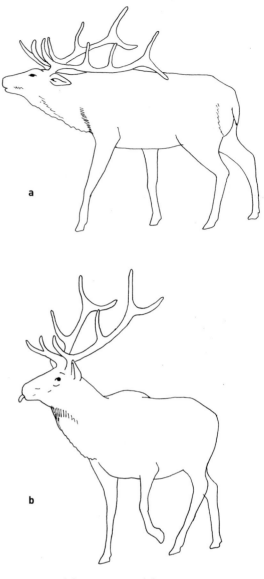

A bull elk in (a) herding and (b) courting postures.

her neck with his front legs hanging down and his weight on her back. His penis is out and searching in an attempt to mount. At first she walks away as he is close to success, and this may happen several times, interrupted by lots of licking. At last he is allowed to mount, and he clasps her with his forelegs, throws his head up and performs a single, powerful thrust. The cow is knocked out from under him and the two separate. After copulation the cow stands with her back arched for up to 30 minutes.

The rutting bulls really feel the pinch of winter with the energy they expend during the rut and their neglect of feeding. They have no time to recover their condition, and their winter survival has a lot to do with the quality and quantity of food they were able to consume throughout the summer. Few bulls retain master status for more than a few years because it is so demanding. Growing antlers has also depleted them of calcium, which some animals attempt to replace once their hormones have subsided by chewing on the antlers of other males, even before they fall off early in the winter.

DEVELOPMENT AND DISPERSAL OF YOUNG

Elk gestation is 8 to 9 months, and calving occurs in early June in most populations. Cows about to give birth remove themselves from their group and steal off to wooded areas for cover. Hidden and alone, the cow gives birth, and when the calf is born the mother cleans up by licking her newborn and eating the afterbirth. She continues to eat the calf's urine and feces for the first few days, to minimize scent, parasites, and flies. Cows sometimes bugle around birthing time and the sound is less resonant and powerful than bulls' bugles. Over a period of a month, the cows of the herd all give birth, but the group never disbands entirely, and a cow's desire to stay apart from the herd doesn't last long. Almost immediately, she will start going back to the herd during the day, leaving her calf hidden under cover where it was born. The cows return to their calves to nurse as often as every 20 minutes at first, although these periods lengthen considerably over the first few weeks. At night the cows bed with their calves.

Newborn elk calves are hiders, and mother and calf remain apart from one another except when suckling. Calves are cryptically colored and give off little scent. They select their own hiding place and freeze, waiting for their mother to return from foraging to allow nursing. A high, nasal whine or "mew" from the mother brings a fawn out of hiding. A cow recognizes her calf from the start, but the calf takes some time to figure out just who its mother is. Their exclusive contact in the first few weeks cements this relationship.

After about 2 weeks, calves join the herd and have grown sufficiently to adopt a strategy of feeding, watching, and fleeing together with the cows. By 3 weeks of age most calves are strong enough to keep up with the herd, but it takes some time for them to internalize the vocalizations, postures, and gaits that the herd uses to communicate with one another. Within a band, elk mothers do not protect their calves from other herd members; they leave them to find their own place within the group. The mother's rank within the herd partially extends to the calves, protecting them from some feeding displacement and other assertions of rank. Yearlings and 2- and 3-year-olds have their own, usually low, rank.

Calves tend to coalesce in groups that feed and play together. These groups are often called crèches when they fix their attention on a single cow rather than each on its own mother. This attention to a single cow could serve to better coordinate their flight if a threat arises. Yet close contact between mother and calf is essential, and whenever they become separated, the cow calls out, moving to the point where she last had contact with her calf. Upon hearing its mother's call, a calf is quick to come to her.

Calves have very high nutritional needs relative to the limited capacity of their small stomachs; they need to grow and develop quickly to be able to withstand their first winter. In order to maximize nutrient intake with small rumen capacity, they have to be more selective about what they eat than larger elk do. They instinctually choose the lowest fiber foods: young leaves, new shoots, and more succulent species. They also eat more frequently than adults, which need more time between meals to digest rougher forage.

INTERACTIONS AMONG ELK

Elk are gregarious, and group size is a function of the season, the openness of the landscape, and the available resources. Herds typically comprise 10 to 30 animals led by an older cow that may not necessarily be the strongest and fittest, but she is experienced and maintains a tight, orderly group. Mostly, herds are congregations of family bands consisting of several breeding cows and their offspring of current and previous years. Males roam independently through the winter and into the summer. As the fall rut approaches, summer herds can swell to between 300 and 400 animals before breaking into harems. Once breeding concludes and migration looms, yearling and young bulls previously driven off during the rut return to join their mother's herd. Winter groups are smaller, looser aggregations of cows, calves, and some bulls. Bulls are most gregarious in the winter while they still have their antlers, the time of the greatest use of open country. As bulls shed their antlers in late winter and early spring, they are subordinate to bulls that still have theirs, so they disperse.

In spring and summer, cows and calves are usually separate from bulls, a situation called sexual segregation. Among elk, scientists believe cows and bulls prioritize predator-avoidance and access to high-quality forage differently, resulting in males and females using different microhabitats. (There is also some evidence that the aggressiveness of bull elk results in females avoiding them on the landscape.) Cows need the safety of the herd to protect their calves and themselves. They choose to stay in areas of high visibility and regular contact. Cow elk end up eating a lower quality (more fibrous) diet in order to stay together as a herd.

Bulls largely forgo foraging during the rut, and after the rut, forage quality is poor in general. The food bulls eat through the summer must sustain them through the huge energetic costs of the rut and carry them through the winter. Bulls, therefore, maximize forage quality, which leads them to wandering alone and avoiding predators as best they can. If a bull has fat reserves remaining after the rut, his situation is not so dire, and he can eat coarse cow forage and remain with the cow herd. Generally, bulls are highly mobile in spring and summer. They seek out high-quality foraging patches and roam into new areas, continuing to do so until the approach of the next breeding season.

INTERACTIONS WITH OTHER SPECIES

Group flight from predators is orderly. The lead cow flees noisily and then turns to face the threat to indicate to others where it is and keep tabs on it. The other females shield the calves from the threat. The calves follow juvenile cows that lead them to safety, while the older cows distract, confront, or monitor the threat.

When females watch predators approach calves in hiding, they become anxious, moving about and stopping eating. A mother elk may bark an alarm to her youngster or attempt to distract the predator away from the area. The calf freezes at its mother's alarm or at the approach of the predator. A bleat from the calf draws the mother back to help. Elk are more likely to run from wolves than to fight them, but they will charge smaller predators such as coyotes, grinding their teeth, boxing with their front limbs, and lowering their heads as if to head-butt their opponent. If the intruder is too large or too numerous to attack, both cow and calf flee, and the mother leads the calf to safety. She will only desert her youngster if hard-pressed. Grizzly Bears, and to a lesser extent Black Bears, eat numerous fawns, sniffing them out where they hide. Cows will defend their young from bears, and sometimes attack them, often to no avail.

Elk avoid cattle-grazed areas during calving (spring and summer). When cattle arrive in Wyoming's Gros Ventre Range in June, elk go to higher country. Elk also occur in Mule Deer range, and although their diets are generally different, winter and other conditions that limit food (such as drought and overgrazing) force them into more direct competition. In those cases, the gregarious and larger elk are able to eat up the food before the deer can get at it. Moose may reduce critical browse supplies for elk in winter. Conversely, winter use of riparian areas by elk could reduce carrying capacity of moose. The core issue in each case is how much of the seasonal ranges the elk have available to them and the condition of the range. Competition with cattle, for example, is most serious on winter-spring range when energy balance is most critical.

Elk have a definite impact on their habitats, and they, in turn, are affected by predators. Heavy elk browsing has been implicated in poor regeneration of willows and trembling aspen in the West. In Yellowstone decades of heavy browsing had eliminated willows from portions of riparian systems in northern areas of the park. With the return of the wolf, however, elk began to shift where they spent their time, weighing the quality of foods they eat against the risk of being caught by predators. The presence of wolves moved the elk enough to allow willow and aspen regeneration in riparian zones that hadn't seen such new growth in decades. With an increase in woody vegetation along streams came other changes, including increased beaver activity and nesting riparian birds.

In areas of high elk density, such as on winter ranges and in calving areas, elk also limit the recruitment, that is, the transition of young aspen seedlings and saplings into the ranks of the mature, canopy-forming trees. Absent the elk, young aspen saplings will grow steadily until their crowns add to the overstory of an aspen stand. Recruitment of new trees drops to about a third of normal levels when heavily browsed. Although the elk can have this effect, they don't appear to threaten aspen across broad areas, just in smaller pockets on the land. The effect of elk on aspen is complex, also involving the extent and intensity of wildfires, which encourage aspen sprouting. The suppression of wildfires may have as great an impact on aspen recruitment as heavy browsing.

Elk are susceptible to brucellosis, a serious bacterial disease affecting cattle, wildlife, and humans. In elk cows it causes miscarriages and still-births. Brucellosis has been largely eradicated among domestic cattle, but persists among wild elk and bison in the Greater Yellowstone Ecosystem of Wyoming, Montana, and Idaho. (These species most likely got the disease from contact with infected cattle in the early 1900s). Some elk have also been diagnosed with chronic wasting disease (CWD). The disease seems to have started among farm-raised herds but now occurs among wild deer. The largest infection of wild animals is in the heart of the Rocky Mountain elk range. Although likened to the similar "mad cow" disease, there is no evidence that CWD is transmissible to humans. Nevertheless, most game management organizations recommend basic precautions for handling meat that could carry CWD. Hunters are recommended to use latex gloves when field dressing and to avoid exposure to bone marrow and brain and spinal tissue, as this is where the disease resides. Cutting the meat from the bone without sawing through bone and exposing marrow or spinal tissue is also recommended. Elk meat is recommended to be thoroughly cooked prior to consumption.

Pronghorn
Antilocapra americana

OTHER NAMES: antelope.

Pronghorns are the fleetest of North American mammals and can attain speeds of 60 miles (96 km) an hour. Their enlarged heart and windpipes virtually pour oxygen into their blood and muscles, allowing them to sustain speeds of 45 miles (72 km) an hour. They can cross the length of a football field in 10 strides and 3.5 seconds.

ACTIVITY AND MOVEMENT

DAILY

Pronghorns spend much of their days walking slowly about their range, foraging as they go. Periodically they lift their head to search for potential threats; their large protruding eyes allow a near-360° field of vision. Their eyes are also set far back in the head, so that they can still see around them when their head is down in short grass. They walk as much as 9.5 miles (15 km) each day, foraging most heavily within several hours of sunup and then again in the evening. During the night pronghorns tend to sleep in the center of their range, reusing the same bedding sites again and again.

During daytime resting bouts they lie up and ruminate. At the same time, they modulate their body temperature by choosing which part of their pelage to expose to the sun. In cold weather they tuck their legs beneath them, exposing only the darker back, absorbing solar heat. Erection of their hairs creates more dead air space for insulation. When it's hot they aim their white rump patch at the sun or lie on their side, exposing the lighter, more reflective fur on the side and belly. When very hot, they will even stick out their tongue to dispel more heat.

When threatened or alarmed, pronghorns run in a rotary gallop. The herd spreads into an ellipse, with the dominant female leading the herd. Running herds are breathtakingly beautiful. Most animals in the herd synchronize their gait, their speed, and even the foot with which they lead, as if they were led by one mind. The mesmerizing rhythm of the running herd inhibits a predator's ability to pick out just one individual upon which to focus its attack.

SEASONAL

Perhaps the most distinctive physical attribute of pronghorns, which places them somewhere between cervids and bovids, is their horns. Like bovids, their horns increase in size each year and are attached to the skull by bony, spikelike extensions projecting up from the head. Unlike bovids, and more like cervids

(which shed their antlers annually), pronghorns shed their horn sheaths each year. The bony projection on the skull remains, but the tough sheath that forms the horn is pushed off by the growth of the new one beneath. Males shed their horns approximately one month after the rut, whereas females with horns may shed them at any time, though most often in the summer. In males the new horn sheath has completely formed by midwinter. Pronghorns molt with the start of spring, and their fur is attractively bright through the summer, and then begins to fade and dull as winter approaches.

Pronghorns may winter up to 100 miles (160 km) away from their summer sites in order to escape deep snows. Seasonal migrations are longest and most arduous for the northernmost populations and those that summer at high elevations. After the fall rut, pronghorns begin to move to wintering areas and form mixed herds of varying size, depending upon forage availability.

Harsh winters take their toll on pronghorns. Males suffer more than females because they enter the winter in a weakened, "rutted out" condition. Males spend the autumn competing for, herding, defending, and mating with females to the near exclusion of feeding. They have already dipped deeply into their biological reserves before winter arrives.

FOOD AND FORAGING

Pronghorns prefer to selectively graze upon forbs, plucking individual leaves with their lips. They typically avoid grasses and so are able to share habitat with large bovids, such as bison, which prefer grasses over forbs. In their northern range, pronghorns browse sagebrush and other woody vegetation during the winter. In the southern portion of

A female pronghorn slips under a cattle fence, reluctant to jump the obstacle. Fences that do not provide adequate space for pronghorns to slip beneath are significant barriers to their movements.

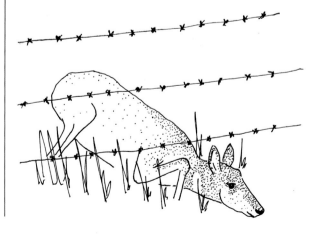

the range, prickly pear cactus is an important part of their summer diet, which provides both water and forage.

The water content of their forage determines whether pronghorns need surface water to survive. When forage has 75 percent water content or more, they do not drink at all. During the hottest and driest times of years, when green forage is depleted, pronghorns may need to drink more than 4 liters every day. During dry months most pronghorns linger within several miles of water sources. The adult males wander the farthest and may occasionally be seen more than 5 miles (8 km) away.

Where snows accumulate, pronghorns graze opportunistically and turn to browse. They can dig with their forelimbs to uncover better forage, and craters dug into the snow become resources for the entire herd. Strict hierarchies allow them to feed with minimal overt aggression. Where possible, pronghorns select areas with minimal snow and wind, providing them easier access to foods and better heat conservation.

Rumination makes many ungulates distinct among mammals, for through a unique digestive tract and process they are able to break down the cellulose in plants that we cannot. In ruminating mammals, chewed plants drop into the rumen—the first chamber of the stomach—which is a melting pot of fermenting bacteria, protozoa, and fungi that work together to break down the cellulose of plants into glucose they can use. But ungulates aren't much interested in the converted glucose that the microorganisms thrive on, but rather in the carbohydrate-rich waste products the microorganisms create in the process.

Having finished the initial bout of feeding, the animal finds a secure place to rest to further digest its meal. The plants it has just eaten are returned to the mouth as a bolus, to be chewed again and mixed with nitrogen-rich saliva, which further fuels the population of microorganisms in the digestive tract upon which the animal depends for survival. These microorganisms ferment the ingested material, and the repeated chewing as well as churning and grinding within the stomachs break down the plant fiber, freeing the nutrients for absorption.

HABITAT AND HOME RANGE

Pronghorns are creatures of open grassland, prairie, and high deserts, and they can be seen throughout the West where suitable habitat and accessibility occur. They range from southernmost Canada south into central Mexico. Researchers have found that home ranges for pronghorns vary so much from area to area, depending upon water, weather, forage, and other factors, that it is not particularly useful to describe the average home range. In their northern

range, large herds are often observed in sagebrush habitats, which provide winter browse. In Colorado sagebrush habitats, densities average approximately 6.25 animals per square mile (2.5 per km²).

COMMUNICATION

Pronghorns have a very small vocal repertoire. When alarmed they make explosive snorts, which travel far and wide across open terrain. A snort is often used to elicit a response from a suspicious, yet unknown, intruder on the landscape. Territorial males also snort in warning to trespassing males.

Pronghorns also erect the hairs on their rump to create a visual flag when they are alarmed. The patch appears both larger and whiter than it actually is, and glands within the patch emit chemical odors, which you can smell if you are close enough. Both the bright rump and odors relay warnings to nearby animals.

A pronghorn flares its rump patch and discharges scent to communicate alarm to other pronghorns nearby. © *Stan Osolinski/OSF/ Animals Animals*

A pronghorn buck deposits scent on a bush with its subauricular glands near the eye. © *Richard Kettlewell/Animals Animals*

Females have two scent glands within the boundaries of their rump patch. Males have these glands as well, along with several others that play important roles in sexual communication. Pronghorns also have interdigital glands between their toes; the secretion is thought to aid in hoof maintenance, but interdigital glands may also play a role in scent communication.

COURTSHIP AND MATING

The breeding season begins as early as July in the southern part of their range, but not until mid-September in the north, and then continues on until early October. Most females mate during their first estrus period. Those that fail to become pregnant

An adult male pronghorn marks his territory with a scrape, urination, and defecation (sometimes called a SPUD).

then come into a second estrus at the end of October and seek a mate at that time.

Territoriality among adult males is central to courtship and breeding in pronghorns. It begins long before the breeding season, providing foraging benefits to doe herds that do not want to compete with bachelor herds in the marginal habitat found in between established males. Aggressive interactions between males increase prior to and during the rut, when bachelor herds attempt to corner and court females.

Dominant bucks mark their territories with scats, urine, and chemical communicators excreted from various glands. Males mark bushes and other tall vegetation with a secretion from the subauricular gland located just anterior to and below their eyes. They also mark with urine and scats in a ritualistic pattern: in sequence, they use stiff forelimbs to scratch the earth, then they urinate on or adjacent to the scrape, and finally they defecate (the whole sequence is sometimes called a SPUD). Bachelor males will also be observed marking in the same way, but outside defended territories.

Resident bucks defend their territories in a predictable progression. When a buck sees an intruder he freezes and stares at it, and he may continue to do so for up to 25 minutes. The length of the stare is often correlated with how far into his territory the intruder has progressed—the farther into the territory, the quicker the action. Next the resident utters a loud, high-pitched snort, or "snort-wheeze," followed by a descending tremolo of decreasing "chugs," during which you can see his sides pumping. Trespassers often take off running when they hear the snorts of the resident male. Snort-wheezes are individually distinct, and pronghorns seem to recognize and respond to the snort-wheezes of their neighbors.

Should an intruder linger after hearing a resident's snort, the resident male hurtles to within 45 to 90 yards (40–80 m) of the trespasser before lowering his head and ears and walking deliberately to within 16.5 to 28 yards (15–25 m). As the resident looms nearer, his gait becomes stiffer and more exaggerated. He abruptly stops and stands broadside, which is a threat position. Other behaviors you might observe while the resident approaches are pauses to thrash vegetation with his horns and pawing the earth with stiff legs followed by urinating and defecating.

Should the intruder still hold his ground, he often matches the displays of the resident, turning broadside to meet the threat. This sometimes escalates into the two males walking parallel to each other for short distances. The pair may continue to exchange combinations of these threats, including lowering the head and ears, walking stiff-legged toward each other, and thrashing vegetation with their horns. Should the trespassing male be so bold as to freeze and stare at the resident, the owner of the territory usually responds with a low, guttural roar and a quick rush to chase or beat the intruder from his territory.

Fighting may ensue if a female in estrus is near. Males lock horns and engage in a rapid and deadly dance, wherein each tries to create opportunities to push his opponent off balance and slip his hooked prongs in to gash at the throat or pierce the chest. Battles are fierce and often lead to serious, if not fatal, wounds. Bucks die each year of punctured lungs and hearts, or disjointed limbs. In one study, 12 percent of fights during the rut resulted in fatalities.

Bachelors are the most aggressive pursuers of females during the breeding season. Even unreceptive females may be chased by more than one bachelor until they find sanctuary in a defended territory and the resident buck chases the bachelors off. Resident males aggressively and often unsuccessfully attempt to keep does within their defended bounds in order to breed. In the short term, dealing with single resident males may be the lesser of two evils for the females, when compared with the constant badgering of bachelors. In the long term, the offspring of stronger resident males may be more attractive to females than those of bachelors.

Resident males split their time between defending their territories and attempting to contain females within their bounds. Males use gullies and other natural features within their territories to hide females from other males. If he is successful a resident buck is able to ward off intruders and keep females around so that several come into estrus while he is with them.

In most cases the females move off to other territories. Does are not forced to breed by males, but rather select males with which to mate. They often jump from territory to territory and repeatedly visit several males before selecting one and allowing him to breed with her.

Males work continuously to keep others at bay and herd their females back into hiding. When one female breaks and runs, he attempts to chase her back, and whether successful or not, within a short time his remaining females have begun to wander. Throw in several bachelors trying to sneak in every few hours, and the territorial male spends most of every day running, chasing, and fighting, trying to maximize his opportunities to mate.

A pronghorn male exhibits the flehmen response when smelling the urine of adult females, especially during the rut. He will scrape and urinate and defecate atop any urine she leaves in his range during the breeding season. When she is in full estrus she emits a potent smell which may draw in other males from the surrounding area. The stench may be so potent as to compel a neighboring male with a territory of his own to temporarily abandon it to invade another male's and court the female in heat.

When a male approaches a doe with the intention to mate, he emits a high-pitched whine and stands erect with his neck held straight up and the hairs of his mane standing at attention. If the female is receptive she stands still and raises her tail; if in estrus she spreads her hind legs slightly. The male then approaches in prancing steps to within 16 feet (5 m), when he starts weaving his head from side to side, emphasizing his subauricular glands, and flicking his tongue in and out. He approaches her with his head outstretched, seeking her vulva while also making a slow sucking sort of noise. Should the female remain still, he mounts her and they mate. After mating, the doe ignores the male completely. Females that are not in estrus or otherwise not receptive lower and twist their head while moving away from the male. He may continue to pursue an unreceptive female and may even knock her down during the chase.

Though territoriality is fundamental in numerous pronghorn populations, males use different strategies when they occur at low densities. When there are fewer females about and spread over a greater distance, it is more efficient for males to defend a harem than a patch of ground.

Once the rut ends, males who may have nearly killed each other over females the week before are suddenly feeding together as if the mating season had never happened. Following their massive expenditures of energy during the rut, the males devote themselves completely to eating. During the breeding season, the larger males invest only approximately 20 percent of their time in foraging, while the smaller females forage for 40 percent of the time. For this reason particularly harsh winters kill more males than females—such are the costs of fighting for mates.

DEVELOPMENT AND DISPERSAL OF YOUNG

Females seek privacy and move away from the herd a day or so before giving birth. After a gestation of about 8.5 months, 8-pound twins are born 9 to 30 minutes apart, although sometimes does have a single fawn. Females act nervous preceding birth and may lie down and rise several times. They may also stand with legs stretched backward, as if encouraging the imminent event. They usually start to give birth on their side and then, as the fawn begins to emerge, stand up to allow the youngster to slide free. Immediately following birth, mothers lick their fawns clean and eat the afterbirth. Fawns nurse for the first time within their first 2 hours, and then mothers lead their fawns away within several hours, since the birth site may draw in predators.

Together the twins weigh approximately 17 percent of their mother's body weight, which is an incredible investment on her part when you consider that most cervids and bovids produce young of only 5 to 9 percent of their weight. For this reason, environmental conditions that have the potential to increase quality of forage—such as whether there are late summer rains or not—directly influence the length of gestation. Gestations are longest when late summers are dry or other conditions lead to lesser quality forage.

Each fawn is left alone for the first time within hours of its birth, and from the first day each twin selects its own bedding site. Fawns instinctively flatten themselves in their beds when potential dangers approach, but keep their eyes open and alert. Does return to their offspring at approximately 3-hour intervals, emitting low grunts to call them out from hiding. Mothers seem to recognize their young by sight. The mother begins to groom her young, which sticks its rump in the air, and she diligently licks its anus and genitalia clean of any urine and feces which might accumulate and attract flies and mammalian predators. Yet this cleaning service may do more than meets the eye. Any infections the fawn may carry are ingested into the mother, whose more robust body in turn produces the appropriate antibodies and then delivers them as medicine within milk in a future nursing.

After nursing, the fawn walks away from its mother to select a bed in which to hide until she calls it again, and in this way a predator that follows the scent of the doe's trail in hopes of finding a fawn never will. When the mother is away she makes sure to lie up in areas at a great enough distance that systematic searches by predators would be unlikely to reveal her fawn. When predators find and kill fawns, mothers may be seen standing over the remains, defending them for an entire day. They may call and search for their now dead fawn for several days.

Fighting male pronghorns compete for access to breeding females. © *Max Allen Photography*

For the first 6 days twins are tended individually and bed in isolation. Thereafter they begin to interact and create sibling bonds. Play is common between siblings and other fawns during the summer months. They become more dexterous as they practice leaps and jumps, and even begin sparring after 3 weeks of age, when they rejoin other females and fawns to form a herd.

Play is most easily observed in the first few hours after sunrise. Individual fawns exhibit ritualistic play patterns. Starting with a twitch, which grows and grows, spreading through their body, they start to buck and leap side to side, arching their neck backward and up toward the sky. They may make several short dashes to warm up, but soon they are charging full speed, ears back, flying like arrows away from their group to a distance of approximately 1,000 yards (910 m) before looping back toward the herd again. As they rejoin the herd they bounce like pogo sticks on all four legs and, panting from the exertion, stop among the adults, who have sensibly ignored the outburst and refused to become engaged. Researchers intrigued with these energy-expending behaviors calculated that fawns use only 20 percent of their remaining energy budget on play after all their survival needs (e.g., feeding) were met, and thus play was actually a minimal use of energy.

Early in the season, does stand passively while the fawns nurse and kick. Within 4 to 6 weeks mothers begin to regulate nursing bouts more strictly and can be seen stepping over their fawns, thus severing their connection and forcing them to become more and more dependent on grazing. Fawns participate as full herd members by 6 weeks of age, when they've already established a dominance hierarchy among themselves.

Fawns are weaned as the rut begins. As females engage in mating antics, groups of fawns can be observed keeping each other company. Females typically breed for the first time at 16 months of age, though on very rare occasions pronghorns will breed in the fall immediately following their spring birth.

INTERACTIONS AMONG PRONGHORNS

From spring through the summer pronghorns move on the landscape in 3 distinctive groups: solitary adult males maintaining territories, female groups with their new fawns and yearlings, and bachelor herds. Male territories are defended from March through October, never overlap, and typically have space between them. Territories vary in size depending upon water access, food quality and quantity, and topography—territories tend to be larger on flat ground, whereas ridges and canyons tend to demarcate smaller areas.

Bachelor herds of 5 to 20 animals are composed of yearling males, 2-year-olds, and older males without territories. They tend to range farther than either adult males with territories or female herds, but must utilize poorer habitat adjacent to and between established male territories. The passive-aggressive behaviors seen within female groups are also displayed within bachelor herds, including foraging displacement and bed displacement (discussed below). The difference is that dominance in bachelor herds is more related to size and weight.

Researchers in Montana revealed that birth order determined social status among females and that fawns born early were dominant over fawns born later. Older fawns are larger than younger fawns, but status established by birth persists into maturity, even if a late-born animal was to grow larger and stronger in time.

Both females with new fawns and those without join together to form a female herd, which often utilizes the range of several male territories and the area between and around them. Dominance within female groups is a fundamental component of pronghorn society. Though more subtle than in males, dominance displays between females are more frequent. Dominant females frequently pressure subordinate animals to move off a foraging site, to give up a day bed, or just to move to a different spot for no apparent gain whatsoever. The dominant animal may do this by just closing in on the subordinate animal, or she may even nudge the animal to help move her on her way. While grazing, subordinate animals remain on the periphery, selecting grazing routes that create the fewest opportunities for encounters with dominant animals.

Female herds mingle with the adult male when they graze within his territory, and thus female herds often appear to have one male member. This relationship provides lactating females access to optimal range under the protection of the resident male, and minimizes female competition for food resources with local bachelor herds.

When fawns and their mothers join the herds, fawns engage in roughly 100 agonistic interactions each day, reinforcing established hierarchies. Unlike adults, who are more subtle, fawns express dominance in dramatic and obvious ways. Dominant animals slam the sides of subordinates to displace them at feeding sites or elsewhere, and they may follow up with a chase, repeatedly butting the subordinate in the hindquarters. Nearby fawns that are also dominant over the one being chased sometimes join in and butt the subordinate from either side as it attempts to flee the area. All the while, its mother typically does not intervene.

Bachelor herds spend their time in two ways. First, they invest tremendous time in feeding, since size and weight are correlated with herd status, and they are preparing their bodies for defending a territory when they are older. Second, they invest considerable time in sparring, further training for defending territories and battling for the right to mate with females in estrus. Sparring can be viewed throughout the year and is instigated by an animal lowering its head and approaching another. A sparring exercise is rarely turned down; the opponent lowers its head and then they engage prongs. Rather than the ears-flat aggressive countenance of fights in the mating season, sparring opponents keep their ears erect and engage in a far less aggressive and energy-expending exercise; typical bouts last 30 to 40 seconds. In fact, larger pronghorns within bachelor herds can be seen holding back when sparring with smaller animals, so as to keep the exercise going. Sparring is a cooperative relationship in which one animal tries to push the other off balance. When one animal succeeds in doing so, the animal in danger of being gored must rapidly throw both hind feet in the direction of its head in an attempt to protect its neck and regain its footing.

Dominance in both female and bachelor herds is perhaps most obvious when they lie up to ruminate. The most dominant animal present must be the first to bed. If not, he or she will oust the transgressor and lie in its bed. This starts a domino effect in which the displaced pronghorn finds a subordinate to oust from its bed and so on and so on, ensuring that the last animal to become comfortable is the least dominant in the herd.

INTERACTIONS WITH OTHER SPECIES

Coyotes are the principal predator of young pronghorns, and coyote abundance has a direct effect on fawn survival. Golden eagles and bobcats also kill fawns, but in lesser numbers. Coyotes very rarely succeed when they hunt adult animals. In fact, healthy adult pronghorns are very rarely killed by any predator. When there are other ungulates about, wolves choose to chase slower prey. Cougars rarely take pronghorns since they are rarely in adequate stalking terrain.

Pronghorns can coexist with cattle, as overgrazing by cattle often increases the forbs that are the preferred foods of pronghorns. Cows will consume some forbs, and one researcher estimated that a single cow consumes the same amount as 38 pronghorns on a given day. Domestic sheep target the same plant species as pronghorns, and in large numbers they eliminate potential forage for pronghorns. They may also spread bluetongue, a disease brought to North America with domestic sheep that can cause mass deaths among pronghorns. In 1984 a small outbreak in Wyoming resulted in 300 dead. Sheep fencing severely restricts pronghorn movements.

American Bison
Bison bison

OTHER NAMES: buffalo, plains bison, woodland bison, wood bison, tatanka (Lakota).

The American Bison is an American icon—a symbol of both wilderness and American history. Perhaps no other animal was so linked to the changes that swept across North America with the arrival of the European settlers. The earliest written accounts by European explorers moving west across North America describe the bison herds as blotting out the prairie grass as far as they could see, and the sounds of the herds like rolling thunder. It is estimated that there were approximately 50 to 60 million bison in North America in the year 1500, when herds wandered coast to coast, and from Florida well into Canada. Then bison were slaughtered by settlers with a remarkable efficiency throughout their range, for meat, tongues (which they sold), hides, and as a means to undermine the native people inhabiting the Great Plains. By the late 1800s there were two remaining wild buffalo herds, the first in northern Canada and the second in Yellowstone National Park, where poachers still killed them with some frequency. Canada was the first to provide federal protection, and then in 1894 President Grover Cleveland signed a new law that made bison killing in Yellowstone an offense with serious ramifications ($1,000 fine or imprisonment). Yellowstone started a second herd with bison bought from the Flathead Indian Reservation, and slowly but surely, through conservation and reintroductions by the American Bison Society and others, the bison was again spread throughout western North America.

ACTIVITY AND MOVEMENT

DAILY

Bison are typically found in open areas, where they graze for 9 to 11 hours each day, resting, loafing about, and ruminating for the remainder. Occasionally bison seek the cover of trees to lie in the shade or escape insects and other disturbances. During the savage storms of the open plains, bison simply face into the wind and rain and endure them. Bison walk slowly, typically staying in a given area for several days before moving several miles to a new location. Sometimes they move at night. Though bison are typically ponderous, they can explode into action if startled or agitated. They may trot to cover ground more quickly, or gallop at speeds up to 37 miles (60 km) an hour when chased. Bison are strong swimmers and ford rivers they encounter to reach new range.

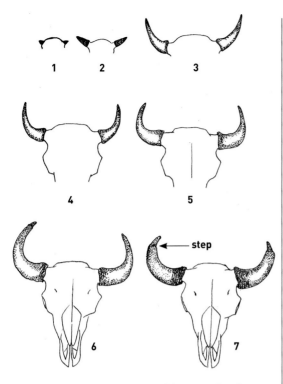

Horn shape at various ages. Bison are 7 to 8 years old when the "step" appears in their horns.

Their sense of smell is acute and seems to aid in the detection of predators. Bison also hear and see quite well; they are able to discern moving objects at a distance of 1.2 miles (2 km), and can distinguish between a man and his horse at 0.6 miles (1 km).

Three behaviors may be observed throughout the year: rolling in dust baths and mud wallows, horning trees, and making and using rubbing posts. Rolling and wallowing are exhibited by all bison, regardless of age and sex. These behaviors alleviate skin irritations, help build up a protective layer of mud against biting flies, and dislodge old fur. Most rolling is done in a dry, dusty patch that likely started as just a small spot on the range and was enlarged over time and with repeated rolling of many buffalo. With enough use, dust baths become conspicuous bare patches on open range that may measure 14 feet (4.3 m) in diameter.

Bison horn trees throughout the year, but bulls horn trees most often just prior to the rut. Females also horn trees, most often just before giving birth to calves in the spring.

Bison rub on trees, boulders, and other objects throughout the year, but this increases slightly during the spring molt, when last year's fur clings in clumps in their new coat. Look for great dislodged tufts of fur adhering to pine and fir trees where bison have rubbed. They also rub on large rocks and boulders. Over time, generations of bison may rub the rock's surface smooth and wear a circular trough around the boulder. Some bison rocks and their encircling depressions can still be found in North Dakota and other parts of the West, where bison have not ranged in well over 100 years.

SEASONAL

Bison migrate with the seasons to take advantage of changes in available forage in various habitats and at differing altitudes. Winter foraging occurs more often in sheltered meadows and in riparian zones where less snow accumulates. Where travel between summer and winter ranges is long, bison follow well-established travel routes and create worn paths on the landscape. Bison that are not restricted by fences may make very long migrations, but most herds today are inhibited from doing so. Weather is a great predator of bison, and severe winters cause high adult mortalities. Late-spring storms kill adults as well as newborn calves. Their annual molt begins as winter turns to spring, but patches of old fur can be seen clinging to the sides of animals until the end of summer. Their new fur is stiff and dark, and their coats are full again by late fall, just in time for winter.

FOOD AND FORAGING

Buffalo are grazing specialists and forage for grasses, sedges, and rushes throughout the year. They forage in grasslands of every kind, from expansive prairies to forest meadows to arid scrublands. Bison consume 15 to 18 pounds (7–8 kg) of greens per day and defecate once per hour, leaving a minefield of patties in their wake. During times of rest and rumination, they regurgitate one bolus at a time, which they chew an additional 38 to 70 times, at a rate of one chew per second, before returning it to the stomach to be further digested.

The imposing musculature of the neck allows buffalo to continue to graze in relatively deep snow, which they clear away with great sweeps of their head. Large bulls are able to clear areas of deeper snow than females, and they may forage in snows up to 3 feet (90 cm) deep. Females graze in areas where snow is less than 2 feet (60 cm) deep. Bison prefer to drink from open water rather than eat snow, and they will break through thin ice if necessary. Where heavy snows or a lack of grasses dictate a switch from winter grazing to some browsing, buffalo eat diverse shrubs, including saltbush and prickly pear.

Compared with cattle, bison more efficiently digest and assimilate native North American forbs and are better able to maximize nutrition in areas of poor forage. Their cold-hardiness and ability to graze in deep snows—and the fact that they produce meat lower in cholesterol, fat, and calories than beef—make them a far superior choice over cattle for farms under normal range conditions, assuming markets pay equal amounts for beef and bison.

HABITAT AND HOME RANGE

Historically bison were widespread in North America, ranging from coast to coast and from Alaska in the north to Mexico in the south. Today, small numbers of free-ranging buffalo herds exist in large preserves sprinkled throughout the West, and the majority live on private ranches.

Though bison were widespread and inhabited a great diversity of habitats in centuries past, they were most abundant in prairies and shrub steppe that provide continuous opportunities for grazing grasses and sedges throughout the year. Wild bison can still be seen in these environments, as well as in mixed forested habitats and tundra in the north, where they seek out open meadows and gaps in forested cover. Bison select areas where recent wildfires open up forest gaps and initiate the growth of grasses and forbs. Controlled burning has been used to improve the quality of bison range through western Canada.

Home ranges of individual bison vary depending upon the quantity and quality of the forage available. Bison are wandering creatures and thus home ranges are traditionally large, though many herds today are restricted by fences and other obstacles. Home ranges for adult females in and around na-

tional parks seem to be largest and vary from 154 to 479 square miles (400–1,240 km^2). Old males seem to move the least and may inhabit a range as small as 66 square miles (170 km^2).

COMMUNICATION

The tail is an important means of communication among bison. In grazing animals it sways peacefully back and forth, and during sexual and aggressive encounters the tail is raised either horizontally or even vertically. The height of the tail is a graded signal, varying along a continuum: the higher it is raised, the greater the intensity of the animal's stress or aggressive intent. Mature bulls generally hold their tails erect when they fight, and submissive animals lower their tails and wag them from side to side. Females often elevate their tail when threatened by a predator or following copulation.

Males of all ages exhibit threat displays and engage in fights throughout the year, most frequently before and during the rut. Females, too, will threaten and charge when they perceive that their calves are threatened. Common visual threat displays include raising the tail, the "broadside threat," a slow advance, the "nod threat," pawing the earth, and sometimes wallowing. A common threat is a combination of pawing the ground, rubbing the head, and wallowing. And nearly every visual display will be accompanied by continuous bellowing. Threat displays communicate power and dominance without

A rolling bison in a well-used patch of earth. Their dust baths make the ground more permeable to rain, and thus are essential to ecosystem health. © *Pawel Strykowski/Fotolia*

A tail-up threat communicates the agitation of this adult bison. © *Megan Wyman*

overt combat, and a study in Alberta found that 73 percent of threat displays did not escalate to physical contact, meaning that a pair can resolve which is dominant in an exchange without fighting most of the time.

The "broadside threat" is a passive threat during which two animals stand parallel to each other to best display their size and proportions. High, humped shoulders, shaggy manes, and bell-like fur hanging from their chins are adaptations that accentuate their powerful profiles during these displays. Even though out-and-out clashes are few, you can be sure that the best bulls have the power to back up their appearances, at least early in the season. As the rut drags on, even the most powerful bulls begin to tire and are occasionally displaced by smaller males.

A "slow advance" by one bison toward another is a very serious threat. If one animal does not assume a submissive posture and move out, expect a fight. Buffalo often nod their head just prior to engaging in a fight and in between physical bouts. A submissive animal may lower its head, turn away, or start grazing.

Bison fighting is fast and fierce, churning the ground into great columns of dust visible for miles across dry, open terrain. Two 1-ton bulls colliding with one another at a full gallop sends colossal concussive ripples through the earth, tremors that can be felt some distance away. Sometimes one bull gallops at an opponent that chooses to stand its ground and absorb the blow. In these cases the impact can be so great that the standing bull is pushed 10 feet (3 m) backward. After initial contact they wrestle with horns locked, trying to attack the other's flanks. Goring with their stout, hooked, and tapered horns can break ribs and puncture organs. Bison injure one another with alarming frequency and severity. In one study 50 percent of dead bison had evidence of healed wounds and cracked ribs acquired in battle.

After males clash on the scarred earth the animals face each other, panting from the exertion, and sometimes roll their eyes upward in their deranged state. Submissive animals may flee the scene, back away slowly while shaking their head side to side, or may quickly turn to grazing. The dominant animal sometimes mounts the loser, as a male mounts a female to copulate.

Bison can be shy and retiring, or aggressive and dangerous. Unfortunately they do not always clearly communicate their intentions to humans, and fatal attacks have occurred with few prior threat displays, or none at all, in both wild and captive animals. Bison have been observed throwing foolish tourists who approach too closely up to 30 feet (9 m) with a quick hook and twist of their shaggy head. Several patterns are clear: The older the bison, the less tolerant and more unpredictable they become; also, females are less predictable during the calving season, as are males during the rut.

Vocalizations among bison vary from bleats in calves to snorts and grunts in adults. Females and calves keep in regular communication through contact calls. The most distinctive voice of bison is the bellow, or roar, of the bull. Males may bellow up to 22 times per minute during the rut, and their roars can be heard many miles away. Males roar while tending females and prior to fights. They may also roar in response to another male's roar or when approaching a bachelor herd. Young males roar more often than older males. A female may roar as well, most often when she feels her calf is threatened.

Like many members of the deer family, bison bulls often urinate in their dust baths and wallows before and during the rut. They may also urinate on themselves and then roll. Scent in the urine can communicate identity, age, status, and reproductive condition. Horning and rubbing also likely deposit scent that conveys information to other bison.

COURTSHIP AND MATING

The mating season may start as early as the end of June and runs through September. In the Yellowstone area breeding peaks from mid-July to mid-August, and in Canada from mid- to late August. Females between 3 and 12 years of age are the most productive, though calving success in wild herds varies considerably: 38 to 88 percent of females successfully wean calves, depending on the quality of available forage, the age of the mother, and their ability to sustain milk production.

Older bulls begin to increasingly visit mixed herds with adult females as the rut approaches, and they spend more and more time with them as the mating season progresses. Bulls also increase their frequency of roaring with the start of the breeding

A male bellows as he approaches a female herd. © *Max Allen Photography*

season and are often heard roaring as they approach a female herd.

Males 7 to 13 years old seek out females in estrus by approaching and smelling them and sometimes licking their genitals or urine. Females enter brief periods of estrus that last 9 to 28 hours and occur about every 3 weeks until they have successfully mated. Bulls exhibit the flehmen response while smelling a female or her urine, curling their upper lip back and extending and arching their neck upward. Bison flehmen throughout the year in response to diverse stimuli, ranging from human urine to rotting carcasses, but more rarely than during breeding. Breeding males are aggressive and insistent, often nudging resting females in order to get them to stand up so that their investigations are more thorough. Although males are the pursuers, females play a role in choosing a mate. They can be observed approaching dominant males and fleeing from younger bachelors. Females may also run through a herd to stir up potential suitors, then stop to watch the males fight it out to see which will gain the opportunity to tend her.

When a male discovers a female in or approaching estrus, he stays with and "tends" her, blocking potential competitors. He moves her to the periphery of the herd, by force if need be, and keeps himself between her and the rest of the herd. His continuous roars and frequent wallowing and pawing communicate his claim and his intention to fight if necessary to protect his prize. That is, unless he is able to sneak her away to a secluded part of their range, in which case he decreases his bellowing so as not to attract any potential competitors. This pair bond is temporary, lasting several minutes to several days—until they have successfully copulated. During this time the male and female maintain an exclusive bond, unless the male is displaced by one more powerful. A female averages 3 to 4 different tending males before she mates. The lucky male at the end makes repeated attempts to mount the female, and she shuns every attempt but one. Tending is an exhaustive exercise since males spend much of the time defending the female from other males. Males often lose 10 percent of their weight during the rut because they have little time to feed themselves.

Look closely to see the urine emerging from the female's hind end and the male's flehmen response, during which he analyzes the scent with his Jacobsen's organ to determine whether she is in estrus. © *Megan Wyman*

Copulation most often occurs at dawn or dusk, or during the dark of night. Their ritualized behaviors might be best described as appearing affectionate. Pairs lick each other and head-butt lightly. The female may even mount the male for short stints, and they may simultaneously wallow together just prior to mating. The male communicates his intention to mount the female by swinging his head onto her backside. Using his chin to steady himself, he rises up and grasps her with his forelimbs and again attempts to mate. The female may hinder the process by trotting forward at the last moment. Successful males hold on and run on their hind feet to maintain the connection. In a moment, it is all over. After copulation, the pair bond dissolves slowly, and some bulls linger to deter another male from mating with the same female. Within several hours, though, he departs and seeks another female in or approaching estrus. The female may stand for several hours, arching her back, lifting her tail, and dribbling urine and semen.

What is described above is characteristic for plains bison, whereas northern wood bison often display a slightly different strategy. Rather than tending individual females, dominant bulls tend to gather small harems, which they defend from intruders. The control of a particular harem is contested often during the breeding season and may switch several times during a single rut.

DEVELOPMENT AND DISPERSAL OF YOUNG

Females approaching birth are noticeably restless. Bison gestation is long, ranging from 262 to 300 days, after which a single calf is born in the spring, between mid-April and June. The female leaves her herd to give birth in isolation where tall grasses, shrubs, or trees provide some protection against predators. If no suitable cover is available, females tend to give birth within the protection of the herd. Occasionally twins are born, but it is rare.

Females more often give birth while lying down, and parturition takes about an hour. Glistening newborn calves weigh 35 to 50 pounds (16–23 kg) and are a bright ochre or reddish tan. Their mother immediately eats the umbilical cord and placenta, and then licks her calf clean. She may continue to lick the calf for several hours, stimulating the newborn animal and initiating the mother-calf bond. Calves are precocial and stand for the first time between 5 and 85 minutes after they are born. Standing is usually followed by the calf's first attempt at nursing.

Females and young join the protection of the herd quickly, but initially the female stands between her calf and the remainder of the herd. Newborns pique curiosity in other herd members, and unrelated bison may be observed approaching, smelling, and licking the calf.

Calves nurse between 6 and 10 minutes per session at unpredictable intervals throughout their youth. They may begin to graze as early as 5 days old and will drink water after just a week. Still, they continue to nurse for 7 to 12 months. Older cows tend to nurse calves even longer and may tolerate nursing calves for up to 2 years.

Within several weeks, calves within a herd begin to cluster together and form a dominance hierarchy that is dependent more upon disposition than size or sex. Play is most common in the youngest calves and becomes less apparent as they age. You might catch them leaping and frolicking about in the open on their own or with other calves, or butting heads with, chasing, and play-mounting each other.

A calf's coat begins to darken at about 2.5 months, beginning with the head and moving down the shoulders to the back. By 8 to 9 months juveniles weigh 300 to 400 pounds (135–180 kg). Young females attain their adult weights more quickly than males, reaching their full size between 4 and 6 years of age. Occasionally a juvenile female will breed at 1 year old, but more often females breed for the first time between 2 and 4 years of age. Males reach adult proportions in about 6 years, and thereafter gain minimal weight each year until they reach their maximum weights between 10 and 12 years of age.

Females aggressively defend their calves from perceived threats. Occasionally adult females adopt orphan calves, and orphaned calves as young as 8 weeks old have been known to survive until adulthood.

INTERACTIONS AMONG BISON

Bison are gregarious by nature and are typically found in large matriarchal herds of calves, yearlings, adult females, young males, and a few older bulls. Older bulls also move about as solitary animals or form small bachelor herds. During the breeding season in Yellowstone National Park, mature males join the matriarchal herds, and several matriarchal herds may merge together to form larger groups of up to 500 animals. Bison likely aggregate to benefit from group defense, and their migratory foraging patterns allow large herds to remain together, letting heavily grazed areas recuperate before a herd returns to it.

Dominance hierarchies are fairly stable over time. Dominance among females clearly correlates with age, yet between mature bulls neither age nor weight appears to be a deciding factor. Individual disposition seems to be a significant variable in determining rank among mature bulls. It is also true that the older the bison, the less tolerant and more unpredictable it becomes.

INTERACTIONS WITH OTHER SPECIES

Bison herds significantly affect the plant communities in which they roam. Rolling, the horning of trees, and constant grazing hinder succession and maintain the grasslands upon which many species depend. The roaming-grazing style exhibited by bison—heavy and intense use for short periods—is helpful to plant regeneration and success. Accumulations of their urine and scats have been shown to increase plant productivity, their wallows allow for greater water percolation into the earth, and their thick fur helps catch and carry seeds, distributing them across the bison's range. Bison damage woody vegetation through rubbing and horning behaviors, though overall their negative impacts on woody vegetation are minimal. They severely damage only 4 percent of vegetation, and cause moderate and light injury to another 25 percent. The exception is for trees in Yellowstone; where high bison densities are contained in a limited area over great lengths of time, bison can significantly damage trees, including large ones.

Bison overlap with the range of every North American deer, but dietary overlap is not great except with elk, which eat more grass than other deer species. Dietary overlap is the primary cause of competition among ungulates, and when it occurs, buffalo tend to be dominant, butting and chasing away their competitors. Increases in the bison population in Wyoming have led to bison-elk competition in the National Elk Refuge, where bison displace and injure elk at feeding stations. Bison have even been known to harass and kill elk calves in Yellowstone National Park.

Pronghorns and bison overlap extensively, but there is little competition between them. Pronghorns eat more forbs and less grass than bison. In a study in Wind Cave National Park, buffalo foraged around the edges of White-tailed Prairie Dog towns where grasses were dominant, while pronghorns fed in the forb-dominant centers of the same towns. Bison are particularly attracted to prairie dog towns, where the activity of these large rodents encourages the growth of higher quality forage. Patches of bare earth exposed by prairie dogs are also attractive for rolling and dust baths.

The wolf is the primary four-legged predator of the buffalo. Wolves primarily prey upon calves, the sick, and the old. Weakened bison are particularly vulnerable to wolves in late winter and early spring, before they have a chance to eat new vegetation and recover their vigor. Wolves chase bison in Yellowstone National Park for an average of 3 miles (4.9 km) per pursuit, but on one occasion a buffalo herd kept running for 24 hours and covered 50.6 miles (81.5 km). When wolves pursue bison, the calves are shifted to the front half of the herd, and adults defend their rear. On occasion a calf is abandoned when it falls behind, but the mother will return to search for it after the threat has passed. Both pronghorns and deer have also been observed seeking protection within a bison herd when threatened by wolves. Bison have also been observed repeatedly harassing resting wolves, forcing them from their beds, as well as pushing them off elk kills in Yellowstone.

Wolf predation has little effect on bison herds throughout their southern range. Isolated bison herds in Canada have been significantly reduced by wolf packs, which may kill a buffalo every 8 days.

Brown Bears also kill calves, juveniles up to 24 months old, and the occasional adult. Bears do not frequently hunt bison, and when they do they are sometimes killed by the buffalo they hunt. Nevertheless, buffalo meat is an important food source for Brown Bears within their range, especially in the spring when bears emerge from their dens and rely upon winter-killed bison carcasses to sustain them until summer. In Yellowstone National Park, the largest component of Brown Bear diets is ungulate meat, and 30 percent of it is bison. Black Bears will also scavenge buffalo carcasses when they can.

Coyotes are not a significant predator of bison, but they can be seen following bison herds in winter. It is suspected that they take advantage of displaced snow cover to hunt small mammals that are active under the snow. Coyotes that follow too closely or enter bison herds are sometimes gored and trampled to death.

Mountain Goat
Oreamnos americanus

Oreamnos **translates** from Latin as "mountain lamb," but Mountain Goats are hardly similar to the idyllic, peaceful lambs of biblical tales. Unlike barnyard goats that butt with their horns, Mountain Goats hook and stab with theirs, and their saberlike tips pierce and puncture skin and muscle alike. Nearly every facet of Mountain Goat society is colored by belligerence and near-constant threat displays and behaviors.

Adult males are sometimes called "billies," females "nannies," and youngsters less than a year old "kids."

ACTIVITY AND MOVEMENT

DAILY

Mountain Goats most actively forage from sunup until midmorning, alternating feeding with resting bouts. They may feed 6 or 7 times, lying up to rest and ruminate in between. A second period of foraging and activity ensues during the evening hours, and they may remain active throughout even the darkest nights.

They select safe sites to bed, with rock faces and accessible escape routes behind and smells and sounds swirling up from below. Before lying down they pause to study their environments carefully for signs of danger. They prepare their beds by pawing and digging with the front feet to create an oval depression, in which they kneel on their front "knees," then lower their hindquarters, and finally roll onto one side. While they are ruminating they often extend one or both forelimbs, and when sleeping during warm weather they tend to extend all their legs to one side. On the hottest days their shaggy coats make them susceptible to overheating, and so they seek shaded beds or lie up on residual snowbanks. Soft grounds suitable for bedding are scarce, so they are reused time and again. Goats within a social group compete for the best of them, and there may be considerable jostling as dominance hierarchies are reinforced. One researcher reported that over one-third of agonistic behaviors they observed in Alberta's mountains were over bedding sites.

Mountain Goats move little on any given day, generally less than half a mile (1 km) for males and just 1 to 1.5 miles (2–3 km) for females. However, they may ascend hundreds of vertical feet while covering little ground horizontally, and they can climb 1,500 vertical feet (450 m) in 20 minutes. It is hypothesized that females with young, who tend to move the farthest, use their mobility as an anti-

Note the difference in horn shapes between male (left) and female (right) Mountain Goats.

predator strategy. Greater movements make them more difficult to find on the landscape.

Goats are plodders built to maneuver in the steepest and most broken terrain and are thus specialized in such a way that limits their potential speed on flatter ground. In a Montana study, goats spent approximately 10 percent of their summer hours in terrain with a slope greater than 60 percent, and somewhat counterintuitively, they increased their use of this steepest terrain during the winter, when snow and ice make tenuous holds more dangerous.

Mountain Goats move like human rock climbers—one limb and then another, securing the position of each before moving the next. Their muscular shoulder humps allow them to hook a hoof over a ledge and pull their body up and over. They have shorter legs than other ungulates, which lowers their center of gravity. The distance between front and hind limbs is shorter, too, as in a Jeep Wrangler, making tight turns possible in narrow spaces. Their hooves splay in a V-shape and have bulbous pads extending below the hoof walls, which increases their traction on all types of ledges. Goats do slip from time to time. If they are able to recover, they flatten themselves against the rock face and claw for any available purchase. During a long-term study in Montana, 17 percent of recorded deaths were due to falling.

Maintenance behaviors may be as simple as scratching and yawning, but Mountain Goats also dust-bathe to relieve itching, rid themselves of insects, and perhaps aid in the removal of shed fur. They typically dust-bathe while lying on their side, with the foot above stretched out and pulling dirt inward to throw over them. Then they switch sides and repeat the process. Witnessing a goat urinating is an opportunity to distinguish between the similar males and females. Females squat and males stretch forward, extending their hind legs.

SEASONAL

Mountain Goats have an annual molt. Adult males start shedding in June and finish up by July. Sub-adult animals and females molt slightly later, ending in August. In July females and yearlings can be separated from males by the remains of their winter fur clinging to their hindquarters. Summer coats are shorter and cooler. Winter coats gradually grow in and are completely full by mid-fall.

During the spring and summer Mountain Goats travel up to several miles to feed at natural salt licks. These salt licks may see densities of 100 Mountain Goats, with aggressive behaviors occurring frequently. In addition to groups around licks, the largest congregations of Mountain Goats can be observed in the early spring, while they linger on their winter foraging areas.

Biting flies and mosquitoes may drive goats to the highest and windiest perches in June and July. Water may be a limiting factor in their summer distributions. In many areas animals linger where snowbanks persist throughout the year, providing a source of water and respite from heat. In the late spring and summer males are solitary or in bachelor herds of up to 6 animals. Females and young form small nursery groups in which they travel and forage. Outside the mating season, males and females generally ignore each other except when salt licks or limited forage bring them in close proximity to each other. Mountain Goats begin their seasonal migration to lower elevations when the first big snow hits in the late fall.

FOOD AND FORAGING

Mountain Goats are intermediate feeders, grazing and browsing depending on season, resources available, and location. Typical summer months are filled with grazing on grasses and sedges, yet in some areas browsing upon willows, dwarf birches, and low shrubs and vines such as whortleberry play larger roles in their diet.

Mountain Goats use natural salt licks heavily in spring and summer. Researchers hypothesize that spring and early summer grasses deplete Mountain Goats of sodium. Alpine vegetation provides less mineral content than do plants growing at lower elevations, and digesting and defecating watery green vegetative growth may speed sodium loss.

During the winter mosses and lichens are an important food source, and goats may be seen scraping ancient lichens off rock surfaces with their lower incisors, or feeding upon the arboreal lichens and mosses that droop lower or drop under the weight of rains, snow, and ice. Mountain Goats also browse a variety of tree buds during the winter, and in some areas bear grass. They also excavate the rhizomes of ferns.

HABITAT AND HOME RANGE

Mountain Goats historically inhabited the alpine and subalpine habitats of the northern Rockies from Montana north into Canada, the Bitterroot mountains in Idaho, and the northern Cascades in Washington, following the coastal ranges through Canada into Alaska. But they've now been successfully introduced to other mountain ranges, where previously great lowland expanses kept them from natural migrations. They can now be seen in the high country of Yellowstone National Park, in Nevada and Oregon, and in several areas of Colorado, most notably on Mount Evans.

Inland, Mountain Goats are strictly creatures of the alpine and subalpine and only dip into the highest forested habitats during winter storms. Coastal populations of Mountain Goats utilize more forested habitats and lower elevations than their inland counterparts.

Mountain Goats seek south- and east-facing slopes in winter, where sun minimizes snow depths and solar melting facilitates its compaction, which makes for easier and more stable mobility. They tend to move to seek out snow-free zones at slightly lower elevations as well. They do not leave their refuges of steep, rocky terrain and may even gravitate to exposed peaks where winter winds keep snow depths down. In a Montana study, goats increased their use of slopes greater than 60 percent from summer to winter, which may be because steeper slopes shed snow.

As spring progresses, Mountain Goats slowly move up the mountains, following shortly behind the receding snowlines and the emerging new growth of vegetation. They may travel as much as 10 miles (16 km) between their summer and winter foraging areas, but more often the distance is much less. Home ranges, which average 7.5 to 19.3 square miles (20–50 km²), including their seasonal migrations, are still relatively small.

COMMUNICATION

Mountain Goat vocalizations do not carry far, so you must be close to appreciate them. Agonistic encounters are often accompanied by low rumblings and guttural roars, and startled animals may snort or emit a soft bleat. Bleats like those associated with domestic sheep and goats are most often heard when females and kids are separated and looking for each other. Females may give a soft bleat during courtship as well. Mountain Goats also communicate with their tails: half-erect means nervous, while fully erect indicates real fear, as when they are sliding out of control.

Males mark bushes during the rut with the glands just behind their horns, which enlarge and exude secretions during the fall. This behavior may also be observed among all age classes and both sexes throughout the year and represents some form of chemical communication we have yet to understand.

Unlike Bighorn Sheep, male Mountain Goats do not engage in colossal head-butting contests. Much of their dominance behavior involves ritualized threat postures and displays. Communicating threats is essential to maintaining dominance among both males and females, and rarely do aggressive behaviors escalate to bloody fights or goring. In one study 95 percent of agonistic encounters were contact-free. However, dominance displays and aggression do result in injuries, but more often from falls than from horns. Dominant animals corral, nudge, push, prod, or hook subordinates over cliffs or onto dangerous ledges, and sometimes the subordinate animals fall. The behaviors described below may be exhibited by either gender, excepting circle fighting, which is exclusive among males.

Mountain Goat displays are somewhat hierarchical in their intensity and significance. A "hard" or prolonged stare is perhaps the most subtle of threats you might observe. Moving up a notch is the lateral display, or "present threat," in which an animal displays its bulk and hump from the side and arches its back to increase its apparent size. The head is lowered and tucked so that the horns point out ominously. During a present threat the tail is tucked,

Circle fighting between two males. Reprinted from *A Beast the Color of Winter: The Mountain Goat Observed* by Douglas H. Chadwick by permission of the University of Nebraska Press. © 1983 by Douglas H. Chadwick.

and if you are close enough you will hear their accompanying rumbling or growling.

The "horn threat" is exhibited when an animal faces an opponent or intruder. The goat tips its head forward to display its horns and point their potentially deadly tips at the opponent. A horn threat may escalate to a bluff charge, or "rush threat," in which the rushing animal lowers its head as if to strike, but stops short of contact. You might also observe a slower version of the bluff charge, wherein the "charging" animal walks rather than runs. Outside the rut, Mountain Goats may progress to contact, which is usually a swift hook or stab with their horns.

During the rut, present threats and bluff charges between males may progress into a "circle fight" in which the two animals circle each other as each aggressor chases the rear end of the other goat. Horn swipes, which are quick attack maneuvers, can inflict nasty puncture wounds to the flanks, and males accumulate thicker and thicker skin in the belly and rear as they age. In older males the skin on the rump may be nearly an inch thick. Even with this protection, contact is rarely made, as the circle fight is more ritualized formality than barroom brawl.

Submissive animals either quickly flee from the dominant, whining as they run, or in milder encounters turn their body or gaze away from the dominant animal. Sometimes a subordinate animal will squat, altogether removing its vulnerable rump from the playing field, and this behavior seems to calm nearly all aggressors.

COURTSHIP AND MATING

Solitary males and small bachelor herds begin to join the groups of females and youngsters in October, but mating doesn't typically occur until late

The Mountain Goat on the right displays a present threat to discourage an approaching animal. Reprinted from *A Beast the Color of Winter: The Mountain Goat Observed* by Douglas H. Chadwick by permission of the University of Nebraska Press. © 1983 by Douglas H. Chadwick.

November and December. In early November males will be seen lingering on the edges of female groups, standing about, watching and waiting, while females adjust to their presence. Males decrease their foraging significantly; some may eat hardly anything for a month. On the periphery of these groups, males mark bushes with the glands behind their horns. With their front hooves they dig rut pits in which they urinate. As they dig deeper they fling the earth up onto their bellies and flanks, and their soiled coats make them easy to differentiate from females even at a great distance.

Very slowly, males close the gap between themselves and the dangerous and moody adult females with which they hope to mate. As females approach estrus, roaring males defend them from other males with displays that occasionally escalate into circle fights. The largest, most dominant males likely mate with the most females, but it is believed that younger, subordinate males mate with a few females as well.

Females are in estrus for a brief 48 hours each year, so males must have gained enough trust to be very close at the right moment. When attempting to mate, a male approaches the female in a "low stretch," bending his knees, remaining parallel to the ground, and flicking his tongue in and out as he stretches his head and exposes his vulnerable neck. He utters a low "buzz" while approaching in a subordinate and servile manner. If responsive, she urinates, and the male noses the urine and then folds back his upper lip in a typical flehmen response. She may even tolerate the male walking directly up to her hind end and licking her genitalia.

More often than not, females are not responsive to soliciting males and turn belligerent instead. Males are sometimes gored in the face, neck, and/ or sides by particularly pugnacious females. Should the female remain receptive, the male will rise up and kick her rear end with his forelegs, and then proceed to mount her. Typically the male mounts the female repeatedly, resting his head upon her back or rump in the intermissions. It is likely that the first series of mounts fail because the female walks away just as the male assumes position. Eventually she allows the male to complete what he's trying so hard to start, and she'll stand her ground and spread her hind legs to aid the process. The actual act of mating is remarkably short and simple given the weeks of investment males have made in courting females. After several good thrusts, they walk their separate ways.

DEVELOPMENT AND DISPERSAL OF YOUNG

Eighty percent of the female population will give birth within a 2-week window in late May and early June after approximately 190 days of gestation. Females retreat to rugged, isolated terrain to give birth alone where cliffy terrain offers protection against predators. Just before giving birth, she hunches and heaves. Typically a single 6.5-pound (3-kg) "kid" is born, although twins are not unusual and triplets have been reported. A newborn kid sports a white coat with a dark dorsal stripe, which fades by the time of its first birthday. After the birth the nannie eats the placenta and licks up any blood that fell during parturition. Then she licks her youngster clean, her tongue stimulating movement in the tiny kid. Once the kid stands, it butts her udders to induce milk flow and nurses for the first time. While nursing, it holds its tiny tail erect and the female turns to lick the anus clean, a ritual that is repeated every time the youngster nurses in the weeks to come.

They remain together for several days, during

The courting male on the right exhibits a low stretch to a potentially dangerous mate. Reprinted from *A Beast the Color of Winter: The Mountain Goat Observed* by Douglas H. Chadwick by permission of the University of Nebraska Press. © 1983 by Douglas H. Chadwick.

which the kid tumbles and falls frequently in its attempts to climb both the mountainsides and its mother. The female always places herself in such a way as to stop any tumbles from becoming fatal falls. On occasion a passing herd may peer over the ledge to look at a newborn goat, and after several days the kid is able to follow her when she returns to the nursery group.

Kids follow their mothers very closely in their first week and nurse at regular intervals, although the frequency of nursing declines rapidly, even in the first few days. One young Mountain Goat that was observed for all the daylight hours of its first few days nursed 17 times for a total of 58 minutes on the first day, 10 times for 31 minutes the second, and 6 times for a total of 20 minutes on the third. By the fourth day, it had begun eating some vegetation.

Kids start feeding on vegetation by 1 week of age, and by 4 weeks are eating plants extensively. Weaning begins slowly, as early as 4 weeks of age, when the mother can be observed stepping over her youngster to terminate nursing, and continues slowly until lactation is finished at about 4 months. Occasionally a kid may still be observed suckling its

Young Mountain Goats jump and frolic in the alpine zone, acquiring the greater balance and coordination that is essential to their future survival. © *Erwin and Peggy Bauer/Animals Animals*

mother at nearly a year old. Throughout their first summer the kids stay very close to their mothers, who protect them from other members of the herd. One study in Washington showed that kids rarely moved more than 3 feet (1 m) from their mothers for their entire first summer.

Play in Mountain Goat kids resembles adult threat behaviors. When less than a year old they will also butt heads with each other, a behavior that stops when their horns are sufficiently developed to do real damage. Kids also wrestle each other with their necks—one will place its head and neck over another and try to force its opponent to the ground. You might also see them playing "king of the mountain," in which one animal attempts to retain the highest position on a boulder or stump. Kids will also play with other animals they encounter, and it's not unusual to see them leaping about with a reluctant marmot or attempting to play with Bighorn Sheep lambs.

Kids often stay with their mother until the following year when she gives birth again, at which time she drives off her youngsters from the previous year. As horns develop and yearlings approach 2 years of age, play-fighting and aggression become more formalized and less violent. Males leave their mother and their nursery group between the ages of 2 and 4. They generally begin to participate in the rut at 2.5, although they don't attain adult size until 4 years of age.

INTERACTIONS AMONG MOUNTAIN GOATS

Mountain Goats may engage in the most intraspecific (goat-to-goat) aggressive encounters of any wild North American ungulate. Goats defend personal territories of approximately 6 to 8 feet (2–2.5 m) in diameter. Other than kids and mating partners, other goats are discouraged from entering this invisible sphere. In one study, each female Mountain Goat was reported to engage in 3.4 hostile encounters per hour, and in large bands a total of 12 to 24 aggressive observations were recorded every hour.

Although not unequivocal, it appears that where food resources are less plentiful, and thus interactions more frequent, females become more aggressive and dominant over males, except during the rut. Females create a rigid social hierarchy that correlates with size, weight, and horn length; often the eldest and largest among them hold the highest ranks. Females then interact with females of similar rank, even though changes in rank within a social group are not uncommon.

Dominance throughout the herd is primarily governed by size, with larger goats displacing and bullying smaller goats. As in pronghorns, this pecking order can sometimes be witnessed when goats

Adult Mountain Goats spar with their lethal horns. © *Victoria McCormick/Animals Animals*

are bedded up. A dominant animal may approach and displace a subordinate from its bed, and the subordinate in turn finds an animal it dominates and does the same thing, instigating a domino effect, which moves down the line in a strange form of musical beds.

The exceptions to the "largest-is-dominant" hierarchy are the adult billies, who are the largest animals within a Mountain Goat community and yet frequently exhibit servility to females and even yearlings, allowing themselves to be displaced from beds and feeding sites. Adult males often wander the landscape alone or form very small bachelor herds. It is suspected that breeding males become more submissive with age so that during the rut they can better interact with females, which are the most dangerously belligerent of the female North American ungulates.

High aggression in Mountain Goats also keeps them well spread out on a landscape where forage is meager in comparison to areas at lower altitudes with longer growing seasons. Yet ungulates also tend to form groups in order to mitigate the burden of watching for predators. In exchange for shared vigilance, individuals are able to invest more time in feeding. Thus we have two opposing forces working on goat herds—aggression keeping them apart, and the benefits of shared vigilance pulling them together. And what we find on the landscape is small clumps of animals in which hierarchies are quite plain and thus agonistic interactions are minimized.

INTERACTIONS WITH OTHER SPECIES

Bighorn Sheep and Mountain Goats can be seen intermingling in the high country and even bedding down in close proximity to each other. Lambs and kids sometimes frolic together, and during their overlapping ruts, confused bighorn rams have been seen pursuing Mountain Goat nannies. Yet for most of the year the two species amicably ignore one another. In the small percentage of exchanges in which dominance is displayed, as in decisions over right of way, Mountain Goats are nearly always dominant.

Observations at salt licks in Montana also revealed that Mountain Goats are dominant over and displace Mule Deer. In turn, elk are dominant over and displace Mountain Goats. Yet a group of goats may stand their ground against a single elk. They paw the earth, lower their horns, and bluff-charge until the elk departs.

Because of the rugged inaccessibility of the terrain Mountain Goats inhabit, they are thought to suffer little predation pressure compared to other ungulates. Grizzlies have been observed ambushing or overtaking goats in lightning sprints, dispatching them with a great swat of their paws. Wolves kill more goats in Alaska than in other parts of North America, and the goats there have been seen clumping together and even circling up, horn tips out and aimed at wolf hunting parties approaching from all sides. Cougars are likely the greatest threat to adult Mountain Goats, given their ability to maneuver in rugged terrain.

Golden and bald eagles are both significant predators of young and adult Mountain Goats. Any whoosh of air or glimpse of an eagle aloft propels Mountain Goats into low squats, to better maintain their center of gravity, or to lean into rock walls when they are on precipices. In their first few days young kids weigh less than 10 pounds (4.5 kg) and can be lifted from the ground by eagles, but more often the eagles use tactics that force animals in precarious positions to lose their footing and fall from cliffs and ledges. In Montana the entwined bodies of a subadult billy and golden eagle were discovered at the base of a cliff. The talons of the eagle were still embedded in the goat, and the horns of the goat fixed in the body of the bird.

Mountain Goat kids have numerous predators, including coyotes, bobcats, golden eagles, lynx, cougars, and Brown and Black Bears. Starvation plays a larger role in kid mortality than predation during their first winter, and harsh winters can be devastating. Hard winters in Montana result in up to 80 percent kid mortality and 40 to 60 percent mortality among yearlings.

Mountain Goats are vigilant in their watch for predators, yet there are gaps in their ability because of morphological and behavioral limitations (the shape of their head and placement of their eyes and where they choose to look). While they are feeding, Mountain Goats often look up and scan their surroundings, and before lying up they study their environment for long periods. Yet Mountain Goats are quite easily approached from above when the wind is right. When goats become aware of something strange nearby they often approach it to investigate. If they identify it as a potential threat, whether human or other predator, they walk nonchalantly away until they are at a safe distance, and then run. Yet if you surprise a goat at very close range, expect lowered horns, bluff charges, or even violence.

Disease and avalanches can kill young and mature goats. Eighteen of 30 carcasses investigated in one study were thought to have been killed in avalanches.

OTHER NAMES: mountain sheep, bighorn, desert bighorn, Sierra bighorn, borrego cimarrón (Mexican Spanish).

The horns of Bighorn Sheep are for pushing, butting, bruising, and concussing their opponents. Although they may not pierce the skin, in combination with a bighorn's weight and speed, they are certain to break bones. It is thought that horns have evolved to help protect the skull, as many of the animals that sport them are born with an instinctive need to butt heads. In the Bighorn Sheep, the corneal and frontal sinuses are expanded to cushion the brain. Head-butting contests are as much a contest of stamina as power—which ram will tolerate the greater abuse?

ACTIVITY AND MOVEMENT

DAILY

Like other ungulates, Bighorn Sheep walk when traveling and foraging. Their form and subsequent movements are something between the Mountain Goat, a rock-climbing specialist, and the deer, fleet runners inhabiting flatter terrain. Bighorn Sheep are both expert climbers that move gracefully in steep, rugged terrain, and swift runners on both flat and broken ground. Yet they neither climb as efficiently as the Mountain Goat, nor run as gracefully or as quickly as deer. Bighorn Sheep balance the two specialties more than any other ungulate in North America.

Bighorn Sheep are diurnal, though they are occasionally active during the night, especially when moonlight provides improved visibility. Each day is divided into foraging and resting, during which rumination also occurs. Feeding bouts may occur from 1 to 6 times per day, though less during cold weather or extreme heat. Feeding occurs most often during the crepuscular hours of dawn and dusk.

Bighorns spend approximately 35 percent of each day in repose. Resting bighorns generally lie down on their sides in lays they dig out with their front feet. They lie in areas with improved visibility either adjacent to or within escape terrain, which is rocky and steep, and gives bighorns an advantage over most predators. Their vision is excellent, and often members of the group lie facing in different directions. As a whole they watch every possible route a predator might use to sneak up on them. They may reuse these resting sites time and again and use them to bed during the night as well. Excavated beds may be enlarged over time; they may be up to 8 inches

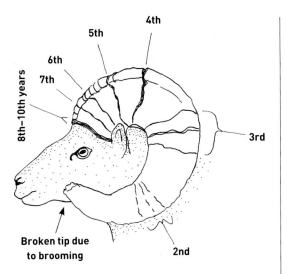

8th-10th years

7th
6th
5th
4th
3rd
2nd

Broken tip due
to brooming

Aging of Bighorn Sheep rams from horns. Drawn after Hansen, in Elbroch, 2006, *Animal Skulls*. Used with permission.

(20 cm) deep, or occasionally more. Look for numerous droppings ringing older, reused beds.

Rocky Mountain Bighorn Sheep sleep with their feet beneath them to conserve heat, while desert sheep sleep on their sides with their feet pointing out during the warmer months to stay cool. In extreme heat some bighorns will remain standing for their rumination bouts. During the warmer months bighorns also select bed sites where breezes are most common and most powerful in order to displace the relentless attacks of biting insects. Bighorns ear-flick and shake their heads more often while lying down. They average 20 ear flicks per minute to ward off biting insects. Standing Bighorn Sheep minimize insect attacks by standing with other sheep, with which they "share" their insect load. Bighorn Sheep also rub trees and rocks to relieve itching and often stretch when feeling secure and content.

SEASONAL

For much of the year bighorns are split into two groups within a range. The adult males 3 years old and older form one group, in which strict dominance hierarchies are established based upon horn size, body weight, and strength. The second group is composed of females, subadults, and young. Their hierarchies are difficult to interpret except that the band is guided by a matriarch, an older female that decides where and when the band travels.

Bands of Bighorn Sheep vary from several animals to 25 or more. Typically, males and females inhabit different areas for much of the year, though they may also overlap somewhat, especially where water resources are limited. The dominant theories of sexual segregation are that males and females have different priorities. Males require optimal forage to ensure health, vigor, and a maximum growth rate to assure their competitiveness in dominance and mating hierarchies. Because they are larger and stronger than females, rams can feed in areas where predation risk is high. And because they need to grow heavier as quickly as possible to compete for females, males are willing to run the risk of encountering predators more than females. Females, on the other hand, select habitat based upon the level of safety it provides their lambs and thus choose to remain in rugged areas of suboptimal forage.

Healthy cold-country bighorns enter their annual molt in early spring, when they actively rub on objects to help dislodge their itchy winter coats. Shedding is dramatic in Bighorn Sheep in cold country, and great mats of fur will dislodge on obstacles they rub. Unhealthy animals retain their coats through the summer before shedding them. Managers use this fact to monitor the health of herds and estimate how many animals in a band are faring poorly. Desert bighorn do not exhibit a dramatic molt like their high-country counterparts.

Over much of the bighorns' range, spring ushers in the start of their seasonal migrations to higher altitudes to feed on new vegetation. Slowly moving up the mountainsides in time with snow recession, they feast on nutrient-rich new growth well into summer. Generally bighorns remain at higher elevations through the spring and summer and then begin to work their way down to lower elevations in the fall, moving just ahead of the snowline that is migrating down the mountains as winter approaches.

In desert regions, however, bighorns migrate in a different fashion, with available water sources driving seasonal movements and behaviors. During the hottest times of year, much of the day is spent bedded to minimize overheating. Desert bighorns purposefully move so that they feed and water almost exclusively on shaded slopes throughout the day.

FOOD AND FORAGING

Bighorn Sheep graze primarily on various species of grass, but they also take sedges and occasionally browse shrubs. As a species, Bighorn Sheep eat a great diversity of vegetation, and one compilation study listed more than 470 different plants eaten across their range. In desert country they eat several species of cacti, yucca, and agave. Bighorns also move great distances to take advantage of natural mineral licks.

Desert bighorns require surface water such as springs and creeks to survive, although sometimes they absorb adequate fluids from the vegetation they eat, or from eating snow. In times of severe drought desert bighorns stomp on and break open barrel cacti to feed on their soft, watery pulp. In some populations desert bighorns remain away from permanent water sources for as long as 7 months out of the year (October to May).

Throughout much of the Southwest, troughs of water, called guzzlers, have been erected to aid Bighorn Sheep recoveries. Bighorn Sheep must drink every 3 to 5 days. When they do, they drink enormous quantities to sustain them until their next visit. One ram drank 7 gallons in a single visit, averaging nearly a gallon of water per minute. Desert honeybees are quick to recognize guzzlers as well, and during the summer they will cover the entire surface of the water in a layer of bee bodies several insects thick. Bighorns must dunk their muzzles through the bees to drink the water, suffer their stingers, and then spit them out in between gulps; at times bighorns are kept at bay by the bees and cannot drink. A wet year provides numerous natural water caches across the landscape, allowing for wider distributions and greater mobility of individual bands.

HABITAT AND HOME RANGE

Bighorns are creatures of dry mountains throughout southwestern Canada, the western United States, northernmost Mexico, and the Baja California peninsula. Their range includes much of the Rocky Mountains, the Sierra Nevadas, and the drier mountain ranges in southern California, Arizona, New Mexico, southern Utah, and Mexico. Their preferred habitats include varied grasslands adjacent to steep terrain, from large river canyons to mountain peaks. Where snows accumulate in winter, bighorns seek areas where snow depths are less than a foot (30 cm) and avoid areas where snow crusts inhibit foraging. They stick to south-facing slopes and other areas where prevailing winds minimize snow accumulation.

In the Southwest, desert bighorns have adapted to inhabit rugged desert regions too dry for deer. In Anza-Borrego State Park in eastern San Diego County, deer are found among the junipers inhabiting the cooler mountains above 3,000 feet (900 m), and bighorns inhabit the hot, rugged terrain below 3,000 feet, even visiting the valley floor, where temperatures reach 120°F (49°C) in the summer.

COMMUNICATION

Several glands of Bighorn Sheep are thought to play significant roles in scent communication. In the corner of their eyes they have large lacrimal glands that ooze visibly and may play a role in dominance interactions. They also have glands on their feet, and some researchers believe scents from these glands are used to mark bedding sites and travel routes.

The vocalizations of bighorns are severely limited, and in the field they are generally silent. They bleat in a deeper tone than domestic sheep when disturbed, agitated, or alarmed. When a female gives an alarm, her lamb immediately returns to her.

Bighorn Sheep rely most upon visual cues to communicate alarm and dominance. Bighorn Sheep that spot a potential predator assume an alarm posture. With their head held high and neck extended, they stare in the direction of the disturbance. They may also paw the earth, snort, or bow their head in the direction of a threat, which communicates to the remainder of the herd the direction and severity of the danger.

Dominance displays include head-butting and staring. These are most easily observed just prior to the rut and in the spring, though they may be seen at any time of year. Bighorn rams follow ritualistic steps leading up to and following physical contests. The more closely matched two rams appear, the longer the displays and clashes will continue before determining which is dominant over the other.

The contest begins when two males exchange stares. Then they turn and walk several steps away from each other before turning back to face one another like gunfighters moving into position in the Old West. They rise up vertically on their hind legs in a "threat jump," then kick forward toward each other on just their hind legs. As the distance between them disappears they fall forward, dropping down to all four feet at the last moment. This compounds the force with which they collide, as does the lowering of their heads and tilting forward of their horns at the very last moment. The impact of their clashing heads and horns echoes like a rifle shot across the landscape. Immediately following

Two bighorn rams rear up in a "threat jump," a ritualized start to ramming their heads together to determine dominance.

Male-male contests are violent and fast, and the echoing sounds of their colliding horns can be heard for miles. © istockphoto.com/Al Parker

the collision the two rams stand side to side, raise their heads high, and freeze in the "present" position, to best display their horns to their opponent. Should neither ram recognize the dominance of the other, the entire process is repeated.

When one ram is defeated it may turn away and begin to feed, or approach the dominant ram and rub his horns on his face or chest. The dominant animal often behaves as if the submissive ram is a female in estrus, bending low, nosing his genital area, kicking him with his forelimbs, and sometimes even mounting him.

Females and juveniles also butt heads in agonistic encounters, but they rarely use the ritualized displays of rams. In desert regions females often fight over water resources. It is hypothesized that this is why their horns are proportionately larger than those of their northern counterparts.

COURTSHIP AND MATING

The mating season, or rut, for Bighorn Sheep is dependent upon climate and strongly correlates with latitude. Mating is timed so that females give birth during the season of explosive vegetation growth; in the south the seasonal rains precede greening, while in the north it's the melting of the winter snows. In much of their northern range mating occurs in mid to late fall and may continue into winter. Depending upon the health of the band and the quality and quantity of forage, every adult female may bear young in a single season, or in a poor year only a tiny fraction of females might do so.

As the rut approaches, male herds begin to merge and intermingle with the females and juveniles. Adult ewes can be identified by their slender horns that curve backward over the posterior of their skull. Mature rams wear massive, heavy horns that curve back, down, and then forward in a spiral. Unlike at other times of year, when males settle dominance

more often through visual displays than violence, pre-rut behaviors are dominated by the clashing sounds of males butting heads, which can be heard over many miles. In pre-rut contests large rams resort to barroom brawls, and size, strength, and mass determine the winners. The majority of rams continue to increase in rank every year until they die. Males peak in weight at 7 to 8 years of age and then might actually begin to lose weight as they age.

As ewes come into estrus, rams begin to approach them and sniff the air immediately behind their vulva in a "low stretch" or bow; their head is held low and extended and their nose turned up. The females usually encourage them by squatting and urinating. Then the ram sniffs both the female's vulva and the urine on the ground before lowering his head slightly and curling his upper lips backward in a flehmen response. If the female is in estrus, the ram proceeds to defend her from other rams and moves into courtship behaviors. Females remain in estrus for 2 weeks, but each female will be receptive to breeding for only an approximately 48-hour window during this time.

Males that breed successfully can be roughly divided into two large categories: dominant rams, which earn the right to breed through sheer mass, strength, and power, and subordinate rams, which successfully manage to sneak in and coerce a female into breeding. Rams have typically established their dominance hierarchy before the rut, and thus top-ranking males are provided easier access to females in estrus. The top one to three rams in a band will father 60 percent or more of the lambs, yet it was once thought that the dominant rams bred almost exclusively.

A dominant ram may defend a single female at a time, or "tend" and defend several females, corralling them into areas on the fringe of the band where he can protect them. Rams increase their contact with a female in estrus by rubbing and butting her vulva with his chest, as well as giving her kicks with his forelegs. He may also nose her, twisting his head upon contact and uttering a bleating vocalization. The female may respond in kind should the male be one of high social rank, and therefore an acceptable mate. The female may also rub the dominant male with her body and/or horns. This increases until the ram mounts the female from behind and success-fully mates with her. The pair may mate repeatedly within a several-hour period, and in one case a pair mated 38 times, each coupling lasting no longer than a minute.

It was realized only recently how successful sub-ordinate rams were at stealing breeding opportuni-ties from the larger, heavier males. "Coursing" rams may work alone or as unified teams to challenge a dominant male defending one or more females. They don't actually attempt to defeat the male, but rather to burst by him. Then they pursue the estrous female on a long, circuitous, and often dangerous route across steep terrain. Dominant rams tend to be too exhausted from long physical contests with other large rams to join in or keep up with the pursuit. A female may aggressively chase off sub-ordinate males or flee to save herself for a more dominant animal. If the chase is unsuccessful, the dominant male inevitably reclaims the female and continues to defend her. The fact that 40 percent of lambs are bred by subordinate males means many such chases result in breeding.

DEVELOPMENT AND DISPERSAL OF YOUNG

Up to a week prior to their parturition, pregnant fe-males abandon their herds and move into the steep-est, most rugged terrain to give birth to their lambs in isolation. Lambing areas are characterized by their scant forage and their hostility, thus providing maximum protection to newborns from terrestrial predators. Research in Arizona revealed that each female returns to the same exact area to birth new lambs year after year, where all other females are excluded.

After a gestation of 172 to 176 days, one lamb is born, although twins are recorded on rare occasions in both wild and captive populations. Females have 2 teats, both of which swell visibly as parturition ap-proaches and remain swollen throughout the lacta-tion period. Lambs are born small, 6 to13 pounds (2.7–6 kg) each, but are precocial and able to stand on their own within 30 minutes. The female cleans her newborn with her tongue and then eats the pla-centa. Within 24 hours the lamb is able to follow the female into an area that provides even better views of potential dangers, in nearly vertical and rugged terrain. A newborn's hooves are initially white and soft, but quickly harden and turn to black. The dried umbilical cord often clings to the lamb for 7 days and can be used to age newborns in the field.

During these first few days of isolation the mother and lamb develop an essential bond, for a female will not nurse an unknown lamb. Within 3 days the female and her new youngster rejoin the band, and the mother smells the rear end of her lamb each time it nurses to make sure it is her own. Lambs suckle their mother approximately 3 times an hour, for 14 to 28 seconds per session. Weaning occurs gradually, but young have been observed grazing as early as 14 days of age. Most youngsters do not begin grazing until much later, and then be-

A young adult male follows a female closely and sniffs her hind end to check whether she might be approaching estrus. © *David Moskowitz/www.david.moskowitz.net*

A dominant male front-kicks a subordinate and rubs his horns along the subordinate's back. Such behaviors maintain the pecking order so vital to the success of dominant males during the breeding season. © istockphoto.com/James Pauls

come completely weaned between 4 and 6 months of age.

Growth is rapid for lambs in their first 6 months. It slows during the winter but resumes a rapid pace in the spring. Lambs regularly play with other lambs and on occasion attempt to engage other animals or adults. They head-butt, play-mount, and chase each other, as well as rise up on their hind legs in threat jumps.

Juvenile females can mate at 18 months, and some do, especially in southern populations where numbers are expanding. More often, females mate for the first time at 2.5 years of age. Males, on the other hand, have little hope of successful breeding until they are 7 to 8 years old, when their bulk and horns will be sufficient to win contests during the rut. Females continue to grow until they are 3 to 4, after which their energetic reserves are completely diverted into lamb production. Males continue to accumulate mass until about 8 years of age.

Subadult females often remain permanently with their maternal group, whereas subadult males tend to stay until they are about 3 years old, when they wander as far as 75 miles (120 km) and across several mountain ranges to join a band of rams in another territory. In this way bands avoid the negative consequences of inbreeding depression.

INTERACTIONS AMONG BIGHORN SHEEP

Bighorn Sheep herds reap the benefits of shared vigilance, reducing an individual's risk of predation while simultaneously providing each more time to forage. Bighorn Sheep with their heads down are more vulnerable to attack than those with their heads up. In females, individual bighorns forage more often as their herd size increases, since they can depend more upon others to alert them when dangers loom near. Lactating females are an exception and invest near-constant and unwavering vigilance regardless of how many other bighorns are nearby.

Densities of Bighorn Sheep influence the health of the herd and the physical condition of individuals. As population densities increase, the average physical size for both males and females decreases. Higher numbers result in greater competition for resources and may also influence the energy reserves allocated to mating competitions versus growth.

INTERACTIONS WITH OTHER SPECIES

Bighorn Sheep forage in relatively open habitat, where they can see with little obstruction, but remain close to steep terrain in which their agility gives them an edge over most predators. Historically, wolves were a significant predator of Bighorn Sheep, and where the two species overlap wolves continue to kill them. When encountered by wolves, adult bighorns have been observed circling up like muskox, with their heads and horns all facing outward.

In some parts of the country coyotes are a significant predator of lambs, and golden eagles, bobcats, and occasionally wolverines also kill lambs. Bighorn females respond differently to coyotes depending upon the terrain in which they face them. When they are in flat terrain they most often flee. When confronted by coyotes in steep, rugged terrain, they are more likely to either stand their ground or even take the offensive. Subadults caught out on flat ground may be corralled by coyote packs away from steeper slopes and subsequently killed. Older adults rarely allow themselves to be corralled and instead plunge through the coyote ranks to assume a higher position in steeper terrain.

Today the natural predator most responsible for influencing bighorn populations is the cougar, which hunts both adults and lambs. In southern bighorn populations under federal and/or state protections, cougar populations are monitored closely and controlled to aid in sheep recovery. In some states cougars are trapped and killed in a circle around managed bighorn populations. In California only select cougars are killed. In the Sierra Nevadas they collared and monitored cougars long enough to determine which of them were killing Bighorn Sheep, and then selectively removed them. In a study in Canada, only 2 of 60 collared cougars sharing bighorn habitat became specialist bighorn hunters. Managers have realized that it is more efficient to maintain deer-hunting cougars on the landscape than to remove them. Removal creates a vacant home range for another cougar to claim, and the next cougar may instead hunt Bighorn Sheep.

Mountain Beaver
Aplodontia rufa

OTHER NAMES: aplodontia, sewellel (Chinook), chehalis (Salish), boomer, mountain rat, whistler, showt'l (Nisqually).

Mountain Beavers are not beavers at all. They are not aquatic rodents, but rather more akin to porcupines in that they climb trees and gnaw wood. *Aplodontia* translates to "simple tooth," which refers to the structure of their cheek teeth. In evolutionary terms Mountain Beavers are the oldest rodent in North America. They are also one of the least studied, and much of their behavior and natural history remains a mystery. *Rufa* means red. The name is derived from their reddish pelts, which Lewis and Clark traded and brought back to the East Coast collections for taxonomic descriptions.

ACTIVITY AND MOVEMENT

DAILY

As if fallen logs and tangled vegetation weren't treacherous enough for the off-trail hiker on the slopes and foothills of the western Cascades, the shallow tunnels of Mountain Beavers provide additional excitement—you'll frequently punch through into them as you explore. The lives of the solitary and fossorial Mountain Beavers revolve around their elaborate burrow systems, which they dig in areas with deep, firm soils with adequate drainage.

Burrow systems have numerous entrances (sometimes more than 20), many of which may be plugged. Open entrances may be concealed by vegetation or exposed with a fan-shaped "step" of debris and dirt, excavated and pushed out from underground. The entire tunnel system may encompass an area 327 feet (100 m) in diameter, with a burrow entrance occurring on average every 18 to 24 feet (6–7 m). Entrances are typically 4 to 8 inches (10–20 cm) in diameter and interconnected belowground by a network of tunnels. Tunnels close to the surface are used for foraging and traveling, whereas the deepest tunnels, which plunge to depths of 3 feet (1 m) below the surface, contain the nest and other chambers. The center of the complex is the large central nest compartment, where up to a bushel of flattened, dried vegetation serves as a mattress. Additional smaller chambers are located nearby, several of which serve as storerooms for food. Other very small compartments serve as trash bins, where vegetation gone bad or discarded remains are placed, and still others near refuse compartments serve as toilets.

On occasion, chambers full of baseball-sized clay balls have also been found in excavations; no one yet knows what purpose they serve. One hypothesis is that Mountain Beavers use them to plug burrows. Another is that they gnaw them to help keep their ever-growing teeth in check. It is also possible that Mountain Beavers ingest clay to counter the effects of plant toxins in their diet, a behavior known among other species of mammals.

Aplodontias are only rarely seen aboveground during the day, but they are often active within the protective confines of their tunnel systems, where air temperatures remain cool and relatively stable through the seasons. They maintain 5 or 6 bouts of activity during a 24-hour period, each of which may last up to 1 to 2 hours. One researcher estimated that Mountain Beavers spend up to 75 percent of their active time in foraging and digesting food and that they must forage regularly because of the poor energetic value of the foods they eat. Under the cover of darkness, aplodontias set out aboveground to forage and collect plant materials to store below. They forage and travel in walks and trots. They climb well, and though their eyesight and hearing are poor, their ability to smell and their tactile senses, enhanced by long whiskers, aid them in explorations underground and in the dark.

SEASONAL

Mountain Beavers do not hibernate, but they often reduce and sometimes altogether stop their aboveground activity during late fall and winter. Mountain Beavers molt once each year, beginning at the end of summer and finishing after several months.

A throw mound of dirt is typical at the entrance to an aplodontia's burrow. © *Mark Elbroch*

A standing aplodontia.

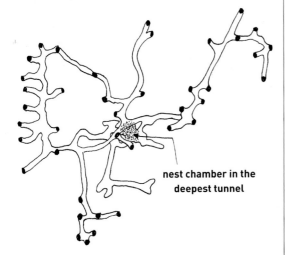

**nest chamber in the
deepest tunnel**

The burrow system of an aplodontia. Most of the main tunnels parallel downed logs aboveground, providing the inhabitant with greater security. Drawn after Macdonald, 2006, *The Encyclopedia of Mammals*. Used with permission.

FOOD AND FORAGING

Mountain Beavers are herbivores that forage on a wide variety of succulent and woody plants. They eat a great diversity of ferns, many of which are toxic to other animals, and sword and bracken ferns are particularly popular fare. Mountain Beavers eat more succulents during the summer months, and then more leaves and buds from fall into spring.

Aplodontias cut, gather, and stack plants to cure at burrow entrances beginning in late summer. Cured ferns and other herbaceous plants are then moved belowground to be cached for later consumption or used for nesting materials. One hypothesis for why aplodontias dry plant materials before caching them is that it retards decay, allowing plants to remain more nutritious and useful for longer periods.

Aplodontias are terrific climbers and spend much of their time from fall through spring climbing shrubs and trees to forage where leaves and buds are most tender—on the outermost growth of branches or the central shoots. Look for twigs that have been bitten off at a 45° angle, browsed, and discarded ("nip twigs") under any number of tree species. Salmonberry, elderberry, vine maple, big-leaf maple, willows, and alders are among their favorites. In the Sierra Nevada mountains, they favor conifers in the winter. When Mountain Beavers descend trees and shrubs, they often do so headfirst. If not too far above the ground they may just let go of the branch to which they are clinging and free-fall to the ground, an effective, if not graceful, means of descent.

In the Pacific Northwest, Mountain Beavers sometimes forage extensively on tree seedlings. In areas where plantations are being started after a logging operation, this conflict may cause intense frustration on the part of the foresters. Up to 25 percent of seedling losses have been attributed to Mountain Beavers. They also debark and/or girdle older saplings when feeding upon the cambium layer beneath the snow and higher up on shrubs and trees when they climb to forage. Aplodontias invade gardens and agricultural areas and at times may cause significant damage.

Mountain Beavers practice coprophagy, meaning they eat their feces for a second run in the digestive tract to maximize energy extraction from a given meal. Soft pellets are produced first. Post-reingestion pellets are smaller and harder. The animal either defecates them directly into latrine compartments or tosses them in with its mouth.

Mountain Beavers rarely wander more than 10 feet (3 m) from burrow entrances when they forage. They clip greens at their base and then may sit, hunched and squirrel-like, and eat while holding the greens in their front forepaws, which have opposable thumbs. Sometimes they sit farther back, like fat prairie dogs, with their hind legs extended outward while they eat. More often Mountain Beavers return to the safety of their burrows to feed underground.

HABITAT AND HOME RANGE

Mountain Beavers inhabit the moist coastal forests at low elevations stretching from southern British Columbia south through Washington and Oregon into northernmost California. Additional populations are found at higher elevations in the Sierra Nevada range and in two small groups along California's coast north of San Francisco Bay, including one on Point Reyes National Seashore.

Aplodontias are especially abundant in newly

A Mountain Beaver reaches for blackberry leaves and stems near Seattle, WA. © *Manlius/123rf.com*

harvested areas or regenerating forests with tangles of dense undergrowth, logs, and other debris littering the area. In drier habitats they seek the moister deciduous slopes near permanent watercourses. Regardless of geographic range, Mountain Beavers require soils of sufficient depth to dig and maintain their extensive burrow systems.

The annual home ranges of Mountain Beavers are little more than the extent of their burrow network plus several square feet of space beyond burrow entrances along the edges. Annual home ranges are much larger than the core areas within which they spend the majority of their time. Home ranges for males and females are very similar, varying from 0.1 to 10.4 acres (0.05–4.2 ha) depending upon habitat and forage quality. Mountain Beavers, however, typically remain within 79 feet (24 m) of their nest chamber and rarely stray beyond 131 feet (40 m). The density of Mountain Beavers in a given location varies depending upon forage availability, and in thick tangled woods, tunnel systems may overlap with each other extensively. From 1 to 5 animals per 2.5 acres (1 ha) have been reported, and densities are highest in areas of young tree stands with open canopies. As forests mature densities somewhat decrease.

COMMUNICATION

The vocal repertoire of the Mountain Beaver appears quite limited. They squeak and squeal when fighting or handled, and they whine when in pain. Growls and chatters have also been recorded, but for much of their lives they are silent. Sometimes they quiver their whiskers in irritation. When cor-

nered they can sit on their haunches, boxing and grabbing with their forelimbs, and bite with their large sharp incisors. If you're aiming to get a close look at one, learn to recognize the sounds of gnashing teeth, which they produce in irritation, often just before they lunge and bite. Aplodontias in agonistic encounters also secrete a white substance at the front edges of their eyes. At this time, researchers believe this may be a product of stress and a means of chemical communication.

Aplodontias regularly rub secretions in and around their nest chamber. They also scent-mark in outward tunnels used by multiple animals at the periphery of their network. Other aplodontias that encounter these scent marks spend a great deal of time investigating them, but do not retreat, so we assume they do not serve as intraspecific barriers.

COURTSHIP AND MATING

In Oregon, the geographic middle of the aplodontia range, estrus may occur between mid-January and the end of April. Within any local population, females tend to synchronize their estrus periods, so the actual duration of mating is only about 2 weeks. The descent and enlargement of the males' testes precedes mating by a month or more, occurring in November or December. The breeding season correlates well with latitude, falling later in the year the farther north you are within the species' range.

DEVELOPMENT AND DISPERSAL OF YOUNG

After a gestation of 28 to 30 days, litters of 1 to 6 animals are born in a nesting chamber underground. A captive female under observation gnashed her teeth and pressed her vulva with her forelimbs 1.5 hours before parturition. During birth she sat back on her haunches and assisted the exit of her 3 young by pressing around the vulva and licking the area to provide greater lubrication.

Newborns are altricial—naked, pink, and blind—but they squeak and begin to nurse within 20 minutes. At 5 days their claws are well developed, and by 7 days soft fur is beginning to cover their bodies. By 15 days each juvenile sports a full gray coat and can crawl about the nest chamber using its front limbs. At 21 days their ear canals are open completely and they can hear. They continue to grow and develop, eating their first solid food between 5 and 6 weeks of age, but it is not until they are approximately 45 days old that they open their eyes and see their world for the first time.

Lactating females increase their consumption of conifers and grasses during the spring, which increases their intake of the proteins necessary to produce milk. Juveniles are weaned after only 6 to 8 weeks, and they begin to emerge from their burrows for the first time at approximately 10 weeks. By 4 months they already weigh 70 percent of their expected adult weight. From here on their growth rate slows considerably. They will be more than a year old before they reach their full adult proportions.

Juveniles may disperse more than a mile (1.6 km), or as little as 27 yards (25 m), and they may either fix up an old abandoned burrow or dig their own. Females sometimes attain estrus at 1 year of age but do not breed for the first time until they are 2 years old.

INTERACTIONS AMONG MOUNTAIN BEAVERS

Mountain Beavers vigorously defend their tunnels around their nests and fight trespassing animals they discover nearby. However, they generally ignore each other aboveground, even when foraging or in other areas where one might expect competition for resources. Several aplodontias will also use shared tunnel systems at the edge of their ranges to move about and explore new areas.

Mountain Beavers are found in clumps on the landscape, meaning that there are congregations of solitary Mountain Beavers sharing excellent habitat interspersed within areas where Mountain Beavers are rare or nonexistent. Vacant territories in good habitat are quickly appropriated by new animals, which may even abandon their own nest and territory to take up residence in the new one. In this way the aplodontia community is a dynamic mosaic of shifting elements.

INTERACTIONS WITH OTHER SPECIES

Numerous species have been recorded using Mountain Beaver burrows and runs. In one study where

Note the well-developed whiskers and claws, so important to Mountain Beavers. © *Wendy Arjo/ USFW*

traps were set in Mountain Beaver runs, Western Spotted Skunks, Long-tailed Weasels, ermines, squirrels, mink, woodrats, voles, pocket gophers, deermice, jumping mice, and Pacific giant salamanders were all caught as well. Other studies have recorded American Badgers, raccoons, Snowshoe Hares, American Martens, Striped Skunks, and numerous other small mammals in their burrows. Thus the networks of tunnels created by Mountain Beavers are a resource for safety, sleeping, raising young, foraging, and hunting for numerous other species.

Coyotes, bobcats, and great horned owls are the principal predators of Mountain Beavers when they are foraging aboveground. Aplodontias may constitute much of the diet of these predators in certain regions of the Pacific Northwest. Skunks, martens, fishers, gray foxes, cougars, golden eagles, goshawks, and weasels also kill aplodontias. Research has also shown that aplodontias avoid areas where scents of predators have accumulated, as a means of reducing predation risk. Downed logs, logging slash, and other woody debris all aid aplodontias in providing refuges from predators while they forage aboveground.

Curiously, research in Washington revealed that a large proportion of predation incidents occurred on Mountain Beavers while they were tucked up in their nests, and the bite wounds at the base of the skull suggested that their main predators were mustelids or spotted skunks. Long-tailed Weasels, ermines, mink, and Western Spotted Skunks are all capable of sneaking belowground to catch Mountain Beavers unawares.

Eastern Gray Squirrel
Sciurus carolinensis, and Allies

OTHER NAMES: cat squirrel, migratory squirrel.

Eastern Fox Squirrel
Sciurus niger, and Allies

OTHER NAMES: stump-eared squirrel, Big Cypress fox squirrel, Delmarva fox squirrel, Sherman's fox squirrel, Carolina fox squirrel, ardilla zorra (Spanish), raccoon squirrel.

There are 6 large tree squirrels (genus *Sciurus*) inhabiting North America north of Mexico: Tassel-eared (Abert's) Squirrel (*S. aberti*), Arizona Gray Squirrel (*S. arizonensis*), Eastern Gray Squirrel (*S. carolinensis*), Western Gray Squirrel (*S. griseus*), Eastern Fox Squirrel (*S. niger*), and Mexican Fox Squirrel (*S. nayaritensis*). The behaviors and natural history of all 6 species are remarkably similar, and yet also distinctive in their own ways. This account will focus on the Eastern Gray Squirrel and Eastern Fox Squirrel, the two most common and most studied species in North America. The genus name *Sciurus* was created from the Greek words *skia* ("shade") and *oura* ("tail") and refers to the luxurious, bushy tail that so dominates our perceptions of squirrels.

ACTIVITY AND MOVEMENT

DAILY

Gray squirrels are expert climbers, and since they can rotate their hind feet 180° to the back, they are able to both ascend and descend trees headfirst. Squirrels only rarely fall, and in one study only 3 of 65 animals displayed healing bones that might have been broken in falls. One researcher witnessed a fox squirrel fall 85 feet (26 m), where it bounced on the ground. The squirrel climbed a nearby tree, perched, and then shook its head, as if dazed. The next day the animal behaved as if it had never fallen at all.

Descending squirrels keep their head up and frequently pause to assess for danger before departing the safety of the tree. Gray squirrels bound while on the ground. When they are exploring and foraging, the bounds are short and slow. When running, they bound at speeds up to 17 miles (27 km) an hour. Fox squirrels walk much more often than gray squirrels and will often be seen exploring cache sites or sniffing for fallen acorns in a slow gait. Tree squirrels are also capable swimmers; they hold their head aloft as they dogpaddle. However, squirrels seek natural bridges over creeks and streams rather than brave the current.

From spring through autumn, squirrels are most active twice each day, and their activity is dominated by foraging. They are busy for several hours following daybreak, and then again during the late afternoon, several hours before sunset. These activity patterns lengthen with the warmth and light, and they may be active up to 70 percent of the daylight hours on summer days. In parts of the country or at the peak of summer, extreme heat may cease squirrel activity completely. Grooming and resting constitute up to 30 percent of daytime activity in the summer and less at other times of year. Feeding activity peaks in the fall, when they spend 75 percent of their time out and about accumulating fat reserves essential for winter survival.

During winter, squirrels do not hibernate but are much less active; they typically have only one bout of foraging and movement per day. Skipping their morning routines, they become active in late afternoon in warmer temperatures and typically remain out for less than 3 hours. Squirrels have several additional methods of warming themselves. To regulate their temperature they manipulate a bundle of blood vessels at the base of their tail that functions like a gate for blood flow. This bundle swells

A nervous fox squirrel tail flicks to convey its alarm. © *Mark Elbroch*

when it blocks blood flow into the tail, which they do to maintain warmth within their core. The release of blood into the tail dissipates heat, cooling the animal when it is hot. When they are cold they also shiver, which increases their body temperature substantially. Like many animals, squirrels also harness radiant heat through sunbathing. During the warmer months squirrels often start each morning with a stint of sunbathing to warm up, and during the winter months they may be seem sunbathing at any time of day when bright sun might provide them a warm reprieve.

Squirrels use leaf and cavity nests as retreats throughout the year. Leaf nests are more commonly built during the warmer months and are of smaller dimensions than those constructed for winter shelters. Nests are typically built upon a platform of twigs out on a tree limb, rather than adjacent to the trunk. The outer framework is formed from interwoven twigs and leaves, and the inside is stuffed with leaf material. The innermost chamber is lined with soft materials, such as dried grasses, shredded bark, and lichens. You might see squirrels stripping the fibrous inner barks from dead branches and trunks at any time of year, as inner nests require periodic upkeep.

During winter months they may build larger leaf nests, but in colder climates squirrels are much more likely to seek out a sturdier retreat. They use abandoned woodpecker holes and any natural tree cavity that provides an adequate entrance, such as those created by wind, heavy snow, or lightning.

FOOD AND FORAGING

Gray and fox squirrels eat a great diversity of plant material, insects and their pupae, amphibians, bird eggs and fledglings, and the occasional small mammal or carrion. Yet the survival of gray and fox squirrels is dependent upon a limited number of large mast-producing trees. Gray squirrels eat hazelnuts, beechnuts, walnuts, pecans, hickory nuts, and the acorns of more than 24 different species of oaks. Squirrels select foods that provide the most nutrition for the amount of energy expended to find and handle them. For gray and fox squirrels it is more efficient to eat white acorns, with their smaller mass, fewer calories, and much softer shells, than the larger, richer walnuts and hickories that are protected by thick, tough shells. Naturally, the abundance of a food resource in a given year also weighs into a squirrel's decision-making, but in general squirrels follow this simple rule when deciding which foods to eat in any particular moment.

Tannins are one of many plant defenses that reduce the edibility and assimilation of seeds and foliage. Tannins are especially concentrated in acorns, a preferred food for both gray and fox squirrels.

Oak trees may be broadly split into two categories: the "black" oaks and the "white" oaks. The acorns of black oaks, including the ubiquitous red oaks, are higher in tannins but also richer in nutritious fats than their white counterparts. Both crops fall to the ground in autumn, but red oak acorns wait until spring to germinate, while those of white oaks begin to germinate right away. To further complicate a squirrel's decisions, individual trees also vary in the quality of mast they produce in any given year. This is why squirrels sample the nuts of many trees early in the harvesting season before making serious investments in harvesting from specific trees.

When a squirrel gathers an acorn, it sits on its haunches and holds it in its front paws. It quickly rotates the acorn beneath its nose, using its keen sense of smell to estimate the tannin content and determine the acorn's health and viability. In an instant the squirrel weighs the species of acorn, the quality of nut, and the tannins within, and decides whether to eat the acorn on the spot or to carry it off to store for the upcoming winter months.

Since red oak acorns germinate in the spring, and are less susceptible to insect infestation, it makes more sense for squirrels to store them for winter use. In addition, the tannins in red oak acorns break down over time and are thus more digestible after a period of storage. Because of the germination tradeoff, gray squirrels most often eat white oak acorns on the spot and store red oak acorns for winter use. Some squirrels have also figured out how to store white oak acorns for future use. They nip and kill the embryo at the tip of the acorn before they bury it so that they don't return to find a sapling.

A great many acorns are infested with the larvae of acorn weevils. Squirrels that encounter infested acorns as they are harvesting eat them immediately, protein-rich larvae and all, rather than storing the acorn for the larvae to eat at its leisure.

When a squirrel has decided to cache an acorn, it jams the acorn into its mouth and bounds off to bury it. Gray and fox squirrels are scatter-hoarders, meaning they make numerous caches all over their home range. The foods of scatter-hoarders are less likely to be found by other animals, and if they are, the loss of a few small caches does not jeopardize the owner's survival. Thus gray and fox squirrels are less territorial than Red Squirrels (which are larder-hoarders), have overlapping home ranges, and share communal scent posts.

A gray squirrel makes hundreds upon hundreds of caches all over its range. We presume it refinds its caches using a combination of sharp spatial memory and then smell to lock onto the exact spot. Squirrels are remarkable in their ability to find their caches and may recover 95 to 99 percent of them. Success rates are lower in areas of dry sand where scents are reduced. Watch squirrels carefully as they make their caches. Sometimes they only pretend to deposit the acorn or nut before moving on to dig what appears to be another cache slightly farther on. Fake caches serve to protect their efforts from animals that might be spying upon them while they work. Squirrels also invest time in shuffling their caches around and may be seen digging up nuts only to move them to another spot and re-cache them. In areas of high squirrel density they might even dig up the caches of other squirrels and move them and cache them as their own.

Gray squirrels also vary their rate of food consumption with the seasons. They eat the least and weigh less during spring and early summer. They begin to consume richer foods at higher rates as late summer turns to fall, which aids in the fat acquisition necessary for winter survival. Squirrels maintain a higher metabolic rate and thus a warmer body temperature than other mammals of comparative size; this is thought to be an adaptation that allows them to remain active in cold temperatures. The limitation is that they must have adequate food resources to keep stoking their internal fire and enough accumulated fat reserves to survive times when foods are scarce. Squirrels consume twice as much food at 39°F (4°C) as they do at 75°F (24°C), in order to stay warm and active.

During the fall, when they are frantically harvesting all the nuts they can, speed seems to be valued over thorough eating. Squirrels are seen eating acorns and other nuts as quickly as possible, wasting much of the edible portions in the process. During this time they often eat only the top half of the acorns, where tannins are less and energy-rich lipids more abundant. With the shift into winter, squirrels eat more slowly and carefully and consume each nut in its entirety. In autumn they eat 32 percent more food than they need to survive, stor-

ing excess energy as fat. This allows them to survive winter storms when they might go without food for perhaps several days in subfreezing temperatures.

In the spring, tree squirrels supplement their diet of stored nuts with emerging buds of many tree species and the early flowers of red maple trees. They also dine on the flowers and fruits of many shrubs and trees, including fruit trees in orchards. Squirrels eat diverse fungi (especially Western Gray Squirrels) in the summer months and are quick to take advantage of undefended crops, such as corn. They eat the seeds and catkins of pines, hemlocks, and spruce trees. Tree squirrels gathering pinecones often exhibit black chins, where the sap released while cutting the cones free has collected and hardened into an impenetrable shell.

In the United States, Eastern Gray Squirrels only rarely debark trees to feed upon the cambium layer, although they often do so in England, where they were introduced. Fox squirrels debark aspens and other species, scraping the sugar-rich cambium layer with their lower incisors.

HABITAT AND HOME RANGE

The Eastern Gray Squirrel is native to the eastern half of the United States and southernmost Canada. The Eastern Fox Squirrel overlaps with this range nearly completely, but it is absent in New England and farther north, and extends farther west to the Rockies. The Western Gray Squirrel inhabits only the Pacific Coast states. Yet all 3 species overlap along the Pacific because both fox and Eastern Gray Squirrels have been introduced in many areas of the western United States and Canada, especially in urban settings. In fact, the fox squirrel is the most easily seen tree squirrel along much of developed coastal California, whereas the native, more reclusive Western Gray Squirrel remains more common in native forests.

Eastern Gray Squirrels are most common in deciduous hardwood forests that produce large mast nuts and where dense understories exist to provide cover while foraging. Forests composed of diverse mast trees (e.g., oaks, hickories, walnuts) allow for greater food abundance and greater squirrel densities. Tree diversity also allows squirrels to switch their diets to take advantage of whichever nuts are most abundant in a given year.

Fox squirrels often share habitats with gray squirrels as described above; they also inhabit large long-leaf pine tracts and other southeastern pine plantations. In comparison to gray squirrels, they successfully inhabit woodlands with minimal understory, where it is believed their larger size makes them less susceptible to predation while out in the open.

Home ranges for Eastern Gray Squirrels are

An Eastern Gray Squirrel arches its back and pats the ground where it has just buried an acorn.

An Eastern Fox Squirrel eats an acorn. © *Mark Elbroch*

A fox squirrel caught in the act of scent-marking a stub along a travel route. It is depositing scent from the oral glands located at the corner of its mouth. © *Mark Elbroch*

larger in areas where foods are scarce and in years of less abundance. Typically a squirrel inhabits less than 12.4 acres (5 ha), though records of 49.4-acre (20-ha) home ranges have been recorded. Males inhabit twice the area of females, which increases their opportunities for mating. Females use only half of their smaller home range while they are raising young.

Squirrel densities correlate with the size of local home ranges. In areas where squirrels have the largest home ranges, they are found at their lowest densities, and where numerous squirrels inhabit the same park or woodlot, their respective home ranges shrink accordingly. In deciduous woods there are typically 1 to 4 Eastern Gray Squirrels per 2.5 acres (1 ha), but where tree cavities and forage are more abundant, densities can be much higher. More than 20 animals per 2.5 acres have been recorded in urban parks.

COMMUNICATION

The tails of tree squirrels are more than just attractive ornaments, and they play vital roles in communication. Squirrels may fluff their tails when disturbed and quickly move to tail flicking, or "flagging," when they are alarmed, investigating a potential threat, or conveying aggression. In tail flicking the tail moves back and forward straight up over their back. Tail shivering conveys nervousness, as when a squirrel approaches a conspecific, and is not to be confused with piloerection (when the hairs of their tail stand on end), which often in-

dicates aggression. Tail waving (side to side) often accompanies social greetings and may also convey nonaggression.

The four common vocalizations of Eastern Gray Squirrels are the *kuk*, buzz, *quaa*, and moan. The *kuk* is a common call conveying mild distress, typically repeated from an elevated perch. Each note is emphasized with the flick of the tail, and all the while the squirrel glares at a potential threat or suspicious object in its range. The buzz denotes mild distress or a startled alarm. The *quaa* is also an alarm conveying stress and wariness and is often repeated from above while the squirrel watches a potential predator, including humans. Gray squirrels also produce a low moan when distressed, and they shriek when terrified, as when caught or nearly caught by a predator, or handled by people.

Squirrels foot-tap with a front paw while they *kuk* or *quaa*, much as a deer stomps a front foot to elicit a response from an as yet unknown entity. Squirrels assume a boxing position, sitting on their back feet to communicate a threat. The hair along their spine stands erect and they narrow their eyes. They also tooth-chatter in aggressive interactions, and they may bluff-charge other squirrels. If they also lay their ears back, they are signaling imminent attack.

Eastern Gray and Fox Squirrels also communicate chemically with urine and secretions from glands in the corners of their mouth. Both sexes smell each other's oral glands while greeting conspecifics, which looks a bit like kissing. Each animal tilts its head to better smell the glands at the corners of the mouth. Squirrels urinate in protected areas under branches, where stains may accumulate over time. Squirrels marking with their oral glands look like they are wiping their cheeks along the side of a branch or knob of wood. They may repeat the act several times, or bounce along to the next knob on the same branch to repeat the process. Males regularly mark trees throughout the year, and females visit these scent posts but rarely leave a mark of their own. Older and more dominant squirrels mark more than younger ones, and a dominant squirrel that witnesses a subordinate making a scent mark may aggressively chase it off and immediately over-mark with his own scent.

In addition to marking knobs and other protrusions along travel routes, gray and fox squirrels chew the bark of large-diameter, dominant trees where they continue to mark for generations. "Territorial stripes" are marked by many squirrels, and their accumulated signs can be impressive, bright stripes of color on the tree visible over long distances. When a squirrel pauses upon a territorial stripe, it slows down and intently smells the area before adding to the sign by chewing the bark with its incisors. It marks the surface with the glands near its mouth by wiping its face across the surface of the exposed bark. In the East, a study compiled data on 64 stripes chewed by gray squirrels on 37 species of trees and found that 90 percent of the stripes fell between 13 and 70 inches (33–178 cm) off the ground. Territorial stripes are almost always placed beneath the leaning side of the trunk, or below a large limb, where they are best protected from weather. Stripes are found on the largest trees in the area with diameters ranging from 13 to 48 inches (33–129 cm).

COURTSHIP AND MATING

There are two breeding seasons each year. The first occurs from December through March, during which time only a small percentage of the females breed. The second is from May through July and is when the majority of females mate. Most females in a given geographic region do not breed twice per year, and when foods are scarce, perhaps none will. When mast crops were plentiful in Ohio, up to 36 percent of females reproduced twice in the following year.

During the breeding season males wake each morning and abandon their nests in search of nearby females in estrus. They can interact with up to 6 females in their first 3 hours, following each of them closely for 20-minute intervals, attempting to move in to smell their genitalia to determine whether they are in estrus and receptive. Females not yet in estrus are aggressive, and they'll whip around to swipe at pursuers with claws and teeth. Males check on nearby females continuously during the breeding season, so as not to miss the single 8- to 20-hour window when a female is in estrus and receptive.

When a female enters estrus, males are generally waiting for her outside her nest in the morning. Males can smell females in estrus and travel from as far away as a half mile (850 m) to join in her pursuit. They chase her relentlessly in an attempt to mate, and it is speculated that it's the presence of a fertile male that induces her ovulation. Each female may develop quite an entourage by the time she is actually ready to mate; in Texas 34 males were observed trailing a single female.

The males form a strict dominance hierarchy, with the most dominant animals closest to the female and defending their positions from others. Fighting between males is fierce and constant, with up to 2,000 interactions per hour within the queue. Males exhibit torn ears, oozing bite wounds, and dislocated tails. Males sometimes become so preoccupied with vying for position that they lose the female completely, after which they all spread out to find her.

Young males may hang about the area of pursuit

An Eastern Gray Squirrel perched adjacent a territorial stripe, where squirrels have been chewing and depositing scent for years. © *Mark Elbroch*

and appear disinterested in the entire affair. They avoid active engagement in the queue, where larger and older squirrels would squash any attempts at mating they might make. But should a female break away from her pursuers, providing the opportunity for a younger satellite animal to sneak in and mate with her, he is quick to do so. If a satellite animal is not near enough when the male queue loses the female, and if the males fail to relocate her quickly enough, she'll chirp from nearby cover or from a perch in the branches above where she has been watching the ensuing pandemonium since her disappearance. The males jump to resume the chase.

When the female is ready and presents herself for copulation, the most dominant male immediately engages with her. Copulation consists of rapid thrusts and persists for 20 to 30 seconds. The male's semen also forms a gelatinous plug that inhibits further copulations with additional males. Immediately following mating, however, both the male and female clean and groom their genitalia, and almost undoubtedly the female removes the copulatory plug. Very often she eats it as well. In about a third of the mating scenarios the same male is allowed to mate a second time after but a brief chase, but rarely is he allowed a third round. She will go on to mate with additional males as well. Once a male has mated he has nothing further to contribute to the raising of the young.

DEVELOPMENT AND DISPERSAL OF YOUNG

Forty-four days after the female successfully mated, she gives birth to a litter of 2 or 3, or occasionally 4, young. Litter sizes are dependent upon available resources, and in one case in North Carolina a gray squirrel gave birth to 8 young. The neonates are pink, bald, and helpless. Their umbilical cords remain attached for the first several days, while they do little but nurse. Their skin begins to darken at about 7 to 10 days, just before their fur coats begin to grow. The hair on their tails starts to fill in at 3 weeks, when their lower incisors also erupt. Their upper incisors erupt 1 week later, and finally their molariform teeth erupt in week 6. Their ears open between 3 and 4 weeks, and their eyes between 4 and 6 weeks. During the same period, their bodies twitch as they crawl about in uncoordinated fashion. Vocalizations develop from squeaks to low growls and then to screams, as youngsters begin to play and wrestle with each other. After 30 days they begin grooming themselves, and by 40 days they start to exhibit the full range of social behaviors.

At any time, the female may move her young to another nest if she is disturbed. She does this by grasping the abdominal area of a young animal in her teeth, and the youngster instinctively grasps her head with its limbs for greater stability. It took a

Mating Eastern Gray Squirrels.

A female gray squirrel moves her young between nests.

fox squirrel an hour to move 5 large young 330 feet (100 m).

At 25 percent fat and 9 percent protein, the incredibly energy-rich milk of gray squirrels fuels the rapid development of the young. Juveniles are weaned when they are between 8 and 10 weeks old, at which point they have increased to 16 times their size at birth and have grown a complete adult pelage. Gray squirrels attain adult proportions within 8 to 9 months, and fox squirrels in 1 year. After weaning, young squirrels exhibit increased aggression and sexual play. Only 25 to 35 percent of youngsters survive until they are 1 year old.

Young females may breed at 5.5 months of age, though 95 percent of females wait until after their first birthday. Males, on the other hand, often breed for the first time at 2 years of age, and even in adulthood may not participate in every breeding cycle. Females may actually breed for 8 or sometimes more years, while males typically breed for 4 to 6.

Males disperse farther than females but typically travel less than 3 miles (5 km). On occasion one will take an epic journey as far as 62 miles (100 km) away from its natal nest. Peak periods of dispersal are between April and May for winter births and July and October for summer litters.

INTERACTIONS AMONG GRAY SQUIRRELS AND AMONG FOX SQUIRRELS

Dominance hierarchies govern gray and fox squirrel societies, and aggression between animals is relatively common. Males are typically dominant over females, and adults dominate yearlings and youngsters. Bigger adults are often dominant over smaller animals, with occasional exceptions to every rule. For instance, while females are raising their young they are intolerant of any intruder and are aggressive to any and all squirrels, regardless of their status within the community. In one study of gray squirrels, only 30 out of 776 agonistic interactions resulted in actual physical combat. However, physical combat is brutal and often results in wounds and severed tails.

Grays, more often than fox squirrels, may take up residence with one or more other squirrels and share a nest. Up to 9 gray squirrels have been recorded sharing a single nest during winter months. Groups are typically single sex, but occasionally of mixed company. Males sharing nests seem to be more transient than females, whereas female groups that nest with each other often do so for long periods. Kinship also influences amicability between females within the group. Mother-daughter and sister-sister bonds result in much more amicable relations than between unrelated or distantly related females.

INTERACTIONS WITH OTHER SPECIES

Eastern Gray Squirrels overlap with the ranges of Eastern Fox Squirrels and Red Squirrels (*Tamiasciurus hudsonicus*). Larger fox squirrels inhabit similar forest habitats and use much of the same foods as gray squirrels, and they appear to be dominant in overt interactions. Female fox squirrels have been observed displacing female gray squirrels at food resources. Red and gray squirrels often split areas by microhabitat, the grays inhabiting the deciduous canopy and the reds inhabiting the conifers. Yet both species occur in mixed forests and overlap. Though gray and Red squirrels often tolerate each other in the field, the dominant and more aggressive Red Squirrel may chase gray squirrels away from localized food resources, such as backyard bird feeders.

Gray squirrels are killed by rattlesnakes and rat snakes, diverse hawks and owls, largemouth bass when they are swimming, raccoons, weasels, mink, martens, fishers, gray and Red foxes, bobcats, housecats, domestic dogs, coyotes, and wolves. Fishers and martens are particularly effective predators, since they climb and can remove squirrels from nests and tree cavities. Hawks, too, are effective hunters of squirrels in trees. However, predation is less an influence on squirrel densities than available food resources.

> ### Red Squirrel
> *Tamiasciurus hudsonicus*

> ### Douglas's Squirrel
> *Tamiasciurus douglasii*

WITH NOTES on Flying Squirrels (*Glaucomys* spp.).

OTHER NAMES FOR RED SQUIRREL: pine squirrel, Hudson Bay squirrel, barking squirrel, boomer.

The frenetic, nervous energy of the Red Squirrel is familiar to anyone who has spent time in coniferous forests across North America. Their loud, scolding alarms are accented with great jerks of their entire body and tail. A Red Squirrel usually stays on the opposite side of a tree trunk from any potential danger, but should you sit still, they will circle around and above you so that they can keep an eye on you while they sound the alarm.

Tamiasciurus is the combination of three Greek words that describe this species well. *Tamias* is "one who hoards or collects," and refers to this animal's tendency to create massive caches of coniferous cones from which it feeds during the winter. *Sciurus* is from the Greek word for squirrel and is created from *skia* ("shade") and *oura* ("tail"), celebrating the massive and beautiful tail belonging to this species and to tree squirrels of the genus *Sciurus*.

Note that this account focuses on the Red Squirrel, but much of what is described is applicable to the very closely related Douglas's Squirrel.

ACTIVITY AND MOVEMENT

DAILY

Much of a Red Squirrel's life is spent in acrobatic tree-climbing. Red Squirrels are expert climbers, and their light weight allows them to move out onto the wispiest of tree limbs. They can swivel their hind feet 180° to the rear and plunge headfirst down the trunk of a tree as quickly as they climb up. Only rarely do Red Squirrels fall, and when they do they usually bounce on the ground with little ill effect. However, some do perish from slips or miscalculated jumps. When they descend a tree they pause often, head extended out from the trunk to scan for danger, before taking to the forest floor to travel or visit a cache site. They move on the ground just as they do on the trunk, in a bounding gait. They use slow, short bounds to explore and forage, and rapid, long bounds are their means of escaping predators or crossing exposed areas to move from one forest patch to another.

Fifty-eight percent of their time is invested in

predator-defense behaviors. This includes visual scanning to identify potential threats and then freezing to watch and determine if what caught their attention justifies an alarm call. Foraging and hoarding take up most of the rest of their time. Whatever is left is invested in maintenance behaviors, including napping, grooming, and scent-marking. Red Squirrels are primarily diurnal and have excellent daytime vision. They also have relatively good nighttime vision and are occasionally active during the night.

Flying squirrels are nocturnal creatures that are only rarely seen in the day. They do not fly, but instead are expert gliders. The folds of excess skin between their front and hind legs on either side of the body that create the opportunity for gliding are called the patagia (singular, patagium); these are supported by thin, stiff pieces of cartilage that articulate with the wrists. Flying squirrels require height for flight and seek the highest trees in their vicinity from which to launch. From up high they spy a destination in the distance and then lean back and forth as if gauging the distance through rudimentary triangulation. Their pelvic girdles are specially adapted to increase the power with which they launch, and they spring with lightning speed. In flight they use their limbs and their flat, rudderlike tail to steer in semicircular fashion. Flying squirrels glide quickly, zigzagging as if in a slalom run, making them difficult to track in low light. Typical flights are about 66 feet (20 m) and terminate low on the trunk of another tree, often just above the ground. Longer glides depend on the slope of the terrain and the height from which they launch, but glides as long as 98.5 yards (90 m) have been recorded.

Just before they land, flying squirrels push their limbs forward and assume a vertical stance, so that they hit the tree trunk with all four feet simultaneously. Upon touchdown they dash to the opposite side of the tree to avoid any aerial predators that may have seen them launch and may be in pursuit. Flying squirrels also land directly on the ground when snows are soft and forgiving, leaving complete body impressions or skid marks to tell the story.

SEASONAL

The daily routines of the Red Squirrel vary from season to season. During the warmer months Red Squirrels are most active twice each day, first in the morning several hours after dawn and again in late afternoon as evening approaches. In the autumn, during the harvest season when they are building the caches that sustain them through the winter, Red Squirrels remain active throughout the day. During the coldest months of winter Red Squirrel activity peaks just once per day during the middle, when temperatures are warmest.

A Northern Flying Squirrel in flight. © *Richard Alan Wood/Animals Animals*

A solid nest that efficiently retains heat is essential for thermoregulation and survival during the coldest winter months, especially for squirrels in the North. Red Squirrels prefer natural cavities for nesting throughout much of their range and are quick to move into holes between 7 and 66 feet (2–20 m) off the ground made by woodpeckers or storm damage in living trees and snags. They may also construct underground nests within the air pockets created by root networks. In warmer climates and during warmer months of the year they also construct leaf and debris nests, which they often build adjacent to the trunk or on occasion in the branches of trees. Most nests are constructed within 100 feet (30 m) of their cone caches and, in the case of underground nests, may be located beneath or within a midden pile of discarded cone debris, which creates warmth as it slowly decomposes. They line their nests with dry grasses, mosses, strips of soft cedar bark, and the dead inner bark of maples and oaks.

Flying squirrels also most often inhabit tree cavities. Unable to carve out their own cavities, flying squirrels depend on rot, lightning, weather, and woodpeckers to create openings in tree trunks and branches. If the core of the tree is rotten and/or softened by carpenter ants and other insects, they may be able to enlarge a nesting chamber within. Abandoned woodpecker nests provide ideal homes for flying squirrels. Cavities are lined with mosses, lichens, and shredded bark for comfort and insulation.

The Red Squirrel's body temperature and metabolism are comparatively higher than those of other mammals and may be an adaptation to remaining active in extreme cold. Yet during the coldest temperatures or harshest storms, Red Squirrels tuck themselves away in the relative safety of their nests. Rarely do they remain in their nests for more than a day. They often construct tunnels through the snow, through which they move undetected between their nests and larders. During cold but sunny bouts, Red Squirrels lie out atop leaf nests or along branches to sunbathe, absorbing the sun's heat.

FOOD AND FORAGING

Red Squirrels eat a great diversity of foods, though they primarily rely upon the seeds of conifers and deciduous trees. Fir, hemlock, pine, and spruce cones are all collected and shelled in identical and systematic fashion. Like humans, squirrels are also right- or left-handed, and this determines how they hold and spin a cone when they begin attacking it at its base, where it attaches to the branch. They chew and sometimes tear through each individual scale one at a time, eat the seeds, and then spin the cone to attack the next scale. Circling upward they remove all the scales and seeds, and then abandon the "cob" of the cone to the midden pile.

Red Squirrels also collect and eat nut crops, including maple seeds, hickory nuts, hazelnuts, walnuts, and acorns. Chewing into hard cones and hard-shelled nuts demands powerful jaws as well as sharp teeth. Red Squirrels that feed on hickory nuts and cones of lodgepole pine have evolved larger and more muscular lower jaws than their counterparts in other regions of the country.

Red Squirrels are larder-hoarders, meaning they gather huge amounts of food during the late summer and fall and cache it in one to several locations near the heart of their territory. Red Squirrels use the "all-in-one-basket" philosophy of hoarding. This makes retrieval of stored food more efficient, but it also means the fruits of their labors are especially vulnerable to pilfering by other animals, including mice, rival squirrels, and massive Brown Bears. The defense of their larders likely accounts for their fierce territoriality.

Some biologists like to differentiate between a *cache*, the actual cones and nuts yet to be eaten, and a *midden*, the discarded remains of food already eaten. In truth, these two may appear together when Red Squirrels cache new cones within the moist, protective layers of old middens created by accumulating refuse. These cool, moist microenvironments inhibit conifer cones from opening, and closed cones minimize pilfering by mice and birds that can't open the cones on their own. At times the larder is completely concealed belowground in a cavity among tree roots and a midden accumulates above it, under a regular perch where the squirrel feeds. Caches and middens accumulate under perches, beneath logs, near stumps, and even surrounding the base of certain trees. Over time, generations of Red Squirrels may use the same cache locations, and accumulated larders and middens can be very massive.

The number of larders maintained by a single squirrel varies between geographic populations and even between individual squirrels. Some squirrels cache all their cones in a single massive larder. Others, particularly those in the northeastern United States and eastern Canada, may cache less than 50 percent of their total reserves in a central location, and then scatter the remainder in smaller caches around their range. This combination strategy of larder- and scatter-hoarding could be a way of offsetting the costs and risks of pursuing either strategy exclusively.

When gathering nuts and cones, Red Squirrels follow basic economic principles and seek the most benefit for the least cost or effort. They manage to weigh the energetic benefit of the seeds in a cone against the cost of carrying it some distance to a larder. In general, Red Squirrels harvest cones with the highest seed-to-cone ratios, the heaviest seeds, the richest seeds, the hardest cones, and those from trees with the densest cone loads.

Red Squirrels trim the cones from branch tips and drop them to the ground below. The sounds of harvesting squirrels are not unlike a rain shower, as the cones drop through the canopy and hit the forest litter with musical raps and thuds. Once a

A Red Squirrel busily nibbles away at a pine nut.
© Robert Roach/Dreamstime.com

A red-breasted sapsucker (*Sphyrapicus ruber*) darts in to defend its sap well from a thieving Douglas's Squirrel. © *Jim L. LeMons (BUGOGRAPHICS)*

squirrel has finished its work in the canopy, it climbs down and begins the arduous and risky work of transporting cones to its caches.

The accumulated wealth of individual Red Squirrels may total several thousand cones and is usually enough to feed a Red Squirrel for several years, thus allowing for a certain degree of pilfering by mice and other competitors. In fact, Red Squirrels often pilfer from each other, more so in some populations than in others. In one study, 28 of 29 Red Squirrels being monitored stole from their neighbors' cone caches. In the end, the average squirrel stole 26 percent of the cones it consumed during the winter and was robbed of 25 percent of the cones it had cached, so things balanced out very well. The rates of theft varied tremendously among the individual squirrels: one adult male stole 15 percent of the cones he ate and lost only 11 percent of his cache to neighbors. A young male in the same area stole 95 percent of the cones he consumed and lost 48 percent of his cache to neighbors.

During the early spring, and sometimes again in the fall, Red Squirrels tap trees for sap. Squirrels are reliable tappers of sugar, red, and striped maples in the East, and of big-leafed maple in the West. They tap yellow birches, serviceberries, and apple trees in the Great Smoky Mountains. To access the sap, squirrels bite into the cambium layer with their head turned sideways. They anchor their upper incisors, and then cut smoothly upward or make a series of slices with the lower incisors. Sap oozes freely from the cut bark. After biting many different places along sapling trunks and along the limbs of mature trees, the squirrel leaves to attend to other business. It returns some time later to lick what remains when most of the water has evaporated, which can condense the sugar content from 2 to 55 percent. Red, Douglas's, and flying squirrels also feed at the wells created by sapsuckers.

In spring Red Squirrels harvest the swollen buds of maples and other trees. They trim the last few inches of branches, and their accumulated feeding can litter forest floors. From late summer into early fall they begin to harvest more mushrooms. More than 45 species of fungus have been reported in their diets, including mycorrhizal, birch polypore, and capped mushrooms. They harvest and hang them along the branches of trees to dry, like poorly placed Christmas ornaments, before stashing them in a cache belowground.

Flying squirrels also relish various fungi and in parts of their range eat little else. They collect and eat mushrooms, as well as steal those hung carefully or stored by Red Squirrels. They regularly forage along the ground for truffles (hypogeous fungi) under coniferous trees, which they locate by scent. Truffles exude chemical cues when they are ripe, making them easier to find, and flying squirrels are perhaps more adept at finding them than trained pigs or hounds. Truffles are especially abundant where ample forest-floor debris holds moisture in the upper layers of the soil. Flying squirrels may cue in on fallen, woody debris to narrow their search for truffles and then use scent to guide them once they are on location. Flying squirrels eat small truffles in their entirety, or sometimes, with the largest ones, eat the soft insides and leave the tough skin like an empty shell. Truffles provide squirrels with nutrition, but they cannot digest the fungal spores and so distribute them throughout their range in their feces.

Red Squirrels also eat fleshy fruits, rosehips, and insects and are active hunters of bird eggs and hatchlings. Occasionally they kill and eat small mammals or adult birds as well. They have been reported eating the kits of cottontails and short-tailed shrews and can be seen gnawing on the carcass of any large ungulate that falls within their range.

Wild Red Squirrels are rarely observed drinking from standing water or eating snow during winter. They have kidney adaptations that allow them to be more water-deprived than gray squirrels, and it is

Northern Flying Squirrels emerge from a nest cavity. © Robert Lubeck/Animals Animals

believed that they can survive several months on only the moisture garnered in their diets.

HABITAT AND HOME RANGE

Red Squirrels are widespread across the northern United States and Canada and in the mountains of more southerly areas. In the East they can be seen north and east of Iowa and then farther south following the spine of the Appalachian Mountains. In the West, Red Squirrels can be found throughout the high country of the Rockies and farther south in the elevated coniferous forests of Arizona and New Mexico. Red Squirrels are "replaced" by the closely related and nearly identical Douglas's Squirrels in the coastal ranges of Washington and Oregon and throughout the Sierra Nevadas in California. In the far north, Red Squirrels range from the Pacific to the Atlantic Ocean and are absent only in the treeless tundra.

Red Squirrels primarily inhabit coniferous and mixed coniferous-deciduous forests. They are less common in deciduous-dominated woodlands. Forests need to be mature enough to produce reliable cone or mast crops, and must have interlocking canopies essential for successful foraging and the evasion of predators.

Home ranges of Red Squirrels are typically circular and revolve around their central larders. The size of their home ranges is driven by food availability, expanding when nut crops fail and retracting when supplemental foods are made available. Home ranges are typically very small at just 0.6 to 2.2 acres (0.24–0.9 ha), but during times of food shortage they may expand to nearly 12.5 acres (5 ha). As home ranges vary, so does squirrel density. Red Squirrel densities vary from 0.3 to 4.5 squirrels per 2.5 acres (1 ha). Selective cutting of large trees in Alaska has resulted in significant reductions in their densities.

COMMUNICATION

In a 100-hour period, a single female Red Squirrel in British Columbia uttered 204 chirp calls, 105 rattle calls, 24 screeches, and a single buzz. Forty-nine of the chirps were responses to the observing biologist, and 5 were in response to the alarm calls of other Red Squirrels. The sixth type of call is the bark, which is given in so many scenarios that it is difficult to interpret its function.

The chirp alarm—a single chirp that might be repeated for up to 30 minutes—is used in response to diverse predators, including raptors and weasels. When a Red Squirrel chirps it is usually conspicuously perched on high, and with each vocalization its tail jerks violently against its back, providing a visual flag to complement the sound. The call is thought to alert nearby squirrels (which are often

A Red Squirrel sounds an alarm and exhibits piloerection of its tail (hair standing on end), which is used to communicate both alarm and threat.

relatives) that danger is near, and also to inform the predator that it has been spotted and won't be able to sneak up on the squirrel for an easy meal.

Rattling is believed to be used in territorial defense, or at least in announcing ownership, and in maintaining spatial distances between squirrels that can't actually see each other. When trespassers hear the rattling call of a territorial resident, they rarely linger or engage in physical chases or combat. During the mating season a dominant male rattles at subordinate males trying to court a female to which he has laid claim. Females also rattle at males, and males usually respond with soft buzzes, which may soothe the female's aggression.

Screeches are also uttered in territorial disputes and may indicate a higher level of agitation than the rattle. A resident screeches when it spots an intruder within its territory, and typically the trespassing squirrel immediately flees back into its own territory. Screeches are the best indicator of forthcoming physical combat. Screeching squirrels often follow up by chasing the intruder from their territory and biting it if they catch up to it.

Buzz calls are associated with appeasement. They are common when one squirrel approaches another and wants to indicate it has no intention of pilfering the other's cache. Males buzz to females they are approaching in hopes of mating, and a female may buzz to her youngsters when returning to the nest after a prolonged absence. After youngsters leave their nest, they use the buzz call to appease their mother when encountering her within her territory.

Growls are used by both sexes during aggressive encounters, including physical fights over territory and mating opportunities, and when females are not ready to mate and must repel approaching males.

Red Squirrels also growl when cornered, just before they bite, and they scream when they are injured.

Red, Douglas's, and flying squirrels also communicate through chemical cues, including those produced by oral glands and urine and scats. Like other tree squirrels, Red Squirrels rub the glands on either side of their mouth on raised objects along their travel routes. These scent posts may aid the resident squirrel in navigating its own home range as well as advertising its territorial ownership to potential trespassers.

Chewing and biting make visual and olfactory signposts. Individual bites are small, but they often accumulate in long lines or "stripes" running along branches and trunks of trees. Each Red Squirrel maintains its own territorial stripe, and after ejecting a trespasser from its territory visits and refreshes it. The squirrel sniffs the stripe's length, pausing often to rub its cheeks on it and add several fresh bites. Stripes can be found on the dead lower branches of conifers. Travel routes from tree to tree are also heavily marked, as are the upper limbs near the nests.

Red Squirrels select where they place scats. Scats accumulate at trail junctions, as where important branches of interposing trees cross, or in areas where squirrels travel to regular food sources. Like foxes and coyotes, squirrels place scats on elevated perches along travel routes. They seem particularly attracted to unusual items within their home range and make a point of using them as regular scent posts. In one instance, the wooden bowl at the corner of a porch that Red Squirrels crossed frequently accumulated 25 scats in relatively short order. They also rubbed their oral glands along the rim of the bowl and chewed it.

COURTSHIP AND MATING

Females are in estrus for only one day, once or twice a year, depending upon locality. In the Northeast and southern portions of their range, Red Squirrels often have 2 litters, one in the spring (March–May) and a second in late summer (July–September). In the West and in the North, Red Squirrels typically have just one litter in early summer. In many mammals, females within geographic populations synchronize their estrous cycles, and they all mate within a relatively short window of time. However, female Red Squirrels each have their own annual estrous cycles that remain consistent throughout their lifetime. Individuals within a geographic population may mate over a several-month period, resulting in a very long breeding season.

Red Squirrels are promiscuous: males and females both mate with multiple partners each breeding season. Dominant males often converge on the territories of females in estrus and engage in "mate chases." Chases are long drawn-out events that are easily witnessed if you are in the woods at the appropriate time. Dominant males, followed by a string of up to 10 subordinate males, chase females up and down trees. Dominant males periodically break from pursuing the female in order to scare off subordinates with growls, bluff charges, a vigorous chase, or physical violence.

During the afternoon on the single day the female is receptive, after hours of chasing and male-male aggression, the female becomes receptive to a suitor. The female typically initiates copulation on the ground or on the lowest branches of a tree. The male mounts from behind, grabs her around her waist, and rests his head upon her back. Copulation occurs several times, each bout lasting several minutes. When copulation is completed, the pair often engage in mutual grooming of their genitalia. Occasionally the male may be reluctant to end their connection, and the female can be seen carrying him piggyback for some distance. When the couple separate and each squirrel goes its separate way, the male plays no further role in caring for the young.

DEVELOPMENT AND DISPERSAL OF YOUNG

After a gestation of 31 to 35 days, Red Squirrels give birth to a litter of 3 to 7 young. Nestlings are born pink, naked (except for a few straggling hairs), and completely helpless. Rich milk fuels rapid development, and by 6 days of age their skin has changed color to a dark hue and fuzz has begun to cover their bodies. Their ears open at 18 days, and their eyes open between 26 and 35 days. Up until this point nestlings do little but nurse, whine, and crawl about in uncoordinated fashion. By 30 days of age

they begin self-grooming and are agonistic toward littermates, using displays such as tooth-chattering and foot-stomping. Young squirrels begin to exhibit both play and scent-marking behaviors between 37 and 45 days old, by which time their fur has grown in completely.

Young squirrels can be seen exploring outside their nest by the time they are 6 to 7 weeks old, during which forays they spend considerable time watching their mother feed. Harvesting and caching do not seem to be completely instinctual, and adult squirrels are much better than young ones; learning may be necessary. They are weaned at approximately 8 weeks and independent by 10 to 11 weeks of age.

Nestling mortality for Red Squirrels is high, and by 10 weeks of age 60 percent of the litter will have likely been lost. Young squirrels lucky enough to be born in a year of peak nut production, when fall foods are plentiful, live an average of 7 months longer than young born in poor crop years. As young animals become more and more independent they forage farther from their mother's territory. They may travel as much as 0.6 miles (1 km) away from her, but in the end tend to settle into their own territories within 1,150 feet (350 m) of their birthplace. The most adventurous youngsters travel farthest from their natal nest and run a greater risk of being killed by a predator. Those that succeed in moving farther away end up being able to establish larger territories than their siblings that stayed closer to their mothers, and they have a better chance at surviving their first winter alone.

In some cases the mother Red Squirrel enlarges

Two Red Squirrels stick out from a nest cavity. Note the chewed edges, which in a live tree may help to keep the hole open, and in dead trees like this one might also be a component in scent-marking.
© Alaska Stock Images/National Geographic Image Collection

As juvenile Red Squirrels mature, they must be increasingly careful around their territorial mother. Here a juvenile tentatively approaches its mother and they touch noses and smell each other's oral glands to confirm their relationship.

her territory as her nestlings become independent, and then bequeaths part of her range to them. A mother may even abandon her home range completely and allow her young to divide it among themselves, while she disperses to a nearby vacancy in a neighboring territory. Approximately 30 percent of each litter survives until they are 10 to 12 months old and ready to mate for the first time.

INTERACTIONS AMONG RED SQUIRRELS

Male and female Red Squirrels are fiercely territorial and actively defend their patches of woods and food caches from all other Red Squirrels as well as from other species. In captive populations, agonistic interactions peak at different times of year for males and females. Male aggression peaks during the mating season in spring, while females are most aggressive toward other squirrels in early summer, when they are lactating and defending their new litters. Red Squirrels rarely fight, but when they do they engage in fierce wrestling matches wherein each opponent tries to bite the other's ears, head, or neck.

Subordinate animals, often young squirrels newly on their own, may establish transient territories in coniferous woodlands for a single winter. They gather only enough resources to survive the winter and then move on to establish a permanent territory in the spring. When an adult with a territory dies, the vacancy is identified by a subordinate animal within hours, and another Red Squirrel immediately moves in and then circles the periphery to establish its claim. These territory takeovers are noisy and raucous affairs, and the newly resident squirrel continues to circle the area's periphery and sound territorial calls for the better part of the first day.

INTERACTIONS WITH OTHER SPECIES

Red Squirrels are prey for diverse predators that attack them both on the ground and from the air. In a study of 14 goshawk nests, 31 percent of the prey items delivered by the parents to nestlings were Red Squirrels. Red Squirrels are also prey for nearly every other raptor with which they share woods. Mammalian predators of Red Squirrels are no less diverse. Nearly all mustelids, from tiny weasels to mink to martens and fishers, hunt and eat Red Squirrels. Martens and fishers may be particularly effective because they can move like squirrels, running both up and down tree trunks in long chases until they catch a squirrel. Bobcats, Canada Lynx, Gray and Red Foxes, and coyotes are also common predators of Red Squirrels.

There is a strong potential for competition between Red Squirrels and other tree squirrels, but the relationships between tree squirrels are not well understood. Despite anecdotes, there is little evidence of direct aggressive competition between red and gray squirrels. Apparently the Red Squirrel's diet is just different enough from the Eastern Gray Squirrel's that they can coexist without much conflict. In contrast, the larger Abert's Squirrels may exclude Red Squirrels from ponderosa pine forests in the southern Rockies. Red Squirrels overlap very little with their close relative the Douglas's Squirrel, suggesting that the two compete.

The vocalizations of Red Squirrels are no doubt heard and understood by other species within their communities. Red Squirrels have in turn been seen responding to the alarm calls of pikas, juncos, and chipmunks with alarm calls of their own, thus spreading the general alarm for nearby predators across species and farther afield.

Red Squirrels are not just prey, they are also significant predators of bird eggs and nestlings. Birds nesting in the canopy and understory are 2 to 3 times more abundant in forests without Red Squirrels as those with them. Red Squirrel predation on bird nests is so significant that they may influence the diversity of birds within a forested system.

Black-tailed Prairie Dog
Cynomys ludovicianus

OTHER NAMES: prairie gopher, prairie marmot, barking squirrel, yap-rat, picket pin, perrito de las praderas (Mexican Spanish).

Prairie dogs were so named by European settlers because they thought their alarm calls sounded like the barks of domestic dogs. When settlers began pushing west across North America, the number of prairie dogs inhabiting North America was estimated to be more than 5 billion. Poisoning, trapping, shooting, and rapid habitat destruction led to their near-complete decimation, and 4 species, including the Black-tailed Prairie Dog, were listed as endangered in the early 1970s. Intensive conservation and management has stabilized Black-tailed Prairie Dog populations. However, today they inhabit less than 2 percent of their historic range.

ACTIVITY AND MOVEMENT

DAILY

Black-tailed Prairie Dogs are diurnal, semi-fossorial rodents that live in colonies, sometimes called towns. Colonies may be vast, stretching several square miles and containing thousands of individuals. Colonies are subdivided into *wards* by boundaries, such as streams or roads, and members of distinct wards rarely if ever interact. Wards appear continuous to the human eye, but they are broken into smaller adjacent territories inhabited by *coteries*, a group of prairie dogs that defend and maintain them. Coteries most often include a single breeding male, several adult females, several yearlings, and the pups of the year. The breeding male is primarily responsible for territorial defense, although all members contribute to boundary disputes. Black-tailed Prairie Dogs are active aboveground from dawn to dusk each day and during fine weather spend 95 percent of daylight hours outside their burrows. They emerge from their burrows shortly after sunup, pausing motionless at the entrance for several minutes to scan for predators before moving out and beginning to forage. Approximately one-third of each day is invested in vigilance and looking for potential predators on the ground and in the air. Prairie dogs sit up or stand on their hind legs to look for danger. They occasionally perch on dirt mounds and other objects to improve their view. Black-tailed Prairie Dogs are unique among prairie dogs in that they cut all high vegetation within their colonies in order to improve visual communication and their ability to detect

Two Black-tailed Prairie Dogs "kiss," or smell each other's oral glands. © Max Allen Photography

predators. Given the great numbers of inhabitants in a colony, there is unlikely a moment in any given day when at least one animal is not looking out for potential dangers, and this shared vigilance is the greatest benefit of their colonial existence.

When temperatures exceed 81°F (27°C), prairie dogs take breaks from foraging and watching for predators and return to their burrows to cool off for 5- to 30-minute intervals. At the end of the day Black-tailed Prairie Dogs enter their burrows for the night. Only under extreme circumstances (e.g., invasion by a badger) will they change burrows during the night.

Black-tailed Prairie Dogs have three kinds of burrows. Escape burrows lack throw mounds (the tailings of dirt that spread out from the openings of some burrows); they are often unconnected to other burrows and are only used for temporary refuge and evasion. Dome and rim craters are two different kinds of burrow entrances and are often both present in the same burrow system. Dome craters, identified by their flat, wide, and round throw mounds, are used for escape, sleeping, and raising young. Rim craters, which are unique to Black-tailed and Mexican Prairie Dogs, are used for all aspects of prairie dog lives. Rim craters are created after heavy rains, when coterie members come together in a communal effort to push and pack mud with their noses, heads, and feet in order to create high and narrow throw mounds reminiscent of volcanoes. They can reach as high as 3.3 feet (1 m). The combination of higher rim craters and lower dome craters creates increased air flow and ventilation through the burrow system. This is vital for moving oxygen and cooler air to coterie members in the deepest parts of the tunnel system. Rim craters also provide a higher vantage point from which to look for trespassing conspecifics and predators, and they reduce the amount of water flowing into tunnels during rainstorms.

All burrow systems within a coterie are shared by its members, and groups often sleep together, especially in cold weather. The only exceptions are those burrows that are claimed for several months each year by females raising their pups. Most burrows have 1 or 2 entrances, but some have 5 or 6. Burrow entrances are 4 to 12 inches (10–30 cm) in diameter and often ringed with droppings. Some of these accumulate during surface foraging and others are ejected from belowground during periodic cleanings. You cannot approach a prairie dog burrow without stepping on scat. The density of burrow entrances in an area varies with terrain, the duration of prairie dog inhabitation, and the size of individual coteries. The range is from 10 to 250 entrances per 2.5 acres (1 ha).

Tunnels often run to 10 feet (3 m) deep and up to 33 feet (10 m) long, though some are deeper and much longer. Burrows contain 1 to 2 large communal nest chambers, each approximately 12 inches (30 cm) high and 20 inches (50 cm) wide. Prairie dogs carry in dry grass to create nests and mattresses for sleeping and to insulate their young. Burrow systems may also have several smaller chambers that animals use to wait out dangers above, to reverse direction, or to navigate around prairie dogs they meet moving in the opposite direction. Burrows are used by generations of prairie dogs; some burrow systems are known to have been active for more than 14 years.

SEASONAL

Whereas some species of prairie dogs hibernate through the winter, Black-tailed Prairie Dogs remain active throughout the year. However, they still rely upon fat reserves to survive the colder months when available food is severely limited. They may even enter short periods of torpor. During cold spells some Black-tailed Prairie Dogs may remain in their burrows for several days, and on occasion during times of severe weather, a group may enter deep torpor and remain belowground for up to a month.

During the winter months Black-tailed Prairie Dogs also delay their emergence from their dens until 1 to 3 hours after sunrise, when temperatures begin to rise, and enter their burrows for the night several hours before nightfall. Burrow systems provide prairie dogs thermal protection at all times of year. Underground temperatures generally remain at 50° to 68°F (10–20°C) in summer and 41° to 50°F (5–10°C) in winter.

The various burrow types of Black-tailed Prairie Dogs: (a) rim crater, (b) dome crater, (c) evasion burrow.

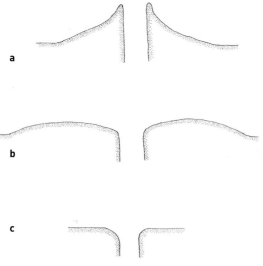

a

b

c

A prairie dog sitting on its haunches, a comical feeding position.

FOOD AND FORAGING

Black-tailed Prairie Dogs are selective herbivores of grasses and forbs that grow within their colonies. During summer they often eat wheatgrass (*Agropyron*), buffalo grass (*Buchloe*), and grama (*Bouteloua*). Foraging prairie dogs move slowly, with their mouths down, clipping and plucking any greenery as they go. Sometimes they sit back on their haunches and stick their hind legs out like a tiny human child. Their bellies protrude comically while they manipulate whatever they are eating in their dexterous forepaws.

During the winter they may chew prickly pear pads, thistle leaves, and various species of roots. Occasionally Black-tailed Prairie Dogs eat insects as well, including cicadas and grasshoppers. They also cannibalize their own kin, both those that have died for other reasons and those they kill themselves.

HABITAT AND HOME RANGE

Black-tailed Prairie Dogs were once widespread, inhabiting a range from Mexico to southern Canada and from New Mexico to Nebraska. Today they persist in isolated islands within their former range, including easy-to-view colonies in several national parks: Wind Cave and Badlands in South Dakota and Theodore Roosevelt in North Dakota. Urban colonies in Santa Fe, New Mexico, and near Boulder, Colorado, are also easy to visit.

Each coterie (breeding group) within a colony defends approximately 0.8 acres (0.33 ha), which on average includes 70 burrow entrances. Tunnel systems do not cross territorial boundaries to allow coteries to intermingle belowground. At high densities each coterie may boast as many as 40 prairie dogs, including new pups, though typical densities are 10 animals per coterie.

COMMUNICATION

The most conspicuous vocalization of Black-tailed Prairie Dogs is the two-syllable *ah-aaah*, which biologists call the "jump-yip," or territorial call. A prairie dog stands upright and throws its head back, arching its back, raising its forefeet, and often lifting off the ground while it gives this piercing two-note call. Territorial calls often instigate a domino effect, with animals in neighboring coteries rising up to jump-yip in a wave that sweeps through the colony. Jump-yips are also made to announce the departure of a predator from an area, signaling that it is again safe to forage.

Anti-predator calls are loud, conspicuous 1- or 2-syllable vocalizations. Upon spotting danger prairie dogs move adjacent to or onto mounds, sit up, and create loud, repetitive, high-pitched "barks." If the danger is imminent, the repetitions increase

A Black-tailed Prairie Dog exhibits a "jump-yip," used in territorial communication as well as alarms. © istockphoto.com/Dave Parsons

A White-tailed Prairie Dog vocalizes an alarm.
© *Max Allen Photography*

but are softer and repeated more slowly. Males also make a vocalization similar to an alarm call just before or just after they mate with females. Prairie dogs whimper, growl, and snarl when cornered or handled.

Amicable behaviors include playing, wrestling, allogrooming, and—like marmots and ground squirrels—frequent "kissing." Prairie dogs approaching each other tilt their heads and nuzzle mouth to mouth, during which each has the opportunity to smell the other's oral glands, located at the corners of their mouths. The perianal glands, located just inside the anus, function within territorial disputes, with opponents exuding strong, skunklike odors during ritualized contests. Individuals convey their aggressive intentions with long stares, raised and flared tails, tooth-chattering, and bluff charges. Their tooth-chattering can be heard as far away as 330 feet (100 m). Territorial animals also chase each other and sometimes fight.

COURTSHIP AND MATING

The breeding season for Black-tailed Prairie Dogs varies with latitude. Breeding occurs in January in Oklahoma, February in Colorado, and early April in Montana. Females are in estrus for only 1 day each year, though on occasion a female that misses the opportunity to mate the first time might come into estrus a second time 2 weeks later.

The breeding season initiates a period of exceptional violence within coteries that is rarely if ever observed at any other time of year. Females fight over nursery burrows, males fight over access to mates, and breeding females sometimes fight with their mates. Fights are vicious and fast. Animals rise up and leap at their attackers with both claws and teeth. They tumble and twist, biting all the while and causing significant injuries. By the end of the breeding season adults are visibly scarred and beaten. The growth of scar tissue can cause hair loss, and their heads can be covered in knobs and welts. Tails are bitten in half, and prairie dogs may sustain serious enough injuries to their limbs to force them to hobble.

The majority of females mate with a single male, which is usually the dominant breeding male in their coterie. A single male may also be dominant in 2 adjacent coteries composed of noninteracting females, or large coteries may have several breeding males, which are most often brothers. In multiple-male coteries, females may breed with 2 different males. The first male to breed with her sires more offspring in the resulting litter than the second. If the first male to mate with her also guards her, he can prevent her mating with another male and ensure that he sires the entire litter. However, such an investment in time is a possible tradeoff, because he

in rate and intensity. Alarming prairie dogs remain next to their burrows, watching the predator approach very close before they dive belowground. In general, Black-tailed Prairie Dogs use the same alarm call for any predator except snakes. The alarm calls used to announce the presence of a snake sound more similar to the jump-yip than their typical alarm barks do. They also use foot drumming to both announce the presence of a snake and to challenge it.

When conspecifics hear alarms they stop what they are doing and try to locate the danger. Often other prairie dogs join in and begin alarming as well. The overwhelming chorus of prairie dogs may deter the predator by letting it know that it has lost the element of surprise; it may also warn other prairie dogs. Territorial barks are similar to alarms might miss the opportunity to mate first with another female in the coterie. Even as she begins to transition out of estrus and turns aggressive, males often linger nearby to chase off or engage any male that dares approach.

When a male smells an estrous female he may begin making mating calls just prior to copulation. Mating calls are similar to alarm barks, but softer and given with less frequency. He frequently approaches and sniffs her vulva before the pair descend into burrows to copulate in one of two ways. Either the female approaches a male, presents him her rear end to sniff, and then saunters down a nearby burrow with him in pursuit, or the male is the aggressor and chases his mate down into a burrow. The average duration that a pair remains submerged is 22 minutes, but the range is from less than a minute to all day. A pair may also repeatedly go belowground to copulate at intervals throughout the day.

After mating, males and females often emerge from underground and begin licking their genitalia. It's an unnatural position for prairie dogs; they often fall over in the process. The male also lingers near the female and may continue making mating calls. He defends her from other males that try to approach her and sometimes carries nesting materials into the burrow. Once estrus passes, the female becomes aggressive and violent toward courting males. Approximately 80 percent of copulations result in litters, with a much higher success rate in adult females than in yearlings.

DEVELOPMENT AND DISPERSAL OF YOUNG

Gestation is 5 weeks, after which 1 to 8 pups (3 on average) are born underground in the safety of a natal burrow during the morning or late afternoon hours. Newborns are naked and their eyes are tightly closed. Fur covers their bodies by 3 weeks of age, and at 5 weeks they open their eyes for the first time. While juveniles remain underground they subsist on their mother's milk, and the female remains close to the burrow when foraging to protect them from other members of the coterie. After 7 weeks they emerge from their burrow for the first time and soon after are completely weaned. When they emerge from their burrow for the first time they average 0.3 pounds (145 g) each. By October each youngster weighs 4 times as much.

After the young have emerged aboveground, communal nursing is common within a coterie. Sometimes a female will even carry her young or lead them into the natal burrow of another female, where they intermingle. Orphaned young will be nursed by other lactating females, and any pup may nurse from any lactating female within the coterie. Multiple females and their mixed litters may also spend nights together in different burrows.

Initially, juveniles spend equal time in play and foraging. They wrestle, climb upon each other and their mother, and roll in nearby grass. They also frequently disappear belowground with an adult female at regular intervals to nurse. As the summer progresses, juveniles forage more and more and eventually stop nursing completely.

Young prairie dogs are called pups until they are approximately 8 months old, then yearlings until approximately 20 months. Thereafter they are considered adults. Young females never disperse and typically spend their entire lives within their natal territory and coterie. The females within a coterie are therefore usually close kin. Males disperse to other coteries within the limits of their colony. Only very rarely do young males successfully disperse across areas between colonies, where they are especially vulnerable to predation.

Approximately 50 percent of young prairie dogs survive beyond their first birthday. Typically males and females mate for the first time during their second breeding season, when they are approximately 23 months old. But about one-third of surviving females breed as yearlings.

INTERACTIONS AMONG BLACK-TAILED PRAIRIE DOGS

Members of a coterie interact frequently and amicably, except during the breeding season. Interactions between individuals in *different* coteries at their borders are often aggressive, dramatic, and can last as long as 30 minutes. The contestants chase each other and sometimes fight. They may sniff each other's anal glands or stand back to back with tails raised and perianal glands everted (sticking out) and exuding strong odors akin to those sprayed by skunks.

The coterie social system of Black-tailed Prairie Dogs could lead to inbreeding, but numerous behavioral mechanisms are in place to mitigate this possibility. Juvenile males always disperse from their natal range, moving away from their mother and sisters before they breed for the first time. Older males also move from coterie to coterie at 2-year intervals, preventing them from mating with their daughters. Further, females in coteries where the dominant male is a father, brother, or son often do not enter estrus and skip a breeding cycle. This usually prevents Black-tailed Prairie Dogs from mating with their closest kin, though they often mate with more distant relatives, including first and second cousins.

Infanticide in Black-tailed Prairie Dogs is remarkably high, accounting for up to 40 percent of lost litters every year. The most common form of infanticide is when lactating females attack and kill

A violent lactating female chases away another Black-tailed Prairie Dog. Females are highly aggressive while their litters are young and still nursing. © Shirley Curtis, courtesy of www.scary squirrel.org

the young of a closely related female within their own coterie. These attacks always occur while the pups are very young and have yet to appear aboveground for the first time. A group of females may invade a neighboring natal burrow while the resident female is off foraging. Should the resident female detect the attack, a vicious fight ensues as she attempts to defend her litter. An attacker may emerge carrying a very young pup that she quickly kills and often eats aboveground. Or she'll emerge with a blood-covered face, which she quickly cleans by rubbing her cheeks in the dirt and then licking her paws and washing.

Aggression in females is rapidly, and almost magically, replaced by amicability when the pups emerge from their natal den at 7 weeks of age. Then females begin to nurse young from any other females within their coterie—even those she may have tried to kill several weeks earlier.

The second most common form of infanticide occurs when a lactating female abandons her own litter. Without her to protect them, the pups become prey to members of her coterie, who quickly move in and eat them. Should a male succeed in taking over a new coterie while pups are very young, he may also kill the youngsters sired by his predecessor. The various forms of infanticide prevent coteries from becoming overpopulated, which would lead to the starvation of all its members.

INTERACTIONS WITH OTHER SPECIES

Black-tailed Prairie Dogs are considered a keystone species, one that has an exceptionally strong influence on its environment. Prairie dog activity alters plant community composition, increases invertebrate and small mammal diversity, and often increases the overall biodiversity in regions at large scales. The vegetation within Black-tailed Prairie Dog colonies is very short, both because they select habitats with short vegetation and because they maintain a manicured landscape to facilitate easier detection of predators. Certain plants thrive within these colonies and only rarely occur outside of them: scarlet globemallow (*Sphaeralcea*), black nightshade (*Solanum*), and the aptly named prairie dog weed (*Dyssodia*). Their foraging and excavating mix topsoil with deeper soils and facilitate greater nitrogen uptake by plants. Prairie dogs also influence the presence of diverse animal species, including pronghorns, elk, coyotes, badgers, mountain plovers, burrowing owls, black widow spiders, and harvester ants, through their influence on the topsoil and vegetation.

Predators of Black-tailed Prairie Dogs are numerous. Coyotes, badgers, and Black-footed Ferrets are significant mammalian predators, while golden eagles, red-tailed hawks, and prairie falcons are their most significant threats from above. Bobcats, foxes, cougars, Long-tailed Weasels, ferruginous hawks, northern harriers, bull snakes, and rattlesnakes also eat them when they can. The critically endangered Black-footed Ferret is completely dependent upon Black-tailed Prairie Dogs for its survival, both for food and for shelter within protected prairie dog towns.

Prairie dogs are not safe by day or night. Coyotes, bobcats, badgers, and raptors attack by day, while Black-footed Ferrets, badgers, and snakes enter their burrows at night. Black-tailed Prairie Dogs sometimes emerge aboveground and plug the burrows in which the predators are hunting, in order to trap them within and slow them down. Prairie dogs in Texas, where snakes are more common, actively defend against them. They sometimes attack gopher snakes (*Pituophis catenifer*), biting them repeatedly until they retreat. They are more cautious with rattlesnakes (*Crotalus* spp.), harassing them in small groups led my males, calling and foot drumming, until the snake leaves the area.

Their colonial existence and multigenerational use of burrow systems create ideal circumstances for parasites to thrive. Numerous species of fleas are common in prairie dog towns, including those that carry bubonic plague. Plague can rapidly wipe out entire colonies in short order and is a leading cause of local extinctions of both coteries and colonies.

Yellow-bellied Marmot
Marmota flaviventris

OTHER NAMES FOR MARMOTS: whistling pig.

Woodchuck
Marmota monax

OTHER NAMES FOR WOODCHUCKS: groundhog, siffleur (Canadian French), wenusk (Cree).

A marmot lifts its head during a sunbathe above a large latrine. The old white scats from previous seasons lie below, and the fresh black scats above. © *Mark Elbroch*

Thousands gather every year on February 2 atop Gobbler's Knob in Punxsutawney, Pennsylvania, to partake in legend and determine the remaining length of winter. Should Punxsutawney Phil see his shadow and run back into his burrow, there remains six weeks of winter, but should he appear from his long winter sleep and linger outside his burrow, winter is wrapping up and spring is just around the corner. Groundhog Day, as the celebration is now known, has its roots in the European religious holiday called Candlemas, which originated in the 4th or 5th century and fell on or near the very same day each year. Traditionally, the emergence of hedgehogs and European Badgers from their burrows were used to predict the length of winter, but in North America new colonists settled for this rodent.

Woodchucks are marmots, and sister species to Yellow-bellied Marmots, Hoary Marmots, and others in North America. Marmots share much in ecology and behaviors, and their definitive variation is in their preferred habitats. Woodchucks are associated with lowlands and farm country in the East, while North American marmots are generally alpine creatures, inhabiting high country throughout the West.

ACTIVITY AND MOVEMENT

DAILY

Marmots are diurnal animals that spend up to 30 percent of each day outside their burrows. As much as 60 percent of their time aboveground is spent sitting or lying around, sunbathing and digesting food. Up to 23 percent of their time is spent foraging, and as much as 15 percent in "vigilance behaviors," when they keep an eye out for potential predators, trespassing neighbors, and transients looking for territories of their own. Marmots periodically lift their heads or stand erect on their hind feet while both grazing and sunbathing to assess the area for danger. In the case of males, they are also looking for intruders, which they aggressively chase out of their territories.

During spring and fall, marmots are active aboveground for one long stretch each day, but twice each day during the summer, to avoid the midday heat. Typical summer days for alpine marmots begin just after sunup, when they emerge from their burrows to sunbathe and warm their bodies after long and often cold nights at high elevations. They orient themselves broadside to the sun on boulders and other perches in order to capture as much warmth as possible. Once they've warmed sufficiently, they invest some time in greeting other members of their community before setting out for their first serious foraging of the day. Marmots waddle in a slow walk while they forage and travel. When exposed or running for cover they move into a bounding gait like squirrels and can attain speeds of 10 miles (16 km) an hour. Marmots also swim and climb trees.

As morning turns to midday they either retire to a perch, where they splay out like throw rugs to sunbathe and absorb the heat in the rocks, or, when temperatures are too hot to linger, they go into their burrows. The day may be filled with periodic bouts of grooming and territorial marking. When a burrow harbors a particularly nasty infestation of fleas, marmots spend considerable time grooming themselves with their teeth. In the afternoon, marmots abandon perches and burrows for their second bout of heavy foraging, which lasts until near sundown, when they retire underground until the following morning.

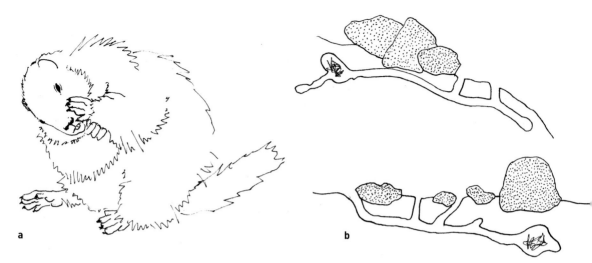

A marmot sits on its haunches and grooms its front legs to remove parasites (a). Two burrow systems of Yellow-bellied Marmots (b). Drawn after Svendsen, 1976, "Structure and location of burrows of yellow-bellied marmot." *Southwestern Naturalist.* Used with permission.

Marmots are semi-fossorial and live throughout the year in burrows they dig themselves. Boulders, root systems, and human structures provide support for burrows, as well as concealment and protection. Such habitat structures often delineate alpine marmot distributions, and family groups are typically distributed on the landscape in relation to boulder outcrops and other protection.

Most burrows are conspicuous affairs, with large entrances and large throw mounds of earth, called "steps," betraying their presence from a considerable distance. Burrows typically have 1 to 3 entrances and are made in well-drained soils on hummocks in fields, slopes, and hillsides. Burrows vary in depth and length, but may be up to 6.5 feet (2 m) deep, where they tend to run parallel with the surface for as long as 43 feet (13 m). There may be 1 or 2 central nesting chambers as large as 16 inches (40 cm) in diameter, which are lined with dry leaves and grasses to provide comfort and insulation. Escape burrows—short, simple tunnels in which they hide while danger passes—are less conspicuous and usually lack a throw mound.

Marmots use multiple burrows within their territories. In Connecticut, woodchucks use 8 different burrows on average, rotating between them every 4 to 6 days. Yellow-bellied Marmots vary in the number of burrows they use, depending upon their densities and the available cover in a given area. Where there are few marmots that hold larger territories, they may each use up to 14 burrows, but where numerous marmots inhabit smaller patches in productive habitat, individual colonies may be restricted to just 3. Burrows are used year after year and often by successive generations. They are constantly renovated, enlarged, and/or cleaned out.

Should you discover a completely new burrow unconnected to any nearby colony, it was likely dug by a subadult animal moving into a new range.

SEASONAL

Marmots put on considerable weight through the summer and become increasingly lethargic as late summer turns to fall. They move slowly, confining their movements to smaller areas near their burrows, and eat less often. All marmots hibernate during winter months to conserve energy during times of food shortage. Marmots do not store food in larders like tree squirrels do, but like bears, they rely upon fat reserves to sustain them as they sleep through the winter. Because marmots hibernate underground for months at a time, they end up spending 80 percent of their lives in the darkness of their burrows.

To avoid spring flooding, woodchucks often move from open fields into woodlands to dig their hibernacula—the chambers in which they hibernate—under canopies on elevated slopes. In flatter terrain they sometimes hibernate in hedgerows, haystacks, or under suburban porches. Alpine marmots may move up to a mile (1.6 km) between summer burrows and winter hibernacula, or dig them within existing burrow systems they use throughout the year. Some marmots hibernate in groups, but both Yellow-bellied Marmots and woodchucks are thought to hibernate in isolation. However, male and female Yellow-bellied Marmots often emerge from the same burrow entrance in spring, so there is a possibility that at least some are social hibernators.

Reduced photoperiod (the amount of light per day) appears to be the trigger that induces marmots to enter their hibernacula within their shared

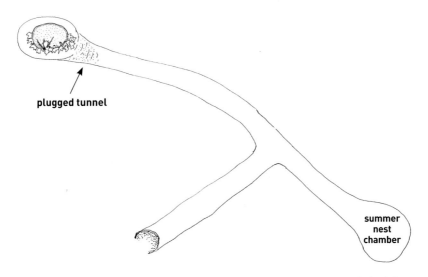

plugged tunnel

summer nest chamber

A top view of a woodchuck's burrow system, to illustrate the animal hibernating in its hibernaculum, dug as a separate chamber from the summer nest.

burrow system). Once inside, they seal themselves within the compartment with a solid layer of earth, feces, and vegetation. Since they seal only the chamber, the plug cannot be detected from the burrow entrance above, and it is difficult to know whether a marmot is sleeping inside. Marmots often hibernate the 7 to 8 months from September to May. At lower elevations where spring warmth arrives sooner, they may emerge as early as mid-February.

Woodchucks inhabit warmer, lower elevations and hibernate for shorter periods. Woodchucks hibernate 3.5 to 6 months in the East, but longer in the far north. Woodchucks emerge in the spring 1 day later for every 10 miles (16 km) you move north. This means woodchucks in Lexington, Kentucky, approximately 350 miles north of Atlanta, should emerge from their winter dens approximately 1 month after their Atlanta counterparts. Global warming has also influenced emergence times. In Colorado, Yellow-bellied Marmots now emerge 23 days earlier than they did in 1976, thanks to warmer April temperatures.

Adult and yearling woodchucks, like other North American marmots, forage heavily throughout the summer months, gaining 0.4 to 0.5 ounces (11–15 g) every day. Hibernation allows for the conservation of energy by minimizing activity. In slumber, marmots require less fuel and so their fat reserves are generally sufficient to last until spring. While in hibernation, adults lose 0.2 to 0.3 ounces (6–9 g) per day, and juveniles lose 0.07 to 0.14 ounces (2–4 g) per day.

Hibernating woodchucks drop their body temperature to just 36°F (2°C) and their heart rate from 130 beats per minute to an average of just 10. They alternate between 4- to 10-day periods of deep torpor, when their heart rates may slow to 3 beats a minute, and periods of arousal lasting 1 to 5 days, when heart rates increase to 95 beats a minute. Periods of torpor become progressively longer through the winter and then start to become shorter in earliest spring, just prior to emergence. This allows intervals of wakefulness when marmots can check current temperatures. Emergence, for all marmots, is temperature-related and occurs during periods of warm weather.

When woodchucks prepare to abandon their hibernacula in spring, their heart rate soars to 220 beats a minute and quickly pumps blood throughout their bodies. Their heart gradually settles into a normal rhythm as their body warms. Male woodchucks and Yellow-bellied Marmots emerge before females, often as early as February. Females and subadults follow a month later, and regardless of age or sex they emerge up to 30 percent lighter than when they entered their hibernacula.

FOOD AND FORAGING

Marmots are generalist herbivores and eat great quantities of whatever grasses, flowers, and forbs are most abundant in their habitat. Marmots generally prefer protein-rich forbs over grasses. Woodchucks favor alfalfa and clovers in the east, and alpine marmots favor lupines and columbines. Marmots feed only within a safe distance from their burrow entrances. When they discover a rich patch of vegetation in an area with little cover, they dig new burrows there to reduce their risk of being killed by a predator while they forage.

As grasses and forbs begin to seed through the summer, marmots in turn harvest them. Seeds are high in polyunsaturated fats, which have been

A woodchuck forages for new growth in a tall shrub. Marmots can climb moderately well, but rarely do so. © *Jahoo/Dreamstime.com*

shown to enable ground squirrels to further lower their body temperature during hibernation, remain longer in torpor, and enter hibernation earlier. Woodchucks eat acorns and other mast crops, and all marmots opportunistically eat insects as they forage, including June beetles, grasshoppers, and snails. They occasionally eat meat, and on rare occasions have been seen carrying chipmunks and other small mammals which they either killed or scavenged. Marmots use salt licks and also harvest salt deposits from roadsides and mineral licks. The succulent green vegetation that dominates their diets provides them with the fluids necessary for survival, but they drink from open water when it is available.

Marmots, more than other rodents, are occasionally subject to incisor malocclusions, meaning the upper and lower incisors do not meet properly to allow self-sharpening and tooth wear. Without abrasive maintenance incisors grow too long, hindering their ability to eat and leading to starvation. Occasionally the teeth grow so long and curve back so far as to pierce the skull before the animal dies.

HABITAT AND HOME RANGE

Marmots are distributed across the Northern Hemisphere throughout North America, Europe, and Asia. Woodchucks are the most widely distributed of the marmots in North America, being found throughout much of the eastern United States and Canada as well as much of western Canada and central Alaska. Woodchucks inhabit open fields and meadows as well as forest edges of all types. They are at home in suburban and country gardens, along golf courses, in agricultural settings, and in highway medians.

Yellow-bellied Marmots are widely distributed throughout the mountains of the western United States and southernmost Canada, inhabiting both forest and open terrain where scattered trees and boulders provide them some cover. Colonies are easily viewed, sprawled out on rock piles in the morning sun where nearby greenery provides them sustenance. In cooler climates they can live at relatively low elevations, inhabiting the edges of open grasslands and meadows much like woodchucks, though in drier habitats. Food availability certainly plays a role in the distribution and persistence of alpine marmot colonies, but predation may be even more influential. Within their range, sites that provide excellent visibility for spotting approaching predators and suitable protective structures in which to hide are good spots to find Yellow-bellied Marmots.

Marmot territories are often 0.5 to 5 acres (0.2–2 ha). In solitary woodchucks, male home ranges generally overlap with the hibernacula of 1 to 3 females.

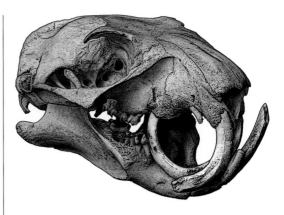

Extreme tooth malocclusion in a woodchuck.

Females expand their home ranges after mating and overlap slightly with other females. The solitary and territorial tendencies of the woodchuck keep it at much lower densities than are seen in more social alpine marmots. Woodchuck densities range from 1 to 6 animals per 5 acres (2 ha), depending upon forage quantity and quality. You can find 12 to 16 Yellow-bellied Marmots living on the same amount of land.

COMMUNICATION

All marmots employ auditory, visual, and chemical forms of communication. Different marmots vary in the degree to which they socialize with other marmots, but in all species, social interactions peak in spring and diminish thereafter. Woodchucks are the least social, and they exhibit the least amicable behaviors, even toward their young. Yellow-bellied Marmots are much more social than woodchucks, but less so than all the other marmot species in North America.

Marmots use three categories of vocalizations: whistles and their variants, screams, and toothchatters. Whistles are alarm calls, and the relative level of danger is conveyed by their repetition. Frequent repetition means high risk, while just one whistle may suffice to alert others of a minor risk. Woodchucks employ a simple high note to signal alarm for any threat and also occasionally make an alarm that sounds something like a muffled bark, as if they were holding their mouths closed. Yellow-bellied Marmots use 3 distinct variations of alarm calls, called whistles, trills, and chucks. The high note, or whistle, is the general alarm call for all predators, while the trill is made while fleeing a predator (or another marmot), and just before disappearing down a burrow. Chucks convey minor alarm and may follow whistles.

Screams and shrieks are made by marmots that are cornered, handled, or under attack. Occasionally a subordinate will shriek while in an exchange with a dominant. Marmot tooth-chatters convey aggression in both defensive and offensive scenarios, and they often precede biting.

Colonial marmots, especially related animals, which share burrows, are often observed exchanging amicable behaviors. These behaviors include allogrooming, wherein partners use their teeth to groom each other's necks, backs, and sides; play-wrestling in younger animals; and "greetings." Marmots, like ground squirrels, approach and greet one another in a way that sometimes resembles kissing. Each animal tilts its head and, while nuzzling nose to nose or cheek to cheek, smells the other's oral glands at the corners of their mouths. In the case of Yellow-bellied Marmots, greetings are sometimes displayed without physical contact. Two marmots may approach one another closely, but then stop and sniff in each other's direction, rather than actually touching nose to nose.

Agonistic interactions are most often observed between marmots from neighboring colonies and include threat displays, chasing, boxing, biting, and avoidance. The simplest visual cue to aggression is an upraised tail. In a display of extreme aggression, marmots arch their back like cats, erect the hair on their tail and flick it side to side, all the while hissing with their mouth open wide ("gaping") and their vicious incisors aimed at their opponent. Aggressive grooming and asexual mounting, where the subordinate is the animal on the bottom, may also be used to convey dominance. Dominant animals sometimes pursue subordinates to the edge of their burrow, and then kick large rocks down on them. They may go so far as to plug the burrow entrance from the outside, temporarily trapping the subordinate within.

Marmots flick their tail up and down while they move and when approaching other marmots. Why they do this is not completely understood, but it may serve to convey their intentions and let the other animal know they are approaching. Adults

A large male Yellow-bellied Marmot deposits scent on a rock near a burrow entrance. He is marking with an oral gland at the corner of his mouth. © *Mark Elbroch*

tail-flick more than juveniles and yearlings, and adult males conspicuously flick their tail up and down and from side to side while patrolling their territory. Adult males wave their tail back and forth when approaching other animals in what appears to be a dominance display. Marmots at the receiving end of a fast-approaching male waving his tail almost always move away, and often at high speed.

Marmots employ their oral glands in marking territories. They rub the sides of their mouth and cheeks on all available objects, including boulders, sticks, fenceposts, tree trunks, human refuse, and shrubby branches of bushes, especially those near their burrow entrances. Marmots mark most often during spring and early summer, and then marking behaviors gradually decline through the summer. In Yellow-bellied Marmots, males mark far more often than females and can be seen investing good portions of their days in moving slowly about their range, marking and re-marking every available surface within 20 feet (6 m) of their burrows. They mark less frequently along their travel routes,

Woodchucks and other marmots lower their head, open their mouth wide to expose their teeth, and arch their back in defensive threats.

A male Yellow-bellied Marmot slides forward on the ground in a scent-marking behavior.

tipping their oral glands into the dirt and rubbing prominent objects at regular intervals as they go. In suitable, soft soils, they place the corner of their mouth in contact with the ground and then slide forward, propelled by their hind feet until they are flat out on the ground. They may push themselves forward a short distance, leaving trough-like trails like otters sliding in snow.

In addition to territory, oral gland secretions may serve to communicate sexual status and other information. Woodchucks of both sexes mark equally, and scent-marking peaks early in the breeding season along with the frequency of agonistic encounters. They have also been observed marking over the scents left by other woodchucks. All marmots also chew branches and trunks of trees near their burrows, where they then rub their oral glands to leave chemical marks.

Yellow-bellied Marmots and woodchucks differ greatly in where they choose to defecate. Woodchucks defecate in underground chambers and cover their scats with dirt, or they defecate atop their throw mounds in front of their burrow entrances, where their scats likewise become covered in dirt. Marmots, on the other hand, defecate throughout their range, as well as in conspicuous and often large latrines atop boulders and other elevated surfaces. Latrines may accumulate hundreds of defecations over time and may include bleached, aged scats from previous years.

COURTSHIP AND MATING

Marmot mating seasons are short and intense, occurring within several weeks of their emergence from winter dens. Females are in estrus once per year for 2 to 3 weeks. Male woodchucks are polygynous and breed with as many females as are within their territories. Shortly after their emergence in spring, male woodchucks lay claim to hibernacula occupied by females and fight to defend them from other males. Once the females emerge, the males guard them against interlopers to ensure their breeding opportunities. Fighting between males is vicious and fast. They grapple, twist, and bite each other on the neck and head, resulting in an accumulation of scars over many years.

Active breeding for woodchucks occurs from late February to late March in the eastern United States and in March and April in eastern Canada. Woodchucks breed annually, and nearly all females in a population breed each year (70 to 80 percent). Other marmots in the West inhabiting lower, warmer elevations may also breed every year, but female Yellow-bellied Marmots at high elevations generally breed only every other year.

Courting male marmots approach females and greet them nose to nose or move directly behind them to smell their posterior. Pairs may or may not chase each other or play-wrestle as part of courtship. When males approach and smell females, they may be aggressively rebuffed. If the female is receptive, she allows the male to mount from behind. He may paw her rear end several times before he pushes her tail aside and rises up to wrap his forelimbs around her midsection. As he thrusts, he grasps the skin and fur on her upper back in his incisors. Mating persists for 30 seconds to 8 minutes and induces ovulation in the female. Sometimes a female approaches and courts a male, standing before him with her tail up in readiness. In solitary woodchucks, females aggressively drive males away after mating has occurred.

DEVELOPMENT AND DISPERSAL OF YOUNG

Gestation in marmots ranges from 30 to 32 days, after which an average of 3 to 4 young are born. In the eastern United States, woodchucks are often born in mid-April, whereas Yellow-bellied Marmots are typically born from mid-May to June. Neonates are born with little hair and light, wrinkly skin, and their eyes and ears tightly closed. Within a week their skin darkens, and by 2 weeks they are covered in a fuzz of fur. By 3 weeks they are crawling, and by 4 they are climbing and ingesting solid foods.

Females nurse their offspring while standing on all four feet, and youngsters lie on their backs beneath them to grasp at nipples. Young marmots remain within their maternal burrows for 20 to 30 days and are weaned shortly after their appearance aboveground, which, depending upon altitude and latitude, is sometime between early June and mid-July. Juveniles that attempt to nurse after weaning are rebuffed by their mother and bitten if they persist in trying.

An adult female Yellow-bellied Marmot refuses to budge while her recently weaned pup attempts to burrow beneath her to access her nipples. She ended the nuisance with a quick nip, and the youngster departed. © *Mark Elbroch*

The earlier the young are weaned, the more they will weigh when they enter hibernation and the greater their chances of survival. Marmots living at higher elevations, which experience shorter growing seasons, wean juveniles at younger ages than do woodchucks. In addition, young Yellow-bellied Marmots living at high elevations grow much faster than those at lower elevations, to compensate for their shorter summers. In this way, litters of Yellow-bellied Marmots from all elevations gain an equal average weight before hibernation.

Play is frequent and common in all young marmots but progressively diminishes as they age. Play is usually preceded by nose-to-nose greetings. Play-fights often start standing upright, and partners box and grapple, arching their necks backward as if to keep their heads out of the fray. In play, they may tumble and roll, and the animal in the top position switches frequently. Playing marmots vocalize softly and nip at each other, but they do not bite. Young males wrestle more than females and end up on top more often when they wrestle their sisters. In alpine marmots, play is also observed in yearlings and occasionally in 2-year-olds. Adult marmots, however, do not play with each other or their young.

Juveniles explore their natal territories on their own, as well as in groups, foraging for longer durations and farther from their natal burrow from week to week. Often juveniles will be seen in one part of their range and the adults in another, though from time to time they intermingle, the young seeking to greet adults after they have been separated.

Woodchuck mothers are more aggressive toward their young than are alpine marmots, encouraging most young woodchucks to disperse at the end of their first summer. A small percentage stay in their natal range until the following year. Yellow-bellied Marmots tend to disperse by the end of their second summer, though this, too, is variable. Adult male Yellow-bellied Marmots become progressively more aggressive toward yearling males, resulting in their eventual dispersal. Young females, however, may or may not disperse, depending upon the aggression directed toward them by their mothers. Male Yellow-bellied Marmots disperse an average of 1.6 miles (2.6 km) and females an average of 0.9 miles (1.4 km). Marmots may move to a new range in a single move, extend their range more slowly until they locate a new range, or hop from one new range to a second to settle down.

Yearling Yellow-bellied Marmots do not breed, and less than half of 2-year-olds breed. In general, female marmots of all species except woodchucks are 3 years old before they breed for the first time. Only a small percentage of yearling female woodchucks breed, but most females in their second year breed and produce litters. Males typically breed for the first time at 2 years of age, when they reach their full adult size.

INTERACTIONS AMONG MARMOTS

Yellow-bellied Marmots live in pairs or loose colonies, where an adult male lives with a harem of several closely related females and their young. Colonies are relatively closed, and female immigrants may move in only when a vacancy is created. When a new animal fills a vacancy and takes up residence, it often experiences high levels of aggression from other members of the colony. Aggression toward it gradually decreases over a year, after which it is treated amicably. In adults, what may appear to be play-fighting often quickly escalates into real fight-

Boxing marmots in a territorial dispute.

ing. Unlike play-fights, true fighting is a blur of violence and biting. Noisy growls and shrieks fill the air as each contestant attempts to maintain the top position.

Adult female Yellow-bellied Marmots vary in their degree of aggression toward their female offspring. In harems, females are often more tolerant and allow female young to remain within the colony. In family groups in which only a single female mates with a single male, mothers are more likely to chase their female offspring away. But if an adult female dies, female yearlings do not disperse and instead remain in residence within the colony.

Colonial living no doubt allows for a degree of incestuous mating, but like prairie dogs, marmots may have behavioral strategies to minimize incest. In a 40-year study in Colorado, 86 percent of females

A young marmot greets its mother after foraging on its own nearby, but out of sight. They smell each other's oral glands to confirm their relationship.

Juvenile Yellow-bellied Marmots play near cover so that they can quickly retreat if they hear an alarm sounded by an adult. © *Mark Elbroch*

died without ever giving birth to a litter, and the age at which females had their first litters ranged from 2 to 6 years. Females delay breeding when social pressures from older, dominant females restrict them from mating. Females that are more social and confident produce more litters per lifetime than those with submissive personalities. On rare occasions Yellow-bellied Marmots commit infanticide, and in these cases, adults are either unrelated or distantly related to the juveniles they kill.

Unlike alpine marmots, woodchucks are usually solitary, except for females with litters. They are typically asocial and territorial. Other than breeding, exchanges between adult animals are agonistic, but neighboring animals fight less often than do those that are less familiar with each other. Males overlap with females but overlap little with other males, and females, too, overlap with males but little with other females. Neighboring animals seem to maintain social relations through strict dominance hierarchies reinforced by indirect signals and displays instead of

physical aggression. Subadult woodchucks are often transient, moving burrows frequently until they locate an open territory to settle into and defend.

Marmots often die in their winter hibernacula for unknown reasons, though starvation, disease, and fungal disease may all play a part. These deaths, and those caused by predation, are what create most territorial vacancies. Among woodchucks, however, human hunting, trapping, and poisoning are often the main sources of mortality.

INTERACTIONS WITH OTHER SPECIES

Marmots share habitat with numerous other grazing mammals, though competition with other species has been little studied. Marmots seem intermediate between pikas and ground squirrels with regard to their dependence upon boulder piles and talus. Pikas live their lives within the talus, foraging as much as possible within its boundaries, and occasionally venture into the fringes of open meadows. Marmots spend more time within meadows, but only in meadows where boulder piles and other refugia are sprinkled across the terrain. In Yosemite National Park marmots are more numerous than Belding's Ground Squirrels in fields interspersed with rock jumbles, and ground squirrels are more numerous than marmots in larger, more open meadows lacking cover.

Marmots have numerous potential predators, and predation is the leading cause of mortality for marmots during the summer months. Should marmots see or hear predators, they whistle alarms. All marmots that hear an alarm immediately stop what they're doing and raise their heads to scan for danger. Often they look in the direction of the alarm to orient themselves to the potential danger. Young marmots are more likely to flee for cover when an adult whistles, and adults respond more dramatically to the calls of juveniles than to those of other adults. Most often marmots return to foraging or sunbathing when they do not themselves detect danger, or they have determined the cause of the alarm and disregarded it. When a 6-week-old Yellow-bellied Marmot gave an alarm at the approach of a yearling Mule Deer, the adults stopped, looked, and then quickly returned to what they were doing. When marmots hear the alarm calls of nearby pikas and ground squirrels, they also sit up to assess the danger and sometimes even respond with alarms of their own.

Coyotes, badgers, and golden eagles are the most common predators of western marmots, but wolves, bobcats, lynx, cougars, and fishers also kill adult animals. In a Colorado study, 58 percent of 80 instances of predation were committed by coyotes. The next most common predators were badgers, American Martens, and Black Bears. Coyotes attempt to catch marmots away from their burrows, while badgers and bears may dig them out. Badgers, which usually prey on juveniles and yearlings, cause high anxiety in Yellow-bellied Marmots. At their approach, marmots alarm repeatedly until the badger is within 10 feet (3 m) of them, and then they disappear into their burrows. American Martens and Long-tailed Weasels also kill young marmots, but they have also been seen being chased off by the larger and fiercer adults protecting their colonies. Woodchucks are killed by foxes, coyotes, domestic dogs, bobcats, fishers, weasels, and mink, as well as by red-tailed hawks and great horned owls.

Abandoned marmot burrows become resources for numerous other species. Cottontails, opossums, skunks, raccoons, weasels, snakes, numerous small mammals, and gray foxes may use them, and Red Foxes may enlarge them to make into dens of their own. Cottontails, raccoons, and skunks are among those documented to use woodchuck burrows even while the resident woodchuck hibernates inside.

Uinta Ground Squirrel
Spermophilus armatus, and Allies

OTHER NAMES: prairie gophers, whistling squirrels, picket pins.

The silhouettes of standing ground squirrels are a common feature of open landscapes throughout the West, as are their sharp, high-pitched alarm calls, which announce your presence to others. There are numerous species of ground squirrels living in North America west of a line drawn roughly north to south through the middle of Lake Erie. They share various physical and behavioral traits, though each is unique in its own way. The Uinta Ground Squirrel is representative of many and is easily seen in several of our most famous and well-visited national parks, namely Yellowstone and Grand Teton. *Spermophilus* comes from the Greek for "seed-loving."

ACTIVITY AND MOVEMENT

DAILY

Ground squirrel burrows are often conspicuous affairs, with a throw mound of dirt and scat lying sprinkled about the vicinity. They excavate tunnels with their well-equipped forepaws, push the dirt beneath them, and then expel it behind them with their hind feet. These burrows fall into one of three categories: nest, escape, and hibernation. Nest burrows are the largest and include tunnels to one or more sleeping chambers, which contain grass mattresses. The main entrance to a nest burrow may be obscured beneath a rock, shrub, log, or other available cover. Nest burrows also include several additional tunnels that lead to just below the earth's surface and function as escape hatches should a predator invade through the "front door." In general, the nest burrows of males are simpler than those of females, and tunnel systems dug in softer soils are more elaborate than those dug in harder ground.

Escape burrows are sprinkled throughout their range and are much simpler in construction. Typically escape burrows are just very short tunnels. They lack any additional chambers and are used only as retreats when they need to flee potential predation. Hibernation burrows, also called hibernacula (singular, hibernaculum), are used during the winter and are discussed below.

Ground squirrels are diurnal and can be seen from shortly after dawn until shortly before dusk each day. Uinta Ground Squirrels forage most intensively within several hours of sunup and again just before sundown. They spend most of their time aboveground feeding, as it is essential that they gain sufficient fat reserves in time to hibernate through the coming winter. At regular intervals ground squirrels stop feeding to either stand or sit up to study their surroundings for potential predators, and they do so with increasing frequency as the summer progresses and they become fatter and slower. Belding's Ground Squirrels are less vigilant at the start of summer when they can run 16.4 feet (5 m) per second, but more so when they've put on enough weight to survive the winter and can run only 11.5 feet (3.5 m) a second. Ground squirrels are also competent climbers and swimmers, but rarely do either.

Maintenance and grooming behaviors can be observed at any time of day. Ground squirrels lick their paws and wrists, then wash their face by dragging their paws backward over their head. They groom their tail and hind legs with their teeth and dust-bathe near burrow entrances or in other sites with suitable loose soils to rid themselves of parasites and maintain their fur. Ground squirrels thermoregulate (control their temperature) by varying their exposure to the sun. Earlier in the spring and summer, ground squirrels sunbathe and remain active aboveground for longer periods in order to harness the heat of the sun. When ambient temperatures exceed 68°F (20°C), they reduce their overall activity aboveground and become more active earlier and later to avoid the hottest hours in the middle of the day. If they begin to overheat, they return to their burrow, where they stretch out on the cool dirt floor to release some body heat into the earth through conduction.

Heart rates of Uinta Ground Squirrels vary over the course of the day and reflect their mindset and behaviors. On average their heart rate during the day is 315 beats per minute; when they rest at night, it decreases to 277. Their elevated heart rate betrays that they indeed know they are trespassing when they wander into unfamiliar territory. While squabbling with another squirrel over territory or dominance, their heart rate can soar to an unbelievable 397 beats per minute.

SEASONAL

Uinta Ground Squirrels are only active for about 4 to 5 months each year and hibernate for the remainder. The exact number of months they remain active correlates with each year's average temperatures and lingering snowpack. Northernmost ground squirrels, like the Arctic Ground Squirrel and those inhabiting higher elevations, such as the Belding's Ground Squirrel in the high Sierra Nevadas of California, are active for the shortest length of time, and southern species living at lower elevations for the longest. Southernmost populations of California Ground Squirrels that inhabit low elevations remain active throughout the year, while their northernmost counterparts hibernate for 6 months.

As fall approaches ground squirrels excavate their hibernacula in inconspicuous locations, smoothing and spreading the excavated earth so that a mound

---

Alertness in ground squirrels can be determined by the straightness of their backs. From left to right, a relaxed ground squirrel, one on alert, and one watching a potential predator.

A ground squirrel gathers grass to create its nest in its hibernaculum.

does not betray them to predators. Hibernaculum tunnels are often several yards long and descend gradually downward before splitting into two chambers. The first, which is lined with vegetation, is where they hibernate, and the second is a latrine. In flatter terrain where water drainage may threaten to flood them, their tunnels are typically J-shaped, hooking upward at the end, to provide a high and dry place to sleep. When finally ready to retire for the winter, ground squirrels enter their hibernacula and plug the entrances behind them.

In Uinta Ground Squirrels, juveniles are the first to disappear into winter burrows, which they begin to do as early as the end of July, with the adults typically following in mid-August. Adult males are the last to hibernate, and every Uinta has typically disappeared belowground by September 1.

As ground squirrels become lethargic and slowly sink into hibernation, their bodies slow and their core temperature drops. While in hibernation, their bodies maintain temperatures only 1 to 2° above ambient temperatures and their heart rates and metabolisms operate at approximately 1 percent of what is normal. In this state they subsist on only 13 percent of the energy required to fuel them when they are awake and active.

At regular intervals through the winter, ground squirrels rouse, coming nearly but not quite awake, and shiver in their nests to raise their body temperatures to normal. Then they maintain these higher body temperatures for several hours to several days, before slowly sinking back into full hibernation. Several hypotheses exist to explain why ground squirrels periodically warm their bodies at considerable cost to their energy reserves. It may be that warm bodies are necessary to produce certain proteins that become depleted in a hibernating state, or that their brains require periodic stimulation. Research has shown that while they are warm, they enter a state of sleep like dreaming, which may be critical mental "exercise."

As spring approaches periodic arousals become more frequent until they finally wake up completely. What triggers their complete arousal is unknown, though it likely has to do with soil temperatures. Once awake, they do not immediately take to the surface, but rather wait several weeks for the weather to turn milder and for snows to recede. In the Uinta and many others, they continue their winter fast until they emerge to feed on grass shoots. Male Uinta Ground Squirrels typically awaken in mid-March but are not seen aboveground until the first week of April. Adult males are the first to emerge, followed by adult females, then yearling females, and finally yearling males. Ground squirrels lose 30 to 50 percent of their body weight during hibernation. In several other species, such as the Columbian Ground Squirrel and the northernmost Arctic Ground Squirrel, males store seeds in a small chamber in their hibernacula. They eat them upon awakening to regain their strength and prepare for the upcoming physical contests that determine their breeding opportunities.

FOOD AND FORAGING

Ground squirrels are primarily herbivores that eat a variety of green vegetation and seeds. Uinta Ground Squirrels graze green grasses and broad-leaved herbs (forbs) throughout the spring and summer months. In a study from northern Utah, Uinta Ground Squirrels fed almost entirely on new shoots of grass for their first 30 days aboveground. As spring and summer progressed, green forbs became an increasingly large percentage of their diets, and as grasses began to seed, they incorporated those seeds into their diets as well. Later the forbs, too, began to seed, and their diets shifted to include this new resource. Seeds are especially important to ground squirrels approaching hibernation. Seeds are high in polyunsaturated fats that enable animals to enter hibernation earlier, and hibernating animals to further lower their body temperatures and remain in torpor for longer periods.

Uinta Ground Squirrels also eat the leaves of sagebrush, various roots, invertebrates, and any foods that tourists might feed them. Numerous ground squirrels also eat carrion. Belding's, California, and Uinta Ground Squirrels are as quick to eat their community members that have fallen prey to automobiles on roads as they are to nibble at carcasses of other animals they discover.

HABITAT AND HOME RANGE

Ground squirrels inhabit large open expanses at every elevation, including alpine meadows, fields, active pastures, grasslands, agricultural areas, and open deserts. The notable exception is the Golden-mantled Squirrel (*S. lateralis*), which inhabits forests at higher elevations throughout the West and is often mistaken for a chipmunk because of the stripes it wears on each side.

The range of the Uinta Ground Squirrel is squeezed between the ranges of several other ground squirrels in the Rocky Mountains. They inhabit parts of Utah, eastern Idaho including the Snake River area, southwest Montana, and western Wyoming. The Uinta Ground Squirrel is widely seen in all varieties of open habitats, from low valleys up to alpine meadows near timberline. In Wyoming they also use shrub-steppe habitats where tall sagebrush and rabbitbrush mix with grasslands. The bushes afford the ground squirrels ample shade in which they forage for longer periods than in more open habitats during hot weather.

Typical home ranges for ground squirrels are 1.5 to 3 acres (0.6–1.2 ha), but range up to 10 acres (4 ha) for the large Arctic Ground Squirrel. Densities of Uinta Ground Squirrels are variable but average 28 animals per 2.5 acres (1 ha) and have been recorded as high as 82, not including new pups. Spring populations are often more than half yearlings (animals born the previous year), and in each population females outnumber males 3 to 2.

COMMUNICATION

There are six distinctive calls used by Uinta Ground Squirrels: chirps, churrs, squeals, squawks, tooth-chatters, and growls. Chirps are challenges to trespassing animals. During the breeding season, males give 2 to 5 short chirps in sequence, most often when another male trespasses on their territory. Neighboring males recognize the calls of residents and respond with chirps of their own. Females produce a higher pitched chirp under similar circumstances, most often in response to approaching animals or visible trespassers within her territory.

Sharp chirps are also used to announce the presence of an airborne predator. Other squirrels that hear such alarms run for their burrows or stand erect and alert to assess the situation for themselves. Churrs are used to announce ground predators, and neighboring squirrels respond with churrs of their own to pass along the message. Uinta Ground Squirrels do not give alarms when they encounter snakes, but California Ground Squirrels do. Studies have revealed that calling California Ground Squirrels are killed and eaten more often than those who remain silent, so why do they bother? Perhaps it is altruism, but some biologists argue that calling

A Uinta Ground Squirrel gives an alarm. © *Ang Ji*

animals are actually protecting their immediate kin and receive some selfish benefit.

Ground squirrels also emit ultrasonic alarms in response to predators, sounds that humans cannot hear. Research in Richardson's Ground Squirrels found that squirrels are more likely to use ultrasonic alarm calls when predators are far away. This makes sense, since ultrasonic alarms carry shorter distances and the squirrel can announce the presence of the predator while remaining undetected. When predators are very close, ground squirrels almost always use normal alarms that humans can hear in the field.

Churrs and trills are often produced by females when another ground squirrel approaches too close, usually within 5 feet (1.5 m), and they strongly communicate that they better back off. Teeth-chattering may be heard during threat displays or after an agonistic encounter. Ground squirrels also use piloerection (when their hairs stand on end) or fanning of their tails as aggressive threats. Squawks and squeals are voiced just prior to being attacked, and while being bitten. Growls are made rarely, most often when they are cornered.

Chemical communication is widely used by ground squirrels, though the means vary across species. Uinta Ground Squirrels, and many other species, establish their territories by rubbing oral glands, located at the corners of their mouths, on the ground and available objects such as rocks and sticks along their boundaries. Many ground squirrels also smell these glands when greeting each other, and they are assumed to aid in individual recognition. Look for ground squirrels coming together nose to nose, or mouth to mouth, often with their mouths open and heads tilted slightly to either side to inspect each other's oral glands. California Ground Squirrels also scent-mark by dragging and rubbing their bodies over objects and in the soft dirt found along road shoulders—likely with anal glands. In many ground squirrels, scats are some-what liberally sprinkled throughout their range, but in Golden-mantled Ground Squirrels they are placed on elevated edges and sometimes in scrapes they dig with their forefeet.

COURTSHIP AND MATING

Uinta Ground Squirrels emerge from their winter dens ready to mate. Males are the first to emerge and immediately set about establishing exclusive territories using scents from their oral glands to form boundaries. They chirp when they see an interloper in their territory, or sometimes they move straight in to engage the trespassing male. Short chases may displace intruders, otherwise they settle dominance with a "boxing" match. Males stand and grab each other, wrestling, rolling, and biting their opponent. Rarely is a male seriously injured during one of these matches; the wrestling alone determines dominance. In other species, including the very closely related Belding's Ground Squirrel, male fighting is vicious and occasionally results in fatalities. Nearly every male Belding's Ground Squirrel in

A pair of Wyoming Ground Squirrels "kiss," and thoroughly smell each other's oral glands. © *Max Allen Photography*

A juvenile Belding's Ground Squirrel dust-bathes, which is also likely a scent-marking behavior.
© David Moskowitz/www.davidmoskowitz.net

a Sierra Nevada study bore wounds and scars from battles during the breeding season.

Females emerge after males, ready to enter estrus, and quickly secure their own territories. Females enter estrus for a single afternoon within 2 to 4 days of emerging from their dens. Yearling females emerge later and may also mate, thus extending the breeding season for as long as 30 days after the first emergence of the males.

During the breeding season, males mate with as many females as possible. They approach females in estrus within their own territories, and females may or may not be receptive. If a female has already mated she usually freezes and adopts what some researchers call a "stay threat" in which she neither approaches nor retreats from the approaching male. If she is receptive, the pair may engage in a bout of "kissing," approaching each other and making contact with their noses, or mouth to mouth, to smell each other's oral glands.

Should the male prove acceptable to the female, Uinta Ground Squirrel pairs move underground to copulate. In Belding's Ground Squirrels and others, you might catch them mating on the surface. Within several hours of mating, a copulatory plug forms in the females of most ground squirrels. If left undisturbed, the plug, which is formed from secretions in the male's semen, mitigates further mating and thus protects his investment from competing males. But females have been observed removing them. After the breeding season males retreat to their own territories and focus solely on gaining weight for the coming winter. Within several days of mating, females become fiercely territorial and redistribute themselves in relation to each other. They are intolerant of every other ground squirrel, including adult males, until the pups are weaned. Thereafter their territorial behaviors diminish dramatically.

DEVELOPMENT AND DISPERSAL OF YOUNG

The majority of Uinta Ground Squirrel litters are born around May 1 of each year. After a gestation of 23 to 26 days, 4 to 6 young are born underground in the relative safety of a nesting chamber. Females 2 to 3 years old are most productive, after which there is a general decline in their litter sizes. The nature of the young and the litter also depends on when they are born. Litters born early in the season are composed of more numerous, smaller pups, which have more time to gain the necessary resources to survive their first winter. Late litters have fewer but heavier pups, to give them a head start in gaining sufficient weight for hibernation.

Newborns grow rapidly for their first 30 to 40 days, and then their growth slows considerably. Juveniles emerge from their dens for the first time at about 3 weeks of age and are weaned soon after. Juveniles can be seen exhibiting numerous adult behaviors once they have emerged aboveground. They begin mounting each other within several days of their emergence, sparring and boxing in their second week, and "kissing" after 3 weeks. They also engage in chases with their siblings more and more often as the summer progresses. As they mature they wander farther and farther from their maternal den and then, after 3 to 4 weeks, dissolve any remaining familial bonds. The young find or dig their own burrows in which to hibernate for their first winter.

Females that dig nest dens in more open terrain with good visibility have greater pup survivorship, though fewer than 50 percent of pups survive their first winter to be seen the following summer. Generally yearling males do not breed. Yearling females may do so, but they are at a disadvantage because they emerge from dens slightly behind older animals and thus struggle to establish territories.

At some point, young ground squirrels disperse to new areas. Males disperse earlier and farther than females, into areas sufficiently free of other ground squirrels where suitable forage can be found. In the Grand Tetons, male Uinta Ground Squirrels dispersed within 3 weeks of their weaning, while females remained in their mother's territory through their first winter. Observations of dispersing Columbian Ground Squirrels likely reveal how most ground squirrels behave while dispersing. They move cautiously, scampering from one refuge to another, using things such as logs and bushes as retreats. Before dashing to their next refuge they scan the landscape for long periods. Some animals actually retrace their routes each evening to their natal dens, and then each day move farther and farther away until they find an available bit of range at a suitable distance.

INTERACTIONS AMONG GROUND SQUIRRELS

Uinta Ground Squirrels are generally clumped in loose communities in open terrain where their numerous burrows, and the ground squirrels themselves, are conspicuous and easy to see. Uinta

Ground Squirrels are fiercely territorial and intolerant of intruders into their community's area. During the first few weeks after they emerge in the spring, aggressive encounters are frequent as territories are established and mating is under way, but then, as the season progresses, disputes occur less often.

Both adult and young ground squirrels may kill other ground squirrels. A female Belding's Ground Squirrel was observed entering the burrow of another female that had recently died, where she killed the undefended young with bites to the head. Males more often eat their victims. In Belding's Ground Squirrels 8 percent of juvenile mortalities are due to infanticide.

INTERACTIONS WITH OTHER SPECIES

Given their high densities and their capacity to produce large litters, ground squirrels are important prey for a number of predators. Coyotes, badgers, bobcats, Long-tailed Weasels, foxes, snakes, and various hawks and eagles are the primary predators of all ground squirrels. The American Badger hunts the Uinta Ground Squirrel throughout the year and readily excavates hibernating ground squirrels and pups in their nest chambers. It also corners adults in their own tunnels. A study in the Grand Teton National Park area showed that Uinta Ground Squirrels are the major food source for coyotes from May through July.

Rattlesnakes prey on ground squirrel species across western North America, and ground squirrels have evolved several behaviors to help mitigate their losses to these well-adapted predators. The first has to do with scent. Ground squirrels locate shed rattlesnake skins and transfer their scent onto themselves by chewing the snakeskin and then licking their fur. Tests with rattlesnakes have revealed that rattlesnakes, whose flicking tongues are sensitive to scent, are less attracted to ground squirrel scents mixed with their own. Thus ground squirrels may be using snake skins as a form of olfactory camouflage.

Rock and California Ground Squirrels, which are both resistant to rattlesnake venom, have also developed harassment and tail-flagging behaviors to force snakes to depart their territories. These ground squirrels harass approaching gopher snakes and rattlesnakes, wagging their tails side to side, every tail hair erect to emphasize the visibility of their tails. They may even kick or throw dirt at the snake to discourage it. When tail-flagging at a rattlesnake, California Ground Squirrels flood their tails with blood. This increases the temperature of the tail, which can be detected by the heat-sensitive sensory pits of the rattlesnake, and surprises the snakes enough to turn them from offensive to defensive posturing.

Eastern Chipmunk
Tamias striatus, and Allies

chipper, chip squirrel, striped squirrel.

There are 25 species of chipmunks in North America, and their ranges and distribution tell a tale of the ecology. The Eastern and Least Chipmunks are the only ones found in the East, and their ranges overlap very little. In the western United States, where habitats are more diverse and physically fragmented, split by mountains, valleys, and deserts, there are 23 others, each limited to a small range in a particular regional habitat. Distinctive diagnoses of most of the western species depend on the study of their bones, particularly the baculum, or penis bone. Some can be identified in the field by their unique calls.

The genus name *Tamias*, which is applied to all the chipmunks, comes from the Greek and means "storer" or "distributor," an exceedingly appropriate reference. The English word *chipmunk*, which used to be *chitmunk*, is a corruption of the Ojibwa name *adjidaumo* (the "o" at the end has a nasal pronunciation) and translates as "headfirst" for its manner of descending trees.

ACTIVITY AND MOVEMENT

DAILY

Eastern Chipmunks are semi-fossorial and strictly diurnal. They often have a single peak of activity around midday and are most active on bright, warm, windless days. Chipmunks are aggressively solitary and watchful not only for predators, but also for trespassers. Their movements radiate from a central point, usually a perch near the burrow mouth. From this point their travels extend out and back as they patrol first one area and then another, spending most of their time in the areas nearer their burrow.

When chipmunks are not active aboveground, they retire to the safety and comfort of underground burrows. Tree cavities are also used as refuges by at least 8 species of chipmunks. In some species, the mother and her youngsters move to a tree nest just before weaning. In one account, a female Eastern Chipmunk likely overwintered in a tree nest and then successfully raised a litter in it the following summer.

Chipmunk burrows have circular entrances approximately 2 inches (5 cm) in diameter. Their holes are clean and tidy, with most of the loose, adjacent soil and vegetation removed. From the entrance, tunnels drop straight down for 6 to 8 inches (15–20

The clean entrance to an Eastern Chipmunk's burrow. © *Mark Elbroch*

cm), after which they more gradually descend to about 2 feet (65 cm) in depth. Tunnels may run parallel to the surface for up to 10 feet (3 m) before terminating in an oval sleeping chamber. These chambers are about 13 inches (32 cm) in diameter and lined with shredded leaves. A chipmunk may live in a burrow for several years, digging new chambers and sealing up the old. It uses a "work hole" to dispose of dirt generated by new digging. It pushes dirt and debris out the work hole, scatters it so as not to draw attention to the site, and then seals the entrance by pushing dirt into it with its nose. Good burrows are precious, and if a resident dies or leaves a good site, its burrow is rapidly taken over by another chipmunk.

Chipmunks are meticulously clean and wash and groom after activities such as digging. Their stature and lifestyle mean they often pick up debris in their fur; as a result, much of every day is spent grooming. A chipmunk can reach every part of its body with its teeth, tongue, and claws. It washes its face in a cat-like manner, moistening its paws and then rubbing its ears and head with them. It washes other areas in similar fashion or licks them directly. It grooms the tail by nibbling it and running it across the tongue through the space behind the front teeth. It scratches with its hind feet like a dog and sometimes shakes like one, too, to remove debris. More often it rolls and wriggles in the moss and leaves to remove little things that might be clinging to the fur.

Chipmunks move with a bounding scamper with their tails held horizontally, unless they are alarmed, when they hold them upright. When for-

A chipmunk grooming its tail.

aging or searching they walk slowly with alternating footfalls, and when curious they keep their hind feet held firmly in place and step toward the object of curiosity with their forefeet. When startled or alarmed they stamp their hind feet and they might jump back at intervals and utter soft trills. Chipmunks climb with a squirrel-like bound, alternately moving both forefeet and both hind; on rare occasions they will even swim.

SEASONAL

Eastern Chipmunks do not hibernate in the winter, but rather enter periods of torpor, a deep sleep. They pass the cold months in successive periods of torpidity and wakefulness. Torpid bouts last up to several days at a stretch. In between these bouts they rouse to urinate and eat stored food. Even as far south as northern Florida, chipmunks enter torpor, which allows their bodies to reduce energy consumption by as much as 85 percent. Some western species are torpid only intermittently or perhaps not at all, depending on the weather.

Adult and juvenile Eastern Chipmunks retreat to their burrows for torpor in late October or early November. They plug their burrow entrances with earth and vegetation and retire to their bedchambers. A sleeping chipmunk curls into a ball, sitting on its tail or lying on its side like a cat. It fluffs its fur for better insulation, and as it enters torpor, its heart rate drops from 350 beats to 4 beats per minute. Its body temperature drops from 98.6°F (37°C) to only 1 or 2 degrees above the ambient temperature in the burrow. Temperatures belowground generally stabilize just above freezing, protecting chipmunks from the dangers of frozen tissue. Unlike hibernators that sustain themselves on body fat, chipmunks awaken periodically and feed on stored seeds and other food.

Some speculate that Eastern Chipmunks also estivate (go dormant in hot weather) in summer. Those who argue against estivation credit their summer disappearances to the demands of maternity, the prevalence at that time of dense, obscuring foliage, and abundant food close to their burrows. Under these conditions a chipmunk would be expected to maximize time in the burrow in hot weather and be difficult to see when moving outside.

FOOD AND FORAGING

Chipmunks can feed as high as 65 feet (20 m) up in trees, but they are most commonly seen foraging and feeding on the ground. They often perch on raised surfaces to process food and keep watch for predators. The discarded remains of acorns or hickory nuts, spaced at regular intervals along old stone walls or on stumps, are sure signs of chipmunks. All chipmunks are mostly vegetarian, but they do eat animal matter such as earthworms, June bugs, worms, grasshoppers, frogs, reptiles, bird eggs, and even small mammals when they can catch them. They occasionally scavenge carrion, and many species have been noted to eat fungi. Truffles, the underground fruiting bodies of some fungi, are highly aromatic when ripe and are a preferred food in some areas.

In spring, Eastern Chipmunks feed heavily on seeds hoarded during the previous year, especially maple and elm. Summer foods consist of berries

The simple burrow system of an Eastern Chipmunk. Note that the back entrance is plugged for a length of the tunnel, which inhibits entry by other animals.

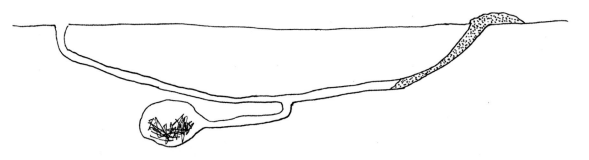

and the flowers, leaves, and buds of wildflowers, supplemented by fungi and invertebrates. Autumn is the time when chipmunks harvest seeds and nuts, especially beechnuts, hazelnuts, hickory nuts, and acorns. When gathering maple and elm seeds, they cut away the vanes and husks and transport the seed pulp to be stashed under the leaves in the bedchamber of their burrows. Chipmunks minimize their travel on hoarding trips by filling their incredibly large and elastic cheek pouches. One chipmunk was found carrying 6 chestnuts in its pouches (each of which is nearly the size of its skull); another carried 31 kernels of corn.

Chipmunks require water, most of which they get from the vegetation they eat, but they also lick water off vegetation and slurp standing water, sucking it up like a horse, instead of lapping it like a dog. Occasionally they even eat snow. During the breeding season they may need as much as a quarter of their body weight in water daily.

HABITAT AND HOME RANGE

Eastern Chipmunks range from Nova Scotia across southern Canada to Manitoba and south to the Gulf States. The primary habitat of chipmunks is woodland. Eastern Chipmunks live throughout the deciduous forests of the eastern United States and Canada. They seek dry ground with good low vegetation cover and well-drained soils. This combination is often found at mature forest edges. They dig their burrows, leaving neat, tidy openings, in brush piles, stone walls, fences, hedgerows, and log piles. Suitable cover for protection from predators is critical to chipmunks.

Chipmunks maintain and aggressively defend the core areas within their larger home ranges. Home range size shrinks in areas of abundant food and may be as small as 1,100 square feet (100 m^2) or as large as 2.5 acres (1 ha). Core areas estimated from radiotelemetry were about 0.2 to 0.4 acres (0.8–0.16 ha), with those of females being larger. Eastern Chipmunks might travel as far as 0.3 miles (500 m) from their burrow during their lifetime, but overall they are rather sedentary. Many maintain the same home range and use the same burrow system for much if not all of their lives.

Good habitat might be able to sustain about 25 animals per acre (10–12 per ha), but other areas support far fewer. Over time, the densities of local populations can also change by a factor of 2 to 5.

A sleeping Eastern Chipmunk. © Breck P. Kent/Animals Animals

An Eastern Chipmunk with swollen cheeks, ready to transport food to its burrow. © *Bruce Macqueen/ Dreamstime.com*

When population densities are high, the stress of food shortages and constantly bumping into and bickering with others causes changes in hormones that inhibit further reproduction.

COMMUNICATION

Chipmunks have expressive voices. Their bright "chip" is easily mistaken for a bird in the spring woods. Each morning, individuals climb up to 6 feet (2 m) to sit on a high perch and sing their morning "songs," which are 10-minute series of chips made once or twice per second. Their songs can be heard up to 600 feet (185 m) away. Their other vocalizations are described as chucks, trills, whistles, chatters, and warbles. The chip is a general announcement call, and when repeated, an alarm for mammalian predators. Chipping calls are often made while in upright postures—those that maximize their view of the surrounding area. The chuck is a male-to-male threat; when vocalized repeatedly, it is an alarm for aerial predators. Chucks are made from coiled, low-alert stances, or while simply standing frozen in place. When anxious, a chipmunk might slouch or coil its back, bringing its paws to the ground and lowering or extending its head in the direction of intended flight. Fleeing

An alert chipmunk.

chipmunks erect their tails and may rapidly emit a multi-note trill just prior to disappearing into their burrows. Females use the trill more than males and most often when they are close to their burrows. That pattern suggests that the females are using it to warn their offspring, not just to express their anxiety at being pursued. Trills are familiar sounds for those who hike in eastern woods, for they are also the sounds made by chipmunks fleeing approaching humans. Males engaged in chases during the breeding season will whistle.

Agonistic encounters are marked by either frozen and fixated stances or attacks. The hackles are raised, the back is arched, the ears laid back, and eyes narrowed. Territorial interactions are accompanied by a chip-trill sound, absent any threatening gestures, which conveys the anxiety of the resident animal. Direct threats include open-mouthed gestures, chuck-trills, short bluff charges, and fights. Fights are a whirlwind of kicking, biting, scratching, and growling. Physical brawls may break and repeat again after a brief chase. When dominance has been established, the subordinate flees without pursuit.

Chipmunks that are comfortable and relaxed will assume a variety of postures, such as upright with forepaws held to the breast, or lying down on the belly, a typical resting position. Calm chipmunks utter soft *cuck cuck* sounds. In moments of indecision chipmunks stop in mid-stride, with one paw raised in the air. When alert they sometimes sit with forepaws on the ground, ears up, and attention fixed, or stand on their hind legs with a straight back. When sizing up a threat they sit and stamp their feet, drumming them independently. A chipmunk's tail is also an active component in mood displays. When relaxed, they hold their tail loosely

around their feet or body. A horizontally straight or slightly extended tail indicates alertness, and when an animal is alarmed, the tail is held upright.

COURTSHIP AND MATING

Eastern Chipmunks breed twice per year. The first round of breeding peaks in March, and the second peaks in June. Males usually emerge from a winter of torpor ready to mate in late January and February. They proceed to tour female territories regularly, and males that encounter one another wrestle in ritualistic tournaments. These tournaments comprise 2 to 10 "jousts" of frenetic wrestling, but without biting, interspersed with breaks during which they pose aggressively. When one animal concedes and escapes, there is no pursuit.

Females begin emerging from their burrows a few weeks after the males and are in estrus within a few days. The males have been active since early each morning, seeking out and congregating in the core areas of estrous females. A female is in estrus for only a few days to a week, but is actively receptive to advancing males for only about 7 hours. Should a male, perhaps overconfident after vanquishing an interloping male, approach a female that is not ready to mate, she beats him severely and drives him far from the area. However, if the female is receptive, a brief courtship and mating ensue. The male trills and nudges her affectionately. A rapid up-and-down movement of the tail communicates his intention to mate; at all other times, chipmunks only shake their tails horizontally. Mating is brief and silent, the male clutching the female's hips with his forepaws as he thrusts. The two remain together for up to 2 hours after copulation, eating and grooming, until the female finally drives him away.

If a receptive female emerges from her den and not one, but several males are about, a mating chase is sure to follow. Four or more males might chase her, a furry bullet train through the debris. At intervals the female will stop to rest, during which she may sneak off undetected as the males fight for priority to mate. When one of the males notices she has departed, he sets off to find her and the race resumes. When only one suitor is left, he will follow her to a place of her choosing for mating. If there are 3 males contesting her, the dominant one is sure to mate. If the number is very high, the dominant male spends so much time fighting off challengers that he doesn't have time to mate. Given the chance, a male will mate several times with the same female. She may also mate with more than one male during her estrus.

DEVELOPMENT AND DISPERSAL OF YOUNG

After mating, the females set to work digging and outfitting their nests. Their diets shift to include more animal protein to support the developing fetuses and subsequent lactation. A pregnant mother retires to her burrow a week or so before parturition, and 3 to 7 blind, hairless young are born in April or May after a month-long gestation. The female emerges within a week of birthing and will continue to emerge occasionally, with the duration of her absences lengthening as weaning approaches.

Even before their eyes open at 4 weeks of age, youngsters begin to walk and will earnestly explore the nooks and crannies of their burrow. After that first month they become increasingly active and finally emerge from the natal den after 5 to 6 weeks. At this point they are about three-quarters of their adult size. They hang about near the burrow entrance, climbing, navigating, forming dominance relationships, and learning to defend themselves through play. One to 3 weeks later the mother bars them from entering the burrow, and they disperse. They reach their adult size at 3 months of age.

Young from the second breeding season are generally born around August. They emerge from their natal burrows in October and may remain active all winter. Their later dispersal may be partially offset by the abundance of acorns and similar hard mast at that time, but they still show lower survival rates than earlier litters.

When young chipmunks disperse, the morning songs of the local population inform the dispersers where and how far they must travel to find space to establish their own burrows. One or 2 females, and occasionally males, will settle in within 165 feet (50 m) of their natal burrow. The others must disperse widely and are subject to much persecution from adults during their travels. Some may find abandoned burrows or territories in which to dig their own burrows within weeks. Those that haven't yet found a home of their own can be found roaming and hiding their food on the surface as late as July.

Males disperse farther than females, many of which stay very close to their mothers. Eastern Chipmunks can show a tremendous amount of tolerance toward female offspring. Some even share their burrow with daughters and granddaughters. Dispersal could help males find competitive access to mates and also avoid the potential of incestuous matings with mothers and siblings.

Most chipmunks aren't sexually mature until their second year of life. Occasionally a female bears a litter in her first summer at the age of 3 months. This is more likely to happen when food is abundant and animals are in especially good physical condition—just the sort of thing that leads to local irruptions, since early breeding means higher than normal population growth.

INTERACTIONS AMONG CHIPMUNKS

The basic social unit of the Eastern Chipmunk is a solitary individual in its burrow. There are some reports of them living in family groups, which is true in a sense, given their low dispersal distances, overlapping home ranges, and general tolerance for one another. However, each animal defends a core area within its home range, through threat displays and aggressive chases that lack physical contact.

There is little social interaction between chipmunks, other than during mating season and near concentrated food sources like bird feeders, where chipmunks tolerate each other as close as 1.5 feet (0.5 m). At these sites, dominance hierarchies determine which animals gain access to the most food. The rank of an animal is influenced by size, sex, age, and experience—those animals with a history of interaction and handling conflict dominate naïve animals. Overall, Eastern Chipmunks live peaceably with their neighbors, spending only about 3 percent of their time in agonistic interactions.

INTERACTIONS WITH OTHER SPECIES

Eastern Chipmunks appear to compete little with Least Chipmunks, especially compared to the intense competition seen among western chipmunk species. Perhaps this is thanks to abundant food and cover in the habitats they share. They may partition food resources. In one study where the Least and Eastern Chipmunks overlapped, only 3 of 16 seed species carried by Least Chipmunks were also found in the pouches of Eastern Chipmunks.

Chipmunks are prey to many species of carnivores, such as foxes, weasels, martens, fishers, bobcats, hawks, and owls. These animals catch them in summer and dig them from their burrows in winter. Two-thirds of hibernating ground squirrels (including, but not limited to, chipmunks) are estimated to die during winter, and though a proportion of deaths are due to predators, most are due to environmental conditions.

Chipmunks occasionally have mites and fleas. Botflies (*Cuterebra emasculator*) lay their eggs in low vegetation and chipmunks sometimes pick them up on their belly fur. The hatching larvae enter a chipmunk's abdomen to incubate, and these invasions can cause oozing, infected sores. Wounds in the groin and under the tail, and the lack of obvious testicles in post-infected males, were once believed evidence that the parasite destroys the testicles, hence the botfly's disconcerting name, *emasculator*. The testes are not, in fact, destroyed by the parasites. They naturally recede into the abdomen outside of the breeding season. Despite the nasty appearance of an infestation, death from botfly infection is rare to unknown. Chipmunks are also one of the primary mammalian vectors of Lyme disease.

American Beaver
Castor canadensis

OTHER NAMES: beaver, castor (Spanish), bievre (French).

The next time someone tells you they've been "busy as a beaver," make sure to ask them, in which season? The expression "busy as a beaver" refers to their constant attention to their dams of sticks, stones, and mud that form ponds along running watercourses. These dams require tremendous effort to keep mostly watertight, but in the North, dam maintenance is a seasonal phenomenon. Winter months are spent doing little but eating stored foods and sleeping and huddling with family members to stay warm inside their dark, gloomy lodges. Even the most egregious couch potato is as busy as northern beavers in winter.

It was once believed that beavers instinctively dammed water like little robots. Researchers have been able to stimulate dam-building in captive beavers simply by playing recordings of running water. The animals detect the sound and respond by hauling mud and debris to the source of the sound, but they seem ignorant of the condition of the water. However, recent research has revealed that there may be a more complex set of variables influencing these behaviors. In times of heavy rainfall and temporary flooding, beavers often ignore the sounds of rushing water and may not build up their dams at all. As if they have preconceived notions about how high the water should be, they wait until water levels drop to normal before resuming dam maintenance.

ACTIVITY AND MOVEMENT

DAILY

During spring, summer, and fall, beavers are active about 12 hours per day, most often from late afternoon into early morning. For most of the daylight hours family members rest together within the lodge, though they can sometimes be roused by intrusive sounds or hunger. While in the lodge or ashore, beavers groom themselves wherever they can reach but rely on family members to groom their backs. The two innermost toes on each hind foot have broad nails that grow with a split down the middle, and they use them in daily grooming activities. The split nails are used like combs to maintain the loft in their coats, which keeps them warm while submerged.

On land, beavers waddle and appear clumsy, though when startled they can retreat to the safety of nearby water in great bounding leaps. In water they swim gracefully with their front feet tucked in tight against their bodies. Their paddlelike hind feet make alternate kicks to propel them forward, and their tails may also flap and contribute to propulsion. Their eyes and ears are located high on their heads, allowing them to see and hear while they swim with their heads and bodies mostly submerged, much like a crocodile. Their lips meet behind their front incisors, allowing them to close their mouths even when carrying or harvesting vegetation underwater.

While diving, blood rushes to a beaver's brain, but overall circulation slows. Beavers can remain submerged for as long as 15 minutes, though dives of 1 to 2 minutes' duration are more typical. Their eyes have nictitating membranes—clear "eyelids" that protect them like goggles while underwater—and their nostrils and ears can be closed to prevent taking in water.

Much of their daily activity in warmer months is devoted to the upkeep and creation of lodges, dams, and the channels necessary to float large logs to work sites. Beaver lodges are familiar wilderness icons and can be massive structures over 10 feet (3

The inside of a beaver lodge, with two entrances and a large central chamber.

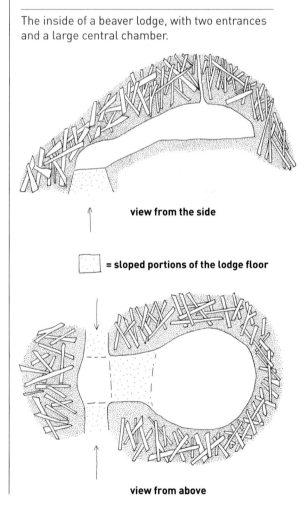

view from the side

☐ = sloped portions of the lodge floor

view from above

An old American Beaver forages on green vegetation. Note its flat, scaly tail. © *Jacob Katz*

m) high and 25 feet (8 m) in diameter. They are built up over time from mud, rotting vegetation, and logs. Beneath the water there are often several entrances that open into "mudrooms"—flat areas where beavers can shake and clean themselves before moving up a sloped tunnel to a single large chamber where the family congregates. Inside the lodge, the relatively smooth, mud-plastered walls seem adorned with eyes, as the rings and cores at the ends of logs are visible between sections of hardened earth. Each beaver maintains a grass-lined bed within the main enclosure, thus much of the inner compartment is covered in vegetation.

Not all beavers use lodges. They are competent diggers, and along riverbanks and lake shores they tend to excavate bank burrows with entrances below water level. Bank burrows tend to be used when moving into new areas or in habitats with deep, moving water. The burrow comprises the living quarters, while a "lodge" of jumbled sticks and logs is constructed above as a fortification against predators.

Beavers are safest in the water and vulnerable on land, where much of their food grows. They con-struct dams across streams because the resulting ponds extend their access to trees either swallowed or approached by rising waters. Beaver dams may be constructed of mud and plant materials dredged and hauled up from beneath the water surface and may measure only a foot (0.3 m) high. More often, dams are complex structures of cut branches and logs filled and cemented with mud, decomposing debris, and rocks found below the surface of the water.

Beavers start a dam by carrying long lengths of wood to the site in their mouths. They secure one end of each of these in the stream bottom with the opposite end facing up into the current. More sticks and branches, often of smaller length, are piled on. These are caught by the longer lengths, creating a lattice upon which mounds and mounds of mud, muck, and other dredged items are placed and packed down by the force of the water and by the beavers themselves until the dam is nearly waterproof. Unlike in children's cartoons, beavers do not pack mud into dams and their lodge with their tail, but they do on occasion comically walk on their hind legs with an armload of muddy debris tucked beneath their chin.

The resulting dams can be massive, ranging up to 10 feet (3 m) high and up to 2,970 feet (850 m) in length. Until recent improvements in remote sensing, beaver dams were one of few animal signs visible from outer space. Beavers sometimes make a series of dams along a water system, creating a series of impoundments called "beaver steps" or "terraces." Structures built by beavers are incredibly resilient, and when people deem it necessary to lower water levels, they often resort to dynamite to punch a hole in a dam.

During times of high water, beavers focus their efforts on dam building and maintenance. In times of lower water they shift their attention to lodge maintenance and ensuring that lodge entrances stay below the water surface, which excludes their most pernicious predators. All members of a colony may contribute to the building of dams and lodges, but they do this independently and not in a coordinated fashion.

SEASONAL

Beginning in late summer, northern beavers store food for the upcoming winter months, when they often become trapped beneath a layer of ice and are unable to forage beyond the limits of their ponds. Beavers stockpile woody plants in a winter cache in two ways. In deep waters they create a floating raft of less palatable branches and then float their preferred foods beneath it to keep them submerged. Winter weather freezes the pond and traps the raft in place, and the beavers retain access to the deeper, tastier vegetation beneath the ice. In shallow waters, beavers drive the butt ends of branches of their preferred foods directly into the muddy bottom of their ponds to hold them in place. Regardless of water depth, look for the tops of branches breaking the water surface near lodges, much like a shrubby garden at their doorstep.

When ice forms in northern winters, beavers huddle together to stay warm in the darkness of their lodge. By swimming and disturbing the water surface, they inhibit ice formation as long as possible so as to maintain access to food on shore. In warmer winters, when ice does not completely close the pond, beavers continue to forage on land, and their distinctive tracks can be seen in the snow.

If the ice forms too quickly for them to maintain holes, they are relegated to a long winter of semi-darkness in the lodge. They make periodic trips beneath the ice in the frigid waters to remove branches from their winter cache. Well-constructed lodges are further insulated by layers of snow and are warmed from within by the bodies of the beavers themselves. Look for their air vents atop the lodge, where their warm breath rises up from below and melts a small passage through the collected snows. As winter wanes and ice recedes, look for beavers

The shrubbery sticking out above the water just beyond the muddy trail running down the side of this lodge is the winter cache of a family of beavers. © *Mark Elbroch*

sunning themselves on the tops of their lodges. No doubt the warmth of the sun is a welcome reprieve after a dark, cold winter in the lodge.

FOOD AND FORAGING

Throughout the year, beavers eat the leaves, barks, and twigs of nearly every woody plant that grows near their watery home. They clearly prefer willows and aspens when they are present, as well as select cottonwoods, alders, birches, maples, blueberries, and sweet fern. Beavers eat between 1 and 4.5 pounds (0.5–2 kg) every day. It takes 60 hours for food to pass through a beaver, and they are able to digest and assimilate a good portion of the cellulose found in vegetation by fermenting it in their guts. While foraging, beavers also intermittently exhibit coprophagy, the act of eating their own feces. They first excrete a soft greenish scat, which they ingest a second time to maximize nutrient assimilation. Their second defecations often resemble pellets of sawdust and are usually deposited in the water in latrines. Common latrine sites include the mouths of slow-moving rivulets entering their ponds and smaller ponds that they no longer maintain.

Beavers are the only North American mammal able to fell large trees, which they do with their heavy, orange-pigmented incisors and massive jaw muscles. While sitting back on their haunches they use their broad, scaly tails for support like a third leg. They can fell a 5-inch (12.7-cm) diameter willow in 3 minutes, and after a period of harvesting they leave half-chewed trees and stumps that resemble varied and beautiful sculptures. Work sites accumulate large wood chips that carpet the work area completely over time. Typically, beavers fell and harvest smaller, younger saplings, but as they move farther from their water source, they may fell larger and larger trees. Beavers are expert loggers, but like all experts they occasionally make mistakes. Occasionally a beaver is killed by the tree it felled, and it is not unusual to find trees the beavers had hoped would fall to the ground hung up in surrounding tree canopies.

Once a felled tree is stripped of its branches, it is cut into manageable chunks and toted off for winter stores or construction. Only the largest pieces will remain, and these will be stripped clean of the cambium layer by feeding beavers, leaving intricate incisor patterns larger than those of porcupine or Snowshoe Hares. Beavers eat the cambium—the inner bark layer between the coarse outer bark and the dead inner wood. This layer is the tissue that transports nutrients and minerals through the tree and is the only portion that provides any nutrition.

Where available during the summer months, beavers live almost exclusively on certain herbaceous, or succulent, plants, including pondweed

A beaver pauses while felling a tree.

(*Potamogeton*), lizard's tail (*Saururus*), and waterweed (*Elodea*). During the winter they also eat the roots, rhizomes, and runners of water lilies (*Nymphaea odorata*). The discarded portions of lily roots float along pond edges during the warmer months, where they resemble old coyote scats. They also harvest cattails and sedges and wear in trails to nearby cornfields, where they harvest entire stalks of ripe corn and transport them back to their watery sanctuary before feeding. Beavers have also been observed feeding upon salmon carcasses in south-central Alaska and California, which they do annually to take advantage of this seasonally abundant resource.

HABITAT AND HOME RANGE

Historically, beavers could be found across North America excepting only the dry deserts of the Southwest, the extreme Arctic region, and peninsular Florida. Their numbers were heavily reduced with the settlement of North America by Europeans and the rise of the booming fur trade. Many local populations became extinct. However, reintroductions and natural dispersals have returned the American Beaver to much of its former range, and today their populations number in the millions.

Beavers inhabit freshwater systems in forested habitats. They are most conspicuous when they inhabit streams and build dams that create ponds, but they also inhabit large rivers and lakes. In these sites they inhabit bank burrows and rarely build dams, making them more difficult to detect. Beaver territories are defined by waterways, and when

A beaver vigorously slaps the water in an attempt to discourage an intruder, simultaneously alerting other nearby beavers of incoming danger. © *McDonald Wildlife Photography/Animals Animals*

exploring on land they remain within 200 feet (60 m) of deep water. Beaver densities vary tremendously with food availability. Typical densities are 1 beaver for every 0.4 square miles (1 km²) of wetland or riparian habitat, with high densities of 3 animals per 0.4 square miles in prime habitat.

COMMUNICATION

Perhaps the easiest beaver communication to witness is the tail-slap. Beavers slap their tails to communicate danger to other beavers and aggression to other species. Upon hearing a tail-slap, members of the colony dive to deeper and safer waters, yet the colony responds differently depending upon which beaver exhibits the behavior. Though males tend to tail-slap more frequently, the colony most often swims to deeper waters if it was an adult female that sounded the alarm. Evidence suggests tail-slapping might also be used to frighten off potential predators or to elicit a response from an as yet unidentified entity. A beaver may approach you when you are canoeing or rafting and slap the water alongside your boat to communicate its distress over your intrusion into its territory. On one occasion a beaver was observed tail-slapping near a Black Bear foraging at the pond's edge. The bear took to the water and began to chase the beaver. Whenever the bear came close to catching it, the beaver would tail-slap, submerge, and then reappear at a safer distance. The bear attempted to catch the beaver four times before the beaver disappeared and never resurfaced and the bear gave up the chase.

Communication between colony members has rarely been observed inside the lodge, so our understanding of these animals is limited to episodes witnessed in the open, when beavers generally act independently of each other. Playful behaviors include wrestling and "dancing," during which two beavers sit back on their haunches and tails and grapple with their forearms. Mutual grooming is common and, along with touching noses, builds and maintains trust between colony members. Beaver kits may be seen whining and begging for food from older siblings and adults, but adults do not tolerate the same behavior from yearlings and quickly discourage them from begging with a violent snap of their head. Aggression between beavers is sometimes observed over food, as when one moves too close to another while sharing a log. Aggressive beavers hiss, grunt, and chatter their dangerous front teeth, but only rarely does aggression escalate to physical fights. Beavers are typically docile toward humans, but will bite if cornered or harassed.

Beavers also communicate using scent from two sources, the anal scent glands and the castor sacs, both of which are located just inside the anus. Secretions from anal scent glands may be deposited alone or in combination with castor secretions and have been shown to communicate kinship and gender. Castoreum is created when urine mixes with organic compounds in the castor sacs; this is deposited on grass tufts, on mounds created from debris dragged up from the bottom of their ponds, and occasionally on dry materials scraped together on land. Once a mound is created—and some are over a foot tall—a beaver walks over it and drags its anus across the top to deposit castoreum. The distinctive odor of castoreum can be smelled at considerable distances, even by the comparably poor noses of humans.

Scent mounds are primarily thought to mark territorial boundaries, since beavers can identify the individual that constructed them. Scent mounds are also most often constructed and maintained in late winter and spring, when transient beavers are roaming about looking to establish their own territories. Transient beavers generally avoid areas where scent mounds exist. Should a trespassing beaver leave a mound within a colony's territory, the resident adult male will obliterate it and/or over-mark it with his own scent. Foreign scent mounds can even elicit hissing and tail-slapping from resident animals as if the interloper himself were still present.

A beaver may create more than 100 mounds within its territory along dams, trails, and the shores of ponds and rivers. The density of scent mounds also increases with the density of beavers in a given area. If a beaver colony is in close proximity to other beaver colonies, they use mounds to create an olfactory fence between them. Males create scent mounds far more frequently than females, though all members of the colony create them.

COURTSHIP AND MATING

Beavers are typically monogamous, though on occasion a male may mate with two females in a colony. Pair bonds endure for their entire lives, or until one of the pair dies, at which point the single animal seeks a new partner. Beavers mate once each year, typically in January or February. Copulation often occurs in the water but may also occur in a bank burrow or lodge. Gestation is typically 15 weeks, and the kits are born in May or June.

DEVELOPMENT AND DISPERSAL OF YOUNG

Females give birth to 3 or 4 kits in the lodge and often in the company of the adult male and other members of the colony. The size of the litter correlates with the health of the female, the availability of foods, and the severity of winter weather. Beaver kits are born covered in fur, with their eyes partially to fully open and their incisors clearly showing. They can walk and swim just moments after birth, and they will nibble at leaves at only 4 days of age. They begin to groom themselves at 1 week and travel outside the lodge as young as 2 weeks old. Mothers continue to groom their kits beyond this time and may be seen flipping them over and over while combing their entire bodies with their claws. Juveniles are completely weaned in 6 to 8 weeks.

Young beavers disperse along waterways at 2 years of age, typically with the birth of a new litter in the spring, when water tables are higher and facilitate safer and easier travel. Typical dispersal distances are 10 miles (16 km) but may be as far as 68 miles (110 km). Young animals do not breed for the first time until their second winter, and they reach sexual maturity between 1.5 and 3 years of age.

Growth in beavers varies geographically. In the far north, beavers grow only in the warmer summer months and stop growing at approximately 3.5 years old. Southern beavers that bask in warmer temperatures for the duration of the year continue to grow throughout the year and may continue to grow for much of their lives.

INTERACTIONS AMONG BEAVERS

Beavers live and work in extended family units of 4 to 8 animals called colonies, maintaining one or more ponds or a section of river or stream. The colony is typically composed of one monogamous, mating pair, their offspring of the previous year, and the newborn offspring of the current year. Thus the mating pair tends to remain in a given territory for a long time, while their young disperse as they mature.

INTERACTIONS WITH OTHER SPECIES

Beavers are not simply inhabitants of their ecosystems—they also shape them through the excavation of canals, harvesting of woody plants, and the building of dams. When beavers dig canals and trenches in order to transport logs and facilitate harvesting farther from the pond, they distribute water across the landscape. They often eat all the hardwoods near their water and extirpate their favorite species. Conifers and other trees they do not harvest increase in prevalence and come to dominate old ponds. This may either hasten or impede the natural process of succession and can create patches of monoculture.

Beaver dams slow currents, reducing erosion above them, but increasing it below. Dams raise water tables, collect soil deposits in ponds, and alter seasonal stream dynamics and temperatures. Flooding kills surrounding trees and other vegetation, creating habitat for numerous insects, cavity-nesting flycatchers, and wood ducks. It also furnishes platforms for the stick nests of egrets and herons. Sediments and organic materials accumulate in beaver ponds and create reservoirs of nitrogen, potassium, calcium, and other minerals on the landscape. Ponds provide habitat for waterfowl, fish, invertebrates, reptiles, and amphibians that propagate in pools, at the expense of those that inhabit faster moving water. Spotted sandpipers, common snipe, blackbirds, Canada geese, mallards, and hooded mergansers are among the birds that increase in density in the presence of beaver ponds. In addition, beaver ponds become vital stopovers for countless bird species during the fall and spring migrations.

Ponds shift aquatic insect assemblages, with a decrease in fast-water species such as black flies, scraping mayflies, and net-spinning caddis flies, and an increase in slow-water caddis flies, dragonflies, and damselflies. Beavers also influence fish diversity on the landscape. There has been concern that beavers may limit trout distribution in warmer climates, because water that sits in beaver ponds absorbs heat. Pond temperatures may increase beyond the thermal tolerances of trout, decreasing available trout habitat in the overall system. In cooler climates, however, trout benefit from beaver ponds and their deeper, warmer eddies during winter. Juvenile coho salmon, too, are found in beaver ponds more often than in any other stream habitat, and juvenile coho in beaver ponds grow faster and larger than juveniles in stream habits uninhabited by beavers.

Moose heavily utilize beaver ponds for summer foraging and to some extent compete with beavers for woody forage in winter. Bears, elk, and deer graze in summers around beaver ponds as well, where lush vegetation often rings the pond. Muskrats move in to feed upon freshwater mussels and pond vegetation, and mink and river otters move into beaver ponds to hunt crayfish and fish.

Beaver dams continue to affect the larger ecological community long after the beavers have moved on. Unmaintained dams allow for a gradual drop in the water level, and rich nutrients in the sediments settle and create an alluvial plain. Plants quickly recolonize the enriched soils to form what are often referred to as "beaver meadows." These meadows remain rich in grasses and forbs and resistant to woody plant invasion owing to the lack of mycorrhizal fungi in new soils.

Both occupied and abandoned beaver lodges provide shelter to numerous species. While beavers are in residence they may share their lodge with muskrats; smaller rodents, from mice to woodrats, may construct nests within their outer walls. While the interior of one winter lodge was being monitored in northern Minnesota, two muskrats shared the inner chamber throughout the winter, until a mink appeared inside the lodge, killed one of them, and dragged it away into the water. The remaining muskrat remained a tenant through the duration of the winter season. Bears sometimes appropriate abandoned lodges for hibernation, and other animals, including wolves and bobcats, use abandoned lodges as dens in which to raise their young.

Other than humans, wolves are the most significant predator of beavers. In some areas, as much as 50 percent of a wolf's summer diet may be composed of beavers. Other predators of adult beavers include cougars, wolverines, otters, coyotes, bobcats, lynx, fishers, alligators, and bears. On an island in Lake Superior, resident Black Bears heavily hunted beavers as they became more abundant, digging into 18 of the 26 known beaver lodges on the island.

Desert Kangaroo Rat
Dipodomys deserti, and Allies

When you are exploring dune habitats in the Southwest, make sure to explore at night, too, for kangaroo rats are not only easy to see but also easy to approach and catch. A kangaroo rat mesmerized by your flashlight's brilliance will often sit quietly and allow you to gently pick it up by the scruff of its neck or be cupped in both hands. They generally won't bite unless they are roughly handled.

The genus name for kangaroo rats is *Dipodomys* and comes from several Greek roots: *di* means "two," *podos* means "feet," and *myos* means "mouse." Thus we have a group of small rodents that hop about on two feet, kangaroo-like, rather than four. Other than humans, kangaroo rats and kangaroo mice are the only mammals in North America that frequently use a bipedal form of locomotion.

ACTIVITY AND MOVEMENT

DAILY

Kangaroo rats are almost strictly nocturnal. They spend their days within their burrow systems, which they sometimes plug to block out predators and the heat of the desert sun. Burrows of Desert Kangaroo Rats are large, conspicuous holes between 3 and 4 inches (7.5–10 cm) high, and sometimes larger. Look for them adjacent to creosote bushes and other dune shrubs. The roots of these plants hold the sand in place, reinforcing the tunnel systems. Tunnels typically remain within several feet of the surface, but they may descend to depths of 5 feet (1.6 m) before they terminate in a nesting chamber and several storerooms for seeds.

Each night they emerge aboveground to forage for two to three hours. Their movements may radiate hundreds of yards in any direction from their burrow entrances as they search out seeds on the landscape. In general, their peak activity is just after dusk, when seeds dropped during the day have not been gathered by competitors and the moon has yet to rise and better reveal them to predators. Moonrise, however, influences foraging, and on evenings when the moon rises early, they may delay their exits from their burrows. A second peak of activity occurs just before dawn, after the coldest part of the night has passed.

Desert Kangaroo Rats live their entire lives at three speeds: slow bounds, hops, and fast jumps. When foraging and exploring, they move on all four feet like rabbits and squirrels, with their hind feet passing to the outside of their front feet in a slow bounding gait. Their tails drag along on the ground behind them as they sniff and search out seeds on

When fleeing, their modified hops become erratic, zigzagging jumps up to 8 feet (2.5 m) in length. Their tails are long and held out behind them, functioning something like a rudder and providing balance. The irregularity of their jumps can confuse predators, as does their ability to fling their tails to one side and change their orientation in midair; changing the position of their bodies enables them to launch in a new direction the moment they touch ground. Should a kangaroo rat be caught away from a burrow, it seeks shelter in any vegetative cover, and then flattens itself in the sand, hoping to be overlooked.

SEASONAL

Their nest is a spherical bed of grasses that keep them warm during the coldest parts of the night and cool during the hottest times of day. When sleeping in their burrows during cool weather, kangaroo rats curl up in tight balls with their heads tucked partially beneath their bodies. During the warmer months they may lie on either their sides or their backs to stretch out and minimize heat retention.

Flash floods sometimes occur in desert habitats, but kangaroo rats are excellent swimmers. Their hind legs are just as useful when navigating strong currents as they are on solid earth. Several species of kangaroo rats are also able to climb trees and shrubs, though they are awkward at it and rarely do so.

FOOD AND FORAGING

Kangaroo rats emerge from their burrows after dark to forage for seeds and insects. They are primarily granivorous, meaning seed-eating, though up to half their diet may be composed of insects and insect larvae during the summer months.

The burrow and trails of a Desert Kangaroo Rat.
© Mark Elbroch

the surface of the sand. They rise up on their hind limbs, lift their tails high, and hop in kangaroo fashion when traveling from place to place. While commuting, they move in straight lines to their destinations on regularly traveled routes, which lie like highways connecting homes to supermarkets.

Postures in kangaroo rats: (a) the elongate form signals curiosity, alertness, and some tension; (b) a relaxed, rounded form; (c) an alert animal. Drawn after Eisenberg, 1963, *The Behavior of Heteromyid Rodents*. University of California Publications on Zoology. Used with permission.

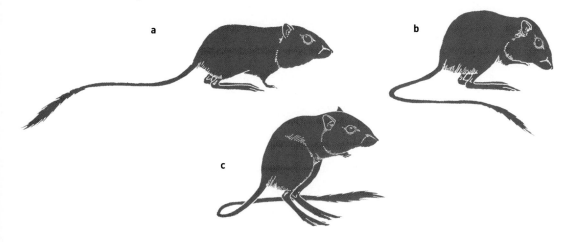

These provide protein and other nutrients and are a critical source of moisture in desert environments. However, proteins also require water to digest, and thus cost them more than dry carbohydrates, upon which they can survive without any water at all. Though larger than chipmunks, Desert Kangaroo Rats sustain themselves on some of the smallest seeds, collected from grasses, forbs, and desert shrubs.

Kangaroo rats locate seeds by scent and then harvest them in one of two ways, either by cutting seed heads and fruits directly from the bush or plant and then extracting the seeds, or by digging up and sifting seeds from the sand. Their shortened forelimbs and sharp, fine claws are useful adaptations for such endeavors. Once they have accumulated the small seeds at their feet, they shovel them into their large, external cheek pouches at incomprehensible speeds—10 armloads per second in Desert Kangaroo Rats. They keep their mouths slightly open between shovel loads to maintain tension on their pouches and keep the seeds from falling out. Rapid seed collection and the ability to efficiently carry seeds to their burrows to eat minimizes a kangaroo rat's foraging time aboveground, where they are extremely vulnerable to predators.

The Desert Kangaroo Rat and other large kangaroo rat species make one large underground seed cache within their burrow system. Other, smaller kangaroo rats and pocket mice scatter numerous smaller caches within their home range, though most often around their burrow entrances. Caching also varies among individuals and can depend on environmental and population conditions. When their population density is high and pilfering by conspecifics is inevitable, Merriam's Kangaroo Rats (*D. merriami*) scatter-hoard all of their seeds in numerous smaller caches near their burrows. When pilfering is less intense, they may scatter-hoard only a portion of their reserves and instead store the remainder in a large cache in their burrows. Both pocket mice and kangaroo rats will steal seed caches from other members of their family, and there are even reports of kangaroo rats digging up and stealing the seed caches of harvester ant colonies.

Kangaroo rats depend on seasonal foods, and caching surplus seeds allows them to survive through times when food is scarce. It also removes food from potential competitors and is thus a competitive strategy for survival. However, the mechanisms of seed storage remain unclear. When researchers collect and store seeds in similar conditions to that of kangaroo rat burrows and other rodents, the seeds tend to germinate. They are still trying to comprehend how their seed stores extend their shelf life and remain a viable long-term food source.

HABITAT AND HOME RANGE

Desert Kangaroo Rats are burrow-dwelling rodents inhabiting the driest, harshest environments in North America. They thrive where even most kangaroo rats cannot, because of their ability to live long periods without any surface water. Deep sand dunes and low shrubs in areas of the scantest rainfall provide them all the refuge they need. Look for their tracks and signs in the sand dunes of the Mojave Desert National Preserve, Death Valley National Park, and other harsh desert environments of southern California, southern Nevada, western Arizona, and northernmost Baja California and Mexico.

The exact size of a Desert Kangaroo Rat's home range is still being determined, but it is roughly 3,200 to 4,300 square feet (300–400 m²). Kangaroo rats are solitary creatures, yet they tend to be clumped in loose colonies across the landscape. They each maintain several burrows within a home range filled with numerous empty burrows. Densities of Desert Kangaroo Rats vary with given regions but range from 3 to 8 animals per acre (0.4 ha) of habitat.

COMMUNICATION

Kangaroo rats have an acute sense of smell and employ scent-marking as a nonconfrontational means of communicating with other kangaroo rats. One method is sand or dust-bathing. When sand bathing, they till up the earth's surface by digging with their forepaws and then slide into the sand, like otters into water. They start with a cheek and run the length of one side of their body across the ground. They also drag their anus along the ground near their burrow or before engaging in a sand bath to deposit secretions from their perineal glands. Kangaroo rats also urinate regularly at scent posts, and Desert Kangaroo Rats create latrines where scats accumulate. At latrines they often rub their cheeks and sides on nearby objects, whether they be the dead branches of a shrub or some novel item such as an abandoned glove. All of these marked areas provide sites where information on neighboring kangaroo rats, including sexual status and availability, can be checked without direct communication or conflict between them.

Vocalizations are poorly documented in free-ranging kangaroo rats. Observers have heard a number of screeching calls and squeals, though their meanings are still a mystery. Animals defending a nest or territory will sometimes give a low growl. Young animals raised in captivity are reported to produce four distinct sounds: faint peeps when being groomed, false suckling noises when removed from the teat, a sharp squeak when roughly handled, and a "scratchy whine" when they

On the left, a kangaroo rat signals submission; on the right, the animal on the left acts submissively to the dominant animal. Drawn after Eisenberg, 1963, *The Behavior of Heteromyid Rodents*. University of California Publications on Zoology. Used with permission.

are separated from the mother or their littermates. Females respond to whines by searching for, finding, and carrying their youngster back to the litter.

The most distinctive means of communication among kangaroo rats is foot-drumming, during which one hind foot repeatedly strikes the ground in rapid succession. Not all kangaroo rats foot-drum, and there seems to be a correlation between body size and the frequency with which they communicate through foot-drumming. The smallest kangaroo rats rarely exhibit ritualized foot-drumming, and among medium-sized kangaroo rats it is only rudimentary. The largest kangaroo rat species often use long series of rapid drumming in varied circumstances, yet even among the largest species, some species foot-drum more than others. Desert Kangaroo Rats foot-drum for a quick 3 to 5 beats and rarely repeat the performance in sequence. Banner-tailed Kangaroo Rats (*D. spectabilis*) include 11 to 23 beats per episode in long sequences that they repeat for long durations. But it is the Giant Kangaroo Rats (*D. ingens*) that win the prize, at 30 to 80 beats per session. However, giants do not often repeat their sequence as many times as Banner-tailed Kangaroo Rats, except when confronting a predator.

Foot-drumming appears to play a role in long-distance displays and may function to establish and advertise territories much like the songs of birds. Banner-tailed and Giant Kangaroo Rats respond to a neighbor's foot-drumming with a round of drumming of their own. These animals recognize the distinctive rhythm of their immediate neighbors, and their response is especially energetic and long when they hear the drumming of an unfamiliar animal. Foot-drumming also tends to precede charges and physical aggression in territorial disputes.

Foot-drumming also plays a role in encounters with predators, including snakes and Kit Foxes. When kangaroo rats spot a snake they rush in, make their presence known, and then back off to a safe distance and begin drumming. Foot-drumming may demonstrate vigor and athleticism or simply alert a predator that it has lost the element of surprise. Either way it seems to tell the predator that the jig is up and encourages them to move on. In some cases, however, hungry snakes cue in on foot-drumming and stalk the animal responsible.

COURTSHIP AND MATING

Numerous kangaroo rat and pocket mouse species follow boom-bust cycles of reproduction. When rainfall is frequent and winter annuals produce ample seeds, females may have several litters in a given year. In droughts, females may raise only a single litter or none at all. The breeding season for Desert Kangaroo Rats typically begins in January, with litters born as early as February, and may stretch until July following moist winters.

Males of some kangaroo rat species foot-drum to compete with other males over mates. Others engage in physical combat. Reproductive behavior starts when a male follows a female in estrus. He finds and follows her by sniffing the sand over which she has just passed; her scent secretions relay her breeding status and condition. If the female is not receptive, she'll respond with physical violence, as if the male were an intruder in her territory. In several species of kangaroo rats, unreceptive females have been observed killing males. However, if she is receptive, she drags her anus along the sand and dust-bathes to advertise her availability and readiness. The male then moves up next to her and grooms her back with his forefeet and teeth. During this grooming the female suddenly freezes in an elongate posture with her tail end raised, or she may charge and strike the male first, and then assume the same position. The male grooms her again and bites the back of her neck as he mounts.

A Desert Kangaroo Rat. Note the tiny front feet with large claws and the much larger hind feet they use to leap about. © *Mark Elbroch*

A successful copulation may take several minutes, and several failed attempts may precede a success. When copulation is complete in Desert Kangaroo Rats and others, a gelatinous plug forms in the female, thwarting any further attempts by competitors to mate with her.

DEVELOPMENT AND DISPERSAL OF YOUNG

The day before the female gives birth she becomes highly active, caching seeds and building up the nest in which she will give birth. After a gestation of 30 to 31 days the female stretches more and more frequently until parturition occurs. During delivery she uses her sharp incisors and tiny forelimbs to pull forth each of her 2 to 3 neonates (sometimes as many as 6). They are born completely naked except for a few tactile hairs, with ears and eyes closed, and lacking incisors.

She licks each young one clean and then consumes her placenta. Desert Kangaroo Rats have also been observed dragging their newborns across the floor of their burrows to break the umbilical cord. The newborns lie on their back and lightly kick at the underside of their mother while they nurse, while simultaneously their mother cleans their undersides of feces and urine. Their ears open at 12 days of age and their eyes at 16 days. Though not exceptionally large at first, in the first 24 days the growth of their hind feet outpaces that of the rest of their body. When the female leaves her burrow to forage during the night, she plugs the entrance behind her to prevent her offspring from wandering and to keep out potential predators.

At approximately 3 weeks of age siblings can be observed grooming each other. Juveniles are weaned between 15 and 25 days, reach sexual maturity in just 60 days, and attain full adult body weight at approximately 85 days of age. After weaning, juveniles begin making excursions beyond the burrow and by 1 month of age are moving considerable distances from the burrow entrance.

INTERACTIONS AMONG KANGAROO RATS

Kangaroo rats are extremely territorial and typically very aggressive, yet there is some evidence suggesting that neighboring animals with familial bonds may be tolerated more often than those who are unrelated. When two animals of the same species encounter each other and territoriality is not at issue, they approach each other slowly, with eyes half-closed, bodies elongated, and ears back. Then they make contact nose to nose, and may turn their heads to join teeth, in what appears like kissing. Alternatively, the animals circle up, nose to anus, and they may move in circular fashion, each chasing the other's behind. Then they follow up by nuzzling each other's cheeks, ears, and heads. If, after a nose-to-nose exchange, one of the pair assumes the dominant, upright position and extends its forelimbs, the other, subordinate animal places its head under the forelimbs of the first, partially closing its eyes.

Aggressive encounters typically start in a somewhat upright position. The more upright they are, the less likely they are to rush their opponent, which may be any small mammal or another member of the same species. Encounters may begin with

A Desert Kangaroo Rat caught away from its burrow hunkers low in an attempt to escape notice.
© *Mark Elbroch*

foot-drumming or, in the case of Desert Kangaroo Rats, kicking sand at the intruder, and then may escalate to physical violence. Desert Kangaroo Rats tend to skip the foot-drumming and rush trespassers with little forewarning. They strike the animal with forelimbs and body. Kangaroo rats box each other, kangaroo-style, punching with the forelimbs, and then grapple and wrestle, rolling about on the desert sands. When one animal finally turns tail and runs, the other pursues and attempts to bite the retreating animal on the rump.

INTERACTIONS WITH OTHER SPECIES

Kangaroo rats and pocket mice coexist in a given habitat through complex relations. Though kangaroo rats dominate smaller pocket mice in direct encounters and drive them away from food sources, pocket mice often pilfer kangaroo rat larders enough to sustain themselves.

Predators of kangaroo rats are diverse. Snakes are among the greatest threats to kangaroo rats, as they can enter their burrows easily and stealthily, and hawks and owls are regular predators while kangaroo rats are out and about. Snakes and owls pose complementary threats to kangaroo rats. Owls strike from a long way off and, as visual hunters, are most effective on moonlit nights when movement betrays their victims. Snakes, on the other hand, are easily avoided if seen by kangaroo rats, so they are most successful hunting kangaroo rats on the darkest nights. One of the unique characteristics of kangaroo rats is their massive auditory bullae, which are bony structures in the ear that house resonating chambers especially suited for hearing and interpreting low-frequency sounds. When placed in complete darkness with an owl or a rattlesnake,

kangaroo rats hear the faintest sounds of their strikes and often escape at the last moment with high, vertical jumps.

Kit Foxes, badgers, and coyotes dig kangaroo rats out of their burrows and opportunistically catch foraging animals. Desert Kangaroo Rats are an important prey species for endangered Kit Foxes, and their tails litter the outside of fox dens each spring. Desert Kangaroo Rats are suspicious of new and mysterious objects in their home ranges and react in predictable manner—by kicking sand at it to see if it responds. Researchers who have attempted to catch these creatures have sometimes found their traps buried by morning.

Sparring, or boxing, form. Drawn after Eisenberg, 1963, *The Behavior of Heteromyid Rodents*. University of California Publications on Zoology. Used with permission.

Meadow Vole
Microtus pennsylvanicus, and Allies

OTHER NAMES: meadow mouse, field mouse.

Meadow Voles play keystone roles in maintaining open fields and delaying natural succession; they are also a fundamental part of the food chain. They influence which trees develop and where they do so within old fields, and they reduce the rate at which trees establish themselves. They selectively girdle and kill specific tree saplings and concentrate their foraging upon seedlings and saplings in areas where they are provided overhead cover. At high densities, voles can essentially stop new trees from establishing in old fields, maintaining the field habitat upon which they and many other species rely. *Microtus* is derived from the Greek roots *micro* ("small") and *otus* ("ear").

ACTIVITY AND MOVEMENT

DAILY

Meadow Voles are active throughout the day and night, and at any given time 50 percent of a Meadow Vole population is active. In areas of dense cover voles are more active during daylight hours than night, and where cover is sparse the opposite is true. Moon cycles influence vole activity, with more activity during the darkness of the new moon and the least activity when the bright full moon is not obscured by cloud cover, betraying their activities to predators. In species living where there is a long dry period each year, such as the California Vole (*M. californicus*), daily activity varies seasonally. When the rains begin in the winter, voles are most active during the day, or at night when cover conditions are less favorable. During the driest times of year, voles are most active at dawn and dusk when dew is more likely to be present.

The front and back legs of voles are equal in size to each other, unlike those of many mice, which have more developed hind legs to propel them forward in bounding gaits. Meadow Voles, and indeed most voles, travel their network of trails in a swift trotting gait. This style of movement is most efficient within the world of voles, where great networks of paths are laid out like streets in a neighborhood. Trails are typically hidden beneath vegetation or snow, and they are kept clean and wear smooth with use. Short legs and trotting makes sense where obstacles are few and within cover where jumping might cause an animal to hit its head. Watching a vole navigate its runway system helps one understand how well suited to their environment they've become. They trot smoothly at lightning speeds, like elongated bullets on tracks. Their bodies flex and bend to make sharp corners with hardly any slowing down, and only contract again into small rounded rodents when they pause to assess for dangers or to forage. Meadow Voles tunnel through green vegetation much like an otter swims through water. Their long, sinuous shapes snake through greenery with amazing speed, creating the tunnels they so need, with periodic stops to pop up through matted grass as if surfacing from water, to quickly assess their environment.

Meadow Voles are competent and comfortable swimmers and are common in moist areas near surface water. If living near calm waters, they may swim on daily foraging trips, accessing food they otherwise could not reach. Where Meadow Voles are comfortable navigating either grass or water, they are not competent climbers. Meadow Voles can climb, but only rarely do so, preferring to forage on the ground. This is in marked contrast to mice and other species of voles that are expert climbers. There are several arboreal vole species in the Pacific Northwest, which may go their entire lives living high in Douglas fir trees and never touch the ground.

SEASONAL

Meadow Voles use nests throughout the year and maintain their foraging patterns throughout the seasons. Voles build their nests within cover that also provides some structural support, and they use any available resources. During the warmer months they might take cover in a tightly matted grass clump or beneath a piece of abandoned

The runs and feeding areas of Meadow Voles exposed by receding snows. The gray rectangle is a small garden plot, the black represents the vole runs, and the two small speckled globular circles are surface nests made of grasses.

A Meadow Vole peeks out from within the green layer of an open meadow. © *Mark Elbroch*

plywood. During the warmer months, voles often build nests in shallow underground cavities, where they are more difficult for their numerous predators to detect. If you follow their trails you are bound to find some that disappear into the earth. Voles create round grass nests about the size of a softball or slightly larger, and they usually have worn trails leading to and from them. Nests often have a latrine near an entrance; voles keep the insides of their nests very clean. The nests themselves are simple affairs and have but one simple central chamber in which they huddle to stay warm.

During winter in the North, where snows may blanket the earth for many months each year, voles often build their nests on the ground, where they are kept safe from detection within a layer of snow. Spring melts reveal them, so look for nests in open fields just after the snows have departed and before they have had time to degrade. Vole nests are almost always made of grass, yet they can be made of other materials as well. One nest in Massachusetts that was discovered after a bobcat had excavated it from the snow was completely constructed from the soft hair and spiky quills of a porcupine, the carcass of which lay rotting several yards away.

Vole activities continue unabated beneath the snow, and they quickly establish a network of runways within the snow layer to facilitate foraging. They also use the snow layer to forage higher than they can during the summer, and evidence in the form of teeth marks high on woody stems will appear when the snows recede. They may also excavate underground passages and use their snow tunnels to accommodate the backfill, as do pocket gophers in the West. When snows melt in the spring, tubes of earth may be seen upon the surface, dissolving quickly in the spring rains.

Meadow Voles disperse throughout the year and, while traveling in search of suitable open habitat, may be seen or caught in forested habitats. Summer dispersers are more frequently female and winter dispersers more often male.

FOOD AND FORAGING

Meadow Voles have been recorded eating a great diversity of forbs, grasses, and sedges in their preferred habitats. Along their runs you will find areas where they have been foraging green shoots and cut them short close to the ground. The tiny feet of Meadow Voles are remarkably dexterous. They nip white clover stalks at their base and then sit back on their haunches to eat the entire stalk and leaves much like we would a very large carrot. Voles also eat a wide variety of root bulbs, from tiny cinquefoils to massive Jerusalem artichokes, and will even store them in underground chambers for the winter months. At other times they will attack and consume roots from below like pocket gophers, and their work can result in entire rose bushes tipping over when touched.

Meadow Voles eat the cambium layer of various woody plants and trees during the winter months, especially when vole populations are high and vole-to-vole competition is intense. They often girdle saplings and the lowest branches of bushes as high up as the snowpack allows them to feed undetected. They feast opportunistically on storm-broken branches that drop to the ground or trees cut to clear trails. The uppermost branches of a tree have a much thinner bark layer that they need to penetrate in order to eat the cambium layer.

Meadow Voles also eat insects and fungi and will occasionally feed from animal carcasses. Voles feed intensively in short bouts throughout the day and alternate these with rest periods. Most often while in repose, voles practice coprophagy. They eat their own feces so that plant materials make a second trip through the digestive tract to be better broken down and assimilated. They do this by bending over to retrieve pellets with their teeth directly from their anus before the feces ever hit the ground.

HABITAT AND HOME RANGE

Meadow Voles are the most widespread of the voles, occurring in the open habitats across Canada and throughout most of Alaska. In the East they are common as far south as Georgia, and in the West they follow the course of the Rocky Mountains into Colorado, where they occur throughout most of the state, and into northern New Mexico. Along the West Coast, the closely related and very similar California (*M. californicus*) and Long-tailed (*M. longicaudus*) Voles occur in similar habitats.

The Meadow Vole, like many closely related species, is a creature of open habitat. Ideal vole habitat includes a dense mat of vegetation, to provide the structure and protection for their tunnel systems, and the diverse greenery upon which they dine. Old fields, fallow pastures, and roadside edges are all inhabited by Meadow Voles. They also thrive in moist habitats such as those near ponds or in riparian areas or bogs.

Home ranges of Meadow Voles vary from 0.04 to 0.86 acres (0.016–0.35 ha), yet they defend only a tiny portion of their range, often only up to 7.7 yards (7 m) in diameter. Summer ranges are smaller than winter; home ranges in meadows are larger than those in marshes; and as vole densities increase, their home ranges decrease.

COMMUNICATION

Scent communication is highly developed in Meadow Voles. It is critical to the process that leads solitary males and females to meet at the appropriate moment when females are in estrus and receptive. Sexual status, health, age, and diet information are all included in scats, urine, and secretions left by rubbing the anogenital region. Both males and females linger longest to investigate scent posts created by the opposite sex. When a Meadow Vole discovers a scent mark of the other sex, it often marks atop or alongside with scents of its own. In this way males and females keep tabs on each other without actually meeting, and when females are in heat, males use their scent marks to track them down. Males may also begin to self-groom their anogenital region after they discover a female's scent, which may increase the broadcast of their own scents or increase the production of the glandular secretions they deposit. Territorial females also scent atop or adjacent to scents of other adult females they encounter, which reinforces territorial boundaries.

Both males and females are attracted to the scent marks left by males rubbing their flanks on objects, but perhaps for different reasons. Females may be sexually driven, while males are aggressively motivated. Male-male agonistic interactions increase around estrous females, and many of their attacks are at the flanks of their opponents. In Montane Voles (*M. montanus*), males attack the glands in their own species as well as those in other voles with which they battle.

Glandular secretions are difficult to see in the field, and so is urine in anything but the driest conditions. Calcareous (calcium-rich) deposits formed by accumulated vole urine can be found in habitats and seasons of infrequent rains. They might be found at cracks in the earth where voles move underground, at burrow entrances, and upon raised objects of earth, where multiple animals mark repeatedly over time. Vole scats also accumulate at trail junctions and upon raised objects along travel routes. Novel objects are often marked with feces, and researchers exploit this behavior to estimate vole numbers. They place small tile squares at intervals along trails and return up to a week later to count the scats placed upon them.

Voles are also particularly vocal during intraspecific agonistic encounters, and you will hear them squeaking and tussling if you sit patiently and quietly in fields where they are numerous. Voles squeak defiantly, bite, and urinate red when under stress or being handled. Voles are brawlers, and nearly every adult will show nicked ears and/or scars from fights.

Infants of several voles have also been recorded producing ultrasonic vocalizations, most often when they are cold and need their mother to either move or warm them.

COURTSHIP AND MATING

Meadow Voles can breed throughout the year, though summer litters are largest when food is most abundant and environmental conditions are most favorable. Fall to spring litters average 14 percent smaller than summer litters, and in some regions Meadow Voles do not produce litters at all during winter months. High winter vole densities result in higher breeding rates. Where seasonality is dramatic, female Meadow Voles may extend the periods in between litters. Breeding females are territorial and aggressive and maintain areas exclusive of other adult females. Yet when females are not breeding, they may intermingle peacefully. Males, on the other hand, are not territorial nor tied to any particular patch of habitat. They overlap the most with other males near estrous females. When a female is in estrus, males become aggressive toward each other and fight for breeding rights.

When a male discovers the scent mark of a female in estrus, he tracks her by scent and moves as fast as he can to catch up with her. Ready males exhibit swollen gonads that drag and bounce along the ground in their frenzy to find the female in heat. Meadow Voles are promiscuous: males and females both breed with more than one partner during a breeding cycle. During copulation, females sometimes run away during intromission (insemination), reducing the amount of sperm that any single male can deliver. In mating with multiple males, a female carries sperm from each, and running away during intercourse may effectively reduce a particular male's contribution to the litter. In a third of all Meadow Vole pregnancies, different males father different offspring within the same litter. This multiple paternity can be advantageous to the female in reducing male aggression toward her and her offspring and broadening their genetic pool. Ovulation in the female is induced by coitus and occurs between 12 and 18 hours after intercourse.

After the birth of a litter, a female may exhibit postpartum estrus, becoming receptive to mating almost immediately. An estrous female will scent-mark more frequently, especially marking atop male scents she locates within her territory. When environmental conditions facilitate large litters and higher survival rates, voles can breed quickly.

DEVELOPMENT AND DISPERSAL OF YOUNG

Gestation is 21 days, after which tiny, pink, hairless young are born in a constructed nest of grasses or other soft vegetation. Typical litters are 4 to 6, though as many as 11 nestlings have been recorded in a single litter. Birth has been observed by several researchers and apparently varies tremendously

Young Meadow Voles in a surface nest of interwoven dry grasses. © *Daniel Bradford*

from animal to animal. In one case, 6 young were born within 40 minutes, after which the female constructed a nest in which she placed her young. At the other end of the spectrum, one researcher reported a vole taking 7 hours to produce a similarly sized litter.

Nestlings begin to grow fur on their fourth day, and they are nearly fully covered by 1 week of age. Their eyes and ears open at approximately 8 days, and they are quickly weaned at 12 to 14 days. Newborns develop rapidly, at a rate matched only by their death rate. By 2 weeks, 40 percent of litters have died or been killed, and within 30 days 90 percent of litters are lost, many of them to predation.

Male infanticide (adult males killing nestlings) has been recorded in several vole species but is poorly understood. Postpartum estrus in females attracts males to them while nestlings are vulnerable.

In Meadow Voles, the father(s) of the litter may be allowed to visit and spend time with the litter, but it appears that unrelated males are more dangerous.

INTERACTIONS AMONG MEADOW VOLES

Meadow Vole populations cycle, with peaks in abundance and density every 2 to 5 years. Four years is the typical interval in the Northeast. As with lemmings, Snowshoe Hares, and other cycling herbivore populations, the driving force behind these fluctuations is still under debate. Is it driven from the bottom up by food availability, or from the top down by predation? In the predation scenario, high predator densities drive vole population crashes, which then result in population crashes of starving predators, during which voles rebound. The increased levels of stress that individuals exhibit at high density may also play a role in cyclic

A Meadow Vole caught and about to be eaten by a great blue heron. © *Rick Leche*

declines, as well as the exhaustion of food supplies, social constraints on reproduction and sexual maturation, and even reductions in immunological competency.

Male and female Meadow Voles live in separate nests and, other than during copulation, generally have little contact with each other. They are aggressive toward each other throughout the year, but even more so when animals are in heat and when population densities are high. Aggressive, dominant males maintain larger ranges but often breed less frequently than subordinate males with smaller ranges. It was once believed that adult males were responsible for suppression of the population's growth through the killing of subadults, but new evidence suggests that adult females are more aggressive toward and kill more juveniles.

INTERACTIONS WITH OTHER SPECIES

Meadow Voles share habitat with numerous small mammals. They exclude other voles, including red-backed and Montane voles, from moist grasslands where they overlap. They also limit deer and White-footed Deermouse distributions within open fields. Meadow Voles also coexist with cotton rats, rice rats, meadow jumping mice, and bog lemmings. Meadow Voles avoid scent marks and areas frequented by short-tailed shrews, which are a capable predator, thus limiting their distribution within any given meadow where shrews are abundant. Adult voles flee from approaching short-tailed shrews, but unless cornered generally survive the encounter. However, shrews can cause significant mortality within a vole population through the killing and consuming of nestlings. Adult female voles often leave their nests unattended while they forage and often flee shrews who attack nests even when young are present.

Voles have remarkably short life spans in the wild. In many populations, voles average 2 to 3 months of life, while in others they may live more than 1 year. Predators of Meadow Voles include nearly every carnivorous animal within their range. Hawks of every size and shape hunt them relentlessly during the day, and owls just as intensely at night. Foxes and coyotes "mouse" for voles throughout the year, digging adults and juveniles from their nests beneath both ground and snow. Weasels are vole specialists and pounce upon them like foxes do, as well as follow them beneath the ground to corner and catch them where larger predators cannot follow. Bobcats, lynx, martens, fishers, skunks, ringtails, housecats, numerous snakes, and many others hunt and eat voles. Even Black and Brown Bears dig up nests to devour the nestlings in a single gulp. Grizzly Bears in Yellowstone also dig up the root caches of voles, stripping them of their winter reserves.

Common Muskrat
Ondatra zibethicus

OTHER NAMES: marsh rat, mush rat, mòskwas (Abenaki), musquash (archaic English).

Muskrats are one of the most common and influential medium-sized mammals in North America and also one of the least known to the average person. Perhaps they remain so mysterious because of their secretive nature and preference for wet, mucky places few of us frequent. Perhaps it's the name "rat," which is off-putting, but muskrats are not true rats, and are most closely related to voles.

Muskrat activity is critical to the life cycle of many marshes, and for decades they have been the intended beneficiaries of extensive wetland management. They have been intensively studied in order to better maintain functional wetlands and manage their populations to support high demands for trapping. Long-term studies of muskrat populations have also contributed to landmark theoretical work in population ecology.

Ondatra is the Iroquois name for this animal and *zibethicus* is Latin for "musky-odored." The common name *muskrat* is descriptive of their appearance and smell, though it probably comes from *musquash*, an English derivative of the Abenaki word *mòskwas*.

ACTIVITY AND MOVEMENT

DAILY

Muskrats swim at and below the surface with alternating kicks of their hind legs and their forefeet drawn up under their chins. When swimming, their scaly, mostly naked tail may scull side to side, but it serves more as a rudder than for propulsion. They swim at the surface at 1 to 3 miles (1.5–5 km) per hour.

On land, muskrats move in a slow walk or a loping hop. There are reports of muskrats climbing wire fences over 2 feet (60 cm) high, and if they aren't able to climb an obstacle, they are likely to jump on or over it. While on land they spend a fair amount of time grooming the fur on which their lives depend. Females groom their suckling young as well as themselves. They lick at wounds and gnaw away infected flesh. Perhaps because of their meticulous grooming, they appear to heal well. Trapped animals sometimes gnaw off their trapped limb to free themselves, and muskrats have been captured that seem healthy other than missing one, two, or even three legs.

Most muskrats and muskrat families maintain several dwellings within their home range, and

A muskrat grooms itself.

primary dwellings are usually surface lodges or bank dens. They seem to prefer bank dens, which may be cooler in summer and warmer in winter than free-standing lodges. Perhaps most important, they are more secure against predators and easier to maintain than lodges. On the other hand, bank burrows require steep banks with abundant vegetation along slow-moving water, and sometimes these conditions are hard to find.

A bank den consists of a complex network of tunnels about 7 inches (18 cm) in diameter that may extend for over 325 feet (100 m) and reach more than 5 feet (1.5 m) below the surface of the ground. Entrances are usually 6 inches (15 cm) below the surface of the water. When water levels drop and entrances become exposed, they may be loosely blocked with clumps of vegetation. If the water level remains low, residents sometimes excavate new submerged entrances deeper down. Initially tunnels extend 10 feet (3 m) or more, angling up and away from the water table before they reach the main network of tunnels. Within the network are one or more chambers with a nest of shredded dry vegetation. The length and complexity of the tunnel system grows over time with successive years of inhabitation and the explorations of many residents. Muskrats are competent diggers, and where water levels are low they may even dig canals to facilitate aquatic access to food and lodges.

The alternative to a bank den is a lodge or "house," a conical or domed heap of vegetation that protects dry nests in one or more internal chambers. It might cover an area as large as 8 feet (2.5 m) in diameter and stand from 1.25 to 4 feet (0.4–1.3 m) tall with walls up to a foot (0.3 m) thick. It looks like a beaver lodge but much smaller, and it isn't made with logs or large sticks. A lodge is home to a pair of muskrats and, often, multiple litters of young. The mother adds a chamber for each new litter, and the older offspring may also create new alcoves. In areas with rapidly fluctuating water levels, a lodge may house multiple nest chambers, each at different heights to ensure that there is always sufficient space to rest in a dry nest above the surface of the water. All lodges typically have one or more "plunge holes" connecting the interior directly to the water.

Feeding huts are nonresidential structures that look like miniature lodges and form a protective cover over and around an internal chamber. They may rise only a foot or so (30–40 cm) above the surface of the water. There are usually 2 to 3 times as many feeding huts as lodges in a muskrat's home range. Other structures, called feeding platforms, are built-up piles of vegetation. They have no enclosed cavities but are simply a high spot built on a slight rise or floating raft where a muskrat can crawl out of the water to eat and rest, leaving an abundance of feces behind.

SEASONAL

Muskrats are primarily nocturnal. In summer they are most active around sunset and sunrise and spend most of their nights out and about. Often they return to their lodges for a few hours in the middle of the night. Muskrats are more active on cooler nights than on hot, muggy ones, but during cold winters they show more daytime activity. When active but not foraging, they patrol their territories and build and maintain their lodges, burrows, and other structures. Building can occur throughout the year but is usually associated with the onset of cooler temperatures in early autumn. Late summer and fall is when the instinctive drive to build seems to kick in for the young born early in the spring. Spring and fall are times of large individual movements as many young and subadult muskrats disperse.

Muskrats remain active all winter, but they move little, usually roaming within 50 feet (15 m) of their lodges or dens. You can tell when a muskrat den is active in the winter by looking for long lines of bubbles trapped under the ice nearby. As the muskrat swims, it exhales these bubbles, and they collect under the ice along their travel routes. Muskrats even scavenge these bubbles at later times, extending their dive times by sneaking a breath while still underwater.

Muskrats spend the winter foraging below the ice and resting and eating in their various structures. In addition to the structures discussed above, in the winter they make another structure called a "push-up." A push-up is a temporary winter feeding hut that starts when a muskrat makes a hole about 6 inches (15 cm) wide in thin ice. Then it dredges up a mass of vegetation from the pond bottom and uses

The lodge of a muskrat in a shallow cattail marsh in southern New Hampshire. © *Mark Elbroch*

it to construct a covered shelter over the hole. This mass encloses a single chamber for feeding and resting. Push-ups are generally small and ephemeral; they collapse and sink as the ice melts.

Access to numerous haulouts is important to being able to swim in cold water. Muskrats must be sufficiently warm before each dive, but the freezing water is quick to suck the heat from their bodies. They haul out frequently to warm up. As winter progresses, carbon dioxide (CO_2) builds up in the air of their lodges and dens and also in their blood. Carbon dioxide stimulates us to breathe; that irresistible urge to gulp in air when you hold your breath is caused by a minute increase in carbon dioxide in your blood. Muskrats are more tolerant of CO_2 than we are, but as it builds up over a winter and they carry less oxygen, their average dive length shortens. Winter home ranges are largely dependent on numerous push-ups and other structures in close proximity to each other, like stepping stones, so that they can frequently rest, warm up, and reach the next stop with only a short dive.

Keeping warm is the critical winter challenge for muskrats, and communal living contributes to the solution. Lodges and dens have ample room for numerous individuals, and when inside they huddle together. Huddling allows others to benefit from heat that would otherwise be lost to the environment and allows individuals to conserve their energy throughout a long, cold winter. Muskrats are

more diurnal in winter to take advantage of sun and warmer temperatures, but with lots of variation among individuals. Variable and independent activity schedules mean that there are almost always one or more individuals in the lodge passively maintaining the warm microclimate inside.

FOOD AND FORAGING

The most common foods of muskrats are the shoots, roots, bulbs, fruits, tubers, stems, and leaves of a variety of aquatic and terrestrial plants. Their actual diets vary by habitat, season, water level, population density, and the presence of predators. The most common foods across their range are bulrush (*Scirpus*), cattail (*Typha*), and arrowhead (*Sagittaria*).

Muskrats are chiefly herbivorous, but they may supplement vegetation with meat. They are highly efficient digesters of plant fiber through bacterial fermentation in the latter portion of their intestines. Dependency on bacteria limits the ability of some herbivores to switch to alternate foods; if they do switch, their bacteria may die. Muskrats can, however, eat quite large amounts of meat without any loss of their fiber-digesting ability. Muskrats need a lot of nitrogen and may supplement their vegetable diets with meat as a nitrogen source, especially in summer. Most muskrat populations are known to eat at least some snails, crayfish, saltwater crabs, freshwater mussels, clams, frogs, turtles, and fish. Stream-, reservoir-, and lake-dwelling muskrats

Note the size of the muskrat's hind feet that serve as paddles when it swims, in comparison to its small front feet. © istockphoto.com/Michael Zurawski

have the most diverse diets and also eat the most animal matter.

Muskrats eat sitting back on their haunches and balancing on their hind feet and tail. This frees their forelimbs to manipulate and deliver food to their mouth. They can't eat while they swim, so they must either stand in shallow water or haul out first. Because of the ever-present threat of predators, they usually retreat to a covered location. Feeding huts, push-ups, and some tunnels are used for eating, but they rarely eat in their lodges or dens. They gather plants by nipping them off at the base or digging them out of the mucky bottoms. Once they've gathered a plant, they swim with it in their mouth to a safe, steady spot to dine. They carry clams to shore in their forefeet. Once ashore, muskrats pry open clam shells by inserting their incisors into the crack between the halves. After they eat the visceral mass of the clam, they cast aside the shell. Middens of discarded shells can accumulate on shore, in shallow water, and outside burrows used for feeding in riverine habitats. In saltwater habitats they'll also dine on crabs, and middens of crab carapaces accumulate just like those of mussel shells.

In the winter, muskrats are largely relegated to feeding on the portions that are available below the ice. Muskrats don't usually store large quantities of food, but they make some small stockpiles. Sometimes, in a crunch, they end up eating portions of their lodges or bedding.

HABITAT AND HOME RANGE

Because of some translocations, muskrats now range throughout most of North America. They are mostly absent from the hotter, drier regions from Texas to California and completely absent from Florida and some surrounding areas.

Muskrats prefer still waters and are most commonly found in fresh water, brackish marshes, lakes, and sloughs. In many parts of their range they are strongly associated with bulrushes, cattails, or cornfields near wetlands. Wherever there is relatively shallow, slow-moving water, excellent sites for semipermanent retreats for safety, and adequate food, you are likely to find muskrats. Mucky, peaty banks and bottoms allow easy digging of tunnels and roots. They also prefer relatively stable water levels since low water exposes them to predators and lowers the availability of food. Muskrats also utilize ocean waters along the coast of Maine and elsewhere, and they may inhabit islands 20 miles (32 km) from the mainland.

Home ranges vary from year to year and location to location. Summer home ranges for marsh-dwelling muskrats are usually up to 210 feet (65 m) in diameter, and often 100 feet (30 m) or less. Average home ranges for pond-dwelling muskrats run up to 275 feet (85 m) in diameter. River-dwelling muskrats often have home ranges covering up to 585 feet (180 m) of riverbank, although they can be twice that.

Populations of muskrats cycle between peaks and declines. Peak densities in bulrush-cattail marshes are around 16 to 24 animals per acre (40–60 per ha) and perhaps as high as 40 per acre (100 per ha). "Normal" densities in the same and various other habitats are usually more like 0.4 to 4 animals per acre (1–10 per ha). Along rivers and streams, densities vary from 0.8 to 80 muskrats per mile of shoreline (0.5–50 per km).

COMMUNICATION

Muskrats are relatively social creatures, and they actively communicate with one another through vocalizations and scent. Young muskrats make a loud, insistent squeaking that draws the attention of their mothers. Quarrels between adults are accompanied by a repetitive *n-n-n-n-n* sound. The same sound accompanies courting between male and females, but louder and at a higher rate of repetition. Adults are also said to squeal, squeak, and snarl at times. When cornered they chatter their teeth, and they have been reported using a tail-slap, like that of a beaver, as an alarm.

Male and female muskrats have paired scent gland on their genitals. Those of the male are more active than the female's, especially during breeding. On the male these glands secrete an oily yellow fluid that is discharged when urinating. Muskrats often defecate randomly, usually in the water, but they also establish latrines or "defecation posts" in prominent locations. Look for their scats to adorn the tops of logs and raised hummocks of vegetation along the water's edge. Multiple animals may deposit hard, brown scat pellets at these posts. At high densities they also construct tiny piles of vegetation and earth at intervals along water edges, upon which they place several scats.

COURTSHIP AND MATING

Muskrats go through numerous estrous cycles in a year, and a healthy, well-fed female can deliver successive litters every month. In the South breeding is essentially continuous, but in the far north it only occurs between June and August. Although males occasionally have more than one mate, females appear to mate exclusively with a single male partner.

Males are generally 1 year or older when they

A muskrat forages in the shallows of a coastal marsh. © istockphoto.com/David Lewis

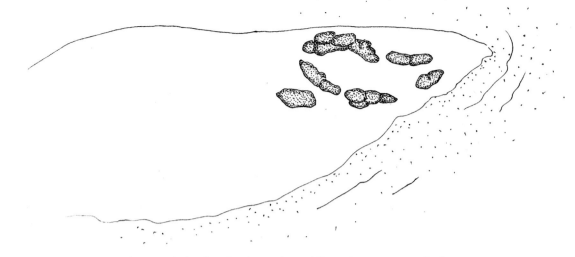

Muskrat scats on a prominent rock that breaks the surface of the water near a pond edge.

begin mating. Females are able to mate as early as 5 to 6 months, but usually do so only in the southern portion of their range. In the North the short summer means females are also 1 year old when they first breed. Breeding activity includes active scent-marking at defecation sites, houses, dens, and along trails. Experiments with captives show that exposure to scents of adult males stimulates estrus in females. The male mates with the female whose home range overlaps with his. Based on observations of captives, copulation appears to occur in shallow water and lasts about 5 minutes.

DEVELOPMENT AND DISPERSAL OF YOUNG

After a gestation of 1 month a litter of blind, naked, helpless young is born. Litter sizes may include 9 to 10 youngsters in the North, but only 3 or so in the South. They are born tiny and altricial, but they grow quickly, quadrupling their weight in the first 2 weeks. By that time they are able to walk, swim, and dive. Even when very young the offspring can cling to the mother's nipples and be carried about if necessary, but a foraging mother will leave her litter covered with debris in the nest when she sets out. As the young grow, the mother moves them by grasping their bellies in her mouth. She can dive while carrying young, but she usually swims holding them up above the surface. By the fourth week the young weigh 6 ounces (180 g) and have stopped nursing. By the time winter arrives, northern muskrats are nearly adult-sized and well equipped to survive the cold.

Young muskrats are cared for by their mother until weaning, after which they are cared for by their father. The father provides the young with food and keeps a vigilant eye while the little ones play, explore, and forage. Males that sire litters with multiple females provide the most care to the litter of their primary mate and very little care to the litters of subsequent mates. Litters of monogamous pairings receive the most paternal care.

By the time the young are weaned the mother is likely expecting a new litter. Weaned offspring may continue to live in the family lodge through the winter; the mother just builds a new chamber for her pending litter. When population density is high competition for space and food is great, and independent young may kill and eat the young of subsequent litters. Parents also sometimes kill their own young. High levels of crowding and intraspecific strife tend to encourage dispersal in the fall in addition to the more typical spring movements.

Spring dispersal occurs in March and April, and 3 times as many males disperse as females. Females are more likely to be allowed to settle in portions of their natal territories. Dispersal within a marsh or from one pond to another is usually between 600 and 1,600 feet (200–500 m) but can be as far as 1 mile (1.6 km). When the population density of muskrats is high, dispersers may have to travel far to find vacant ground for territories of their own.

INTERACTIONS AMONG MUSKRATS

Muskrats are territorial, especially during the breeding season. In the winter they are more tolerant of each other, and they may share lodges and huddle for warmth. The typical spatial pattern is for muskrats to exclude others of the same sex but to allow their territories to overlap with muskrats of the opposite sex. Usually this means that a male territory overlaps those of a few females.

Muskrats are aggressive and readily fight their rivals. Aggressive interactions, as indicated by wounds found on trapped muskrats, increase dramatically among mature animals 2 years and older. Muskrats also interact and fight more when populations are high and suitable habitat is densely populated. High levels of agitation, restlessness, and intolerance are associated with reduced breeding success and are considered one of the means by which populations are reduced when too high. Attempts at fur-farming muskrats by raising them in semi-natural, enclosed pens failed because of the aggressiveness of the muskrat toward its own kind. In one case, a large wetland tract was fenced and stocked with breeding muskrats that immediately set about fighting one another. In short order, 75 of 86 animals were dead.

INTERACTIONS WITH OTHER SPECIES

Muskrats, especially the young, are prey for a wide variety of mammalian and avian predators. Mink, raccoons, harriers, cottonmouths, foxes, coyotes, weasels, badgers, bald eagles, otters, and barn, barred, and great horned owls are all known predators of muskrats. In some areas, raccoons do extensive damage to lodges as they tear them open to access young in the nests. Various large fish like gar and bowfin have also been implicated as predators of muskrats, as have snapping turtles and bullfrogs.

Mink are commonly considered a significant predator of muskrats. Mink are smaller than mature muskrats, but they can still kill them. Muskrats swim better than mink, and if they see one coming will flee for deep water. Young muskrats in the nest are most vulnerable to mink, because the mink can easily access submerged tunnel entrances and other muskrat refuges.

Trappers have long maintained that mink and muskrat populations rise and fall together, and recently much attention has been directed at investigating the possibility that mink control muskrat populations. Analysis of the numbers of mink and muskrat pelts harvested across Canada from 1925 to 1949 show that both species' populations fluctuate through cycles of high and low numbers. Across most of Canada, muskrat populations go through 8- to 9-year cycles. The mink, too, follow 8- to 9-year cycles with their peak abundances and lowest lows coming a few years after the same in muskrats. This pattern is highly suggestive of a predator-prey system in which mink become abundant when muskrats increase but then subsequently kill and eat muskrats excessively, causing them to decline. Then mink, too, begin dying off for lack of food. In northeastern Canada, muskrat cycles are every 4 years and seem unrelated to mink. Anecdotal evidence suggests that predation by Red Foxes could be driving the muskrat declines there. The discovery of parallel cycles in the numbers of mink and muskrat is interesting, but far from conclusive. Changes in habitat, disease, and other factors could also contribute to their population cycles.

In addition to being prey, muskrats are also predators. Their feeding on clams and mussels has a significant effect on their populations. Muskrats

A muskrat grips fresh forage in its teeth as it paddles to safety to feed. © istockphoto.com/Robin Arnold

prefer larger clams and mussels, and where they feed intensively, larger ones become scarce. They forage for them in shallow water and can often completely deplete shallow shorelines of clams. In areas where some species of mussels are larger than others, muskrats target and have a greater impact on the larger species. Overall, their feeding alters the structure and dispersal of clam and mussel populations. Selective predation on larger individuals, if consistent and thorough, could become an evolutionary pressure against large size for those species.

Muskrat lodges are used by a wide range of other animals as homes and resting sites. Geese, ducks, and other water and sea birds use muskrat houses as nest platforms. Over a 2-year period in a marsh in Wisconsin, more than 70 clutches of snapping turtle eggs were found in muskrat houses. A bobcat was even once found inside a muskrat house, sadly with all four feet frozen into the ice. Mink often occupy muskrat dens and lodges, usually after they have been abandoned, but perhaps after the mink entered and killed and ate the residents.

Nutria (or coypu), a muskratlike animal from South America, can compete with and exclude muskrats from marshes. Nutria were introduced to the United States by fur ranchers, and released or escaped animals have established feral populations in the southeastern and northwestern United States and British Columbia. The diets of muskrats and nutria are broadly similar, and the larger nutria displace muskrats from shared habitat. With low demand for their fur, nutria are likely to flourish in many areas in coming years.

Muskrats have a pronounced impact on their habitats. Foraging and lodge-building can alter the distribution and abundance of aquatic plants and can speed succession from an emergent wetland dominated by plants growing thickly in the water to a marsh characterized by large expanses of open (plantless) water. As muskrats remove emergent vegetation for food and building materials, they allow more light to reach down into the water, stimulating species diversity among plants and their attendant invertebrate communities. In some cases, muskrats denude huge areas of surface and root-level vegetation. These "eat-outs" persist until water levels drop low enough to expose the mucky bottoms to increased oxygen and sunlight, which stimulates new germination and the re-emergence of the marsh plant community. Eat-outs are more common in the Southeast than the North, where winter likely limits muskrat density and shorter summers limit the potential for such tremendous feeding. Although dramatic, eat-outs are likely a natural element in a marsh's life cycle and lead to new regeneration and greater species diversity in the marsh as a whole.

Woodrats
Neotoma spp.

OTHER NAMES: packrat, trade rat.

There are 12 species of woodrats inhabiting North America north of Mexico. Collectively, they are often called packrats because they collect novel items that they discover in their environments to construct and adorn their outer nests, or middens. Old cow dung, rifle shells, bones, bottle caps, palo verde beans, bits of charcoal, small mammal skulls, chewed acorn hulls, antlers, plastic bags, rusty nails, and feathers are just a few of the items you might see jutting out between sticks in a woodrat nest. The common definition of a midden is a refuse pile, which in archaeological contexts is a collection of shells and/or bones used to study prehistoric cultures and settlements. Today, archaeologists and climatologists study not just prehistoric human middens but also those of woodrats.

Woodrats urinate atop their nests, and as their urine crystallizes it cements their assorted structural elements and collected items in place, protecting them from the elements. Woodrats are numerous in dry climates, where they often build their nests in protected rock alcoves; some nests have remained undisturbed for thousands of years. In the absence of moisture, plant and animal items collected by woodrats mummify over time and become fossil debris, preserved indefinitely. Successive generations use the same nests, providing a vital record of past environmental conditions for scientists to analyze.

Fossilized pollen, plant remains, and animal bones in woodrat nests aid in the reconstruction of prehistoric plant and animal communities; they also provide information about climate changes in the area local to the nest. Excavations and analysis of plant remains in Bushy-tailed Woodrat (*N. cinerea*) middens have revealed changes in plant communities and periods of warming and cooling dating back 3,500 years. In the Sonoran and Chihuahuan deserts, dry climates preserve animal and floral remains even longer, and excavated woodrat middens have been dated to as far back as 45,000 years. Fossilized ants found in middens betray local climate and moisture changes, and fossilized plant and animal remains, including bats, shrews, and cotton rats, have contributed much to our understanding of the dynamics of wildlife communities.

ACTIVITY AND MOVEMENT

DAILY

Woodrats are nocturnal, leaving their nests about 30 minutes before complete darkness and remain-

A White-throated Woodrat pauses above its stick nest nestled in a prickly pear cactus. © *Paul and Joyce Berquist/Animals Animals*

ing active until 30 minutes before sunrise. Woodrats are least active on nights of the full or three-quarter moon and most active during times of intermediate moonlight. They may decrease their rounds during deep cold or rain, and on occasion they forage briefly during the day. Desert-dwelling White-throated (*N. albigula*) and Desert (*N. lepida*) Woodrats confine their movements to the coolest parts of the night to avoid overheating.

Woodrats are expert climbers and readily take to branches and limbs when traveling and foraging. They appear unhurt by the dense spines of cholla cactus when they climb on them and transport segments of the plant back to their lodges. They simply groom themselves and remove any spines they happen to pick up from the cholla. They walk when exploring, trot when traveling, and run in rapid bursts up to 11 miles (17 km) an hour to cover exposed areas where predators might catch them. When walking or running, their tail is held straight out behind them and extended horizontally.

Adults respond quickly to danger by racing along memorized runs in the vicinity of their nests. They sometimes climb a tree to better view potential danger, going all the way to the top if it affords a commanding view. Mothers with young carry them to safety attached to their nipples; if a youngster falls

off, the mother grabs it and carries it in her mouth. When they need to, they retreat to their houses, or into rock crevices or under bushes and shrubs, to hide.

Woodrats tend to move in a relatively small area around their nests. They usually build their nests in relatively homogeneous habitats, where everything they need is found close at hand. Where they inhabit rocky outcrops, they commute farther from home to forage and seek mates. Eastern Woodrats (*N. floridana*) in Kansas move up to 1,070 feet (329 m) per night, but many never venture that far from their nests for their entire lives. Males travel farther than females, and sexually mature males travel the farthest of all.

During the day, woodrats typically remain in their nest (though they often make an appearance if you disturb it). Their nests are elaborate, conspicuous, and often large, and they provide them and their litters protection from predators and extremes of temperature. Woodrat nests appear in every form and every location. They often build them where there is structural support provided by tree trunks and branches, cacti, yucca leaves, abandoned buildings, rock crevices, hollow logs, or abandoned furniture. Some are also free-standing under forest canopies or constructed up to 26 feet (8 m) aboveground in tree cavities; others may be supported in branches or tucked into holes on cliffs. Construction materials include any material at hand, such as sticks and branches, cow dung, stones, parts of cacti, or any other suitable debris. White-throated Woodrats often build nests in prickly pear cacti, and they appear as loose collections of debris surrounding the living pads of the plant. Desert Woodrats also create untidy-looking nests, whereas others, including the Big-eared (*N. macrotis*) and Dusky-footed (*N. fuscipes*) Woodrats, use larger sticks and other items in their constructions, and their nests appear more tidy, interwoven, and sound.

Nests on the ground away from rocks and crevices are domed and sometimes 6 feet (2 m) in diameter and more than 5 feet (1.5 m) high. They are often used by successive generations and may accumulate several cubic yards of material with time. One nest built along a fallen log measured over 13 feet (4 m) long and 6.5 feet (2 m) wide. Captive Desert Woodrats have been observed adding 200 to 359 new items to their nests each night. They pick up and carry small items to the site in their mouth; they drag larger items. Paths around the house are cleared of debris for ease of movement. Runways radiate out from the nests toward reliable foraging areas and are essential for quick escape from predators.

Woodrats inhabit one or more nests at a time. There are up to 6 entrances passing through the prickly outer barrier, accessing the inner sanctum. There may be sleeping chambers in the outer debris, but the actual nest of soft materials in which they usually sleep is sometimes tucked in a crevice or in a burrow belowground. The inner nest is either a cup or complete sphere of soft grasses or shredded bark approximately 6 to 10 inches (15–25 cm) in diameter. Some large nests contain up to 3 small grass nests in different locations in the larger interwoven fortress.

SEASONAL

In September and October woodrats start caching food, which they do not do in spring and summer. As they forage they discriminate food based upon perishability. They consume the moist foods on the spot and cache the dry ones, eating them later in their houses. These stores, which are usually larger for large woodrats than for smaller species, may last 25 to 271 days.

FOOD AND FORAGING

Overall, woodrats are foraging generalists that consume a wide variety of mast and herbaceous vegetation. However, within each geographic region woodrats tend to specialize on specific foods

The 5-foot-tall nest of a Big-eared Woodrat in southern California. © *Mark Elbroch*

more than others. Seventy-nine percent of the summer diet of Desert Woodrats inhabiting the Gulf of California is ironwood leaves (*Olneya*), whereas coastal California populations subsist almost entirely on white sage plants (*Salvia*). In areas where Desert Woodrats can find turbinella oaks (*Quercus turbinella*), acorns dominate their diets. Big-eared and Dusky-footed Woodrats are oak specialists and much larger than Desert Woodrats. Where Big-eared overlap with Desert Woodrats they force them to shift their diets from acorns to other items.

In Kansas, the primary food for Eastern Woodrats is osage orange fruits and leaves. In various locations, they also eat the fruit of poison ivy; seeds of palmetto; bark, fruit, and seeds of sumac; seeds of redbud; mushrooms; grapes; walnuts; acorns; and some corn and wheat. White-throated Woodrats feed primarily upon cactus joints and fruit (*Opuntia* spp.) and the fruit and seeds of yuccas and junipers. Desert Woodrats feed on cacti, agaves, yuccas, juniper, and acorns. Woodrats are able to safely ingest the oxalic acid in cacti that poisons many other animals.

Most woodrats are thought to be strictly vegetarian, but there are records of woodrats eating bird eggs and the occasional insect. Desert Woodrats eat other woodrats and smaller rodents they discover caught in traps. Females of several woodrat species cache and eat bones as mineral supplements.

Woodrats do not require open water to drink; they gain sufficient moisture from dew and vegetation. White-throated and Desert Woodrats turn to foraging on yuccas and cacti during the driest times of year or during droughts to gain enough moisture to survive. They consume up to 60 percent of their body weight in cacti every day, and when droughts are hardest they can radically influence the life cycles of succulents in specific areas. During a drought year in Anzo Borrego State Park in southern California, Desert Woodrats girdled and killed nearly every flower stalk of desert agave (*Agave deserti*) over an entire mountainside.

HABITAT AND HOME RANGE

Woodrats occur throughout the United States except for the Northeast and Alaska; they are largely absent from Canada. They are associated with warmer and often drier climates, and most species occur in the western half of the United States. White-throated Woodrats exist in varied habitats from southeastern California east to central Texas, and from central Mexico north to southern Utah and Colorado. They are particularly associated with prickly pear cacti, living at the elevations where they are most abundant. They are also abundant where prickly pear can be found interspersed in pinyon pine–juniper habitats throughout the Southwest.

Desert Woodrats inhabit the driest and hottest parts of western America, including the Baja peninsula, southern California, and the deserts stretching north through Nevada and into southeastern Oregon. Desert Woodrats make their home in the Mojave and Great Basin deserts and persist with relatively less vegetative structure than other woodrats.

Woodrats inhabit home ranges of 0.04 to 0.64 acres (160–2,600 m^2). Since these estimates are two-dimensional and don't account for all the climbing that woodrats do in forested habitats, they likely underestimate the true size of their home ranges. Subadults have larger home ranges than adults, and males have larger home ranges than females because they roam in search of mates.

Densities for White-throated Woodrats have been recorded from 1 to 8 animals per 2.5 acres (1 ha). The number of nests on a site provides rough estimates for the number of woodrats in an area. Ninety-one percent of 1,700 nests were occupied in a study straddling the border of New Mexico and Arizona. Densities are largely regulated by the number of suitable sites in which to construct nests and remain safe from predation, as well as by local food abundance and quality. Densities for Desert Woodrats have been recorded as low as 1 and as high as 30 animals per 2.5 acres (1 ha), where rocks and cover were abundant.

COMMUNICATION

Other than breeding interactions, woodrats are antisocial and rely upon chemical communication as their primary means of communicating with each other. They have conspicuous ventral abdominal glands that deposit secretions that stain their fur. The gland grows largest in males and is often poorly developed in females. During the breeding season, male ventral glands swell and likely communicate much about sexual status, dominance, and territoriality. Males rub their ventral glands on rocks, sticks, nest entrances, and travel routes, sometimes exhibiting a perineal drag, wherein they splay their hind legs and literally drag their hind ends to deposit scent marks. Males also mark as an act of dominance, marking more frequently near the nests of subordinates than their own. Subordinate males mark less frequently than dominants, and they avoid marking near the nests of dominants.

Females, more often then males, roll to scent-mark, digging up earth with their forelimbs and then rubbing their cheek, shoulder, hind leg, and sides into the ground. Males scent with their ventral glands in response to finding the ventral rubs of other males, but roll to mark when they encounter the rolls of females.

Woodrats form large latrines of scats and urine near nests and along travel routes. Scats and urine may occur together, but are often separate. Scat latrines can be impressive, with small tubular scats flowing forth from beneath rocks like rivers, covering several square feet and accumulating several inches deep. When woodrats claim abandoned shacks, the entire floor often becomes covered in a layer of their feces. Woodrats also form latrines upon elevated surfaces along travel routes, which likely serve some communicative function. Their feces are sometimes soft, like black tar, sticking well along elevated travel routes.

Urine, too, is placed regularly at specific locations, and in certain species these areas become very conspicuous. Perhaps they are easiest to find in the Bushy-tailed Woodrat, which marks the sharp edges of rocks along its travel routes. The accumulated urine builds up a white calcareous deposit easy to see at a distance against the often dark rocks some woodrats inhabit. They can be confused with the white stains created by roosting raptors, but they are often horizontal in orientation rather than vertical.

Scent-marking in woodrats is neither well understood nor well studied. In the cotton rats (*Sigmodon* spp.), which inhabit the southern half of the United States and Mexico, and in smaller voles, scent-marking has proved incredibly complex. Cotton rats select sites to urinate and defecate depending upon their social rank within their community, and their reaction to scats and urine of other cotton rats is also dependent upon the same hierarchy.

Woodrats make loud squeaking noises when aggressive or fighting. They make a chattering noise by grating their teeth together, and they rattle and slap their tails in the debris when agitated.

Foot-drumming is common and may be a means of communication between woodrats. They drum when disturbed in their nests, as well as in alarm when confronting snakes and Gila monsters. When drumming, they beat their feet on the ground so quickly as to make a sound like the low hum of an engine. They sometimes drum for more than a minute at a time, and at frequent intervals if the threat persists. If you have woodrats in your attic, you may hear their drumming when you move about and disturb them.

COURTSHIP AND MATING

Woodrats are polygynous, and males seek out females in estrus in the breeding season, locating them via scent marks females leave in their territories. The timing of breeding seasons in woodrats varies with species and geographic climate. California White-throated Woodrats breed during the moist season, from January to July, while in Mexico they breed throughout the year. Southern California Desert Woodrats breed November to March,

but they skip breeding altogether during years of intense drought. Eastern Woodrats breed from March to October in Oklahoma and February to August in Kansas.

Female woodrats can have many estrous cycles annually, with each estrous period lasting 4 to 6 days. They enter estrus again shortly after giving birth, and thus may have several litters or more per year. In Kansas, Eastern Woodrats average 2 to 4 litters per year. During times of food abundance, woodrats breed early and often and their population can grow rapidly. Typically breeding is unsuccessful when woodrats are less than 1 year old, but females may reach sexual maturity as young as 3 to 6 months.

Mating has been observed and documented in captivity and is similar across species. Upon greeting, paired Eastern Woodrats sniff each other's ventral glands and genitalia. The pair may spar and fight for dominance, and if the female wins, she may kill the male before he escapes (mortalities are likely uncommon in wild woodrats). If the male is dominant, then mating may proceed. The now-dominant male proceeds to follow the female, drumming his feet, wiggling his ears, and sniffing and licking her perineal region. His romantic gestures soon soothe her, and she becomes docile and assumes a position that allows him to mount. Should he be slow to take advantage of the opportunity, she follows him around licking his scrotum. The male mounts from behind and makes a series of short, quick thrusts. Afterward the female attempts to walk away, but the pair remain joined by a copulatory lock, as seen in dogs, for approximately 30 seconds. The Desert Woodrat is an exception and may be the only woodrat not to end its mating in a copulatory tie. When the pair disengage, the male departs and has nothing further to do with raising the litter.

DEVELOPMENT AND DISPERSAL OF YOUNG

Gestation in woodrats ranges from 30 to 38 days and varies within species more than across species. If a female is pregnant and still nursing a previous litter, she may delay implantation of the newly fertilized embryos and successfully extend her gestation by 3 to 14 days. This allows her to postpone the more energetically costly phases of gestation until after she has weaned earlier pups and no longer needs to produce milk.

Female Eastern Woodrats give birth standing on their hind legs and tails, holding their forefeet aloft. They drop their chin, close their eyes, and arch their back, exhibiting muscular contractions of their abdomen. In contrast, White-throated Woodrats exhibit no contractions and often remain on all four feet. Females lick each neonate as it emerges and then eat the placenta.

An intimate look at a White-throated Woodrat. © *Paul and Joyce Berquist/Animals Animals*

Young Desert Woodrats in an internal grass nest, inside the sturdy framework of their larger home.
© Dagmar/Animals Animals

Litters vary from 1 to 5 pups, and litter size depends upon food availability and quality. Newborn woodrats are altricial, but they can roll around and make uncoordinated movements with their limbs. Whiskers and claws are present, but they are otherwise naked and gray-skinned with pink muzzles. Their eyes and ears are closed, but their incisors are erupted and splayed with an opening between them. When they nurse, a nipple fits perfectly between these teeth, and they lock onto it so tightly as to require considerable force to detach them. Their mother separates them by dragging them in circles and pushing them away with her feet, until they finally let go.

Young woodrats develop relatively slowly for such a small mammal. During their first week the mother uses her forefeet to compress the abdomens of each pup to induce excretions, and then cleans up after them. In their second week their ears begin to open and their backs are covered in fur. Not until into their third week in the nest do their eyes open and the gap between their incisors close, so that they are unable to lock onto their mother's nipples while nursing. By this time they also sport complete coats and can run around. They eat solid food at 3 weeks and begin foot-thumping by 4 weeks. They are weaned at approximately 1 month, but they remain in the vicinity of the nest for 2 to 3 months before they disperse. Females may reach sexual maturity as early as 3 months, and males by 4, but they usually aren't successful breeders until they are 1 year old. Woodrats attain adult size at approximately 8 months of age.

INTERACTIONS AMONG WOODRATS

Home ranges of individual woodrats may overlap completely or not at all, but they are never amicably social. Woodrats are individualistic and territorial, and both sexes aggressively defend their nests from conspecifics. Adults dominate subadults and chase them away from food. Lactating females are especially aggressive.

Captive males placed in the same cage approach each other, touch noses, and launch into fights. They fight upright, boxing with their forepaws, while tilting their heads backward to avoid each other's punches. Occasionally they bite, and sometimes the opponents interlock and grapple, until the loser ends up on its back. Captive animals have been known to force entry into another's cage and kill it, yet other researchers report their captive colonies living together peaceably.

Woodrat species overlap in range in various parts of the country, and larger species generally dominate smaller ones. In trials with captive animals, Big-eared Woodrats that encountered Desert Woodrats chased them down and killed them.

INTERACTIONS WITH OTHER SPECIES

Woodrats are food for diverse predators. Great horned owls feast on them by night, as do spotted skunks, weasels, foxes, bobcats, coyotes, badgers, and raccoons. Snakes hunt them in their nests and, should they venture out in the day, hawks kill them as well. Predators probably account for the low survival in some populations. For example, of 27 Eastern Woodrats caught and tagged in Kansas as juveniles, only 6 survived until adulthood, and only 3 survived long enough to breed. Young in the nest are particularly vulnerable to snakes.

Woodrat foraging, nesting, and excavations increase soluble salts, bicarbonate, and nitrate in soils, and thus influence what plants can inhabit the areas around their nests. Not only do they influence their environments, their nests provide shelter and entire worlds for numerous other animals. Cottontails, mice, snakes, tree frogs, toads, lizards, shrews, and other small mammals find refuge within nooks and crannies in the outer and inner structures of occupied nests. Opossums and skunks rest in vacated houses. Mice are the most common associates of woodrats and are competitors for and thieves of their food. Woodrat houses are also homes for numerous insects and invertebrates, including ticks, fleas, and numerous other parasitic bugs. Thirty-two species of pseudoscorpions have been found living with and eating the ectoparasites of woodrats. Woodrats also work to rid themselves of parasites. The leaves of California bay laurel trees contain chemicals that repel insects. Dusky-footed Woodrats place bay leaves, which they nibble to release the fumigants, near their nests, which decreases the survivorship of some ectoparasites by up to 73 percent.

Woodrat houses are also common hosts to blood-sucking assassin bugs (*Triatoma* spp.), sometimes called kissing or conenose bugs. These species are the principal transmitter of Chagas' disease, which can be fatal in humans if left untreated. Worried about this disease, some landowners destroy woodrat houses on their properties. Sixty-seven of 79 White-throated Woodrat houses surveyed contained assassin bugs, but only 1 in 68 bugs collected from Desert Woodrat nests actually carried the disease. Whereas assassin bugs are common in woodrat nests, the risk that they will give you Chagas' disease is very slim. Woodrats are occasionally a carrier for hantavirus, but only rarely; White-footed Deermice are the primary carriers.

North American Deermouse
Peromyscus maniculatus

WITH NOTES on California Deermouse (*P. californicus*).

Although "mice" are common in legends, fairy tales, modern storybooks, movies, and cartoons, these characters are often some caricature of the non-native House Mouse (*Mus musculus*) and share little about the secret lives of our North American mice. Here we shall focus on the North American Deermice (*Peromyscus maniculatus*) and its relatives. They are country mice, inhabiting the woods and fields, foraging for a variety of plant and animal foods, and nesting in trees. Anyone who lives in rural areas or visits cabins beyond suburbia will be familiar with them, since they are as quick to move into houses and steal food as are House Mice in more urban habitats. *Peromyscus* is most commonly said to be derived from the Greek words *pera* for "small pouch" and *myskos* for "little mouse," referring to the mouse's small internal cheek pouches. *Maniculatus* is a diminutive adjective from the Latin word for "hand" (*manus*), and so translates into "little hand."

ACTIVITY AND MOVEMENT

DAILY

Deermice are nocturnal and are more active on dark rather than bright moonlit nights. On some days their peak activity is right after sunset, while on others it is later in the night. When they emerge for the night they move about quickly on runs and trails emanating from their nests. Generally, deermice do not make obvious, worn runs like voles, but they use the same pathways over and over. In woodlands they often use downed wood like elevated highways. On the prairie they visit and forage in a different portion of their home ranges on successive nights, returning to the nest on the same path used for the outward trip.

Deermice explore at a walk and may also trot, a gait like a fast walk. They commonly bound like rabbits when they need to, as can be seen from their tracks in snow in which the hind feet land forward and to the outside of the front feet. Deermice are also agile climbers and, depending on the subspecies, are commonly active in trees. The long mobile tail is not prehensile, but it does help balance the mouse and is often draped across the twig or branch it is climbing. Deermice can also leap several feet (0.6 m), which, given their tiny size, is an impressive feat.

Deermice are inquisitive and curious. As with

An agile deermouse deftly negotiates twigs in a brush pile. © *Mark Elbroch*

other generalists, an attraction to novel experiences is likely a means of discovering new foods and opportunities. The exploring deermouse adopts a tense, elongated posture with its body held low to the ground and extended to its maximum length. Its ears are erect, and it sniffs and probes each new object of interest. Even its tail, which is lined with fine muscle, is tensed and extends stiffly outward or bows slightly. Deermice move in short runs and sniff and inspect their surroundings on braced feet. They may also frequently stand up on their hind legs and nod or wave their head slightly as if testing the air. As they become familiar with their surroundings, they relax and once again move in a slower walk or hop.

When not active, deermice rest in nests on the ground or up in trees. In some areas, 8 out of 10 of their nests are up to 50 feet (15 m) aboveground,

where they use hollows and abandoned bird and squirrel nests. They are quick to commandeer abandoned bird nests, which they roof over with an interwoven lattice, and then build a soft nest within. Ground nests are in logs, stumps, fenceposts, under rocks, in root channels, and in nearly any other covered, protected spot, including old boots and drawers in garages and unused cabins. Each nest has one or two entrances, and if there is a burrow or other spaces adjoining the nest, they may be used for latrines and food caches.

North American deermice build nests tucked into crevices, cracks, and hollows, but California Deermice (*P. californicus*) make huge nests, using half a bushel or more of grass, weeds, and small sticks, tucked under a fallen log or some such place on the ground. Inside is a chamber lined with fine grass. California Deermice are also commonly found nesting inside the built-up "houses" of woodrats.

Deermouse nests are ball-shaped, about 6 to 8 inches (15–20 cm) wide, and are made of grass, leaves, and various plant matter with an inner lining of fur, feathers, and finely shredded plant material, like the dry, inner bark of trees and shrubs. They gather material for building the nest in their mouth, sometimes using the paws to help gather it up. When removing inner bark that still clings to a dead limb, for example, the mouse bites and tugs with up-and-down jerks of its head.

Deermice sleep inside their nest curled in a ball with their head under their body and their tail usually curled around them. When they wake, deermice stretch and yawn. They extend all of their limbs in turn and lengthen out the body. Then they scratch and wash themselves. They start by sitting crouched on their hind feet and licking their forefeet while rolling them rapidly under their mouth. They use their forepaws to wipe first along their snout and then continue wiping the head and face by reaching back to the ears and wiping forward. In between wipes, they repeatedly lick their hands and bob their heads. They groom their body by cleaning directly with their mouth while combing and parting the fur with their forepaws. They lick their genital area clean and lick their tail along their entire length. They also scratch with their hind feet and then clean their claws in their mouth.

SEASONAL

Where winters are cold and snowy, deermice confine most of their activity to the airspace under the snow. A blanket of snow forms a layer of insulation that keeps the ground at a warmer temperature than the air temperature above. Latent heat in the earth then melts the bottom of the snow and creates a subnivean ("below the snow") space, with a floor of earth and a roof of snow. In this world they continue their lives much as they do in the summer. Sometimes they move above the snow by climbing up where a tree pokes through, and their trails can be seen dotting the surface of the snow heading to another tree or hole where they disappear once more. Deermice rely upon snow cover to protect them from frigid temperatures. When there are only a few inches of snow, and not enough to provide adequate cover and insulation, many mice perish.

Deermice hoard food during the growing season to keep themselves fueled while food is scarce. In autumn they begin carrying seeds and nuts in their mouths or their internal cheek pouches to cache sites in nooks and crannies, such has stumps, logs, abandoned bird nests, hollow logs and trees, stone walls, or in a chamber adjoining a ground nest. Deermice dig with rapid scratching of the forefeet and can make or enlarge holes for caching food. A single deermouse may store up to 3.2 quarts (3 L) of food for a winter's use.

In winter, deermice keep warm by huddling in a common nest, in groups of 2 to 5, sharing their body warmth. On several occasions researchers have found groups of wintering North American Deermice that also included the very similar White-footed Deermice (*P. leucopus*) in the same nest. Although they do not hibernate, deermice may enter torpor for brief periods during cold spells.

FOOD AND FORAGING

Deermice are omnivorous, and insects and other invertebrates often form the majority of their diet. Seeds and arthropods (insects, spiders, etc.) are their staple foods throughout their range. Local and seasonal abundances determine the proportion of different foods in the diet. In moist forests, deermice consume a wide variety of seeds, berries, buds, nuts, and fungi. Green vegetation, such as clover and various grasses, is common in the diet, but in relatively small proportions. In southeastern Idaho, crested wheatgrass seeds make up a large portion of

A deermouse chewing at the base of a freshly fallen acorn. © *Mark Elbroch*

the diet, and when they are less abundant, caterpillars are the most important food. North American Deermice and White-footed Deermice are principal predators of gypsy moths (*Lymantria dispar*), an introduced pest that can defoliate huge tracts of forest when their populations boom. The deermice prey heavily on gypsy moth pupae and also eat the caterpillars after skinning off their irritating, hairy skin and gutting them.

Deermice sniff out their food on and below the surface, pick it up in their mouths, and either eat it in place or carry it to a safe location to eat or cache. A feeding deermouse sits upright and holds and manipulates food in its forepaws. It opens acorns and other hard-shelled nuts and seeds by chiseling away a hole in the shell and then inserting its incisors to scoop out the meat. Deermice are also quick to gather up the early dropping acorns, which are often infected with acorn weevil larvae. They chew small holes in the base of the acorns to liberate the soft, protein-rich pupae. Intermittently, they set down their meal and wash their face before continuing to eat.

HABITAT AND HOME RANGE

North American Deermice are the most widely distributed species in North America. They range from tree line in Alaska and Canada southward into Mexico, excepting only the extreme southeastern United States. They inhabit nearly every ecological community within that range, but are most common in woodlands, bushy shrubland, and prairies.

The lack of clear habitat preferences may be true for the species as a whole, but subspecies of deermice often have more consistent preferences. Two subspecies, known as the Prairie (*P. m. bairdii*) and Woodland (*P. m. gracilis*) Deermice, have been the subject of classic studies on habitat selection. Prairie Deermice prefer grassy habitats and avoid wooded areas even if they have grassy ground cover. The Woodland Deermice, on the other hand, avoid open grassland. When individuals of both types are placed in an outdoor pen with open grass on part of it and woods on the other part, they sort themselves accordingly.

The size of the deermouse home range is directly related to food supply, season, and population density, among other factors. At the small end, home ranges in young oak-pine forest in Arkansas average 0.08 acre (0.03 ha). In contrast, home ranges in mesquite woodland in New Mexico average 4.7 acres (1.2 ha). Deermice may have several nest sites within their home range that serve as resting stations and refuges as they roam. Normal population densities in Canada range from 1 to 7 animals per acre (2–17 per ha) but are subject to periodic irruptions and declines.

COMMUNICATION

Deermice communicate through much direct physical contact. They approach one another cautiously and can discourage approaches by other mice by assuming a threat posture: bracing themselves on all four feet in a low stance similar to the exploratory pose (tense and elongated), but with their ears erect and their head lifted to expose their incisors. They move neither forward nor back, but dart their head at their opponent. Deermice also use an upright threat posture, standing on the hind feet and swiping at another mouse with head and forepaws. They also use the upright stance as a defensive posture.

If faced with a threat and not wanting to fight, a deermouse signals its submission with laid-back ears and closed or partially closed eyes. A California Deermouse signals submission by slowly turning away from an aggressor and uttering a low mewing sound, which inhibits further attacks. A deermouse that is bested in a fight and cannot flee protects itself by signaling total defeat. It does so by lying still, usually on its back, exposing its vulnerable belly, while squealing and holding its forepaws rigidly extended toward the victor, warding off further attack.

In addition to squealing in defeat, deermice squeak during aggressive interactions. The squeaks are graded signals, meaning they vary along a spectrum of intensity. They range from prolonged squeaks during fights to explosive, sharp squeaks, sometimes described as a metallic *chit*, made by females defending their nests. Young deermice make a distress call when cold, hungry, or disturbed, but this tendency diminishes as their bodies and abilities to look after themselves develop.

A nonvocal sound that deermice use is foot-pattering or drumming. When disturbed, the mouse rapidly drums one of its forefeet, making a soft, whirring sound. Foot-drumming is especially common in the Cactus Deermouse (*P. eremicus*) and the Pinyon Deermouse (*P. truei*), and when an individual drums, nearby mice may go on alert, perking up their ears or freezing in place.

Urine and scats are important means of scent communication among deermice. Deermice do not defecate in their nests, instead scattering them about their home ranges and forming latrines near the nest. In captivity they tend to defecate in a certain corner of their cage, which is where they also retreat to groom themselves. Some urine is deposited wherever the animal wanders, "painting" its range with its own scent. Captive deermice, more than some other *Peromyscus* species, urinate in conspicuous locations such as in doorways between enclosures, maximizing the chances that other mice encounter the scent. Deermice drag their preputial glands (located in front of the genitals) to make

The defensive posture of a deermouse as it is approached by another mouse.

marks when exposed to a new environment and immediately after a fight.

Extensive work with laboratory mice (*Mus musculus*) shows that dominant mice urinate constantly as they wander. Subordinates mark less and in fewer areas. The chemicals in the urine directly affect the biology of nearby mice. The urine scents of mature males speeds up sexual development in females and retards that of young males. Exposure to male urine scents after mating improves the chances of successful pregnancy in mature females.

COURTSHIP AND MATING

The mating systems of *Peromyscus* deermice vary from monogamous to polygamous or even promiscuous. California Deermice are exclusively monogamous. They form lasting pair bonds, and there is no genetic evidence of extra-pair breeding, which is common among many other monogamous species. The males remain with females throughout the breeding season and help take care of the young, keeping them warm and protecting them. North American Deermice form pairs during breeding, with males and females sharing nests for a short period. The pair bond doesn't last as long as in California Deermice, and the male offers no parental care. When a female deermouse bears a litter, the male that mated with her may go off in search of another female.

The mating season spans a period from March to September, sometimes longer. If conditions are favorable (ample food and protection from bad weather), deermice may mate year-round, even as far north as Pennsylvania. When males are sexually active, they are also very aggressive, and while searching for females they fight with one another when they cross paths. North American Deermice mate and produce litters repeatedly throughout the year. Females can produce litters approximately once a month for the duration of the breeding season. Theoretically, a single female could produce up to 28 young in just 4 months, but few adults or young live long enough to attain these numbers. Two to 4 litters of 3 to 5 young each are more typical, and only half or less of the young survive to independence.

Deermice seeking mates sniff them out. Approaching another, a deermouse adopts the exploratory pose, reaching forward attentively with its nose and whiskers. Moving in, they sniff each other and often end up nose to nose. Their heads may be tilted away from each other as they bring their noses and mouths together in a position called "kissing." Especially in the breeding season, they sniff all over each other's bodies but focus on the anal region. Encounters between deermice also include allogrooming (grooming each other). In breeding deermice, the male often puts his paws up on the female, nibbles and tugs at the fur on her shoulders, and investigates and licks her genital region. If he grooms her too roughly, she runs, and he chases her.

During courtship, the female California Deermouse lies down on her belly with her nose down on the ground. She turns her face away from the male and half-closes her eyes while he grooms the side of her face. Then he moves on and grooms her flanks, and when he gets to her tail, she gets up and walks away, with him following. All of this contact, as well as exposure to one another's scents, likely elicits sexual receptivity if the female is not already in estrus when they meet.

Sexual encounters typically begin with a brief sniffing encounter, and then the male focuses his attention on the female's hindquarters. He sniffs and sniffs, and if she walks away, he follows, keeping his nose close to her. At some point after their initial contact, the male stops sniffing, grooming, and following the female and tries to copulate. Moving behind her, he nibbles at her rump and mounts. If she is not yet receptive, she repulses him with a squeak and a jab of her head or just moves away, causing his mount to fail. He does not give up so easily, but follows her and tries to mount again. When the female allows it, the male mounts, thrusts rapidly for a second, and then dismounts and separates from her. Females in estrus often adopt the lordotic posture—back arched downward and hips up—which entices a male to mount if necessary. After copulation, both deermice groom and clean their genital areas, and after several minutes, they mate again. The process is repeated as fertilization sometimes requires multiple copulations.

DEVELOPMENT AND DISPERSAL OF YOUNG

Gestation lasts 23 days, after which 4 to 5 young are born, although litters range from 3 to 7. The female enters estrus immediately after giving birth and becomes pregnant while nursing her current litter.

Pregnancies carried while nursing an earlier litter often last 27 or 28 days.

Young are pink, naked, blind, and helpless at birth, but their growth is rapid. Hair is evident in a few days, but their eyes do not open for 2 weeks. During their third week their mother is usually preparing for the birth of a new litter, and the earlier offspring are abruptly weaned. Female California Deermice don't breed immediately after giving birth, and the period of parental care is longer. Young California Deermice may not wean until about week 6. Deermice are independent at 1 month and are sexually mature at 2 months; the young conceived early in the spring are able to breed by fall. Their offspring are important contributions to overwintering populations.

During their first few weeks of life, the squeaks of distress made by young pups solicit adult attention. They squeak if they are cold, hungry, or otherwise disturbed. If a pup is inadvertently dropped out of the nest, it squeaks and is picked up and returned to safety. Suckling young cling tightly to the nipples of their mothers and can even be carried by her in that fashion, but usually she detaches them before leaving the nest. When carrying pups from place to place the mother typically carries one at a time, fully cradled in her jaws. Older and larger pups are carried by the loose skin of their backs and necks. In addition to nursing her young and making sure they are together and safe in the nest, the mother warms them with her body and grooms them, licking them with bobbing head movements and patting their little bodies with her forefeet.

Male deermice sometimes remain with their mates and use the natal nest even when young are present, but they contribute no parental care. A male California Deermouse, however, does everything the female does to care for the young, short of lactating. One of their most important jobs is to warm the young by huddling over them in the nest. Experimental evidence shows that male care in addition to that of females increased pup survival nearly 3 times over what is achieved by a mother working alone. Relative to other *Peromyscus*, the California Deermouse has smaller litters, fewer litters per year, and slower-developing offspring. Those conditions appear to make male parental investment that much more important. Since California Deermice do not produce as many young, the fitness of the adults depends on a high rate of survival among their offspring, and that requires care.

Before long, the young are old enough to be looking after themselves much of the time and they no longer squeak for help from the female (or male). Older young even quarrel over food with parents. A sneaky youngster sometimes leans in toward its feeding mother with submissive, half-closed eyes and tries to pinch her food in its incisors and run off. The mother often turns away, using her hip to block any youngster's approach and may move off to eat in private. She does not aggressively repel her offspring, and if they manage to nip a bit of her meal, they eat right next to her.

Dispersal usually follows weaning, but dispersal is not limited only to juveniles. Depending on local competition for food and other resources, adults may disperse as well. Spring and fall are times when population densities peak for many *Peromyscus* species. Males tend to disperse early, and in one study, nonbreeding males dispersed in the spring and summer. In the fall, after the breeding season had ended, juveniles and breeding males dispersed. Deermice of both sexes sometimes disperse over the winter. Most travel less than 500 feet (154 m) before settling into a new area.

INTERACTIONS AMONG DEERMICE

Deermice are not typically territorial in regard to their home ranges, but females are strongly defensive of their nests and the immediate vicinity around them. The California Deermouse is the more territorial, and males and females both drive off interlopers, especially members of their same sex. The White-footed Deermouse, one of the least sociable and most pugnacious *Peromyscus* species, is known for its practice of infanticide. Females and males both kill pups. Males that have sired pups of their own kill pups outside of their own home ranges, and females kill unfamiliar pups encountered outside of their own nests. In both cases, reducing the reproductive success of other deermice improves their own relative success, contributing to their fitness.

Most aggression is expressed between males during the breeding season and females defending their nests with young inside. Males are intolerant of each other, and adults in general are intolerant of juveniles during the breeding season and drive them out of their home ranges. Adults typically kill juveniles in interaction experiments in cages intended to simulate dispersal. Group huddling in winter is only possible once breeding and rearing are over.

When deermice meet, they approach one another in the stiff, elongated exploratory posture and move to sniff and feel each other. Nose-to-nose contact is common, as is sniffing of the anal region. Lingering contact is rare between males because fighting usually ensues immediately. If a contact doesn't lead to aggression, because one animal shows submission (narrowed eyes and laid-back ears), then grooming follows. Sometimes the grooming, which is done by the dominant mouse, is amicable, and sometimes it is aggressive. Aggressive grooming includes vigorous use of the teeth and hair-pulling, usually with the aggressor at a right angle to the other. Other amicable behaviors that can be observed include sitting in close contact with one another (huddling) and, as with males seeking to mate, one mouse following the other.

If a meeting leads to aggression, it may start with the threat posture (standing on all fours, incisors exposed), which can rapidly turn into a whirlwind of fighting and chasing. Mostly this is seen between males during the mating season and in nest defense. Nest defense includes a hunched upright posture, hazing with head and forefeet, and, in some species, one or a series of explosive squeaks or *chits*.

When deermice fight, they rush and wrestle, leap and evade, and engage in long chases. They rear up on their hind feet and box at each other, striking with their forepaws and darting their heads at one another. Commonly, they just rush right in from the first contact. Most of the time one animal flees and the aggressor chases, trying to bite his rival on the rump and tail. Females commonly flee from over-aggressive approaches of breeding males, causing chases. The chasing male tries to mount the fleeing animal regardless of its sex. Chasing is the most common male-male interaction in the breeding season. If neither flees the initial threatening contact, they clasp each other, belly to belly, and, locked together, they roll about, each trying to gain the upper position. They chew at the other's fur and usually don't make any sounds, and it ends after a minute or two when the two break apart and one flees while the other chases. The chases are usually rocket-fast across the ground with occasional high leaps to avoid biting attacks.

California Deermice fight by springing together, scuffling briefly, and then jumping away. This kind of fighting, plus the ability to inhibit aggression with the mewing cry, allows California Deermice to manage their interactions with less violence than among other deermice. In experiments in

A deermouse pauses, its massive eye attempting to capture any potential danger. © *Mark Elbroch*

which two pairs of California Deermice were put in the same cage for a week, they fought initially, but soon settled into a dominance relationship and got along relatively peacefully. Fighting-related injuries were not observed. In similar experiments with other *Peromyscus* species, they often kept fighting all week, never settling into a stable relationship. Weaker males lost up to half their tails to repeated biting. Often, the level of aggression increases with population density, and when there are more deermice about, fights are more common and fierce.

INTERACTIONS WITH OTHER SPECIES

Deermice are a fundamental prey species for most predators across North America.

Despite their tremendous similarities and overlapping ranges, different *Peromyscus* species do not interbreed in the wild and compete with one another only mildly if at all. If they do compete, it is mitigated by slight differences in habitat use and preference. In a study in Virginia there was no evidence of competition between deermice and White-footed Deermice in terms of displacement in space, habitat, or diet. When either species was experimentally removed, neither remaining species flourished, as is expected if competition is inhibiting them.

Relationships with various other small mammals are unclear. Reports conflict as to the degree and direction of competition between *Peromyscus* mice and Meadow Voles or short-tailed shrews. Where deermice live alongside Ord's Kangaroo Rat (*Dipodomys ordii*), the latter can exclude deermice from open habitats. Aggressive fights and displays are seen under experimental conditions when the two species encounter one another, and laboratory trials indicate that Grasshopper Mice (*Onychomys* spp.) can and will kill deermice.

Deermice, and to a lesser extent White-footed Deermice, are carriers of hantavirus. Hantavirus infections cause a respiratory disease called Hantavirus Pulmonary Syndrome that produces flu-like symptoms in humans and can lead to death. It is spread when virus-containing particles from rodent urine, droppings, or saliva are stirred into the air. You can protect yourself by keeping your home and other spaces clean and free of rodents. Infection occurs when you breathe in virus particles, so it is important to avoid actions that raise dust, such as sweeping or vacuuming where rodents have been active. When you need to clean out an old shed or cabin littered with deermice droppings, *first* spray all surfaces with a bleach-water mix, to kill the virus. Wait until the surface is dry, and then sweep and clean as normal. *Check with local health authorities for further information on prevention of exposure.*

North American Porcupine
Erethizon dorsatum

OTHER NAMES: porkie, quill-pig.

The porcupine cannot throw or shoot its quills, but they are easily shed. Porcupines have a distinctive layer of musculature just below their skin with which they can raise and lower their quills and let them go when they come into contact with a predator. The quills are 0.8 to 4 inches (2–10 cm) long, with barbed tips that make them difficult and painful to remove. The barbs are angled in such a way that if the quills are left unattended, they dig deeper and deeper into an animal as it moves. Should the quills avoid large bones and vital organs, with enough time they can work their way straight through an animal and come out the other side. The quills are covered with a mildly antibiotic fatty compound that likely reduces the risk of infection if a porcupine happens to get stuck with its own quills.

The porcupine's quills are a necessary protection given its ponderous meanderings in areas with diverse carnivores. Porcupines do an amazing job of eking out a living on the least nutritional foods in some of the harshest climates in North America. Their lethargic lifestyle is the cost of feeding on low-quality browse and aids in energy conservation. Yet their distinctive armor and ability to survive on poor forage allow them to exploit vast areas of low-quality woodlands as home across the continent.

ACTIVITY AND MOVEMENT

DAILY

Porcupines are nocturnal and crepuscular. On the ground, they move in a slow walk, and their feet move independently beneath their skirts of overhanging hairs and quills. They resemble mobile pin cushions, with their spiky backs swinging loosely from side to side. Their tails sometimes drag on the ground, leaving marks like those made when dragging a broom, but more often they hold them aloft and straight out behind them. If harassed, they can move into a trot or shuffling lope, though when threatened their tendency is actually to stand their ground, spinning in place to keep a predator at bay, or to seek a refuge in which they can bury their vulnerable noses. Porcupines can manage only feeble jumps, but they can swim and are known to cross small bodies of water.

Observations of captive porcupines show that they can be very playful. Youngsters are more playful than adults, but individual personality makes a big difference, too. As the observed captives reached 1 and 2 years of age, some became conspic-

When a porcupine is disturbed or frightened, it raises its quills, and suddenly they are much more apparent. © *Mark Elbroch*

uously fat, and their playfulness waned accordingly. Solitary play includes mock-defensive behavior wherein the animal makes all the instinctive actions of defense, but without an aggressor. The porcupine will hide its face, raise its quills, and back up toward an imaginary threat, striking out with its tail. Young ones will also jump up and down and whirl about. Playing porcupines also walk and run about and gnaw on all manner of things. In captivity they seem to like to gnaw and claw at metal objects as if they enjoy the ringing sounds. Porcupines are also seen lying on their backs and manipulating objects with all four feet.

Groups of captive porcupines will explore, manipulate, and gnaw on things together. They also wrestle and roughhouse. They twist, bite, and struggle against one another with much loud whining and complaint. In one wrestling match, a small but particularly rambunctious young male bit a larger young female hard enough on the back to paralyze her hindquarters; she died a few hours later.

The most amazing form of play is the "exercise dance." Up to three porcupines at a time have been seen doing this together in a common cage. It is most often seen among mature porcupines; in animals over 2 years of age, this was the only type of play seen. In the exercise dance, the porcupine stands up on its hind legs and tail and rocks rhythmically side to side. With each rocking motion, the hind feet are raised up and stomped down again. The arms swing and the head and shoulders rotate with the swaying motion. Individuals vary in their stance and motion, but the basics are the same. In the captives in whom this was observed, it might be done day after day in the same spot in the cage. If lightly disturbed, the porcupine will pause but remain standing and then resume dancing. If annoyed, it will quit altogether.

SEASONAL

In winter, porcupines move very little. They hole up in their dens, emerging for nocturnal foraging bouts in coniferous trees and rocky cliffs. Dens are in rocky crevices where they are available, but are also found in the banks of ephemeral streams, in hollow trees and logs, and in similar inaccessible areas. When suitable denning is not available, they may use a "station tree," wintering in the upper foliage of a hemlock or spruce. Dens are often used year after year, and rivers of scat sprinkled with shed quills and reeking of their "piney" urine scent may spill forth from the entrance. Some dens become so choked with scat from successive winter denning that the animals must nearly tunnel their way through it to get in or out.

The area around a den will have several feeding runs radiating outward. In winter the snow may be quite packed down, stained with urine, and littered with feces and quills. Runs may extend visibly up trees, with a heavily used tree showing clawing and wear from repeated visits of the porcupine. You can find their distinctive runs in the snow if you are in the woods in winter. Short-legged porcupines have to wade along, plowing a trough through the snow, and thus they keep their commuting short. They expend tremendous effort walking through snow and are often easy to locate at their destination, resting in the crown of a tree or beneath cover in their den.

Whereas in winter they seek shelter on hillsides where conifers dominate the canopy, as the weather warms, porcupines may relocate to new quarters nearer meadows and other summer foods. With spring they also become increasingly active in the daytime and forage on green vegetation and young browse on the ground. In the middle of summer their activity is spread evenly over day and night.

FOOD AND FORAGING

Porcupines are herbivorous. The content of their diets varies by season and geography and might include an occasional snack on an animal carcass. They can ferment wood fiber in their guts as well or better than many ruminants, and they are highly efficient at metabolizing nitrogen, a nutrient criti-

A porcupine napping in a tree. Porcupines often rest with their hind end, and their defensive quills, facing the trunk of the tree, which is the direction from which a predator is most likely to appear.
© Sara Robinson/Fotolia.com

cally lacking in their highly fibrous diet. Porcupines feed on a mixture of tree cambium (inner bark), foliage, and broad-leaved herbs. In winter they subsist on cambium and coniferous foliage. They typically feed on bark in the upper reaches of a healthy, mature tree, both on the trunk and at the ends of branches. They quickly strip away the outer bark to expose the cambium, allowing the debris to fall freely to the ground. Then they plant their upper teeth against the tree and pivot the head so that the lower teeth remove the cambium in a small triangular patch in five or six passes. The resulting pattern is a pleasing cross-hatch evoked by the contrasts of dark and light wood. Preferred trees vary regionally but include eastern hemlock and sugar maple in the Northeast, eastern white pine in the Great Lakes area, paper-shell pinyon pine in Texas, and yellow pine in the West.

Seasonal shifts in diet are a function of the changing availability of food items, and also the changing chemical composition within them. During spring in the Northeast, the swollen buds of sugar maple are abundant and high in nitrogen. They are the porcupine's primary spring food, but once they burst into new leaves, they develop high concentrations of tannins, chemical defenses against herbivory, and the porcupines abandon them. Porcupines are also particularly fond of sap, and they will raid maple syrup buckets left unattended.

Porcupines discriminate among individual trees, ignoring some and feeding heavily on others of the same type, apparently sensing individual differences in palatability. In a particular tree they eat only the most nutritive portions of the foliage—the leaf blades—ignoring the leaf stems and terminal twigs. They feed in trees by pulling a branch in toward their mouth and nipping it off with their teeth. They eat the leaves and drop the remaining twig to the ground. The accumulation of these "nip-twigs" is a telltale sign of porcupine feeding.

Spring is also truffle (underground fungi) season, and porcupines feed heavily on them when they are abundant. Porcupines locate ripe truffles by scent. They dig shallow holes up to 6 inches deep from which they pluck the truffles.

In the warm seasons they feed on deciduous and herbaceous foliage, spending plenty of time on the ground. In summer they might eat roots, seeds, and catkins, as well as stems and leaves of various plants, sitting back on their haunches and manipulating foods with their forepaws. They eat prickly pear cactus, raspberry canes, cattails, and low-bush blueberry in various portions of their range. Apples and other fruits are a favorite harvest in late summer. They prefer apples low in acid and will eat every fruit from one tree while ignoring another full of tart apples right next to it.

In autumn they feed heavily on acorns and beechnuts. Sitting high in a tree, they grab and nip off the ends of branches with acorns, which they strip clean of nuts before dropping them to the ground. Twigs nipped by porcupines retain their withered leaves and are scattered through the canopy, hung up by other branches when they were dropped. When nut crops fall, porcupines forage for them on the ground. In years with abundant nut crops they forage on acorns and beechnuts well into winter, digging through the snow layer to consume nuts they locate by smell.

Some of the defensive plant compounds porcupines eat disrupt their sodium metabolism. Poor mineral metabolism and a generally mineral-poor diet drive porcupines to seek salt. Some of that drive can be satisfied by feeding on aquatic plants high in sodium. They eat water lilies (*Nuphar* spp.), aquatic liverwort (*Riccia fluitans*), and arrowhead (*Sagittaria* spp.), which they can harvest by swimming but seem to prefer to gather from shore or while wading. When this doesn't provide them enough sodium, they resort to chewing unconventional "foods": mud and sand along river bottoms, hikers' backpacks, rubber tires, plywood and other lumber, antlers and bones, and carrion.

HABITAT AND HOME RANGE

Porcupines inhabit a great diversity of habitats across their range. Their range extends from tree line in northern Canada and Alaska down to the desert scrub of New Mexico and western Texas. They are absent from the driest desert habitats of southern California and Arizona and parts of the Midwest and southeast United States. Food influences habitat selection, as does safety. In the Great Basin Desert, studies show that smaller porcupines will occupy areas with poor forage if they offer more protection from predators, leaving more open areas to the larger porcupines.

Home ranges vary with geographic region, but male ranges are consistently larger than those of females. An average female may have an annual home range of 0.1 square miles (0.25 km²) or more, whereas males average 0.3 square miles (0.73 km²). Male home ranges do not vary much from year to year, but they vary greatly between individuals. Home range is positively correlated with male reproductive success, so either more successful males command larger ranges, or maintaining a larger home range affords more mating opportunities. The area a porcupine uses in winter is only a fraction of that used in summer. In the Adirondacks of New York, porcupines are usually captured within 1 mile (1.6 km) of their winter dens during the summer. In winter they foraged within 330 feet (100 m) of their den.

A porcupine forages on wildflowers and other green vegetation. Note its long, fingerlike toes and large claws. © *Mark Elbroch*

The highest population densities reported are 41 animals per square mile (16 per km²) in mixed hardwood-hemlock forests in Michigan, and 108 animals per square mile (42 per km²) in central Massachusetts, where eastern hemlocks, oaks, and rocky outcrops provide abundant food and denning opportunities. Densities as low as 2.5 animals per square mile (1 per km²) occur in portions of Arizona and the Upper Peninsula of Michigan.

COMMUNICATION

Porcupines are individualistic, and their communication is limited. In the wild, frequent urination and defecation contribute to a distinctive odor of porcupines near an active feeding site or den and along well-used runs. Active urine-marking increases in the spring as part of courtship (see below).

Porcupine vocalizations have been described as grunts, snuffles, whines, and hoots. During the mating season males utter piercing whines, and females advertise their estrus with high-pitched calls. Aggressive encounters between males and courtship encounters between male and female include sharp grunts and cries. Some porcupine calls can be heard over 650 feet (200 m) away and can be used to track them to their dens. The most common sound from porcupines is the loud sound of chewing.

The North American Porcupine's first line of defense (after the bright color of its quills, perhaps) is a loud tooth-chattering. They vibrate their incisors against one another and clack their cheek teeth, making an eerie clatter. They also stomp their feet and shake their bodies, which can incidentally make the quills rattle. When severely stressed they emit a strong, repellent odor. The odor comes from a patch of bare skin on the upper surface of the base of the tail called the rosette. This area of glandular skin is usually only a little smelly, but when the animal is cornered or pursued closely it can exude a vivid stench. In a confined space the stink will make your eyes water and nose run, and it serves as an efficient deterrent against predators, at least humans.

COURTSHIP AND MATING

Breeding takes place in September, October, and November, before the onset of winter, with the most-northerly populations breeding earlier than others. In Texas and the southwestern United States, where winters are mild and summers very hot, courtship and breeding have been observed continuing into December and early January. As the breeding season begins, large male home ranges may expand farther to include the home ranges of more females. Most likely following females' scents on the ground and in the air, males roam in search of potential mates. Often a male will arrive before the female is receptive to mating and he will have to guard her from competitors. Typically perched on a lower branch than she in the same tree, he fights off other males that attempt to ascend the tree trunk. Males around an estrous female may be seen with scores of quills jammed in their snouts, and the torn-up ground littered with thousands of shed and bitten quills testify to their battles for breeding access. Successful males must be able to repel all challengers over a long period, and they tend to be older, larger, and more densely quilled than other males.

Whichever male prevails against his challengers will stay near the female and intermittently spray her with urine. The urine may contain hormones that induce estrus, thereby synchronizing her receptivity with his presence. When the male first approaches, she makes sharp squawks and keeps him at a distance. As she warms up to his attentions she allows him to come closer and closer. They may rub noses and exchange softer vocalizations. The final stage of courtship involves copious "urine-hosing." Unlike normal urination, the male shoots urine at the female through his erect penis with tremendous force, thoroughly dousing her. Biologists believe the urine must contain hormones necessary for successful mating.

When she is receptive, which may only occur after exposure to a guarding male for several days, the two will mate—carefully—on the ground. The female lays her quills tightly to her back, lifting her hindquarters and arching her tail over her back to afford a relatively safe surface for the male's chest and paws.

DEVELOPMENT AND DISPERSAL OF YOUNG

Gestation lasts 7 months, and a single young is born in April or May in a protected maternal den or a makeshift nest on the ground. A newborn weighs about 1 pound (450 g) and is precocial, emerging fully quilled, open-eyed, and able to defend itself with tail-slaps. Porcupine newborns glisten with viscous fluids, which keep their quills soft and malleable, and blink their eyes at their surroundings. They and their quills dry within several hours, after which their quills stiffen and are ready for action. Newborns are capable crawlers, but they cannot climb for several weeks. The mother spends her days resting in the canopy of trees near her feeding sites while her baby hides nearby on the ground. The pair reunite at night when the mother comes down to feed.

Young porcupines hide in any number of different places, but a hollow at the base of their mother's feeding tree is the most common. They apparently follow their mother from one tree to the next and find the best hiding spot they can nearby. Once a

A walking porcupine. © *Mark Elbroch*

youngster can climb, mother and young may forage in the same or different trees. As the juvenile ages, the distance over which they separate grows, but they reunite frequently to nurse for the first 4 months. When darkness falls and the mother is ready to forage, she seeks out her baby. The hungry youngster squeaks and mews as it approaches its mother and makes contented *mmmm* sounds while it suckles. The mother makes purr-like sounds that have been likened to the opening and closing of a zipper. If the youngster does not suckle for 3 nights in a row, the mother will stop lactating. If the female becomes separated from her young for more than a week, the next time they meet she will treat it with aggression as if it were a stranger.

Juveniles nurse exclusively for their first 2 weeks, after which they eat green vegetation and continue to nurse into their fifth month. The young spend their first summer in their mother's home range. It is a long period of dependency, and despite the attention the mother gives in terms of feeding her baby, she will offer no action in its defense. The youngster must defend itself from the start. As summer wanes and the next breeding season is dawning, the young leave their mother's orbit. Female offspring

actually disperse, while males tend to hang around in or near their mother's home range, establishing themselves and increasing their own ranges as they grow.

Female dispersal is uncommon in mammals; male dispersal is the norm. Among porcupines, females may be territorial to protect the necessary resources to sustain themselves while nearly always either pregnant or lactating. Mothers cannot tolerate continuous competition from their daughters, and so they must go. Males have lower survival rates than females, so there is more opportunity for a young male to move into or take over part of a vacated home range near where he was born.

INTERACTIONS AMONG PORCUPINES

In New York, females are fiercely territorial against other females, while male home ranges overlap with those of females and other males. In Nevada, females are not territorial, while males are. Female home ranges in Nevada are one-third the size of those in New York. The reasons for the differences are unknown, but it could be related to greater clumping of resources in the desert. When food resources occur in dense pockets, it becomes difficult for females to exclude others. For males, this may provide an opportunity to monopolize an aggregation of potential mates by fighting off their rivals.

Porcupines fight one another vigorously. Large old males show a high incidence of past injuries from fierce mate-guarding battles. The increased movement and fighting during the breeding season may contribute to why males have a higher rate of mortality than females. Harsh winter conditions can result in death of both males and females, but the weakened condition of males following the breeding season makes them even more vulnerable to mortality. Other injuries found on wild porcupines appear to be caused by falls.

INTERACTIONS WITH OTHER SPECIES

Predators of porcupines include coyotes, bobcats, cougars, Black Bears, fishers, martens, great horned owls, and others. Coyote scats are often found containing large numbers of quills, which somehow maneuver through the coyote without causing it any major trouble. The fisher is the most infamous predator of porcupines. Although the tales of fisher-porcupine battles are usually exaggerated, fishers do have instinctual abilities for unique attacks that are effective at killing porcupines while at the same time protecting themselves from their quills. Cougars were thought to have caused the near extirpation of porcupines in areas of Nevada and Idaho. The porcupine generally needs only to protect its vulnerable face from attack since its quills defend its body. Cougars, however, seem to ignore the quills and bat the porcupine regardless, accepting quills in the forelimbs as a consequence.

A porcupine's defensive behaviors include climbing as high as possible in a tree and keeping its back to the threat, or moving out on thin branches, facing away from the tree trunk and the threat. On the ground, they seek to guard their face by burying it in a hole or hollow. They will face into dirt banks on a steep hillside or use the hollows under stumps when no better refuge is available. The tail is also a weapon used for slapping predators and can deliver a debilitating faceful of quills.

Humans are a major predator of porcupines, largely for being a legitimate or perceived nuisance. Porcupines do some damage to standing timber and also to human artifacts such as car tires and wooden structures. As a result, they are killed as pests. Given their reliance on quills and not speed for defense, they are often killed by cars when crossing roads or feeding on salt along roadsides.

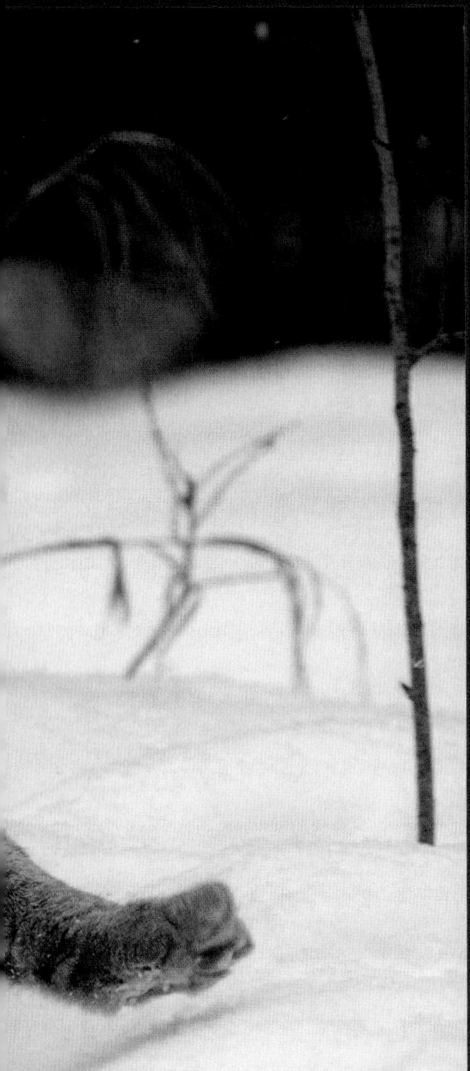

ACKNOWLEDGMENTS

Thank you to Lisa White and all those at Houghton Mifflin Harcourt who allowed us this opportunity. Thank you to Anne Hawkins for deftly negotiating another contract and for her continued friendship, humor, and support.

Kurt and I would like to thank the following wildlife professionals for taking the time to review species accounts and provide us feedback that made the accounts stronger: Sarah Allen (seals), Wendy Arjo (aplodontia), Paul Beier (cougar), Tasha Belfiore (pocket gopher), Brian Cypher (Kit and Swift Fox), Cristina Eisenberg (wolf), Adam Fergusen (spotted skunks), Katie Fleer (ground squirrels), Janet Foley (woodrats), David Garshelis (Sea Otter), Stanley Gehrt (opossum), John Hadidan (raccoon), Eric Hellgren (peccary), David Hirth (White-tailed Deer), Jen Hunter (skunks), Linda Ilse (porcupine), Ryan Jenkinson (sea lion), Luanne Johnson (Striped Skunk), Mark Jorgensen (Bighorn Sheep), Jacob Katz (beaver), Doug Kelt (kangaroo rat), Bill Kilpatrick (shrews, bats), Sara Krause (gray squirrel), Bill Lidicker (voles), John Litvaitis (bobcat), Carolyn Mahan (chipmunks), Lui Marinelli (muskrat), Rachel Mazur (Black Bear), Bruce McClellan (Brown Bear), Colleen McDonough (armadillo), Connie Millar (pika), Jessie Quinn (badger), Naomi Rose (orca), Ben Sacks (coyote, gray fox), Jaya Smith (flying squirrel), Mark Statham (Red Fox), Victor Van Ballenberghe (moose), Dirk Van Vuren (marmots and woodchuck), Floyd Weckerly (elk), Mason Weinrich (humpback whale), Heiko Wittmer (caribou), Megan Wyman (bison). Unfortunately, several accounts were cut in the interest of size.

Thank you also to the many who shared images of mammals free of charge: Max Allen, Wendy Arjo, Tom Beatty Jr., Ken Catania, Brian Cypher, Roberta Davenport, Tanguy Debier, Jerry Dragoo, Ryan Jenkinson, Jacob Katz, Jerel Kolling, Rick Leche, Kevin Mack, Dave Moskowitz, Doug Smith, Dave Stiles, Todd Weed, Davis Wyatt, Megan Wyman.

Sustaining the effort to create a project of this size required support from many. First and foremost I want to thank Kurt Rinehart, for friendship, for professional collaborations, and for honest dialogue and authentic cowriting. It continues to be a pleasure to work and share adventures with you. While I've been running like a gerbil in a wheel to keep up with my work at UC Davis, many have encouraged me, and at times even carried me: Heiko Wittmer, Jacob Katz and Kendra Johnson, Bjorn Erickson and Lisa Matsubara, Allison Olliver, Jen Hunter, Maria Santos, Katie Fleer, Phil Sandstrom, Marit Wilkerson, Karthik Ram, Kristy Deiner, Tomiko Wong, Doug Kelt, Walter Boyce, and all those others faithful to Sophia's.

A core group of people have continued to support me through the years, and the recent ones have been no exception: Keith Badger, Nancy Birtwell, Fred Vanderbeck, Susie Rinehart, Mike Pewtherer, Jonathan Talbot, Julie Stowell, Kalani Souza, Mike Kresky, Louis Liebenberg, George Leoniak, Mike Puzzo, Nate Harvey, and Keely Eastly. And my amazing family, my parents, V and L, my sister Annie, Trevor, and wicked Tessa. A special thanks to Lizzie, who passed on this year, but whose support for me and my work continues.

Thank you to the animals. A special thanks to the cougars that give chase, tolerate my abuse, and continue to instill me with wonder. This project humbled and inspired me—there is so much to learn about mammal behavior, and so much we as a larger community do not know. Certainly an exciting lifetime of learning, and adventure.

Mark Elbroch

First and foremost, my work on this book has been dependent on my wife, Susie, whose love, support, and forbearance allowed me to pursue this project. A project like this always grows beyond your expectations and without Susie I would never have made much progress. Thanks to my son Cole and daughter Hazel who share my passion for the natural world. I also owe a debt of gratitude to my good friend and collaborator Mark Elbroch. Lisa White of Houghton Mifflin Harcourt and Anne Hawkins of John Hawkins and Associates were critical to this book's success. Thanks to Terri Donovan and Dave Hirth for their continuing support of my professional development. I am forever indebted to my parents, Richard and MJ Rinehart, my siblings, Rick Rinehart and Allison Dancy; Lyn Caldwell; Faith Catlin; John Griesemer; Kathy Parshley; Rhoda Ackerman; and my friends, coworkers, and students at the Mountain School in Vershire, Vermont. Thanks for helping make this possible.

It was fun, interesting, and exciting work. Spending so much time looking not only at the lives of North American mammals, but also at the work and experiences of thousands of passionate scientists and naturalists, left me with a deepened respect and admiration for their efforts.

Kurt Rinehart

GLOSSARY

agonism. Conflict and/or competition between two or more animals. Often used to describe aggressive or combative behaviors. (*adj.*, agonistic)

allogrooming. Mutual grooming, in which two animals groom each other at the same time.

allopatric. Describing two animals with completely separate geographic ranges—meaning they do not share habitat. *Opposite of sympatric.*

altricial. Describing young born helpless and naked, or nearly so. Altricial young require substantial care from their parents to survive. *Opposite of precocial.*

aposematic coloration. Bright or contrasting colors that warn potential predators that an animal is noxious or dangerous (as in skunks). Sometimes nondangerous species mimic the aposematic coloration of others to benefit from the protection it provides.

apparent competition. Competition between two prey species mediated by a common predator. Apparent competition occurs when one prey species indirectly increases predation on a second prey species.

benthic. Pertaining to the bottom of a lake or ocean.

bovid. Any member of the cow family (Bovidae).

canid. Any member of the dog family (Canidae).

carnivore. Any animal, such as a shrew, that feeds primarily on other animals. In taxonomic terms, it also refers to mammals in the order Carnivora, including felids, canids, ursids, pinnipeds, mustelids, skunks, and procyonids.

cervid. Any member of the deer family (Cervidae).

commensalism. An ecological interaction between two animals in which one individual benefits and the other is neither helped nor harmed.

communication. An interaction between two animals during which one individual sends a signal and the other perceives it and reacts in some way.

competition. Interactions between two or more individuals over control of or access to some scarce resource. Forms of competition include *exploitation*, *interference*, and *apparent competition*, each further defined in this glossary.

conspecific. An animal of the same species as another.

coprophagy. The act of eating one's own feces. This is common in rodents and lagomorphs that run plant material through their digestive tract twice to better assimilate its nutrients.

copulatory plug. A solid plug formed from the male ejaculate that forms a barrier in a female's vagina, temporarily preventing additional mating by other males. It should be noted that in many species the female removes the plug so that she can mate with other males.

copulatory tie. A condition in which a mating pair remain joined as a result of the bulbous glandis at the base of the penis swelling after ejaculation and becoming lodged in the vagina. Typical of canid intercourse; males often step over the female's hind end and the pair remain stuck together, facing opposite directions.

core area. That part of the home range most used by an animal. In species that have home ranges that somewhat overlap with home ranges of conspecifics, the core area is also defined as the portion of their home range that does not overlap with those of others.

courtship. Ritualized or stereotyped behaviors that initiate or lead to mating.

crèche. A communal nursery in which young animals are watched over by one or more adult females while the other mothers are foraging.

delayed implantation. In the reproductive cycle of some species, a mechanism by which the fertilized egg does not implant immediately in the uterus, but instead becomes dormant and remains in suspended animation. After a certain period, the egg implants and resumes its development, culminating in birth. This delay in implantation decouples mating from gestation periods and allows young to be born at times of year that provide them the best opportunities to survive.

dispersal. The act of a young animal leaving its natal range to find and establish a territory of its own.

dominant. An animal that has established authority or leadership over another animal during an exchange. *Opposite of subordinate.* (*n.*, dominance)

estivation. Warm-weather dormancy or torpidity analogous to hibernation.

estrous. Relating to estrus or to a female that is entering or has entered estrus.

estrus. Generally, the cycle by which females are prepared biologically for reproduction. Specifically, the time within the reproductive cycle, near ovulation, when females are receptive to male attempts to mate and when fertilization is possible.

exploitation competition. Competition in which one animal uses up a scarce resource before its competitor can.

felid. Any member of the cat family (Felidae).

forb. A broad-leaved, nonwoody flowering plant as distinct from a grass or sedge; dandelions, clover, and buttercups are forbs.

form. The shallow depression created by a rabbit or hare in which it rests and hides.

fossorial. Describing an animal adapted to a life underground; a fossorial animal typically digs and maintains a burrow or a system of tunnels.

frugivore. An animal that primarily eats fruit.

granivore. An animal that primarily eats seeds, nuts, and other mast.

habitat. The physical environment in which an organism or community lives, including all the living and nonliving resources and influences that shape that space. In common usage, the term is applied to plant communities or land-cover types (such as forest and wetland), implying an environment that generally provides habitat for certain species.

herbivore. An animal that feeds primarily on vegetation.

hibernation. A survival strategy in which an animal becomes dormant to pass the winter months, significantly slowing its metabolism and dropping its body temperature to save energy and remain inactive for longer periods more efficiently.

home range. The area delineated by an animal's movements over a given amount of time; for many mammals, this is often a year, producing an *annual home range.*

insectivore. A specialist carnivore than feeds primarily on invertebrates.

interference competition. Competition involving direct interactions like physical fights, attacks, or threats between two animals both seeking access to the same resource.

interspecific. Between two species or groups of animals. *Opposite of intraspecific.*

intraspecific. Within the same group or species of animals. *Opposite of interspecific.*

juvenile. A young, incompletely developed animal, usually one that has not yet attained sexual maturity (that is, a prepubescent) or has not dispersed to establish its own range.

keystone species. A species with a disproportionate impact on increasing the biodiversity of the eco-

logical community in which it lives relative to its biomass.

lactation. The period following birth during which the female produces and secretes milk from the mammary glands.

lordotic posture. A position assumed by a female to solicit mating, in which the spine is arched downward and the pelvis rotated upward to expose the genitalia.

mast. A fruit or nut produced by a tree or shrub. A *mast year* is a year in which the fruit or nut crop is higher than normal, and it is usually followed by a year in which mast production is much lower than normal.

monestry. Having a single estrous cycle per year. *Opposite of polyestry.*

monogamy. A mating system in which a single male mates with a single female.

mustelid. Any member of the weasel family (Mustelidae).

omnivore. An animal that eats both vegetation and other animals.

optimal foraging. Any behaviors that optimize the energy gained from eating against the energetic costs of foraging. Optimal foraging theory predicts that animals select locations, foods, and hunting strategies that maximize the ratio of energy gained to energy expended (benefits vs. costs).

over-mark. To deposit scent atop the scent mark of a conspecific or other animal.

parasitism. An ecological relationship in which one animal benefits to the detriment of another. A *social parasite* does this indirectly, for example by stealing food collected by another individual.

pelage. A mammal's coat of fur.

pelagic. Pertaining to the open ocean, distant from landmasses.

perianal glands. Paired glands found just inside the anus, used in scent-marking and olfactory communication.

perineal. Pertaining to the region of the body between the anus and the genitalia.

philopatric. Referring to animals that exhibit site fidelity, returning repeatedly to the same areas to breed or feed.

piloerection. The raising of the hair so that it stands on end.

pinniped. Any mammal with flippers; a general term that describes all seals, sea lions, and walruses.

piscivore. A specialist carnivore that feeds primarily on fish.

polyestry. Having more than one estrous cycle per year. This includes species that cycle regularly throughout the year and those that experience several cycles within a narrower reproductive season. *Opposite of monestry.*

polygamy. A mating system in which one partner dominates access to two or more partners of the opposite sex.

polygyny. A mating system in which one male dominates access to two or more females.

precocial. Describing young born with fur and with the eyes open. Precocial young require less care from their parents to survive and are mobile immediately after birth. *Opposite of altricial.*

predation. The extreme form of parasitisim, wherein one animal kills and consumes another.

procyonid. Any member of the raccoon family (Procyonidae).

promiscuity. A mating system in which any male or female may mate with any other male or female.

recruitment. The proportion of juveniles in a local population of animals that survive to adults, remain in the same area, and reproduce themselves. Recruitment is one way in which a population may grow and is in contrast to a population sustained by the immigration of animals from other areas.

rendezvous site. A social meeting place for families and extended networks, such as wolf packs. Often considered an aboveground den.

resident. An individual that lives in a particular place. Among many species, this class implies potential dominance over conspecifics in that same space.

riparian. Pertaining to the bank of a stream or river. The width of the riparian zone is variable and often characterized by moisture-dependent vegetation.

ritual. A behavior that may have originated to fulfill other purposes but now acts as a communication signal.

semi-fossorial. Describing an animal that spends a great deal of time beneath the ground, as chipmunks and marmots do.

sexual dimorphism. The disparity in size and/or shape between the sexes within a single species.

sign. Any mark or indication of an animal's presence or behavior. Typical examples include scat (feces), scratchings or gnawings on trees, digging sites, discarded food remains, etc. Tracks are a form of sign but are usually considered separately (as in the phrase "tracks and signs").

signal. A sign that serves as a means of communication.

stereotyped. Describing an innate sequence of behaviors that unfold reflexively in the presence of the appropriate stimulus.

subadult. Usually, a sexually mature individual that is not able to function socially as an adult. This stage often occurs when large size is required for establishing home ranges or breeding.

subnivian. Below the snow. It usually refers to a zone at the base of a snowpack where latent heat from the ground forms an open space usually 0.4 to 1.6 inches (1–4 cm) high.

subordinate. An animal that is subject to the authority or leadership of another animal in an exchange. *Opposite of dominant.*

superfetation. The formation of a fetus while another fetus is already present in the uterus.

sympatric. Describing two animals with overlapping geographic ranges—meaning they share the same space. *Opposite of allopatric.*

tandem marking. Coordinated urine scent-marking by mated pairs in the period before and during estrus. Commonly observed in canids, including coyotes and wolves.

territory. The defended area established and maintained by an individual animal; in the case of social species, the area defended by a mating pair, pack, or herd.

torpor. A decrease in metabolic activity and body temperature more profound than simple rest but less extreme than hibernation. Torpor can be as brief as a few hours or as long as several months.

transient. An animal without a territory.

ungulate. Any hoofed animal.

ursid. Any member of the bear family (Ursidae).

vibrissae. Whiskers; specialized hairs on the face used to gain information from the environment, as during communication and foraging.

weaning. The process in which a mother slowly or abruptly stops providing milk to her young.

SELECTED BIBLIOGRAPHY

Ackerman, B. B., F. G. Lindzey, and T. P. Hemker. 1986. "Predictive Energetics Model for Cougars" in S. D. Miller and D. Everett, eds., *Cats of the World: Biology Conservation, and Management*. National Wildlife Federation, pp. 333–352.

Adams, J. R., J. A. Leonard, and L. P. Waits. 2003. Widespread occurrence of a domestic dog mitochondrial DNA haplotype in southeastern US coyotes. *Molecular Ecology* 12:541–546.

Aho, K., N. Huntly, J. Moen, and T. Oksanen. 1998. Pikas (*Ochotona princeps*) as allogenic engineers in an alpine system. *Oecologia* 114:405–409.

Allen, D. L. 1938. Notes on the killing technique of the New York weasel. *Journal of Mammalogy* 19:225–229.

Amstrup, S. 2003. "Polar Bear (*Ursus maritimus*)" in G. Feldhamer, B. Thompson, and J. Chapman, eds., *Wild Mammals of North America: Biology, Management, and Conservation*, 2nd ed. Baltimore: Johns Hopkins University Press, pp. 587–610.

Amstrup, S. C., I. Stirling, T. S. Smith, C. Perham, and G. W. Thiemann. 2006. Recent observations of intraspecific predation and cannibalism among polar bears in the southern Beaufort Sea. *Polar Biology* 29:997–1002.

Anderson, A. E., and O. C. Wallmo. 1984. *Odocoileus hemionus. Mammalian Species* 219:1–9.

Anderson, E., and M. Lovallo. 2003. "Bobcat and Lynx (*Lynx rufus* and *Lynx canadensis*)" in G. Feldhamer, B. Thompson, and J. Chapman, eds., *Wild Mammals of North America: Biology, Management, and Conservation*, 2nd ed. Baltimore: Johns Hopkins University Press, p. 758–786.

Anthony, H. E. 1916. Habits of *Aplodontia. Bulletin of American Museum of Natural History* 25:53–63.

Arjo, W. M., R. E. Huenefeld, and D. L. Nolte. 2007. Mountain beaver home ranges, habitat use, and population dynamics in Washington. *Canadian Journal of Zoology* 85:328–337.

Armitage, K. B. 2003. "Marmots (*Marmota monax* and Allies)" in G. Feldhamer, B. Thompson, and J. Chapman, eds., *Wild Mammals of North America: Biology, Management, and Conservation*, 2nd

ed. Baltimore: Johns Hopkins University Press, pp. 188–211.

Atwood, T. C., and E. M. Gese. 2008. Coyotes and recolonizing wolves: Social rank mediates risk-conditional behaviour at ungulate carcasses. *Animal Behaviour* 75:753–762.

Aubry, K. B., K. S. McKelvey, and J. P. Copeland. 2007. Distribution and broadscale habitat relations of the wolverine in the contiguous United States. *Journal of Wildlife Management* 71: 2147–2158.

Audet, A. M., C. B. Robbins, and S. Larivière. 2002. *Alopex lagopus. Mammalian Species* 713:1–10.

Baker, R. J., R. D. Bradley, and L. R. McAliley. 2003. "Pocket Gophers (Geomyidae)" in G. Feldhamer, B. Thompson, and J. Chapman, eds., *Wild Mammals of North America: Biology, Management, and Conservation*, 2nd ed. Baltimore: Johns Hopkins University Press, pp. 276–287.

Ball, L. C., and R. T. Golightly. 1992. Energy and nutrient assimilation by gray foxes on diets of mice and Himalaya berries. *Journal of Mammalogy* 73:840–846.

Ballard, W. B., L. N. Carbyn, and D. W. Smith. 2003. "Wolf interactions with non-prey" in L. D. Mech and L. Boitani, eds., *Wolves: Behavior, Ecology and Conservation*. Chicago: University of Chicago Press, pp. 259–271.

Ballard, W. B., D. Lutz, T. W. Keegan, L. H. Carpenter, and J. C. deVos. 2001. Deer-predator relationships: A review of recent North American studies with emphasis on mule and black-tailed deer. *Wildlife Society Bulletin* 29:99–115.

Balph, D. M., and D. F. Balph. 1966. Sound communication of Uinta ground squirrels. *Journal of Mammalogy* 47:440–450.

Bangs, P. D., P. R. Krausman, K. E. Kunkel, and Z. D. Parsons. 2005. Habitat use by desert bighorn sheep during lambing. *European Journal of Wildlife Research* 51:178–184.

Barash, D. P. 1973. Territorial and foraging behavior of pika (*Ochotona princeps*) in Montana. *American Midland Naturalist* 89:202–207.

Barash, D. P. 1989. *Marmots: Social Behavior and Ecology*. Stanford, CA: Stanford University Press.

Bauer, E., and P. Bauer. 1995. *Elk Behavior, Ecology, Conservation*. Stillwater, MN: Voyageur Press.

Bazin, R. C., and R. A. MacArthur. 1992. Thermal benefits of huddling in the muskrat (*Ondatra zibethicus*). *Journal of Mammalogy* 73:559–564.

Beer, J. R., and C. F. MacLeod. 1966. Seasonal population changes in the prairie deer mouse. *American Midland Naturalist* 76:277–289.

Beier, P., D. Choate, and R. H. Barrett. 1995. Movement patterns of mountain lions during different behaviors. *Journal of Mammalogy* 76:1056–1070.

Beier, P. 1991. Cougar attacks on humans in the United States and Canada. *Wildlife Society Bulletin* 19:403–412.

Bekoff, M. 2001. *Coyotes: Biology, Behavior, and Management*. Caldwell, NJ: Blackburn Press.

Bekoff, M., and E. M. Gese. 2003. "Coyote (*Canis latrans*)" in G. Feldhamer, B. Thompson, and J. Chapman, eds., *Wild Mammals of North America: Biology, Management, and Conservation*, 2nd ed. Baltimore: Johns Hopkins University Press, pp. 467–481.

Bekoff, M., M. Tyrrell, V. E. Lipetz, and R. Jamieson. 1981. Fighting patterns in young coyotes: Initiation, escalation, and assessment. *Aggressive Behavior* 7:225–244.

Belan, I., P. N. Lehner, and T. Clark. 1978. Vocalizations of the American pine marten, *Martes americana*. *Journal of Mammalogy* 59:871–874.

Belant, J. L., K. Kielland, E. H. Follmann, and L. G. Adams. 2006. Interspecific resource partitioning in sympatric ursids. *Ecological Applications* 16:2333–2343.

Ben-David, M., R. T. Bowyer, L. K. Duffy, D. D. Roby, and D. M. Schell. 1998. Social behavior and ecosystem processes: River otter latrines and nutrient dynamics of terrestrial vegetation. *Ecology* 79:2567–2571.

Beneski, J., and D. Stinson. 1987. *Sorex palustris*. *Mammalian Species* 296:1–6.

Bengtson, J. L., and S. M. Fitzgerald. 1985. Potential role of vocalizations in West Indian manatees. *Journal of Mammalogy* 66:816–819.

Best, T. L. 1996. *Lepus californicus. Mammalian Species* 530:1–10.

Best, T. L., N. J. Hildreth, and C. Jones. 1989. *Dipodomys deserti. Mammalian Species* 339:1–8.

Betancourt, J. L., T. R. V. Devender, and P. S. Martin, eds. 1990. *Packrat Middens: The Last 40,000 Years of Biotic Change*. Tucson: University of Arizona Press.

Bissonette, J. A. 1982. Ecology and social behavior of the collared peccary in Big Bend National Park, Texas. Scientific Monograph Series No. 6. U.S. Dept. of the Interior, National Park Service, Washington, DC.

Bleich, V. C. 1999. Mountain sheep and coyotes: Patterns of predator evasion in a mountain ungulate. *Journal of Mammalogy* 80:283–289.

Blossom, P. M. 1932. A pair of long-tailed shrews (*Sorex cinereus cinereus*) in captivity. *Journal of Mammalogy* 13:136–143.

Blumstein, D. T., and J. C. Daniel. 2004. Yellow-bellied marmots discriminate among the alarm calls of individuals and are more responsive to the calls from juveniles. *Animal Behaviour* 68:1257–1265.

Blumstein, D. T., A. Ozgul, V. Yovovich, D. H. Van Vuren, and K. B. Armitage. 2006. Effect of predation risk on the presence and persistence of yellow-bellied marmot colonies. *Journal of Zoology* 270:132–138.

Blundell, G., M. Ben-David, and R. T. Bowyer. 2002. Sociality in river otters: Cooperative foraging or reproductive strategies? *Behavioral Ecology* 13:134–141.

Bodkin, J. L. 2003. "Sea otter (*Enhydra lutris*)" in G. Feldhamer, B. Thompson, and J. Chapman, eds., *Wild Mammals of North America: Biology, Management, and Conservation*, 2nd ed. Baltimore: Johns Hopkins University Press, pp. 735–743.

Boonstra, R. 1984. Aggressive behavior of adult meadow voles (*Microtus pennsylvanicus*) towards young. *Oecologia* 62:126–131.

Boonstra, R., X. Xia, and L. Pavone. 1991. Mating system of the meadow vole, *Microtus pennsylvanicus*. *Behavioral Ecology* 4:83–89.

Born, E. W., S. Rysgaard, G. Ehlmé, M. Sejr, M. Acquarone, and N. Levermann. 2003. Underwater observations of foraging free-living Atlantic walruses (*Odobenus rosmarus rosmarus*) and estimates of their food consumption. *Polar Biology* 26:348–357.

Bornhold, B. D., C. V. Jay, R. McConnaughey, G. Rathwell, K. Rhyna, and W. Collins. 2005. Walrus foraging marks on the seafloor in Bristol Bay, Alaska—a reconnaissance survey. *Geo-Marine Letters* 25:293–299.

Bouskila, A. 1995. Interactions between predation risk and competition: A field study of kangaroo rats and snakes. *Ecology* 76:165–178.

Bowyer, R. T. 1986. Antler characteristics as related to social status of male southern mule deer. *The Southwestern Naturalist* 31:289–298.

Bowyer, R. T., V. C. Bleich, X. Manteca, J. C. Whiting, and K. Stewart. 2007. Sociality, mate choice, and timing of mating in American bison (*Bison bison*): Effects of large males. *Ethology* 113:1048–1060.

Bowyer, R. T., and D. W. Kitchen. 1987. Significance of scent-marking by Roosevelt elk. *Journal of Mammalogy* 68:418–423.

Bowyer, R. T., D. R. McCullough, and G. E. Belovsky. 2001. Causes and consequences of sociality in mule deer. *Alces* 37:371(332).

Bowyer, R. T., V. Van Ballenberghe, and J. G. Kie. 2003. "Moose (*Alces alces*)" in G. Feldhamer, B. Thompson, and J. Chapman, eds., *Wild Mammals of North America: Biology, Management, and Conservation*, 2nd ed. Baltimore: Johns Hopkins University Press, pp. 931–964.

Boyce, M. S. 1989. *The Jackson Elk Herd: Intensive Wildlife Management in North America.* Cambridge, MA: Cambridge University Press.

Brinck, C., R. Gerell, and G. Odham. 1978. Anal pouch secretion in mink *Mustela vison*: Chemical communication in Mustelidae. *Oikos* 30:68–75.

Broadbooks, H. E. 1974. Tree nests of chipmunks with comments on associated behaviour and ecology. *Journal of Mammalogy* 55:630–639.

Bruseo, J. A., and R. E. Barry, Jr. 1995. Temporal activity of syntopic *Peromyscus* in the central Appalachians. *Journal of Mammalogy* 76:78–82.

Burke da Silva, K., L. K. Donald, M. W. Daniel, D. L. Kramer, and D. M. Weary. 1994. Context-specific alarm calls of the eastern chipmunk, *Tamias striatus*. *Canadian Journal of Zoology* 72:1087–1092.

Buskirk, S. W., S. H. Alton, G. R. Martin, and A. P. Roger. 1994. *Martens, Sables, and Fishers: Biology and Conservation.* Ithaca, NY: Comstock and Associates Publishing.

Byers, J. 2003a. "Pronghorn (*Antilocapra americana*)" in G. Feldhamer, B. Thompson, and J. Chapman, eds., *Wild Mammals of North America: Biology, Management, and Conservation*, 2nd ed. Baltimore: Johns Hopkins University Press, pp. 998–1009.

Byers, J. 2003b. *Built for Speed: A Year in the Life of Pronghorn.* Boston: Harvard University Press.

Byers, J. A., and M. Bekoff. 1981. Social, spacing, and cooperative behavior of the collared peccary, *Tayassu tajacu*. *Journal of Mammalogy* 62:767–785.

Campbell, K. L., and R. A. MacArthur. 1996. Digestibility of animal tissue by muskrats. *Journal of Mammalogy* 77:755–760.

Careau, V., J. F. Giroux, and D. Berteaux. 2007. Cache and carry: Hoarding behavior of arctic fox. *Behavioral Ecology and Sociobiology* 62:87–96.

Carraway, L. N., and B. J. Verts. 1993. *Aplodontia rufa. Mammalian Species* 431:1–10.

Carroll, C. 2007. Interacting effects of climate change, landscape conversion, and harvest on carnivore populations at the range margin: Marten and lynx in the northern Appalachians. *Conservation Biology* 21:1092–1104.

Casteel, D. A. 1966. Nest building, parturition, and copulation in the cottontail rabbit. *American Midland Naturalist* 75:160–167.

Catania, K. C. 1999. A nose that looks like a hand and acts like an eye: The unusual mechanosensory system of the star-nosed mole. *Journal of Comparative Physiology A: Neuroethology, Sensory, Neural, and Behavioral Physiology* 185:367–372.

Catania, K. C. 2006. Olfaction: Underwater "sniffing" by semi-aquatic mammals. *Science* 444:1024–1025.

Catania, K. C., J. F. Hare, and K. L. Campbell. 2008. Water shrews detect movement, shape, and smell to find prey underwater. *Proceedings of the National Academy of Sciences* 105:571–576.

Chadwick, D. H. 1983. *A Beast the Color of Winter.* San Francisco: Sierra Club Books.

Chapman, J. A., J. G. Hockman, and M. M. Ojeda. 1980. *Sylvilagus floridanus. Mammalian Species* 136:1–8.

Chapman, J. A., and J. A. Litvaitis. 2003. "Eastern Cottontail (*Sylvilagus floridanus* and Allies)" in G. Feldhamer, B. Thompson, and J. Chapman, eds., *Wild Mammals of North America: Biology, Management, and Conservation*, 2nd ed. Baltimore: Johns Hopkins University Press, pp. 101–125.

Churchfield, S. 1990. *The Natural History of Shrews.* Ithaca, NY: Comstock Publishing Association, Cornell University Press.

Clark, T. W., E. Anderson, C. Douglas, and M. Strickland. 1987. *Martes americana. Mammalian Species* 289:1–8.

Clark, W. K. 1951. Ecological life history of the armadillo in the eastern Edwards Plateau region. *American Midland Naturalist* 46:337–358.

Cleveland, C. J., M. Betke, P. Federico, J. D. Frank, T. G. Hallam, J. Horn, J. Lopez, G. F. McCracken, R. A. Medellin, A. Moreno-Valdez, C. G. Sansone, J. K. Westbrook, T. H. Kunz. 2006. Economic value of the pest control service provided by Brazilian free-tailed bats in south-central Texas. *Frontiers in Ecology and the Environment.* 4:238–243.

Clucas, B., D. H. Owings, and M. P. Rowe. 2008. Donning your enemy's cloak: Ground squirrels exploit rattlesnake scent to reduce predation risk. *Proceedings of the Royal Society of Biology* 275:847–852.

Collen, P., and R. J. Gibson. 2000. The general ecology of beavers (*Castor* spp.), as related to their influence on stream ecosystems and riparian habitats, and the subsequent effects on fish—a review. *Reviews in Fish Biology and Fisheries* 10:439–461.

Coltman, D. W., P. O'Donoghue, J. T. Jorgenson, J. T. Hogg, C. Strobeck, and M. Festa-Bianchet. 2003. Undesirable evolutionary consequences of trophy hunting. *Nature* 426:655–658.

Conway, C. H. 1952. Life history of the water shrew (*Sorex palustris navigator*). *American Midland Naturalist* 48:219–248.

Copeland, J. P., and J. S. Whitman. 2003. "Wolverine (*Gulo gulo*)" in G. Feldhamer, B. Thompson, and J. Chapman, eds., *Wild Mammals of North America: Biology, Management, and Conservation*, 2nd ed. Baltimore: Johns Hopkins University Press, pp. 672–682.

Coppedge, B. R., and J. H. Shaw. 1997. Effects of horning and rubbing behavior by bison (*Bison bison*) on woody vegetation in a tallgrass prairie landscape. *American Midland Naturalist* 138:189–196.

Côté, S. D., A. Peracino, and G. Simard. 1997. Wolf, *Canis lupus*, predation and maternal defensive behavior in mountain goats, *Oreamnos americanus. Canadian Field-Naturalist* 111:389–392.

Côté, S. D., and M. Festa-Bianchet. 2003. "Mountain Goat (*Oreamnos americanus*)" in G. Feldhamer, B. Thompson, and J. Chapman, eds., *Wild Mammals of North America: Biology, Management, and Conservation*, 2nd ed. Baltimore: Johns Hopkins University Press, pp. 1061–1076.

Côté, S. D., T. P. Rooney, J.-P. Tremblay, C. Dussault, and D. M. Waller. 2004. Ecological impacts of deer overabundance. *Annual Review of Ecology, Evolution, and Systematics* 35:113–147.

Currier, M. J. 1983. *Felis concolor. Mammalian Species* 200:1–7.

Cypher, B. L. 2003. "Foxes (*Vulpes* species, *Urocyon* species, and *Alopex lagopus*)" in G. Feldhamer, B. Thompson, and J. Chapman, eds., *Wild Mammals of North America: Biology, Management, and Conservation*, 2nd ed. Baltimore: Johns Hopkins University Press, pp. 511–546.

Cypher, B. L., and N. Frost. 1999. Condition of San Joaquin kit foxes in urban and exurban habitats. *Journal of Wildlife Management* 63:930–938.

Darden, S. K., and T. Dabelsteen. 2008. Acoustic territorial signalling in a small, socially monogamous canid. *Animal Behaviour* 75:905–912.

Darden, S. K., L. K. Steffensen, and T. Dabelsteen. 2008. Information transfer among widely spaced individuals: Latrines as a basis for communication networks in the swift fox. *Animal Behaviour* 75:425–432.

Dasmann, R. F., and R. D. Taber. 1956. Behavior of Columbian black-tailed deer with reference to population ecology. *Journal of Mammalogy* 37:143–164.

Davis, H., and A. S. Harestad. 1996. Cannibalism by black bears in the Nimpkish Valley, British Columbia. *Northwest Science* 70:88–92.

Dearing, M. D. 1997. The manipulation of plant toxins by a food-hoarding herbivore, *Ochotona princeps. Ecology* 78:774–781.

DeMaster, D., and I. Stirling. 1981. *Ursus maritimus. Mammalian Species* 145:1–7.

Derner, J. D., J. K. Detling, and M. F. Antolin. 2006. Are livestock weight gains affected by black-tailed prairie dogs? *Frontiers in Ecology and the Environment* 4:459–464.

de Vos, A., P. Brokx, and V. Geist. 1967. A review of social behavior of the North American cervids during the reproductive period. *American Midland Naturalist* 77:390–417.

Dochtermann, N. A., and S. H. Jenkins. 2007. Behavioral syndromes in Merriam's kangaroo rats (*Dipodomys merriami*): A test of competing hypotheses. *Proceedings of the Royal Society of Biology* 274:2343–2349.

Donaldson, G. M., G. Chapdelaine, and J. D. Andrews. 1995. Predation of thick-billed murres at 2 breeding colonies by polar bears and walruses. *Canadian Field-Naturalist* 109:112–114.

Dooley, J. L., Jr., and R. D. Dueser. 1990. An experimental examination of nest-site segregation by two *Peromyscus* species. *Ecology* 71:788–796.

Edwards, J., M. Ford, and D. Guynn. 2003. "Fox and Gray Squirrels (*Sciurus niger* and *S. carolinensis*)" in G. Feldhamer, B. Thompson, and J. Chapman, eds., *Wild Mammals of North America: Biology, Management, and Conservation*, 2nd ed. Baltimore: Johns Hopkins University Press, pp. 248–267.

Egoscue, H. J. 1979. *Vulpes velox. Mammalian Species* 122:1–5.

Eide, N. E., J. U. Jepsen, and P. Prestrud. 2004. Spatial organization of reproductive Arctic foxes: Responses to changes in spatial and temporal availability of prey. *Journal of Animal Ecology* 73:1056–1068.

Eisenberg, J. F. 1962. Studies on the behavior of *Peromyscus maniculatus gambelli* and *Peromyscus californicus parasiticus. Behaviour* 19:177–207.

Eisenberg, J. F. 1963. The Behavior of Heteromyid Rodents. *University of California Publications on Zoology*, vol. 69.

Elbroch, M. 2003. *Mammal Tracks and Sign: A Guide to North American Species*. Mechanicsburg, PA: Stackpole Books.

Ellis, J. E., and M. Travis. 1975. Comparative aspects of foraging behaviour of pronghorn antelope and cattle. *Journal of Applied Ecology* 12:411–420.

Emslie, S. D., M. Stiger, and E. Wambach. 2005. Packrat middens and late Holocene environmental change in southwestern Colorado. *The Southwestern Naturalist* 50:209–215.

Erb, J., M. S. Boyce, and N. C. Stenseth. 2001. Spatial variation in mink and muskrat interactions in Canada. *Oikos* 93:365–375.

Eshelman, B. D., and C. S. Sonnemann. 2000. *Spermophilus armatus. Mammalian Species* 637:1–6.

Estes, J. A. 1980. *Enhydra lutris. Mammalian Species* 133:1–8.

Estes, J. A., M. T. Tinker, T. M. Williams, and D. F. Doak. 1998. Killer whale predation on sea otters linking oceanic and nearshore ecosystems. *Science* 282:473.

Fagen, R., and J. M. Fagen. 1996. Individual distinctiveness in brown bears, *Ursus arctos* L. *Ethology* 102: 212–226.

Fair, J., and L. Rogers. 1990. *The Great American Bear*. Minocqua, WI: Northword Press, 192 pp.

Fairbairn, D. J. 1978. Dispersal of deer mice, *Peromyscus maniculatus*. Proximal causes and effects on fitness. *Oecologia* 32:171–193.

Farias, V., T. K. Fuller, R. K. Wayne, and R. M. Sauvajot. 2005. Survival and cause-specific mortality of gray foxes (*Urocyon cinereoargenteus*) in southern California. *Journal of Zoology* 266:249–254.

Fay, F. 1985. *Odobenus rosmarus. Mammalian Species* 238:1–7.

Fedriani, J. M., T. K. Fuller, R. M. Sauvajot, and E. C. York. 2000. Competition and intraguild predation among three sympatric carnivores. *Oecologia* 125:258–270.

Feldhamer, G. A., J. A. Rochelle, and C. D. Rushton. 2003. "Mountain beaver (*Aplodontia rufa*)" in G. Feldhamer, B. Thompson, and J. Chapman, eds., *Wild Mammals of North America: Biology, Management, and Conservation*, 2nd ed. Baltimore: Johns Hopkins University Press, pp. 179–187.

Ferkin, M. H., and R. E. Johnston. 1995. Meadow voles, *Microtus pennsylvanicus,* use multiple sources of scent for sex recognition. *Animal Behaviour* 49:37–44.

Ferkin, M. H., S. G. Mech, and C. G. Paz-Y-Miño. 2001. Scent marking in meadow voles and prairie voles: A test of three hypotheses. *Behaviour* 138:1319–1336.

Ferron, J. 1983. Scent marking by cheek rubbing in the northern flying squirrel (*Glaucomys sabrinus*). *Canadian Journal of Zoology* 61:2377–2380.

Fournier, F., and M. Festa-Bianchet. 1995. Social dominance in adult female mountain goats. *Animal Behaviour* 49:1449–1459.

Fox, M. W. 1971. Socio-infantile and socio-sexual signals in canids: A comparative and ontogenetic study. *Zeitschrift fuer Tierpsychologie* 28:185–210.

Fox, M. W. 1975. "Evolution of social behavior in canids" in Fox, M. W., ed., *The Wild Canids: Their Systematics, Behavioral Ecology and Evolution*. New York: Van Nostrand Reinhold, pp. 429–459.

Francke, O. F., and G. A. Villegas-Guzman. 2006. Symbiotic relationships between pseudoscorpions (Arachnida) and packrats (Rodentia). *Journal of Arachnology* 34:289–298.

Franzmann, A. W. 1981. *Alces alces. Mammalian Species* 154:1–7.

Franzmann, A. W., and C. C. Schwartz. 1997. *Ecology and Management of the North American Moose*. Washington, DC: Smithsonian Institution Press.

Frase, B. A., and R. S. Hoffman. 1980. *Marmota flaviventris. Mammalian Species* 135:1–8.

Fritzell, E. K., and K. J. Haroldson. 1982. *Urocyon cineroargenteus. Mammalian Species* 189:1–8.

Frommolt, K.-H., M. E. Goltsman, and D. W. MacDonald. 2003. Barking foxes: Field experiments in individual recognition in a territorial mammal. *Animal Behaviour* 65:509–518.

Fuller, A. K., D. J. Harrison, and J. H. Vashon. 2007. Winter habitat selection by Canada lynx in Maine: Prey abundance or accessibility? *Journal of Wildlife Management* 71:1980–1986.

Fuller, T. K., and B. L. Cypher. 2004. "*Urocyon cinereoargenteus*" in C. Sillero and D. W. Macdonald, eds., *Canids: Species Status and Conservation Action Plan*, 2nd ed. Gland, Switzerland: International Union for the Conservation of Nature and Natural Resources, pp. 92–97.

Garant, Y., and M. Crete. 1997. Fisher, *Martes pennanti*, home range characteristics in a high density untrapped population in southern Quebec. *Canadian Field-Naturalist* 111:359–364.

Gardner, A. L., and M. E. Sunquist. 2003. "Opossum (*Didelphis virginiana*)" in G. Feldhamer, B. Thompson, and J. Chapman, eds., *Wild Mammals of North America: Biology, Management, and Conservation*, 2nd ed. Baltimore: Johns Hopkins University Press, pp. 3–29.

Garshelis, D. L., C. B. Johnson, and J. A. Estes. 1999. Otter-eating Orcas: Killer whale predation on sea otters may be key to declining otter populations. *Science* 283:176(171).

Gehrt, S. D. 2003. "Raccoon (*Procyon lotor*) and Allies" in G. Feldhamer, B. Thompson, and J. Chapman, eds., *Wild Mammals of North America: Biology, Management, and Conservation*, 2nd ed. Baltimore: Johns Hopkins University Press, pp. 611–634.

Gehrt, S. D. 2005. Seasonal survival and cause-specific mortality for urban striped skunks in the absence of rabies. *Journal of Mammalogy* 86:1164–1170.

Gehrt, S. D., and E. K. Fritzell. 1998a. Duration of familial bonds and dispersal patterns for raccoons in south Texas. *Journal of Mammalogy* 79:859–872.

Gehrt, S. D., and E. K. Fritzell. 1998b. Resource distribution, female home range dispersion and male spatial interactions: Group structure in a solitary carnivore. *Animal Behaviour* 55:1211–1227.

Gehrt, S. D., and E. K. Fritzell. 1999. Behavioural aspects of the raccoon mating system: Determinants of consortship success. *Animal Behaviour* 57:593–601.

Geist, V. 1982. "Adaptive Behavioral Strategies" in D. E. Toweill and J. W. Thomas, eds., *Elk of North*

America: Ecology and Management. Mechanicsburg, PA: Stackpole Books, pp. 219–277.

Geist, V. 1998. *Deer of the World: Their Evolution, Behaviour, and Ecology.* Mechanicsburg, PA: Stackpole Books.

Gende, S. M., and T. P. Quinn. 2004. The relative importance of prey density and social dominance in determining energy intake by bears feeding on Pacific salmon. *Canadian Journal of Zoology* 82:75–85.

Genoways, H. H., and J. H. Brown, eds. 1993. *Biology of the Heteromyidae.* American Society of Mammalogists: Special Publication No. 10.

George, S. L., and K. R. Crooks. 2006. Recreation and large mammal activity in an urban nature reserve. *Biological Conservation* 133:107–117.

Gerhardt, F. 2005. Food pilfering in larder-hoarding red squirrels (*Tamiasciurus hudsonicus*). *Journal of Mammalogy* 86:108–114.

Gese, E. M., and R. L. Ruff. 1997. Scent-marking by coyotes, *Canis latrans*: The influence of social and ecological factors. *Animal Behaviour* 54:1155–1166.

Gese, E. M., and R. L. Ruff. 1998. Howling by coyotes (*Canis latrans*): Variation among social classes, seasons and pack sizes. *Canadian Journal of Zoology* 76:1037–1043.

Gese, E. M., T. E. Stotts, and S. Grothe. 1996. Interactions between coyotes and red foxes in Yellowstone National Park, Wyoming. *Journal of Mammalogy* 77:377–382.

Gettinger, R. D. 1984. A field study of activity patterns of *Thomomys bottae*. *Journal of Mammalogy* 65:76–84.

Getty, T. 1979. An observation on *Tamias striatus* reproducing in a tree nest. *Journal of Mammalogy* 60:636.

Getty, T. 1981. Structure and dynamics of chipmunk home range. *Journal of Mammalogy* 62:726–737.

Getz, L. L. 1961. Factors influencing the local distribution of shrews. *American Midland Naturalist* 65:67–88.

Getz, L. L., C. M. Larson, and K. A. Lindstrom. 1992. *Blarina brevicauda* as a predator on nestling voles. *Journal of Mammalogy* 73:591–596.

Getz, L. L., and B. McGuire. 2008. Factors influencing movement distances and home ranges of the short-tailed shrew (*Blarina brevicauda*). *Northeastern Naturalist* 15:293–302.

Gilbert, F. F. 1969. Analysis of basic vocalizations of the ranch mink. *Journal of Mammalogy* 50:625–627.

Gleason, J. S., R. A. Hoffman, and J. M. Wendland. 2005. Beavers, *Castor canadensis*, feeding on salmon carcasses: Opportunistic use of a seasonally superabundant food source. *Canadian Field-Naturalist* 119:591–593.

Goldstein, M. I., A. J. Poe, E. Cooper, et al. 2005. Mountain goat response to helicopter overflights in Alaska. *Wildlife Society Bulletin* 33:688–699.

Gorman, M. L., and R. D. Stone. 1990. *The Natural History of Moles.* Ithaca, NY: Cornell University Press.

Gorman, T. A., J. D. Erb, B. R. McMillan, and D. J. Martin. 2006. Space use and sociality of river otters (*Lontra canadensis*) in Minnesota. *Journal of Mammalogy* 87:740–747.

Gorman, T. A., J. D. Erb, B. R. McMillan, D. J. Martin, and J. A. Homyack. 2006. Site characteristics of river otter (*Lontra canadensis*) natal dens in Minnesota. *American Midland Naturalist* 156:109–117.

Green, G. I., and D. J. Mattson. 2003. Tree rubbing by Yellowstone grizzly bears, *Ursus arctos*. *Wildlife Biology* 9:1–9.

Gremillion Christensen, C., and G. H. Waring. 1980. The "chuck" sound of the nine-banded armadillo (*Dasypus novemcinctus*). *Journal of Mammalogy* 61:737–738.

Grinell, J., J. Dixon, and J. Linsdale. 1937. *Fur-bearing Mammals of California, Vol. 1 and 2.* Berkeley: University of California Press.

Gunther, K. A., and D. W. Smith. 2004. Interactions between wolves and female grizzly bears with cubs in Yellowstone National Park. *Ursus* 15:232–238.

Gurnell, J. 1987. *The Natural History of Squirrels.* New York: Facts on File, Inc.

Halls, L. K. 1984. *White-Tailed Deer: Ecology and Management.* Mechanicsburg, PA: Stackpole Books.

Halpin, Z. T., and T. P. Sullivan. 1978. Social interactions in island and mainland populations of the deermouse, *Peromyscus maniculatus*. *Journal of Mammalogy* 59:395–401.

Hamer, D., and S. Herrero. 1990. Courtship and use of mating areas by grizzly bears in the Front Ranges of Banff National Park, Alberta. *Canadian Journal of Zoology* 68(12):2695–2697.

Hamlin, K. L., and L. L. Schweitzer. 1979. Cooperation by coyote pairs attacking mule deer fawns. *Journal of Mammalogy* 60:849–850.

Harper, J. Y., and B. A. Schulte. 2005. Social interactions in captive female Florida manatees. *Zoo Biology* 24:135–144.

Harrington, F. H., and C. A. Asa. 2003. "Wolf Communication" in L. D. Mech and L. Boitani, eds., *Wolves: Behavior, Ecology and Conservation.* Chicago: University of Chicago Press, pp. 66–103.

Hart, F. M., and J. A. King. 1966. Distress vocalizations of young in two subspecies of *Peromyscus maniculatus*. *Journal of Mammalogy* 47:287–293.

Hartman, D. S. 1971. "Behavior and Ecology of the Florida Manatee (*Trichechus manatus latirostris*) at Crystal River, Citrus County." PhD dissertation, Cornell University.

Hartman, G. D., and T. L. Yates. 2003. "Moles (*Talpidae*)" in G. Feldhamer, B. Thompson, and J. Chapman, eds., *Wild Mammals of North America: Biology, Management, and Conservation*, 2nd ed. Baltimore: Johns Hopkins University Press, pp. 30–55.

Hassrick, J. L., D. E. Crocker, R. L. Zeno, S. B. Blackwell, D. P. Costa, and B. J. Le Boeuf. 2007. Swimming speed and foraging strategies of northern elephant seals. *Deep Sea Research Part II: Topical Studies in Oceanography* 54:369–383.

Hayes, A. R., and N. J. Huntly. 2005. Effects of wind on the behavior and call transmission of pikas (*Ochotona princeps*). *Journal of Mammalogy* 86:974–981.

Heffelfinger, J. 2006. *Deer of the Southwest: A Complete Guide to the Natural History, Biology, and Management of Southwestern Mule Deer and White-Tailed Deer.* College Station: Texas A & M University Press.

Hellgren, E. C., and J. A. Bissonette. 2003. "Collared Peccary (*Tayassu tajacu*)" in G. Feldhamer, B. Thompson, and J. Chapman, eds., *Wild Mammals of North America: Biology, Management, and Conservation*, 2nd ed. Baltimore: Johns Hopkins University Press, pp. 867–876.

Hemmes, R. B., A. Alvarado, and B. L. Hart. 2002. Use of California bay foliage by wood rats for possible fumigation of nest-borne ectoparasites. *Behavioral Ecology* 13:381–385.

Henry, J. D. 1977. The use of urine marking in the scavenging behaviour of the red fox (*Vulpes vulpes*). *Behaviour* 61:82–105.

Henry, J. D. 1993. *How to Spot a Fox.* Boston: Houghton Mifflin.

Herrero, S. 1985. *Bear Attacks: Their Causes and Avoidance.* New York: The Lyons Press.

Hickman, G. C. 1983. Influence of semiaquatic habit in determining burrow structure of the star-nosed mole (*Condylura cristata*). *Canadian Journal of Zoology* 61:1688–1692.

Hirth, D. H. 1977. Social behavior of white-tailed deer in relation to habitat. *Wildlife Monographs* 53:3–55.

Hirth, D. H., and D. R. McCullough. 1977. Evolution of alarm signals in ungulates with special reference to white-tailed deer. *The American Naturalist* 111:31–42.

Hockman, J. G., and J. A. Chapman. 1983. Comparative feeding habits of red foxes (*Vulpes vulpes*) and gray foxes (*Urocyon cinereoargenteus*) in Maryland. *American Midland Naturalist* 110:276–285.

Hodson, J. 2003. Habitat associations of American marten (*Martes americana*) in the Rabbit Lake watershed, Temagami, Ontario. Conservation thesis submitted to the University of Toronto.

Hogg, J. T., and S. H. Forbes. 1997. Mating in bighorn sheep: Frequent male reproduction via a high-risk "unconventional" tactic. *Behavioral Ecology and Sociobiology* 41:33–48.

Holbrook, S. J. 1979. Vegetational affinities, arboreal activity, and coexistence of three species of rodents. *Journal of Mammalogy* 60:528–542.

Holloway, G. L., and J. R. Malcolm. 2007. Nest tree use by flying squirrels (*Glaucomys sabrinus* and *G. volans*) in central Ontario. *Journal of Mammalogy* 88:226–233.

Hoogland, J. L. 1995. *The Black-Tailed Prairie Dog: Social Life of a Burrowing Mammal.* Chicago: University of Chicago Press.

Hoogland, J. L. 1996. *Cynomys ludovicianus.* *Mammalian Species* 535:1–10.

Howe, R. J. 1977. Scent-marking behavior in three species of woodrats (*Neotoma*) in captivity. *Journal of Mammalogy* 58:685–688.

Howe, R. J. 1978. Agonistic behavior of three sympatric species of woodrats (*Neotoma mexicana, N. albigula,* and *N. stephensi*). *Journal of Mammalogy* 59:780–786.

Huff, J. N., and E. O. Price. 1968. Vocalizations of the least weasel, *Mustela nivalis. Journal of Mammalogy* 49:548–550.

Hunter, J. S. 2009. Familiarity breeds contempt: Effects of striped skunk color, shape and local abundance on wild carnivore behavior. *Behavioral Ecology* 20:1315–1322.

Hurly, T. A., and S. A. Lourie. 1997. Scatterhoarding and larderhoarding by red squirrels: Size, dispersion, and allocation of hoards. *Journal of Mammalogy* 78:529–537.

Husa, S. L. 1978. *Trichechus manatus. Mammalian Species* 93:1–5.

Hwang, Y. T., S. Larivière, and F. Messier. 2007. Energetic consequences and ecological significance of heterothermy and social thermoregulation in striped skunks (*Mephitis mephitis*). *Physiological and Biochemical Zoology* 80:138–145.

Ilse, L. M., and E. C. Hellgren. 2001. Demographic and behavioral characteristics of North American porcupines (*Erethizon dorsatum*) in pinyon-juniper woodlands of Texas. *American Midland Naturalist* 146:329–338.

Ivins, B. L., and A. T. Smith. 1983. Responses of pikas (*Ochotona princeps*) to naturally occurring terrestrial predators. *Behavioral Ecology and Sociobiology* 13:277–285.

Jokela, J., and P. Mutikainen. 1995. Effect of size-dependent muskrat (*Ondatra zibethica*) predation on the spatial distribution of freshwater clam, *Anodonta piscinalis* Nilsson (*Unionidae*, Bivalvia). *Canadian Journal of Zoology* 73:1085–1094.

Jordan, R. H. 1974. Threat behavior of the black bear (*Ursus americanus*). *International Conference Bear Research and Management* 3:57–63.

Kaiser, J. 1998. Sea otter declines blamed on hungry killers. *Science* 282:390.

Kamler, J. F., and W. B. Ballard. 2002. A Review of Native and Nonnative Red Foxes in North America. *Wildlife Society Bulletin* 30:370–379.

Kanda, L. L., T. K. Fuller, and P. R. Sievert. 2006. Landscape associations of road-killed Virginia opossums (*Didelphis virginiana*) in Central Massachusetts. *American Midland Naturalist* 156:128–134.

Kastelein, R. A. 2002. "Walrus" in W. Perrin, B. Wursig, J. Thewissen, eds., *Encyclopedia of Marine Mammals*. San Diego: Academic Press, pp. 1294–1300.

Keefe, J. F., and D. E. Wooldridge. 1967. *The World of the Opossum*. Philadelphia: Lippincott.

Keeley A. T. H., and B. W. Keeley. 2004. The mating system of *Tadarida brasiliensis* (Chiroptera: Molossidae) in a large highway bridge colony. *Journal of Mammalogy* 85:113–119.

King, C. M. 1983. *Mustela erminea*. *Mammalian Species* 195:1–8.

King, C. M., and R. A. Powell. 2007. *The Natural History of Weasels and Stoats: Ecology, Behavior, and Management*. New York; Oxford: Oxford University Press.

Koehler, G. M., G. H. Maurice, and S. H. Howard. 1980. Wolverine marking behavior. *Canadian Field-Naturalist* 94:339–341.

Komers, P. E., K. Roth, and R. Zimmerli. 1992. Interpreting social behavior of wood bison using tail postures. *Z. Säugetierk* 57:343–350.

Koprowski, J. L. 1993. Sex and species biases in scent marking by fox squirrels and eastern gray squirrels. *Journal of Zoology* (London) 230:319–323.

Koprowski, J. L. 1994a. *Sciurus niger*. *Mammalian Species* 479:1–9.

Koprowski, J. L. 1994b. *Sciurus carolinensis*. *Mammalian Species* 480:1–9.

Kovach, A. I., and R. A. Powell. 2003. Effects of body size on male mating tactics and paternity in black bears, *Ursus americanus*. *Canadian Journal of Zoology* 81:1257–1268.

Krausman, P., and R. Bowyer. 2003. "Mountain Sheep (*Ovis canadensis* and *O. dalli*)" in G. Feldhamer, B. Thompson, and J. Chapman, eds., *Wild Mammals of North America: Biology, Management, and Conservation*, 2nd ed. Baltimore: Johns Hopkins University Press, pp. 1095–1115.

Krohn, W. B., D. E. Kenneth, and B. B. Randall. 1995. Relations among fishers, snow, and martens: Development and evaluation of two hypotheses. *Forestry Chronicle* 71:97–105.

Krupnik, I., and R. G. Carleton. 2007. Pacific walruses, indigenous hunters, and climate change: Bridging scientific and indigenous knowledge. *Deep-Sea Research* 54:2946–2957.

Kruuk, H. 2006. *Otters: Ecology, Behaviour, and Conservation*. New York: Oxford University Press.

Kucera, T. E. 1978. Social behavior and breeding system of the desert mule deer. *Journal of Mammalogy* 59:463–476.

Kunz, T. H., and M. B. Fenton, eds. 2003. *Bat Ecology*. Chicago: University of Chicago Press.

Kwiecinski, G. C. 1998. *Marmota monax*. *Mammalian Species* 591:1–8.

Labisky, R. F., and M. C. Boulay. 1998. Behaviors of bobcats preying on white-tailed deer in the Everglades. *American Midland Naturalist* 139:275–281.

Lair, H. 1990. The calls of the red squirrel: A contextual analysis of function. *Behaviour* 115:254–282.

Laist, D. L., and J. E. Reynolds, III. 2005. Influence of power plants and other warm-water refuges on Florida manatees. *Marine Mammal Science* 21:739–764.

Larivière, S. 1999. *Mustela vison*. *Mammalian Species* 608:1–9.

Larivière, S. 2001. *Ursus americanus*. *Mammalian Species* 647:1–11.

Larivière, S. 2003. "Mink (*Mustela vison*)" in G. Feldhamer, B. Thompson, and J. Chapman, eds., *Wild Mammals of North America: Biology, Management, and Conservation*, 2nd ed. Baltimore: Johns Hopkins University Press, pp. 662–671.

Larivière, S., and F. Messier. 1996. Aposematic behaviour in the striped skunk, *Mephitis mephitis*. *Ethology* 102:986–992.

Larivière, S., and M. Pasitschniak-Arts. 1996. *Vulpes vulpes*. *Mammalian Species* 537:1–11.

Larivière, S., and L. R. Walton. 1997. *Lynx rufus*. *Mammalian Species* 563:1–8.

Latour, P. B. 1981. Interactions between free-ranging, adult male polar bears: A case of adult social play. *Canadian Journal of Zoology* 59:1775–1783.

Le Boeuf, B. J., D. E. Crocker, D. P. Costa, S. B. Blackwell, P. M. Webb, and D. S. Houser. 2000. Foraging ecology of northern elephant seals. *Ecological Monographs* 70:353–382.

Lehmer E. M., L. T. Savage, M. F. Antolin, and D. E. Biggins. 2006. Extreme plasticity in thermoregulatory behaviors of free-ranging black-tailed prairie dogs. *Physiological and Biochemical Zoology* 79:454–467.

Lehner, P. N. 2001. "Coyote Communication" in M. Bekoff, ed., *Coyotes: Biology, Behavior and Management*. New Jersey: The Blackburn Press, pp. 127–162.

Lindzey, F. G. 2003. "Badger (*Taxidea taxus*)" in G. Feldhamer, B. Thompson, and J. Chapman, eds., *Wild Mammals of North America: Biology, Man-*

agement, and Conservation, 2nd ed. Baltimore: Johns Hopkins University Press, pp. 683–692.

Lingle, S., and S. M. Pellis. 2002. Fight or flight? Antipredator behavior and the escalation of coyote encounters with deer. *Oecologia* 131:154–164.

Linsdale, J. M., and P. Q. Tomich. 1953. *A Herd of Mule Deer: A Record of Observations Made on the Hastings Natural History Reservation.* Berkeley: University of California Press.

Litvaitis, J. A., A. G. Clark, and J. H. Hunt. 1986. Prey selection and fat deposits of bobcats (*Felis rufus*) during autumn and winter in Maine. *Journal of Mammalogy* 67:389–392.

Litvaitis, J. A., J. P. Tash, and C. L. Stevens. 2006. The rise and fall of bobcat populations in New Hampshire: Relevance of historical harvests to understanding current patterns of abundance and distribution. *Biological Conservation* 128:517–528.

Loeser, M. R., S. D. Mezulis, T. D. Sisk, et al. 2005. Vegetation cover and forb responses to cattle exclusion: Implications for pronghorn. *Rangeland Ecology and Management* 58:234–238.

Logan, K. A., and L. L. Sweeney. 2001. *Desert Puma: Evolutionary Ecology and Conservation of an Enduring Carnivore.* Washington, DC: Island Press.

Lomolino, M. V., and G. A. Smith. 2004. Terrestrial vertebrate communities at black-tailed prairie dog (*Cynomys ludovicianus*) towns. *Biological Conservation* 115:89–100.

Long, C. A. 1973. *Taxidea taxus. Mammalian Species* 26:1–4.

Lotze, J., and S. Anderson. 1979. *Procyon lotor. Mammalian Species* 119:1–8.

Loughry, W. J. 1988. Population differences in how black-tailed prairie dogs deal with snakes. *Behavioral Ecology and Sociobiology* 22:61–67.

Loughry, W. J., P. A. Prodohl, C. M. McDonough, and J. C. Avise. 1998. Polyembryony in armadillos: An unusual feature of the female nine-banded armadillo's reproductive tract may explain why her litters consist of four genetically identical offspring. *American Scientist* 86:274–276.

Lutton, L. M. 1975. Notes on territorial behavior and response to predators of the pika, *Ochotona princeps. Journal of Mammalogy* 56:231–234.

MacArthur, R. A. 1980. Daily and seasonal activity patterns of the muskrat *Ondatra zibethicus* as revealed by radiotelemetry. *Holarctic Ecology* 3:1–9.

MacCracken, J. G., V. Van Ballenberghe, and J. M. Peek. 1997. Habitat relationships of moose on the Copper River Delta in coastal South-Central Alaska. *Wildlife Monographs* 136:3–52.

Macêdo, R. H., and M. A. Mares. 1988. *Neotoma albigula. Mammalian Species* 310:1–7.

Mackie, R. J., J. G. Kie, D. F. Pac, and K. L. Hamlin.

2003. "Mule Deer (*Odocoileus hemionus*)" in G. Feldhamer, B. Thompson, and J. Chapman, eds., *Wild Mammals of North America: Biology, Management, and Conservation,* 2nd ed. Baltimore: Johns Hopkins University Press, pp. 889–905.

Maher, C. R. 2004. Intrasexual territoriality in woodchucks (*Marmota monax*). *Journal of Mammalogy.* 85:1087–1094.

Marín, A. I., L. Hernández, and J. W. Laundré. 2003. Predation risk and food quantity in the selection of habitat by black-tailed jackrabbit (*Lepus californicus*): An optimal foraging approach. *Journal of Arid Environments* 55:101–110.

Marinelli, L., and M. Francois. 1993. Space use and the social system of muskrats. *Canadian Journal of Zoology* 71:869–875.

Marinelli, L., F. Messier, and Y. Plante. 1997. Consequences of following a mixed reproductive strategy in muskrats. *Journal of Mammalogy* 78:163–172.

Marsden, H. M., and C. H. Conaway. 1963. Behavior and the reproductive cycle in the cottontail. *Journal of Wildlife Management* 27:161–170.

Marsden, H. M., and N. R. Holler. 1964. Social behavior in confined populations of the cottontail and the swamp rabbit. *Wildlife Monographs* 13:3–39.

Mateo, J. M. 2007. Ecological and hormonal correlates of anti-predator behavior in Belding's ground squirrels (*Spermophilus beldingi*). *Behavioral Ecology and Sociobiology* 62:37–49.

Mattson, D. J. 1997. Use of ungulates by Yellowstone grizzly bears, *Ursus arctos. Biological Conservation* 81:161–177.

Mattson, D. J., R. R. Knight, and B. M. Blanchard. 1992. Cannibalism and predation on black bears by grizzly bears in the Yellowstone ecosystem, 1975–1990. *Journal of Mammalogy* 73:422–425.

Mazur, R., and V. Seher. 2008. Socially learned foraging behaviour in wild black bears, *Ursus americanus. Animal Behaviour* 75:1503–1508.

McBee, K., and R. J. Baker. 1982. *Dasypus novemcinctus. Mammalian Species* 162:1–9.

McCord, C. M., 1974. Selection of winter habitat by bobcats (*Lynx rufus*) on the Quabbin Reservation, Massachusetts. *Journal of Mammalogy* 55:428–437.

McCracken, G. F. 1996. Bats aloft: A study in high altitude feeding. *Bats* 14:7–10.

McCracken, G. F., and M. K. Gustin. 1991. Nursing behavior in Mexican free-tailed bat maternity colonies. *Ethology* 89:305–321.

McDonald, D. 2006. *The Encyclopedia of Mammals.* London: The Brown Reference Group.

McDonough, C. M. 1997. Pairing behavior of the nine-banded armadillo (*Dasypus novemcinctus*). *American Midland Naturalist* 138:290–298.

McDonough, C. M., and W. J. Loughry. 1997a. Influences on activity patterns in a population of nine-banded armadillos. *Journal of Mammalogy* 78:932–941.

McDonough, C. M., and W. J. Loughry. 1997b. Patterns of mortality in a population of nine-banded armadillos, *Dasypus novemcinctus*. *American Midland Naturalist* 138:299–305.

McGrew, J. C. 1979. *Vulpes macrotis*. *Mammalian Species* 123:1–6.

McIntire, E. J., and D. S. Hik. 2002. Grazing history versus current grazing: Leaf demography and compensatory growth of three alpine plants in response to a native herbivore (*Ochotona collaris*). *Journal of Ecology* 90:348–359.

McLaren, B. E., B. A. Roberts, N. Djan-Chekar, and K. P. Lewis. 2004. Effects of overabundant moose on the Newfoundland landscape. *Alces* 40:45–59.

McManus, J. J. 1974. *Didelphis virginiana*. *Mammalian Species* 40:1–6.

McMillan, B. R., M. R. Cottam, and D. W. Kaufman. 2000. Wallowing behavior of American bison (*bos bison*) in tallgrass prairie: An examination of alternate explanations. *American Midland Naturalist* 144:159–167.

McNay, M. E. 2002. A Case History of Wolf-Human Encounters in Alaska and Canada. Alaska Department of Fish and Game, Technical Bulletin 13.

Meagher, M. 1986. *Bison bison*. *Mammalian Species* 266:1–8.

Mech, L. D. 1999. Alpha status, dominance, and division of labor in wolf packs. *Canadian Journal of Zoology* 77:1196–1203.

Mech, L. D., and L. Boitani, eds. 2003. *Wolves: Behavior, Ecology and Conservation*. Chicago: University of Chicago Press.

Mech, L. D., J. R. Tester, and D. W. Warner. 1966. Fall daytime resting habits of raccoons as determined by telemetry. *Journal of Mammalogy* 47:450–466.

Mech, L. D., R. T. McIntyre, and D. W. Smith. 2004. Unusual behavior by bison, *Bison bison*, toward elk, *Cervus elaphus*, and wolves, *Canis lupus*. *Canadian Field-Naturalist* 118:115–118.

Melquist, W. E., and M. G. Hornocker. 1983. Ecology of river otters in west central Idaho. *Wildlife Monographs* 83:3–60.

Michener, Gail R. 2004. Hunting techniques and tool use by North American badgers preying on Richardson's ground squirrels. *Journal of Mammalogy* 85:1019–1027.

Michener, G. R., and A. N. Iwaniuk. 2001. Killing technique of North American badgers preying on Richardson's ground squirrels. *Canadian Journal of Zoology* 79:2109–2113.

Miksis-Olds, J. L., P. L. Donaghay, J. H. Miller, P.

L. Tyack, and J. A. Nystuen. 2007. Noise level correlates with manatee use of foraging habitats. *Journal of the Acoustical Society of America* 121:3011–3020.

Miller, B. J., et al. 2007. Prairie dogs: An ecological review and current biopolitics. *Journal of Wildlife Management* 71:2801–2810.

Miller, E. H. 1985. Airborne acoustic communication in the walrus, *Odobenus rosmarus*, National Geographic Researcher 1:124–145.

Minta, S. C. 1993. Sexual differences in spatio-temporal interaction among badgers. *Oecologia* 96:402–409.

Minta, S. C., K. A. Minta, and D. F. Lott. 1992. Hunting associations between badgers and coyotes. *Journal of Mammalogy* 73:814–820.

Mitchell, S. C. and R. A. Cunjak. 2007. Stream flow, salmon and beaver dams: Roles in the structuring of stream fish communities within an anadromous salmon dominated stream. *Journal of Animal Ecology* 76:1062–1074.

Mizelle, J. D. 1935. Swimming of the muskrat. *Journal of Mammalogy* 16:22–25.

Molvar, E. M. and R. T. Bowyer. 1994. Costs and benefits of group living in a recently social ungulate: The Alaskan moose. *Journal of Mammalogy* 75:621–630.

Monty, A.-M., and R. E. Emerson. 2003. "Eastern woodrat (*Neotoma floridana* and Allies)" in G. Feldhamer, B. Thompson, and J. Chapman, eds., *Wild Mammals of North America: Biology, Management, and Conservation*, 2nd ed. Baltimore: Johns Hopkins University Press, pp. 381–393.

Mooring, M. S., T. A. Fitzpatrick, I. C. Fraser, J. E. Benjamin, D. D. Reisig, and T. T. Nishihira. 2003. Insect-defense behavior by desert bighorn sheep. *Southwestern Naturalist* 48:635–643.

Müller-Schwarze, D., and S. Heckman. 1980. The social role of scent marking in beaver (*Castor canadensis*). *Journal of Chemical Ecology* 6:81–95.

Murdoch, J. D., K. Ralls, B. Cypher, and R. Reading. 2008. Barking vocalizations in San Joaquin kit foxes. *Journal of Mammalogy* 89:1087–1093.

Murray, A. L., A. M. Barber, S. H. Jenkins, and W. S. Longland. 2006. Competitive environment affects food-hoarding behavior of Merriam's kangaroo rats (*Dipodomys merriami*). *Journal of Mammalogy* 87:571–578.

Murray, D. L., and S. Boutin. 1991. The influence of snow on lynx and coyote movements: Does morphology affect behavior? *Oecologia* 88:463–469.

Neale, J. C., and B. N. Sacks. 2001. Food habits and space use of gray foxes in relation to sympatric coyotes and bobcats. *Canadian Journal of Zoology* 79:1794–1800.

Nolte, D. L., G. Epple, D. L. Campbell, and J. R.

Mason. 1993. Response of mountain beaver to conspecifics in their burrow systems. *Northwest Science* 67:251–255.

ODFW. 2005. *The Importance of Beaver* (Castor canadensis) *to Coho Habitat and Trend in Beaver Abundance in the Oregon Coast Coho ESU.* ODFW (7) Beaver Final Report, Part 4.

O'Donoghue, M., S. Boutin, C. J. Krebs, G. Zuleta, D. L. Murray, and E. J. Hofer. 1998. Functional responses of coyotes and lynx to the snowshoe hare cycle. *Ecology* 79:1193–1208.

Oli, M. K., and K. B. Armitage. 2003. Sociality and individual fitness in yellow-bellied marmots: Insights from a long-term study (1962–2001). *Oecologia* 136:543–550.

Olsen, R. W. 1969. Agonistic behavior of the short-tailed shrew (*Blarina brevicauda*). *Journal of Mammalogy* 50:494–500.

O'Shea, T. J., and L. B. Poche, Jr. 2006. Aspects of underwater sound communication in Florida manatees (*Trichechus manatus latirostris*). *Journal of Mammalogy* 87:1061–1071.

Ostfeld, R. S., and C. D. Canham. 1993. Effects of meadow vole population density on tree seedling survival in oil fields. *Ecology* 74:1792–1801.

Ouellet, J. P., and J. Ferron. 1988. Scent-marking behavior by woodchucks (*Marmota monax*). *Journal of Mammalogy* 69:365–368.

Ough, W. D. 1982. Scent marking by captive raccoons. *Journal of Mammalogy* 63:318–319.

Ovsyanikov, N. G., L. L. Bove, and A. A. Kochnev. 1994. The factors causing mass death of walruses on coastal rookeries. *Zoologichesky Zhurnal* 73:80–87.

Parker, J. D., C. C. Caudill, and M. E. Hay. 2007. Beaver herbivory on aquatic plants. *Oecologia* 151:616–625.

Pasitschniak-Arts, M., and S. Larivière. 1995. *Gulo gulo. Mammalian Species* 499:1–10.

Peacock, M. M., and A. T. Smith. 1997. Nonrandom mating in pikas, *Ochotona princeps*: Evidence for inbreeding between individuals of intermediate relatedness. *Molecular Ecology* 6:801–811.

Peek, J. M. 2003. "Wapiti (*Cervus elaphus*)" in G. Feldhamer, B. Thompson, and J. Chapman, eds., *Wild Mammals of North America: Biology, Management, and Conservation*, 2nd ed. Baltimore: Johns Hopkins University Press, pp. 877–888.

Peek, J. M., R. E. LeResche, and D. R. Stevens. 1974. Dynamics of moose aggregations in Alaska, Minnesota, and Montana. *Journal of Mammalogy* 55:126–137.

Pelletier, F., and M. Festa-Bianchet. 2006. Sexual selection and social rank in bighorn rams. *Animal Behavior* 71:649–655.

Pelton, M. R. 2003. "Black Bear (*Ursus americanus*)"

in G. Feldhamer, B. Thompson, and J. Chapman, eds., *Wild Mammals of North America: Biology, Management, and Conservation*, 2nd ed. Baltimore: Johns Hopkins University Press, pp. 547–555.

Persson, J., T. Willebrand, A. Landa, R. Anderson, and P. Segerstrom. 2003. The role of intraspecific predation in the survival of juvenile wolverines. *Wildlife Biology* 9:21–26.

Petersen, K. E., and T. L. Yates. 1980. *Condylura cristata. Mammalian Species* 129:1–4.

Peterson, R. O., and P. Ciucci. 2003. "The Wolf as Carnivore" in L. D. Mech and L. Boitani, eds., *Wolves: Behavior, Ecology and Conservation*. Chicago: University of Chicago Press, pp. 104–130.

Peterson, R. O., A. K. Jacobs, T. D. Drummer, L. D. Mech, and D. W. Smith. 2002. Leadership behavior in relation to dominance and reproductive status in gray wolves, *Canis lupus. Canadian Journal of Zoology* 80:1405–1412.

Phillips, G. E., and G. C. White. 2003. Pronghorn population response to coyote control: Modeling and management. *Wildlife Society Bulletin* 31:1162–1175.

Pierce, B. M., and V. C. Bleich. 2003. "Mountain Lion (*Puma concolor*)" in G. Feldhamer, B. Thompson, and J. Chapman, eds., *Wild Mammals of North America: Biology, Management, and Conservation*, 2nd ed. Baltimore: Johns Hopkins University Press, pp. 744–757.

Powell, R. A. 1981. *Martes pennanti. Mammalian Species* 156:1–6.

Powell, R. A. 1993. *The Fisher: Life History, Ecology, and Behavior,* 2nd ed. Minneapolis: University of Minnesota Press.

Powell, R. A., S. W. Buskirk, and W. J. Zielinski. 2003. "Fisher and Marten (*Martes pennanti* and *Martes americana*)" in G. Feldhamer, B. Thompson, and J. Chapman, eds., *Wild Mammals of North America: Biology, Management, and Conservation*, 2nd ed. Baltimore: Johns Hopkins University Press, pp. 635–649.

Prange, S., and S. D. Gehrt. 2007. Response of skunks to a simulated increase in coyote activity. *Journal of Mammalogy* 88:1040–1049.

Prange, S., S. D. Gehrt, and E. P. Wiggers. 2003. Demographic factors contributing to high raccoon densities in urban landscapes. *Journal of Wildlife Management* 67:324–333.

Probert, B. L., and J. A. Litvaitis. 1996. Behavioral interactions between invading and endemic lagomorphs: Implications for conserving a declining species. *Biological Conservation* 76:289–295.

Quinn, J. H. 2008. The ecology of the American badger *Taxidea taxus* in California: Assessing conservation needs on multiple scales. PhD dissertation, University of California, Davis.

Ralls, K., and P. J. White. 1995. Predation on San Joaquin kit foxes by larger canids. *Journal of Mammalogy* 76:723–729.

Ramsay, M. A., and I. Stirling. 1984. Interactions of wolves and polar bears in northern Manitoba. *Journal of Mammalogy* 65:693–694.

Randall, J. A. 1997. Species-specific footdrumming in kangaroo rats: *Dipodomys ingens, D. deserti, D. spectabilis. Animal Behaviour* 54:1167–1175.

Randall, J. A. 2001. Evolution and function of drumming as communication in mammals. *American Zoologist* 41:1143–1156.

Reepa, R. L., C. D. Marshall, and M. L. Stolla. 2002. Tactile hairs on the postcranial body in Florida manatees: A mammalian lateral line? *Brain, Behavior and Evolution* 59:141–154.

Regehr, E. V., N. J. Lunn, S. C. Amstrup, and I. Stirling. 2007. Effects of earlier sea ice breakup on survival and population size of polar bears in western Hudson Bay. *Journal of Wildlife Management* 71:2673–2683.

Reich, L. M. 1981. *Microtus pennsylvanicus. Mammalian Species* 159:1–8.

Reynolds, H. W., C. C. Gates, and R. D. Glaholt. 2003. "Bison (*Bison bison*)" in G. Feldhamer, B. Thompson, and J. Chapman, eds., *Wild Mammals of North America: Biology, Management, and Conservation*, 2nd ed. Baltimore: Johns Hopkins University Press, pp. 1009–1060.

Rideout, C. B., and R. S. Hoffmann. 1975. *Oreamnos americanus. Mammalian Species* 63:1–6.

Riedman, M. L., and B. J. Boeuf. 1982. Mother-pup separation and adoption in northern elephant seals. *Behavioral Ecology and Sociobiology* 11:203–215.

Rieucau, G., and J. G. Martin. 2008. Many eyes or many ewes: Vigilance tactics in female bighorn sheep *Ovis canadensis* vary according to reproductive status. *Oikos* 117:501–506.

Ripple, W. J., and R. L. Beschta. 2004. Wolves and the ecology of fear: Can predation risk structure ecosystems? *BioScience* 54:755–766.

Robinson, D. E., and E. D. Brodie, Jr. 1982. Food hoarding behavior in the short-tailed shrew *Blarina brevicauda. American Midland Naturalist* 108:369–375.

Rock, K. R., E. S. Rock, R. T. Bowyer, and J. B. Faro. 1994. Degree of association and use of helper by coastal river otters, *Lutra canadensis*, in Prince William Sound, Alaska. *Canadian Field-Naturalist* 108:367–369.

Rode, K. D., S. D. Farley, and C. T. Robbins. 2006. Behavioral responses of brown bears mediate nutritional impacts of experimentally introduced tourism. *Biological Conservation* 133:70–80.

Roemer, G. W., C. J. Donlan, and F. Courchamp. 2002. Golden eagles, feral pigs, and insular carnivores: How exotic species turn native predators into prey. *Proceedings of the National Academy of Sciences* 99:791–796.

Ronald, K., and B. L. Gots. 2003. "Seals (*Phocidae, Otariidae*, and *Odobenidae*)" in G. Feldhamer, B. Thompson, and J. Chapman, eds., *Wild Mammals of North America: Biology, Management, and Conservation*, 2nd ed. Baltimore: Johns Hopkins University Press, pp. 789–854.

Rosatte, R., and S. Larivière. 2003. "Skunks (Genera *Mephitis, Spilogale*, and *Conepatus*)" in G. Feldhamer, B. Thompson, and J. Chapman, eds., *Wild Mammals of North America: Biology, Management, and Conservation*, 2nd ed. Baltimore: Johns Hopkins University Press, pp. 692–707.

Rosell, F., O. Bozser, P. Collen, and H. Parker. 2005. Ecological impact of beavers *Castor fiber* and *Castor canadensis* and their ability to modify ecosystems. *Mammal Review* 35:248–276.

Roze, U. 1989. *The North American Porcupine.* Washington, DC: Smithsonian Institution Press.

Roze, U., and L. M. Ilse. 2003. "Porcupine (*Erethizon dorsatum*)" in G. Feldhamer, B. Thompson, and J. Chapman, eds., *Wild Mammals of North America: Biology, Management, and Conservation*, 2nd ed. Baltimore: Johns Hopkins University Press, pp. 371–380.

Rundus, A. S., D. H. Owings, S. S. Joshi, E. Chinn, and N. Giannini. 2007. Ground squirrels use an infrared signal to deter rattlesnake predation. *Proceedings of the National Academy of Sciences* 104:14372–14376.

Russell, F. L., D. B. Zippin, and N. L. Fowler. 2001. Effects of white-tailed deer (*Odocoileus virginianus*) on plants, plant populations and communities: A review. *American Midland Naturalist* 146:1–26.

Rychlik, L., and E. Janecewicz. 2002. Prey size, prey nutrition, and food handling by shrews of different body sizes. *Behavioral Ecology* 13:216–223.

Sacks, B. N. 2005. Reproduction and body condition in California coyotes (*Canis latrans*). *Journal of Mammalogy* 86:1036–1041.

Samelius, G. 2004. Foraging behaviours and population dynamics of arctic foxes. *Arctic* 57:441–450.

Sandegren, F. E., E. W. Chu, and E. V. Judson. 1973. Maternal behavior in the California sea otter. *Journal of Mammalogy* 54:668–679.

Sanderson, E. W., et al. 2008. The ecological future of the North American bison: Conceiving long-term, large-scale conservation of wildlife. *Conservation Biology* 22:252–266.

Sanderson, G. C. 1949. Growth and behavior of a litter of captive long-tailed weasels. *Journal of Mammalogy* 30:412–415.

Schartz, C. C., S. D. Miller, and M. A. Haroldson. 2003. "Grizzly Bear" in G. Feldhamer, B. Thompson, and J. Chapman, eds., *Wild Mammals of North America: Biology, Management, and Conservation*, 2nd ed. Baltimore: Johns Hopkins University Press, p. 561.

Schwartz, M. K., K. L. Pilgrim, K. S. McKelvey, E. L. Lindquist, J. J. Claar, S. Loch, and L. F. Ruggiero. 2004. Hybridization between Canada lynx and bobcats: Genetic results and management implications. *Conservation Genetics* 5:349–355.

Shackleton, D. M. 1985. *Ovis canadensis*. *Mammalian Species*. 230:1–9.

Shannon, J. S. 1989. Social organization and behavioral ontogeny of otters (*Lutra canadensis*) in coastal habitat in northern California. *Bulletin of Nature Otter Specialist Group* 4:8–13.

Shapiro, J. 1949. Ecological and life history notes on the porcupine in the Adirondacks. *Journal of Mammalogy* 30:247–257.

Sheffield, S. R., and C. M. King. 1994. *Mustela nivalis*. *Mammalian Species* 454:1–10.

Sheffield, S. R., and H. H. Thomas. 1997. *Mustela frenata*. *Mammalian Species* 570:1–9.

Shipley, C., M. Hines, and J. S. Buchwald. 1981. Individual differences in threat calls of northern elephant seal bulls. *Animal Behaviour* 29:12–19.

Shipley, B. K., and R. P. Reading. 2006. A comparison of herpetofauna and small mammal diversity on black-tailed prairie dog colonies and noncolonized grasslands in Colorado. *Journal of Arid Environments* 66:27–41.

Siepielski, A. M. 2006. A possible role for red squirrels in structuring breeding bird communities in lodgepole pine forests. *Condor* 108:232–238.

Silverberg, J. K., P. J. Pekins, and R. A. Robertson. 2003. Moose responses to wildlife viewing and traffic stimuli. *Alces* 39:153–160.

Smith, A., and M. Weston. 1990. *Ochotona princeps*. *Mammalian Species* 352:1–8.

Smith, W. P. 1991. *Odocoileus virginianus*. *Mammalian Species* 388:1–13.

Snyder, D. P. 1982. *Tamias striatus*. Mammalian Species 168:1–8.

Sowls, L. K. 1997. *Javelinas and Other Peccaries: Their Biology, Management, and Use*. College Station: Texas A & M University Press.

Spencer, W. D., and W. J. Zielinski. 1983. Predatory behavior of pine martens. *Journal of Mammalogy* 64:715–717.

Spritzer, M. D., N. G. Solomon, and D. B. Meikle. 2006. Social dominance among male meadow voles is inversely related to reproductive success. *Ethology* 112:1027–1037.

Stahler, D. R., D. W. Smith, and D. S. Guernsey. 2006. Foraging and feeding ecology of the gray wolf (*Canis lupus*): Lessons from Yellowstone National Park, Wyoming, USA. *Journal of Nutrition* 136:1923S–1926S.

Stankowich, T., and R. G. Coss. 2008. Alarm walking in Columbian black-tailed deer: Its characterization and possible antipredatory signaling functions. *Journal of Mammalogy* 89:636–645.

Steele, M. 1998. *Tamiasciurus hudsonicus*. *Mammalian Species* 586:1–9.

Steele, M., and J. L. Koprowski. 2001. *North American Tree Squirrels*. Washington, DC: Smithsonian Institution Press.

Stempniewicz, L. 2006. Polar bear predatory behaviour toward molting barnacle geese and nesting glaucous gulls on Spitsbergen. *Arctic* 59:247–251.

Stewart, B. S., and R. L. DeLong. 1995. Double migrations of the northern elephant seal, *Mirounga angustirostris*. *Journal of Mammalogy* 76:196–205.

Stirling, I., and E. H. McEwan. 1975. The caloric value of whole ringed seals in relation to polar bear ecology and hunting behavior. *Canadian Journal of Zoology* 53:1021–1027.

Stoddart, L. C., R. E. Griffiths, and F. F. Knowlton. 2001. Coyote responses to changing jackrabbit abundance affect sheep predation. *Journal of Range Management* 54:15–20.

Strand, O., A. Landa, J. D. C. Linnell, B. Zimmermann, and T. Skogland. 2000. Social organization and parental behavior in the arctic fox. *Journal of Mammalogy* 81:223–233.

Svendsen, G. E. 1976a. Structure and location of burrows of yellow-bellied marmot. *Southwestern Naturalist* 57:398–399.

Svendsen, G. E. 1976b. Vocalizations of the long-tailed weasel (*Mustela frenata*). *Journal of Mammalogy* 57:398–399.

Svendsen, G. E. 2003. "Weasels and black-footed ferret (*Mustela* species)" in G. Feldhamer, B. Thompson, and J. Chapman, eds., *Wild Mammals of North America: Biology, Management, and Conservation*, 2nd ed. Baltimore: Johns Hopkins University Press, pp. 650–661.

Sweanor, L. L., K. A. Logan, and M. G. Hornocker. 2005. Puma responses to close approaches by researchers. *Wildlife Society Bulletin* 33:905–913.

Sweitzer, R. A., and J. Berger. 1992. Size-related effects of predation on habitat use and behavior of porcupines (*Erethizon dorsatum*). *Ecology* 73:867–875.

Sweitzer, R. A., S. H. Jenkins, and J. Berger. 1997. Near-extinction of porcupines by mountain lions and consequences of ecosystem change in the Great Basin Desert. *Conservation Biology* 11:1407–1417.

Swihart, R. K. 1991. Modifying scent-marking behavior to reduce woodchuck damage to fruit trees. *Ecological Applications* 1:98–103.

Swimley, T. J., T. L. Serfass, R. P. Brooks, and W. M. Tzilkowski. 1998. Predicting river otter latrine sites in Pennsylvania. *Wildlife Society Bulletin* 26:836–845.

Tannerfeldt, M., B. Elmhagen, and A. Angerbjörn. 2002. Exclusion by interference competition? The relationship between red and arctic foxes. *Oecologia* 132:213–220.

Taylor, W. P. 1943. The gray fox in captivity. *Texas Game and Fish* 1:12–13, 19.

Toweill, D. E., and J. W. Thomas, eds. 1982. *Elk of North America: Ecology and Management.* Mechanicsburg, PA: Stackpole Books.

Tumlison, R., and J. Jones. 1987. *Felis lynx. Mammalian Species* 269:1–8.

Van Ballenberghe, V. 2004. *In the Company of Moose.* Mechanicsburg, PA: Stackpole Books.

Van der Wal, R. 2006. Do herbivores cause habitat degradation or vegetation state transition? Evidence from the tundra. *Oikos* 114:177–186.

Van Djik, J. 2008. Wolverine foraging strategies in a multiple-use landscape. PhD dissertation, Norwegian University of Science and Technology, Trondheim.

Van Vuren, D. H. 2001. Predation on yellow-bellied marmots (*Marmota flaviventris*). *American Midland Naturalist* 145:94–100.

Verts, B. J. 1967. *The Biology of the Striped Skunk.* Chicago: The University of Illinois Press.

Verts, B. J., and L. N. Carraway. 2002. *Neotoma lepida. Mammalian Species* 699:1–12.

Wade-Smith, J., and B. J. Verts. 1982. *Mephitis mephitis. Mammalian Species* 173:1–7.

Walmo, O. C. 1981. *Mule and Black-tailed Deer of North America.* Lincoln: University of Nebraska Press.

Weckerly, F., K. McFarland, M. Ricca, and K. Meyer. 2004. Roosevelt elk density and social segregation: Foraging behavior and females avoiding larger groups of males. *American Midland Naturalist* 152:386–399.

Weir, R. D. 1994. Landscape habitat use by fishers in central British Columbia. *Northwest Science* 68:156.

Whitaker, J. O. 2004. *Sorex cinereus. Mammalian Species* 743:1–9.

Wiig, O., I. Gjertz, D. Griffiths, and C. Lydersen. 1993. Diving patterns of an Atlantic walrus *Odobenus rosmarus rosmarus* near Svalbard. *Polar Biology* 13:71–72.

Wilkins, K. T. 1989. *Tadarida brasiliensis. Mammalian Species* 331:1–10.

Willner, G. R., G. A. Feldhamer, E. E. Zucker, and J. A. Chapman. 1980. *Ondatra zibethicus. Mammalian Species* 141:1–8.

Wilson, D. R., and J. F. Hare. 2006. The adaptive utility of Richardson's ground squirrel (*Spermophilus richardsonii*) short-range ultrasonic alarm signals. *Canadian Journal of Zoology* 84:1322–1330.

Wishner, L. A. 1982. *Eastern Chipmunks: Secrets of Their Solitary Lives.* Washington, DC: Smithsonian Institution Press.

Wolfe, J. L. 1966. Behavior and dominance relationships of the eastern chipmunk, *Tamias striatus. American Midland Naturalist* 76:190–200.

Woods, C. A. 1973. *Erethizon dorsatum. Mammalian Species* 29:1–6.

Woods, S. E. 1980. *The Squirrels of Canada.* Ottawa, Canada: National Museum of Natural Sciences, National Museums of Canada.

Wright, J. D., and J. Ernst. 2004a. Effects of midwinter snow depth on stand selection by wolverines, *Gulo gulo luscus*, in the boreal forest. *Canadian Field-Naturalist* 118:56–60.

Wright, J. D., and J. Ernst. 2004b. Wolverine, *Gulo gulo luscus*, Resting sites and caching behavior in the boreal forest. *Canadian Field-Naturalist* 118:61–64.

Yahner, R. H. 2003. "Pine Squirrels (*Tamiasciurus hudsonicus* and *T. douglasii*)" in G. Feldhamer, B. Thompson, and J. Chapman, eds., *Wild Mammals of North America: Biology, Management, and Conservation*, 2nd ed. Baltimore: Johns Hopkins University Press, pp. 268–275.

Yamaguchi, N., R. J. Sarno, W. E. Johnson, S. J. Brien, and D. W. Macdonald. 2004. Multiple parenting and reproductive tactics of free-ranging American minks, *Mustela vison. Journal of Mammalogy* 85:432–439.

Yensen, E., and P. W. Sherman. 2003. "Ground Squirrels (*Spermophilus* and *Ammospermophilus* species)" in G. Feldhamer, B. Thompson, and J. Chapman, eds., *Wild Mammals of North America: Biology, Management, and Conservation*, 2nd ed. Baltimore: Johns Hopkins University Press, pp. 211–231.

Yom-Tov, Y., S. Yom-Tov, D. MacDonald, and E. Yom-Tov. 2007. Population cycles and changes in body size of the lynx in Alaska. *Oecologia* 152:239–244.

Zager, P., and J. Beecham. 2006. The role of American black bears and brown bears as predators on ungulates in North America. *Ursus* 17:95–108.

Zielinski, W. J., N. P. Duncan, and E. C. Hellgren. 2004a. Diets of sympatric populations of American martens (*Martes americana)* and fishers (*Martes pennanti*) in California. *Journal of Mammalogy* 85:470–477.

Zielinski, W. J., R. L. Truex, G. A. Schmidt, F. V. Schlexer, K. N. Schmidt, and R. H. Barrett. 2004. Resting habitat selection by fishers in California. *Journal of Wildlife Management* 68:475–492.

Zimen, E. 1981. *The Wolf: A Species in Danger.* New York: Delacorte Press.

INDEX

Index pages in bold refer to text graphics.